PSYCHOPATHY

PSYCHOPATHY
Antisocial, Criminal, and Violent Behavior

Edited by

THEODORE MILLON
ERIK SIMONSEN
MORTEN BIRKET-SMITH
ROGER D. DAVIS

THE GUILFORD PRESS
New York   London

© 1998 The Guilford Press
A Division of Guilford Publications, Inc.
72 Spring Street, New York, NY 10012
www.guilford.com

Paperback edition 2003

Printed in the United States of America

This book is printed on acid-free paper.

Last digit is print number: 9   8   7   6

Library of Congress Cataloging-in-Publication Data

Psychopathy : antisocial, criminal, and violent behavior / edited by
   Theodore Millon . . . [et al.].
      p.   cm.
   Includes bibliographical references and index.
   ISBN 1-57230-344-1 (hc.)   ISBN 1-57230-864-8 (pbk.)
   1. Antisocial personality disorders. 2. Psychopaths. I. Millon,
   Theodore.
   RC555.P785 1998
   616.85′82—dc21   98-6845
                                                             CIP

Contributors

Morten Birket-Smith, MD, Department of Psychiatry, Bispebjerg University Hospital, Copenhagen, Denmark

Ronald Blackburn, PhD, Department of Clinical Psychology, University of Liverpool, Liverpool, England

Jeremy W. Coid, MD, FRCPsych, Academic Section of Forensic Psychiatry, St. Bartholomew's and the Royal London School of Medicine and Dentistry, London, England

David J. Cooke, PhD, Douglas Inch Centre, Glasgow; Department of Forensic Psychology, Glasgow Caledonian University, Glasgow, Scotland

Murray Cox, MD, FRCPsych, (deceased), Crowthorne, England, Department of Forensic Psychotherapy, Broadmoor Hospital; Shakespeare Institute, University of Birmingham, Birmingham, England

Alv A. Dahl, MD, DrMedSc, Research Department, Aker Hospital, Division of Psychiatry, University of Oslo, Oslo, Norway

Roger D. Davis, PhD, Institute for Advanced Studies in Personology and Psychopathology, Coral Gables, FL

Bridget Dolan, PhD, CForensicPsychol, Department of Forensic Psychology, Henderson Hospital, Sutton, Surrey, England

Darwin Dorr, PhD, Department of Psychology, Wichita State University, Wichita, KS

Lisa Ekselius, MD, PhD, Department of Neuroscience, Psychiatry, Uppsala University Hospital, Uppsala, Sweden

H. J. Eysenck, PhD, (deceased), Institute of Psychiatry, University of London, London, England

Carl B. Gacono, PhD, Private Practice, Austin, TX

John Gunn, MD, FRCPsych, Department of Forensic Psychiatry, Institute of Psychiatry, University of London, London, England

Heidi Hansen, MD, Chief Psychiatrist, Danish Department of Prisons and Probation, Copenhagen, Denmark

Robert D. Hare, PhD, Department of Psychology, University of British Columbia, Vancouver, British Columbia, Canada

117646

Per Jensen, MD, Department of Psychiatry, University of Copenhagen, Copenhagen, Denmark

Otto F. Kernberg, MD, Director, Personality Disorders Institute, New York Hospital—Cornell Medical Center, Westchester Division, White Plains; Department of Psychiatry, Cornell University Medical College, New York; Columbia University Center for Psychoanalytic Training and Research, New York, NY

Joachim Knop, MD, Department of Psychiatry, Gentofte University Hospital, Hellerup; Institute of Preventive Medicine, University of Copenhagen, Copenhagen, Denmark

David T. Lykken, PhD, Department of Psychology, University of Minnesota, Minneapolis, MN

Donald R. Lynam, PhD, Department of Psychology, University of Kentucky, Lexington, KY

Peter McGuffin, MB PhD, FRCPsych, Department of Psychological Medicine, University of Wales College of Medicine, Cardiff, Wales, UK

J. Reid Meloy, PhD, Department of Psychiatry, School of Medicine, University of California, San Diego; School of Law, University of San Diego, San Diego, CA

Theodore Millon, PhD, DSc, Institute for Advanced Studies in Personology and Psychopathology, Coral Gables, FL; Department of Psychology, University of Miami, Miami, FL; Department of Psychiatry, Harvard Medical School, Boston, MA

Erik Lykke Mortensen, PhD, Institute of Preventive Medicine, University of Copenhagen, Copenhagen, Denmark

Joel Paris, MD, Department of Psychiatry, McGill University, Montreal; SMBD—Jewish General Hospital, Montreal, Quebec, Canada

William H. Reid, MD, MPH, Private Forensic Practice, Horseshoe Bay, TX; Department of Psychiatry, University of Texas Health Science Center, San Antonio, TX

Henry Richards, PhD, Clinical Heuristics, Inc., Silver Spring, MD; Friends Research Institute, Baltimore, MD

Niels Peter Rygaard, PhD, Private Practice, Aarhus, Denmark

Larry J. Siever, MD, Department of Psychiatry, Mount Sinai School of Medicine, New York, NY

Erik Simonsen, MD, Institute of Personality Theory and Psychopathology, Roskilde, Denmark

Michael H. Stone, MD, Department of Clinical Psychiatry, Columbia University, New York, NY

Anita Thapar, MB PhD, Department of Psychiatry, University of Manchester, Royal Manchester Children's Hospital, Manchester, England

Hans Toch, PhD, School of Criminal Justice, University at Albany—State University of New York, Albany, NY

Per Vaglum, MD, PhD, Department of Behavioural Sciences in Medicine, University of Oslo, Oslo, Norway

Lars von Knorring, MD, PhD, Department of Neuroscience, Psychiatry, Uppsala University Hospital, Uppsala, Sweden

Thomas A. Widiger, PhD, Department of Psychology, University of Kentucky, Lexington, KY

Preface

Psychopathy was the first personality disorder to be recognized in psychiatry. Early this century, according to the German psychiatrist Kurt Schneider, psychopathy referred to all kinds of personality disorders (psychopathic personalities) as extreme variants of normal personality. Since then it has been given many different labels or terms: the unscrupulous man, *manie sans delire,* moral insanity, psychopathic inferiority, sociopathy, character deficiency, the manipulative personality, and, lately, in DSM-IV and ICD-10, Antisocial Personality Disorder and Dissocial Personality Disorder.

The most characteristic traits in psychopaths are their superficial charm, egocentricity, incapacity for love, guiltlessness, lack of remorse and shame, lack of insight, and failure to learn from experience.

Although still a controversial issue among clinicians and researchers, there seems to be a renewed interest in the concept of psychopathy. First, the concept has shown reliability, descriptive validity, and utility in clinical, correctional, and forensic settings. Second, a growing body of developmental, biological, and psychodynamic research has strengthened the construct and the predictive validity of the term. Third, personal and sociocultural factors in recurrent violence in society have received the attention of the general public, including the question of treatment versus punishment. Psychopathy is often the primary cause of physical and sexual abuse as well as being present in all kinds of criminality, and the cost to society and the consequences in personal suffering are no doubt huge.

The use of the psychopathy concept in clinical settings has for different reasons faded away in many countries in Europe. Nevertheless, there is a close and inverse relationship between psychopathy and borderline diagnoses, which was illustrated in a study in Denmark. Patients who would have earlier been diagnosed as having psychopathic deviances are now often labeled borderline.

The ambivalence toward classification of psychopaths is exposed in current classification systems, where the criteria of antisocial personality disorder in the DSM system, for instance, are too biased toward criminality, too descriptive, and too socioeconomically skewed to be clinically useful, while the ICD system maintains similar criteria with more psychodynamic implications.

Current DSM classification of psychopaths probably puts too much emphasis on criminal behavior, as many psychopaths do not become criminals in a strict sense. But noncriminal psychopaths may, at the psychological level, be equally exploitative, deceptive, and irresponsible. A parallel to criminality in daily life is the behavior of the succesful, manipulative, narcissistic personality, who by charm and intuition knows how to exploit the emotions, needs, and weaknesses of others for his or her own benefit. Thus, we tend to reserve the term psychopath for the "unsuccesful" psychopath.

Psychopathy is often comorbid with other psychiatric syndromes, such as substance abuse, malingering, somatization, suicidal behavior, anxiety, depression, and schizophrenia. The prognosis for these syndromes is very much dependent on the presence or absence of psychopathy, although they may also be seen as a part of the same underlying psychological and biogenic deficit as psychopathy.

The search for the developmental origins of psychopathy has indicated that a significant proportion of children from chaotic and disorganized family environments will develop into criminal, antisocial adults. Lack of parental bonds of affection, as well as maternal deprivation and having a sociopathic father are regarded as predictors of psychopathy. Similar recent research has validated the existence of a biological understructure in psychopathy. Twin and adoption studies have shown a partly genetic etiology, and brain imaging has identified dysfunctions and lesions in the frontal and temporal regions of the brain. Dysregulation in the serotonergic system is associated with homicidal, suicidal, and impulsive behavior as well as with difficulties in language. Affective processing, lack of inhibitory anxiety, and failure to be responsive to aversive consequences in psychopaths may in a similar way have biological correlates. The psychodynamics of psychopaths has been described and explored by many psychotherapists, and instruments such as the Rorschach test have been used for assessing defense mechanisms. Failure of object constancy, superego deficits, and inadequate control of aggressive impulses have been major focuses of attention.

Psychopathy is perhaps the most difficult personality disorder to treat. One important reason for this is that psychopaths often do not consider themselves to be suffering, although depression or anxiety arising from social failure, confinement, or substance abuse may help to foster a therapeutic alliance. Therapeutic alliances are enhanced by demographic similarity, some personal affinity, and a therapist's positive perception and understanding of a patient. The most common countertransferences on the other hand are moral condemnation and a therapist having the illusion that he or she can effect a change that has never been possible before. An antitherapeutic moralistic stance is often facilitated by strong feelings of sympathy and empathy for the victim(s) of the psychopath. Specialized residential treatment programs that provide firm structure, here-and-now confrontations regarding interpersonal behavior, structured work programs, and close supervision by the staff seem to be the most effective. Medication is often abused by psychopaths and failure to take medication might deter their motivation to be tested, but recent promising studies of a variety of anti-impulsive and antiaggressive agents suggest better options. Time seems to be an important predictive factor in treatment, because antisocial behavior appears to diminish with age.

The Institute of Personality Theory and Psychopathology (IPTP) was founded in 1989, although it was originally created by Erik Simonsen and Niels Strandbygaard in 1984 as a Millon study group under the Danish Psychiatric Society. In collaboration with Theodore Millon the study group organized the First International Congress on the Disorders of Personality in Copenhagen in 1988 and shortly thereafter the group was restructured as an institute. The IPTP is now affiliated with the International Society on the Study of Personality Disorders (ISSPD). The aim of the institute is to contribute to research and postgraduate education in the field of personality disorders. The close collaboration between the IPTP and the ISSPD has through the years encouraged the IPTP to organize international meetings.

Following a very succesful Scandinavian Symposium on borderline conditions (*Proceedings of the Scandinavian Symposium on Borderline Conditions, Acta Psychiatrica Scandinavica*, 89[Suppl. 379], 1994) the Board of the IPTP decided to hold an international meeting on psychopathy. The IPTP saw the borderline and psychopathy concepts as of equal importance in personality disorder research and of equally significant clinical relevance. Outstanding researchers and clinicians from Scandinavia, Great Britain, and the United States and Canada were invited to summarize and update our knowledge of different aspects of psychopathy: concept and classification, etiology, epidemiology, and treatment.

The Scandinavian countries, not the least Denmark, have contributed to research on psychopathy and antisocial behavior, especially with regard to family transmission, psychophysiology, and special treatment programs.

Initially it was intended that the proceedings of the symposium be published as a journal supplement. As an alternative we came up with the idea of extending our close collaboration with Professor Millon by doing a book on the topic. In this way it also became possible to include other well-respected researchers as authors. The idea was that the book was to cover a broad range of clinically relevant topics, updated with regard to scholarship. We are pleased that Consulting Senior Editor Herb Reich, of The Guilford Press, supported our project and put the work forward for publication.

We wish to thank the chapter authors for their contributions and collegial cooperation, which made this book possible. Although occasioned with deep regret, the book contains the last chapters written by H. J. Eysenck and Murray Cox, both of Great Britain. Both died this past summer. We also want to thank secretary Dorit Mortensen for her great help in organizing the symposium. The symposium was generously supported by Lundbeck Pharma A/S, and IPTP wishes to express its gratitude for the kind assistance.

ERIK SIMONSEN
MORTEN BIRKET-SMITH
Institute of PersonalityTheory
  and Psychopathology (IPTP)
Roskilde, Denmark
May 1998

Contents

I

HISTORY AND VIEWPOINTS

1

Historical Conceptions of Psychopathy in the United States and Europe

THEODORE MILLON
ERIK SIMONSEN
MORTEN BIRKET-SMITH

Because of the extensive and divergent literature on the topic, the present review of the concepts and theories of the psychopathic personality pattern is more detailed than usual. This pattern's origins and clinical characteristics have been formulated and reformulated innumerable times over the past two centuries. Throughout this checkered history, the notion of a psychopathic character has served to designate a rather varied collection of behaviors that have little in common other than being viewed as repugnant to the social mores of the time. Despite disagreements concerning the notion's nature and origins, few clinicians today will fail to "get the picture" when they hear the designations "sociopath" or "antisocial personality."

Descriptions of the features that now characterize the antisocial personality can be traced back to earliest times. Theophrastus, a student of Aristotle, was well known for his apt portrayal of personality types. One of them, "The Unscrupulous Man," corresponds closely to our current conception of the antisocial character. As best it can be translated, Theophrastus wrote:

> The Unscrupulous Man will go and borrow more money from a creditor he has never paid. . . . When marketing he reminds the butcher of some service he has rendered him and, standing near the scales, throws in some meat, if he can, and a soup-bone. If he succeeds, so much the better; if not, he will snatch a piece of tripe and go off laughing. (Quoted in Widiger, Corbitt, & Millon, 1991, p. 63)

EARLY 19TH-CENTURY CONCEPTIONS

Attention was drawn to the clinical features of the antisocial personality when doctors and philosophers at the end of the 18th century engaged in the age-old arguments con-

3

cerning free will and whether certain moral transgressors are capable of "understanding" the consequences of their acts. It was Philippe Pinel (1801/1962), referring to a form of madness known at the time as *la folie raisonnante,* who noted that certain of his patients engaged in impulsive and self-damaging acts, despite the fact that their reasoning abilities were unimpaired and they fully grasped the irrationality of what they were doing. Describing these cases under the name *manie sans délire* ("insanity without delirium"), he was among the first to recognize that madness need not signify the presence of a deficit in reasoning powers. As Pinel (1801/1962) described it, "I was not a little surprised to find many maniacs who at no period gave evidence of any lesion of understanding, but who were under the dominion of instinctive and abstract fury, as if the faculties of affect alone had sustained injury" (p. 9). Until Pinel forcefully argued the legitimacy of this psychopathological entity, it was universally held that all mental disorders were disorders of the mind; since "mind" was equated with "reason," only a disintegration in the faculties of reason and intellect would be judged as insanity. However, beginning with Pinel, there arose the belief that one could be insane (*manie*) without a confusion of mind (*sans délire*).

Benjamin Rush, the well-known American physician, wrote in the early 1800s of similar perplexing cases characterized by lucidity of thought combined with socially deranged behaviors. He spoke of these individuals as possessing an "innate, preternatural moral depravity" in which "there is probably an original defective organization in those parts of the body which are preoccupied by the moral faculties of the mind" (1812, p. 112). Rush appears to have been the first theorist to have taken Pinel's morally neutral clinical observation of defects in "passion and affect" and turned it into a social condemnation. He claimed that a lifelong pattern of irresponsibility was displayed by these individuals, without a corresponding feeling of shame or hesitation over the personally destructive consequences of their actions. Describing the features characterizing this type, Rush (1812) wrote:

> The will might be deranged even in many instances of persons of sound understandings . . . the will becoming the involuntary vehicle of vicious actions through the instrumentality of the passions. Persons thus diseased cannot speak the truth upon any subject. . . . Their falsehoods are seldom calculated to injure anybody but themselves. (p. 124)

In 1824 the Danish physician Carl Otto returned to Copenhagen after visiting several of the European universities. Otto published several books and three medical journals, and was an enthusiatic phrenologist who had been inspired by the visit of Franz Joseph Gall and his coworker Spurzheim to Copenhagen in 1805 (Otto, 1825). In addition, Otto was appointed the successor of Professor Howitz as physician at the municipal prison of Copenhagen. This gave him the opportunity to examine and treat hundreds of convicts, and in the 1827 volume of the medical journal *Hygaea* (Otto, 1827a) he gave a thorough description of the health of the convicts, the cells, the sparse food, and the disciplinary penalties, such as "putting in irons" and "bread and water." Otto advocated for better conditions for the convicts, and in his descriptions of criminal cases he pointed out the need for individual considerations when the penalty was meted out. He proposed the use of phrenological examinations in forensic psychiatry as a means to distinguish between the sane and the insane:

> If this science [phrenology] was taken as a guide in the conviction of the criminal, you would not, as is now commonly the practice, convict criminals equally harshly, when

they are entirely different in sanity. . . . Many a criminal who now falls under the axe of the executioner would have been judged insane and merely unsuitable to remain in society. (Otto, 1827b, p. 32; our translation)

Applying phrenology, Otto gave a surprisingly modern description of the psychopathic mind. He devoted a whole paper to the concept of the mental organ *dølgeattrå* ("secretiveness") (Otto, 1827b). In general, according to phrenological theory, the mental organs were divided into four classes: those common to both humans and animals, the emotions, the intellectual organs, and the higher organs. *Dølgeattrå* was one of the organs common to both humans and animals, as were the organs for sexual drive, aggression, self-defense, and affection for the offspring. Otto defined the function of *dølgeattrå*, and its relation to personality disorder, in terms that remind us of present theories of impulse regulation:

Its function seems to be to suppress and regulate the external expressions of other mental organs—the behavioral expressions of all those thoughts, emotions, and dispositions that prompt us to act—until the intellect judges that it is suitable for these expressions to take place. . . . If too strong, badly controlled, and given an incorrect direction, *dølgeattrå* produces major abuse. It results in an inclination to shamming, to intrigues, to cunning politics, and to thinking it wise to shroud plans and intentions in an impenetrable fog. Slyness and cunning are then assumed to be wisdom and pretended to be practical cleverness. The mental character will have an inclination to lies, hypocrisy, and sly charades as the best means for obtaining a goal or conducting a plan. (Otto, 1827b, p. 376; our translation)

In Otto's view, the activities of a mental organ had their roots in inborn tendencies and were modulated during development. When the relations between the organs were close to equilibrium, as in most people, the environment would greatly influence and modify behavior. Correspondingly, the tendency to criminal behavior was not due to the activity of any single organ, but rather to a dysfunctional interplay of several organs, which again was related to each individual's peculiar constitution and development.

As evident from the dates mentioned up to this point, the British alienist J. C. Prichard (1835)—credited by many as having been the first to formulate the concept of "moral insanity"—was in fact preceded in this realization by several theorists; nevertheless, he was the first to label it as such and to give it wide readership in English-speaking nations. Although he accepted Pinel's notion of *manie sans dé lire,* he dissented from Pinel's morally neutral attitude toward these disorders and became the major exponent of the view that these behaviors signified a reprehensible defect in character that deserved social condemnation. He also broadened the scope of the original syndrome by including under the label "moral insanity" a wide range of previously diverse mental and emotional conditions. All of these patients ostensibly shared a common defect in the power to guide themselves in accord with "natural feelings"—that is, a spontaneous and intrinsic sense of rightness, goodness, and responsibility. Those afflicted by this disease were swayed, despite their intellectual ability to understand the choices before them, by overpowering "affections" that compelled them to engage in socially repugnant behaviors. As Prichard (1835) described it:

There is a form of mental derangement in which the intellectual functions appear to have sustained little or no injury, while the disorder is manifested principally or alone in the state of the feelings, temper or habits. In cases of this nature the moral or active principles of the mind are strangely perverted or depraved; the power of self-government is lost or greatly impaired and the Individual is found to be incapable, not of talking or reasoning upon any subject proposed to him, but of conducting himself with decency and propriety in the business of life. (p. 85)

The separation between insanity due to defects in reasoning and insanity owing to defects in "natural affections," espoused by Prichard, led to a major and long-standing controversy among British legal scholars and alienists. The discussion returns to this controversy after a few comments on the terminology of the day.

1. The word "moral" was imposed upon Pinel's concept by both Rush and Prichard. Pinel's syndrome signified the inability to restrain the affections (emotions) without a corresponding loss of reasoning; it was entirely neutral with regard to conventional notions of morality. Immersed in the British philosophical doctrine of "natural rights," which stressed both the state's and the individual's responsibility for social action, Rush and Prichard took Pinel's neutral clinical observation and transformed it into an entity consisting of moral censure and social depravity. In seeking to counter this intrusion of irrelevant philosophical and moralistic values upon clinical judgments, a distinguished British psychiatrist of the later 19th century, Daniel Hack Tuke (1892), proposed that Prichard's label be dropped and the syndrome renamed "inhibitory insanity," thereby recapturing the essence and moral neutrality of Pinel's original formulations.

2. Prichard's entity of "moral insanity" has little in common as a clinical syndrome with contemporary notions of psychopathy or antisocial personality. So diverse were the disorders subsumed in Prichard's category that almost all mental conditions, other than mental retardation and schizophrenia, would be so diagnosed today. If we sorted the "morally insane" into contemporary categories, the syndrome would be depleted so severely as to leave but a minor fraction that could be characterized by current notions of antisocial behavior.

Prichard did make one important positive contribution, in that he was the first theorist to have differentiated the prognosis of long-standing clinical traits from those that arise in response to transient stresses. He stated this original idea as follows:

When the disorder is connected with a strong natural predisposition, it can scarcely be expected to terminate in recovery. Such we must conclude to be the case in those instances in which the phenomena bear the appearance of an increase or exaltation of peculiarities natural to the individual, and noted as remarkable traits in his previous habits. If, however, this morbid state of mind has been the effect of any external and accidental cause, which admits of removal, or if the individual can be extracted from its influence or helped defend against it, there is reason to hope that the disorder will gradually subside. (1835, p. 122)

In 1841, Harald Selmer, often called the father of Danish psychiatry, published a book called *Om Psykiatriens Tilstand i Danmark (On the Conditions of Psychiatry in Denmark)*. Still a doctor in training, he criticized the dire conditions in Danish mental institutions at the beginning of the century: "Most of them are organized like prisons for criminals rather than as residences for suffering people, and with the only intention of confinement and preventing escape" (p. 2; our translation). In 1846 Selmer stated that the relation between society and insanity was fundamental, and that it was therefore duty of the society to establish psychiatric institutions and offer moral treatment for the insane. The conditions for the insane did not improve quickly, though; as late as 1841, Hübertz (cited in Gadelius, 1933) found 133 cages for unruly mental patients in the provinces of Denmark. The criminal mentally disturbed (including psychopaths) and quite a number of other patients were still kept in prisons and penitentiaries, where improvement in the conditions was even slower.

Physiognomy, a theory originally developed by I. C. Lavanter in the 1770s, had some support in Denmark in the second half of the 19th century. Sophus Schack wrote several books, including *Physiognomiske Studier* (*Physiognomic Studies*) (1858), in which he correlated the characteristics of the face with personality traits:

> Depraved people—yes, even major criminals—often hide under smooth, seemingly calm and guilt-free features, while sharply defined, wrinkled, serious and even repulsive lineaments not seldom cover thoughts and feelings of the most noble kind. . . . The perfect villain [has] a smooth face with absolutely calm and unpassionate features. (p. 97; our translation)

Although Schack believed in predisposition and heredity, he pointed out:

> While our budding abilities and characteristics are given us by nature clean and unpolluted, but of unequal intensity from the hand of nature, they are gradually brought to rise or fall, since the original power, the conscience, and the upbringing on the one hand, and weakness, bad guidance, and unlucky cicumstance on the other, have their effect. (p. 101; our translation)

The concept of moral insanity continued as a major source of contention and preoccupation in England and on the Continent for more than 70 years. In contrast to Daniel Hack Tuke, Henry Maudsley (1874), another leading British psychiatrist of the period, not only sided unequivocally with Prichard but argued for the existence of a specific cerebral center underlying "natural moral feelings." His views concerning the morally insane were stated thus: "As there are persons who cannot distinguish certain colours, having what is called colour blindness, so there are some who are congenitally deprived of moral sense" (p. 11). To the notion that there were cerebral deficits among the morally depraved were added several anthropological "stigmata," as proposed by Lombroso (1872–1885) and Gouster (1878). If we dismiss the primitive physical anthropology, what is striking about Lombroso's exposition is how closely it corresponds to the current DSM criteria for antisocial personality disorder. Lombroso was explicit in proposing the idea of a "born delinquent," whereas the DSM only implies a similar notion. According to Lombroso, constitutionally disposed criminal types displayed a notably large and projective lower jaw, outstretched ears, retreating forehead, left-handedness, robust physique, precocious sexual development, tactile insensibility, muscular agility, and so on. Behaviorally, they were emotionally hyperactive, temperamentally irascible, impetuous in action, and deficient in altruistic feelings. Gouster's list of stigmata parallels other aspects of the DSM antisocial personality criteria. Most similar is the symptom cluster he described as characterized by moral perversion from early life, as evidenced in headstrong, malicious, disobedient, irascible, lying, neglectful, and frequently violent and brutal behaviors; Gouster also noted a delight in intrigue and mischief, and a tendency toward excesses in seeking excitement and passion.

LATE 19TH-CENTURY AND EARLY 20TH-CENTURY CONCEPTIONS

Toward the end of the 19th century, German psychiatrists turned their attentions away from the value-laden theories of the English alienists and toward what they judged to be observational research. Prominent among this group was J. L. Koch (1891), who proposed that the label "moral insanity" be replaced by the term "psychopathic inferiority," under which he included "all mental irregularities, whether congenital or acquired, that influence a man in his personal life and cause him, even in the most favorable cases, to seem not fully in possession of normal mental capacity" (p. 67; our translation). The term "psychopathic," a generic label for all personality disorders until recent decades, was selected by Koch (1891) to signify his belief that a physical basis existed for these impairments. Thus, he stated: "They always remain psychopathic, in that they are caused by organic states and changes which are beyond the limits of physiological normality. They stem from a congenital or acquired inferiority of brain constitution" (p. 54; our translation). As Prichard had done, Koch included a wide group of conditions in his category of psychopathic inferiority, only a small portion of which would be considered within our current rendering of an antisocial or sociopathic syndrome. His subgroups of "psychopathic disposition" (*Zartheit*), noted by tension and high sensitivity; "psychopathic taint" (*Belastung*), seen clinically in those with peculiarities, egocentricities, and impulsive fury; and "psychopathic degeneration," manifested predominantly in borderline mental states, all rested on presumptive physical defects, none of which Koch admitted could be structurally or physiologically verified.

The concept of a "constitutionally inferior" type was introduced into the American psychiatric literature at the turn of the century by Adolf Meyer (1904), shortly after his arrival from Germany. Although he followed Koch's ideas in the main, Meyer sought to separate psychopathic cases from psychoneurotic disorders, both of which were grouped together in Koch's "psychopathic inferiority" classification. Meyer was convinced that the etiology of the neuroses was primarily psychogenic—that is, colored less by inherent physical defects or by "constitutional inferiorities." The line of distinction he drew between these groups remained clear and sharp for many years in American nosology. The label "inferiority," however, did not fare as well, since its deprecatory connotation was anathema to both the verbalized social values and the medical practices of the day. "Constitutional psychopathic state" and "psychopathic personality" evolved as the two popular American designations through the first half of the 20th century.

It is necessary to step back again in this review to bring into sharper focus the fact that for the first three decades of the 20th century, the label "psychopathic" conveyed nothing more than Koch's contention that the individual's personality was physically rooted or constitutional. Furthermore, the term "inferiority" implied nothing more, insofar as specific clinical characteristics were concerned, than the observation that these personalities deviated unfavorably from the norm. In time, the term took on a more specific cast, assuming the features connoted by the designation "moral insanity"—the historical precursor that Koch sought to escape. Recall that the meaning of the category *manie sans délire*, as originally formulated by Pinel, had nothing whatsoever to do with the value judgments ascribed to it by Prichard in his construction of "moral insanity." Similarly, Koch's effort to obviate the moral pejoratives in Prichard's conception was slowly undermined as his designation gradually evolved to mean quite the opposite of what he intended. This fascinating transmutation of the meaning of a diagnostic label is not unique in the history of clinical science. Moreover, to add further insult to the injury of having "psychopathy" so misconstrued, Koch's intent that a physical etiology for these syndromes be clearly affirmed was undone in later years when the designation was changed to "sociopathy," a means of signifying its now ostensible social origins. The shifting sands of our terminologies and theories in this field should give us good reason to question current formulations that appear to be throwbacks to earlier, discarded notions. Although the label "antisocial personality" may seem less pejorative than "constitutional psychopathic state" or "psychopathic inferiority," it does hark back to its ancestral fore-runner, "moral insanity."

A formal psychological construct representing the clinical features of domination and cruelty can be traced to the late 19th-century writings of Krafft-Ebing (1867/1935, 1882/1937). Drawing upon the letters and short stories of the Marquis de Sade—an 18th-century French nobleman and author whose novels extolled the administration of pain and sexual dominance, as well as the association of cruelty and humiliation with sexual pleasure—Krafft-Ebing (1882/1937) introduced the term "sadism," as well as its counterpart, "masochism." He defined masochism as "the experience of sexual, pleasur-able sensations (including orgasm) produced by acts of cruelty, bodily punishment, af-flicted on one's own person or when witnessed in others, be they animals or human be-ings" (p. 80). Krafft-Ebing wrote of an "innate desire to desire to humiliate and hurt" that was characteristic of all humans. He speculated that this sadistic force was stimulat-ed by the natural shyness or innate coyness of women (p. 82) and was especially trouble-some if the male was hypersexual. He noted: "Sexual emotion, if hyperaesthetic, might degenerate into a craving to inflict pain . . . under pathological conditions, man's active role of winning women may become an unlimited desire for subjugation" (1882/1937, p. 214). Krafft-Ebing believed that the only adequate explanation for the lustful quality seen in these acts was the involvement of the sexual drives. He reasoned that the roots of sadism lie in an exaggeration of normal male sexual impulses, of which aggressive ten-dencies are a natural component. However, he noted that if such impulses were to be found in a psychopathic individual, the likelihood of acting out these urges more broadly was greatly increased. Phrased differently, psychopathy, though oblique to the sadistic tendency, could act as a catalyst in the actualization of broad-based destructive urges.

In 1895, Schrenck-Notzing introduced the term "algolagnia" to describe the sado-masochistic phenomenon. The term comes from the Greek and translates roughly into "pain enjoyment." What was special about his proposal was the view that the pain expe-rienced was in effect pleasurable—an acquired synthesis that fused normally contrasting emotional or affective experiences. The term "algolagnia" did not become popular and was not revived until the work of Havelock Ellis (1898/1933). In contrast to his prede-cessors, who focused on cruelty and hostility, Ellis considered sadism as an expression of love. To him, "Sadism and masochism may be regarded as complementary emotional states; they cannot be regarded as opposed states. The sadist desires to inflict pain, but in some cases, if not in most, he desires it to be felt as love" (pp. 261–262).

The threads of this historical review return to the decades shortly before and after the turn of the century with the descriptions provided by Emil Kraepelin; the successive editions of his important work, *Psychiatrie: Ein Lehrbuch* (*Psychiatry: A Textbook*), re-flect the changing emphases given to the psychopathic syndrome. In the second edition of this major work (1887), Kraepelin identified the "morally insane" as suffering congenital defects in their ability to restrain the "reckless gratification of . . . immediate egotistical desires" (p. 281; our translation). The fifth edition, in 1896, referred to these conditions as "psychopathic states" for the first time, asserting that these constitutional disorders display themselves as lifelong morbid personalities. The next edition, published in 1899, referred to psychopathic states as one of several forms of degeneration, along with such syndromes as obsessions, impulsive insanity, and sexual perversions. Retaining the theme of degeneration in his seventh edition of 1903–1904, Kraepelin now referred to these states as "psychopathic personalities," by which he meant "those peculiar morbid forms of personality development which we have grounds for regarding as degenerative. The characteristic of degeneration is a lasting morbid reaction to the stresses of life" (p. 547; our translation).

In 1904, Kraepelin identified four kinds of persons who had features akin to what we speak of today as antisocial personalities. First, were the "morbid liars and swindlers" who were glib and charming, but lacking in inner morality and a sense of responsibility to others; they made frequent use of aliases, were inclined to be fraudulent con artists, and often accumulated heavy debts that were invariably unpaid. The second group included "criminals by impulse"—individuals who engaged in such crimes as arson, rape, and kleptomania, and were driven by an inability to control their urges; they rarely sought material gains for their criminal actions. The third type, referred to as "professional criminals," were neither impulsive nor undisciplined; in fact, they often appeared well mannered and socially appropriate, but were inwardly calculating, manipulative, and self-serving. The fourth type, the "morbid vagabonds," were strongly disposed to wander through life, never taking firm root, lacking both self-confidence and the ability to undertake adult responsibilities.

By the eighth edition of his work, the fourth volume of which was published in 1915, Kraepelin described psychopaths as deficient in either affect or volition. He separated them into two broad varieties: those of morbid disposition, consisting of obsessives, impulsives, and sexual deviants; and those exhibiting personality peculiarities. The latter group was differentiated into seven classes: the excitable (*Erregbaren*), the unstable (*Haltlosen*), the impulsive (*Triebmenschen*), the eccentric (*Verschobenen*), the liars and swindlers (*Luegner und Schwindler*), the antisocial (*Gesellschaftsfeinde*), and the quarrelsome (*Streitsuechtige*). Only the latter three possessed features similar to current notions of the antisocial. As noted previously, liars and swindlers were "naturally cheats and occasionally thieves"; sexual offenses were common to them, and they were "uncertain and capricious in everything." Quarrelsome personalities were "in constant trouble"; they always thought others were against them, and their judgment was "warped and unreliable" (our translations). Last, antisocial personalities, the explicit and prime forerunners of our contemporary nomenclature, were

> the enemies of society . . . characterized by a blunting of the moral elements. They are often destructive and threatening . . . [and] there is a lack of deep emotional reaction; and of sympathy and affection they have little. They are apt to have been troublesome in school, given to truancy and running away. Early thievery is common among them and they commit crimes of various kinds. (Partridge, 1930, pp. 88–89)

The details described by Kraepelin in the final edition of his monumental text are almost identical to the diagnostic criteria spelled out for the younger antisocial personality (i.e., the young person with conduct disorder) in the DSM. Were Kraepelin's views the final word? Apparently many of his contemporaries thought not.

In the late 19th century in Denmark, physiognomy evolved into craniography as used by Knud Pontoppidan. Pontoppidan (1895) described in detail the features of his patients—for example, detailed measures of the head of a young man with an abnormal personality, and the facial features of an "anatomically degenerated," eccentric man. These descriptions had a strong resemblance to the *Konstitutionsschema* of Kretschmer in his *Körperbau und Charakter* (1936), to be published several decades later. Pontoppidan (1895) also included in his *Psychiatriske Forelæsninger og Studier* (*Psychiatric Lectures and Studies*) several pathographs of "abnormal personalities." According to Pontoppidan, the prognosis for abnormal personality was just as poor as in other forms of degeneration (see below), but he stressed the importance of social events as precipitating factors. In his psychiatric lectures Pontoppidan did not specifically use the diagnosis of psychopathy, but gave a thorough description of different antisocial behaviors. In discussing different forms of "wanderlust" in abnormal personalitites, he wrote:

> When you hear nowadays about individuals who declare that they want to see the "whole wide world," these are undoubtedly certain pathological individuals: either melancholics (*melancholia errabunda*) or defective characters, who without any plan give in to an undefined feeling of discomfort, disharmonic mood, an instinctive drive to wander. (p. 95; our translation)

Back in 1857, the French psychiatrist M. Morel (had published an influential book on the theory of degeneration. Although the *folies héréditaires* constituted just one of several classes of mental disorders in Morel's nosology, the concept of the degeneration of families appealed to several later Danish psychiatrists, notably Pontoppidan and Fritz Lange. In his book *Slægter* (*Families*), Lange (1904) took Morel's concept of degeneration for granted. He stated that degeneration of a family might begin with a concussion, poisoning, abuse of alcohol or narcotics, malnutrition, general physical weakening, or epileptic seizures, or possibly even with "lack of mental freedon, low and mean thinking, brutality of the mind and lowness of the character. Often a small and insignificant deviation—an error by nature—will commence the inevitable process of disintegration of the mind and degeneration will be accomplished in just a generations" (p. 83; our translation). In earlier work, Lange (1883) had classified family dysfunction in concordance with Morel's "moral insanity," as the mildest form of the degenerative mental disorders. He was opposed to the general view of the morally insane as individuals who did evil for the sake of evil; instead, he perceived the morally insane person as a poor, deficient individual, with a faulty and poorly developed ability to reflect: "He is neither in the moment nor in the situation able to place himself freely and superiorly in a position of evaluation and judgment . . . and will never be able to acquire the solid sum of experience" (p. 159; our translation).

In 1894 Lange elaborated his ideas in *De vigtigste Sindssygdomsgrupper i Kort Omrids* (*A Brief Description of the Major Mental Disorders*). In his section on degenerative mental disorders, he described "insanity of puberty," "impulsive insanity," and "moral insanity." In Lange's view, individuals suffering from moral insanity were definitely carriers of a severe degenerative disposition. Although violent and criminal behavior were commonly seen, not all suffering from moral insanity would be in opposition to social norms and authorities. Lange also pointed out the periodical course of the disorder, with remissions and exacerbations, and note that "emotional abnormalities" (e.g., hypochondriasis, depressions, submanic excitations, rudimentary compulsions, and delusions) were fairly common. In his view, the prognosis for moral insanity, like that for other degenerative disorders, was poor: "Only the calm and disciplined atmosphere of the institution for the insane . . . can ease the condition and lead the patient into a more calm and smooth course" (p. 164; our translation).

CONCEPTIONS FROM WORLD WAR I TO THE 1940s

K. Birnbaum (1909), writing in Germany at the time of Kraepelin's later editions, was the first to suggest that the term "sociopathic" might be the most apt designation for the majority of these cases. To him, not all delinquents of the degenerative psychopathic type were either morally defective or constitutionally inclined to criminality. Birnbaum asserted that antisocial behavior only rarely stems from inherent immoral traits of character; rather, it reflects most often the operation of societal forces that make the more acceptable forms of behavior and adaptation difficult to acquire. This social conditioning thesis did not become a prominent alternative in psychiatric circles until the later 1920s, largely gaining serious consideration through the writings of Healy and Bronner (1926) and Partridge (1930) in the United States. In the interim decades, psychopathy was conceived internationally in the manner most explicitly stated in the British Mental Deficiency Act of 1913; still wedded to Prichard's conception of moral insanity developed some 80 years earlier, it was judged a constitutional defect that manifested "strong vicious or criminal propensities on which punishment has had little or no deterrent effect" (Prichard, 1835)

The prime theorist in post-World War I German psychiatry was Kurt Schneider, whose major work, *Die Psychopathischen Personlichkeiten* (*The Psychopathic Personalities*), went through many editions (the first appeared in 1923, the ninth in 1950). Schneider stressed the belief that many criminals were delinquent in youth and largely incorrigible. However, he stated that in addition to those who progressed into criminal activity, many of this type could also be found in society at large. Moreover, Schneider observed that many of these individuals were unusually successful in positions of either political or material power. Schneider anticipated a number of contemporary problems concerning these "psychopaths," and referred to the views of alienists who preceded him by many decades but who faced similar issues. He wrote

> that the term moral insanity was likely to be much used in forensic medicine and [it is] dramatically urged on all those concerned with the criminal law to watch out lest the pleas of moral insanity wrested the sword of justice from their hands.
>
> It does not seem to us proper in Court cases to put forward a pleas of diminished responsibility in such personalities simply because this may be the only way to get admission into institutional custody. . . . It seems to us a functional matter of principle that judgments on the matter of culpability should not rest on considerations of legalistic expediency. (1950/1958, pp. 131–132)

Notable also was Schneider's division between a more *passive* affectionless variety (more like what we call today the schizoid type) and the more *active* antisocial type. He described these "psychopathic" personalities as follows:

> We mean personalities with a marked emotional blunting mainly but not exclusively in relation to their fellows. Their character is a pitiless one and they lack capacity for shame, decency, remorse and conscience. They are ungracious, cold, surly, and brutal in crime. . . . The social moral code is known, understood but not felt and therefore [this] personality is indifferent to it. (1950/1958, p. 126)

Schneider (1923) likewise concluded that the aggressive and impulsive characteristics described by Kraepelin were found in a variety of different psychopathic personalities. His description of the "explosive psychopath" comes closest to our current thinking regarding a sadistic personality. However, like Kraepelin, he viewed the feature of hostile explosiveness as an unspecific type of reaction, an important hallmark of a subgroup of otherwise diverse personalities. He commented that Kraepelin's notion of an "irritable personality" failed to reflect the "outgoing nature of the discharge." Schneider also referred to the work of Baer (1893), who spoke of the "impulsively violent type," but he rejected Baer's notion that criminal conduct was necessarily associated with explosiveness. A quote from Schneider describing his conception of these individuals may be informative:

They tend to make an unholy row for the slightest of reasons or they will hit out without warning, reactions which have been well labeled short-circuit reactions. . . .

There are many links with other psychopathic personalities—the blustering hyperthyme, the morose or paranoid depressive and the labile personality. . . . These and associated drunkenness often cause explosive personalities to be hospitalised. In addition, as is well known in states of violent affect, consciousness becomes blurred and at times these explosive excitements may develop into psychogenic twilight states.

These "hotheads" often present a social problem in their disturbed marriages, [in] their incapacity to care for their children properly and in their criminal outbreaks. (1950/1958, p. 110)

In his 1929 book on the heredity of mental disorders and on endeavors for racial improvement, the Danish psychiatrist August Wimmer estimated that 2,000 out of 9,500 patients admitted to his psychiatric ward during 1920–1927 had the diagnosis "constitutional psychopathy." He criticized the classification of psychopathy into cyclothymic, schizoid, and epileptoid psychopathy for being too simple, and included diagnoses of hysterical, explosive, instable, sexually perverted, asocial, and antisocial psychopathy. Dismissing the degeneration theory that had previously been popular in Denmark, Wimmer described psychopathy as being inherited according to Mendel's laws of heredity, although aspects of Lambroso's theories of the "born criminal" or "born delinquent" (who's inclination to crime was supposed to be an atavistic return to prehistoric human types) were also evident in Wimmer's work. Like many other Danish psychiatrists at that time, he advocated for racial improvements through prohibition of marriage, forced abortion, and sterilization. He wrote:

[The aim of these measures is] to prevent the birth of individuals who, due to hereditary taint such as insanity, are exposed to disease and mental abnormity, and [are condemmed] to live a more or less unhappy or pitiful life to little happiness and benefit for themselves. . . . Sterilization of certain insane persons and psychopaths, especially those who are moral degenerates or overt criminals; of certain debilitated individuals and epileptics; of certain chronic alcoholics; and maybe of other individuals with hereditary neurological and other physical disorders—this is a thought that deserves a high degree of open-minded discussion. (1929, pp. 81, 87; our translation)

In a 1974 review of the previous 50 years of research and theory on the "elusive category" of the psychopathic personality, the well-known British psychiatrist Sir Aubrey Lewis commented as follows:

These reveal a preoccupation with the nosological status of the concept . . . its forensic implications, its subdivisions, limits [and] the propriety of identifying psychopathic personality with antisocial behavior. The effect of reading solid blocks of literature is disheartening; there is so much fine-spun theorizing, repetitive argument, and therapeutic gloom. (pp. 137–138)

Nearly 70 years ago the same issues were in the forefront—notably, whether the psychopathic personality was or was not synonymous with overt antisocial behavior. Partridge's (1930) detailed review of the conceptions of the psychopath then prevalent began as follows:

Ideas relating to psychopathic personality are scattered widely throughout psychiatric and criminological works. Much that has been written is somewhat incidental to the study of delinquency as a whole; some relate to the various types of mental disorders in which deviations of personality are involved. (p. 53)

In addressing the issue of whether psychopathy and antisocial behavior are one and the same, Partridge wrote:

> There is comparatively little attention paid to [psychopathological] personality deviations which, though distinct, are not expressed in antisocial behavior.
>   There is an assumption that at least some types of chronic misbehavior are the visible extensions, so to speak, of deep [personality] ledges. (1930, p. 75)

In reporting on the covariations found between diagnosed psychopathy and recorded histories of criminal or delinquent behavior, he noted:

> The proportionate importance of the psychopath in the production of the total of delinquency has been given some attention. Some, we have seen, find a very large proportion of psychopathic personality in criminal groups or delinquents in general, some seem to find only a small one. (1930, p. 93)

In the conclusion of his analysis, Partridge wondered whether the tendency of nosologists to focus on antisocial behaviors, at the expense of the deeper personality structure and its nonsociopathic variants, simply reflects the fact that these behaviors are "obvious." He wrote:

> One reason why there has arisen confusion about the so-called psychopaths is that, in these cases, the personality deviations become *apparent* at an early age in a distinct form. . . . The main difference . . . [is] that the sociopathic forms are more objective, merely in their manifestations or adjustment patterns—at least more fully revealed. (1930, pp. 98–99)

As the novel concepts and theories of psychoanalysis took root in the 1920s, preliminary and scattered notions concerning the "character" of psychopaths began to be published by clinicians oriented by this school of thought. Most were prompted to this task by an intriguing paper of Freud's (1916/1925), entitled "Some Character-Types Met With in Psycho-Analytic Work"; here Freud described "peculiar acts" that appear out of character for an individual. In exposing the dynamics of a subgroup of these cases, referred to as "criminality from a sense of guilt," Freud wrote:

> Analytic work then afforded the surprising conclusion that such deeds are done precisely *because* they are forbidden, and because by carrying them out the doer enjoys a sense of mental relief. He suffered an oppressive feeling of guilt, of which he did not know the origin, and after he had committed a misdeed the oppression was mitigated. (1916/1925, p. 342)

This paper served as the impetus for a number of subsequent clinical reports by other analysts. Among these authors were August Aichorn, Wilhelm Reich, Karl Abraham, and Franz Alexander.

Perhaps the first attempt at an analytically based examination of delinquent behavior was made by Aichorn (1925). Stressing the observation that surface controls imposed by treatment are rarely sufficient to withstand the unconscious forces of the patient, Aichorn wrote:

> When we look at dissocial behavior, or symptoms of delinquency, as distinct from delinquency, we see the same relation as that between the symptoms of a disease and the dis-

ease itself. This parallel enables us to regard truancy, vagrancy, stealing, and the like as symptoms of delinquency, just as fever, inflammation, and pain are symptoms of disease. If the physician limits himself to clearing up symptoms, he does not necessarily cure the disease. The possibility of a new illness may remain; new symptoms may replace the old. . . . When a psychic process is denied expression and the psychic energies determining it remain undischarged, a new path of discharge will be found along the line of least resistance, and a new form of delinquency will result. (pp. 38–39)

Particularly sensitive to variations in the background of delinquent behaviors, Aichorn asserted that either extreme indulgence and overvaluation or excessive harshness and depredation can set the groundwork for a child's renunciation of social values. Viewing these as defects of the superego, Aichorn noted that these children are not disposed to internalize parental norms and will be inclined to seek immediate gratifications through impulsive behaviors.

Writing also in 1925, Abraham (1925/1927) articulated his view of the development of antisocials in his analysis of "an impostor." In the following brief quote, he would appear to join Aichorn in recognizing conditions that give rise to narcissistic traits on the one hand, and antisocial traits on the other:

We often come across the results of early pampering, which intensifies the child's demands for love to an extent which can never be adequately satisfied (narcissistic). Among delinquents (antisocial) we are more likely to come across a different fate of the libido in early childhood. It is the absence of love, comparable to psychological undernourishment, which provides the pre-condition for the establishment of dissocial traits. An excess of hatred and fury is generated which, first directed against a small circle of persons, is later directed against society as a whole. (p. 304)

In what he first termed "instinct-ridden characters" and later called the "impulsive character," Reich (1925) asserted that the "superego" of these personalities fails to gain expression under the ego's unyielding controls, and subsequently cannot adequately restrain the id's seduction when faced with instinctual temptations, hence resulting in the free expression of impulses. Contrasting the impulsive character with what he and others termed the "neurotic character" (essentially the compulsive personality), Reich wrote:

As we differentiated between the neurotic symptom and the neurotic character, we must now separate compulsive acts, in the sense of uncontrollable compulsive deeds, from the general behavior of the impulsive character. Whereas the former appears as a circumscribed foreign body within an otherwise ordered personality and is condemned by it, the . . . impulsive individual is . . . only rarely recognized as pathological. . . . The actions of the impulsive individual never appear as senseless as do those actions of the compulsion neurotic and they are rationalized to a much greater degree. (pp. 251–252; our translation)

In commenting on papers presented by more traditional psychiatrists, Coriat (1927), an American psychoanalyst, described the "constitutional psychopathic" as an antisocial character who is fixated at infantile levels, has unresolved Oedipal conflicts, and has never learned to replace the ego ideals of childhood with the ego ideals of society. Partridge (1927), employing psychoanalytic concepts, perceived the demands of the psychopath as stemming from unfulfilled oral needs.

The leading British theorist of the 1930s, D. K. Henderson (1939), allied himself with Partridge's basic conclusions but felt that a useful distinction could be drawn among three subtypes: (1) the predominantly aggressive, (2) the predominantly passive or inadequate, and (3) the predominantly creative. Original at the time was Henderson's suggestion that these individuals feel themselves to be outcasts, rarely understood by others, and stigmatized and scapegoated unjustly. Because of his prominence in British circles, certain of Henderson's views gained quick attention and stirred much debate. Notable among the issues he raised was his inclusion of a passive/inadequate type, considered by most of his psychiatric colleagues to be more properly diagnosed as neurotic; even more controversial was his proposal of a "creative psychopath," a brilliant, aggressively active, but erratic and moody person, exemplified by such individuals as Lawrence of Arabia. As elsewhere, controversy raged not over matters of empirical substance or theoretical logic, but as a consequence of terminological confusion and issues of syndromal scope.

In 1939, the Danish theorist Hjalmar Helweg published his *Den Retslige Psykiatri i Kort Omrids* (*Forensic Psychiatry*), in which he related his classification of psychopathy to those of such authors as Kraepelin and Prichard. He included both personality abnormalies and symptoms such as kleptomania and pyromania in his definition of constitutional psychopathy which he described as "a constitutional abnormality in the sense that it is inborn or acquired so early that it determines the development of the character" (p. 127; our translation).

As late as 1948, the discussion of constitutional psychopathy was still open in Scandinavia. Regnér, from Sweden, claimed that many so-called constitutional psychopaths probably in fact suffered from fixed misadaptations to the environment during childhood, based on a constitution that in itself should not be called psychopathic. Stürup (1948) spoke of individuals who due to unlucky circumstances in their surroundings ended up being detained as psychopaths, while Helweg (1948) warned against the perception that psychopathy was something a person attained, writing: "A constitutional psychopath is something that you are. To a degree, you have certain more or less inappropriate ways of reacting that manifest themselves by influences that the normal person would resist" (p. 112; our translation)

Important epidemiological research was also carried out in Denmark during this period. Strömgren (1938) found the prevalence of psychopathy to be 1.17% in a census study of the population of the island of Bornholm, and found the 10-year prevalence of psychopathy to be 4.61% in a rural county of Denmark. Fremming (1947) viewed psychopathy as constitutional, due either to genetic influence or in some cases to lesions of the central nervous system sustained prenatally, perinatally, or during infancy. In an epidemiological study, he diagnosed 122 psychopaths (65 males and 57 females), resulting in a prevalence of 3%. Most of the male psychopaths were socially unstable, while the female psychopaths more often were mood-labile. Fremming (1948) also stated that eugenic measures (sterilization) should be recommended, or even mandatory, in cases of psychopathy.

To return to the psychoanalysts, it was not until the work of Franz Alexander (1923/1930, 1930, 1935), that the first assessment of psychopathy and criminal behavior was undertaken from a thoroughgoing psychoanalytic perspective. In Alexander's book *Psychoanalysis of the Total Personality* (1923/1930), he distinguished several levels of personality psychopathology; a similar thesis was presented in a 1930 paper, "The Neurotic Character." Four levels of pathology were proposed: neuroses, neurotic character, psychosis, and true criminality. They were arranged in this sequence to reflect diminishing levels of the ego's ability to restrain unconscious impulses, the neurotic displaying the greatest capacity and the criminal the least. The neurotic character was believed by Alexander to be the underlying personality of psychopaths. As he saw it, neurotic characters act out their conflicts rather than transforming them intrapsychically. He wrote:

They live out their impulses, many of their tendencies are asocial and foreign to the ego, and yet they cannot be considered true criminals. It *is* precisely because one part of such an individual's personality continues to sit in judgment upon the other . . . that his total personality is easily differentiated from the more homogeneous, unified and antisocial personality of the criminal. The singular and only apparently irrational drive to self-destruction met with in such people indicates rather definitely the existence of inner self-condemnation.

Their conduct arises from unconscious motives which are not directly accessible to their conscious personality. . . . Admonition, encouragement or punishment coming from the environment is as useless as his own resolution, "I am beginning a new life tomorrow."

A large proportion of such individuals, neurotically driven by unconscious motives, now to commit a transgression, then to seek punishment, sooner or later fall foul of the law. . . .

[Their] lives are full of dramatic action . . . something is always happening, as if they were literally driven by the demonic compulsion. . . . Here is where the adventurers belong whose manifold activities give expression to an underlying revolt against public authority. They always manage to be punished unjustifiably from their highly subjective point of view. (1923/1930, pp. 11–15)

Lest the analytic model of the psychopath be viewed as naive, it may be helpful to quote at some length from Alexander's later study, *The Roots of Crime* (1935). The quotation indicates his thorough awareness that antisocial behaviors reflect an inextricable interplay among intrapsychic processes, social forces, and constitutional dispositions.

The chief difference between neurosis and criminal behavior is that in the neurosis the emotional conflict results in symbolic gratifications of unsatisfied urges, whereas in criminal behavior it leads to overt misdeeds. Those needs which are frustrated by economic conditions . . . cannot be satisfied as easily by the symbolic gratifications of fantasy as can the emotional tensions of love and hate. The emotional conflicts and deprivations of childhood, the resentments of parents and siblings, find a powerful ally in resentment against the social situation, and this combined emotional tension seeks a realistic expression in criminal acts and cannot be relieved by mere fantasy products that are exhibited in neurotic symptoms.

We found that criminality in some cases is a direct expression of a protest against certain deprivations, a reaction of spite against certain members of the family, the expression of jealousy, envy, hostile competition, all of which are strengthened by early sufferings or the lack of love and support on the part of adults. But, we must add, intense hostilities in such cases frequently create strong guilt feelings, which in turn lead to an unconscious need for punishment. . . .

Certain unacquired bases of the instinctive life (constitution), apart from the environmental influences, must be partly responsible for the fact that similar emotional conflicts may, depending on the make-up of the individual, result either in criminality or in neurosis. The introverted nature of the neurotic, his readiness to content himself with gratifications in fantasy and to renounce real satisfaction, seems to be founded on some constitutional factor. And, on the other hand, certain individuals are characterized by a more robust, expansive instinctual life which contents itself only with outgoing behavior. (1935, pp. 278–279)

The last paragraph is of special interest, in that it presages in almost exact detail the views of later, vigorously antianalytic critics such as Eysenck (see Chapter 3, this volume). Alexander was the first prominent psychoanalyst to devote a significant portion of his attention to antisocial behavior. Subsequent, similarly inclined writers (Bartemeier,

1930; Wittels, 1937; Karpman, 1941; Fenichel, 1945; Friedlander, 1945; Greenacre, 1945; Allen, 1950; Levy, 1951) also sought a rationale for the development of these behaviors with reference to intrapsychic processes and early parent–child relations.

A formulation similar to that presented by Alexander was set forth during this period by L. Bartemeier (1930):

> The neurotic character is more bold and daring than the neurotic personality. He does not allow society to intimidate him into mere fantasy but dramatizes his primitive impulses in real action. . . . He maintains a social spite against civilization and its restrictions. The life of such a person . . . is made up of socially ruthless indulgences and subsequent insistences upon punishment. These people only commit crime with emotional conflict while true criminals experience no such stress. (p. 516)

Wittels (1937) differentiated neurotic psychopaths from "simple" psychopaths; the former, fixated ostensibly at the phallic stage, fear their bisexual impulses, whereas the latter directly indulge their bisexuality. Karpman (1941) also distinguished two variants of psychopathy, the "idiopathic" and the "symptomatic." The former were judged to be the true psychopaths in that they are constitutionally guiltless, insensitive to the feelings of others, and disposed to acquisitiveness and aggression; moreover, no psychogenic history appears to account for their antisocial inclination. Karpman's symptomatic group was composed of neurotics "parading" as psychopaths; they were seen as akin to Alexander's neurotic characters and were not considered true psychopaths because their actions were thought to stem from unresolved unconscious difficulties. Levy (1951) proposed another subdivision to represent what he saw as clearly different forms of early experience. Termed by Levy the "deprived" psychopath and the "indulged" psychopath, they are similar in conception to Millon's (1969) distinction between "antisocial" and "narcissistic" sociopaths, the former being a product of a harsh upbringing, and the latter a result of parental overvaluation.

Following the line of thinking first presented by Reich, Fenichel (1945), a renowned psychoanalytic scholar, sought to clarify the distinction between the antisocial's impulsiveness and the neurotic's compulsions. He, too, emphasized the failure of the superego to be effective in its efforts to control the impulses of the id. In that same year, Friedlander (1945), another psychoanalytic theorist, stressed the fact that the character structure of psychopathic youngsters remains under the dominance of the pleasure principle, unguided by an adequately developed superego. A thoughtful analysis of delinquent acting out by Eissler (1949) portrayed their behaviors as designed to restore feelings of omnipotence that have been severely injured in childhood. Having suffered these injustices or deprivations, these youngsters feel deeply betrayed, and hence become mistrustful, narcissistic, self-inflating, material-seeking, and addicted to risk and excitement.

A nonanalytic, yet incisive and thorough, clinical characterization of the antisocial personality was provided by H. Cleckley in his book *The Mask of Sanity*, first published in 1941. Attempting to clarify problematic terminologies, and seeking to counter the trend of including ever more diverse disorders under the rubric of "psychopathy," Cleckley proposed replacing the term with the label "semantic dementia" to signify what he viewed as the syndrome's prime feature—the tendency to say one thing and to do another. More important than his proposal of a new nomenclature, which attracted little following, was the clarity of Cleckley's description of the psychopath's primary traits: guiltlessness, incapacity for object love, impulsivity, emotional shallowness, superficial social charm, and an inability to profit from experience. No less significant was Cleckley's assertion that these personalities are found not only in prisons but in society's most respected roles and settings. Cleckley (1941) illustrated this thesis with several examples of "successful" businessmen, scientists, physicians, and psychiatrists. He wrote:

> In these personalities . . . a very deep seated disorder often exists. The true difference between them and the psychopaths who continually go to jails or to psychiatric hospitals is that they keep up a far better and more consistent outward appearance of being normal.
>
> The chief difference . . . lies perhaps in whether the mask or facade of psychobiologic health is extended into superficial material success. (pp. 198–199)

MID-20TH-CENTURY CONCEPTIONS

A passage concerning the evolving history of psychopathy, written by Cameron and Margaret in 1951, is as apt today as it was then:

> The residue of this tortuous and perplexing historical development is unfortunately still with us. For example, the popular labels for social deviation now . . . seem merely to be a restatement of the outmoded category of "constitutional psychopathic inferiority." They do not refer to new concepts. Moreover, the accounts of psychopathic behavior given by present-day behavior pathologists are still likely to be accusations rather than descriptions. The evaluative attitudes of nineteenth-century psychiatry continue to tinge our modern classifications; and the psychopath stands accused of crime, of exploitation and of inability to profit from corrective procedures.
>
> The background of "psychopathic personality" in nineteenth-century psychiatry, although relevant as past history, need not dictate the present and future development of the concept. Nor can we afford to perpetuate the implication that social deviation is morally bad. We cannot ignore the effects of parental emphasis, of others' reactions and of self-reactions in training a growing child to socially deviant behavior. (pp. 190–191)

This plea that we progress beyond the perspective of moral and social judgments as a basis for clinical concepts is as relevant today as it was when written.

Among the notable developments at midcentury were the pioneering treatment efforts of psychiatrist Georg K. Stürup at the Herstedvester Detention Center in Denmark. Stürup was appointed the head of this institution in 1942 and kept his post for over 30 years. In his 1951 book *Krogede Skæbner* (*Crooked Fates*), Stürup gave a brief history of the institution, and in his 1968 book *Treating the "Untreatable,"* he described his work as a psychiatrist and the treatment implemented at Herstedvester. The aim of this treatment was rehabilitation through strengthening of self-respect and responsibility; Stürup's principle was not to make treatment mandatory, but to motivate the convicts and make treatment available when they were motivated. Psychotherapy was described as "integrated individualized group therapy," but the treatment program also made use of the milieu of the institution. (In addition, psychopharmacological and operative treatment was used, including castration of sexual offenders.) Stürup concluded the 1968 book with this statement: "The prime condition must be, that anybody participating in the treatment of personality disorders [including psychopathy] in advance believes that he can obtain something by his effort" (p. 247). The work of Stürup is described in more detail by Hansen in Chapter 28 of this volume.

A social/interpersonal model paralleling psychiatric concepts of the antisocial personality was formulated most clearly in the work of Leary (1957). In what he referred to as "adjustment through rebellion," Leary outlined a common motivation for several personality disorders. The subgroup he referred to as "distrustful" comes closest to what we consider today to be the typical aims and behavior of the antisocial. In his insightful portrayal, Leary wrote:

> Pain and discomfort are traditionally associated with alienation from others, but for these subjects this discomfort is less than the anxiety involved in trustful, tender feelings. For the person who has experienced past rejections or humiliations there are certain comforts and rewards in developing a rebellious protection. The essence of this security operation is a malevolent rejection of conventionality. Trust in others, cooperation, agreeability, and affiliation seem to involve a certain loss of individuality. Giving or sharing or trusting requires a sacrifice of pure narcissism and some relinquishing of the critical function. The rebellious adjustment provides a feeling of difference and uniqueness which is most rewarding to some individuals. [They experience] a rebellious freedom, a retaliatory pleasure in rejecting the conventional, a delight in challenging the taboos, commitments, and expectations which are generally connected with a durable affiliative relationship. (p. 270)

The discussion now turns to the often overlooked but important empirical work of research psychologists. For example, Eysenck (1957, 1967) offered evidence for the thesis that psychopaths possess an inherited temperamental disposition to extraversion that inclines them to acquire antisocial behaviors. According to the learning theory espoused by Eysenck, extraverts condition slowly and therefore, in contrast to normals, are able to acquire the values and inhibitions of their social group to only a minimal degree. Eysenck's thesis leaves many details of psychopathic development unclear, and laboratory evidence for its central assumptions is scanty at best. (However, see Eysenck, Chapter 3, this volume, for further discussion.)

Whereas Eysenck's theory rests on the assumption of innate constitutional dispositions, other learning theorists who have studied aggressive sociopathic behavior couch their interpretations solely in terms of vicarious learning and reinforcement. Thus, Bandura and Walters (1959), following a social learning model that is fairly similar in content to the views of many analysts, gave primary attention to the role of parent–child interactions. For example, hostile parents in some cases may serve as models that the child imitates and uses as a guide to establish antisocial relationships with others. In other cases, parents may mete out rewards and punishments in a manner that produces a style of superficial affability cloaking fundamentally devious attitudes. A series of extensive studies by Quay and his associates (Quay, 1964; Quay & Werry, 1979) focused on delinquent populations and used multivariate statistical techniques to identify distinct clusters or types. Four characteristic patterns were obtained repeatedly across a variety of population samples: conduct disorder, anxiety–withdrawal, immaturity, and socialized–aggressive disorder.

An empirical approach of special note is the work of Robins (1966) and her colleagues, which attempted to unravel the juvenile antecedents of adult psychopathy and antisocial behavior. What is noteworthy in these findings is the close correspondence they show to the behaviors specified as characteristic of psychopathic personalities 50 years earlier by Kraepelin. What made these data so historically important was that they comprised, in almost every detail, the diagnostic criteria promulgated in the DSM-III definition of antisocial personality disorder (American Psychiatric Association, 1980). Despite the history of alternative models and theories available for consideration, the DSM-

III Task Force voted to base its diagnostic guidelines on this single, albeit well-designed, follow-up study of delinquency cases referred to one child guidance clinic in a large midwestern city.

LATE 20TH-CENTURY CONCEPTIONS

A psychoanalytic theorist of the 1970s, B. Bursten (1972), proposed that the essential features of classical sociopaths are their need to bolster their self-esteem by being contemptuous of others and "needing to put something over them." Referring to this pattern as "the manipulative personality," Bursten wrote:

> This conceptualization begins to throw some light on why the sociopath seems not to learn from experience; we are looking at the wrong experience. Frequently these people are quite bright and do learn. They are quite adept at assessing social situations. Indeed it is their very sharpness and their ability to size up a situation which inspires simultaneously our admiration and our anger.
>
> They have well learned from experience what to expect in certain social situations. Nevertheless, the psychopath's behavior has baffled us because we have misunderstood the main purpose of his behavior. (1972, p. 319)

Of particular note also is Bursten's effort to counter the moral and judgmental implications of the "antisocial" label by substituting what he viewed as a value-free designation. He phrased his proposal as follows:

> By describing such people as manipulative personalities, we get further away from the mixture of psychiatric concepts and concepts involving offenses against society. The manipulation is an interpersonal event resting in great measure on the internal dynamics of the manipulative personality; whether he comes into conflict with society is now immaterial as far as the diagnostic category is concerned.
>
> What the shift from antisocial personality to manipulative personality can add is the further separation of the personality configuration from the social conflict. For indeed, there are many people who are internally driven to manipulate and who do not get into serious conflict with society. People with similar character structures may manifest their dynamic processes in a variety of ways [depending on] the options for expression which society offers them.
>
> The category . . . includes some successful businessmen, politicians, administrators . . . as well as those who come into open conflict with society. (1972, p. 320)

Bursten's specific proposals for the manipulative personality are highly debatable, but his desire to protect personality diagnoses from value judgments and his assertion that these personalities are to be found in all sectors of social life are both relevant and appropriate.

Drawing inspiration from the psychoanalytic framework, but more in keeping with the ideas formulated by Karen Horney, Erich Fromm (1973) contributed his own views concerning the role of sadism from both an individual and a cultural perspective. Fromm placed primary emphasis on the role of historical and societal influence in both the development and manifestation of sadism. As he noted: "Social groups tend to reinforce all those characteristic elements that correspond to [sadistic cruelties], while the opposite elements become dormant" (p. 333). Fromm recognized the specific conditions in which specific behaviors manifest themselves in stating the following:

There is no simple relation between environment and character. This is because the individual character is determined by such individual factors as constitutionally given dispositions, idiosyncrasies of family life, exceptional events in a person's life . . . environmental factors . . . also . . . religious or philosophical–moral traditions, small town and big cities. (pp. 296–297)

In what Fromm spoke of as "exploitative–sadistic" character, he found a "passion" to exploit and control. In such people, the sadistic impulse is constantly active, waiting only for proper situations and a fitting rationalization in order to be acted out. Like Horney, Fromm took exception to the association between sexuality and sadistic behaviors. He wrote:

Sadism (and masochism) as sexual perversions constitute only a fraction of the vast amount of sadism in which no sexual behavior is involved. Nonsexual sadistic behavior, aiming at the infliction of *physical* pain up to the extreme of death, has as its object a powerless being, whether man or animal.

Mental cruelty, the wish to humiliate and to hurt another person's feelings, is probably even more widespread than physical sadism. This type of sadistic attack is much safer for the sadist; after all, no physical force but "only" words have been used. On the other hand, the psychic pain can be as intense or even more so than the physical.

I propose that the core of sadism, common to all its manifestations, is *the passion to have absolute and unrestricted control over a living being.* To force someone to endure pain or humiliation without being able to defend himself is one of the manifestations of absolute control, but is by no means the only one. . . . Most sadism is malevolent. Complete control over another human being means crippling him, choking him, thwarting him. (pp. 283, 289; emphasis in original)

Although adhering to the fundamentals of analytic thought, as well as being appreciative of Fromm's concepts of sadism and masochism, Shapiro (1981) has taken exception to the view that sadism may not have a degrading ambition as a central element. Shapiro writes:

The aims of sadism are, as I said, not only to make the victim suffer but especially to humiliate or degrade him, to make him feel helpless or powerless, to "put him in his place" or "show him who's boss." In the mildest case, the sadist wishes to make his victim feel ridiculous and small; in the most extreme case, to abuse him in such a way as to destroy his self-respect, break his will, and make him give in. These are aggressive aims of a special kind.

This view accounts for many aspects of sadism: for example, the important fact that the sadistic person regularly chooses his victims from those who are subordinate to him, the comparatively powerless, those he can control. . . . There are aspects of sadism, of cruelty, that, it seems to me, cannot plausibly be explained by any degree of interest in mere control of another individual. An aggressive satisfaction—a satisfaction in the other's suffering as such, perhaps even a hatred—is an essential and undeniable part of sadism. (p. 103)

Avery (1977) has used the sadistic–masochistic pairing in a different way from those of his predecessors, albeit one that is still anchored to the analytic metapsychology. To Avery, these relationships are conducted under strict rules: a mutual trading of blows; the provocation of punishment; and the introduction of guilt, in which both partners know precisely what the "bursting point" is of their object ties. Seeking to understand the logic that keeps the pairing bonded, Avery writes:

> The thesis that now emerges is that dissolution is imminent and, should it occur, the weaker, needier partner will suffer the greater loss.
>
> As in a poker game, it costs something to challenge this thesis. Submission to the threat means one has accepted the subordinate, more painful, position. However, the pain is borne within the boundaries of a relationship. To challenge or call the threatener is to possibly win—that is, to become dominant if the threat is not substantiated. Should the threat of a decision materialize, however, one has risked the ultimate risk—separation. (p. 102)

In addition to developing his views in a manner consistent with his psychoanalytic perspective (see above), Shapiro (1965) has enriched his theory with an important cognitive dimension. Although not addressing the antisocial personality directly, Shapiro elaborates the major characteristics of what he terms "impulsive styles"; many of these styles reflect central characteristics of what we term the antisocial in our current nomenclature. Shapiro describes the cognitive elements of these individuals as follows:

> In many respects, the psychopath is the very model of the impulsive style. He exhibits in a thorough and pervasive way what for others is only a direction or tendency. He acts on a whim, his aim is the quick, concrete gain, and his interests and talents are in ways and means. (p. 157)

> Lack of planning is only one feature of a style of cognition and thinking in which active concentration, capacity for abstraction and generalization, and reflectiveness in general are all impaired. (p. 147)

> If we say that the impulsive person's attention does not search actively and analytically, we may add that his attention is quite easily and completely captured; he sees what strikes him, and what strikes him is not only the starting point of a cognitive integrative process, but also, substantially, it is its conclusion. (pp. 150–151)

Another model of contemporary thought has sought to anchor "psychopathic" behaviors to developmental learning and psychological dynamics. Proposed by Millon (1969) in his formulation of the active–independent personality, the following descriptions and criteria served as the initial working draft in 1975 for what was ultimately labeled by the DSM-III Task Force as the "antisocial personality" (American Psychiatric Association, 1980). The abstract but clinically oriented draft criteria (Millon, 1975) may prove useful to the reader:

> This pattern is typified by a self-assertive, temperamentally hostile and socially forceful and intimidating manner. There is pride in self-reliance[,] unsentimentality and hard-boiled competitive values. Malicious personal tendencies are projected outward, precipitating frequent outbursts of explosive anger. Vindictive gratification is obtained by humiliating and dominating others. A rash willingness to risk harm is notable as is a fearlessness in the face of threats and punitive action. Frank antisocial behaviors (e.g., truancy, non-traffic arrests, frequent fighting) are common among adolescent and post-adolescent aggressive personalities, as well as in certain socioeconomic subpopulations. However, the majority of these personalities do not exhibit flagrant antisocial behaviors, finding a sanctioned niche in conventional roles. (p. 7)

The eventual DSM-III criteria for antisocial personality disorder, and their successors in DSM-II-R and DSM-IV, are discussed and debated in several other chapters of this book. (Toch, in Chapter 9, outlines the DSM-IV criteria in some detail.)

Otto Kernberg (1970, 1984, 1989), as he has done with many other personality disorders, presents a thoroughgoing analysis and reconceptualization of the antisocial personality. Integrating the views of many of his psychoanalytic predecessors, Kernberg recommends a hierarchical differentiation among individuals of an antisocial nature, aligning them from the most to the least severely disordered. He sees all antisocial personalities as possessing the fundamental features of the narcissistic personality, plus possessing unusual pathology in their sense of morality—that is, their superego functions. He gives special attention to the syndrome he terms "malignant narcissism," a personality pattern characterized by a combination of (1) a narcissistic personality disorder; (2) antisocial behavior; (3) ego-syntonic aggression or sadism directed either toward others or toward oneself, the latter producing a perverse sense of triumph in self-mutilation or suicide; and (4) a strong paranoid orientation.

Kernberg (1989) describes the typical symptoms of antisocial personality disorder as follows:

> These patients typically present a narcissistic personality disorder. The typical symptoms of the narcissistic personalities are, in the area of *pathological self-love*: excessive self-reference and self-centeredness; grandiosity and the derived characteristics of exhibitionism, an attitude of superiority, recklessness, and overambitiousness; overdependency on admiration; emotional shallowness.... Regarding the area of *pathological object relations*, these patients' predominant symptoms are inordinate envy (both conscious and unconscious); devaluation of others as a defense against envy; exploitativeness reflected in greediness, appropriation of others' ideas or property, and entitlement.... The *basic ego state* of these patients is characterized by a chronic sense of emptiness, evidence of an incapacity to learn, a sense of aloneness, stimulus hunger, and a diffuse sense of meaninglessness of life.
>
> In addition, all of these patients present some degree of *superego pathology*. Ordinary superego pathology of narcissistic personalities includes the incapacity to experience mournful, self-reflective sadness; the presence of severe mood swings; [and] a predominance of "shame" as contrasted to "guilt" in their intrapsychic regulation of social behavior. (pp. 559–560)

Still another contemporary analyst of note is Michael Stone (1993), who has explored not merely the "annals of crime" as these relate to personality, but the biographies of rather notorious and violent individuals, which he has drawn upon to examine his notions of psychopathy. In reviewing his examination of these individuals, Stone writes:

> Forensic specialists mention several attributes, personality traits among them, noted with unusual frequency in persons who murder. Rebelliousness and aggressivity are common, as are mendacity, entitlement, and social isolation. Murderers are typically beset by surpluses of hatred and impulsivity. These attributes, especially when fueled by alcohol, conduce to *ragefulness*, characterized by episodic outbursts of violent behavior directed against others. (p. 454)

In describing the many forms in which "callousness" is expressed, Stone (1993) points out numerous character types who do not seem especially amenable to therapeutic efforts. Among these highly destructive persons are the following:

> Despotic bosses whose abrasiveness and insensitivity make torture chambers of the workplace are known all too well....
>
> Certain explosive tempered, violent persons stop short of murder, but come to our attention (or to the attention of the authorities) because of pathological jealousy and wife-battering....

Power-mad narcissistic leaders constitute a truly untreatable group. . . . Mendacious psychopaths who cheat and betray, relying on their charm and acting skill to "con" and exploit others, may be said, as is true of power-mad leaders, to inhabit the realm of evil. . . .

The realm of evil is defined by the presence of malice; the active desire to harm others . . . enough to bring about, possibly, the psychological death of the victim. (pp. 451–452)

Aaron Beck and his colleagues, approaching the subject of the antisocial personality from their particular cognitive orientation, do not modify the conventional view of the characteristics of the disorder, but do address the dysfunctional beliefs that shape many aspects of the antisocial's behavior. Beck, Freeman, and Associates (1990) write:

These personalities view themselves as loners, autonomous, and strong. Some of them see themselves as having been abused and mistreated by society, and therefore justify victimizing others because they believe that they have been victimized.

The *core* beliefs are "I need to look out for myself," "I need to be the aggressor or I will be the victim." The antisocial personality also believes that "Other people are patsies or wimps," or "Others are exploitative, and therefore I'm entitled to exploit them back." This person believes that he or she is entitled to break rules—rules are arbitrary and designed to protect the "haves" against the "have nots." (pp. 48–49)

Antisocial patients' automatic thoughts and reactions are frequently distorted by self-serving beliefs that emphasize immediate, personal satisfactions and minimize future consequences. The underlying belief that they are always right makes it unlikely that they will question their actions. Patients may vary in the degree of trust or mistrust they have in others, but they are unlikely to seek guidance or advice on any particular course of action. . . . Their behavior tends to be objectionable and even infuriating to others. Instead of evaluating the potential helpfulness of such input, [antisocial] patients tend to dismiss input from others as irrelevant to their purposes. In addition, antisocial distortions tend to show a loss of future time perspective. (p. 154)

Continuing the interpersonal tradition, Benjamin (1974, 1993) has furnished an extended series of analysis of numerous personality disorders. In her characterization of the interpersonal dimensions of the antisocial personality, she notes the following as core characteristics:

There is a pattern of inappropriate and unmodulated desire to control others, implemented in a detached manner. There is a strong need to be independent, to resist being controlled by others, who are usually held in contempt. There is a willingness to use untamed aggression to back up the need for control or independence. The [antisocial personality] usually presents in a friendly, sociable manner, but that friendliness is always accompanied by a baseline position of detachment. He or she doesn't care what happens to self or others. (1993, p. 203)

The interpersonal analysis of [the antisocial personality] suggests that the "criminality" depicted by the DSM can be characterized as inordinate autonomy taking, addiction to control, and lack of attachment to self or others. These dimensions also describe the "antisocial" lawyers, doctors, and politicians not diagnosable by the DSM. Like the criminals described by the diagnostic manual, individuals within these higher-socioeconomic-status groups misuse their positions in the service of control for control's sake. They have no regard for the impact of their actions on other people. (1993, p. 209)

A rather dispassionate approach to the characterization of the antisocial personality may be achieved best by methods that seek to coordinate the traits of each syndrome as objectively as possible. Thus, the five-factor approach espoused by Costa and Widiger (1994) achieves this goal by virtue of a statistical rather than a clinical and hence subjective manner. In their summary of the traits found to underlie antisocial personality disorder, they write:

> The diagnostic criteria essentially provide a set of behavioral examples of excessively low conscientiousness and low agreeableness. . . . Persons who are low in conscientiousness tend to be aimless, unreliable, lax, negligent, and hedonistic; the most extreme variants of these tendencies describe the indulgent and irresponsible antisocial individual. The antisocial person, however, is also manipulative, exploitative, vengeful, criminal, and ruthless, which are aspects of antagonism (particularly the facets of excessively low straightforwardness, altruism, compliance, and tendermindedness). (p. 45)

The work of Hare and his associates (e.g., Hare, 1986) has drawn upon Cleckley's formulation of the "psychopathic personality," reconceptualizing Cleckley's descriptive texts in the form of the Psychopathy Checklist (PCL) and its revision, the PCL-R. Two correlated factors have emerged from this work. The first factor appears to represent a narcissistic personality variant of the psychopathic pattern, including tendencies toward selfishness, egocentricity, superficial charm, and a lack of remorse and empathy. The second factor appears more directly related to those with an overtly antisocial lifestyle; it includes early periods of delinquency, low frustration tolerance, frequent substance abuse, a parasitic lifestyle, impulsivity, and frequent illegal or criminal behaviors.

Hare's work appears to support the ideas of both Kernberg and Millon concerning the two major features of the psychopathic lifestyle. It represents Millon's view that psychopathy has at its core a deficiency in concerns for others, with a *passive* variant in the narcissist's self-focus and an *active* variant as seen in the self-focus of the antisocial. Similarly, these data reflect Kernberg's recognition that the antisocial and the narcissist share essential and major features in common, despite aspects of dissimilarity in their overt behaviors (notably the prominent lack of conscience or morality in the antisocial).

Reference to the biogenic origins of the antisocial personality has been made by many investigators seeking to uncover the underlying biophysical correlates of the disorder. However equivocal these results may be, biological theorists continue to explore its potential subtsrates (see Siever, Chapter 14, this volume). Siever and his associates (Siever & Davis, 1991; Siever, Klar, & Coccaro, 1985) have formulated the following thesis regarding the antisocial syndrome. Siever et al. (1985) write:

> In antisocial personality disorder . . . the impulsive characteristics take the form of repetitive behaviors that conflict with social constraints, for example, stealing, lying, and fighting behaviors that are normally suppressed or inhibited in the service of societal rules. Clinically, these behaviors are often conceptualized in terms of a failure of social learning or internalization of societal constraints in the course of development—that is, a faulty superego or capacity for experiencing guilt. A number of studies suggest that such individuals may demonstrate lowered cortical arousal and more disinhibited motoric responses to a variety of stimuli. Thus, patients with antisocial personality disorder may be considered to be more likely to act than to reflect prior to their taking action, so that internalization of societally sanctioned controls may be more problematic. (p. 43)

A similar notion has been formulated by Cloninger (1987) in his efforts to deduce the underlying neurobiological elements of this personality. He writes:

Antisocial personality is defined here as the personality variant characterized by the basic response characteristics of high novelty seeking, low harm avoidance, and low reward dependence. This combination is associated with second-order traits of impulsive–aggressive, oppositional, and opportunistic behavior. This description is essentially identical to the traditional concept of the "primary psychopath" described by Cleckley and others. (p. 584)

A final noteworthy development in recent decades has been epidemiological research that has utilized the uniquely reliable government registers in Denmark as data sources for studying psychopathy and criminality. Most of these studies have been or are being carried out (some of the work is still ongoing) as collaborative Danish–American projects sponsored by the U.S. National Institute of Mental Health. Denmark is a country that is particularly well suited to the conduct of population studies, both because of the reliability of the government records and because the population is ethnically homogeneous, with little migration or mobility. Space limitations prohibit a full review of this research, but some of the most notable studies are mentioned here.

Fini Schulsinger (1972) addressed the issue of psychopathy in an adoption research design. From a sample of 5,483 Copenhagen adoptees, he identified 57 adoptees hospitalized with the principal diagnosis of psychopathy. He matched them with 57 control nonpsychopathic adoptees and examined the frequency of hospital admissions among their biological and adoptive relatives. Twice as many biological relatives as adoptive relatives of psychopathic adoptees suffered themselves from psychopathy. No major environmental factors could be demonstrated.

Mednick and collaborators (Hutchings & Mednick, 1977; Hodgins, Mednick, Brennan, Schulsinger, & Engberg, 1996) have conducted several studies concerning predictors and genetics of criminal behavior and the association between psychopathy and crime. These studies were commenced in the mid-1970s and are still continuing. The studies resulted from merging data from several Danish government data sources: the Central Personal Register, the National Register of Psychiatric Admissions, the Adoption Register, and the National Criminal Register. The studies of criminality in the adoption sample suggested both a genetic component and an environmental component in serious crime. In the Hutchings and Mednick (1977) study, a sample of 14,427 male and female adoptees from all adoptions in Denmark between 1924 and 1947 was entered into a cross-fostering analysis; the final sample consisted of 4,065 adopted males. The highest proportion of adoptees with one criminal conviction was found in the group with both biological and adoptive criminal parents. Criminality in both an adoptive and a biological parent increased the risk of registered criminality, but the biological parent seemed more important, since the next highest proportion of males with one conviction was found in the group in which only the biological parents were criminal. Naturally, crime is a sociological concept, and an important part of variance in criminal behavior is of course determined by socioeconomic factors. The genetic component is probably related to several personality traits, such as lack of cognitive skills, impulsivity, sensation seeking, aggressiveness, and hyperactivity, and will covary with other conduct problems. Several Danish long-term follow-up studies of high-risk populations have underlined the predictive power of these risk factors for a broader spectrum of mental disorders, including psychopathy and substance abuse. (See Knop, Jensen, & Mortensen, Chapter 20, this volume, for a detailed discussion of the comorbidity of alcoholism and psychopathy.)

In a recent very large Danish birth cohort study of 358,180 individuals born between 1944 and 1947 Hodgins et al. (1996) screened the subjects at the age of 43 for any admission to psychiatric wards within Denmark and for arrests and convictions. The relative risk of conviction was calculated by comparing each diagnostic group to nondisordered groups never admitted to a psychiatric ward. The relative risk for psychopathic females was 6.45, and that for male psychopaths was 5.27. The absolute percentage of female subjects registered for at least one crime *and* admitted to a psychiatric ward with the principal diagnosis of psychopathy was 13.6%, and that for male subjects was 32.4%.

The lifetime risk for psychopathy is difficult to calculate, as psychopaths are reluctant to seek treatment. In the Danish birth cohort study described above (Hodgins et al., 1996), the lifetime risk up to the age of 43 for an admission to psychiatric wards with a principal diagnosis of psychopathy was 2.2% for females and 1.9% for males. Simonsen and Mellergård (1988) examined the distribution and change of prevalence rates among patients with personality disorders admitted to Danish psychiatric hospitals from 1975 to 1985, using data from the National Register of Psychiatric Admissions. The percentage of cases diagnosed as pseudoneurotic or pseudopsychopathic borderline personalities increased from 5% to 20%, whereas the percentage of cases diagnosed with classical psychopathic personality disorder decreased from 22% to 7%. The overall percentage of admissions with a personality disorder remained the same through this 10-year period. The same trend was shown for the first-time-admitted personality disorder patients. According to the authors, it appeared that those who had previously been diagnosed as psychopathic deviants were now being labeled as borderlines. This was most strikingly seen in men. Women presently diagnosed as borderlines would likely have been called psychopathic, immature, or hysterical 10 years earlier.

CONCLUSION

Psychopathy was the first personality disorder to be recognized in psychiatry. The concept has a long historical and clinical tradition, and in the last decade a growing body of research has supported its validity, from both a psychodynamic and a neurobiological point of view. Danish psychiatry's long tradition of psychopathy research and treatment affirm the need to continue the concept. However, psychologists and psychiatrists must not simply condemn these patients, but must seek to understand them. To quote the distinguished Danish psychiatrist Georg Stürup (1951): "Don't forget these people. They have no one, yet they are people. They are desperately lacking and in terrible pain. Those who understand this are so rare; you must not turn your back on them" (p. 212; our translation).

REFERENCES

Abraham, K. (1927). Character-formation on the genital level of the libido. In K. Abraham, *Selected papers on psychoanalysis*. London: Hogarth Press. (Original work published 1925)

Aichorn, A. (1925). *Wayward youth*. New York: Viking.

Alexander, F. (1930). *Psychoanalysis of the total personality*. New York: Nervous and Mental Disease Publications. (Original work published 1923)

Alexander, F. (1930). The neurotic character. *International Journal of Psycho-Analysis, 11,* 282–313.

Alexander, F. (1935). *The roots of crime*. New York: Knopf.

Allen, F. (1950). The psychopathic delinquent child. *American Journal of Orthopsychiatry, 20,* 223–265.

American Psychiatric Association. (1980). *Diagnostic and statistical manual of mental disorders* (3rd ed.). Washington, DC: Author.

Avery, N. (1977). Sadomasochism: A defense against object loss. *Psychoanalytic Review, 64,* 101–109.

Baer, A. (1893). *Anthropological study of the delinquent.* Leipzig, Germany: Barth.

Bandura, A., & Walters, R. H. (1959). *Adolescent aggression.* New York: Ronald Press.

Bartemeier, L. H. (1930). The neurotic character as a new psychoanalytic concept. *American Journal of Orthopsychiatry, 1, 512–519.*

Beck, A. T., Freeman, A., & Associates. (1990). *Cognitive therapy of personality disorders.* New York: Guilford Press.

Benjamin, L. S. (1974). Structural analysis of social behavior. *Psychological Review, 81,* 392–425.

Benjamin, L. S. (1993). *Interpersonal diagnosis and treatment of personality disorders.* New York: Guilford Press.

Birnbaum, K. (1909). *Die psychopathischen Verbrecker.* Leipzig: Thieme.

Bursten, B. (1972).The manipulative personality. *Archives of General Psychiatry, 6,* 318–321.

Cameron, N., & Margaret, A. (1951). *Behavior pathology.* Boston: Houghton Mifflin.

Cleckley, H. (1941). *The mask of sanity.* St. Louis, MO: C. V. Mosby.

Cloninger, C. R. (1987). A systematic method for clinical description and classification of personality variants. *Archives of General Psychiatry, 44,* 573–588.

Coriat, R. C. (1927). Discussion of the "constitutional psychopathic inferior." *American Journal of Psychiatry, 6,* 686–689.

Costa, P. T., & Widiger, T. (Eds.). (1994). *Personality disorders and the five-factor model of personality.* Washington, DC: American Psychological Association.

Eissler, K. R. (Ed.). (1949). *Searchlights on delinquency: Essays in honor of August Aichorn.* New York: International Universities Press.

Ellis, H. (1933). Auto-erotism: A psychological study. *Alienist and Neurologist, 19,* 260–299. (Original work published 1898)

Eysenck, H. J. (1957). *The dynamics of anxiety and hysteria.* New York: Praeger.

Eysenck, H. J. (1967). *The biological basis of personality.* Springfield, IL: Charles C Thomas.

Fenichel, 0. (1945). *The psychoanalytic theory of neurosis.* New York: Norton.

Fremming, K. H. (1947). *Sygdomsrisikoen for sindslidelser og andre abnormtilstande.* Copenhagen: Munksgård.

Fremming, K. H. (1948). *Arvelige faktorers betydning for sindslidelæsernes opståen.* Menneske og Miljø, 2, 63–69.

Freud, S. (1925). Some character-types met with in psycho-analytic work (E. C. Mayne, Trans.). In *Collected papers* (Vol. 4, pp. 318–344). London: Hogarth Press. (Original work published 1916)

Friedlander, K. (1945). Formation of the antisocial character. *Psychoanalytic Study of the Child, 1,* 189–203.

Fromm, E.(1973). *The anatomy of human destructiveness.* New York: Holt, Rinehart & Winston.

Gadelius, B. (1933). *Human mentality in the light of psychiatric experience.* Copenhagen: Levin & Munksgaard.

Gouster, M. (1878). Moral insanity. *Review of Scientific Medicine, 38,* 115–131.

Greenacre, P. (1945). Conscience in the psychopath. *American Journal of Orthopsychiatry, 14,* 495–509.

Hare, R. D. (1986). *The Hare Psychopathy Checklist.* Toronto: Multi-Health Systems.

Healy, W., & Bronner, A. (1926). *Delinquents and Criminals: Their making and unmaking.* New York: Macmillan.

Helweg, H. (1939). *Den retslige psykiatri i kort omrids.* Copenhagen: Hagerup.

Helweg, H. (1948). Psykopathibegrebets uundvaerlighed. *Menneske og Miljø, 3–4,* 105–112.

Henderson, D. K. (1939). *Psychopathic states.* London: Chapman & Hall.

Hodgins, S., Mednick, S. A., Brennan, P. A., Schulsinger, F., & Engberg, M. (1996). Mental disorders and crime: Evidence from a Danish birth cohort. *Archives of General Psychiatry, 53,* 489–496.

Hutchings, B., & Mednick, S. A. (1977). Criminality in adoptees and their adoptive and biological parents: A pilot study. In S. A. Mednick & K. O. Christiansen (Eds.), *Biosocial bases of criminal behavior.* New York: Gardner Press.

Karpman, B. (1941). On the need for separating psychopathy into two distinct clinical types: Symptomatic and idiopathic. *Journal of Clinical Psychopathology, 3,* 112–137.

Kernberg, O. F. (1970). Factors in the psychoanalytuc therapy of narcissistic patients. *Journal of the American Psychoanalytic Association, 18,* 51–85.

Kemberg, O. F. (1984). *Severe personality disorders.* New Haven, CT: Yale University Press.

Kemberg, P. (1989). Narcissistic personality disorder in childhood. *Psychiatric Clinics of North America, 12,* 671–294.

Koch, J. L. (1891). *Die psychopathischen Minderwertigkeiten.* Ravensburg, Germany: Maier.

Kraepelin, E. (1887). *Psychiatrie: Ein Lehrbuch* (2nd ed.). Leipzig: Abel.

Kraepelin, E. (1896). *Psychiatrie: Ein Lehrbuch* (5th ed.). Leipzig: Barth.

Kraepelin, E. (1899). *Psychiatrie: Ein Lehrbuch* (6th ed.). Leipzig: Barth.

Kraepelin, E. (1903–1904). *Psychiatrie: Ein Lehrbuch* (7th ed.). Leipzig: Barth.

Kraepelin, E. (1915). *Psychiatrie: Ein Lehrbuch* (8th ed., Vol. 4). Leipzig: Barth.

Krafft-Ebing, R. (1935). *Moral insanity: Its recognition and forensic assessment.* (Original work published 1867)

Krafft-Ebing, R. (1937). *Psychopathia sexualis.* New York: Physicians and Surgeons Books. (Original work published 1882)

Kretschmer, E. (1936). *Körperbau und Charakter* (11th ed.). Berlin: Springer-Verlag.

Lange, F. (1883). *Om arvelighedens indflydelse i sindssygdommene.* Copenhagen: Gyldendal.

Lange, F. (1894). *De vigtigste sygdomsgrupper kort omrids.* Copenhagen: Gyldendal.

Lange, F. (1904). *Slægter.* Copenhagen: Gyldendal.

Leary, T. (1957). *Interpersonal diagnosis of personality.* New York: Ronald Press.

Lewis, A. (1974). Psychopathic personality: A most elusive category. *Psychological Medicine, 4,* 133–140.

Levy, D. M. (1951). Psychopathic behavior in infants and children. *American Journal of Orthopsychiatry, 21,* 223–272.

Lombroso, C. (1872–1887). *L'uomo deinquente.* Turin, Italy: Bocca.

Maudsley, H. (1874). *Responsibility in mental disease.* London: King.

Meyer, A. (1904). A review of recent problems of psychiatry. In A. Church & F. Peterson, *Nervous and mental diseases* (4th ed.). Baltimore: Williams & Wilkins.

Millon, T. (1969). *Modern psychopathology: A biosocial, approach to maladaptive learning functioning.* Philadelphia: W. B. Saunders.

Millon, T. (1975). *Proposals for the Personality Disorder section.* Unpublished DSM-III draft description and criteria.

Morel, M. (1857). *Traité de dégénérescences physiques, intellectuelles et morales de l'espèce humaine.* Paris: Ballière.

Otto, C. (1825). *Phraenologien eller Galls og Spurzheims hjerne—og organlaere.* Copenhagen: Brummer.

Otto, C. (1827a). Oversigt over de året 1826 i tugt-rasp og forbedringshuset behandlede syge. *Hygaea, 1,* 305–357.

Otto, C. (1827b). Phrenologiens Studium and Betragtningerorer Dølgeattraa. *Tidsskrift for Phrenologien, 1,* 1–612.

Partridge, G. E. (1927). A study of 50 cases of psyschopathic personality. *American Journal of Psychiatry, 7,* 953–974.

Partridge, G. E. (1930). Current conceptions of psychopathic personality. *American Journal of Psychiatry, 10,* 53–99.

Pinel, P. (1962). *A treatise on insanity* (D. Davis, Trans.). New York: Hafner. (Original work published 1801)

Pontoppidan, K. (1895). *Psychiatriske forelaesninger og studier II.* Copenhagen: T. Lind.

Prichard, J. C. (1835). *A treatise on insanity and other disorders affecting the mind.* London: Sherwood, Gilbert & Piper.

Quay, H. C. (1964). Personality dimensions in delinquent males as inferred from the factor analysis of behavior ratings. *Journal of Research in Crime and Delinquency, 1,* 33–37.

Quay, H. C., & Werry, J. S. (Eds.). (1979). *Psychopathological disorders* (2nd ed.). New York: Wiley.

Reich, W. (1925). *Der Triebhafie Charakter.* Leipzig: Intenationaler Psychoanalytischer Verlag.

Robins, L. (1966). *Defiant children grown up.* Baltimore: Williams & Wilkins.

Rush, B. (1812). *Medical inquiries and observations upon the diseases of the mind.* Philadelphia: Kimber & Richardson.

Schack, S. (1858). *Physiognomiske studier.* Copenhagen: Wøldike.

Schneider, K. (1923). *Die psychopathischen personlichkeiten.* Vienna: Deuticke.

Schneider, K. (1958). *Psychopathic personalities* (9th ed., M. Hamilton, Trans.). London: Cassell. (Original work published 1950)

Schrenk-Notzing, A. Von. (1895). *Hypnotismus.* Leipzig: Vogel.

Schulsinger, F. (1972). Psychopathy: Heredity and environment. *International Journal of Mental Health, 1,* 199–206.

Selmer, H. (1841). *Om psykiatriens tilstand i Denmark.* Copenhagen: Reitzel.

Selmer, H. (1846). *Almindelige grundsætninger om dårevæsnets indretning.* Copenhagen: Reitzel.

Shapiro, D. (1965). *Neurotic styles.* New York: Basic Books.

Shapiro, D. (1981). *Autonomy and rigid character.* New York: Basic Books.

Siever, L. J., & Davis, K. L. (1991). A psychobiological perspective on the personality disorders. *American Journal of Psychiatry, 148,* 1647–1658.

Siever, L. J., Klar, H., & Coccaro, E. (1985). Biological response styles: Clinical implications. In L. J. Siever & H. Klar (Eds.), *Psychobiological substrates of personality* (pp. 38–66). Washington, DC: American Psychiatric Press.

Simonsen, E., & Mellergård, M. (1988). Trends in the use of the borderline diagnosis in Denmark from 1975 to 1985. *Journal of Personality Disorders, 2*(2), 102–108.

Stone, M. H. (1993). *Abnormalities of personality.* New York: Norton.

Strömgren, E. (1938). *Beitrage zur psychiatrischen erblehre.* Unpublished doctoral dissertation, Copenhagen.

Stürup, G. K. (1948). Sexualforbrydelse og kastration. *Menneske og Miljo, 3,* 112–118.

Stürup, G. K. (1951). *Krogede skæbner.* Copenhagen: Munksgaard.

Stürup, G. K. (1968). *Treating the "untreatable."* Baltimore: John Hopkins University Press.

Tuke, D. H. (1892). *Dictionary of psychological medicine.* Philadelphia: Blakiston.

Widiger, T., Corbitt, E. M., & Millon, T. (1991). Antisocial peronality disorders. In A. Tasman & M. Riba (Eds.), *Review of psychiatry* (Vol. 11). Washington, DC: American Psychiatric Press.

Wimmer, A. (1929). *Sindssygedommenes arvegang og raceforbaedrende bestraebelser.* Copenhagen: Levin & Munksgaard.

Wittels, F. (1937). The criminal psychopath in the psychoanalytic system. *Psychoanalytic Review, 24,* 276–283.

2

Psychopathy: An Elusive Concept with Moral Overtones

JOHN GUNN

I have always been fascinated by the challenge of using psychiatric techniques to treat difficult, antisocial people. From my very first months in psychiatry, I began voluntary work in a community setting with antisocial, aggressive "down-and-outs." Groups for heavy drinkers; accommodation for people who were rejected by hostels and other drop-in centers and day care facilities for the most unlikeable of ex-prisoners—all claimed my attention.

Later, I became more focused on people who are more seriously antisocial, whether they have committed sexual assault, have engaged in other forms of violence, or have caused psychological distress to others. This led to an interest in the associations between mental state (especially delusional phenomena) and antisocial behavior. However, my primary interest has always rested with those who are not obviously deluded or hallucinated, but who other people can see are "not quite right in the head"—who are in some way behaving neurotically, compulsively, or impulsively, and who have little or no insight into their behavior.

In all my work, I do not use the noun "psychopath," the adjective "psychopathic," or the phrase "psychopathic disorder." In my opinion, these terms serve to confuse and mislead. At times the disease concept of "psychopathic disorder" has seemed attractive. It puts the most despised of mentally disordered people squarely into a medical framework. Yet the term has been dropped from the major classifications. Perhaps the concept is a bit like that of the "privy," the "water closet," the "lavatory," the "toilet," or the "restroom": If we change the name, it will not seem so horrid and embarrassing.

REIFICATION

A more fundamental problem is that whereas the privy really exists and can be visited, measured, and even painted, psychopathic disorder does not exist. So often, diseases are conceptualized as real things that exist inside their hosts. Yet diseases do not exist in the way in which patients exist, or in the way in which a bacterium exists. The equating of abstract concepts with real objects is called "reification."

In his book *The Mismeasure of Man,* Gould (1981) took pains to illustrate the way in which reification has led us to conflate a series of cognitive skills into a single concept of "intelligence" and then to regard this shorthand symbol as a thing in itself, which can be measured, studied, and used to divide people into categories. "Intelligence" is in fact a descriptive abstract concept that we impose on ourselves and others as a shorthand way of describing a wide range of our brain characteristics that we believe are correlated. We are familiar with the ways in which intelligence is actually measured by testing people, often against the clock, in a variety of cognitive, visual, and other language tasks. We are always intrigued when individuals do well in one so-called subtest but not in another, but yet we still end up with a global concept and a number. Admittedly this number has its uses (although those uses may be more limited than is sometimes supposed), but what the number does not have is physical properties that would enable it to be identified and studied in any structural sense.

Diseases do not exist, either. For example, "tuberculosis" does not exist. The tubercle bacillus exists, damaged lungs exist, damaged bones exist, and people who suffer damaged lungs and damaged bones exist; "tuberculosis" is an imposed abstraction that makes conversation flow more easily, but is a poor basis for scientific inquiry. The conquest of the scourge created by the tubercle bacillus depended upon a study of the causative agent and its life cycle, the study of the damage it causes to tissue, the symptoms to which damaged tissues give rise, the study of the way in which the causative agent is transferred from one individual to another, and the study of mechanisms that make one individual more susceptible to damage than another.

Does it matter if we continue to think of "tuberculosis" as a thing in itself, as a structure? Not a lot, perhaps, because the pathology related to it is well understood, and treatment is not likely to be impaired by this philosophical error. Nevertheless, thinking of diseases as entities that invade or take hold of people tends to lead to the kind of medicine patients often complain about. They notice when a doctor is more interested in some abstraction he or she calls a "disease" than in them and their suffering. Moreover, they may have a point, because a mistaken conceptual approach can lead to a stereotyped approach to treatment that ignores or misses the important variations among patients.

Reification matters more in psychiatry, because pathology in most psychiatric conditions is ill understood, and the conceptual analogy is further from actuality than in other branches of medicine. If we think of "tuberculosis" as a real thing that invades somebody, we are reasonably close to a working understanding, because the tubercle bacillus is real and does invade. If we think of "melancholia" in the same terms, we are miles away from the mark: There is no invader, and we have only the sketchiest understanding of the neurophysiological mechanisms of the disease. It may even be that there are several pathways to the symptoms we tend to put together and call "melancholia."

PSYCHOPATHIC DISORDER

Things get worse as we move further into the depths of psychiatric uncertainty. We have no understanding of the pathological mechanisms involved in "psychopathic disorder." Worse still, a close look at the abstract concept tells us that we are also entering a moral discourse. "Psychopathic" is almost synonymous with "bad"—a powerful subjective concept that is unhelpful in medical science. Patients may be harder to treat if they are called "psychopaths" or any other name that is synonymous with "badness" and that invites rejection. "Oh he's just a psychopath!" means "I don't like him; I regard him as a bad guy." It is perfectly possible to treat good and bad people in a similar fashion, but it is very difficult to do so. In medicine, the morality of a patient's symptoms or behavior ought to be irrelevant.

In 1974, the eminent British psychiatrist Sir Aubrey Lewis wrote a paper entitled "Psychopathic personality: A Most Elusive Category." The synopsis of his paper tells us that

> for 150 years the diagnostic concept at first called "moral insanity" has been troubling psychiatric nosologists. Initially emphasis was laid on the affective disturbance in this condition, which was unaccompanied by intellectual impairment. Then its conformity to the idea of degenerative process became prominent. At various times its relation to epilepsy, hereditary disease, vice, and crime, has held the stage. Latterly [i.e., in 1974], little advantage has been taken of the information provided about personality by the investigations of psychologists. (p. 133)

Lewis was making the point that all the notable writers of psychiatry have toyed with the term "psychopathic disorder" and come to no profound conclusions. He ended thus:

> The conclusion of the whole matter is somewhat gloomy. The diagnostic groupings of psychiatry seldom have sharp and definite limits. Some are worse than others in this respect. Worst of all is psychopathic personality, within its wavering confines. Its outline will not be firm until much more is known about its genetics, psychopathology, and neuropathology. (p. 139)

All kinds of diagnostic classifications and interesting diseases were evoked by the best thinkers of the 19th century, who noted signs and symptoms, and clustered these together into syndromes that they hoped might have some meaning. There were, for example, a number of different kinds of anemia, based on different symptoms such as skin color, breathlessness, and the like. However, the pathology underlying "anemia," which in itself is simply a descriptive term, was not understood until the physiology, the biochemistry, and above all the pathology of blood were understood. Once the pathology was clear, then signs and symptoms, despite being of great importance to the patient and providing him or her with entrance into the world of medicine, actually became less important from a diagnostic and therapeutic perspective. The doctor needed to know—and was now able to tell—whether an anemic patient's symptoms were due to iron deficiency or vitamin B12 deficiency, for example. The pathology of these conditions is different, and each is treatable with the right method.

In itself, the abstract tag "anemia" did not get science very far; knowledge of the underlying cell structure and its composition was needed. In modern medicine, we begin with pathology and we move to mechanisms. My concern is that the elusive concept of "psychopathic disorder" will not help us do that. It will impede us.

MORAL DEFECTS, UNTREATABILITY, AND EVIL BRAINS

"Psychopathic" literally means "psychically damaged," and the term was introduced into 19th-century Germany to cover all forms of psychopathology. It was later narrowed to refer to psychic anomalies that were not mental diseases, and Schneider (1950/1958) followed Kraepelin (1915/1921) in describing a typology of psychopathic personalities. It is of some interest that Schneider explicitly excluded antisocial behavior from the criteria for abnormal personality. Psychopathic personalities were those abnormal personalities who caused suffering to themselves or to others. This classification was never widely adopted in the United Kingdom, where the influence of Prichard's (1835) notion of "moral insanity" became prominent. He defined this as "a morbid perversion of natural feelings, affections, inclinations, temper, habits, moral dispositions, and natural impulses, without any remarkable disorder or defect of the intellect or knowing and reasoning faculties, and particularly without any insane illusion or hallucination." This definition eventually led to the "moral imbeciles" of the English Mental Deficiency Act of 1913, and the "moral defects" of the Mental Deficiency Act of 1927 (Gunn, 1993).

I contended there that this moral excursion away from the more straightforward clinical approach adopted in the original German literature, although understandable and, in the beginning, quite open, has created extra difficulties in this field over and above the problems inherent in any so-called "personality disorder." These moral considerations have led to a remarkable British curiosity: the "untreatable psychopath." In all the textbooks of medicine, surgery, pediatrics, gynecology, psychiatry, and neurology combined, there are hundreds and hundreds of labels for human conditions that doctors are interested in. Some are said to be more amenable to remedy than others, and some are so destructive that they go on relentlessly dragging the patient down in spite of modern treatments, but nowhere in any of these books is there a suggestion that a doctor's care and concern should be any less for the more serious and the more lethal conditions than for those that will clear up with treatment. In English law, however, there is the most remarkable exception to this otherwise laudable medical approach. A clause in the Mental Health Act 1983 states that on occasions psychopathic disorder may be "untreatable," and therefore that individuals with this disorder may be excluded from some of the benefits available to other patients. Now this "untreatability" only comes into play when compulsory hospitalization is being considered, but, surely it is a distinct oddity to enshrine in law a distinction between patients who can be given all the benefits of a health service and those who cannot, based on a highly subjective "treatability" criterion.

How has this come about? The term "psychopathic disorder," a largely moral term, is a trigger for rejection. Patients labeled in this way are excluded from all sorts of arrangements and are often dealt with via punitive rather than therapeutic responses. It is even the case that patients with other diagnoses (e.g., schizophrenia) may come to be labeled "psychopathic" when their behavior becomes particularly truculent, aggressive, or in some way antisocial. In such cases we are sometimes told that the patients have a "dual diagnosis." In these situations the label "psychopathic" is not usually being applied to assist with the understanding of the patients' psychopathology, or to provide some new physiological hypothesis for the patients' problems. Rather, it is simply used as a mechanism to reject these patients, who, we are told, would fit into the system if it were not for their antisocial behavior.

It is of passing interest that the term has not always been used in this pejorative manner by all observers. Scott (1963) defined a "psychopath" as "one whose persistently antisocial or asocial behavior cannot be primarily attributed to mental subnormality or psychosis, and stimulates society to treat him" (p. 2). Even this apparent swimming against the tide was, however, not all it seemed, for later in his career Scott (1970) argued that psychopathic patients should be treated in prisons, not hospitals.

These days, the Hare Psychopathy Checklist—Revised (Hare, 1991) is commonly used to identify people as psychopaths. On this scale individuals have to be rated for such characteristics as glibness, superficial charm, a grandiose sense of self-worth, a need for stimulation, a proneness to boredom, pathological lying, cunning, manipulative behavior, lack of remorse, shallow affect, callousness, a lack of empathy, a parasitic lifestyle, poor behavioral control, promiscuity, lack of realistic long-term goals, impulsivity, irresponsibility, a failure to accept responsibility, and criminal versatility, among others. All these characteristics are heavily loaded with evaluation. A specially trained rater who applies 15 of these concepts to a patient also calls the patient a "psychopath"; most other people would call this patient a "really bad person." The rater is probably also saying that he or she does not like the patient, and if the rater is a clinician, there is a good chance that he or she will add, "And I do not want this person in my clinic." In England, there is also a good chance that the therapist will declare the object of all this invective "untreatable."

Now, of course, many of the people who score highly on the Hare scale have done terrible things, and they may go on doing terrible things. It is hard to like them, and the Hare scale's description may be, at least in part, an apt one. From both the scientific and the therapeutic perspective, however, it would be more helpful if we could describe unpleasant patients in more neutral terms. The value-laden language makes the treatment task even more difficult than it is to begin with. The scale has a second problem: In seeking to identify the devil in the machine, and viewing "psychopathy" as a real, invading monster, the clinical scientist is led away from understanding the patient's problems. It is possible that grandiosity, impulsivity, and promiscuity are highly correlated. If so, they should be represented by one measure, but if they are not, then they are characteristics that are each worth studying in their own right. For example, grandiosity could be due to a neurotransmission error, impulsivity to a structural brain lesion, and promiscuity to training and education.

At one time, I would have said that we all understand that "badness" is not a real thing. I would have suggested that it is relatively easy to see that when we use this term, when we simplify the language, we are simply pointing the finger and describing someone along the most powerful semantic dimension—that of "good" and "bad." I had to change my mind about this at the beginning of 1996, however, because of a startling editorial ("Pandora and the Problem of Evil," 1996) published in the *Lancet*. It suggested that evil will be soon discovered to be a lesion in the brain somewhere! This editorial actually stated that "to deny the possible existence of evil is as scientifically arrogant as claiming that no new phylum of living things could be discovered" (p. 1). The research to discover this thing called "evil," we were told, will be done on the preserved brains of those afflicted. In this way, "evil" will become classifiable and may even prove reversible!

THE WAY FORWARD

The important issue is not whether to label a particular kind of offender as "bad" or "mad," or even whether he or she fulfills some criteria for a personal or legal definition of "psychopathic disorder." What is necessary is for the clinician to understand the range of problems in the patient who comes or is sent to treatment because of the distress and disability of being, for example, too aggressive or too impulsive to be acceptable to society.

As noted above, Lewis said that in 1974 "little advantage has been taken of the information provided about personality by the investigations of psychologists" (p. 133). Although this is less true than it was, it is still true to a large extent. It is probably also true that the conceptual trap of reifying psychopathic disorder is largely a medical problem, not shared by psychologists. Two different psychological approaches may be of value to us in this regard. The first is the dynamic approach. It is likely that the topic of psychopathic disorder has remained elusive in part because it is confused with morality in the way indicated above. Although this is unhelpful, it is perhaps to be expected. Persistent or serious offenders against social mores are easily categorized in some kind of outgroup, whatever the basis for their behavior. Unfortunately, such a reaction can lead to bad treatment or no treatment at all. Psychoanalysis can be constructive here. According to the psychoanalytic view, recognizing that negative feelings about a patient are subjective and based on matters irrelevant to the treatment is an important step in overcoming such negative feelings, so that treatment can go forward.

The second approach is described in more detail in a previous paper (Gunn, 1988), but its essence is to set out a dimensional profile of the problems that confront a patient and those he or she comes into contact with. Traditionally psychiatry is concerned with such things as anxiety, depression, obsessionality, sleeping, eating, and thought disorder. Evaluating these phenomena assists greatly in the understanding of a patient's disabilities and gives strong clues about treatment. Furthermore, this type of trait approach to assessment is essential for serial measures of progress over time. Yet though these familiar traits are very useful, they are insufficient. Other key traits, such as impulsiveness, irritability, aggressiveness, sadism, self-esteem, and grandiosity, also need to be evaluated.

All this seems pretty banal and obvious, and yet this type of trait analysis is often not attempted with patients who are lumbered with the label "psychopathic personality." A negative halo leads directly to a global label, which in turn leads to negative ideas about treatment and often to frank rejection. Once the pejorative label is dropped, once the term "psychopathic" is out of the way, the notion of "untreatability" can also be tempered or dropped. If individual elements of pathology (e.g., low mood, anxiety, irritability, and sadistic fantasies) are identified, and if these individual traits are measured and monitored, treatment programs can be set up and the effectiveness of particular treatment strategies can be measured. A particularly important aspect of the treatment of patients who are difficult and potentially violent is the level of security they require. A full personal functional analysis will enable security matters, as well as treatment matters, to be attended to in a rational manner and measured over time, so that security can be relaxed when some progress has been made.

If a trait-pathological approach is applied to antisocial patients, not only can treatment be more productive, but descriptive pathology—the first step in understanding causal mechanisms—can come into its own. For example, is there a pathology of excessive aggressiveness? No, there is not a single pathology of excessive aggressiveness; there are many pathologies. Some violent people are responding to mood changes, others to delusions, and still others to hallucinations; some have intense irritability and anger; some are substance abusers. Violence is an integral part of any social system, and the unskillful use of violence is what we are interested in. This lack of skill may derive from a variety of causes, ranging from clear-cut mental pathology to inadequate or inappropriate training in the use of violence. (See also Gunn, 1991.)

With modern developments in neuroimaging, it may be possible to relate particular discrete aspects of pathology (e.g., impulsiveness) with particular functional variations or abnormalities revealed by a scanner. With luck, the term "psychopath" can soon be consigned to history books, novels, films, and the vernacular. Doctors and psychologists will identify and treat the abnormalities underlying antisocial behavior in any given individual with new insights and greater effectiveness.

Blackburn (1988) has given one of the most lucid critiques of the confusion created by regarding psychopathy as a homogeneous entity. His conclusion is worthy of note:

> It must be concluded that the current concept of psychopathic or antisocial personality remains a 'mythical entity'. The taxonomic error of confounding different universes of discourse has resulted in a diagnostic category that embraces a variety of deviant personalities. Such a category is not a meaningful focus for theory and research, nor can it facilitate clinical communication and prediction. Indeed, a disorder defined by past history of socially deviant behaviour is permanently fixed, and cannot provide a point of reference for clinical intervention. Such a concept is little more than a moral judgement masquerading as a clinical diagnosis.
>
> Given the lack of demonstrable scientific or clinical utility of the concept, it should be discarded. This is not to argue that socially deviant behaviour is unrelated to personality characteristics, but the nature of such a relationship is a question for theory and research. . . . Our understanding of how the attributes of the person contribute to socially deviant or other problematic behaviour will only progress when we have an adequate system for describing the universe of personality deviation. Focus on an ill-conceived category of psychopathic personality has merely served to distract attention from the development of such a system. (p. 511)

The treatment of patients with antisocial problems can be a very rewarding activity. The patients are fascinating, vary enormously, and respond to a wide variety of treatment strategies. They have very little in common with one another, other than the negative feelings they engender in other people. If such patients are to be helped, they require an individual functional analysis based on an understanding of their pathology, as well as an individualized treatment program.

We should not be disheartened that the elusive category Aubrey Lewis wrote about in 1974 has remained elusive for over 20 years more. We can learn from this important fact in itself. We can ask potentially heuristic questions, such as "Are we on the wrong track." Research techniques are developing rapidly. When we can understand the structural pathology of traits such as impulsivity and the developmental path to "manipulative behavior" (whatever that is), we will become very uninterested in psychopathy, and we will be of greater use to a group of unhealthy patients who are otherwise outside the current framework of medicine.

REFERENCES

Blackburn, R. (1988). On moral judgements and personality disorders: The myth of the psychopathic personality revisited. *British Journal of Psychiatry, 153,* 505–512.

Gould, S. J. (1984). *The mismeasure of man.* New York: Norton.

Gunn, J. (1988). Personality disorder: A clinical suggestion. In P. Tyrer (Ed.), *Personality disorders.* London: Wright.

Gunn, J. (1991). Human violence: A biological perspective. *Criminal Behaviour and Mental Health, 1,* 34–54.

Gunn, J. (1993). What's in a name?: A psychopath smells just as sweetly. *Criminal Behaviour and Mental Health, 3,* iii–vii.

Hare, R. D. (1991). *The Hare Psychopathy Checklist—Revised.* Toronto: Multi-Health Systems.

Kraepelin, E. (1921). *Manic–depressive insanity and paranoia.* Edinburgh: Livingstone. (Original work published 1915)

Lewis, A. (1974). Psychopathic personality: A most elusive category. *Psychological Medicine, 4,* 133–140.

Pandora and the problem of evil [Editorial]. (1996). *Lancet, 347,* 1–2.

Prichard, J. C. (1835). *A treatise on insanity and other disorders affecting the mind.* London: Sherwood, Gilbert & Piper.

Schneider, K. (1958). *Psychopathic personalities* (9th ed., M. Hamilton, Trans.). London: Cassell. (Original work published 1950)

Scott, P. D. (1963). Psychopathy. *Postgraduate Medical Journal, 39,* 12–18.

Scott, P. D. (1970). Punishment or treatment: Prison or hospital? *British Medical Journal, 2,* 167–170.

3

Personality and Crime

This chapter argues for a central role for personality in mediating between the genetic and environmental forces that act as causal agents on the one hand, and the criminal behavior that is to be explained on the other. Such a causal chain must of course also incorporate the biological/hormonal intermediaries between DNA and personality. In addition, we require an explanation for the specific behaviors that make up antisocial conduct, and it is suggested that this is to be found in Pavlovian conditioning. A review of the evidence relating to these theories suggests a fairly definite framework, which also leads to some suggestions concerning the reduction of criminality.

SOCIOLOGICAL VERSUS PSYCHOLOGICAL THEORIES OF CRIME

Crime has been an ever-present problem throughout recorded history. Almost as old have been two contrasting ways of explaining it, as well as of attempting to reduce its impact. Sociologists blame social factors, such as unemployment and poverty (Taylor, Walton, & Young, 1973), whereas psychologists are more likely to look at personality and intelligence as causal factors (Eysenck & Gudjonsson, 1989). This difference in interest has resulted in very one-sided approaches to the problem, although it must be obvious that both sides are concerned with very relevant causes of criminal behavior. Social conditions cannot be dismissed. The breakdown of communism in the Soviet Union resulted in a tremendous increase in crime, but can hardly have affected the genetics, personality, and intelligence of the Russian and other indigenous populations. Psychological differences cannot be dismissed. Whatever the social conditions, some people resort to crime and others do not, even though both groups are similar in income, prospects, and employment.

However, the situation is not as symmetrical as it might seem. The first point is that sociological theories are not usually put in a way that makes them testable. If unemployment is a powerful factor, does it work immediately? Is there a delay, and if so, how long—5 years, 10 years, 20 years? Similar questions can be asked about poverty. And how do we define poverty? Is it absolute or relative? Arbitrary assumptions are usually

40

made when sociologists are confronted with contrary evidence, but still there is no theory precise enough to permit exact quantitative predictions. Such facts as are available certainly do not support common-sense ideas of this kind. Differences in personal wealth—a favorite sociological cause of crime—have declined considerably since the turn of the century, but crime has gone up several hundred percent. Poverty? From 1979 to 1987, there has been a particularly steep rise in crime, but poverty has decreased dramatically (Eysenck & Gudjonsson, 1989). Unemployment? Some authors have analyzed U.S. crimes and found an inverse relation between unemployment and crime. Gross national product, an indicator of national wealth? Ellis and Patterson (in press) found it to correlate positively and highly with criminality in a sample of 13 industrial nations (.68 with total theft). The evidence, if anything, is strongly opposed to sociological theories. Naturally, poverty, unemployment, and wide differences in wealth are undesirable and ought to be eradicated or at least diminished; however, doing so might increase rather than diminish crime, counterintuitive as such a prediction, might seem. Possibly, of course, the regression is curvilinear. That is, perhaps great poverty, great unemployment, and great differences in wealth lead to low crime (as, e.g., in the early days of the Weimar Republic?); middling poverty, medium unemployment, and middling differences in wealth lead to high crime (as in the United States of America?); and little poverty, little unemployment, and few differences in wealth lead to low crime (as in Switzerland?). My point is that sociological theories are hunches rather than theories–not based on thorough statistical analysis of historical records, and too inexact to be testable.

The second argument against sociological theories is that social "causes" of crime, even if they could be proved to exist, must act through psychological pathways. Individuals react differentially to poverty, unemployment, and inequality; clearly, the personality and intelligence of the individuals concerned filter objective conditions and determine their perception. Poverty may cause some people to rebel against society, blame the government, and seek refuge in crime, while others blame themselves, their lack of cognitive ability, their ignorance, and their lack of skill, and regard unemployment as just punishment. This great diversity of reactions to stress is well documented (Lazarus & Folkman, 1989); to disregard relevant factual knowledge is unscientific in the extreme. Ultimately sociology must be a part of psychology, because it studies a limited set of factors that affect human behavior through psychological mechanisms.

THE NATURE OF PERSONALITY

To correlate personality and crime, and discover the causal pathways involved, we must have a good theory of personality. What would constitute such a theory? Figure 3.1 shows my own understanding of the evidence. Taxonomy (i.e., the correlational analysis of large numbers of traits in many different populations) tells us that there are three major dimensions of personality (Eysenck & Eysenck, 1985): psychoticism (P), extraversion (E), and neuroticism (N). These will be considered presently. The causal chain begins with DNA—that is, the genetic structure underlying individual differences. (The evidence shows clearly that most of the variance for individual differences in personality is due to genetic causes (Eaves, Eysenck, & Martin, 1989). DNA, of course, cannot directly influence behavior, just as social conditions cannot do so, and we must look for biological intermediaries in the central and autonomic nervous systems. These two sources of individual differences constitute the distal and proximal antecedent conditions for individual differences.

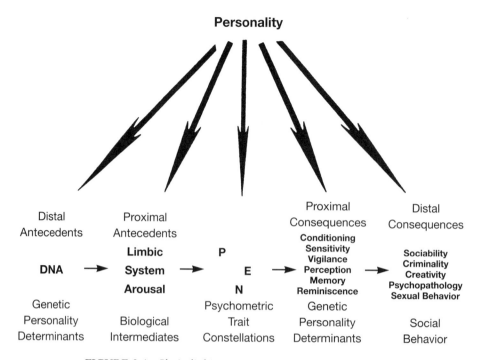

FIGURE 3.1. Chain linking DNA, personality, and criminality.

We next turn to the proximal and distal consequences. If our theory is truly scientific, we should be able to predict with considerable accuracy the outcome of experimental studies of proximal consequences and differential social behavior patterns (e.g., criminality), which are the distal consequences. Ideally, such a scheme should serve to link together in a factual chain all the variables considered. It should also enable us to predict the individual effect of social conditions on people differing in P, E, and N.

P, E, and N are essentially dimensions of personality built in a hierarchical manner upon the predicted and observed correlation between primary (more elementary) traits. Figures 3.2, 3.3, and 3.4 show the elements of such systems; there is, of course, strong empirical evidence for the relations shown in these figures (Eysenck, 1991). It is in these terms that I shall discuss the relation between crime and personality.

Before turning to a discussion of the relation of crime to the other links in this chain, I will briefly deal with the studies supporting the view that genetic causes play an important part in antisocial and criminal behavior. This simple fact is no longer in doubt (Raine, 1993). There are two major sources of evidence. The first relies on twin studies looking for concordance between monozygotic (MZ, or identical) and dizygotic (DZ, or fraternal) twins. The former share 100% heredity, the latter on the average only 50%; hence if one twin is a criminal, the likelihood that the other twin is also a criminal (concordant) is much higher for MZ than for DZ twins. Thirteen such studies have been carried out in many different countries (from Norway to Japan, from Germany to the United States), with predicted results in all. For 262 MZ twin pairs, the concordance rate was 51.5%; for 375 DZ twin pairs, the concordance rate was 20.6% (i.e., less than half). This would suggest a heritability for crime of 64%. Studies of MZ twins brought up in

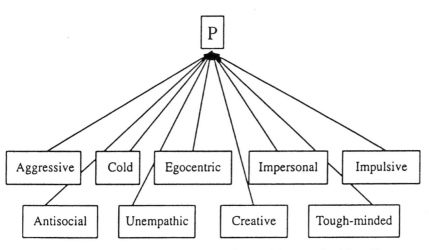

FIGURE 3.2. Traits correlating together to define psychoticism (P).

separation have also shown good concordance for antisocial criminal conduct (Raine, 1993).

The other source of evidence is the study of adopted children, who may come from criminal or noncriminal biological families and may be adopted into criminal or noncriminal families. The question is simply whether their later criminal behavior resembles more that of their biological families (heredity) or that of their adopted families (environment). Two reviews (Raine, 1993; Eysenck & Gudjonsson, 1989) have surveyed the literature. With one exception, all 15 studies find evidence for some genetic predisposition; again, researchers in different countries have discovered congruent evidence. This genetic predisposition relates to property crimes, but not to violent crimes. Why this should be so is not clear.

Bohman, Cloninger, Sigvardsson, and von Knorring (1982) state the conclusions we may come to: "It is important to realize that there are no genes for criminality, but only genes coding for structural proteins and enzymes that influence metabolic, hormonal and

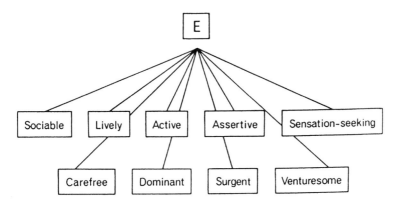

FIGURE 3.3. Traits correlating together to define extraversion (E).

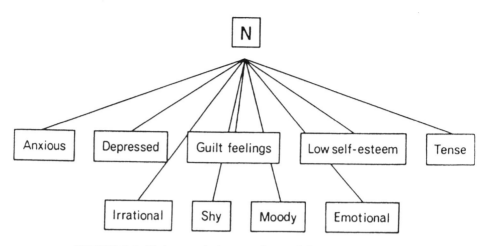

FIGURE 3.4. Traits correlating together to define neuroticism (N).

other physiological processes, which may inadvertently modify the risk of 'criminal' behavior in a particular environment" (p. 1234).

THE PSYCHOPHYSIOLOGY OF CRIME

We must next turn to the proximal antecedents of criminal activity—that is, the metabolic, hormonal, and other physiological processes involved in antisocial and criminal behavior. This is a complex undertaking; Raine (1993) took almost 400 pages to summarize the literature, which is now even more extensive than it was then. But essentially we may differentiate two approaches. The first is concerned with specific relationships. Thus Raine et al. (1994) demonstrated that, as suggested by previous work, murderers (as compared with matched controls) had significantly lower glucose metabolism in both lateral and medial prefrontal cortex areas. They suggested that deficits localized in the frontal cortex may be related to violence. There are many such specific studies linking specific psychophysiological data to crime (or, more usually, certain restricted types of crime).

Another example is an isolated gene that was found to underlie highly aggressive behavior characteristics in a particular Dutch family. The same gene was found to be manipulable in mice, and to be associated there too with highly aggressive behavior. The advent of molecular genetics has led us to the point where we may be able (as in this case) to discover the specific action of single genes, although in the great majority of cases behavior is of course governed by groups of genes, rather than by single genes (Brunner, Nelen, Breakfield, Ropers, & Dost, 1993).

Other fairly special relations are differences in testosterone and in monoamine oxidase (MAO). Persons indulging in various criminal activities tend to be characterized by high testosterone and low MAO (Zuckerman, 1991; Raine, 1993). The former is probably linked with the well-known fact that women are much less likely than men to indulge in criminal conduct, and that when commit crimes, these are usually sex-related crimes (i.e., prostitution), which are essentially victimless and arbitrarily defined as crimes by society. MAO is related to the catecholamine, including norepinephrine, dopamine, and epinephrine, which in turn are related to psychosis. I shall return to this topic in the next section, in connection with the P dimension. Here let me only say that, of the neurotransmitters, serotonin is characteristically lower in antisocials, whereas dopamine goes the other way.

Of particular interest, and more relevant to the title of this chapter, are more general psychophysiological concepts that are theoretically tied to major personality variables. I shall return concentrate here on the concept of cortical arousal, because for many years this has played a major part in personality theory (Strelau & Eysenck, 1987; Zuckerman, 1991). Cortical arousal is a state of the organism in which the brain is wide awake, attentive to outside stimuli, and working at maximum pace, concentrating and fixing attention on central features of interest. Low arousal indicates lack of interest, sleepiness, lack of attention, and loss of vigilance. The most clearcut measure of low arousal is electroencephalographic (EEG) alpha that is slow and with high amplitude; in high arousal the EEG alpha rhythm is fast with low amplitude. I linked this concept with the personality dimension of E, in the sense that extroverts characterized are by poor arousal/arousability, and that for that reason they require stronger stimulation (sensation seeking) than introverts (Eysenck, 1967). There is now a good deal of evidence to support this view (Eysenck, 1990; Zuckerman, 1991). Later work has suggested that the P dimension, too, is characterized by poor arousal/arousability.

I have mentioned the arousal syndrome specifically because it is most clearly related to antisocial and criminal activity, and to personality. This special relationship will be discussed in the next section.

CRIME AND THE THREE MAJOR PERSONALITY DIMENSIONS

We have now arrived at the central portion of Figure 3.1—namely, the psychometrically defined major dimensions of personality. I have suggested that antisocial conduct and crime should be positively associated with P, E, and N, for various reasons (Eysenck, 1977; Eysenck & Gudjonsson, 1989); the evidence from numerous studies has on the whole upheld these predictions. P is always involved; E is more involved in young samples, N in older ones. Why were these predictions made? My main concern was with the causal problem. It is often asked, "Why do people act antisocially and commit crimes?" I felt that this question put the cart before the horse. It seems perfectly rational to act in one's own interest, and to take whatever one wants or needs. Babies and young children certainly do so, and so do animals. The real question, rather is this: "Why do most of us behave in a socially desirable fashion?" This is not an easy question to answer.

We may reply, "Because of the police officer on the beat, and the judge on the bench," but that does not make sense, even though it must play a part. As Napoleon said, "You can do anything with bayonets except sit on them," and if social rules were really widely disregarded (as they are in some no-go areas even in our society), social behavior breaks down completely. The police are dependent on social agreement; what causes that agreement? It cannot be reason and knowledge. Research has shown that criminals know what is right and wrong as well as anybody—they just prefer the wrong to the right. My answer was along rather different lines. I suggested that we behaved well because our consciences would trouble us if we did not; this is not an original notion, because it agrees with common-sense and religious teaching. However, I went on to suggest a natural history origin of this mysterious conscience, at variance with the religious notion of a God-implanted moral sense.

Conscience, I suggested, is a conditioned response (CR) acquired according to Pavlovian principles. Every time we transgress, we are punished by our parents, our teachers, our peers; often, when we act in a socially approved fashion, we are lauded or rewarded. Each such occasion serves to reinforce our doing the right, socially approved thing, and not to do what is wrong. This huge amount of conditioning experience we conceptualize as "conscience," and we use language to generalize and tie together these varied experiences. Why, then, do we find differences between people in the degree of socially approved behavior? There are three possibilities, which are mutually exclusive:

1. The conditioning experiences are missing. A permissive society fails to install the required conscience by falling down on its duty, and parents, peers, and teachers leave a child without proper reinforcers.

2. The wrong experiences are reinforced. Some parents encourage their children to act aggressively, to steal, to behave antisocially. Such encouragement is undoubtedly more prevalent now than it used to be, perhaps accounting for the growth in crime.

3. The third possibility is perhaps the most interesting. Low arousal makes conditioning less likely to occur, so that high-E and high-P persons, exposed to similar conditioning experiences of a social kind as low-E and low-P persons, should have problems aggregating these experiences into a properly functioning conscience. Hence they should have less resistance to the actual given antisocial behaviors of our animal nature. There is considerable evidence for this theory, both from animal experiments and from human studies as well. On the human side, we can experimentally test people's "conditionability" (i.e., the speed with which they form CRs). There is overwhelming evidence that antisocial and criminal people show relatively poor conditionability compared with ordinary people; a good review is given by Raine (1993). Fundamentally, this constitutes a natural philosophy theory of antisocial conduct that explains a great deal of the known facts, and that has found strong experimental support.

Note that conditioning, experimentally studied, comes into the "proximal consequences" part of Figure 3.1, with criminality coming into the "distal consequences" part. The prediction comes via the "proximal antecedents" aspect (i.e., the psychophysiology of arousal) and via the personality theory central to the figure. We are thus dealing with a complex theory that can be tested (and has been tested) in many of its ramifications; here, of course, only a very cursory survey can be given.

Arousal has effects on criminality that can be studied directly, and not only via conditioning. Thus Raine, Venables, and Williams (1990) studied the relationship between experimental measures of arousal at age 15 and criminality at age 24. They showed that on all measures used, future criminals showed less arousal in the experimental situation than future noncriminals did. All three response systems (electrodermal, cardiovascular, and cortical) were equally involved.

To complete this survey, let me only say that of the large number of studies done directly to test the predicted relationship between P, E, and N and crime, most have given strong support to the theory. P in particular, has always distinguished very significantly between criminals and noncriminals, as has N (with adults) and E (with youngsters). The reason for N's acting as a predictor is properly related to its drive properties, which multiply the action tendencies present. There may also be other reasons, such as emotion's overruling reason in high-N subjects; they tend to be aggressive and impulsive.

The conditioning paradigm must of course be taken together with the social realities mentioned, such as lack of conditioning experiences or the wrong conditioning experiences in a child's life. Parents who practice the child-rearing philosophy of permissiveness have abandoned the practices that used to act as reinforcers, so it is not surprising that antisocial and criminal behavior is now much more common. Society consciously avoids putting into practice those mechanisms that have ensured social conformity in the great majority of children; hence a much weaker conscience than we used to implant is now common. It is often said that these theories must be wrong because there cannot have been any change in the genetic basis of the population to account for the increase in crime. But that is not what is suggested. The theory suggests an interaction between social and psychophysiological factors, not a 100% biological chain of causation.

WHAT CAN BE DONE?

Socially, the main concern of psychological studies relates to the question of how to reduce crime and recidivism. Rehabilitation of criminals, once one of the major aims of justice, became a dirty word during the 1970s (Rothman, 1980), and the belief spread that "nothing works." This is one of many myths that shroud the whole field of criminology. Consider prison. It is often said to be useless, but 50% of criminals sent to prison do not reoffend—is the glass half full or half empty? Probation officers often quote statistics to show that criminals on probation do not reoffend more frequently than criminals sent to prison, but the statistics are meaningless because there is no random element involved; criminals given probation are chosen as being the least likely to reoffend!

Quite generally, it may be said that modern penal practices are usually the opposite of what psychology would recommend. The effects of prison depend on the conditioning history of the criminal, and that is being manipulated in a direction almost guaranteed to lower the preventive use of incarceration. Very young offenders cannot be touched by the law. Young offenders are cautioned any number of times, instead of being punished. Youths are usually given probation several times before being sent to prison. In other words, the conditioning process associates the unconditioned stimulus (UCS) with the unconditioned response (UCR) of (effectively) no punishment; consequently, the CR to the conditioned stimuli (CSs) tempting the crime will be giving in to temptation, there never having been any attempt to build up a conscience through appropriate punishment. There is ample evidence for "latent inhibition" (Lubow, 1989)—that is, in the fact that when a CS is not followed by a proper UCR, it will be more difficult to form the proper links later. Thus psychology suggests that at most one caution should be given on the occasion of the first offense, but that serious punishment should follow the next offense. Thus the restricted usefulness of prison in rehabilitation is understandable as a consequence of earlier misplaced lenience.

Is there any evidence that severity of treatment (UCR) is effective? The evidence from animal work is entirely in favor, but human evidence is almost entirely circumstantial. Thus the election of a new mayor of New York who was perceived as "tough on punishment," following a weak liberal mayor, led to a very pronounced reduction in crime. Psychological research has mainly concentrated on studying correctional treatment, with encouraging results (Andrews, Zinger, et al., 1990; Gendreau & Ross, 1987). The large body of empirical study has shown that behavioral approaches based on learning theory are most effective. "Traditional psychodynamic and non-directive client-centered therapies are to be avoided within general samples of offenders" (Andrews, Bonta, & Hoge, 1990). The best studies show very acceptable levels of reduction in recidivism.

However, psychology does not encourage the belief that any single measure, such as increasing severity of punishment, would have a large effect. The evidence suggests, rather, that there are many causes of criminality, each only contributing a rather small amount of variance to the total of criminality. Correlates of later criminality can be found in early childhood: Troublesome behavior in kindergarten is predictive of later police contacts! Poor childbearing practices and poor parental supervision are the most important precursors of future criminality, as might be expected from conditioning theory (Farrington, 1987). Of course, genetic factors cannot be ruled out in this connection, but they cannot account for all the connections found. Furthermore, as Zigler, Taunis, and Black (1992) have pointed out, "Major reports over the last decade have constantly shown that some early childhood intervention programs have lasting effects on social competent behaviors" (p. 999). Zigler et al. discuss several such programs where final delinquency was the outcome investigated, and concluded that in early childhood intervention programs may reduce "juvenile delinquency and pre-delinquent behavior" (p. 1002).

School, of course, also exerts a civilizing influence and has been studied in some detail (Farrington, 1992), although not as exhaustively as parenting. Rutter, Maugham, Mortimore, and Ouston (1979) have published the most carefully controlled account of an empirical study, looking at effects independently of intake factors (usually the most crime:prone pupils in primary school go to the most crime=prone secondary schools). There have been no accounts of intervention studies, so any conclusion would be premature.

Finally, it is important also to look at prenatal and perinatal factors (Farrington, 1994). Low birth weight, a relatively small baby, and perinatal complications (e.g., forceps delivery, asphyxia, a long duration of labor, or toxemia in pregnancy) have been shown to predict later conduct problems and delinquency in children. As an example, it has been found that delivery complications significantly predicted later violent offending for males, as well as property offenses.

ACKNOWLEDGMENT

A similar version of these ideas may be found in *Psychology, Crime and Law,* 1996, 2, 143–152.

NOTE

1. Deceased, September 1997.

REFERENCES

Andrews, D., Bonta, J., & Hoge, R. (1990). Classification for effective rehabilitation: Rediscovering psychology. *Criminal Justice and Behavior, 17,* 19–52.

Andrews, D., Zinger, I., Hoge, R., Bonta, J., Gendreau, P., & Cullen, F. (1990). Does correctional treatment work? A clinically relevant and psychologically informed meta-analysis. *Criminology, 28,* 369–404.

Bohman, M., Cloninger, C., Sigvardsson, S., & von Knorring, A.-L. (1982). Predisposition to petty criminalities in Swedish adoptees: Genetics of environmental heterogeneity. *Archives of General Psychiatry, 39,* 1233–1241.

Brunner, W., Nelen, M., Breakfield, O., Ropers, H., & Dost, B. (1993). Abnormal behavior associated with a point mutuation in the structural gene for monoamine oxidase A. *Science, 262,* 578–581.

Eaves, L., Eysenck, H. J., & Martin, N. (1989). *Genes, culture and personality.* New York: Academic Press.

Ellis, L., & Patterson, J. (in press). Crime and religion: An international comparison among thirteen industrial nations. *Personality and Individual Differences.*

Eysenck, H. J. (1967). *The biological basis of personality.* Springfield, IL: Charles C Thomas.

Eysenck, H. J. (1977). *Crime and personality.* London: Routledge & Kegan Paul.

Eysenck, H. J. (1990). Biological dimensions of personality. In L. A. Pervin (Ed.), *Handbook of personality* (pp. 244–270). New York: Guilford Press.

Eysenck, H. J. (1991). Dimensions of personality: 16, 5 or 3? Criteria for a taxonomic paradigm. *Personality and Individual Differences, 12,* 773–790.

Eysenck, H. J., & Eysenck, M. W. (1985). *Personality and individual differences.* New York: Plenum Press.

Eysenck, H. J., & Gudjonsson, G. (1989). *The causes and cures of criminality.* New York: Plenum Press.

Farrington, D. P. (1987). Early precursors of frequent offending. In Q. J. Wilson & G. C. Loury (Eds.), *From children to citizens: Vol. 3. Families, schools, and delinquency prevention* (pp. 27–51). New York: Springer.

Farrington, D. P. (1992). Psychological contribution to the explanation, prevention and treatment of offending. In F. Losel, D. Bender, & T. Bliesenet (Eds.), *Psychology and law* (pp. 35–51). Hawthorne, NY: Walter de Gruyter.

Farrington, D. (1994). Delinquency prevention in the first few years of life. *Justice of the Peace,* 531–533.

Gendreau, P., & Ross, R. (1987). Recidivation of rehabilitation: Evidence from the 1980s. *Justice Quarterly, 4,* 24–37.

Lazarus, R., & Folkman, S. (1989). Latent inhibition and conditioned attention theory. Cambridge, England: Cambridge University Press.

Raine, A. (1993). *The psychopathology of crime.* New York: Academic Press.

Raine, A., Bucksbaum, M., Stanley, J., Lottenberg, S., Abel, L., & Stoddard, J. (1994). Selected reductions in pre-frontal glucose metabolism in murderers. *Biological Psychiatry, 36,* 365–373.

Raine, A., Venables, P., & Williams, M. (1990). Relationships between central and autonomic measures of arousal at age 15 years, and criminality at age 24 years. *Archives of General Psychiatry, 47,* 1003–1007.

Rothman, D. (1980). *Conscience and Convenience: The asylum and its alternatives in progressive America.* Boston: Little, Brown.

Ruttter, M., Maugham, B., Mortimore, P., & Ouston, J. (1979). *Fifteen thousand hours.* London: Open Books.

Strelau, I., & Eysenck, H. J. (1987). *Personality dimensions and arousal.* New York: Plenum Press.

Taylor, I., Walton, P., & Young, J. (1973). *The new criminology.* London: Routledge & Kegan Paul.

Zigler, I. E., Taunis, C., & Black, K. (1992). Early childhood intervention: A primary presentation for juvenile delinquency. *American Psychologist, 47,* 997–1006.

Zuckerman, M. (1991). *Psychobiology of personality.* Cambridge, England: Cambridge University Press.

4

Psychopathy and the Contribution of Personality to Violence

RONALD BLACKBURN

Current concepts of "psychopathy" and its synonyms represent attempts to attribute the harmful social rule-breaking to a particular type of person. Formulations of the proto-typical traits of "psychopathic personality" by North American writers such as Cleckley (1976) and Gough (1948) have emphasized egocentricity and impulsive self-gratification in the context of a callous disregard for the feelings of others. The antisocial personality disorder (APD) category of DSM-IV (American Psychiatric Association, 1994) similarly aims to identify a consistent, thoroughgoing pattern of ignoring and violating the rights of other people.

Callous violation of the rights of others can take many forms, but it is particularly likely to entail psychological or physical aggression. Although neither Cleckley nor Gough explicitly refers to aggressive traits, it is commonly assumed that psychopathy embodies the relationship between abnormal personality and aggression. In the 1983 Mental Health Act for England and Wales, the category of "psychopathic disorder" is defined as "a persistent disorder or disability of mind . . . which results in abnormally aggressive or seriously irresponsible conduct on the part of the person concerned" (Mental Health Act 1983, p. 2). This is a legal concept and not a clinical category, but several clinical conceptions also emphasize aggression. McCord and McCord (1964), for example, describe the psychopath as "an asocial, aggressive, highly impulsive person, who feels little or no guilt, and is unable to form lasting bonds of affection with other human beings" (p. 5). For Millon (1981), "aggressive personality" is preferable to the term "antisocial personality," the cardinal traits being hostile affectivity, social rebelliousness, vindictiveness, and disregard for danger. Aggression is also among the traits defining APD in DSM-DIV (irritability and aggressiveness, as indicated by repeated physical fights or assaults; American Psychiatric Association, 1994) and dissocial personality disorder in ICD-10 (a very low tolerance for frustration and a low threshold for discharge of aggression, including violence; World Health Organization, 1992).

An understanding of the psychological attributes of psychopaths might therefore be expected to illuminate the contribution of personality characteristics to violence. However, most current concepts of psychopathy have evolved with little reference to the empirical literature on either personality or aggression, and lack a theoretical basis for linking the two. In this chapter, I propose that psychopathy can be understood in terms of an established theory of personality that provides such a link, and I describe research with mentally disordered offenders in support of this argument. In this theory, psychopathy is construed as a *dimension* of personality, and I will therefore first discuss reasons for questioning the utility of current categorical concepts of psychopathic or antisocial personality.

PSYCHOPATHY AND PERSONALITY DISORDER

The current equation of "psychopathic" with "antisocial" reflects a transmogrification of the meaning of the adjective from "psychologically damaged" (i.e., psychopathological) to "socially damaging," and is the result of historical differences between European and North American psychiatry (Millon, 1981; Pichot, 1978). In German psychiatry, "psychopathic personality" became a generic term denoting a heterogeneous group of abnormal personalities defined by personality deviation, not antisocial behavior (Schneider, 1950/1958). Paradoxically, Schneider's psychopathic personalities are now essentially the wider class of personality disorders in current psychiatric classifications. In England, however, use of the term "psychopathic" owes more to the 19th-century notion of "moral insanity" and has referred to antisocial individuals defined by social deviance rather than by personality. This is apparent in the Mental Health Act category of psychopathic disorder described earlier, for which the only defining feature is the aggressive or irresponsible conduct from which a "mental disability" is inferred. Although this is a legal category, it is still commonly used in clinical practice to identify "psychopaths." However, this description makes little contact with current North American concepts of psychopathy, and research has clearly established that legal "psychopaths" are heterogeneous in personality (Blackburn, 1975; Coid, 1992).

The APD category as introduced in DSM-III (American Psychiatric Association, 1980), also follows the moral insanity tradition, insofar as psychological abnormality is inferred from social deviance. This category was influenced by the work of Robins (1978), who objected to inferential trait concepts, but its adoption in DSM-III also reflected the "nothing works" view of offender rehabilitation. Millon (1981) described this category as an "accusatory judgment," and its adequacy in identifying psychopathic personality has been questioned by others (Blackburn, 1988; Hare, Hart, & Harpur, 1991). Although antisocial acts may be *consequences* of personality traits, they belong in a different universe of discourse from that of personality dispositions (Blackburn, 1988). They do not therefore provide a logical basis for inferring personality deviation.

Cleckley's concept of psychopathic personality is a hybrid, in that personality traits define a specific antisocial type. Nevertheless, operationalization of this construct through the development of the Psychopathy Checklist—Revised (PCL-R; Hare, 1991; 1996) has served to establish its validity. The PCL-R measures a unitary construct, and extreme scores reliably discriminate the more recalcitrant offender or forensic psychiatric patient. Further discrimination can be achieved by the subdivision of scores into two oblique factor scales—Factor 1 measuring a callous and remorseless style of relating to others, and Factor 2 a socially deviant lifestyle (Harpur, Hare, & Hakstian, 1989). Factor 1 identifies the central personality characteristics of psychopathy described by Cleckley and others; Factor 2 represents the unsocialized behaviors assessed by APD.

Research with the PCL-R appears to support the utility of a relatively specific concept of psychopathy, but several issues about the relationship of this concept to the classification of personality disorders remain unresolved. Despite criticisms of the recent categories of APD, Cleckley (1976) considered the DSM-II version "a recognizable entity in a fairly large group of different and distinct disorders" (p. 134). Hare and Hart (1993) similarly describe psychopathy as "a specific form of personality disorder . . . similar in many respects to the category antisocial personality disorder" (p. 104). However, the conceptualization of psychopathy as one of several discrete categories of personality disorder raises the question not only of how specific the category is, but also of whether it is more appropriately construed as a dimension than as a categorical entity.

The relationship of the PCL-R to personality disorders other than APD has received only limited attention, but traits held to define psychopathy are not specific to a single disorder in the current classifications. In DSM-IV, for example, such traits are among the criteria for several personality disorders in addition to APD—notably histrionic (superficial charm, insincerity, egocentricity, manipulativeness), narcissistic (grandiosity, lack of empathy, exploitativeness), borderline (impulsivity, suicidal gestures), and paranoid (mistrust) personality disorders. Cleckley's "distinct entity" therefore seems to encompass more than a single category of disorder. Correlations of the PCL-R with DSM-III-R personality disorders in prison and forensic psychiatric samples also reveal relationships of psychopathy to several disorders (Hart & Hare, 1989; Hart, Forth, & Hare, 1991; Hart, Hare, & Forth, 1994). In these studies, the PCL-R was significantly associated with more than half of the personality disorders, particularly the narcissistic, histrionic, borderline, and paranoid disorders, as well as APD. These data question the assumption that psychopathy is one of several distinct categories of personality disorder, and seem more consistent with the view that psychopathy is a superordinate personality dimension pervading many disorders (Blackburn, 1988, 1993a).

In a taxometric analysis of the PCL-R, Harris, Rice, and Quinsey (1994) found evidence for a taxon, apparently supporting the notion of psychopathy as a discrete entity. This conclusion, however, is equivocal, because the discriminating items were primarily the social deviance items of Factor 2 of the PCL-R. Evidence favoring a dimensional concept, on the other hand, comes from factor-analytic studies of deviant personality traits, which consistently yield a dimension equivalent to psychopathy. For example, Presly and Walton (1973) and Tyrer and Alexander (1979) identified a factor described as "sociopathy" or "social deviance," which was defined by such traits as egocentricity, callousness, impulsivity, and conscience defect. A similar factor emerges in more recent North American studies of DSM-III personality disorders. These identify three or four factors, one of which is defined by narcissistic, histrionic, and borderline personality disorders, as well as APD (Kass, Skodol, Charles, Spitzer, & Williams, 1985; Hyler & Lyons, 1988; Zimmerman & Coryell, 1990). These are the disorders found to be most closely associated with the PCL-R. The remaining factors in these studies are also relatively consistent. One relates to submissiveness or passive dependence and is defined by dependent and avoidant personality disorders, while another is defined by schizoid and schizotypal personality disorders. Where a fourth factor is extracted, it is typically defined by DSM-III compulsive personality disorder.

Tyrer (1988a) has argued that the DSM aim of identifying mutually exclusive *categories* of personality disorder was a "mirage." The recurring patterns of comorbidity indicated by factor-analytic research reflect the organization of underlying dimensions

(Clark, Watson, & Reynolds, 1995), and a dimensional approach to personality disorders has been advocated increasingly in recent years (e.g., Blackburn, 1988; Tyrer, 1988a; Widiger & Frances, 1994; Livesley, Schroeder, Jackson, & Jang, 1994). It has also been proposed that the dimensions most relevant to personality disorders are the "Big Five" personality factors of agreeableness, neuroticism, extraversion, conscientiousness, and openness to experience (Livesley et al., 1994; Widiger & Frances, 1994; Wiggins & Pincus, 1994). The sociopathic, dependent, schizoid, and compulsive factors described above are proposed to be variants of the first four of the Big Five dimensions, respectively. In these terms, psychopathy would be expected to be closely related to agreeableness, or rather to its opposite extreme, disagreeableness or antagonism. This proposal is considered later in the chapter.

Dimensional description is consonant with the assumption that personality dysfunctions differ quantitatively rather than qualitatively from normality, and it is manifestly not the case that egocentricity, callousness, impulsivity, and so forth are the exclusive property of those processed by the criminal justice system or the mental health system. However, categorical or typal descriptions have advantages for many purposes, and may summarize multidimensional patterns. In research reported below, our strategy has been to identify naturally occurring types through empirical methods that take account of these patterns.

AGGRESSION AND PERSONALITY DISORDER

"Violence" denotes the forceful infliction of physical injury, and "criminal violence" is the illegitimate injury of an unwilling victim. Violent crime, however, constitutes only a small part of the phenomenon of "aggression," which covers the intentional infliction of harm more generally (Berkowitz, 1993; Blackburn, 1993a). Humiliating others through verbal abuse, for example, is functionally equivalent to hitting them. Tedeschi (1983) argues that human aggression is more appropriately conceptualized as "coercive power" (i.e., the use of threats or punishments to control social interaction). This emphasizes the interpersonal context of harmful behavior, and "aggression" is used interchangeably with "coercion" in the current discussion. This can be distinguished from the emotional state of "anger," which is relatively independent of aggression. Although most extreme aggression is probably motivated by anger, aggression is not a necessary consequence of heightened anger, nor is all aggression accompanied by such a state (Novaco, 1994). These terms can be further distinguished from "hostility." Some authors use the terms "hostility" and "aggression" interchangeably, but the present discussion follows Buss (1961) in limiting hostility to negative evaluations or attitudes of resentment, mistrust or hate.

People clearly vary in the extent to which they experience and express anger or behave aggressively, and a single *act* of aggression is not necessarily indicative of an aggressive *disposition*. An "act" is an intentional, goal-directed behavior performed by a person in a specific situation. A "disposition" is a tendency or capacity to engage in acts of a particular class, and is inferred from the regularity with which acts in the class are performed. Dispositions or traits are, then, probabilistic tendencies describing average behavior over time and setting. They describe what people *can* do, not what they necessarily *will* do, because tendencies are only realized as acts under specific conditions. An aggressive disposition therefore makes violence more likely but is not sufficient for a violent act. In predicting violence, for example, we may at best judge the strength of an aggressive disposition, and can rarely forecast the situational contexts in which that disposition may eventuate in an extreme act of aggression (Blackburn, 1993a). Conversely, violent crimes may often be committed by people who are not habitually aggressive, but who committed their offenses because of situational factors, temporary stress, or mental disorder. Populations of violent offenders are, then, likely to be heterogeneous in personality, as will be shown below.

Harmful acts occur in a variety of contexts and can rarely be attributed to a single causal factor. In general terms, the attempt by one person to inflict damage on another can be characterized as a complex sequence of interpersonal exchanges in which the situation, the meanings attached to it by the participants, their emotional state, and their expectations and interpretations of each other's behavior are among the more salient determinants of a harmful outcome. However, these proximal contributions to aggression are in turn mediated by the preexisting attributes of the actors. People may create or invite aggressive confrontations, and bring with them generalized beliefs or expectancies about the self and others and habitual styles of coping with interpersonal problem situations. An aggressive disposition or tendency as indicated by a history of frequent verbal or physical attacks on others is therefore a function of cognitive and affective attributes that make aggressive acts more likely. Such characteristics represent the persisting products of prior experiences that mediate new experiences.

Reference to such attributes seems necessary to account for the relatively high degree of consistency of individual aggressiveness across the lifespan (Huesmann, Eron, Lefkowitz, & Walder, 1984; Olweus, 1979). Longitudinal studies have also established links between early aggressive behavior and later criminal violence (e.g., Farrington, 1989; Robins, 1978). These studies find that early aggression is associated with later socially deviant behavior more generally, justifying the notion of an antisocial personality "syndrome" in which aggressive traits are a prominent feature.

In DSM-IV, direct indicators of an aggressive disposition are among the criteria for APD, as noted earlier. However, they also characterize paranoid personality disorder (quickness to react angrily or to counterattack) and borderline personality disorder (difficulty controlling anger), although they are not necessary to these diagnoses. The category of sadistic personality disorder—proposed in an appendix to DSM-III-R (American Psychiatric Association, 1987), but omitted from DSM-IV—also directly identified coercive personality traits likely to be associated with violence (Widiger & Trull, 1994). This category was described as a consistent pattern of vicious, humiliating, and aggressive behavior, and was defined by such criteria as using physical cruelty or violence to establish dominance in a relationship; humiliating or demeaning people in the presence of others; controlling others through intimidation; and being fascinated by violence, weapons, martial arts, or torture. Widiger and Trull (1994) suggest that the current classification of personality disorders is insufficient to clarify the role of maladaptive personality traits in the development of violent behavior. However, direct indicators of an aggressive disposition do not tell us which attributes of the person contribute to violence, and indirect signs may be equally predictive. The PCL-R includes only one item directly relevant to aggression (poor behavioral controls). Nevertheless, the PCL-R not only correlates with prior history of violence among offenders (e.g., Serin, 1991; Blackburn & Coid, in press), but also predicts violent criminal recidivism (e.g., Harris, Rice, & Cormier, 1991; Serin, 1996).

Psychopathic traits therefore appear to be conducive to aggression, but there has been only limited exploration of the psychological processes involved. The traditional view is that psychopaths lack affective responses of empathy or guilt that restrain or inhibit aggressive impulses. This is reflected in such traits as callousness, shallow affect, and grandiose sense of self-worth. However, this inhibitory concept assumes an instinct model of aggression, which has now been discredited (American Psychological Association, 1990). If there is no internal source of aggressive energy to be inhibited, we must inquire how aggressive "impulses" originate and why psychopaths are more disposed to manifest them. An alternative model holds that aggression is initiated by cognitive appraisals of threat and attributions of malevolence (Ferguson & Rule, 1983; Novaco, 1994; Zillmann, 1979). Such appraisals are more likely when individuals have a hostile "working model" of their social world. The view developed here is that the callous indifference to the feelings of others that exemplifies psychopathy has more to do with interpersonal beliefs than with affective deficits.

PERSONALITY DISORDER IN MENTALLY DISORDERED OFFENDERS

My research has centered on the contribution of personality deviation to antisocial behavior and violence, and particularly on the utility of the North American concept of psychopathic personality in this context. This work has been undertaken with adult male mentally disordered offenders detained in English maximum-security hospitals ("special hospitals") because of presumed dangerousness. Some of this research is confined to patients in the legal category of psychopathic disorder, but many forensic psychiatric patients described by the English Mental Health Act as "mentally ill" also have comorbid personality disorders. Tyrer (1988b), for example, found that 56% of mentally ill patients met criteria for personality disorder on the Personality Assessment Schedule. Using the Millon Clinical Multiaxial Inventory (MCMI; Millon, 1983), we also identified personality disorder in 65% of mentally ill patients (Blackburn, Crellin, Morgan, & Tulloch, 1990). The two medicolegal categories are also not differentiated by Hare's PCL-R (Howard, 1990; O'Kane, Fawcett, & Blackburn, 1996). Several of our studies therefore include patients from both legal categories.

Much of this research has operationalized psychopathic traits by means of self-report scales. Self-reports tap aspects of experience and self-image not always apparent to an observer, but typically correlate only modestly with clinical ratings of psychopathy (Hare, 1991). Hare therefore questions their usefulness in assessing psychopathy among offenders. However, because psychopathy is a theoretical construct rather than a palpable entity, there can be no "true" operational measure, and there are both methodological and philosophical objections to the assumption that observer ratings are necessarily more valid assessments of personality than self-ratings (Gifford, 1994). Nevertheless, we have attempted to establish the generalizability of our findings by using observer ratings in several studies.

An Empirical Classification of Personality Types among Mentally Disordered Offenders

A primary aim of this research has been to reduce the heterogeneity of the mentally disordered offender population by multivariate analyses of personality test data. My initial studies were guided by Megargee's (1966) hypothesis that violent offenders can be divided into "overcontrolled" and "undercontrolled" types. Undercontrolled offenders, according to Megargee, have weak inhibitions against aggression, and hence respond aggressively with some regularity. They are also likely to be identified as psychopaths.

Overcontrolled offenders, in contrast, have strong inhibitions, and aggress only when anger arousal is sufficiently intense to overcome inhibitions. They are therefore expected to attack others rarely but with extreme intensity, and should be found more commonly among those who have been extremely assaultive. Supporting the hypothesis, I found that extreme assaultives among mentally disordered offenders were significantly more controlled, inhibited, and defensive on the Minnesota Multiphasic Personality Inventory (MMPI) than were moderate assaultives (Blackburn, 1968). They were also less likely to have a prior criminal record or to be diagnosed clinically as psychopaths.

The theory was later tested further through cluster analysis of MMPI profiles of homicidal patients (Blackburn, 1971). This, however, produced two undercontrolled and two overcontrolled types. One undercontrolled type was defined by the "49" profile associated in clinical lore with psychopathic personality (i.e., combined elevations on the Psychopathic Deviate and Hypomania scales); the other was characterized by a highly deviant profile with abnormal scores on most clinical scales. Of the overcontrolled groups, one was defined by a defensive "hypernormal" pattern, the other mainly by marked social introversion.

I subsequently developed the Special Hospitals Assessment of Personality and Socialisation (SHAPS; Blackburn, 1979a, 1987), which focuses more specifically on psychopathic traits such as impulsivity and hostile interpersonal attitudes, but which also contains measures of two of the Big Five dimensions, neuroticism and extraversion. The earlier fourfold typology is consistently reproduced by cluster analyses of the SHAPS. The four profile types are apparent among patients in the legal category of psychopathic disorder (Blackburn, 1975), but also constitute the main patterns of personality deviation among mentally disordered offenders as a whole (Blackburn, 1986). I describe the four classes as (1) "primary psychopaths" (P; impulsive, aggressive, hostile, extraverted, self-confident, low to average anxiety); (2) "secondary psychopaths" (S; hostile, impulsive, aggressive, socially anxious, withdrawn, moody, low in self-esteem); (3) "controlled" (C; defensive, controlled, sociable, nonanxious); and (4) "inhibited" (I; shy, withdrawn, controlled, moderately anxious, low self esteem). The groups are differentiated by the personality disorder scales of the MCMI (Blackburn, 1996a), the P group being predominantly narcissistic, histrionic, and antisocial, while the S group is antisocial, passive–aggressive, avoidant, schizoid, dependent, and paranoid. The I group is also schizoid, avoidant, schizotypal, and passive–aggressive, but has low scores on the antisocial scale. Patients in the C group score highest on the compulsive scale, but show the fewest signs of personality disorder more generally.

The classification has been replicated in research in the English prison system on "normal" murderers (McGurk, 1978) and violent offenders (Henderson, 1982). The typology is therefore robust and represents the main personality types identifiable through self-report in prison and forensic psychiatric populations. The same patterns are also recovered from cluster analysis of MCMI personality disorder scales, reflecting common underlying dimensions (Blackburn, 1996a).

The groups differ on a number of nontest variables. Patients in the S group, who are characterized by the most deviant personality profiles, are also typically most deviant in other respects. The electroencephalographic abnormalities claimed in the older clinical literature to be common among psychopaths are most likely to be found in this group (Blackburn, 1979b; Howard, 1984), and in a delinquent sample, Gillham (1978) found that S patients reported the least vivid emotional imagery. P patients differ from S patients in having higher levels of cortical and autonomic arousal (Blackburn, 1979b), and score highest on Zuckerman's Sensation Seeking Scale (Blackburn, 1978). Although patients in the C group show few distinctive characteristics that would not be anticipated from their denial of strong emotional reactions or socially improper behavior, the I group is characterized by poor social skills (Henderson, 1982).

The groups also differ in aggression and criminality. In one study (Blackburn, 1975), P and S patients were found to have earlier criminal careers than C and I patients, but the P group had the most convictions for violent crimes. These findings have been replicated in recent unpublished work (Table 4.1). It will be noted that P and S patients have more convictions than C and I patients, and have been convicted from an earlier age, but whereas S patients have the most convictions for acquisitive offenses (theft, burglary), P patients have the highest level of convictions for violence. P and S patients also describe themselves as more dominant in both threatening and affiliative settings, but the differences between psychopathic and nonpsychopathic groups are more apparent in threatening situations (Willner & Blackburn, 1988). On the other hand, S patients describe the most intense anger in response to verbal or physical threat (Blackburn & Lee-Evans, 1985).

Research therefore supports the validity of this empirically derived classification in discriminating classes of personality deviation among offenders. The members of the first group have been identified as *primary* psychopaths because they are distinguished by traits that approximate the characteristics held to define the psychopath by McCord and McCord (1964) and Cleckley (1976). In particular, their hostile alienation from others, impulsivity, aggression, and relative absence of anxiety or social inhibition are consistent with this concept. Findings that this group is distinguished by narcissism, sensation seeking, interpersonal dominance, and violent criminality strengthen this interpretation. The secondary psychopaths share some of these traits, but differ in showing extreme social anxiety and traits of schizoid, avoidant, and passive–aggressive personality disorders. It seems likely that they will also meet broader clinical criteria for borderline personality disorder. The differences between the two groups accord with the distinction made by Lykken (1957), who proposed that Cleckley psychopaths could be divided according to high and low trait anxiety. However, some recent work suggests that primary psychopaths are more likely than secondary psychopaths to be identified as psychopaths by the PCL-R (Blackburn, 1996b). The label "secondary psychopath" may therefore be misleading, but its referent is nonetheless a clinically distinct and deviant group that seems to be prevalent among violent offenders.

TABLE 4.1. Criminal History of Mentally Disordered Offender Groups

	Group				
Convictions	P (*n* = 31)	S (*n* = 32)	C (*n* = 42)	I (*n* = 30)	*F* (3, 131)
Age at first	18.26	15.97	21.36	20.73	4.06**
Total	14.13	16.72	9.31	8.83	3.11*
Theft/burglary	5.13	9.03	4.36	4.43	2.78*
Violence	3.52	1.84	1.83	1.77	2.77*
Robbery	0.16	0.28	0.14	0.10	<1.0
Sex	0.65	1.13	0.43	0.30	1.38
Criminal damage	0.81	0.97	0.79	0.37	<1.0
Arson	0.52	0.16	0.26	0.13	<1.0

Note. P, primary psychopath; S, secondary psychopath; C, controlled; I, inhibited.
**$p < .01$; *$p < .05$.

Psychopathy and the Dimensions of Personality

In addition to discriminating types of abnormal personality, a further aim of my research has been to identify the personality dimensions contributing to these differences and to determine their relationship to empirically established dimensions of normal personality variation. When this research began, there was agreement that the dimensions of neuroticism and extraversion accounted for much of this variation, but considerable disagreement beyond that. More recently, however, a relative consensus has emerged that the Big Five factors can account for most variation in normal personality. It is also proposed that personality disorders represent extreme variants or combinations of these five factors (Widiger & Frances, 1994). Of particular interest in the present context is whether traits of psychopathy are accounted for by the Big Five.

In an attempt to discriminate aspects of aggression and hostility and their relationship to neuroticism and extraversion, I conducted a factor analysis of a number of personality measures in a sample of mentally disordered offenders (Blackburn, 1972). Three oblique factors of aggression, hostility–neuroticism, and extraversion emerged. The aggression factor was defined by scales of overt aggressiveness, acting out, resentment, and impulsivity, and negatively by Megargee's overcontrol scale. It correlated positively with hostility–neuroticism but was independent of extraversion. It seems likely that this factor has some relationship to what is now identified as agreeableness versus antagonism, but these results indicated two higher-order factors.

Several scales from that study are included in the SHAPS. The same two higher-order factors underlie the 10 SHAPS scales (Blackburn, 1979a, 1986). The first is defined by impulsivity, aggression, and hostility (and negatively by the Lie scale), and labeled "psychopathy" or "antisocial aggression." The second factor is defined by introversion, social anxiety, and proneness to dysphoric mood, and is labeled "withdrawal versus sociability." These factors have been found consistently across several samples of mentally disordered offenders. They appear to correspond to 45° rotations in the two-dimensional space of neuroticism and extraversion (Kassebaum, Couch, & Slater, 1959), and in that respect are equivalent to Gray's (1987) impulsivity and anxiety dimensions. Whether the first factor also incorporates agreeableness–disagreeableness remains to be tested.

The two dimensions account for the fourfold typology described earlier. The P and S groups fall toward the impulsive/aggressive extreme of the first factor, but lie at opposite extremes on the withdrawal dimension. The C and I groups fall toward the nonaggressive extreme of the first factor, but are also differentiated by the withdrawal dimension. The aggression and withdrawal factors may be construed as rejection versus acceptance of others and of self, respectively (Blackburn, 1987). In these terms, primary and secondary psychopaths are similar in rejecting others, but differ in self-concept and self-esteem.

These factors are virtually identical to the two largest factors in the MCMI personality disorder scales (Blackburn, 1996a), the aggression factor corresponding to an MCMI dimension defined by APD and paranoid, passive–aggressive, and borderline disorders. A similar dimension emerged from a recent factor analysis of interview ratings of the DSM-III personality disorders in a large sample of violent prisoners and mentally disordered offenders (Blackburn & Coid, in press). Of four factors extracted, the first was defined by high loadings on APD and paranoid, passive–aggressive, narcissistic, borderline, and histrionic disorders. Its interpretation as a broad dimension of psychopathy was supported by a correlation of .75 ($p < .001$) with the PCL-R. Correlations with self-report measures, however, were consistent with the proposal that personality disorder dimensions are variants of the Big Five dimensions, the psychopathy dimension being apparently related to agreeableness.

The aggression and withdrawal factors found in self-report scales also have their counterparts in behavior rating data (Blackburn, 1979b). The assumption that the aggression factor is closely related to psychopathy was supported by the finding of a significant correlation ($r = .60$, $p < .001$) between ratings of this factor and observer ratings of Cleckley's criteria of psychopathy (Blackburn & Maybury, 1985). We also demonstrated that relationships between the behavior ratings formed a circular array corresponding to the interpersonal circumplex.

The "interpersonal circumplex" or "interpersonal circle" is a well-established scheme for describing interpersonal styles (Leary, 1957; Kiesler, 1996; Wiggins & Pincus, 1994), the two dimensions defining this space being (1) the degree of power or control in social interactions (dominance vs. submission), and (2) the kind of affiliation (hostility vs. nurturance). Figure 4.1 shows a simplified version of the circular arrangement and the descriptions we apply to the octants around it. In our analysis, the aggression or psychopathy factor aligned with the coercive–compliant axis (BC-JK), Cleckley ratings being clustered around the hostility axis. The representation of psychopathic traits in the circumplex is illustrated by rating items falling within the hostile–dominant quadrant, which include "blames others," "lies easily," "demands attention," "impulsive," and "threatens others with violence" (Blackburn & Renwick, 1996). Using different measures with Canadian prisoners, Harpur et al. (1989) found that the PCL-R also projects onto the hostile–dominant quadrant of the circumplex.

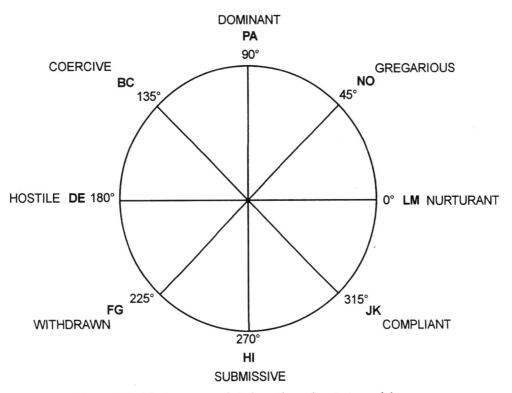

FIGURE 4.1. The interpersonal circle, and our descriptions of the octants.

The theoretical implications of these findings are developed in the next section. The point to be emphasized here is that analyses of self-report scales, interview ratings, and observer ratings converge in identifying a personality dimension defined by impulsivity, aggression, and hostility that is strongly related to established operational measures of psychopathy. The association of this dimension with the hostile–dominant quadrant of the interpersonal circumplex provides a link with the Big Five dimensions of personality, because the circumplex measures two of these dimensions (Wiggins & Pincus, 1994). Agreeableness is represented by the compliant–coercive axis, and extraversion by the gregarious–withdrawn axis.

Psychopathy, then, seems to be closely related to the dimension of agreeableness. This is consistent with the antagonistic and callous attributes defining the disagreeableness pole of this dimension. It is conceivable that other personality dimensions, such as neuroticism and conscientiousness, also have some role in psychopathic traits, although Harpur, Hart, and Hare (1994) found that agreeableness was the only dimension of the Big Five that correlated significantly with the PCL-R in a small sample of prisoners. Nevertheless, because psychopathy is identified particularly by such interpersonal characteristics as indifference to the effects of behavior on others, lack of affectional bonds, and manipulation or exploitation, its apparently close association with the interpersonal dimension of agreeableness–antagonism is perhaps not surprising. This suggests that interpersonal theory is particularly relevant to an understanding of psychopathy.

A COGNITIVE INTERPERSONAL MODEL OF PSYCHOPATHY

The Interpersonal Circle and Interpersonal Style

Current interpersonal theory originates in the work of Sullivan (1953) and Leary (1957). Sullivan saw the appropriate focus of psychopathology as social interactions and relationships rather than socially decontextualized individual behavior, and believed that most psychiatric problems are the outcomes of early distortions in relationships that are perpetuated into adult life. Leary developed these ideas further in a theory of personality based on findings that the relationship between interpersonal behaviors is represented by a circular array around the dimensions of dominance and nurturance, as described earlier. These dimensions represent the themes most commonly negotiated in social encounters, and the varying blends of these in interpersonal exchanges account for the circular ordering. Wiggins (1991) proposes that these interpersonal dimensions are concrete representations of the metaconcepts of "agency" (dominance) and "communion" (nurturance) that pervade many personality theories. Agency (vs. passivity) is manifested in strivings for mastery and power as a differentiated individual. Communion (versus dissociation) is manifest in strivings for intimacy and solidarity with a larger social or spiritual entity.

The units of interpersonal analysis may be dyadic interactions at the microanalytic level, but the circumplex also represents personality traits, or "interpersonal styles." Adaptive behavior calls for a repertoire of interpersonal skills represented at all parts of the circle. However, as a result of developmental experiences, people tend to acquire a distinctive style emphasizing a particular area of the circle. The more consistent or extreme a style, the narrower the range of interactions on which the person relies. This follows from the circumplex structure, in which segments of the circle are positively associated with adjacent segments and negatively associated with opposite segments. A person with an extreme dominant style, for example, is someone whose interactions are marked by a high frequency of dominant exchanges. Such a person will also show coercive and gregarious characteristics quite often, but submissive, withdrawn, or compliant behavior infrequently. The individual's behavior will hence be rigid and inflexible.

This notion of inflexible interpersonal styles is consistent with the concept of personality disorders as inflexible traits, and because these disorders are defined prominently by interpersonal dysfunction, many researchers have suggested that the interpersonal circle provides a basis for describing and classifying them. However, recent work indicates that personality disorders are more comprehensively described by the Big Five personality dimensions (Soldz, Budman, Demby, & Merry, 1993; Widiger & Frances, 1994; Wiggins & Pincus, 1994), only two of which are represented by the interpersonal circle. Nevertheless, interpersonal dysfunction seems to be central to APD and to histrionic, narcissistic, dependent, avoidant, and schizoid personality disorders (Wiggins & Pincus, 1994). As suggested above, psychopathy is a dimension corresponding broadly to the coercive–compliant axis of the circle, and can be construed in terms of a coercive interpersonal style.

Interpersonal Style, Personality Disorder, and Antisocial Behavior

In recent work, we expanded our earlier findings by developing a nurse rating scale to measure the interpersonal circle (Blackburn & Renwick, 1996). This instrument is called the Chart of Interpersonal Reactions in Closed Living Environments (CIRCLE), items being grouped into eight scales to mark the circle octants (see Figure 4.1). The four personality types described earlier are significantly discriminated by these scales (Blackburn, 1993b). Primary psychopaths are the most coercive, but they are also the most dominant and gregarious. Secondary psychopaths are also coercive, but they are more withdrawn and submissive. Both groups, then, exhibit interpersonal styles likely to promote conflict with others. However, in terms of Wiggins's distinctions, secondary psychopaths seem less "agentic" than primary psychopaths, reflecting their social anxiety and low self-esteem.

Studies using self-ratings of interpersonal style support the general proposition that personality disorders can be differentiated by the interpersonal circle (e.g., Soldz et al., 1993). This has been replicated by the finding of significant associations between CIRCLE ratings and most of the MCMI personality disorder scales (Blackburn, 1998). Of interest here is the location of APD and paranoid, passive–aggressive, narcissistic, and histrionic disorders, which were shown earlier to be related to a broad dimension of psychopathy. All of these disorders project onto the hostile–dominant quadrant, APD being closely related to the coercive octant, and histrionic and narcissistic disorders to dominance.

The association of psychopathy and acting-out disorders with hostile–dominant interpersonal styles suggests that criminal behavior may also be related to the circle. We therefore recently examined the relation of CIRCLE ratings to criminal history in mentally disordered offenders (Blackburn, in press). Within mentally ill patients, there is only a weak relation between interpersonal style and criminality. Among patients in the legal category of psychopathic disorder, however, there are several relatively strong correlations (Figure 4.2). A coercive interpersonal style is clearly associated with more persistent criminality as reflected in total number of convictions, convictions for stealing, and earlier age at first conviction. However, violence falls in the dominant–nurturant quadrant. These findings suggest that general criminality is associated with a coercive style, but that

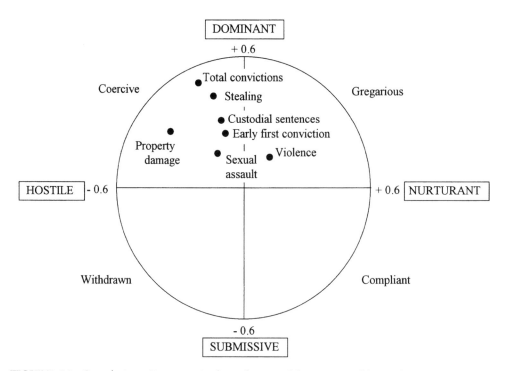

FIGURE 4.2. Correlations (Spearman's rho) of criminal history variables with the coordinates of the Chart of Interpersonal Reactions in Closed Living Environments (CIRCLE) (*n* = 59).

violent criminality is more likely when the individual also has a more dominant style. Further data are needed to confirm this, but it will be recalled that primary psychopaths, who are the most dominant individuals, also tend to have more convictions for violent offenses.

These data lend some support to the proposal that psychopathy is primarily an interpersonal dimension associated with the hostile–dominant quadrant of the interpersonal circle and with the personality dimension of agreeableness. Because the interpersonal circle assesses only two of the Big Five dimensions of personality, discrimination within socially deviant populations needs to take account of *intra*personal factors. For example, work with the PCL-R suggests an association of psychopathy with low levels of anxiety or neuroticism (Hare, 1991). Nevertheless, interpersonal theory has implications for the explanation of psychopathy, as well as for possible intervention strategies (Kiesler, 1996).

Interpersonal Style, Cognition, and Personality Disorder

Explanations of psychopathy have commonly emphasized affective deficits and associated psychophysiological or neuropsychological processes (Blackburn, 1993a). However, the cognitive revolution has demonstrated that cognitions are emergent properties with the causal power to determine emotional and social responses (Sperry, 1993). Although a biological basis to personality dimensions is generally acknowledged, an explanation of psychopathy may more readily be found in dysfunctional cognitions, and interpersonal theorists propose a process-oriented model underpinned by research in social cognition.

Interpersonal styles express fundamental motivational concerns (Wiggins, 1991), and the traits that define personality disorders can be understood in terms of what is communicated in interpersonal transactions. Wiggins's analysis suggests that concerns about power and status in social hierarchies (agency) in the context of rejection or avoidance of intimacy (communion) are central to a coercive style and hence to psychopathy. Millon (1981) offers a similar account, proposing that the aggression of aggressive personalities is a preemptive counterattack in the face of anticipations that others will exploit, dominate, and brutalize them. These conceptions imply that much of the behavior of psychopaths is motivated by interpersonal *beliefs*.

According to interpersonal theory, a particular behavior "pulls" a reaction from the other person, within a limited range, and this is governed by principles of complementarity (Kiesler, 1996). Along the dominance–submission axis, complementarity is reciprocal (i.e., a dominant response pulls a submissive reaction), whereas along the hostile–nuturant axis, the relation is corresponding or congruent (i.e., a hostile response invites a hostile reaction). These will be combined for different behaviors around the circle. For example, hostile dominance is likely to elicit hostile submission. The effect of a rigid interpersonal style will be for the person to produce many anticomplementary reactions that are aversive to other people.

Carson (1979) argues that the persistence of interpersonal styles across the lifespan and across situations can be understood in terms of expectancy confirmation processes. He proposes a causal relation among expectancies, interpersonal style, and the behavior of others. Cognitive dissonance is avoided by eliciting behavior from the other in accord with the concept of the self and one's role in the interaction. A particular overture involves verbal and nonverbal behavior that sends a message about the relationship. This invites a complementary response from the other, which, if forthcoming, provides feedback confirming the relationship.

In accounting for dysfunctional interpersonal styles, Carson (1979) suggests that early interactions may create strong expectations of how others are likely to react to oneself, and that these biased expectations subsequently become self-fulfilling prophecies. Similar proposals are advanced by attachment theorists (Ainsworth & Bowlby, 1991). Behavior is directed toward others to elicit a complementary reaction, which then confirms the expectations. For example, a hostile person expects hostile reactions from others and behaves in a way that produces them. People with strong expectations are thus likely to create interactions that minimize the chance of disconfirming experiences. Extreme interpersonal styles should therefore be associated with particular kinds of expectancies. For example, the coercive style proposed to characterize psychopathy would be expected to be associated with expectations of both hostile submission and hostile dominance, according to Carson, and a relative lack of skills for eliciting other reactions. Lack of empathic concern and manipulation of others would readily follow from such beliefs. Friendly dominance, on the other hand, should be associated with expectations of friendly submission.

As a preliminary test of this hypothesis, we constructed a simple measure of social expectations that asks patients how often they expect others to avoid them, criticize them, behave in a hostile way, be sympathetic, and so on (Blackburn, 1993b). Three factors were found in the items, reflecting expectations that others will be hostile–dominant or "challenging" ("argue," "wind you up," "be sarcastic"), friendly–submissive or "attentive" ("be friendly," "be sincere," "confide"), and hostile–submissive or "yielding" ("do things your way," "be fearful," "admit you are right"). There are highly significant differences ($p < .001$) between our four personality types on these factors. Secondary psychopaths are most likely to expect others to challenge them, but not to be attentive or yielding. Primary psychopaths, on the other hand, do not expect others to be challenging, but expect attention and also expect others to be more yielding. The results are broadly in line with the model. Primary psychopaths, who are the most hostile–dominant and friendly–dominant, expect others to be both hostile–submissive and friendly–submissive. Secondary psychopaths, who are more submissive, expect others to be hostile–dominant.

CONCLUSIONS

Psychopathy can be conceptualized as a broad dimension of personality disorder linked to the dimensions of personality, and in particular to agreeableness–antagonism. Hostility and aggression are central to this dimension. However, psychopaths are heterogeneous when other personality dimensions are considered, and our research has distinguished subgroups of primary and secondary psychopaths among violent offenders. Primary psychopaths are more persistently violent, but secondary psychopaths, who are characterized by poor self-esteem, are equally prevalent among dangerous offenders.

Psychopathic traits are represented within the interpersonal circumplex, and it is proposed that psychopathy is a manifestation of attempts to maintain coercive control of the social environment, supported by negative expectations of others. In these terms, psychopaths create conditions of interpersonal conflict in order to maintain their world view. Social-cognitive processes may therefore provide a key to understanding the violence of psychopaths.

REFERENCES

Ainsworth, M. D. S., & Bowlby, J. (1991). An ethological approach to personality development. *American Psychologist, 46*, 333–341.

American Psychiatric Association. (1980). *Diagnostic and statistical manual of mental disorders* (3rd ed.). Washington, DC: Author.

American Psychiatric Association. (1987). *Diagnostic and statistical manual of mental disorders* (3rd ed., rev.). Washington, DC: Author.

American Psychiatric Association. (1994). *Diagnostic and statistical manual of mental disorders* (4th ed.). Washington, DC: Author.

American Psychological Association. (1990). The Seville statement on violence. *American Psychologist, 45*, 1167–1168.

Berkowitz, L. (1993). *Aggression: Its causes, consequences, and control.* New York: McGraw-Hill.

Blackburn, R. (1968). Personality in relation to extreme aggression in psychiatric offenders. *British Journal of Psychiatry, 114*, 821–828.

Blackburn, R. (1971). Personality types among abnormal homicides. *British Journal of Criminology, 11*, 14–31.

Blackburn, R. (1972). Dimensions of hostility and aggression in abnormal offenders. *Journal of Consulting and Clinical Psychology, 38*, 20–26.

Blackburn, R. (1975). An empirical classification of psychopathic personality. *British Journal of Psychiatry, 127*, 456–460.

Blackburn, R. (1978). Psychopathy, arousal, and the need for stimulation. In R. D. Hare & D. Schalling (Eds.), *Psychopathic behavior: Approaches to research* (pp. 157–164). Chichester, England: Wiley.

Blackburn, R. (1979a). Psychopathy and personality: The dimensionality of self-report and behaviour rating data in abnormal offenders. *British Journal of Social and Clinical Psychology, 18,* 111–119.

Blackburn, R. (1979b). Cortical and autonomic arousal in primary and secondary psychopaths. *Psychophysiology, 16,* 143–150.

Blackburn, R. (1986). Patterns of personality deviation among violent offenders: Replication and extension of an empirical taxonomy. *British Journal of Criminology, 26,* 254–269.

Blackburn, R. (1987). Two scales for the assessment of personality disorder in antisocial populations. *Personality and Individual Differences, 8,* 81–93.

Blackburn, R. (1988). On moral judgements and personality disorders: The myth of the psychopathic personality revisited. *British Journal of Psychiatry, 153,* 505–512.

Blackburn, R. (1993a). *The psychology of criminal conduct: Theory, research and practice.* Chichester, England: Wiley.

Blackburn, R. (1993b). Psychopathic disorder, personality disorders and aggression. In C. Thompson & P. Cowen (Eds.), *Violence: Basic and clinical science* (pp. 101–118). Oxford: Butterworth–Heinemann.

Blackburn, R. (1996a). Replicated personality disorder clusters among mentally disordered offenders and their relation to dimensions of personality. *Journal of Personality Disorders, 10,* 68–81.

Blackburn, R. (1996b). Psychopathy and personality disorder: Implications of interpersonal theory. In D. J. Cooke, A. E. Forth, J. Newman, & R. D. Hare (Eds.), *Issues in criminological and legal psychology: No. 24. International perspectives on psychopathy* (pp. 18–23). Leicester, England: British Psychological Society.

Blackburn, R. (1998). Relationship of personality disorders to ratings of interpersonal style in forensic psychiatric patients. *Journal of Personality Disorders, 12,* 77–85.

Blackburn, R. (in press). Criminality and the interpersonal circle in mentally disordered offenders. *Criminal Justice and Behavior.*

Blackburn, R., & Coid, J. W. (in press). Psychopathy and the dimensions of personality disorder in violent offenders. *Personality and Individual Differences.*

Blackburn, R., Crellin, M. C., Morgan, E. M., & Tulloch, R. M. B. (1990). Prevalence of personality disorders in a special hospital population. *Journal of Forensic Psychiatry, 1,* 43–52.

Blackburn, R., & Lee-Evans, M. (1985). Reactions of primary and secondary psychopaths to anger evoking situations. *British Journal of Clinical Psychology, 24,* 93–100.

Blackburn, R., & Maybury, C. (1985). Identifying the psychopath; The relation of Cleckley's criteria to the interpersonal domain. *Personality and Individual Differences, 6,* 375–386.

Blackburn, R., & Renwick, S. J. (1996). Rating scales for measuring the interpersonal circle in forensic psychiatric patients. *Psychological Assessment, 8,* 76–84.

Buss, A. H. (1961). *The psychology of aggression.* New York: Wiley.

Carson, R. C. (1979). Personality and exchange in developing relationships. In R. L. Burgess & T. L. Huston (Eds.), *Social exchange in developing relationships* (pp. 247–269). New York: Academic Press.

Clark, L. A., Watson, D., & Reynolds, S. (1995). Diagnosis and classification of psychopathology: Challenges to the current system and future directions. *Annual Review of Psychology, 46,* 121–153.

Cleckley, H. (1976). *The mask of sanity* (6th ed.). St. Louis, MO: C. V. Mosby.

Coid, J. W. (1992). DSM-III diagnosis in criminal psychopaths: A way forward. *Criminal Behaviour and Mental Health, 2,* 78–94.

Farrington, D. P. (1989). Early predictors of adolescent aggression and adult violence. *Violence and Victims, 4,* 79–100.

Ferguson, T. J., & Rule, B. G. (1983). An attributional perspective on anger and aggression. In R. G. Geen & E. I. Donnerstein (Eds.), *Aggression: Theoretical and experimental reviews* (Vol. 1, pp. 70–97). New York: Academic Press.

Gifford, R. (1994). A lens-mapping framework for understanding the encoding and decoding of interpersonal dispositions in nonverbal behavior. *Journal of Personality and Social Psychology,* *66,* 398–412.

Gillham, R. (1978). *An investigation of imagery in psychopathic delinquents.* Unpublished BSc dissertation, University of Aberdeen, Scotland.

Gough, H. G. (1948). A sociological theory of psychopathy. *American Journal of Sociology, 53,* 359–366.

Gray, J. A. (1987). Perspectives on anxiety and impulsivity. *Journal of Research in Personality, 21,* 493–509.

Hare, R. D. (1991). *The Hare Psychopathy Checklist—Revised.* Toronto: Multi-Health Systems.

Hare, R. D. (1996). Psychopathy: A clinical construct whose time has come. *Criminal Justice and Behavior, 23,* 25–54.

Hare, R. D., & Hart, S. D. (1993). Psychopathy, mental disorder, and crime. In S. Hodgins (Ed.), *Mental disorder and crime* (pp. 104–115). Newbury Park, CA: Sage.

Hare, R. D., Hart, S. J., & Harpur, T. J. (1991). Psychopathy and the DSM-IV criteria for antisocial personality disorder. *Journal of Abnormal Psychology, 100,* 391–398.

Harpur, T. J., Hare, R. D., & Hakstian, A. R. (1989). Two-factor conceptualisation of psychopathy: Construct validity and assessment implications. *Psychological Assessment: A Journal of Consulting and Clinical Psychology, 1,* 6–17.

Harpur, T. J., Hart, S. D., & Hare, R. D. (1994). Personality of the psychopath. In P. T. Costa & T. A. Widiger (Eds.), *Personality disorders and the five-factor model of personality* (pp. 149–173). Washington, DC: American Psychological Association.

Harris, G. T., Rice, M. E., & Cormier, C. A. (1991). Psychopathy and violent recidivism. *Law and Human Behavior, 15,* 625–637.

Harris, G. T., Rice, M. E., & Quinsey, V. (1994). Psychopathy as a taxon: Evidence that psychopaths are a discrete class. *Journal of Consulting and Clinical Psychology, 62,* 387–397.

Hart, S. J., Forth, A. E., & Hare, R. D. (1991). The MCMI-II and psychopathy. *Journal of Personality Disorders, 5,* 318–327.

Hart, S. D., & Hare, R. D. (1989). Discriminant validity of the Psychopathy Checklist in a forensic psychiatric population. *Psychological Assessment: A Journal of Consulting and Clinical Psychology, 2,* 338–341.

Hart, S. D., Hare, R. D., & Forth, A. E. (1994). Psychopathy as a risk marker for violence: Development and validation of a screening version of the revised Psychopathy Checklist. In J. Monahan & H. J. Steadman (Eds.), *Violence and mental disorder: Developments in risk assessment* (pp. 81–99). Chicago: University of Chicago Press.

Henderson, M. (1982). An empirical classification of convicted violent offenders. *British Journal of Criminology, 22,* 1–20.

Howard, R. C. (1984). The clinical EEG and personality in mentally abnormal offenders. *Psychological Medicine, 14,* 569–580.

Howard, R. C. (1990). Psychopathy Checklist scores in mentally abnormal offenders: A re-examination. *Personality and Individual Differences, 11,* 1087–1091.

Huesmann, L. R., Eron, L. D., Lefkowitz, M. M., & Walder, L. O. (1984). Stability of aggression over time and generations. *Developmental Psychology, 20,* 1120–1134.

Hyler, S. E., & Lyons, M. (1988). Factor analysis of the DSM-III personality disorders: A replication. *Comprehensive Psychiatry, 29,* 304–308.

Kass, F., Skodol, A. E., Charles, E., Spitzer, R. L., & Williams, J. (1985). Scaled ratings of DSM-III personality disorders. *American Journal of Psychiatry, 142,* 627–630.

Kassebaum, G. C., Couch, A. S., & Slater, P. E. (1959). The factorial dimensions of the MMPI. *Journal of Consulting Psychology, 23,* 226–236.

Kiesler, D. J. (1996). *Contemporary interpersonal theory and research: Personality, psychopathology, and psychotherapy.* New York: Wiley.

Leary, T. (1957). *Interpersonal diagnosis of personality.* New York: Ronald Press.

Livesley, W. J., Schroeder, M. L., Jackson, D. N., & Jang, K. L. (1994). Categorical distinctions in the study of personality disorder: Implications for classification. *Journal of Abnormal Psychology, 103,* 6–17.

Lykken, D. T. (1957). A study of anxiety in the sociopathic personality. *Journal of Abnormal and Social Psychology, 55,* 6–10.

McCord, W. M., & McCord, J. (1964). *The psychopath: An essay on the criminal mind.* New York: Van Nostrand.

McGurk, B. J. (1978). Personality types among normal homicides. *British Journal of Criminology, 18,* 146–161.

Megargee, E. I. (1966). Undercontrolled and overcontrolled personality types in extreme antisocial aggression. *Psychological Monographs, 80* (Whole No. 611).

Mental Health Act 1983. (1983). London: HMSO.

Millon, T. (1981). *Disorders of personality: DSM-III, Axis II.* New York: Wiley.

Millon, T. (1983). *Millon Clinical Multiaxial Inventory* (3rd ed.). Minneapolis: Interpretive Scoring Systems.

Novaco, R. W. (1994). Anger as a risk factor for violence. In J. Monahan & H. J. Steadman (Eds.), *Violence and mental disorder: Developments in risk assessment* (pp. 21–59). Chicago: University of Chicago Press.

O'Kane, A., Fawcett, D., & Blackburn, R. (1996). Psychopathy and moral reasoning: Comparison of two methods of assessment. *Personality and Individual Differences, 20,* 504–514.

Olweus, D. (1979). Stability of aggressive reaction patterns in males: A review. *Psychological Bulletin, 86,* 852–875.

Pichot, P. (1978). Psychopathic behaviour: A historical overview. In R. D. Hare & D. Schalling (Eds.), *Psychopathic behaviour: Approaches to research* (pp. 55–70). Chichester, England: Wiley.

Presly, A. S., & Walton, H. J. (1973). Dimensions of abnormal personality. *British Journal of Psychiatry, 122,* 269–276.

Robins, L. (1978). Sturdy predictors of adult antisocial behaviour: Replications from longitudinal studies. *Psychological Medicine, 8,* 611–622.

Schneider, K. (1958). *Psychopathic personalities* (9th ed., M. Hamilton, Trans.). London: Cassell. (Original work published 1950)

Serin, R. C. (1991). Psychopathy and violence in criminals. *Journal of Interpersonal Violence, 6,* 423–421.

Serin, R. C. (1996). Violent recidivism in criminal psychopaths. *Law and Human Behavior, 20,* 207–217.

Soldz, S., Budman, S., Demby, A., & Merry, J. (1993). Representation of personality disorders in circumplex and five-factor space: Explorations with a clinical sample. *Psychological Assessment, 5,* 41–52.

Sperry, R. W. (1993). The impact and promise of the cognitive revolution. *American Psychologist, 48,* 878–885.

Sullivan, H. S. (1953). *The interpersonal theory of psychiatry.* New York: Norton.

Tedeschi, J. T. (1983). Social influence theory and aggression. In R. G. Geen & E. I. Donnerstein (Eds.), *Aggression: Theoretical and empirical reviews* (Vol. 1, pp. 1–25). New York: Academic Press.

Tyrer, P. (1988a). What's wrong with DSM-III personality disorders? *Journal of Personality Disorders, 2,* 281–291.

Tyrer, P. (1988b). *Personality disorders: Diagnosis, management and course.* London: Wright.

Tyrer, P., & Alexander, J. (1979). Classification of personality disorder. *British Journal of Psychiatry, 135,* 163–167.

Widiger, T. A., & Frances, A. J. (1994). Toward a dimensional model for the personality disorders. In P. T. Costa & T. A. Widiger (Eds.), *Personality disorders and the five-factor model of personality* (pp. 19–39). Washington, DC: American Psychological Association.

Widiger, T. A., & Trull, T. J. (1994). Personality disorders and violence. In J. Monahan & H. J. Steadman (Eds.), *Violence and mental disorder: Developments in risk assessment* (pp. 203–206). Chicago: University of Chicago Press.

Wiggins, J. S. (1991). Agency and communion as conceptual co-ordinates for the understanding and measurement of interpersonal behavior. In W. M. Grove & D. Cicchetti (Eds.), *Thinking clearly about psychology: Essays in honor of Paul E. Meehl* (Vol. 2, pp. 89–113). Minneapolis: University of Minnesota Press.

Wiggins, J. S., & Pincus, A. L. (1994). Personality structure and the structure of personality disorders. In P. T. Costa & T. A. Widiger (Eds.), *Personality disorders and the five-factor model of personality* (pp. 73–93). Washington, DC: American Psychological Association.

Willner, A. H., & Blackburn, R. (1988). Interpersonal style and personality deviation. *British Journal of Clinical Psychology, 27,* 273–274.

World Health Organization. (1992). *The ICD-10 classification of mental and behavioural disorders: Clinical descriptions and diagnostic guidelines.* Geneva: Author.

Zillmann, D. (1979). *Hostility and aggression.* Hillsdale, NJ: Erlbaum.

Zimmerman, M., & Coryell, W. (1990). DSM-III personality disorder dimensions. *Journal of Nervous and Mental Disease, 178,* 686–692.

5

Evil Intent: Violence and Disorders of the Will

HENRY RICHARDS

This chapter attempts to integrate several views of psychopathic personality disorder (PPD) by locating it as a distinct taxon within a broad spectrum of disorders, the paranoid–narcissistic spectrum. The disorders in the proposed spectrum have phenomenological and behavioral similarities, a common etiological linkage to pathological narcissism, and a common structural reliance on derivatives of aggression as a central organizing principle.

The title of this chapter suggests that in the severe cases in this spectrum, normal guilt and self-esteem are rarely, if ever, experienced. *Mens rea,* guilty intent, does not exist on the subjective level for such individuals. Instead, pathological identifications and renunciations, both at the unconscious level of object relations and at the conscious level of belief systems and values, engender intentions centered on aggression and destructiveness. This evil intent, or ill will, becomes essential to the individual's self-cohesion. These extreme cases exhibit an inversion of normal conscience, which punishes good intentions and rewards evil actions and intentions (Svrakic, McCallum, & Milan, 1991). Such disorders of the will significantly attenuate the individual's freedom to "choose life" over destructiveness. Articulating this spectrum concept will require exhuming and revitalizing the relationship between psychopathy and paranoid phenomena, especially the projection of potential negative self-evaluations, as well as restoring angry affect and hostile mood as cardinal features of paranoia.

Rather than investigating the specifics of violence or its prediction, this chapter will explore several factors common to personalities in the proposed spectrum that make their potential for violence particularly salient, compared to the potential of other personality types. These factors include impediments to developing the will to be morally responsible, an abnormal or defective moral conscience, ineffective inhibitory mechanisms, the habitual use of aggressive and destructive strategies, and unique motivational and catalytic dynamics in which self-regulation hinges largely on the use of aggression.

In order to lay the groundwork for placing PPD within a broader spectrum context, an elaboration of PPD as a fully developed and distinct therorotype (Rychlak, 1981) is presented in the next section, followed by sections discussing pathological narcissism, paranoid phenomena, and approaches to the construction of spectrum formulations. The paranoid–narcissistic spectrum and its implications for psychopathy are then explored.

AN INTEGRATIVE REVIEW OF THE MANY FACES
OF THE PSYCHOPATH

This brief review focuses on the features and formulations of psychopathy that contribute to the integrative image of the psychopath and the related spectrum formulation advanced in this chapter. More comprehensive and inclusive reviews are available elsewhere (Hare, 1970). The psychopath has been perceived alternatively as a person with an inordinate amount of aggressive drive, as an individual with a defective superego, as a malignant narcissist, as a barely sealed-over psychotic masked as a person with character disorder, and, more recently, as suffering from a subtle dementia. Of course, numerous combinations of these views have been proposed. For example, Fenichel (1945) emphasized the distortions of early identifications and spoke of "instinct-ridden characters." Friedlander (1945) emphasized the pleasure principle orientation of the psychopath, which suggested both disinhibition and deficient reality orientation. Earlier in this century, Aichorn (1925/1935) noted the contribution of narcissism, Oedipal configurations, and the failure of incorporating parental ideals as necessary precursors to a developed superego in psychopaths. Horney (1945) eloquently described the use of exploitation and sadism to increase a sense of power and importance. Her understanding of the use of aggression and destructiveness in the service of self-enhancement foreshadowed the seminal work of Bursten (1972) on the manipulative personality.

By 1950 this line of theory stressing narcissistic pathology in the development of psychopathy was well established, with Levy (1951) distinguishing between individuals who had experienced two extremes of narcissistic injury: the deprived psychopath, who had often experienced a harsh upbringing; and the indulged psychopath, who had often experienced parental overvaluation. This formulation parallels Millon's (1981) aggressive and narcissistic subtypes of the independent personality orientation. Although Millon's system does not use PPD as a nosological prototype per se, he and his coworkers continue to develop subtypes of personality disorders, including subtypes of antisocial personality disorder (APD). A range of severities appears to be implied as obtaining among these subtypes. Millon's "malevolent antisocial" and "covetous antisocial" subtypes (Millon with Davis, 1996) have similarities with PPD as treated here. The degree of inflexibility and interpersonal incapacity apparently exhibited by these subtypes suggests that they are more structurally defective than the mainstream APD prototype.

Although structural defects have been cited often as cardinal features in many formulations of the psychopath, the most extreme view of these—the view of the psychopath as a sealed-over or concealed psychotic—has neither been used frequently in combination with other views, nor developed very far in its own right. Cleckley (1941, 1976) considered psychopathy as a type of concealed psychosis hidden under a "mask of sanity," which was revealed primarily though the disintegrating effects of strong emotion (aggressive or libidinal), as well as in "semantic dementia"—an inherent disjoint relationship between word and deed.

Like his brilliant clinical descriptions, Cleckley's image of a mask of sanity covering semantic dementia is profound. This image suggests that the 19th-century thinkers who proposed psychopathy as a form of *delirium sans dementia* were on to something important. Cleckley suggested that psychopaths have a selective dementia that involves affect and language. This dementia is difficult to detect because the psychopath adaptively simulates normal reality orientation, normal affect, and interpersonal attachment. Only the shallowness of higher social affects, the absence of guilt and loyalty, and the inability to appreciate consequences indicate a concealed disregard for the value of reality and a misunderstanding of consensual meanings. Studies indicating a negative relationship between traditionally diagnosed stable psychotic syndromes, such as schizophrenia and psychopathy, may have prematurely closed this line of theory development, due to an oversimplification of what was traditionally conveyed by the idea of a sealed-over or covert psychotic disorder. These terms traditionally conveyed more than the delayed onset or the late detection of severely impaired reality testing and first-rank symptoms. They implied what would be referred to now as "borderline personality organization" or "borderline personality structure," following Kernberg's (1975) revitalization of such concepts. Studies indicating normal performance of psychopaths on traditional neuropsychological tests might have threatened a similar preemption of the pursuit of a specific dementia or neurodynamic defect. However, the increasing sophistication, multidisciplinary collaboration, and technological advances of cognitive and psychophysiological investigations continue to open more paths headed in this direction.

Robert Hare's (1991) Psychopathy Checklist—Revised (PCL-R), a highly reliable and valid rating instrument for measuring psychopathy, builds explicitly on Cleckley's clinical criteria. Coming from a background in experimental psychophysiology, Hare may have based his choice of these criteria in part on Cleckley's implicit assumption of a neurophysiological defect in psychopaths. Cleckley's "semantic dementia" continues to provide a link between earlier formulations and recent advances in studying groups of psychopaths identified through Hare's PCL-R, such as the learning, language, and physiological differences that discriminate psychopaths from normals and from nonpsychopathic individuals with APD (Hare, 1991). Although psychopaths appear not to be impaired on traditional neuropsychological tests (Hart, Forth, & Hare, 1990), a kind of evaluative semantic aphasia in psychopathy is being investigated through psycholinguistic and cognitive experiments involving emotional response style, attributions, and moral reasoning (Rieber & Vetter, 1994).

Studies demonstrating these differences are now readily found in the scientific literature. For example, in a recent study, psychopaths inappropriately substituted attributions of happiness or indifference for appropriate guilt in judging the emotions of protagonists of emotional vignettes, but appropriately attributed happiness, sadness, and embarrassment to protagonists (Blair, Sellars, Strickland, & Clark, 1995). In another study utilizing narratives (Blair, Jones, Clark, & Smith, 1995), aggressive transgressions and transgressions of moral convention were indistinguishable to all of the psychopathic subjects ($n = 20$), whereas all of the nonpsychopaths ($n = 20$) made the appropriate distinction; these results suggest that psychopaths understand the letter of the law, but not its spirit. Abnormal processing of emotional stimuli in psychopaths has been demonstrated, using startle reflex modulation (Patrick, Bradley, & Lang, 1993) and models of fear image processing (Patrick, Cuthbert, & Lang, 1994). In these studies, abnormal processing of emotionally arousing stimuli occurred independently of affective self-report, suggesting the dissociation of affective and semantic processing in a manner consistent with Cleckley's hypothesis of an inherent disjoint relationship between word and deed in psychopathy. A recent review of the effects of functional separation of brain hemispheres due to brain damage noted that the pattern of loss of empathic skills, sense of familiarity related to bonding, and alexithymia, especially when right-hemispheric contributions were inhibited, was highly suggestive of the pattern of deficits and dissociated affective processing in psychopathy (Henry, 1993). Based on their findings of abnormal language evoked response potentials in psychopaths, Williamson, Harpur, and Hare (1991) speculated that internalized speech mechanisms implicated in the development of the conscience, following Luria (1973), may be impaired in psychopaths. They further speculated that the psychopath may, by necessity, develop alternative strategies to compensate for an inability to intuit the emotional valence of words from context. Hare and colleagues, using advanced diagnostic imaging technology to record ongoing brain functioning, continue to find convergent evidence for abnormal affective functioning patterns in psychopaths (e.g., subvocalization similar to that found in the learning of reading), in the absence of detectable tissue abnormalities (R. D. Hare, personal communications, November 4, 1996).

Working from within a different research tradition, Gacono and Meloy (1993) and others have garnered Rorschach evidence of patterns in conscious cognitive style, unconscious defensive processes, and physiological responses that differentiate psychopaths from nonpsychopathic individuals with APD and from normals. These differences include more severely disordered attachments and narcissistic fixation at the expense of object relatedness, combined with orienting and coping responses that are more pathognomonic than those of nonpsychopathic criminals. Simultaneously, there is a relative absence of performance deficits related to anxiety or conflict.

Meloy (1988; see also Meloy & Gacano, Chapter 6, this volume) has formulated a coherent integration of ideas related to such physiological differences and cognitive deficits in psychopaths with related psychodynamic concepts. His formulation stresses failures in narcissistic processes, superego defects, and innate predispositions toward impulsivity and aggression. Meloy speculates that a biological basis may account for the attachment failure and malignant identification of the psychopath. He views this as occurring along two causal paths. The first path begins with a deficit in the ability to attach or bond, which is perhaps most cleanly conceptualized as an early defect involving heretofore unspecified neurological strata or a polythetic configuration of genes. The second causal path begins with a defect resulting in an overabundance of aggressive drive, or with a defect in inhibitory functions, or both. The effects of infantile and early childhood experience, combined with biological predispositions, set the stage for the development of psychopathy.

In following this formulation, and in later charting the development of pathological superego and conscience structures, I believe it is important to make clear distinctions between "introjection" and "identification"—concepts often used inconsistently and with varying degrees of precision in the psychodynamic literature. Meissner (1979) made the distinction between two kinds of internal objects: introjects and identifications. He viewed introjections as functioning closely with libidinous and aggressive drive states, whereas identifications function independently of these vicissitudes. As superego stand-ins for drives, introjections are closely allied to the defensive projection of threatening or unacceptable impulses. Introjections modify the superego and may work counter to ego development. Identifications, on the other hand, modify ego structure directly and share in conscious behavior. In Kernberg's terminology, it would appear that identifications become metabolized and generalized aspects of the ego, whereas introjections remain fragmentary, drive-charged, and personified aspects of the superego.

In Meloy's formulation, it appears that the psychopath does not fail in the attachment process because of an inability to identify; rather, the psychopath develops abnormal identifications. These identifications are overimbued with the nonmetabolized (personified and polarized), early introjections of the archetypal experience of the stranger selfobject, instead of being informed primarily by the reality components of rewarding and frustrating parental interactions. Grotstein (1982) defines the stranger selfobject as "the unconscious pre-awareness of the enemy which is believed to be both within ourselves and to have an external counterpart" (p. 63). The identification with the stranger selfobject is later enacted as a predator–prey relationship, which relies on projection and reincorporation of aggression in a process similar to the paranoid process described by Meissner (1978). The persistence of these primitive, unmodified introjections may account for the psychopath's increased openness to fantasy (Harpur, Hart, & Hare, 1994) as a means of gaining gratification from the superego derivatives of these introjects, which are defined in the next formulation to be reviewed as constituting a "mirror conscience"—the antithesis of the normal moral conscience.

Meloy's (1988) intriguing discussion of the psychopath as a predator (i.e., as a human functioning from the "reptilian brain") is a creative combination of clinical, scientific, and popular notions. However, this animal image obscures the depth of psychopathic deviance. It is not that psychopaths *are* predators, but that they themselves deeply *identify with,* and will to possess and to become, the destructive, aggressive, evil intentions and malicious powers that have been historically attributed to the "ignoble beasts," especially serpents (Midgley, 1978).[1]

Also working from within the object relations and self-psychological traditions, Svrakic et al. (1991) have specified a spectrum relationship between narcissistic personality disorder (NPD) and APD, based on the shared etiology for these two disorders in pathological narcissism and what they refer to as a two-level self-structure. They emphasize the high degree of symptom overlap among all of the personality disorders, due to the ubiquity among them of borderline personality organization, and view APD and NPD as pathologies of narcissism organized at the borderline level of personality structure. Kernberg (1984) has contributed the most to the understanding of the meaning of such structural deficits in the personality disorders in general, and in the malignant narcissist subtype that has often been equated with PPD in particular. In Kernberg's schema of progressive structuralization, the level of predominant defense and the degrees of integration, coherence, and realism within the self, or representational world, are interdependent and reciprocally related. These facets of structure are determined by the degree to which repression and its allied mechanisms have replaced splitting and its allied mechanisms (Kernberg, 1975). "Splitting," the polarization and antagonism of mental contents at the same level of consciousness, can be contrasted with "repression," which isolates dissonant contents at different levels of consciousness. Effective repression facilitates integration and coherent complexity at the level of conscious awareness.

Kernberg is not the only theorist contributing to Svrakic et al.'s integration. In something like a Kohutian iteration of Cleckley's "mask" image, Kernberg and Cleckley see both the narcissistic and antisocial personalities as having a two-level self-structure. The real self of these personalities is alone, empty, unable to learn, inferior, and insecure. This real face is hidden by an overlay of a mask—a grandiose facade in the case of the narcissist, or a destructive facade in the case of the antisocial personality. In Svrakic et al.'s model, the differences in facade self between NPD and APD result from differences in superego development. The narcissist's superego is not fully developed and consists primarily of sadistic superego forerunners, or fragments, that intrude upon ego functioning in the form of nonpsychotic paranoia, obsessiveness, remnants of moral behavior, and a circumscribed capacity for guilt. In contrast,

> The superego of an antisocial person has not been arrested at the stage of superego precursors, but is rather a fully developed organizer that gratifies destructive behaviors and punishes positive behaviors. Such superego is best described as a "mirror" image of normal superego. This may explain the fact that the identity of a "negative hero" supports and increases the self-esteem of most antisocial persons. (Svrakic et al., 1991, p. 422)

It appears that in their view, the antisocial personality has the better-organized but more deviant pathology. Svrakic et al. have coined the term "destructive self" to designate self-concepts organized around idealized aggression, as are found in the antisocial personality. In the disorders in their spectrum, the facade self appears to be a defense to protect the person from experiencing the real self and to relate to the external world through the mechanism of projective identification. Therefore, the narcissist, who experiences a self that is "really" inferior and insecure, engages others in order to gain their admiration, whereas the destructive personality, who views the real self as weak and victimized, seeks the experience of domination and destructive power. Svrakic et al. view the talents and valued attributes of the child (e.g., attractiveness), and the degree of receptiveness of the family environment, as factors that channelize the facade self in the direction of the narcissist or the destructive. This formulation is similar to Millon's (1981) view that passive, entitled strategies versus active, appropriative strategies differentiate the narcissistic and antisocial personalities, respectively.

Svrakic et al. (1991) indicate that destructives differ among themselves in the degree of integration of the self, by which they primarily appear to be referring to the hierarchical subordination of the real self (which is nonadaptive) to the facade self (which has adaptive capacities). Poorly integrated destructives are in almost constant conflict within themselves and others, due to intrusions of real-self experiences into consciousness and consequent nonadaptive behaviors. These lower-level destructives never develop effective facade selves that can successfully adapt to the external world. Better-organized destructives, whom they equate with psychopaths, increase self-esteem and effectively gain real-world benefits through their destructive acts, thus further shoring up the defective real self and presumably improving adaptation. The most organized of destructives in this formulation are capable of never allowing the real self to be disruptive or exhibited, which enables them to become successful "professional criminals." Although Svrakic et al. do not explicitly indicate this, it appears that their "mirror conscience" shores up repressive mechanisms enough to permit containment of the real self through projective identification and acting out of aggressive and libidinal wishes.

Svrakic et al.'s introduction of the term "destructive personality," which has been adopted for use in the paranoid–narcissistic spectrum, clarifies many of the conceptual and practical confusions caused by the term "antisocial personality." The idea of a sense of conscience that is the antithesis to the normal conscience is also of great significance. However, designating this concept with the term mirror conscience, despite the vivid imagery, risks confusing the new concept with many already existing terms and their connotations. For example, such terms as "mirror transference" and "empathic mirroring" have become ubiquitous among therapists, almost without regard to theoretical orientation. More importantly, the mirror has been the perennial icon of self-awareness and self-monitoring, of normal conscience and its ability to strengthen the ego in right conduct, and of psychological reflection and the psyche itself. These ancient associations should not be darkened or confused by identifying the mirror as the icon of a severe pathological process or structure.[2] The concept of a sense of conscience that rewards destructive fantasies and acts is adopted for use in the integration offered in this chapter, but it is referred to as the "inverse conscience," whereas the mirror as symbol is conserved in its traditional iconology as described above. A further elaboration is made to the inverse conscience, beyond the lexical change, by suggesting a process through which the inverse conscience might develop.

PRELIMINARY INTEGRATION

An attempt at integrating these disparate theoretical formulations and wide-ranging empirical investigations is offered, at the risk of overinclusiveness. The best candidate to serve the basis for such an integrative attempt is the view that psychopathy is a semantogenic disorder—a disorder arising from the incomprehension and misconstruing of evaluative, affective, and ultimately moral meanings. In this complex semantogenic process, abnormalities in brain functional organization (of unknown origin) interact with environmental assaults and deprivations, and with neurodynamics (Sacks, 1989) that result from coping with having psychopathic deficits in the midst of a social world of normality, where emotions and evaluations are paramount. What follows is an integrative attempt at describing this psychopathic development from such a complex interaction of causal factors.

Abnormal emotional processing and affective learning abnormalities, such as abnormal fear responses and defective passive avoidance learning (Newman & Wallace, 1993), arise early in the life of the psychopath, probably resulting from the reciprocal interaction of biological inheritance and the quality of parental care. These abnormalities culminate in severe limitations in developing the consensual meanings related to attachment, such as empathy, values, and morality. These deficits may make it impossible for such infants and children to tolerate (let alone incorporate) the emotional and evaluative reality of their parents and others, which is perceived as being intrusively and ruthlessly imposed upon them, almost from the beginning of life. For reasons that I attempt to address below, aggressive introjects and identifications begin to displace introjections and identifications based on parental ideals. This displacement is the first critical step in the development of the inverse conscience. The few identifications with parental values that are incorporated in this early phase are later subordinated or discarded, as psychic cathexis. Interpersonal emphasis is increasingly diverted from parental models to those of powerful siblings, to persons outside the family circle, and eventually to peers, older youths, and mentors selected because they are destructive or psychopathic, or because they present the opportunity to exercise aggressive or destructive trends.

In later childhood and adolescence, simulation of higher social affects (and related motives) and manipulative deception are learned operantly as the psychopath attempts to fit in and gain concrete rewards and social advantage. At the interpersonal level, conscious deception and the related attitude of contempt for the deceived other begin to predominate over other kinds of interactions. Through the process of projective identification, psychopaths enact (using others as props, supporting actors, and "fifth business") the betrayal, belittlement, and banishment of their own internal experience, which results from their outsiders' perspective on the normal caring and meaning they observe in others. To a psychopath, normal caring appears transparently unreal because it is grounded in normal attachment and other affectively charged experiences and symbols. These meanings are not simply inscrutable to the psychopath. Because of the powerful reward value that attachment and affect clearly have for others, their meanings are provocative—always alluring, and always frustrating and exiling. Our sweetest fruits *are* sour grapes to the psychopath. The psychopath tries to crash the party but is always on the outside looking in. The psychopath's deviant affective life and evaluative semantic aphasia set the stage for profound and repetitive narcissistic injuries, which perpetuate primitive solipsism. Normal reciprocal demands from others are increasingly perceived as malevolent intrusions and further contribute to the development of the inverse conscience. Without the normal reciprocal inhibitory relationship among affiliation, empathy, and fear, the psychopath is stripped of the internal violence inhibition mechanisms (Blair, 1995) common to other humans—mechanisms that are tenuous in our species, compared to other large social predators (Lorenz, 1963).

Physical violence and violent recidivism may be more closely related to impulsivity than to psychopathy per se (DeJong, Virkkunen, & Linnoila, 1992; Reid, 1995), although psychopaths are often impulsive. Nonetheless, accepting the idea of the inverse conscience implies that there is no internal obstacle to physical violence for the severe psychopath, unless violence is seen in a given situation as the lesser of two evils. The inverse conscience provides a great incentive to engage in violence, in all of its modes, against persons, organizations, values, and ideals. As identification of the actual self with the idealized, destructive self is realized through aggressive action, fantasies of grandiosity and omnipotence may induce superconfidence, which in turn may contribute to impulsive and brazen acts. In short, success is likely to ruin the psychopath, but only after extensive destructiveness has been visited upon others.[3]

The account of the development of psychopathy offered so far leaves begging the question of how psychopathic identifications, such as that with the predator/enemy introject, develop in the first place. It would appear that, other than aggressively rejecting parental inputs, the infant would have no other alternative but to develop a superego and later a conscience primarily determined by parental models. How does something like the predator/enemy introject appear on the developmental scene to provide a source of pathological identification? The answer to this question is tied up in the Gordian knot that forms the nexus between genetic inheritance and object relations theory. From the explanatory thread of genetic inheritance, constitutional factors may predispose the infant toward having an inordinately high aggressive drive. This will have its primary effect on ego development, resulting in poor cohesion of the ego and impulsivity. Other inherited structures that might directly affect superego development have been posited, such as Laforgue's primitive superego ("The Relativity of Reality," 1940, as cited in Campbell, 1981), which was seen as placing limits on and guiding the development of brain organization toward certain functions and goals and away from others. Also, Jung's collective unconscious contains archetypes that influence ego and superego development. The predator/enemy introject could be such a "wired-in" archetype, stored in the genetic archive of all humans.

But why would the prepsychopathic infant begin to identify with and realize such an archetype? The answer may be found in the object relations thread of the knot. In the Kleinian narrative of development, the infant's early incorporation of external reality has an inherent oral quality, which in the paranoid–schizoid position is tinged with aggression and annihilation anxiety. Since the incorporations that result in the formation of the superego take place prior to self–other differentiation, the prepsychopathic infant may begin to idealize the aggressive component of the incorporative experience as a magical weapon to be used against, or as a protection from, the parents, whose evaluations and affects are perceived as intrusive and cruel. These perceptions may reflect a reality of parental abuse or incompetence, but are more likely related to basic attachment and affective processing deficits. However, like the effect of inordinate aggression on the ego, idealizing the aggressive component of incorporation would result in a superego that would be inherently unstable (if not actually untenable), wherein ideals would annihilate ideals. Psychobiology, inheritance of psychic deep structure in the form of something like archetypes, and object relations alone all fail to explain cases of psychopathy in which the inverse conscience appears to be at least superficially stable. However, if the idealization of the inordinate aggressive component activated a wired-in archetype, such as the predator/enemy, a source of stable but highly pathological superego development would be established. Also, the semantogenic origin of psychopathy would be established at the preverbal level, since the adoption of this particular archetype for the purpose of identification in infancy is a fatal misconstruing of meaning. If such an archetypal bundle of information (in the Aristotelian sense of having the ability to in-form, or shape psychic structure) exists, it must have evolved in order to aid the young in recognizing and evading predators and to enable adults to mimic more aggressive animal predators when dealing with threatening out-species, large game animals, and human outgroup enemies. Directing the archetype toward one's parents or parental ideals in infancy or early childhood is a fundamental semantic error.

Once this critical event of adopting a destructive attitude toward parental ideals takes place, the process of negation of the ego provides a model of how the systematic development of the inverse conscience could proceed in later eras of life. In negation of the ego (Campbell, 1981), an individual adopts a negative and antagonistic attitude toward a powerful object and then strives to differentiate from the object by becoming its opposite. If a process of negation of the superego occurs in the psychopath, the result would be a vicious cycle of moral development: The psychopath would idealize the aggressive component of incorporating parental values, which in turn would activate the predator/enemy introject and identifications with it, thereby fueling further elaborations of the inverse conscience and more distorted meanings. Alternative and countercultural contacts (including those with criminals) would further consolidate these identifications, as would actual injustices suffered at the hands of authority figures, or hypocrisy or inconsistency detected in such figures.

In this proposed integration, psychopathy results from the confluence of developmental failures in attachment, communication, affective attunement, and meaning formation. Grotstein (1995) has posited a similar confluence in the development of primitive psychotic conditions. In such conditions, symbolism and imagination, ineffectively mediated by language, fail to provide a protective, humanizing buffer against the empty, inhuman nature of reality, thus creating what he refers to as "orphans of the 'real.'" Psychopathy can therefore be usefully compared and contrasted to both schizophrenia and autism—disorders involving disruptions or developmental errors in similar biopsychosocial functions, although comparatively subtle and delimited in the case of psychopathy, rather than the gross and pervasive defects of the psychotic disorders. If the neurodynamics of psychopathy are in some important way like the neurodynamics of schizophrenia and autism, then we might look first to paranoid schizophrenia for parallels, because of the focus on self, threat, and aggression found in this disorder. The psychopathic equivalents of the negative signs of schizophrenia are related to the inability to be caring, by which is meant the psychological capacities of empathy and attachment, the ontological capacity of being for the sake of others (Heidegger, 1926/1962), and the theological capacity for living through values developed from and subordinated to an ultimate concern (Tillich, 1952). The positive signs of psychopathy are seen in ill will or evil intent: hatred, envy, and destructiveness as inherent aspects of maintaining the self-structure. These two sets of features come together in the deviant identifications and idealizations that make up the inverse conscience.

Integrative models of psychopathy as a semantogenic disorder can be cross-fertilized and further informed by models of schizophrenia as a disorder of social cognition, communication, and metarepresentation of intentions and motives (Steffy, 1993). For example, Wirth (1992) has proposed such a model for schizophrenia, in which the temporal cortex and amygdala provide crucial information for the content of social-cognitive propositions, including the attribution of reward values (good–bad, nice–nasty) and subtle nuances of affects to objects, while the interaction of these areas with the frontal cortex provides the needed metarepresentational context, including the representation of the mental states of self and others. Similar neural processing loops may be involved in the development of psychopathy.

When these ideas of semantic dementia and a related failure of a protective semantic barrier are applied to the moral behavior of psychopaths and schizophrenics, very different scenarios for the neurodynamics of conscience are suggested. The typical schizophrenic may have more moral sense than can be tolerated, given the individual's integrative limitations and gross imaginal, perceptual, and semantic deficits. On the other hand, the typical psychopath may have a moral sense that is so far eroded by some more specific deficit (such as an evaluative aphasia) that the person is permanently outside the internal arena of moral conflict and related distress. In the journey of self-cohesion, the schizophrenic attempts to integrate ideals (various components of the will) within the context of distorted thinking and feeling. The pervasive illness dooms the schizophrenic to become Oedipus, who orphans himself to isolation, guilt, and shame. On the same road, the psychopath's perversion of ideals murders both meaning and caring, leaving the psychopath without conflict, comfortable in an unhumanized world. To change metaphors, paranoid schizophrenics hear strange, accusative, threatening voices; psychopaths are deaf to the voice of conscience. Schizophrenics know the music of morality, although they sometimes jumble the words; psychopaths parrot the right words, but to a different tune. The psychopaths' mute eloquence exposes severe structural defects that are only subtle when we are looking the wrong way.

Of course, this brief review and attempt at preliminary integration do not exhaust all of the possible views of psychopathy. The basic argument of this chapter is that the image of the psychopath will not be complete until it is placed in context with images of related disorders. The next two sections of this chapter will review in more depth the nature of pathological narcissism, its relationship to paranoid phenomena, and the convergence of these two dimensional aspects of psychopathology in a spectrum formulation that includes both Svrakic et al.'s (1991) destructive personality disorder and PPD.

PATHOLOGICAL NARCISSISM

Most personality-disordered individuals are egocentric in the sense that they view the world from a narrow, idiosyncratic perspective, focused nonadaptively on exaggerated or denied needs and sensitivities. Personality disorders that are essentially narcissistic, however, are more than self-centered; they are self-reflexive. Interpersonal relationships and environmental goals are pursued in order to shape and control self-representations. Thought, fantasy, and action turn back on the self and are primarily focused on repairing, preserving, or enhancing the rewarding and anxiety-reducing aspects of a reflexive arch between the actual self and the ideal self. Following Stolorow's (1975) definition of narcissistic mental activity, the narcissistic personality gives psychological and behavioral priority to maintaining the structural cohesiveness, temporal stability, and positive affective coloring of the self-representation at almost any cost. Taking this broader view of narcissism increases its relevance to all the personality disorders, but results in its being intimately linked to NPD, APD, PPD, and paranoid personality disorder.

The most obvious cases of narcissism are typified by grandiosity and "pronoia"—a term coined by Kirmayer (1983) in describing distortions that go beyond the well-documented self-serving bias of normal individuals and that result in unrealistic positive expectations of efficacy, success, and acceptance from others. Because their attention appears to be on others, cases of narcissism involving paranoia (where the form of self-confirming distortion involves an unrealistic anticipation of rejection and attack from others, rather than admiration) are not as obvious, especially when premorbid passive–aggressive and compulsive styles predominate in states that operate in nonthreatening areas of functioning, or during times of relative security. In either the pronoid or paranoid narcissist, affect may be highly constricted or congruent with the cognitive processing bias—that is, expressing either the euphoria and exuberance of the confident narcissist, or the hostility, irritability, or fearfulness of the paranoid style. Both pronoia and paranoia serve to create a sense of coherence from chaos and confusion.

Since the proposed spectrum relies on the assumption of the existence of facets of pathological narcissism, a recent empirical investigation of narcissistic traits as seen from several theoretical schemes is of particular interest, in that distinct dimensions of narcissism were detected (several of which remained coherent across three different sets of criteria for narcissism). Perry and Perry (1996) assessed the coherence, homogeneity, and convergence of narcissistic features as specified by Kernberg (1975, 1982), Akhtar and Thompson (1982), and DSM-III-R (American Psychiatric Association, 1987). These three systems were judged in an earlier review to be well enough articulated as theories to suggest clear empirical rating schemes (Ronningstam & Gunderson, 1988). Subjects were individuals endorsing various symptomatic complaints who had been recruited for a broader study of borderline personality organization. Experienced clinicians rated the narcissistic traits of subjects under each of the three systems from audiotaped psychodynamically oriented interviews that explored symptoms, motives, conflicts, and defenses. Acceptable interrater reliability was found for all three systems. The systems were moderately homogeneous in regard to internal consistency. As expected, the three systems were highly interrelated. The combined DSM-III-R criteria were correlated .84 with both of the other systems. Akhtar and Thompson's system correlated .85 with Kernberg's criteria.

Factor analyses (principal components with varimax rotation) of the three-systems resulted in a three factor solution for DSM-III-R, and four factors for the other systems. All three systems had a factor interpreted by the authors as grandiosity and overdependence on admiration (12.4% to 33.2% of variance), a factor of exploitation and indifference to others (17.0% to 38.9% of variance), and a factor of hypersensitivity and poor self-esteem regulation (6.5% to 11.6% of variance). Fourth factors unique to Akhtar and Thompson's system and to Kernberg's system, respectively, were a factor describing pathological love and sexuality (9.7% of variance) and "a factor describing emotional neglect, containing features broadly shared with borderline personalities" (8.4% of variance; Perry & Perry, 1996, p. 15). In discussing these findings, the investigators suggested a formulation based on empirical convergence of the three factor structures:

> The factor structures we obtained suggest that more than one process is involved in the development of narcissistic pathology. Furthermore, their independence suggests that individuals may develop narcissistic traits in one, two, or up to five areas. This could yield different character types. For instance, the classic psychopath described by Cleckley . . .

may score high on two or three of the core factors with emphasis on lack of empathy and antisocial features. By contrast an occupationally successful narcissistic person may score highest on the factor of grandiosity and fantasies of success, while the Don Juan character scores highest on interpersonal exploitativeness and Akhtar and Thompson's factor of promiscuity, infatuation and inability to remain in love. (Perry & Perry, 1996, p. 17)

Although this summary addresses the issue of severity and structural level, the formulation is very similar to one I have proposed (Richards, 1993), working from considerations regarding theory construction and theory integration.

It is important to note, in both the Akhtar and Thompson and Kernberg factor analyses, that exploitation of others was the primary component of narcissism, explaining over twice the variance of the grandiosity factors in the respective systems. This view of the narcissist as primarily exploitative, contemptuous, demeaning toward others, and having antisocial features, and only secondarily being grandiose, has obvious implications for a proposed spectrum linking narcissism, antisocial personality, and psychopathy. This relationship was reversed for the DSM-III-R factor analysis, suggesting that the DSM-III-R criteria may overrepresent the grandiosity component of narcissism through an insufficient sampling of the full domain of NPD.

The factors that emerged from the Kernberg criteria are especially relevant to the formulations posed in this chapter. Factor I, which accounted for most of the explained variance (28.1% of total variance), was interpreted by Perry and Perry as exploitation and indifference to others. Factor II (12.4% of total variance) was interpreted as grandiosity and overdependence on admiration. Factor III (8.4% of total variance) was interpreted as "a factor describing emotional neglect, containing features broadly shared with borderline personalities" (p. 10). Factor IV (8.4% of variance) was interpreted as hypersensitivity and poor self-esteem regulation, although the largest contributor to the five-item factor was the criterion of a general paranoid orientation in severe cases of narcissism. The other four items, all of which loaded positively on this factor, were shame-regulated behavior, incapacity to learn, devaluation of others, and severe mood swings. Since the first three of these are relevant to paranoid dynamics as traditionally discussed in the psychodynamic literature, the factor could just as well have been described as paranoid orientation and emotional dysregulation. An examination of the composition of the other factors suggests that only Factor II, interpreted by Perry and Perry as grandiosity and overdependence on admiration, was not clearly related to paranoid dynamics. Removing the variance explained by grandiosity would yield 43.0% of the variance being construable as relevant to paranoid dynamics, or 77.6% of the explained variance in the Kernberg criteria for narcissism.

NARCISSISM AND PARANOID PHENOMENA

Millon (1981), in discussing the relationship between the paranoid personality disorder and other personality types, has implied the existence of a paranoid dimension of personality:

In mixed cases, the paranoid dimension is often an insidious and secondary development, fusing slowly into the fabric of an earlier and less dysfunctional coping style. Although paranoid-like features may be exhibited in almost every other personality disorder, they tend to become integral components of only four of the patterns previously described: the narcissistic, the antisocial (aggressive), the compulsive, and the passive–aggressive. (p. 375)

Meissner (1979) has detailed the paranoid process as active in a range of normal and abnormal states of mind he refers to as the "paranoid spectrum." His work underscores the fact that paranoid phenomena are organized around aggression in all of its forms, from violence to sadomasochistic dynamics to lingering hostile mood. In Meissner's view, paranoia has its roots in the desperate attempt to maintain self-esteem, to control the self, and to master an environment that is viewed as hostile and chaotic. He differentiates psychopaths from paranoid personalities primarily by the object-specific focus of the aggression of the latter, compared to the general pervasive aggression and hostility of the former. Meissner has also stressed the importance of projection and projective identification in paranoid phenomena, and has pointed out the same kind of reversal of passive to active found in Svrakic et al.'s (1991) dual-level formulation of a narcissistic spectrum.

Klein (1957) had earlier proposed that paranoid states are a fundamental part of normal psychological development. Splitting and projection follow the infant's experience of satisfaction or frustration with the mothering experience. Internalization of a satisfying experience (the good breast) results in the capacity to feel supported or comforted without external support or in the presence of external frustrations. This capacity is ultimately expressed as the ability to experience self-satisfaction and positive, comforting solitude, and to tolerate indifference, separation, and frustration in relationships (i.e., lack of manipulative control of the selfobject). Internalization of the frustrating experience (the bad breast) results in rageful affects, preventing the development of tolerance for frustration and causing a sense of persecution. This sadistic attitude is defended against through manic and counterphobic defenses, resulting in the perception of threat from others and the initiation of provocative (and confirmatory) interactions toward them, in the process of projective identification. Projective identification involves the displacement of disowned aspects of the self to others and the later controlling of these disowned self-fragments through establishing perceived or actual complementary interactions and role relationships.

More recently, the idea that paranoid phenomena of various levels of severity may be related to various kinds and degrees of disturbances in narcissism has recently been reintroduced and refined, both in psychodynamic work (Aronson, 1989; Garfield & Havens, 1991) and in cognitive research (Trower & Chadwick, 1995). Although coming from a tradition that relies more on unconscious dynamics, this view of paranoia is similar to the "bad me" paranoid type identified by Trower and Chadwick (1995). In their cognitive dynamic formulation, the "bad me" paranoid unconsciously views the world as rightfully punishing toward the self, which is viewed as guilty or shameful, due to the anticipation and defense against a negative self-evaluation stemming from the dissonance between the actual and ideal self-concepts. This type of paranoid contrasts in their formulation with the "poor me" paranoid, who views the world as basically unfair and persecutory toward the self, stemming from the anticipation of the discomfort of rejection and frustration of needs viewed as legitimate. This depiction of guilty and guiltless types of paranoid personality, related to the degree of incongruity between the ideal self and the actual self, closely parallels the finding of guilty and guiltless types of narcissistic and antisocial personalities, which are often confused with individuals with and without grandiosity. It also illustrates the dichotomies and splits in basic attributes between self and others (good–bad, weak–strong, etc.) which are typical of the projective mechanisms of paranoid, narcissistic, and antisocial personalities.

SPECTRUM FORMULATIONS

In the context of examining the relationship between schizophrenia and personality disorders, Meehl (1962) proposed that nosological spectra should be developed in order to link apparently distinct disorders through their sharing of cardinal features and underlying causes. Although the most common usage of the spectrum approach relates to the affective disorders, several spectrum formulations addressing personality disorders have been proposed (Grinker, 1966; Eysenck & Eysenck, 1977; Stone, 1980; Zuckerman, 1983; Cloninger, 1987; Siever & Davis, 1991). Spectrum formulations transcend schemes such as the DSM personality disorder clusters by sorting disorders into ordinal or hierarchical arrays based on their relationship to levels or facets of common underlying causal factors. Spectrum formulations are applied polythetically, meaning that no single feature or index is required for inclusion in a spectrum; rather, the sameness of the overall causal and clinical gestalt to a schematic paradigm description recommends inclusion in the spectrum (Cantor, Smith, French, & Mezzich, 1980).

Several criteria for establishing a spectrum relationship have been specified following biological typology, such as the criteria that spectrum components should demonstrate significant comorbidity and familial aggregation (Cloninger, Reich, & Guze, 1975; Reich, Cloninger, & Guze, 1975). In determining the viability of a spectrum formulation, no *a priori* requirement should be made concerning the magnitude of feature overlap or causal connection among its constituents. Since spectrum concepts are primarily heuristic, their usefulness as tools of theory construction—for generating testable hypotheses about individual disorders, relationships among disorders, and their underlying causes—is at stake, rather than their immediate validation. Construct validation attempts should therefore evaluate the discovery and communication functions of heuristic formulations, in addition to evaluating the spectrum's congruence with empirical findings (Skinner, 1986). Disorder prototypes may be viewed profitably within more than one nosological scheme, including multiple spectrum formulations, so long as each scheme or formulation links meaningful phenomenological characteristics across disorders to one or more causal processes.

Spectrum formulations may be particularly appropriate at our current stage of understanding personality disorders, since it appears that a single cause (e.g., neglectful or harsh child rearing) often results in multiple effects (various personality disorders), and there is little clarity at present about the factors that may mediate these differences. For the same reason, spectrum formulations that link Axis I disorders (clinical syndromes) with the personality disorders may be particularly useful. For example, spectrum categorizations can help make sense of the isomorphisms (similarities often observed as muted versions or mirror-image reversals) among a patient's major mental disorder symptoms, his or her premorbid personality characteristics, and the various subclinical personality characteristics of the patient's biological relatives. Such isomorphism may suggest that just as fault lines indicate geological structures that will predictably separate, given various kinds and levels of seismic activity, personality characteristics insinuate the probable direction and extent of collapse toward various clinical syndromes in the event of personality decompensation.

Several psychobiological spectra have recently been proposed that would link many of the personality disorders, but not the paranoid disorders or NPD. For example, Siever and Davis (1991) developed a heuristic scheme designating four spectra that would link both Axis I and Axis II disorders. Their model included spectra based on etiologies of pathology due to failures of psychobiological functions related to cognitive perceptual organization, impulsivity/aggression, affective instability, and anxiety/inhibition. The paranoid disorders and NPD were notably absent from this application of spectra concepts to the personality disorders. This may be because the self-structural deficits that are primary in NPD and paranoid personality disorder are not explainable from a simple biology-centered approach.

THE PARANOID–NARCISSISTIC SPECTRUM

In an earlier work, I proposed three disorder spectra—the schizotypal–schizophrenic, the cycloid–affective, and the paranoid–narcissistic spectra—to group various Axis I and Axis II disorders (Richards, 1993). The compound names of the spectra reflect a mixed dimensional–prototypical approach. Following Millon (1981), each spectrum's name is composed of a personality decompensation as the prototype/anchor of the spectrum, and a primary pathological process, which is the dimensional aspect of the grouping. The vulnerability of personality disorders to deterioration and disintegration along certain fault lines to other levels and types of disorders is implicit in this terminology. Also, the defining exemplar/anchor approach incorporates Millon's view that personality is more central to overall functioning than are behavioral symptoms and clinical syndromes. Severity is important to this approach. In the most severe cases, the differences between the Axis I and Axis II disorders, and among the various spectra groupings, begin to break down. For example, the "fingerprint" patterns of cognitive, affective, and narcissistic disturbances that differentiate disorders more clearly at the less severe levels are often found together in the decompensated cases of the personality disorders and the severe cases of the major mental illnesses.

Disorders within the paranoid–narcissistic spectrum are conceived of as linked through their sharing of pathological narcissism as both a cardinal descriptive feature and a critical etiological factor. Aggression, either directed inwardly or outwardly, also plays a critical role in these disorders. Paranoid personality disorder is the defining exemplar/anchor, meaning that paranoid personality disorder both manifests the cardinal features shared in the spectrum and is also analogous to the median case of severity of the group, with other disorders falling above or below it in prototypicality and severity. A revised version of the paranoid–narcissistic spectrum is presented here. The revision more explicitly incorporates the principle of aggression's serving an integrating/cohesive function of the self, and differences in structural organizational level within each personality disorder type. To limit this discussion to the personality disorders, the spectrum is arrayed as follows: NPD, negativistic personality disorder, destructive personalities disorder (APD), paranoid personality disorder, PPD, and sadistic personality disorder. As with most disorders, intelligence, age, and other moderating factors may contribute greatly to the adaptiveness of the individual. Each of these disorders may exist at higher or lower levels of structural organization, although one level may be modal. Following Millon's (1981) view of personality decompensation, a lower layer could be added to this spectrum, consisting of decompensated personality disorder with aggressive–paranoid patterns of disorganized, maladaptive behaviors.

It is important to note that personality types that show increasing fragmentation or loss of cohesion stemming directly from aggressive affects are not included in the spectrum. Therefore, destructive personality types constituted at Kernberg's neurotic and borderline levels of structural organization are included in the spectrum, whereas borderline personality disorder as formulated in DSM-IV (American Psychiatric Association,

1994) is not included. Persons with the latter disorder often display excessive anger, hostile affect and general negative affectivity, projective mechanisms, and manipulative behavior; however, they decompensate when, or soon after, these affects are aroused. These personalities are incapable of using aggression effectively in self-enhancing or self-reparative modes for very long because of conflicting principles of organization based in dependency and guilt.[4]

The degree of cohesiveness, or integrity of the self, is not synonymous with the severity of deviance or pathology of structural organization. When therotypes are arrayed by severity of overall self-pathology and pathology of conscience, both of these dimensions must be considered. Highly deviant self-structures and consciences may also be highly cohesive and efficient in the management of drives, anxiety, threats, and the like. In regard to the conscience, the degree to which punishment anxiety and other guilt-like affects cause conflict-driven behaviors or intrude more directly into consciousness is largely determined by the degree to which integrative structures, such as identifications and motivating values, predominate over such structures as unmetabolized and personified introjects (Kernberg, 1975; Meissner, 1979) or disintegration products (Kohut, 1977).

Table 5.1 summarizes the relationship of personality disorders in the paranoid–

TABLE 5.1. Personality Disorders within the Paranoid–Narcissistic Spectrum

Attribute	Basic personality disorder therotype					
	Narcissistic	Negativistic	Destructive (antisocial)	Paranoid	Psychopathic	Sadistic
Aggressive style	Contrived, self-inflation, denigration of others	Apprehensive subversion	Rebellious contempt	Provocation, peremptory attack	Malicious predation	Sadism
Balance of integrating versus fragmenting internal objects	*Identification*: Consolidation predominates	*Introjection*: Fragmentation predominates	*Identification*: Consolidation predominates	*Introjection*: Fragmentation predominates	*Identification*: Consolidation predominates	*Introjection*: Fragmentation predominates
Superego development	Immature/ fixated	Immature/ fixated	Deviant	Defective	Perverse	Defective and perverse
Structure of conscience	Normal conscience with lacunae	Normal conscience with lacunae	Distorted conscience	Shattered conscience	Inverse conscience	Shattered inverse conscience
Quality/ function of conscience	Solipsistic; seeks to purge intrusion of imperfections	Accusatory; seeks to reverse intrusive guilt	Dissentient; justifies actions	Retributive; vindicates self	Annihilative; idealizes aggression	Vicious, inhumane; idealizes sadism
Significant destructive behaviors	Interpersonal exploitation	Sabotage, self-defeat, explosive anger	Instrumental and expressive crime, self-destructiveness	Preemptive attack, retribution for betrayal	Strategic conquest and predation	Infliction of prolonged anguish, torture, zombieism

narcissistic spectrum to themes of particular relevance to moral development and destructive behaviors, although in these disorders it is difficult to separate themes or issues related to the conscience from the total personality. The disorders are arrayed in order of increasing pathology (the combination of the degree of deviance and the degree of efficiency or cohesion) from left to right. The rows beneath the disorder therotypes show, sequentially, (1) the relationship of each disorder to the aggressive style that maintains self-cohesion; (2) the coherence, integrity, and consistency of the conscience as related to the balance between integrating (identifications) versus fragmenting (introjects) internal objects; (3) the resulting level of superego development; (4) the related structure of the conscience; (5) the quality of conscience-directed behavior; and (6) modal destructive behaviors.

As illustrated in this table, personalities with trends toward coherent and consistent consciences alternate with personalities with trends toward fragmented consciences. It is assumed that these trends toward cohesion or fragmentation also reflect the typical organization structure of the personality, not only the conscience, since the conscience or superego is crucial to overall self-cohesion or its relative absence. The disorders in the table can be seen, therefore, as paired: A personality having a more stable moral stance is paired with a less consistent but closely related disorder. The row entitled "Superego development" merits further comment. It indicates whether the superego is immature/fixated, deviant, or perverse, and reflects the severity of the structural pattern of the conscience itself (compared to that of the mature normal conscience, which consists of well-coordinated identifications, ideals, and values that have become appropriately generalized). The deviant conscience incorporates dissident and alternative values, such as those found in criminal subcultures. The defective conscience is ineffective. The perverse conscience is assumed to result from the previously described process of negation of the superego.

The row entitled "Structure of conscience" describes the result of the superego development. Garfield and Havens (1991) have offered an intriguing analogy that captures this distinction in regard to the self as a whole. They describe the configuration of the self in paranoia as being like a shattered windshield that is partially dislodged from its frame. The webbing of the glass that holds the fragments together is analogous to the webbing of narcissism. The self does not disintegrate, but is in a new dysfunctional form because the view of the outside world is "distorted and treacherous to negotiate" (p. 168). I would like to return to the classic icon of the shattered mirror to serve as the icon of the structure of the conscience. The conscience allows the ego to observe the self and the praiseworthiness or blameworthiness of behavior, as in the idiomatic conscience probe: "How can you look at yourself in the mirror?" The shattered mirror is analogous to the sense of conscience that results when self disintegration products (Kohut, 1977) or unmetabolized introjects (Kernberg, 1992; Meissner, 1980) predominate over integrative forces, primarily affirmative identifications and motivating values. The therotypes that are indicated as having shattered consciences in Table 5.1 have the same kind of reflexive disfunction as Garfield and Haven's external, projection-oriented windshield. Therefore, moral issues in general are viewed in a fragmented, distorted way, with little continuity of the overall image. The individual sections of clear images contribute to an overall chaotic, fragmentary vision of self and morality.

These relationships can be further illuminated through an analysis of the object relations that typify each disorder and the spectrum as a whole. An object relations account of aggression must consider the degree of self–other differentiation and the degree and nature of polarized attributions perceived at the object level between the aggressor and the target of the aggression. These relationships will be developed in depth in a future contribution. For the purposes of the present chapter, it is important to note that for all of the disorders that constitute this spectrum, self–other differentiation is superficial, tending toward the solipsistic. As the severity in the array increases, the mere existence of the other is viewed increasingly as an intrusion. Kohut put it as follows:

> The enemy, however, who calls forth the archaic rage of the narcissistically vulnerable is seen by him not as an autonomous source of impulsions, but as a flaw in a narcissistically perceived reality. He is a recalcitrant part of an expanded self over which he expects to exercise full control and whose mere independence or otherness is an offense. (Kohut, 1972, p. 385)

When this kind of perception is expressed without mitigation, it can fairly be typified as psychotic. In most human affairs, the reality orientation of the group is poor, although reality testing is good when attention is called to negative consequences to the self or when self-interest is not at stake at all. Bursten (1989) has added to our understanding of the narcissistic pleasure of lying and deception in the psychopath; however, the psychopath's argument with reality goes beyond the pleasure of conning others. In addition to this solipsism, extreme dichotomous splits such as good–bad, strong–weak, and masculine–feminine typify the object relations of personality disorders across this spectrum. Specific patterns of split attributes and their projection to various objects (self, other, male, female, strangers, authority figures, etc.) differentiate the various specific disorders. The mechanism of projective identification, through which these splits are externalized, is essential to the ability of these personalities to maintain self-cohesion. Similarly, aggression is central to self-cohesion and to projective processes in these disorders. The disorders, paired by stability of the conscience, are now briefly discussed in the context of the spectrum.

In contrived self-inflation, which is prototypical of the narcissist, aggression is turned against the real self in favor of identification with the idealized, grandiose facade self. Through the process of projective identification, this results in self-centered disregard, derogation, or exploitation of others. The reality component related to this style is the childhood experience of being valued for specific, often precocious talents or abilities. The negativist engages in apprehensive subversion, due to conflicting and alternating identifications with both the aggressor and the victim; this individual may at times demonstrate a range of self-destructive and self-defeating behaviors, and at other times explosive and decisive violence. These patterns may reflect the reality of extremely inconsistent parental attitudes toward, or effective influence on, aggression and self-assertion. Many negatives also tend to perceive the good as changeable and fickle, and the bad as stable and predictable—attributions that further fuel vacillating behaviors.

In rebellious contempt, prototypical of the destructive personality, the aggressive component is turned primarily toward others. Aggression provides narcissistic repair through identification with the power aspect of aggression, appropriation of the goodness of the victim, or attribution of responsibility to the victim. The destructive's violence is always justified as a morally neutral necessity of power differences, as a punishment deserved by the object, or as a response to the perpetrator's previous or anticipated victimization (usually reflecting biography). This dynamic results in frequent instrumental and expressive crimes. Some self-punishing and self-defeating behaviors also may be observed, indicating that the split between powerful/bad and weak/good attributions is not maintained. Since high levels of emotional arousal and external stress may tend to support and increase these defensive self–other splits, and situations that normally support personality integration may tend to decrease them, this personality type is prone to self-destruction in periods of relatively little external stress. The paranoid struggles to maintain a positive self-image despite the presence of unacceptable motives, characteristics, and identifications, given a learning history filled with unpredictability, criticism, and abuse. Adjustment is tentative and rigidly defended. Aggression toward self and others is high, and repression is inadequate to develop or maintain a more successful narcissistic style. Projection of fantasy-based negative contents gradually eclipses accentuating positive and unrealistic self-attributions. Eventually the positive self-image can only be maintained at the expense of viewing others as bad and destructive. The results are a "jump to conclusions" cognitive style, and aggression toward others that is provocative and preemptory.

The psychopath identifies without conflict with the aggressor, who is viewed as powerful, bad, and ideal. In extreme cases, early attachment problems may engender identification with fantasies of animal predators or archetypal evil demigods. This idealization of evil results in the paradox of an inverse conscience. Normal moral conscience can be seen as resulting from superego identifications with good and powerful objects. In normals, behavior that would be condoned by good and powerful objects increases self-esteem, security, and self-cohesion, whereas behaviors that would be condemned by good and powerful objects induce guilt, insecurity, and the anticipation of punishment. In an inverse conscience, the identification with bad and powerful objects increases self-esteem, security, and self-cohesion. The sadistic personality adds the element of idealized sadism to the inverse conscience. The actual self can experience the consummation of narcissistic identity with the ideal self only when it is persecuting others through inducing pain, suffering, and the conscious awareness of being the object of malicious destruction—dynamics that may reflect the reality of the sadistic personality's extreme background of powerlessness, abuse, and invalidation during childhood.

The present conceptualization of the psychopath differs from Svrakic et al.'s view of the psychopath as a subcategory of the destructive personality, which exhibits an inverse conscience. In the present spectrum of progressive narcissistic pathology, the psychopath is the first type with an intact inverse conscience. However, in any of the more deviant types exhibiting the inverse conscience to some extent, fragments of more normal superego precursors—based on nonaggressive and rewarding part-attachments—may intrude into consciousness, during moments of poor self-cohesion. These guilt fragments are likely to fuel increased destructiveness aimed at exorcising the experience of being haunted by such good ghosts, which spoil coherence of the self through aggression. An alternative to destructiveness as purgation of the good is to seek the experience of the oceanic merger that identifies the self with the universal. Thus we find the occasional attachment of psychopaths to their mothers, combined with religious mysticism and, more frequently, with a compulsion to adopt self-created identities, making them their own parents.[5]

VIOLENCE AND DESTRUCTIVENESS AS ADDICTIVE

The paranoid–narcissistic spectrum was originally proposed in the context of developing a self-state theory of experience in psychopathology, especially in cases comorbid with psychoactive substance use. Self-states and addictive phenomena are particularly relevant to disorders in the spectrum, especially in regard to the self-regulatory and self-reparative use of destructiveness and violence.

Self-states are similar to mood states, but are more extensive and have a cyclical relationship. Pathological extremes in self-states are posited as modes of experiencing organized around a triad of structural components: (1) problematic primary affects and drives, (2) problematic representations of self and other, and (3) habitual defenses against the catastrophic realization and conscious experience of the painful aspects or consequences of the other two structural components. An individual's self-states and the relationships among them constitute the organization of the self as a supraordinal psychological structure. The dominant self-state at any point in time determines the perception of and behavior toward self and environment in the areas of cognitive approach, affective coloring, interpersonal stance, and ongoing construction of meaning or value.

An addicted person, according to the self-state theory of addiction, is a person whose relationship with drugs (particularly a drug or drug category of choice) results in experiencing cycles of self-state extremes. The term "cycle of addiction" describes the tendency to use drugs in a manner that perpetuates the maladaptive inclination for one of these extreme self-states to be the dominant organizer of experience and behavior at any given point in time, thereby temporarily shoring up self-cohesion while undermining the long-term adaptive integration of self and experience. These dynamics of addiction—especially when applied to the potential for aggression and violence as addictive activities, and the tendency for psychoactive substances to undermine inhibitory mechanisms and to facilitate both aggressive and paranoid states—are particularly important for all of the disorders in this spectrum. These personalities are already prone to these states and experience them as ego-syntonic.

IMPLICATIONS

Many theoretical implications of the proposed spectrum and integrative view of the psychopath have been noted in the course of presenting these ideas and their foundations. Among the most important is that although many of the personality disorders are discrete enough to demonstrate taxonomy, they are nonetheless fuzzy sets that are highly interrelated, and may profitably be viewed from the perspective provided by superordinal groupings (such as spectra). These broader categories may have as much relevance to a particular case as a single discrete disorder may, if not more. Placing the case within the context of a spectrum may be particularly valuable for heuristic purposes early in the process of making diagnostic, focused assessments and treatment decisions, when there is not yet enough information to substantiate a specific personality disorder. Similarly, the spectrum approach may be helpful later, when fine-tuning or reformulation of the case is needed. However, approaches to higher-order categories or dimensions that overlook the discrete, nodal aspect of personality may prove misleading for extreme personality disorders, where a confluence of patterns results in unique, emergent features. The approach recommended in this chapter provides the unifying perspective of a multifaceted dimensional process (aspects and levels of paranoid–narcissistic dynamics), with an anchoring point in a group exemplar (paranoid personality disorder), while preserving the unique qualities of specific disorder therotypes (NPD, APD, etc.).

The immediate implications for forensic practice and criminal justice policy of the spectrum concept and image of the psychopath presented here lie in reframing some of the goals and practices of risk assessment for dangerousness and destructiveness. The Hare PCL-R appears to be the best candidate for a measure to serve as the foundation for assessment of violent recidivism, and the presence of any personality disorder has been shown to add additional significant predictive power over that provided by the PCL-R (Webster, Harris, Rice, Cormier, & Quinsey, 1994). The formulations offered in this chapter suggest that the diagnosis of a personality disorder in this spectrum may indicate an increased risk for dangerousness over that predicted by psychopathy as measured by the PCL-R, and by the diagnosis of personality disorders not in this spectrum.

The particular relevance of these personalities to violence, aggression, and rule breaking suggests that correctional versions of such psychological tests as the Millon Clinical Multiaxial Inventory—III might be more useful if they were explicitly structured to incorporate these relationships. For example, the automated output for scales related to personality disorders could be placed in order of self-enhancement through aggression, with other scales indicating moderating or exacerbating factors (such as impulsivity, compulsivity, and structural organization) clustered together.

Finally, in regard to reframing assessments, more inclusive assessments should address such factors as the individual's level of moral reasoning, the structure of the conscience, any indications of underlying superego structures (such as primary identifications and related beliefs), and an estimate of the likelihood of further growth in moral development with and without intervention. Informing these kinds of judgments is exactly what assessment of personalities in this spectrum should do.

This chapter's emphasis on the conscience and its underpinnings, and on state factors, also has important implications for personality assessment. Personality disorders are routinely dealt with in research and clinical practice as if traits were at the ideal level of discourse, assessment, and intervention. State-level descriptions (Horowitz, 1979, 1988; Richards, 1993; Horowitz, Milbrath, Ewert, Sonneborn, & Stinson, 1994) should be added to trait-level and situation-specific descriptions to provide a comprehensive understanding of the causes and meaning of violence. It may be that some destructive behaviors are motivated by the conscience or the superego. Since many individuals with the disorders of the will described in this chapter have poorly integrated consciences, their self-guides (the conscience and ideal self) may have the same spotty, nonspecific weaknesses that have been observed for ego functioning in borderline organizational structure.

The manifestation of self-states, which are dominated by various aspects of superego functioning (such as diffuse superego weakness or partitioned, partly dissociated superego fragments), may alternate in response to stress or specific situational factors, such as involvement in activating interpersonal situations. In exacerbating circumstances, these changes may result in behavior that more closely approximates disorders of a higher degree of severity than the individual's typical mode of functioning. The reverse may occur in circumstances that promote integration or activation of more benign superego states. If this is the case, some crimes may only be committed (or may only take on expressive destructive or sadistic aspects) during the activation of specific self-states that are colored by a transient configuration of the self, in which deviant, defective, or perverse aspects of the conscience predominate. The self-state model of addiction would predict that some individuals may exhibit a habitual addictive pattern of violence or destructiveness that is related to cyclical extremes in states of mind driven by aspects of a divided, unintegrated conscience.

As an example, evidence of the alternation of self-states dominated by different aspects of conscience was observed in an incarcerated psychopath during treatment for substance abuse, which, among other things, both engages the self-ideal and appeals to the conscience or sense of values.[6] Through her treatment, she was able to gain perspective on the aspect of herself that has been referred to in this chapter as the "inverse conscience." In a psychotherapy group session, she revealed that while committing a habitual act of violence she had previously felt "good," and recalled thinking that she "ought to be" or "should be" pistol-whipping her armed-robbery victim. As treatment progressed, she responded to a confrontation with a work supervisor in an untypically, nonviolent and nonvindictive way. She reported that the incident caused her to "lose my peace," and she became disoriented to the point that her altered state was noticed and commented on by the custodial staff. The patient's remark, repeated several times, was telling. This client had previously relied on a kind of inverted conscience, which demanded righteous retribution and appropriation for having suffered perceived injustices and deprivations. This sense of inverted conscience was made concrete in her pistol, and also may have represented a form of protest against and rejection of male sexual domination and exploitation. Acting on some newly developing sense of conscience had caused her to "lose her peace." In street parlance, a handgun is often called a "piece"—a term that is also used pejoratively in reference to a woman as an object of sexual exploitation. Her new behavior may have meant that she could no longer rely on the old selfobject and value system that the "piece" had represented. Some new or previously inaccessible aspect of conscience had surfaced, initially causing disorientation and a sense of vulnerability.

The research implications of the concepts proposed in this chapter begin with the need for investigating the relationships of the individual disorders from a new perspective, as well as for beginning a systematic investigation of the nature of the conscience, and of the affective and evaluative processing across and within the disorders. Applying the self-state model of personality and conscience to the personality disorders within a theoretically derived spectrum could be investigated though combining methods for investigating group differences (such as narratives involving moral issues and responses to evaluative and affect-laden words) with methods for investigating state-specific factors, such as mood state induction techniques. Finally, a more aggressive attempt should be made to initiate clinical applications of established laboratory techniques related to empathy, affective processing, ability to make moral distinctions, and object relational measures relevant to aggressive behavior.

ACKNOWLEDGMENTS

Preparation of this chapter was supported in part by National Institute on Drug Abuse R01 Research Grant No. DA09646-03, "Effective Addiction Treatments for Female Offenders," awarded to Friends Research Institute (Henry Richards, Principal Investigator). Jay Casey, Patuxent Institution, Jessup, Maryland, contributed thoughtful comments in response to earlier drafts of this chapter. Debra Kafami, Patuxent Institution, provided general comments as well as editorial assistance. Kevin McCamant, Patuxent Institution, provided clinical case material, in addition to providing comments on earlier drafts.

NOTES

1. One philosophical discussion concluded that psychopaths are the moral equivalent of animals, but should be treated as human because of their sentience, and treated as moral beings for utilitarian reasons. The author concluded that psychopaths are outside the realm of obligation, and therefore have no moral rights (Murphy, 1972).

2. On the mythopoetic level, the use of the mirror to denote a perverse narcissistic process is also somewhat off base. Narcissus fell in love not with his mirror image, but with his watery im-

age, which in its very substance invoked the rejected water nymph, Echo. Echo cursed Narcissus to an inanimate existence as a flower because of his inability to return her cries of adoration, which he mistakenly attributed to his own image. This brief retelling of the myth points out the semantogenic aspect of the narcissistic disorders.

3. If the formulation presented here appears to some readers to be describing the *Beowulf* poet's Grendel, rather than any real human being, I would like to cite the recent attempt of convicted murderer Richard Allen Davis at his sentencing hearing (Curtius, 1996) to morally destroy the father of his victim, Polly Klaas, as a case in point of a psychopathic evil greater than those of monster myths. Davis quoted his murder victim as implicating her father in an earlier sexual assault. Also, a reading of the biographies of a few of the psychopaths in the upper region of Stone's (1993) array of murderers by intensity of evil (narcissism and sadism combined) should correct any impression of an overreaction, at least for such severe cases.

4. In regard to violence, the borderline is apt to cling to his or her objects in hostile dependency, thereby smothering them, whereas the psychopath is more apt to cannibalize the object, or stand on the corpse to gain a better predatory view of the horizon and flaunt the destructive triumph. The psychopathic murderer inherits from the victim, and is renewed and is confirmed by the victim's destruction. The borderline murderer is orphaned without legacy, and may attempt or commit suicide.

5. This pattern reminds us that Oedipus was an anonymous murderer of a stranger and that, in the sexual sense, he became his own father. Perhaps the greatest sin of pride and resentment committed by Milton's Satan in *Paradise Lost* is to have claimed to have sprung from the ground like a turnip, as being self-created; thus he denies the reality of his creatureness, and his reliance on the ontological ground of God's caring creativity.

6. This case example was provided by Kevin McCamant, PhD, who encountered the case while providing services to incarcerated women in a substance abuse research project.

REFERENCES

Aichorn, A. (1935). *Wayward youth.* New York: Viking. (Original work published 1925)

Akhtar, S., & Thompson, J. A. (1982). Overview: Narcissistic personality disorder. *American Journal of Psychiatry, 139,* 12–20.

American Psychiatric Association. (1987). *Diagnostic and statistical manual of mental disorders* (3rd ed., rev.). Washington, DC: Author.

American Psychiatric Association. (1994). *Diagnostic and statistical manual of mental disorders* (4th ed.). Washington, DC: Author.

Aronson, T. (1989). Paranoia and narcissism in psychoanalytic theory: Contributions of self psychology to the theory and therapy of the paranoid disorders. *Psychiatric Review, 76*(3), 329–351.

Blair, R. J. (1995). Cognitive developmental approach to morality: Investigating the psychopath. *Cognition, 57*(1), 1–29.

Blair, R. J., Jones, L., Clark, F., & Smith, M. (1995). Is the psychopath "morally insane"? *Personality and Individual Differences, 19*(5), 741–752.

Blair, R. J., Sellars, C., Strickland, I., & Clark, F. (1995). Emotion attributions in the psychopath. *Personality and Individual Differences, 19*(4), 431–437.

Bursten, B. (1972). The manipulative personality. *Archives of General Psychiatry, 26,* 318–321.

Bursten, B. (1989). The relationship between narcissistic and antisocial personalities. *Psychiatric Clinics of North America, 12*(3), 571–584.

Campbell, R. J. (1981). *Psychiatric dictionary* (5th ed.). New York: Oxford University Press.

Cantor, N., Smith, E., French, R., & Mezzich, J. (1980). Psychiatric diagnosis as prototype categorization. *Journal of Abnormal Psychology, 89,* 181–193.

Cleckley, H. (1941). *The mask of sanity: An attempt to reinterpret the so-called psychopathic personality.* St. Louis, MO: C. V. Mosby.

Cleckley, H. (1976). *The mask of sanity* (6th ed.). St. Louis, MO: C. V. Mosby.

Cloninger, C. R. (1987). A systematic method for clinical description and classification of personality variants. *Archives of General Psychiatry, 40,* 659–668.

Cloninger, C. R., Reich, T., & Guze, S. (1975). The multifactorial model of disease transmission: III. Familial relationship between sociopathy and hysteria. *British Journal of Psychiatry, 127,* 23–32.

Curtius, M. (1996, September 27). Klass killer sentenced to die, stuns court. *Los Angeles Times.*

DeJong, J., Virkkunen, M., & Linnoila, M. (1992). Factors associated with recidivism in a criminal population. *Journal of Nervous and Mental Disease, 180*(9), 543–550.

Eysenck, H. J., & Eysenck, S. B. (1977). *Psychoticism as a dimension of personality.* New York: Carne & Russak.

Fenichel, O. (1945). Neurotic acting out. *Psychoanalytic Review, 32,* 197–206.

Friedlander, K. (1945). Formation of the antisocial character. *Psychoanalytic Study of the Child, 1,* 189–203.

Gacono, C. B., & Meloy, J. R. (1993). Some thoughts on Rorschach findings and psychophysiology in the psychopath. *British Journal of Projective Psychology, 38*(1), 42–52.

Garfield, D., & Havens, L. (1991). Paranoid phenomena and narcissism. *American Journal of Psychotherapy, 65,* 161–171.

Grinker, R. (1966). "Open-system" psychiatry. *American Journal of Psychoanalysis, 26*(2), 115–128.

Grotstein, J. S. (1982). Newer perspectives on object relations theory. *Contemporary Psychoanalysis, 16,* 479–546.

Grotstein, J. S. (1995). Orphans of the "real": I. Some modern and postmodern perspectives on neurobiological and psychosocial dimensions of psychosis and other primitive mental disorders. *Bulletin of the Menninger Clinic, 59*(3), 287–311.

Hare, R. D. (1970). *Psychopathy: Theory and research.* New York: Wiley.

Hare, R. D. (1991). *The Hare Psychopathy Checklist—Revised.* Toronto: Multi-Health Systems.

Harpur, T. J., Hart, S. D., & Hare, R. D. (1994). Personality of the psychopathy. In P. T. Costa, Jr. & T. A. Widiger (Eds.), *Personality disorders and the five-factor model of personality* (pp. 149–175). Washington, DC: American Psychological Association.

Hart, S. D., Forth, A. H., & Hare, R. D. (1990). Performance of criminal psychopaths on selected neuropsychological tests. *Journal of Abnormal Psychology, 99,* 374–379.

Heidegger, M. (1962). *Being and time* (J. Macuarrie & E. Robinson, Trans.). New York: Harper. (Original work published 1926)

Henry, J. P. (1993). Psychological and physiological responses to stress: The right hemisphere and the hypothalamo-pituitary-adrenal axis. An inquiry into problems of human bonding. *Integrative Physiological and Behavioral Science, 28*(4) 369–387.

Horney, K. (1945). *Our inner conflicts.* New York: Norton.

Horowitz, M. J. (1979). *States of mind.* New York: Plenum Press.

Horowitz, M. J. (1988). *Introduction to psychodynamics.* New York: Basic Books.

Horowitz, M. J., Milbrath, C., Ewert, M., Sonneborn, D., & Stinson, C. (1994). Cyclical patterns of states of mind in psychotherapy. *American Journal of Psychiatry, 151*(12), 1767–1770.

Kernberg, O. F. (1975). *Borderline conditions and pathological narcissism.* New York: Jason Aronson.

Kernberg, O. F. (1982). An ego-psychology object relations theory approach to the narcissistic personality. In L. Grinspoon (Ed.), *Psychiatry 1982: The American Psychiatry Association annual review* (Vol. 1, pp. 510–523). Washington, DC: American Psychiatric Press.

Kernberg, O. F. (1984). *Severe personality disorders.* New Haven, CT: Yale University Press.

Kernberg, O. F. (1992). *Aggression in personality disorders and perversions.* New Haven, CT: Yale University Press.

Kirmayer, L. J. (1983). Paranoia and pronoia: The visionary and the banal. *Social Problems, 31*(2), 170–179.

Klein, M. (1957). *Envy and gratitude: A study in unconscious sources.* New York: Basic Books.

Kohut, H. (1972). Thoughts on narcissism and narcissistic rage. *Psychoanalytic Study of the Child, 27*, 360–400.

Kohut, H. (1977). *The restoration of the self.* New York: International Universities Press.

Levy, D. (1951). Psychopathic behavior in infants and children. *American Journal of Orthopsychiatry, 21*, 223–372.

Lorenz, K. (1963). *On aggression* (M. K. Wilson, Trans.). New York: Harcourt, Brace & World.

Luria, A. R. (1973). *The working brain: An introduction to neuropsychology* (B. Haigh, Trans.). New York: Basic Books.

Meehl, P. E. (1962). Schizotaxia, schizotypy, schizophrenia. *American Psychologist, 17*, 827–838.

Meissner, W. W. (1978). *The paranoid process.* New York: Jason Aronson.

Meissner, W. W. (1979). Internalization and object relations. *Journal of the American Psychoanalytic Association, 27*, 345–360.

Meissner, W. W. (1980). The problem of internalization and structure formation. *International Journal of Psycho-Analysis, 61*, 237–248.

Meloy, J. R. (1988). *The psychopathic mind: Origins, dynamics, and treatment.* Northvale, NJ: Jason Aronson.

Midgley, M. (1978). *Beast and man: The roots of human nature.* Ithaca, NY: Cornell University Press.

Millon, T. (1981). *Disorders of personality: DSM-III, Axis II.* New York: Wiley.

Millon, T., with Davis, R. (1996). *Disorders of personality: DSM-IV and beyond.* New York: Wiley–Interscience.

Murphy, J. G. (1972). Moral death: A Kantian essay on psychopathy. *Ethics, 82*, 284–298.

Newman, J. P., & Wallace, J. F. (1993). Psychopathy and cognition. In K. S. Dobson & P. C. Kendall (Eds.), *Psychopathology and cognition* (pp. 293–349). New York: Academic Press.

Patrick, C. J., Bradley, M. M., & Lang, P. J. (1993). Emotion in the criminal psychopath: Startle reflex modulation. *Journal of Abnormal Psychology, 102(1)*, 82–92.

Patrick, C. J., Cuthbert, B. N., & Lang, P. J. (1994). Emotion in the criminal psychopath: Fear image processing. *Journal of Abnormal Psychology, 103(3)*, 523–534.

Perry, P. D., & Perry, J. C. (1996). Reliability and convergence of three concepts of narcissistic personality disorder. *Psychiatry, 59*, 4–19.

Reich, T., Cloninger, C. R., & Guze, S. (1975). The multifactorial model of disease transmission: Description of the model and its use in psychiatry. *British Journal of Psychiatry, 127*, 1–10.

Reid, W. H. (1995). Impulsivity and aggression in the antisocial personality. In E. Hollander & D. J. Stein (Eds.), *Impulsivity and aggression* (pp. 175–182). Chichester, England: Wiley.

Richards, H. J. (1993). *Therapy of the substance abuse syndromes.* Northvale, NJ: Jason Aronson.

Rieber, R. W., & Vetter, H. (1994). The language of the psychopath. *Journal of Psycholinguistic Research, 23(1)*, 1–28.

Ronningstam, E., & Gunderson, J. (1988). Identifying criteria for narcissistic personality disorder. *American Journal of Psychiatry, 29*, 545–549.

Rychlak, J. (1981). *A philosophy of science for personality theory* (2nd ed.). Malabar, FL: Krieger.

Sacks, O. (1989). Neuropsychiatry and Tourette's. In J. Mueller (Ed.), *Neurology and psychiatry: A meeting of minds* (pp. 156–174). Basel: Karger.

Siever, L., & Davis, K. (1991). A psychobiological perspective on the personality disorders. *American Journal of Psychiatry, 148*, 1647–1658.

Skinner, H. A. (1986). Construct validity approaches to psychiatric classification. In T. Millon & G. L. Klerman (Eds.), *Contemporary directions in psychopathology: Toward the DSM-IV* (pp. 307–329). New York: Guilford Press.

Steffy, R. A. (1993). Cognitive deficits in schizophrenia. In K. S. Dobson & P. C. Kendall (Eds.), *Psychopathology and cognition* (pp. 429–469). New York: Academic Press.

Stolorow, R. D. (1975). Toward a functional definition of narcissism. *International Journal of Psychoanalysis, 56*, 179–185.

Stone, M. H. (1980). *The borderline syndromes.* New York: McGraw-Hill.

Stone, M. H. (1993). *Abnormalities of personality: Within and beyond the realm of treatment.* New York: Norton.

Svrakic, D., McCallum, K., & Milan, P. (1991). Developmental, structural, and clinical approach to narcissistic and antisocial personalities. *American Journal of Psychoanalysis, 51*(4), 413–432.

Tillich, P. (1952). *The courage to be.* New Haven, CT: Yale University Press.

Trower, P., & Chadwick, P. (1995). Pathways to defense of the self: A theory of two types of paranoia. *Clinical Psychology: Science and Practice, 2*(3), 263–278.

Webster, C. D., Harris, G. T., Rice, M.E., Cormier, C., & Quinsey, V. L. (1994). *The Violence Prediction Scheme: Assessing dangerousness in high risk men.* Toronto: University of Toronto, Centre of Criminology.

Williamson, S., Harpur, T. J., & Hare, R. D. (1991). Abnormal processes of affective words by psychopaths. *Psychophysiology, 28,* 260–273.

Wirth, C. D. (1992). *The cognitive neuropsychology of schizophrenia.* Hove, England: Erlbaum.

Zuckerman, M. (1983). *Biological bases of sensation seeking: Impulsivity and anxiety.* Hillsdale, NJ: Erlbaum.

6

The Internal World of the Psychopath

J. REID MELOY
CARL B. GACONO

The heart of darkness of the psychopath is well known in both the world literature and real life. Biblical scripture captured its essence in Psalms 10:7–9:

> His mouth is full of curses and lies and threats; trouble and evil are under his tongue. He lies in wait near the villages; from ambush he murders the innocent, watching in secret for his victims. He lies in wait like a lion in cover; he lies in wait to catch the helpless; he catches the helpless and drags them off in his net. His victims are crushed, they collapse: they fall under his strength.

Likewise, in late 1996 the U.S. public was horrified and enraged when Richard Allen Davis, the convicted sexual murderer of 12-year-old Polly Klaas, read a prepared statement during his televised courtroom death sentencing. He was certain he had not sexually molested his victim, because before he killed her she had turned to him and said, "Don't do me like my dad" (*People v. Davis*, 1996).The cruelty of this utterance, with her father and grandmother sitting in the courtroom, was beyond the pale.

Yet psychopaths have inner lives, as we all do. They experience thoughts, fantasies, emotions, and impulses, and defend against them, as we all must. Between their highly problematic social behavior, which is at times exceedingly dangerous, and their psychobiological anomalies, which are crystallizing in the light of recent research (Hare, 1991; Raine, 1993), are their psychodynamics. We have spent the last decade attempting to measure these (Gacono & Meloy, 1994).

INSTRUMENTS AND METHODS EMPLOYED IN OUR RESEARCH PROGRAM

A psychological test is defined by its reliability, validity, and norms. The Rorschach was selected as our dependent measure because of its historical status as one of the most frequently used psychological tests (Piotrowski & Keller, 1992), and the enormous empirical work done by Exner and his colleagues (Exner, 1993, 1995) during the past 30 years to validate and norm the instrument. It is also particularly suited to studying antisocial populations because it has very low face validity (i.e., it is an ambiguous stimulus) and partially bypasses volitional controls. Unlike self-report measures, which Hare (1991) has argued are inherently unreliable with psychopaths, the Rorschach is uniquely situated to empirically "map" the psychostructure and psychodynamics of these subjects. The scoring methods we applied to the Rorschach data included the Comprehensive System (Exner, 1993) and several psychoanalytic measures of defenses (Cooper & Arnow, 1986; Lerner & Lerner, 1980) and object relations (Kwawer, 1980).

Our independent measures—a diagnosis of antisocial personality disorder (APD) and a measure of psychopathy—define the two historical avenues of research concerning antisocial individuals. First, the most recent metamorphosis of the APD diagnosis in DSM-IV (American Psychiatric Association, 1994) marks the relatively young "social deviancy" tradition for understanding chronic antisocial behavior. It is the accepted diagnostic label in the United States and Canada. Second, the construct of psychopathy marks the much older "personality" tradition for understanding these individuals, and has been successfully operationalized by Hare and his colleagues in the Psychopathy Checklist—Revised (PCL-R; Hare, 1991). We applied the criteria derived from both the social deviancy and personality research traditions to the subjects in our studies.

Our methodology was quite simple. We selected nonrandom samples of convenience from various outpatient, jail, prison, hospital, and forensic hospital populations throughout the United States who met criteria for APD (or, in the samples of children and adolescents, conduct disorder [CD]). In a proportion of our samples, we also scored subjects for degree of psychopathy on the PCL-R (Hare, 1991), using the research convention of a score of $\geq$ 30 to label a subject a "primary" or "severe" psychopath. We then gathered a Rorschach protocol from each subject, administered according to the Comprehensive System (Exner, 1993). Data were gathered from archival cases from our own clinical and forensic practices (both public and private sectors), the professional work of colleagues, and doctoral dissertation samples. In all cases, the interjudge reliability (both percentage of agreement and kappa coefficients) of our independent and dependent measures was satisfactory.

SUBJECTS OF OUR RESEARCH

Between 1982 and 1992, we gathered Rorschach data on 380 antisocial children, adolescents, and adults of both genders, reflecting our desire to measure internal psychological characteristics at various stages of development and across the sexes. The geographical distribution of our aggregate sample included the states of California, Iowa, Wyoming, Illinois, Florida, and Massachusetts, as well as the District of Columbia. Our subjects were mostly whites, but included a representation of blacks and Hispanics. Eighteen percent of our aggregate sample were females ($n = 69$).

Although we think our study has a certain external validity, or generalizability to other samples when matched for diagnosis, age, and gender, it remains limited in several ways. Our samples were not randomly selected; moreover, among the data gathered from clinical and forensic practices where there were no reliability tests, the known diagnoses may have introduced an examiner bias into the psychological testing. Finally, all of these subjects were antisocial *failures*. That is, they were usually institutionalized at the time of testing, and consequently our research may not accurately capture the internal structure and dynamics of the *successful* antisocial or psychopathic individual. This fact hampers most extant work on psychopathy, and the limits of generalizability will need to be tested with future community samples.

OUR HYPOTHESES

The specific hypotheses we tested were shaped by three general questions that guided our work. First, could the Rorschach test discriminate between psychopathic and nonpsychopathic antisocial samples, and also among DSM Cluster B personality disorders? Second, could the test empirically generate quantitative data from which we could infer, based upon validity studies, certain psychostructural and psychodynamic properties of antisocial individuals? And third, could the Rorschach data provide further construct validity for the term "psychopathy," and empirically validate certain theoretical psychoanalytic constructs concerning antisocial behavior (Kernberg, 1975; Meloy, 1988)? We believe that our work has answered all three questions in the affirmative.

Our purpose in the remainder of this chapter is to review our findings in some detail for those clinicians and researchers whose intellectual curiosity and, perhaps, emotional demeanor draw them to understand more fully the meaning of psychopathy and the motivations of such individuals. We are mindful, however, that most readers of this chapter will not be familiar with Rorschach terminology and the clinically validated meaning of certain Rorschach ratios, percentages, and derivations; we will attempt to surmount this difficulty by briefly explaining the meaning (validity) of each index to which we refer, and invite the reader to consult other texts for validation studies of the index (Exner, 1986, 1991, 1993).

OUR FINDINGS

Our earliest studies focused upon Rorschach measures of attachment, anxiety, aggression, and narcissism, and were implemented to test, through small-group comparison designs, several theories that had been advanced in both the psychoanalytic (Kernberg, 1975, 1984; Meloy, 1988) and nonpsychoanalytic research (Cleckley, 1941; Hare, 1991).

Attachment and Anxiety

Chronic emotional detachment in psychopaths was explicitly discussed by Bowlby (1944) and has been generally accepted by clinicians (Reid, Dorr, Walker, & Bonner, 1986). Likewise, minimal anxiety was one of the first empirical correlates that distinguished "primary" from so-called "secondary" psychopaths (Lykken, 1957). In a series of studies, we used the Rorschach to measure these two constructs in samples of CD children and adolescents and of APD inmates (Weber, Meloy, & Gacono, 1992; Smith, Gacono, & Kaufman, 1997; Gacono & Meloy, 1991; Gacono & Meloy, 1994). The Rorschach variables we used were T (the perception of texture through the use of shading) and Y (the perception of shading). The former variable is a measure of attachment capacity or affectional relatedness; the latter variable is a measure of felt helplessness or anxiety.

All four groups produced lower scores on the attachment (T) measure than normals

(Exner, 1991). Attachment deficits were found in 88% of CD children, 86% of CD adolescents, 71% of antisocial female inmates (with APD or other Cluster B diagnoses/traits), and 91% of APD male inmates who were also primary psychopaths. Although chronic emotional detachment is not specific to antisocial individuals, we think that it is a necessary (but, alone, insufficient) psychobiological substrate for the development of a pattern of chronic antisocial behavior and, in its extreme form, psychopathy. Bowlby (1944) first postulated this in his sample of "affectionless" delinquents, and Meloy (1988, 1992) has developed the "biopsychoanalytic" idea that without normative attachment, there is no subsequent avenue for psychological identification with others (the precursor of empathy) and the internalization of values (the precursor of conscience).

Findings with the Rorschach measure of anxiety (Y) were less conclusive, although the male antisocial samples appeared to be less anxious than normals, particularly when we compared psychopathic to nonpsychopathic male inmates. Our Rorschach findings with this small sample comparison (Gacono & Meloy, 1991) thus parallel the psychophysiological results of Lykken (1957) many years ago, and add construct validity to other laboratory evidence (Ogloff & Wong, 1990). Self-report measures of anxiety are less clear (Hare, 1991), but there does seem to be a robust negative correlation between Factor 1 of psychopathy (what Meloy, 1992, labeled "aggressive narcissism") and such instruments as the State–Trait Anxiety Inventory (Spielberger, 1968).

In one carefully controlled and diagnostically rigorous study comparing hospitalized teenagers, we found that a sample of dysthymic adolescents was significantly more likely to bond, more anxious, and more interested in others as whole, real, and meaningful individuals than a same-age sample of CD adolescents (Weber et al., 1992). These findings, consistent with the development and pathogenesis of antisocial behavior (Robins, 1966; Millon with Davis, 1996), had a real-world anchor in the finding that the CD adolescents had absent mothers significantly more often than the dysthymic adolescents. Anxiety has long been associated with attachment pathology (Ainsworth, 1989), and we would expect concordance between these psychologically and biologically based constructs, respectively.

Aggression

Psychological test measures of aggression or violence have been notoriously weak (Monahan, 1981). Early in our research we noticed that virtually all of our antisocial samples—whether children, adolescents, or adults—produced virtually *no* aggression responses to the Rorschach (Gacono, 1988; Heaven, 1988).[1] This was unexpected, since the conventional wisdom and a little empirical research (Exner, 1993) have argued that aggression responses to the Rorschach are measures of real-world aggressive behavior.

We initially hypothesized that our adult subjects were just censoring their responses; for instance, we guessed that a male psychopathic inmate might look at the first inkblot, perceive two men raping and mutilating a woman, think about where he was and what he was doing, and respond, "It's a bat." When the CD children in our research, who were mostly of the solitary–aggressive type (DSM-III-R), also did not produce as many aggression responses as their normal peers, we needed a better formulation. The early work of Rapaport, Gill, and Schafer (1946) gave direction to our search for an explanation. They wrote that aggression on the Rorschach implied "a great tension of aggressions within the subject" (p. 460), and with Ferenczi's (1930) theory of alloplastic adaptation, the explanation took shape. We would expect less tensions of ego-dystonic aggression in antisocial subjects, because their aggressive impulses would be ego-syntonic and therefore acted out more readily than those of normals. With less tension of ego-dystonic aggression—that is, less control of unwanted impulse through various conscious maneuvers and unconscious defenses—there would be less need to symbolize aggression during Rorschach testing.

As a part of this investigation, we developed more refined measures of aggression on the Rorschach, the most striking being our SM (sadomasochism) measure. It is scored when the subject articulates a morbid, devalued, or aggressive response and shows pleasurable affect at the same time. This one experimental measure did significantly discriminate between psychopathic and nonpsychopathic inmates (Meloy & Gacono, 1992), and contributes to a small but growing body of research that correlates sadism and psychopathy (Gacono, Meloy, Sheppard, Speth, & Roske, 1995; Hart, Forth, & Hare, 1991). Subsequent independent researchers have demonstrated interjudge reliability and some criterion validity for these additional aggression scores: Aggressive content (AgC), aggressive past (AgPast), and aggressive potential (AgPot) (Riquelme, Occupati, & Gonzales, 1991; Margolis, 1992; Ephraim, Occupati, Riquelme, & Gonzales, 1993). We wrote:

> The various indices of aggressive responses to the Rorschach appear to be a rich source for understanding the structure and dynamics of an individual's intrapsychic aggression. Links to real-world behavior are suggestive, especially with individual cases, but have not been nomothetically demonstrated with any certainty. (Gacono & Meloy, 1994, p. 278)

Pathological Narcissism and Level of Personality Organization

Psychoanalytic theory, particularly the developmental–object relations school, hypothesizes three levels of personality organization—neurotic, borderline, and psychotic—that horizontally demarcate various character pathologies, such as psychopathic, histrionic, and narcissistic. Kernberg (1984) refined this model by focusing upon differences in object relations, defenses, and reality testing across these three levels, and idiographic Rorschach studies have supported his theory (Meloy, Acklin, Gacono, Murray, & Peterson, 1997). Meloy (1988) applied the theory to psychopathy and integrated it with psychobiological research.

We completed several early studies to nomothetically test certain components of this theory, and found that psychopathic subjects produced significantly more borderline-level object relations than nonpsychopathic subjects on the Rorschach (Gacono, 1990; Gacono & Meloy, 1992). Gacono (1990) also measured defenses, and even though there was no significant difference between psychopathic and nonpsychopathic inmates (all of whom were diagnosed with APD), both groups utilized pre-Oedipal defenses, the most common being devaluation. Although the empirical measure of reality testing (X–%) on the Rorschach has not yet been subjected to a comparative research design, the data from our aggregate sample for this particular variable strongly suggest that it is impaired; it is much worse than that of normals, but not as grossly impaired as that of psychotics.[2]

Psychopathic character has also been viewed as an aggressive variant of narcissistic personality disorder (Kernberg, 1975; Meloy, 1988), and our Rorschach research has empirically found, using the reflection response and the personal response,[3] that psychopathic inmates are more pathologically narcissistic than nonpsychopathic inmates

(Gacono, Meloy, & Heaven, 1990). When we compared psychopaths to outpatients with other Cluster B personality disorders, the pathological narcissism in psychopaths was similar to that found in outpatients with narcissistic personality disorder, but significantly greater than that in outpatients with borderline personality disorder (Gacono, Meloy, & Berg, 1992). An important treatment finding from this latter study was the presence of both anxiety and attachment capacity in the narcissistic personality disorder subjects, despite their narcissism—positive prognostic indicators not found among the psychopaths. Subsequent research has supported the utility of the Rorschach in diagnosing narcissistic psychopathology (Hilsenroth, Handler, & Blais, 1996; Hilsenroth, Fowler, Padawer, & Handler, 1997). Formative pathological narcissism has also been found in CD adolescents (Smith et al., 1997), but this characteristic is not apparent in CD children (Gacono & Meloy, 1994). These results are in line with developmental theory that narcissistic defenses, such as devaluation and omnipotence, have not yet consolidated in childhood (Kernberg, 1975).

These Rorschach findings provide some empirical validity for two hypotheses generated by psychoanalytic theory: First, the psychopath is organized at a borderline level of personality, showing expectable part-object relations, pre-Oedipal defenses, and impaired reality testing; and second, the psychopath is a "malignant narcissist," characterized by an aggression and sadism not seen in the more benign narcissistic disorders (Kernberg, 1975, 1984).

The Antisocial and Psychopathic Reference Groups

As our samples of antisocial subjects grew, we realized that our Rorschach data could provide valuable reference group information for clinicians and researchers working in forensic settings, and could be descriptively compared to the Comprehensive System normative groups (Exner, 1993). Our aggregate sample of 380 individual Rorschachs clustered into six groups: CD children ($n = 60$), CD adolescents ($n = 100$), antisocial females ($n = 38$), APD males ($n = 82$), APD males with schizophrenia ($n = 80$), and sexual homicide perpetrators ($n = 20$). The analysis and interpretation of the data focused upon development, gender similarities and differences, and the comorbidity of an Axis I major mental disorder (schizophrenia). The following sections review the findings for each of our six reference groups.

CD Children

The CD children's group ($n = 60$), two-thirds of whom were solitary–aggressive (the DSM-III-R subtype most consistent with "fledgling psychopathy"; Lynam, 1996), were gathered in northern and southern California treatment settings. Ages ranged from 5 to 12, with a mean age of 9 years. IQ was normally distributed.

Unlike normal children, the CD sample were "high-lambda" subjects. This refers to the Rorschach proportion of pure form responses, and is a measure of simplistic, item-by-item problem solving unrelated to intelligence. The children were also predominantly "extratensive," an esoteric Rorschach term that describes a field-dependent, trial-and-error approach to problems. It is related to but not identified with extraversion, a biologically rooted personality dimension (Eysenck, 1967) common in criminals.

Although emotions were expectedly unmodulated (as in normal children), they were markedly avoided in others, and felt less often in the self. There was a greater propensity toward emotional explosiveness, measured by the Pure C (color without form) response, one of the few temporally unstable major Rorschach variables (Exner, 1993). The CD children were less anxious (Y) than normals, and chronically emotionally detached (T). The emotional life of the CD child, inferred through the Rorschach, correlates with Anna Freud's (1936/1966) focus upon shallow affect and the defense of acting out.

The cognitive problems of the CD children were severe, which was all the more surprising since we carefully screened out any clinically psychotic subjects. Formal thought disorder (WSum6 Special Scores; see Meloy & Singer, 1991), perceptual unconventionality (X+%, F+%, Xu%), and impaired reality testing (X–%) were all evident, suggesting that the *process* of perception and association is abnormal in CD children, but that it may be masked by more obvious behavioral problems. Thirteen percent of our sample were diagnosed with attention-deficit/hyperactivity disorder (ADHD). Our cognitive data for CD children provide construct validity for Lynam's (1996) thesis that the CD children at greatest risk for adult psychopathy are those with the most hyperactivity, impulsivity, and attentional problems.

The CD children thought about other people less often than normal children, and when they did the mental representations were uncooperative, somehow spoiled by morbidity or aggression, or strikingly malevolent. Their conception of others was more fantasy-based and part-object-dominated (fewer whole-human [H] responses than normals)—an empirical measure of pre-Oedipal object relations that remains throughout life for the antisocial individual.

The majority of the CD children also evaluated themselves negatively when compared to others (the egocentricity index)—an unusual finding in normal 9-year-olds (5%; Exner, 1993). The grandiosity of adolescent and adult psychopathy is not evident in CD children, and pathological narcissism appears to load on Factor 2 rather than Factor 1 in a children's version of the PCL-R (P. Frick, personal communication, October 1995). This interpersonally damaging transition from devaluation of the self to devaluation of others as the child grows is a poignant reminder of the concealed pain of CD (Willock, 1986).

CD Adolescents

The CD teenagers in our studies (*n* = 100) were gathered in residential treatment settings in California and Iowa, and averaged 15 years of age. Most were males (79%), and IQ was normally distributed.

The developmental pathways toward adult antisocial behavior were evident, but differences emerged when we compared the boys and girls. The simplistic problem-solving style (high lambda) continued to mark both genders, a Rorschach measure that can also be interpreted as a defense against affect. Most subjects were chronically emotionally detached (T), and were minimally anxious (Y), but the boys avoided emotion in others more readily (affective ratio) and modulated their own emotion less than the girls (FC:CF+C). Both genders were less affectively modulated than normals, and showed a greater propensity for emotional explosiveness than normals.[4] Adolescence also signaled the emergence of chronic anger in a large proportion of CD subjects, although cognitive–emotional impulse control in our sample, measured by the Rorschach indices D and Adjusted D, was normal.

Cognitive improvements were evident in the CD adolescents as compared to CD children, but reality-testing impairment (X–%) and formal thought disorder did not go away. CD adolescent boys were more inattentive ("underincorporative" in Rorschach jargon, a measure probably related to ADHD) and grandiose than adolescent girls; the girls were more likely to evidence a passive-dependent problem-solving style (passive movement responses greater than active movement responses).

The CD adolescents' internal representations of self and objects were largely devoid of whole-human responses, and the majority of the subjects produced no present aggression responses, underscoring a point we have made earlier in this chapter: Tension of ego-dystonic aggression is not expected in an acting out population. The internal object relations were also evidently borderline (Kwawer, 1980).

Our hypothesis concerning a shift from self-devaluation to grandiosity (and therefore other devaluation) between childhood and adolescence received support in this sample, most obviously among the boys. The proportion of low egocentricity ratio (EgoC) decreased to 47% (a measure of negative comparison to others), and reflections (Rf or Fr) increased to 37% (a measure of pathological narcissism). This change was less apparent in the girls.

The Comprehensive System also has several "constellation indices" (groupings of certain variables that have been empirically constructed through discriminant-function analyses to measure certain disorders). In the CD adolescent sample, one out of three girls was positive on the DEPI, a measure of affective or mood disorder. This important empirical finding suggests that depression needs to be clinically considered in all CD-diagnosed adolescent females—in spite of, or perhaps because of, the severity of their acting out.

Antisocial Females

Our small sample of antisocial women ($n = 38$) was composed of inmates at the Wyoming Prison for Women and individual forensic cases from our practices. Diagnostic heterogeneity marked this group, with subjects meeting criteria for APD or other Cluster B diagnoses or traits. All the women scored ≥ 20 on the PCL-R, and had an average age of 29 ($SD = 6.5$). This group was too small to be considered anything other than a nonrandom descriptive sampling of incarcerated female offenders.

The core personality characteristics of the antisocial females suggested a simplistic, rigid, item-by-item problem-solving style (high lambda, pervasive extratensive or introversive) and volitional psychological resources below the norm for nonpatient females (Exner, 1993). Cognitive problems abounded, with indices suggesting perceptual unconventionality (X+%, F+%), borderline reality testing (X–%), and moderate although pervasive formal thought disorder (WSum6 Special Scores). Despite the clinical exclusion of psychotic diagnoses from this sample, a refined measure of perceptual and associational abnormality such as the Rorschach could pick up these "borderline-level" difficulties (Kernberg, 1975).

The emotional lives of these antisocial women were more dysphoric than those of antisocial men. Poor affect modulation and a tendency toward emotional explosiveness were the same as in the APD males, however, and located both samples at a 5- to 7-year-old developmental level (Exner, 1993). The women avoided affect in others, perhaps to manage their own coarse and tumultuous feelings, and were normatively anxious. More than one-third showed signs of a diagnosable mood disorder (positive DEPI), just as the CD adolescent girls did.

Interpersonal and affectional relatedness was expectedly diminished. The women were not dependent and did not expect cooperation from others. Their capacity for attachment was minimal, and they did not internally represent others as whole, real, and meaningful objects (Pure H responses). Although the women were not pathologically narcissistic (reflection responses), they were also not psychologically minded and compared themselves to others in a too harsh or too positive light.

These affectional and interpersonal variables, particularly the virtual absence of attachment, find construct validity in the work of Strachan (1993). She found in her sample of 75 incarcerated female offenders (mean PCL-R score = 24.49) that psychopathy ratings were strongly related (.62, *p* < .001) to the failure to parent offspring, even when the effects of drug abuse and prostitution were removed. Taylor (1997) has validated these findings in a larger sample of female jail detainees, using the screening version of the PCL.[5]

We also compared our sample to an outpatient group of borderline personality disorder females (*n* = 32; Gacono & Meloy, 1994). The antisocial females were significantly less bonded than the borderline females, but there was no difference in egocentricity, pathological narcissism, anxiety, or reality testing between the groups. The borderline females, however, were more internally conflicted, showing more aggression and blood content in their Rorschachs. We wrote in summary:

> Both groups are significantly psychopathologic when affect states, object relations, and perceptual accuracy are measured. The damage, dysphoria, and anxiety of both groups is only distinguished by the borderline female's capacity to bond and a greater amount of affect, positive treatment indicators that also portend a tumultuous tie to the psychotherapist. Object relations will be pre-Oedipal in both groups, but much more apparent in the borderline female. Symbiotic rather than autistic developmental themes are likely. Both groups will be characterologically rigid, self-absorbed, and likely to express a narcissistic sense of entitlement: the borderline female's wish to be taken care of, the antisocial female's wish to take. (Gacono & Meloy, 1994, p. 108)

APD and Psychopathic Males

We gathered Rorschach data from APD men (*n* = 82) in prisons and forensic hospitals throughout California. Half of the subjects were randomly chosen during the course of doctoral dissertations, and the other half were pulled nonrandomly from our forensic practices. All subjects were carefully screened for a diagnosis of APD (DSM-III-R), and for the absence of any diagnosis of mental disorder, organic brain disorder, or mental retardation. Average age of the sample was 30 (*SD* = 7).

Forty percent of our sample (*n* = 33) were psychopaths (PCL-R scores ≥ 30). Although we analyzed the entire sample in our book (Gacono & Meloy, 1994), we would like to focus here on the 33 psychopaths we extracted from the larger group.

The psychopaths solved problems in a simplistic, item-by-item manner, missing interpersonal and emotional nuances. The "high-lambda" nature of these subjects, as found in their Rorschachs, validates empirical and clinical evidence that psychopaths' skills at short-term manipulation far exceed, and may blind them to, the long-term self-destructive consequences of their actions. Rorschach indices of impulse control (D, Adjusted D) also indicated that the psychopaths were typically *not* impulsive—a finding that contradicts other research (Hare, 1991). We think this may be due to the three domains of measurable impulse control (cognitive, emotional, and motor), which are somewhat independent of each other. The Rorschach measures cognitive–emotional control; other measures may focus solely on motor control (e.g., PCL-R item 14). Although psychopaths have below-average volitional psychological resources, we caution those who examine these subjects not to assume the existence of impulse control problems. Psychopaths may instead use their unmodulated affect, such as angry explosiveness, to deliberately control others in their environment, reinforcing their fantasies of omnipotent control. Our data support this hypothesis.

The affective lives of our psychopaths were marked by chronic anger and explosiveness (space responses and pure color responses). They avoided emotion in others (low affective ratio), and did not experience deeply felt, strongly socialized, whole-object-related emotions, such as guilt or remorse (an absence of vista responses). They were chronically emotionally detached (no texture response) and highly defended against their own affect (elevated lambda). When they did feel emotion, which was less often than normals (low sum color responses), their emotion was grossly unmodulated (FC:CF+C ratio); when coupled with their pathological narcissism (reflection responses), their feelings were likely to be "presocialized" ones, such as rage, excitement, boredom, persecutory anxiety, or envy. Emotions necessitating the perception of others as whole objects—empathy, sympathy, gratitude, reciprocal pleasure, or mutual eroticism—were starkly absent.

The psychopaths, moreover, had little interest in others as whole objects (pure human responses). People were part-objects (selfobjects in Kohutian theory), defined by the psychopaths' present desires. They did not expect cooperativeness from others (few, if any, COP responses), and they were not troubled by tensions of ego-dystonic aggression because of their proclivity to act out when they felt like it. Sexual preoccupation was apparent (sex response), shaped by hedonic calculation and suffused with aggression.

Our psychopaths were pathologically narcissistic, grandiose, and self-focused individuals (reflection response, whole-area to human movement ratio, egocentricity index) who unconsciously identified with predatory objects (Meloy, 1988). Their relationships were defined by dominance, not affection (personal responses, no texture response). These latter Rorschach measures empirically support the hypothesis that psychopaths engage in predatory rather than affective violence (Meloy, 1988; Serin, 1991; Williamson, Hare, & Wong, 1987).

The content of the psychopaths' internalized object relations was indicated by a plethora of Kwawer's (1980) Rorschach categories called narcissistic mirroring, violent symbiosis, symbiotic merging, and boundary disturbance—typical of borderline personality organization, and found at least once in 91% of our psychopathic protocols. As we wrote concerning the difference between a general APD sample and a psychopathic sample, "trends are in the direction of a less conflicted sense of self and a more smoothly functioning grandiosity" (Gacono & Meloy, 1994, p. 172).

The cognitive impairments of these psychopaths were pervasive. Moderate formal thought disorder was measurable, and indicated a propensity of the psychopaths to become tangential or circumstantial in the service of self-aggrandizement (deviant responses with personal responses). This suggests a psychodynamic basis (narcissism) for formal thought disorder in psychopaths, rather than a structural basis (physical brain impairment) for the more severe formal thought disorder seen in schizophrenia.

The psychopaths' reality testing was impaired at a borderline level (X−%), virtually the same as the female antisocials' was, and they were more likely to abuse fantasy than APD males in general (human movement passive greater than active). We are not sure of the meaning of this latter finding, but it may be related to the rehearsal of acts of predation in fantasy.

Although our actual sample of adult male psychopaths was small, the data are remarkably consistent with other behavioral and trait measures of psychopathy recorded in different samples, with different measures, by different research groups. We are especially intrigued by the pervasive cognitive deficits of the psychopaths evident on the Rorschach—findings often missed, perhaps with the exception of proverb interpretation, in a routine mental status exam.

APD Schizophrenics

Our sample of schizophrenic patients (n = 80) with a comorbid diagnosis of APD, all committed or incarcerated in California maximum-security hospitals or prisons, gave us an opportunity to measure the mutual relationship between an Axis I major mental disorder and Axis II character pathology.

The schizophrenic APD males (mean age = 31, SD = 10) showed severe formal thought disorder (WSum6 Special Scores) and grossly impaired reality testing (X–%), like other nonforensic reference groups of hospitalized schizophrenics (Exner, 1993). Chronic antisocial behavior, however, appeared to organize the schizophrenia psychologically—a testament to the impact of character pathology on a biochemically based major mental disorder. For instance, APD schizophrenics were less anxious (Y) than, but just as chronically emotionally detached (T) as, other schizophrenics. They were, however, significantly more narcissistic (reflection response) than other schizophrenic patients. The schizophrenic APD males did not modulate affect well, experienced it in a weak form, were highly defended against it, and avoided it in others. Their acute and chronic impulse control was normal, at least when they were not psychotic.

Clinicians working with this population should be very careful, especially if schizophrenic patients are also psychopaths, and not just diagnosed with APD. The delusions of schizophrenic patients may bring a certainty and a relentlessness to the expected predatory violence if they are also psychopaths (Meloy, 1988). The psychiatric dilemma with these patients is also immense, since the successful medication of the Axis I disorder may result in a better-organized psychopath.

Sexual Homicide Perpetrators

Our smallest sample—20 sexual homicide perpetrators (mean age = 34, SD = 9)—gave us an opportunity to explore the similarities and differences between this group, only defined by an extreme and aberrant *behavior,* and psychopaths in general. Since the publication of our book, this sample has increased (n = 38), with no significant changes in our earlier-published findings (Meloy, Gacono, & Kenney, 1994).

The sexual homicide perpetrators, when compared to a random sample of nonsexually offending psychopaths, were no different in measurable narcissism, anger, formal thought disorder, and borderline reality testing. They did distinguish themselves, however, by being suggestively more dysphoric, significantly more obsessional (feral movement responses),[6] and paradoxically better able to form whole, real, and meaningful representations of others in their minds than the psychopaths. Attachment was abnormal, and mostly absent; but, unlike the psychopaths, about one-third of the sexual homicide perpetrators were abnormally hungry for an attachment (elevated texture responses). The sexual homicide perpetrators also expected more cooperation from others than the psychopaths did.

We were left with the distinct empirical impression that sexual homicide perpetrators, among whom there will always be some degree of psychopathy (Geberth & Turco,

1997), are a much more emotionally disturbed and conflicted group than psychopaths who have never committed such an extremely aggressive sexual crime.

CONCLUDING REMARKS

Although the behavior of psychopaths is often enigmatic, their internal worlds are measurable and understandable. Nomothetic Rorschach data help us to discern how chronically antisocial individuals think and feel, and the characteristic ways in which they organize, adapt to, and defend against their perceptions, associations, emotions, and impulses. Our work appears to be quite convergent with other efforts to study and measure both psychopathy in particular (Hare, 1991) and chronic antisocial behavior in general (Lykken, 1995; Millon with Davis, 1996; Raine, 1993; Stone, 1993). Perhaps Brittain (1970) said it best when he wrote that "we cannot treat, except empirically, what we do not understand; and we cannot prevent, except fortuitously, what we do not comprehend" (p. 206).

NOTES

1. The aggressive movement score (Ag) in the Comprehensive System is used "for any movement response involving two or more objects in which the action is clearly aggressive . . . the aggressive action must be occurring" (Exner, 1993, p. 172).

2. The X–% is the proportion of responses that have a minus form level, meaning that "the answer is imposed on the blot structure with total, or near total disregard for the structure of the area being used in creating the response. Often arbitrary contours will be created where none exist" (Exner, 1993, p. 152). The face validity of this measure should be apparent, if reality testing is understood to be the ability to distinguish clearly between internal stimuli (fantasy) and external stimuli (the constraints of the actual percept).

3. The reflection response is scored when an object seen is reflected because of the symmetry of the blot. It is interpreted as a measure of egocentricity (Exner, 1993), and occurs in about 50% of the Rorschach protocols of psychopaths (Gacono & Meloy, 1994). Only 5% of normals produce one or more reflection responses. The personal response is scored whenever the subject refers to personal knowledge or experience as part of the basis for the response. It is likewise elevated among psychopaths (> 3), and we think that it is fundamentally a self-aggrandizing mechanism in psychopaths to maintain their grandiosity during the testing (Gacono, Meloy, & Heaven, 1990).

4. These various indices are premised on the "color–affect hypothesis," which Rorschach (1921/1942) proposed in his original work. The developmental Rorschach literature generally supports this hypothesis, but much more *experimental* research is needed to establish the validity of this assertion. The coarseness and rapidity of emotional expression also constitute a clinically indirect measure of empathy (partially measured on the Rorschach by human movement [M] responses): The more a normal child realizes the impact of emotional expression on others (e.g., explosive feelings may frighten or anger others), the greater the likelihood that feelings will be monitored as they are felt and expressed in a volitionally controlled and modulated manner. Most people colloquially refer to this as "emotional maturity."

5. An interesting biochemical correlate that awaits testing is the relationship between vasopressin and oxytocin levels and psychopathy in samples of postpartum antisocial and normal women.

6. This empirical finding confirms an old clinical and forensic observation that sexual homicide, particularly if it is repetitive, has an obsessive–compulsive dimension to it. Our data also lend

support to the notion that medications used for obsessive–compulsive disorder may also be useful in the treatment of extreme sexual aggressors whose behavior is ego-dystonic.

REFERENCES

Ainsworth, M. (1989). Attachments beyond infancy. *American Psychologist, 44,* 709–716.
American Psychiatric Association. (1994). *Diagnostic and statistical manual of mental disorders* (4th ed.). Washington, DC: Author.
Bowlby, J. (1944). Forty-four juvenile thieves: Their characters and home-life. *International Journal of Psycho-Analysis, 25,* 19–53.
Brittain, R. (1970). The sadistic murderer. *Medical Science and Law, 10,* 198–207.
Cleckley, H. (1941). *The mask of sanity.* St. Louis, MO: C. V. Mosby.
Cooper, S., & Arnow, D. (1986). An object relations view of the borderline defenses: A Rorschach analysis. In M. Kissen (Ed.), *Assessing object relations phenomena* (pp. 143–171). Madison, CT: International Universities Press.
Ephraim, D., Occupati, R., Riquelme, J., & Gonzales, E. (1993). Gender, age and socioeconomic differences in Rorschach thematic content scales. *Rorschachiana, 18,* 68–81.
Exner, J. E. (1986). *The Rorschach: A Comprehensive System* (2nd ed.). *Vol. 1. Basic foundations.* New York: Wiley.
Exner, J. E. (1991). *The Rorschach: A Comprehensive System* (2nd ed.). *Vol. 2. Interpretation.* New York: Wiley.
Exner, J. E. (1993). *The Rorschach: A Comprehensive System* (3rd ed.). *Vol. 1. Basic foundations.* New York: Wiley.
Exner, J. E. (1995). *Issues and methods in Rorschach research.* Mahwah, NJ: Erlbaum.
Eysenck, H. J. (1967). *The biological basis of personality.* Springfield, IL: Charles C Thomas.
Ferenczi, S. (1930). Autoplastic and alloplastic. In *Final contributions to the problems and methods of psychoanalysis.* New York: Basic Books.
Freud, A. (1966). *The ego and the mechanisms of defense* (C. Baines, Trans., rev. ed.). New York: International Universities Press. (Original work published 1936)
Gacono, C. B. (1988). *A Rorschach analysis of object relations and defensive structure and their relationship to narcissism and psychopathy in a group of antisocial offenders.* Unpublished doctoral dissertation, United States International University, San Diego.
Gacono, C. B. (1990). An empirical study of object relations and defensive operations in antisocial personality. *Journal of Personality Assessment, 54,* 589–600.
Gacono, C. B., & Meloy, J. R. (1991). A Rorschach investigation of attachment and anxiety in antisocial personality. *Journal of Nervous and Mental Disease, 179,* 546–552.
Gacono, C. B., & Meloy, J.R. (1992). The Rorschach and the DSM-III-R antisocial personality: A tribute to Robert Lindner. *Journal of Clinical Psychology, 48,* 393–405.
Gacono, C. B., & Meloy, J. R. (1994). *Rorschach assessment of aggressive and psychopathic personalities.* Hillsdale, NJ: Erlbaum.
Gacono, C. B., Meloy, J. R., & Berg, J. (1992). Object relations, defensive operations, and affective states in narcissistic, borderline, and antisocial personality. *Journal of Personality Assessment, 55,* 270–279.
Gacono, C. B., Meloy, J. R., & Heaven, T. (1990). A Rorschach investigation of narcissism and hysteria in antisocial personality disorder. *Journal of Personality Assessment, 55,* 270–279.
Gacono, C. B., Meloy, J. R., Sheppard, K., Speth, E., & Roske, A. (1995). A clinical investigation of malingering and psychopathy in hospitalized insanity acquittees. *Bulletin of the American Academy of Psychiatry and the Law, 23,* 387–398.
Geberth, V., & Turco, R. (1997). Antisocial personality disorder, sexual sadism, malignant narcissism, and serial murder. *Journal of Forensic Sciences, 42,* 49–60.

108   PART I. HISTORY AND VIEWPOINTS

Hare, R. D. (1991). *Manual for the Hare Psychopathy Checklist—Revised.* Toronto: Multi-Health Systems.

Hart, S., Forth, A., & Hare, R. (1991). The MCMI-II as a measure of psychopathy. *Journal of Personality Disorders, 5,* 318–327.

Heaven, T. (1988). *Relationship between Hare's Psychopathy Checklist and selected Exner Rorschach variables in an inmate population.* Unpublished doctoral dissertation, United States International University, San Diego.

Hilsenroth, M., Fowler, C. Padawer, J., & Handler, L. (1997). Narcissism in the Rorschach revisited: Some reflections upon empirical data. *Psychological Assessment, 9,* 113–121.

Hilsenroth, M., Handler, L., & Blais, M. (1996). Assessment of narcissistic personality disorder: A multi-method review. *Clinical Psychology Review, 16,* 655–683.

Kernberg, O. (1975). *Borderline conditions and pathological narcissism.* New York: Jason Aronson.

Kernberg, O. (1984). *Severe personality disorders.* New Haven, CT: Yale University Press.

Kwawer, J. (1980). Primitive interpersonal modes, borderline phenomena and Rorschach content. In J. Kwawer, P. Lerner, H. Lerner, & A. Sugarman (Eds.), *Borderline phenomena and the Rorschach test* (pp. 89–109). New York: International Universities Press.

Lerner, P., & Lerner, H. (1980). Rorschach assessment of primitive defenses in borderline personality structure. In J. Kwawer, P. Lerner, H. Lerner, & A. Sugarman (Eds.), *Borderline phenomena and the Rorschach test* (pp. 257–274). New York: International Universities Press.

Lykken, D. (1957). A study of anxiety in the sociopathic personality. *Journal of Abnormal and Social Psychology, 55,* 6–10.

Lykken, D. (1995). *The antisocial personalities.* Hillsdale, NJ: Erlbaum.

Lynam, D. (1996). Early identification of chronic offenders: Who is the fledgling psychopath? *Psychological Bulletin, 120,* 209–234.

Margolis, J. (1992). *Aggressive and borderline level content on the Rorschach: An exploration of some proposed scoring categories.* Unpublished doctoral dissertation, California School of Professional Psychology, Berkeley.

Meloy, J. R. (1988). *The psychopathic mind: Origins, dynamics and treatment.* Northvale, NJ: Jason Aronson.

Meloy, J. R. (1992). *Violent attachments.* Northvale, NJ: Jason Aronson.

Meloy, J. R., Acklin, M., Gacono, C., Murray, J., & Peterson, C. (1997). *Contemporary Rorschach interpretation.* Mahwah, NJ: Erlbaum.

Meloy, J. R., & Gacono, C. B. (1992). The aggression response and the Rorschach. *Journal of Clinical Psychology, 48,* 104–114.

Meloy, J. R., Gacono, C. B., & Kenney, L. (1994). A Rorschach investigation of sexual homicide. *Journal of Personality Assessment, 62,* 58–67.

Meloy, J. R., & Singer, J. (1991). A psychoanalytic view of the Comprehensive System "special scores." *Journal of Personality Assessment, 56,* 202–217.

Millon, T., with Davis, R. (1996). *Disorders of personality: DSM-IV and beyond.* New York: Wiley–Interscience.

Monahan, J. (1981). *The clinical prediction of violence.* Beverly Hills, CA: Sage.

Ogloff, J., & Wong, S. (1990). Electrodermal and cardiovascular evidence of a coping response in psychopaths. *Criminal Justice and Behavior, 17,* 231–245.

People v. Davis, C.R. No. 186000 (Santa Clara Co. Super. Ct.), Sept. 26, 1996.

Piotrowski, C., & Keller, J. W. (1992). Psychological testing in applied settings: A literature review from 1982–1992. *Journal of Training and Practice in Professional Psychology, 6,* 74–82.

Raine, A. (1993). *The psychopathology of crime.* San Diego: Academic Press.

Rapaport, D., Gill, M., & Schafer, R. (1946). *Diagnostic psychological testing.* New York: International Universities Press.

Reid, W., Dorr, D., Walker, J., & Bonner, J. (1986). *Unmasking the psychopath.* New York: Norton.

Riquelme, J., Occupati, R., & Gonzales, E. (1991). *Rorschach study of the content normative data for nonpatient subjects from the greater Caracas area according to Exner's Comprehensive System.* Unpublished manuscript.

Robins, L. (1966). *Deviant children grown up.* Baltimore: Williams & Wilkins.

Rorschach, H. (1942). *Psychodiagnostics.* New York: Grune & Stratton. (Original work published 1921)

Serin, R. (1991). Psychopathy and violence in criminals. *Journal of Interpersonal Violence, 6,* 423–431.

Smith, A., Gacono, C. B., & Kaufman, L. (1997). A Rorschach comparison of psychopathic and nonpsychopathic conduct-disordered adolescents. *Journal of Clinical Psychology, 53,* 289–300.

Spielberger, C. (1968). *The State–Trait Anxiety Inventory.* Palo Alto, CA: Consulting Psychologists Press.

Stone, M. H. (1993). *Abnormalities of personality.* New York: Norton.

Strachan, C. (1993). *The assessment of psychopathy in female offenders.* Unpublished doctoral dissertation, University of British Columbia, Vancouver.

Taylor, C. (1997). *Attachment and psychopathy in female offenders.* Unpublished doctoral dissertation, California School of Professional Psychology, San Diego.

Weber, C., Meloy, J. R., & Gacono, C. B. (1992). A Rorschach study of attachment and anxiety in inpatient conduct-disordered and dysthymic adolescents. *Journal of Personality Assessment, 58,* 16–26.

Williamson, S., Hare, R., & Wong, S. (1987). Violence: Criminal psychopaths and their victims. *Canadian Journal of Behavioural Science, 19,* 454–462.

Willock, B. (1986). Narcissistic vulnerability in the hyper-aggressive child: The disregarded (unloved, uncared-for) self. *Psychoanalytic Psychology, 3,* 59–80.

7

Antisocial Character and Behavior: Threats and Solutions

I have devoted a significant portion of my professional life to understanding violence and antisocial behavior, and to treating or rehabilitating its perpetrators. I have commented on and treated not only the "badness" of those perpetrators, but also their needs, their defects, their illnesses, and even their sadness (Reid, 1978). I have great respect for those who work in the tradition of such clinicians as Georg Stürup and Karl Menninger, to empathize with the deep needs of chronic, characterological criminals and mend their broken psyches. Met individually, in the clinical arena, we may work with them as patients who deserve care even as we care for their victims.

That is not the purpose of this chapter. Here I will speak frankly about *societal* cost from, and response to, characterological antisocial behavior and criminal violence. The chapter does not refer to persons whose behavior arises primarily from Axis I DSM-IV disorders such as schizophrenia or major depression, but rather to those whose *style* of life and conduct is both abhorrent to society and under their conscious control. The concepts in this chapter sound uncomplicated at first; many readers will simply compare it to "get tough" or "law and order" diatribes. I ask such readers to be patient and read further. The points to be made are both more complex and more effective. I ask that my readers consider the philosophical issues impartially until the end, and keep their momentary stereotypic reactions in check.

The sheer variety of antisocial syndromes and behaviors—with their many causes and many effects—complicates discussions of, and proposed actions for dealing with, troublesome social conduct. Some kinds of violence are seen as "fair game" for conservative societal action to decrease crime; others are seen as special because of the status of the perpetrator or setting (e.g., some juvenile offenders, abused women, persons with mental illness). Our social rules and conscience will not let us apply a straightforward "lock 'em up" ideology. Nevertheless, it may be useful for criminologists, mental health professionals, and social academics—not just stereotypic "law and order" conservatives—to homogenize our views and responses to antisocial conduct and to view antisocial behavior more generically.

THE COSTS OF PSYCHOPATHY AND OTHER ANTISOCIAL SYNDROMES

It is easy to list the financial costs of crime and injuries to victims. If these were the only costs to people and society, our problem would not be so great; many other kinds of injury cost money and are managed without controversy. How we deal with people who purposefully hurt us is a special matter. Other, arguably deeper costs of tolerating widespread psychopathy and antisocial behavior include loss of day-to-day freedoms, eroding social values, decreasing attention to personal responsibility, flawed developmental models for children and youths, evolution of skewed social controls, and expanding entitlements that diminish the productive portion of society. Several of these will be discussed briefly below. Each owes some of its importance to what we may call collectively a "numbing" phenomenon: the fact that U.S. citizens and society began a generation ago to view these costs as somehow *normal*, as simply "the way things are."

Freedom of Living

Chronic antisocial behavior has taken a great deal from our day-to-day freedoms. There has always been crime, just as there probably have always been psychopaths. Nevertheless, it is tempting to say that fear of predation has rarely been such a pervasive part of U.S. life as in the past two decades. The elderly cannot walk on most city streets without some level of anxiety, sometimes outright fear. Parks designed, built, and paid for by ordinary citizens are often given over to the antisocial or predatory element, and even when they are not given over in fact, many people still cannot use them because they worry that harm will come to them. More and more homes and businesses have become defensive bastions, with bars on windows and carefully controlled access. New homes built in the United States almost always contain provisions for electronic burglar alarms (or, in many, the alarms themselves).

Sometimes the loss of freedom is small, such as in the case of a man on a subway afraid to ask a teenage boy to turn down his "boom box," or a woman who keeps her windows locked on a hot day for fear of assault or theft. Many larger losses are subtle, but nonetheless limiting and sometimes life-threatening, such as difficulty shopping because storekeepers and cab drivers refuse to do business in dangerous neighborhoods.[1] The psychopaths, thugs, and predators thus take greatly from us *even when they are not present*, and we see and fear them even in people—such as teenagers listening to radios on a subway—who are not always dangerous to us.

Eroding Social Values

As we must live in a particular environment, we become accustomed to it, even defensive of it. In this era of instant news and ubiquitous access to (even unwanted) information, we begin to adapt. Soon many people—because it is easier than wrestling to uphold social virtue, or because it seems that this battle is being lost—adopt the premise that the ever-present antisocial environment is now part of a normal and appropriate life. It would be inaccurate to say that they have *accepted* that premise, since for the most part they have not compared the moral and immoral side by side and chosen the immoral; rather, they have *adopted* what they now believe is the world in which they must live. Some rage against it, bitterly citing older, better values; however, the pendulum is inexorably pushed away.

Flawed Developmental Models

One of the most ominous results of societal adaptation to life in an antisocial environment is the fact that children have no memory of what came before. They automatically see eroded social values as part of their "normal" environment, much as an abused child sees a brutal family as normal until he or she begins to experience the broader world. Unfortunately, when one's society, not one's individual household, is the problem, there is no "broader world." Pockets of moral values may be difficult for children and adolescents to find, are unlikely to appear serendipitously, and in any case are not very competitive in the contest for youthful attention. It is thus inevitable that a child's sense of what is and is not socially acceptable is shaped by a world that accepts antisocial behavior as a "natural" part of life. Although the problem is not yet a matter of developing an aberrant "conscience" in this first generation without a memory of other social values, the child develops easily into either predator or apathetic potential prey.

In the second generation, social and personal damage multiplies in both quality and quantity. The child's early models are themselves predators or potential prey. This means that his or her most important developmental information, gathered from birth to age 6, is filtered through already changed parents. The attitudes thus created are now not formed from mere social experience, but embedded in the roots of ego and superego. They may now be called "characterological," feel deeply normal to the person, and are very difficult to change. When this happens to a large segment of the population, as it has and is happening in the United States, the *societal* mores thus created—for good or bad; whether mores of predation, acceptance, predestination, or apathy—are as deeply inculcated as are "character" attributes in the individual. At that point, we become a nation of people who do not even know that something is wrong.[2]

Decreasing Personal Responsibility

Society's *expectation* that each of us will take responsibility for his or her actions—in this case, antisocial ones—is an enormous determinant of whether or not we commit antisocial acts, and of whether or not there is broad, reliable social modeling for adults and children alike. Furthermore, a consistent social expectation of appropriate behavior significantly increases proper conduct among those who might not otherwise adhere to societal norms, such as children, the severely mentally ill, and persons with mental retardation.

Personal responsibility depends greatly on a healthy sense of guilt. Treating guilt as a mere offshoot of internal conflict encourages people—both patients and others—to ignore it as a warning of social problems ahead. Once we can ignore guilt, it becomes easy to ignore the things that should make us guilty, such as breaking the law, deliberately harming others, or ignoring their needs and wishes.

I have come to appreciate the futility, even folly, of many mental health professionals' views of social appropriateness and morality. Children and adolescents need to learn that guilt is usually a sign that they are doing something wrong; moreover, they should be unambivalently corrected by adults through education, discipline, or modeling. It is time that psychiatrists and psychologists acknowledge a preference for what is *right* in their treatment of children, adolescents, and adults, and not treat antisocial or guilt-inducing behavior as if it were a personal choice rather than a developmental and social imperative.

Every cost of psychopathy just discussed is, in large part at least, a cost U.S. society has brought upon itself. During the past three decades, we—the citizens of this precious representative democracy—have *allowed* our dangerous surroundings and destructive developmental models to evolve. We have contributed to the decline of guilt, and thus of the things from which guilt protects us. We have, as a nation, *promoted* an environment in which the good are fodder for the bad.

NATURAL-BORN PSYCHOPATHS

The costs of chronic and widespread psychopathic[3] behavior are not some nonjudgmental natural phenomena in which the fittest survive. North America is not "nature red in tooth and claw," in which there is no right or wrong in being predator or prey in some oddly natural order of things. We control our social destiny as no animals and no other humans in history have done. We are rational people choosing to deny our own responsibility for personal and social well-being.

I dislike anthropological comments, now pop social science, that compare psychopaths to wolves and speak of some misinterpreted Darwinian survival of the fittest. Such academic wags are engaging in what seems to be the opposite of anthropomorphism[4] It is tempting to say that our masses have somehow become baitfish for the psychopathic shark, or sheep for the antisocial wolf, but this is not quite the case. In modern society, human predators are not acting out of some instinct, and their prey are not genetically predestined to become part of a figurative food chain. To say that most human predators are acting animalistically, out of some natural but hypertrophied survival or territorial imperative, is to give them more credit than they are due, and to deny them the responsibility that we are entitled to demand for their actions.

I agree that we can see remnants of our phylogeny in our brains and behaviors, but it is a mistake to search there for all answers to behavioral questions. Sadistic, amoral, or intraspecies violence (not related to mating contests or, in a few species, competition for food) is not often found in nature. It has little evolutionary value. Thus predatory sexual violence, for example, cannot be correctly termed "animalistic," since no "animals" engage in it. Preying upon the elderly or disabled of one's own species, a hallmark of psychopathic opportunism, has almost no parallel in mammalian nature. Human psychopathy involves human experience and human choice.

If the human predators, psychopaths and others, are not to be seen as "animals," should they then be seen as "only human," part of the "human condition"? And should they be treated according to the Golden Rule: "Do unto others as you would have them do unto you"? Should our lofty principles and sense of ethics cause us to treat them with understanding and forgiveness alone? Of course not.

OUR SENSE OF FAIRNESS IS KILLING US

One of the biggest obstacles to finding answers to chronic antisocial behavior and violent crime, and at the same time one of the least appreciated, is our sense of fairness.

Law-abiding U.S. citizens are heavily invested in the premise that all people value the tenets of our Constitution. Many go further, and believe that a very liberal interpretation of the Constitution is important to protecting our republic and its representative democracy.

Chronic criminals and psychopaths do not value the same rules and tenets, except for themselves. Instead, they use them against us. They thus *take from us* in a very serious way—by turning our deep convictions (and guilts about going against those convictions) to their own ends. We hobble ourselves, but not the crooks, with our rules. In this, one of our most dangerous games, the playing field is wildly tilted in favor of the opponent.

But isn't our fairness in the face of adversity a mark of our civilization? Isn't this what separates us from the animals, and even from the very criminals we seek to control? Don't we need that sense of fairness to keep our society intact?

No. First, life is full of situations in which we need to do something distasteful, try to do it within our rules of law and ethics, and somehow accomplish the goal. Most of us agree that we need to slaughter animals from time to time. We do it as humanely as possible, but we get it done. And we do it in such a way that our needs for food, safety, efficiency, and profit are met. We also agree that some public health needs are important enough to require suspension of some rights of people who have not been convicted of any crime; this suspension is sometimes based merely on the possibility that they may become ill and represent a danger to others. We require that certain people with infections be reported, treated, and in some cases prevented from infecting others (via quarantine or even incarceration).

But we shrink from controlling the criminal or probable criminal, even when the danger is far more obvious. We are so bound by the tenets of fairness and basic equality upon which we have founded systems of Western law (and some, but not all, Western religion) that we steadfastly prevent ourselves from seeing some exceptions to those tenets. We recognize that there *are* exceptions—for children and a few other groups—but we fail to apply them to psychopaths and other chronically predatory people until the damage has been done.

Firm Action Need Not Threaten Our Democracy or Our Ethics

We wrestle endlessly with the question of who is the greater danger: those who would openly subvert society and overthrow it, or those who we fear would weaken it by suspending our rights, one by one, in the name of protecting us from some internal threat. While we have been interminably discussing this weighty issue, the psychopaths, who don't trouble themselves with contemplation, have been gaining ground. It is not a just a question of finding a solution that protects us from violence while guarding against the possibility that we will throw the Constitution out with the crooks. Our philosophical struggle with the issues has become truly obsessive. We are frustrated, but complacent. Reformers disagree, obstruct each other's actions, and accomplish virtually nothing in the way of real solutions. If this were an invasion, with clouds of war gathering on the horizon, would we be so complacent?

There is no "if." To fail to act is to make our world ever smaller—to give up our streets, parks, stores, and schools to predators who neither believe in nor adhere to the rules we hold dear for ourselves. To fail to act is to continue to limit our freedoms at the hands of those who laugh at our naiveté. *To fail to act may be to lose our democracy.*

"They" Are Different from "Us"

I have no wish to dehumanize people when I say that those who purposely endanger others in our streets, parks, and schools, even our homes, are qualitatively different from the rest of us. I care less and less about *why* they're not the same as the rest of us; the enemy is at our door. Most of our energy must be diverted to immediate defense, not merely to studying his motivations. There is no (reasonable) ethic which requires that we treat him as we treat other adults; indeed, to do so is foolish. If we treat him as if he were like us, *we will continue to fail,* and he will continue to take from us.

SOLUTIONS

North American social scientists and mental health professionals expend great effort trying to understand, in greater and greater detail, the types and motivations of various antisocial perpetrators. Violence motivated by character disorder, mental illness, neurophysiological irritability, intoxication, gang initiation, "macho" defensiveness, monetary gain, or simple meanness has varying roots in various settings. A scholar or social scientist may need such studies (and may have energy to spare for pursuing them), and the search for basic information may certainly have long-range rewards; however, the answer to most violent crime does not require such intellectual hairsplitting. There are ways to stop much of the violent and psychopathic behavior without having to understand or cure those roots.

1. Expect Responsibility

We are so busy finding reasons for criminals' and psychopaths' not controlling their behavior—often making them into the victims of childhood abuse or neglect, intoxication, social ills, unemployment, youthful misjudgment, or mental illness—that we fail to realize that almost all individuals, even those under great duress, can control their behavior if they are expected to do so. Since we often do not expect people to control their behavior, it is no surprise that we must bear the consequences of behaviors they do not control.

What an insult to the perpetrator! If a woman kills her husband, we often say she was too weak or victimized to think of any alternative. If a teenage boy kills an innocent baby in a drive-by gang shooting, we actually entertain the notion that his act was predetermined by his upbringing, social situation, or youthfulness, and that he didn't mean to do it. If a mentally ill person lashes out at someone with a knife, we become so frightened of his or her mental illness that we don't consider the possibility that the *person,* not the illness, may be to blame (and we thus support a fear of all mentally ill persons). If a woman drives the getaway car in a bank robbery, and then isn't caught for a couple of decades, many want to believe that she is less blameworthy when she finally is caught than she was at the time of the crime. When a pedophilic murderer has served a few years of his sentence and seems to be acting civilized (in a prison far from small children or other victims), parole boards—often with support from a psychologist or psychiatrist—want to believe he is rehabilitated or sufficiently punished for release, perhaps to make room for someone else.[5]

I am impressed by the enormous number of very ill or socially deprived people who *can* control their behavior when they are expected to do so. Even psychotic individuals rarely run red lights or relieve themselves in front of other people. The most blatant criminals can almost always control themselves long enough to wait until their victims are helpless or alone before they start mugging them. Very little violence is knowingly committed in the presence of a police officer. Provided both we and the perpetrators *expect* the latter to be held accountable, they almost always can be considered responsible for their acts and the consequences of what they do. If they know this from consistent experience in ordinary society, they are, as a group, far less likely to engage in antisocial behavior.

2. Guarantee Consequences

The wages of sin, to paraphrase the old joke, are pretty good nowadays. In the first place, one's chances of being swiftly and surely punished are almost zero. If punishment comes at all, it is unlikely to be very serious. If the sentence *is* severe, appeals, bonds, "good time," mandatory release dates, and the like are the rule even for many heinous crimes. For people who are about to commit crimes or otherwise abuse others—especially those who rely on external controls (rather than morals or empathy for others) to guide their conduct, and who do not see very far into the future—these facts combine to make the probability of punishment seem so remote that it doesn't really exist.

In the unlikely event that punishment does eventually arrive, the perpetrator may not even associate it with his or her antisocial act. When months or years pass before sentencing, with myriad intercurrent events, any cause-and-effect (or even temporal) association is lost. The perpetrator often blames the judge, the victim, the lawyer, or just bad luck for the discomfort of incarceration. No meaningful connection is made between the behavior and the consequence.

Readers who protest, "If that happened to me, I'd be terrified of going to prison; I'd know why I was being punished," must remember the primary premise of this chapter: We must stop identifying with the chronic criminal, and stop allowing him to manipulate our misplaced guilt about treating him as he is: qualitatively *different* from the rest of us.[6]

Remember, normal people have an internal guide, or conscience, that brings the probability of punishment into their minds and blends it seamlessly with their views of the world. The psychopathic person has little or no such conscience, and we must not delude ourselves that he has one, no matter how much we wish it were so. He is not like us, and to treat him as if he were is self-destructive folly. We must not make the mistake of trying to put ourselves in the criminal's shoes, or of thinking, "There but for the grace of God go I." If we had been in the same situation as the crook, we would not have committed the crime!

We feel guilt and shame; he feels little or none. We live from day to day with the consequences of our actions; we go to work so that we can buy the things we need; we avoid violence because we don't want its (internal or external) consequences. The psychopathic person, regardless of his age or situation, does not expect to live with those consequences—either because he does not feel them *or because he does not expect them.* As a society, we can do little to change psychopathic lack of empathy and guilt, but we can increase perpetrators' expecting of consequences. Few people have such profound brain or personality deficits that they cannot respond to a predictable environment. The problem is that which they have come to expect from the rest of society.

When we expect something, we prepare for it. If I am hungry and given food every time a bell rings, I will salivate at the sound of the bell alone. If I am required to pay rent to remain in my home, I will either prepare to pay the rent or prepare to move. If I expect something bad to happen should I clobber a little old lady for a couple of dollars, I will avoid clobbering her. The anticipated "something bad" may be internal (such as guilt or shame) or external (such as being arrested or beaten up by bystanders).[7]

This internal picture of consequences that we nonperpetrators generate is made possible by our past experience with similar situations. For most of us, that experience comes not from actual clobbering of little old ladies but from others' teaching and examples, and from the internalizing of thousands of fantasy situations that generate enough anxiety to cause us to anticipate discomfort or punishment. Lack of a warm family upbringing does not preclude a future adolescent or adult world with meaningful consequences for behavior, however. Not all one's "experience" must come from family or school (although it's best if most early experience does). Early learning is a powerful shaper of later behavior, but we also respond to the world around us. People can be positively conditioned by their adolescent and adult environment, as well as their infant and childhood experiences. Increasing the likelihood, timeliness, and importance of the *negative* consequences for criminal behavior will decrease the behavior. By the same token, decreasing any of these—or increasing the likelihood and importance of the *positive* consequences of such behavior—will increase it to a certain extent.

"But," says the reader once more, fighting my logic with every socially liberal fiber of his or her body, "courts have increased sentences for violent crimes, and being in prison is a negative consequence!"

Many of the principles invoked here are qualitative, not quantitative. Small changes in quantity may not produce significant change in behavior (e.g., changes in length of prison sentence do not alter the frequency of most criminal behavior, except to the extent that the criminal is in prison and not able to commit crimes). We must go beyond simple stimulus–response paradigms and observe the effect of the reinforcement *schedule* (see below).

For people who are not antisocial, the possibility of bad consequences of violent acts is pretty real and frightening. This is so, in part, because many of the bad consequences are internal (e.g., guilt). We tend to forget that the probability of external bad consequences (e.g., prison) is pretty low. We may *imagine* that the probability is high, because we dread prison or being caught, or because our internal controls need some reinforcement. But the crook, intoxicated person, social misfit, or rebellious teenager very often does not feel that internal guilt, and lacks the ability to think ahead to the possibility of losing his job or going to prison. Empathy for the victim—a prerequisite for a mature sense of guilt over another's suffering—just isn't there.

In short, a potential perpetrator has to be reminded over and over of the consequences of his violence. We need a law enforcement/criminal justice system that moves rapidly, and one whose negative actions for the perpetrator are easily predictable for even the dense or addled mind. This means more than intellectual awareness of the possibility of punishment. It means a visceral expectation, a matter of such unconscious certainty that the thought of consequences becomes as natural as the thought of looking both ways at a busy intersection.[8]

The key to the effectiveness, and anticipation, of consequences is a combination of their *timing, reliability,* and *severity.* Drunk driving is rare in Scandinavia because consequences are serious, justice is swift, and punishment is fairly certain. On the other hand, in Eastern Europe the consequences of drunk driving are severe, but the probability of getting caught is low (and one has ample opportunity to bribe the police); the drunk driving problem there is enormous. In regard not only to drunk driving but to crime in general, we in the United States often lack all three—timing, reliability, and severity of consequences—but our timing and reliability are particularly poor. We would not mortally wound our Constitution and democratic way of life if we greatly enhanced both, even at the cost of some of the severity. Our "freedom of living" (see above) may depend on our willingness to do so just as soon as we can.

3. Provide Predictable Punishment, without Delay

I have already discussed timeliness, and the relative inability of psychopathic people to anticipate far-off consequences of their behavior or to associate consequences (once they arrive) with behavior months or years in the past. Rapid trial or other adjudication is one step toward correcting this; however, we should realize that shortening trial delays only slightly may not help very much. The psychopath feels little difference between 3 months and 6. His perception of time is more primitive, in the Piagetian sense, than that. If judicial resolution cannot come within days or weeks, it is important to focus on pretrial consequences, even though the defendant is presumed not guilty. Thus jail awaiting trial, electronic monitoring, impounding of offense-related materials and equipment (e.g., the defendant's car pending trial for drunk driving), and the like, should be routine. Such measures also decrease the defendant's own motivation to delay adjudication. "Speedy trial" was originally conceived to benefit the accused.

In addition to timeliness, *reliability* of consequences is extremely important to any chance that antisocial behavior will be discouraged. Surer sentencing, little or no parole, and limiting use of extenuating circumstances in sentencing arguments after conviction are all relevant. Indeterminate sentencing, unless clearly linked to measurable treatment or rehabilitation objectives, is far too ambiguous for those with a chronically antisocial style. Once again, what seems logical to the rest of us is simply not relevant to the psychopathic individual. It is far better to be predictable and unambiguous about the beginning, middle, and end of the judicial and correctional process. This does not mean rigidly holding to a release or end-of-probation date when the person's behavior convincingly suggests that he is dangerous, however. We understand enough about sexual predators, for example, to know that they should not be released unless or until their behavior can be externally (or biologically) controlled.

4. Separate Known Predators from the Rest of Society

I am sometimes amused—but more often frustrated—by those who protest the building of more prisons in the United States. Their arguments are so easily refuted that I shall spend only a little time on them here. First, the frequent comparison of U.S. incarceration numbers with those of other countries is superficial and self-serving. Most of us are not willing to replace our social system with that of some other country.

Second, to those who balk at the cost of building and maintaining large prisons and other incarceration environments, one can only say that the cost of allowing chronically antisocial persons to remain at large is far greater. I do not care whether the prison is viewed as a "country club" or a "dungeon"; just keep the crook off my street.

Third, those who say that prisons do not rehabilitate, or that they may foster further criminal careers, are missing the point. There are many theories of the purpose of incarceration: Quaker reflection, punishment, organized rehabilitation, containment, and others. Failing at one purpose (such as rehabilitation) should not weaken arguments for others, including the just-mentioned keeping the criminal off the street.

Fourth, those who say that our criminal justice and correctional systems discriminate against some people are also missing the point. Both predatory behavior and victim costs are equal-opportunity concepts. Nothing in this chapter suggests economic or racial bias either in law enforcement or in consequences for antisocial behavior. I *do* suggest more appropriate attention to fairness to neighborhoods and broad social costs, even beyond attention to physical victims. Our efforts toward achieving that fairness must not be stayed by spurious claims based in some other social agenda.

5. Don't Imbue Children with Full Adult Rights

My final premise addresses children's behavior and children's rights. The thesis is consistent: The above-described principles of reasonable expectation and the rights of citizens not to be victims apply to youthful perpetrators as well as adults. But there is a further, crucial point to be made with respect to children: To imbue them with all adult rights and choices is inappropriate (sometimes tragically so) and cheats them of healthy personal and social development. Children are not adults. We limit their access to adult activities, and, depending on age and a few other factors, prevent them from taking adult responsibility for many kinds of decisions and behavior (e.g., whether or not to attend school, consent to medical treatment, make contracts, drink alcohol, serve in the military, work certain hours, drive automobiles, or even have sex).

There are competing interests for the child (and sometimes for society, which finds both a general interest in protecting children and a responsibility to protect the rights of all citizens) when we wish at once to protect the child's person, protect his rights, and hold him responsible for his behavior. At present, the tensions of those competing interests pull so strongly toward protecting the child's or adolescent's rights that we often hurt both him and society. It is no wonder that limiting adult prosecution of reasonably culpable minors, for example, has not lowered the crime rate, has not made our neighborhoods safer, has not reduced the costs to victims, and has not protected civil rights in any but the most superficial way.

Children and adolescents are at once ill equipped to make adult decisions and harmed by having to make them. We must not leave them to their own immature decision processes. Adolescents, especially, are torn by their efforts to mature. Their developing psyches force them to demand independence even as they yearn for guidance and the simpler times of childhood. We must not be seduced by those demands for independence as if they were mature; they are not. We must not confuse their heartfelt cries for adult rules and responsibilities with true adulthood. Structure, even when the rules are not perfect, is far healthier and less frightening than the absence of structure. Adults must provide that structure, withdrawing it in gradual steps as the child, and later adolescent, becomes ready to practice being (but not yet to *be*) an adult.

The expectation that children and adolescents will behave in some ways like adults (e.g., not hurting others, being sensitive to them, taking responsibility for behavior, and bearing appropriate consequences for that behavior) occurs in a context of adult guidance. In the best of cases, this comes from parents, from other family members, and later from school and culture. When one or more of these fails or is not present, society (e.g., in the form of school or court) has both the right and the duty to be an unambivalent substitute, and to direct a child or adolescent away from antisocial behavior. The "duty" refers to shaping and preparing the child for successful adulthood. The "right" refers to protecting others and society from both the current and future costs of his antisocial behavior. Schools must not tolerate one child's disrupting another's opportunity for education or development. Neighborhoods must be able to discipline appropriately when the child or adolescent infringes on the rights of others. Law enforcement agencies and courts must be allowed to guide juveniles firmly and hold them responsible at the same time, without being hamstrung by strident accusations from those who believe children's rights should allow children's tyranny.

As good parents know, this is hard today, but rewarding tomorrow. Unambiguous structure and guidance lead to a reassured child—one who senses a predictable and secure environment instead of a frighteningly chaotic one. Sometimes, eventually, he even thanks you.

NOTES

1. Similarly, in February 1997, a 77-year-old African-Methodist-Episcopal church in Chicago's low-income Cabrini–Green area was likely to close its doors because members had been "scared away for years" by some people in the rough neighborhood ("Church at Cabrini Hoping to Survive," 1997).

2. Consider Russian and East European society after the recent fall of totalitarianism. Although a few people thrived, with the opportunities provided by capitalism, most became very anxious, not knowing how to live—or even to survive—without a socialist regime. Although they complained of lack of freedoms before the sweeping political change, two generations of strict socialism since 1946 had been sufficient (for many at least) to erase concepts of self-determination and confidence in their independent abilities. The results have been (1) widespread support for a return to a socialist system (out of societal insecurity and anxiety as well as economic need); and (2) uncontrollable predation by criminals and other antisocial people, who find little to stand in their way.

3. "Psychopathic" is used in this chapter simply to describe a kind of chronic antisocial style or behavior. It does not always (or even usually) refer to persons who meet diagnostic criteria for psychopathy or antisocial personality, and should not be taken to mean that all psychopath*ic* people are "psychopaths."

4. "Anthropomorphism" is the imbuing of animals with human characteristics—soothing for pet owners and profitable for Walt Disney, but not an accurate representation of the real world. Neither is its opposite: seeing human civilization in animalistic terms.

5. Each example is from an actual case.

6. Note the purposeful use of the singular "he" or "him" from this point on in my discussion. (I use the masculine pronoun for the sake of simplicity, though psychopathic behavior is rapidly becoming an equal-gender-opportunity field.). We may view *groups* of criminals or psychopaths as "different," as stereotypes deserving unthinking prejudice, but my premise is that *individuals* are arrested, stand trial, are sentenced, and tell their stories to clinicians and the media. If we treat the entire group of antisocial persons with mindless bias, then my argument would be vulnerable to examples of reformed criminals—a burglar turned home security expert or a murderer turned prison evangelist—to support misguided optimism for the larger group. We must be able to look into the face of an individual offender, hear his convincing excuses and promises about the future, and still say to ourselves, "This person is not like me. His chronic hurting of others prevents him from deserving my trust or my regard. I do not believe him, and I must protect myself and my community from him."

7. Note that for purposes of changing antisocial behavior, it does not matter whether the reinforcers are internal or external. Indeed, this chapter focuses on the importance of consistent *external* reinforcers, both to guide currently antisocial persons and to create a consequential milieu for developing infants' and children's internalization.

8. "Aha," says the still-resisting reader. "This author advocates social controls so draconian they'll make *1984* seem tame. Does he want video cameras on every street? Transmitters and identity numbers affixed to our foreheads? Brain implants connected to our pain and pleasure cen-

ters?" No. I want to avoid all that by changing things now rather than letting them deteriorate. If we allow them to get much worse, a frightened and frustrated public will almost certainly call for very harsh social controls. At that point, I fear, someone far more draconian than I will seize the opportunity, ride a populist wave to power, and do real damage to our republic.

REFERENCES

Church at Cabrini hoping to survive. (1997, February 16). *Chicago Sun-Times*, Metro, p. 11.

Reid, W. H. (1978). The sadness of the psychopath. *American Journal of Psychotherapy, 32*(4), 496–509.

8

The Case for Parental Licensure

DAVID T. LYKKEN

> Wait. Are they going to let me just walk off with him? I don't know
> beans about babies! I don't have a license to do this. . . . I mean
> you're given all these lessons for the unimportant things—piano-
> playing, typing. You're given years and years of lessons in how to
> balance equations, which Lord knows you will never have to do in
> normal life. But what about parenthood? . . . Before you can drive a
> car you need a state-approved course of instruction, but driving a
> car is nothing, nothing, compared to . . . raising up a new human
> being.
>
> —ANNE TYLER (1988, p. 127)

We are suffering in the United States from an epidemic of crime, violence, and other social pathology. In 1993 nearly 5 million Americans were murdered, raped, robbed, or assaulted, and 19 million more were victims of property crimes. Although the U.S. Justice
Department's National Crime Victimization Survey (NCVS; Bureau of Justice Statistics,
1994) shows only a modest rise in the rate of victimization of the (mostly middle-class)
citizens surveyed since the NCVS was begun in 1973, these data are misleading. The
NCVS undersamples those citizens most vulnerable to crime: the homeless, people who
happen to be in hospital or in jail at the time of the survey, and especially those residents
of inner-city neighborhoods and housing projects where the mostly female NCVS interviewers are reluctant to venture.

The Federal Bureau of Investigation's (FBI's) Uniform Crime Report, on the other
hand, indicates that index crime and especially violent crime has been increasing sharply
since about 1960 (FBI, 1994). The Uniform Crime Report is a compilation of crimes reported and arrests made by police departments nationwide. The number of crimes reported to the FBI per 100,000 people in the population—that is, the crime *rate*—tripled
from 1960 to 1992 (FBI, 1994). The rate of violent crime—murders, aggravated assaults,
forcible rapes, and robberies with violence—more than tripled by 1980, decreased slightly until about 1984, and then continued its climb to nearly *five times* the 1960 rate by
1992.

Most violent crimes are committed by young males aged 15 to 25 (FBI, 1993). Part of the increase beginning in 1960 was due to the baby boomers' moving into that age of higher risk. But by 1975 they were beginning to move out of that age bracket, and the crime rate should have dropped again, but it did not. Another reason to have expected a decrease in violent crime was the increase in the proportion of the population who are elderly: The proportion of people over 65 has increased 20% since 1960 (National Center for Health Statistics, 1993b). We often think of seniors as more vulnerable, but the fact is that young people are 10 to 15 times more likely to be victims of violent crimes than are people over 65 (Bureau of Justice Statistics, 1994, Table 20).

There has been much made in the news recently of the fact that big-city violence has decreased a few percent each year since 1993. But there were some 190,000 inmates in U.S. prisons in 1965, whereas in 1998, due to much more active policing (e.g., Anderson, 1997) and especially to stricter sentencing practices, there are 1,300,000 men in prison in the United States (Bureau of Justice Statistics, 1998) (a higher proportion of our male population is imprisoned than that of any other nation) and 81% of them have been convicted of at least one previous crime (Beck et al., 1993). Prison surveys in Wisconsin and New Jersey agreed in finding that the typical inmate reports having committing an average of 12 property or violent crimes during the year prior to imprisonment (Beck et al., 1993, p. 20). There are a lot of predators out there, but when more than a million of them are sequestered for years at a time, that fraction of the total at least is out of action.

But replacements are waiting in the wings. The rate of violent crime committed by juvenile offenders in 1990 was, for black youngsters aged 12 to 17, double the already high rate in 1965, while the rate for white juveniles was *four times* higher than in 1965 (FBI, 1993). These are muggings, rapes, drive-by shootings, gang-style executions—crimes of violence committed by boys too young to meet psychiatry's criteria for the diagnosis of antisocial personality disorder; most of these criminals are juvenile sociopaths. ("Sociopath" is defined later in this chapter.) The homicide rate among teenagers has trebled in the United States since the 1960s (Fuchs & Reklis, 1992). Juveniles from 10 to 17 years old now account for nearly one-fifth of all arrests for violent crime (Snyder & Sickmund, 1995, p. 47). According to the Centers for Disease Control (1993), which also regards violence in America as having the characteristics of an epidemic, homicide is the third most frequent cause of deaths in the U.S. workplace; indeed, it is the *most* common cause of workplace death for women (Centers for Disease Control, 1993). From Maine to California, juvenile corrections facilities (many of them relatively new) are overcrowded and dangerous, and most of the inmates have been there before. The adult prison system is so crowded that in Florida (among other states), admitting each 100 newly convicted felons requires giving early release to 100 current inmates—many of whom rob and rape and kill again during the period when, but for the forced early release, they would have been safely incarcerated.[1]

NATURE VIA NURTURE

The last several decades of behavior-genetic research has demonstrated that most psychological traits that can be reliably measured owe from 25% to about 75% of their total variance to genetic differences (e.g., Bouchard, Lykken, McGue, Segal, & Tellegen, 1990). How is it that genetic differences can possibly determine, or even partly determine, psychological tendencies that seem obviously to depend on learning? The best guess is that the genes affect the mind largely indirectly, by influencing from infancy onward the kinds of learning experiences one is likely to have (Plomin, DeFries, & Loehlin, 1977; Scarr & McCartney, 1983). Children with different genotypes elicit different reactions from their social environment, seek out different experiences, and may react differently even to the same experiences. For example, an active youngster who frequently elicits parental admonitions to "Do this" or "Stop doing that" may respond coercively. If the parent then backs off, this may initiate a series of similar experiences in which the child learns to resist parental control by increasingly aversive counterattack—a sequence Patterson and his colleagues refer to as the "three-step dance" (Patterson, 1982; Patterson, Reid, & Dishion, 1992). This child's more passive, less aggressive sibling is likely to have quite different experiences with the same parent and to be shaped differently in consequence—that is, if the sibling *is* less active and aggressive.

The Psychopath

Since the beginnings of psychiatry in the early 19th century, it has been recognized that there are persons whose persisting antisocial behavior cannot be understood in terms either of psychosis or neurosis, or of antisocial rearing or environment. Benjamin Rush (1745–1813), the first American psychiatrist, described patients with "innate preternatural moral depravity" (Rush, 1812). Kraepelin, in the 1907 edition of his influential textbook, first used the term "psychopathic personality" to describe the amoral criminal type, and since Cleckley (1941), these individuals whose innate temperaments make them intractable to socialization have been called "psychopaths." Based on the particular temperamental peculiarity involved, I think one can identify numerous species and subspecies of psychopaths (see Lykken, 1995, pp. 31–38)—including, for example, the "distempered" type, of which the "choleric" and the "hypersexed" would be representative subspecies. The "primary" or "Cleckley" psychopath has been the most extensively studied, and I argued long ago (Lykken, 1957) that nothing more exotic than relative fearlessness accounts for at least one subspecies of primary psychopathy. Findings from the subsequent 40 years of research (reviewed in Lykken, 1995, pp. 133–165) provide consistent and rather impressive support for the low-fear hypothesis or for its modern incarnation as the Fowles–Gray theory of a weak behavioral inhibition system (Fowles & Missel, 1994; Gray, 1987).

An example of this taxon is "Monster" Kody Scott, also known as Sanyka Shakur (Shakur, 1993). Kody was a fearless boy (Horowitz, 1993, p. 32) initiated at age 12 into the Eight-Tray Gangster Crips in south central Los Angeles, where he shot his first victim that same night. Kody never knew his father, who is said to have been a professional football player. On the other hand, another fearless psychopath, Christopher Boyce (the Falcon in Lindsey's [1979] *The Falcon and the Snowman*), was the son of a retired FBI agent with a large, well-socialized family. After being sentenced to a long term for selling secrets to the Soviets, Boyce managed a daring escape from a high-security prison and remained at large for more than a year, robbing a series of banks, in spite of the most vigorous manhunt in the history of the U.S. Marshals' Service (Lindsey, 1983).

Not all persons who can await painful electric shocks with dry palms and inner calm are psychopaths, of course. The low-fear hypothesis says only that youngsters of this stamp will be difficult to socialize because they respond poorly to punishment, and parents tend to rely on punishment in disciplining children. One theory of conscience development (see Zahn-Waxler & Kochanska, 1988, for a survey) holds that the child, fearful of the all-powerful big people, learns to introject their attitudes and values so as to be able to predict their reactions and thus keep out of trouble. All this is less likely to happen in a relatively fearless youngster. Kochanska (1991, 1993) has shown that skillful parental discipline at age 2 predicts effective conscience development by ages 8 to 10, but not in temperamentally less fearful children. On the other hand, fortunately, no theory of psychopathy denies that these individuals are responsive to praise or to feelings of pride and self-esteem. Clever parents rely on pride and positive reinforcement to create in their low-fear child a socialized self-concept that the youngster values and is motivated to sustain. With patience and luck, they may be able to raise that child to become a hero rather than a psychopath.

Most other theories of psychopathy (reviewed in Lykken, 1995, or in Raine, 1993) postulate some congenital peculiarity—either in temperament, as in the low-fear theory, or in brain function, as in the frontal lobe dysfunction theories of Newman, Kosson, and Patterson (1992). The pure-case psychopath is relatively rare, and therefore no adequate adoption or twin study has been done to estimate the heritability of this (these) condition(s). There is no doubt, however, that children differ congenitally and markedly in temperament (Kagan, 1994) and that Kagan's "uninhibited" children are at greater risk for delinquency and crime than those he classifies in infancy as "inhibited." As might be expected, therefore, genetic studies of criminality (e.g., Cloninger & Gottesman, 1987) or of antisocial personality (e.g., DiLalla, Gottesman, & Carey, 1993; Grove, Eckart, Heston, & Bouchard, 1990) indicate substantial heritability (.30 to .40) for these heterogeneous categories, of which psychopaths form a relatively small component.

Most crimes are committed by the relatively small proportion of unsocialized young males who are chronic offenders. The evidence reviewed briefly above suggests that this proportion is rapidly increasing. Because psychopaths, as usually defined, have an innately deviant temperament, it is unlikely that there has been a sudden surge in their relative numbers. Although it is true that unsocialized people are generally inclined to breed carelessly (and to be dreadful parents), the sharply increased incidence of young chronic offenders cannot reasonably be attributed solely to dysgenic reasons.

The Sociopath

Since most criminals do not quality as psychopaths, it is convenient to have a name for the larger fraction who have grown up unsocialized primarily because of environmental rather than genetic reasons. I have suggested (Lykken, 1995) the term "sociopath" for this purpose. The most plausible explanation of our present crime wave is that there has been an increase in the proportion of the current cohort of young males who are sociopaths. This is supported by the fact that the proportions of all males aged 15 to 25 who were arrested for violent crimes increased nearly 140% from 1965 to 1992 (FBI, 1993).

To account for this epidemic of sociopathy and crime, we have to find some possibly causal social factor that also has increased inexorably over the same span of time. When we look at the usual suspects, such as poverty and joblessness, they do not seem to fill the bill. During this century, the crime rate has actually been higher in good times than in bad (Rubinstein, 1992). There has indeed been a sharp increase over these decades in the numbers of children living in poverty with single mothers who either never married or were abandoned by their husbands. I shall argue, however, that such conditions—like the guns, gangs, and drugs that go with them—are themselves a consequence of a first cause: namely, parental malfeasance.

There is no question that the drug problem has increased greatly in recent decades, and that the drug trade is associated with a lot of the violence we read about. When Minneapolis broke its homicide record in 1995, at least half of the victims and half of the shooters were young black men, immigrants from other states, who were involved one way or another in the drug business. But suppose we were to admit that our $20 billion a year "war on drugs" has been lost. Suppose we were to take the step of legalizing drugs, so that any adult with a special picture ID credit card could buy them in modest quantities in any liquor store, with the Drug Enforcement Agency's computer keeping track of each purchase. There would still be a small illegal trade in drugs for juveniles, but billions of dollars would be removed from the underworld economy. The brightest and most entrepreneurial of inner-city young men would no longer be lured away from entry-level jobs at $300 a week to risky but promising jobs selling drugs—jobs that pay $1,000 a week tax-free and have great possibilities for promotion. Most of the drug trade incentive for violence would dry up. But it is important to remember that the people doing that actual violence are people who have grown up to be unsocialized, aggressive, feral, and violent. A few of them are psychopaths, but most are phenocopies of psychopathy—sociopaths. If the drug business dried up, they would find other employment, and it would not be at McDonald's.

Another social change that began in the 1960s and is a candidate explanation for our crime epidemic is another epidemic—that of illegitimacy and fatherless rearing. Nationwide, the proportion of American children born out of wedlock increased from about 5% in 1960 to about 30% in the early 1990s (Eckholm, 1992; Fuchs & Reklis, 1992; Murray, 1993). For black Americans, this change began earlier. In 1925 in Harlem, some 85% of black families were headed by males "and in most of the female-headed households, the woman was not a teenager but over the age of 30" (Wilson & Herrnstein, 1985, p. 480). "In every census from 1890 to 1960 the percentage of African American households with two parents remained essentially unchanged at about 80%" (Westman, 1994, p. 187). According to Lemann (1993), "a generation of historical scholarship . . . stands in refutation of the idea that slavery destroyed the Black family" (p. 30). Yet black illegitimacy had increased to 25% by 1965, leading Daniel Patrick Moynihan (1969) to make his celebrated prediction:

> From the wild Irish slums of the 19th Century Eastern seaboard to the riot-torn suburbs of Los Angeles, there is one unmistakable lesson in American history: a community that allows a large number of young men to grow up in broken families, dominated by women, never acquiring any stable relationship to male authority, never acquiring any set of rational expectations about the future—that community asks for and gets chaos. Crime, violence, unrest, unrestrained lashing out at the whole social structure—that is not only to be expected; it is very near to inevitable. (p. 44)

White illegitimacy has now caught up to and passed what the black rate was in 1965, when nearly twice as many black as white babies were born out of wedlock. Now the ratio is reversed: Twice as many white as black births are illegitimate (U.S. Bureau of the Census, 1995). In 1960 about 3.5% of the total high-risk group of 15- to 25-year-old males were born out of wedlock, and nearly 30% had parents who were divorced (there was a sharp peak in the divorce rate during and just after World War II, so that many of the older baby boomers came from broken homes). By 1994 the illegitimacy proportion in this group had risen from 3.5% to 13.4%, and the proportion left fatherless by divorce had more than doubled (National Center for Health Statistics, 1993a, 1993b).

The Role of Family Environment

Twin and adoption studies have indicated that being reared together in the same family does not tend to make siblings more alike psychologically (Plomin & Bergeman, 1991; Plomin & Daniels, 1987; Rowe, 1994). Scarr (1992) goes so far as to suggest that at least in the broad reaches of the middle class, parents are fungible. Most such parents, through their parenting actions as well as by means of the neighborhood and school environments that they provide for their children, make it possible for the "genetic steersman" within each child to seek out those compatible experiences that will create a phenotype that expresses the child's unique genotype reasonably well. This means, among other things, that siblings reared in the same family will tend to resemble one another as adults in proportion to their genetic similarity—monozygotic (MZ) twins about twice as strongly as dizygotic (DZ) twins or ordinary siblings, and unrelated foster siblings not at all. This is what study after study seems to show.

However, it is easy to overinterpret these findings. Unrelated foster siblings reared in a middle-class home in Minnesota will be no more similar as adults than random pairs of middle-class Minnesotans of the same age and sex. But they will be a lot more similar than pairs in which each member is chosen randomly from all over the United States or from the world at large. Those fungible Minnesota parents will have provided each foster child with adequate nutrition, middle-class educational opportunities, and middle-class socialization experiences. Therefore, each pair will tend to differ in weight, in educational attainment, and in their histories of minor misbehaviors about as much as random pairs of Minnesotans—but they will tend to differ less in weight and education than pairs in which one member grew up in Bangladesh or the Sudan. And they will tend to differ less in their histories of criminal behavior than pairs in which one member was raised in Iowa City and the other in the Robert Taylor housing project in Chicago.

Most children of such fungible middle-class parents will become tolerably socialized along the way toward law-abiding, tax-paying adulthood. This would be true even if their name tags had been randomly shuffled in their hospital nurseries, so that they went home with the wrong parents. But it would not be true if those nurseries included the babies of abusive, addicted, immature, or unsocialized parents. Some such infants who happened to get middle-class name tags in the shuffling would tend to grow up less well socialized than their middle-class neighbors, because such infants would tend to carry genes making them harder than average to socialize. Some of those scions of middle-class parents who went home with underclass mothers would remain wholly unsocialized, because poor parenting would make them more susceptible to peer group influence, and their peer group would be likely to be unsocialized.

Most behavior-genetic research has drawn its samples from the broad reaches of the middle class, where, as Scarr (1992) points out, the variance in parental effectiveness is relatively small. If these studies were to sample instead from the segment of society that generates the preponderance of sociopaths, then one might expect to see a significant fraction of the variance in socialization attributable to common family variance. One way to include the criminogenic stratum of society into our analyses is to do twin and adoption studies of the similarity of sibling pairs in which each pair includes a criminal or sociopathic proband. Recent research of this kind by O'Connor and colleagues (cited in Rutter, 1996) shows a clear influence of common family environment; the DZ correlation for criminality is 80% of the MZ value (.65 vs. .81), and unrelated siblings correlate .27. A study of the large Vietnam Era Veteran Twin Registry (Lyons, 1996) found a strong influence of shared family environment on self-reported early criminal behavior, which in unselected samples is a good predictor of adult criminality. In their widely cited review, Loeber and Dishion (1983) found that parental (mis)management and the child's conduct disorder are the best predictors of delinquency. Latent class analysis of data from the Virginia Twin Study of Adolescent Behavioral Development (Silberg et al., 1996) yielded a group labeled "pure conduct disorder," constituting 9% of the sample, in which virtually all of the variance (97%) was associated with shared family environment.

It is important to note also, however, that these studies also find a large component of variance attributable to heredity. Aggressive, impulsive, adventurous youngsters are obviously more likely to resist socialization by incompetent parents than are children with timid or docile temperaments. Figure 8.1 illustrates the differences between psychopathy and sociopathy, and shows how I believe these two troublesome syndromes are related to genetic factors and to parenting. The bell-shaped curve at the left of the figure indicates that most people are in the broad middle range of socialization, with a few saintly people very high on this dimension, whereas a few more (the criminals) are very

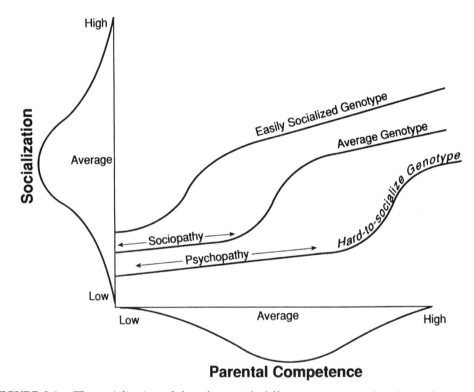

FIGURE 8.1. The socialization of three boys with different genotypes, plotted as a function of parental competence. The top curve represents Pat, a boy with easy-to-socialize temperament, who is likely to make it even with relatively incompetent parents. Hard-to-socialize children like Mike, represented by the bottom curve, are likely to become psychopaths unless their parents are unusually skillful or unless strong socializing incentives are provided from other sources in their rearing environments. By definition, the great majority of youngsters have average genotypes like Bill, represented by the middle curve. If Bill's parents are average or better in their parenting skills, or if Bill's peer group is uniformly well socialized, then Bill will turn out all right. But if Bill's parents are incompetent and neither the extended family nor the peer group compensates for their ineptitude, then Bill is likely to become a sociopath. Adapted from Lykken (1995). Copyright 1995 by Lawrence Erlbaum Associates. Adapted by permission.

low. The horizontal axis represents parental competence, and the curve at the bottom assumes that most parents are average, some are incompetent, and a few are super parents.

The top curve in the body of the figure represents what might happen to a child (I will call him Pat) whose innate temperament makes him truly easy to socialize; he is bright, nonaggressive, moderately timid, with a naturally loving disposition. Like all little boys, he starts out life essentially unsocialized—and if his parents are totally incompetent, his neighborhood a war zone, and his peers all little thugs, Pat might remain marginally socialized. But boys like Pat tend to avoid conflict and chaos; they are attracted by order and civility; and they tend to seek out socialized mentors and role models. With even poor parenting, the Pats of this world tend to stay out of trouble.

Rosa Lee, the subject of a Pulitzer Prize-winning series by *Washington Post* reporter Leon Dash (1996), began stealing at age 9, quit school in the seventh grade, married at 16, left her abusive husband soon after, and then proceeded to have eight children by five different men. Rosa Lee worked as a waitress, a prostitute, and a small-time drug dealer. She had shoplifted since age 10 and taught her grandson to shoplift when he was about the same age. She introduced one daughter to prostitution at age 13, and several of her children followed her example of heroin addiction. Two of the eight children, however, raised under the same squalid conditions as the other six, were boys like Pat; somehow they stayed out of trouble, found socialized role models outside the home, and became self-supporting family men.

The middle curve in Figure 8.1 represents Bill, a boy with an average genetic makeup—moderately aggressive, moderately adventurous. Because he is average, we can safely anticipate that average parents living in an average neighborhood will be able to raise Bill to be an average, law-abiding citizen. Incompetent parents living in a disruptive neighborhood, however, will not succeed with Bill, who will remain a sociopath. Although two of Rosa Lee's offspring matured like Pat, the other six grew up to be sociopaths like Bill.

Mike, the bottom curve in the figure, is really difficult to socialize; he may be fearless, impulsive, or hostile and aggressive. The great majority of parents would find Mike too much to cope with, a perennial source of worry and disappointment. Mike's curve goes up on the far right of the figure because really talented parents (or, more likely, a truly fortuitous combination of parents, neighborhood, peer group, and subsequent mentors) can sometimes socialize even these hard cases.

The important fact that I was not clever enough to symbolize in Figure 8.1 is this: The Bills in each generation, because they are average, are vastly more numerous than either the Pats or the Mikes. Most youngsters have average genetic temperaments like Bill; therefore, even though only a minority of parents are truly incompetent, the total number of Bills (and Marys) who reach adolescence and adulthood still unsocialized—the number who become criminal sociopaths—is much larger than the number of psychopaths like Mike. Moreover, in part because unsocialized people tend to become incompetent parents themselves, the number of sociopaths is growing faster than the general population. Indeed, it is growing faster than we can build reform schools and prisons.

It is unfortunate that many incompetent parents have difficult temperaments themselves, so that their offspring tend to be doubly disadvantaged: by their parents' genes, as well as by their parents' neglect, abuse, or ineptitude. Therefore, as is suggested in Figure 8.2, "psychopath" and "sociopath" are overlapping categories. It is a safe guess that the average sociopath has temperamental characteristics somewhere between average and psychopathic on the horizontal or "difficult-to-socialize" axis in Figure 8.2. As the figure also indicates, the pure-case psychopath is relatively rare, while the incidence of sociopathy is much higher—vastly higher than in ancient times or in traditional cultures of today. As the circumstances of child rearing depart further from those to which our species is evolutionarily adapted, the incidence of sociopathy can be expected to increase.

Socializing Children

To begin at the beginning, we are social animals. During the Pleistocene era, our ancestors were dependent upon the collective wisdom, vigilance, assistance, and resources of the extended-family bands in which they lived. To be excluded from the band would likely have been fatal, which means that those who were excluded (or who excluded themselves) did not become our ancestors. By natural selection, those destined to be ancestors gradually augmented their preexisting primate propensities for social living with talents that included the ability to acquire language, to develop a restraining conscience, to learn empathy and altruism, and to respect the elders and others in authority. They acquired an ability to learn to work and hunt cooperatively, to accept responsibility, and probably also a tendency to admire prosocial role models (Wright, 1994).

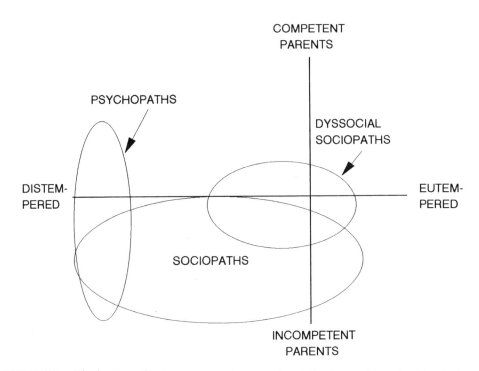

FIGURE 8.2. The horizontal axis represents the ease of socialization as determined by the innate temperament, with "eutempered" representing the child who is normally harm-avoidant, nonaggressive, careful, and considerate. The "distempered" extreme represents the child who is so fearless, impulsive, aggressive, or choleric as to be nearly incorrigible to socialization. The sociopaths are the largest group by far; they have all had relatively incompetent parenting, and many of them have also begun life with relatively "difficult" temperaments. Hence there is considerable overlap between psychopaths and sociopaths. Some people with average temperaments and average parents do get into trouble with the law, of course, including those Moffitt (1993) refers to as "adolescence-limited" offenders. The ellipse toward the right center of the figure represents this group. Adapted from Lykken (1995). Copyright 1995 by Lawrence Erlbaum Associates. Adapted by permission.

But, like our nascent capacity for language, these other socialization talents need to be elicited, shaped, and reinforced during childhood by the adult community. We can suppose that child rearing during the Pleistocene was a communal function, with parents playing an important role, but with the consistent and important help of the uncles, aunts, the older cousins, and other members of the band. Because the socialization of each child was important both to the child and to its elders, our ancestors acquired the talents both to become socialized themselves and, as adults, to assist in the socialization of others. That is, in the communal environment of evolutionary adaptation, we can reasonably assume that our ancestors *did* become socialized and that there was little intramural crime, just as there is comparatively little crime today in those remaining hunter–gatherer societies organized along traditional lines.

For example, in her important study of mental illness in traditional societies, Harvard anthropologist Jane Murphy (1976) found that the Yupic-speaking Eskimos in northwest Alaska have a name, *kunlangeta,* for the

> man who, for example, repeatedly lies and cheats and steals things and does not go hunting and, when the other men are out of the village, takes sexual advantage of many women—someone who does not pay attention to reprimands and who is always being brought to the elders for punishment. One Eskimo among the 499 on their island was called kunlangeta. When asked what would have happened to such a person traditionally, an Eskimo said that probably "somebody would have pushed him off the ice when nobody else was looking." (p. 1026)

In our environment of evolutionary adaptation, the entire band or tribe participated in the socialization of the children. In those remaining villages, small towns, and rural communities where there is as yet little crime, much the same sort of arrangement prevails today. Good parents, who are able to maintain the affection and respect of their children and whose offspring admire them and value their good opinion, can be reasonably certain that their values and ways of socialized behaving will be adopted by the next generation. The children of less effective, less competent parents will be more likely to adopt the customs and values of the peer group; however, if the community is small, close-knit, and well socialized generally, this will achieve the same result. In urban or suburban middle-class communities, the offspring of less competent parents will be somewhat more at risk. Most of the available peer group will be well socialized because their parents are, but as the community grows in size and in mutual estrangement, the likelihood increases that there will be a few neglected, undisciplined, or feral children in the peer group—faux-adult role models to whom a child not closely tied to home and parents may be drawn, and by whom that child will be influenced (see Moffitt, 1993).

What I am suggesting here is a kind of contagion model. Children with neglectful or otherwise ineffective parents are at risk of "infection" if there are one or more unsocialized children in their local peer group. Suppose we have 100 neighborhoods with 10 children in each, and only 10% of the 100 groups are thus far infected. I shall assume that 5 children in each of the 10 affected peer groups had competent parents and were thus able to resist infection, yielding 50 or 5% of the total of 1,000 children on the road to delinquency. Now we add 300 additional children, 5% of them unsocialized, distributed at random among the 100 local groups. If, say, 10 previously uninfected peer groups each receive one or more of the 15 new out-of-control youngsters, then we soon have a total incidence of (at least) 115 little delinquents—an increase of 130%, although the total number of children increased by only 30%.

In an important recent paper, Harris (1995) argues that the environmental component of socialization is primarily mediated by the peer group. Her thesis depends in part on the fact discussed above: In samples from the general population, the environmental component of the variance in most psychological traits, including socialization, is largely of the unshared variety (i.e., experiences other than those shared by siblings growing up in the same family). But when we talk about crime and delinquency, we are not (yet) talking about all or even most of the general population, but about only a few percent of children and of families. Suppose we could measure law-abidingness in the offspring of families in which at least one child had become a chronic delinquent and then criminal. Suppose further that we have temperament measures on all biological parents and offspring, and that our sample contains a sufficient number of twins, siblings, and half-siblings to permit a powerful genetic analysis. Then, as indicated by the studies cited earlier, we should be likely to find both a significant genetic component and also an important proportion of variance attributable to shared family environment. According to Snyder and Sickmund (1995, p. 175), 53% of juveniles currently in custody have at least one family member, often a sibling, who is also in custody; Wiig (1995) found that 70% of 135 child felons in Minneapolis had at least one criminal parent or sibling. Thus, crime does run in families. Often this criminogenic shared environment will also include a bad neighborhood populated by sociopathic peers. I would argue, however, that selecting the neighborhood in which to rear one's children—or choosing not to have children unless and until one can escape a bad neighborhood—is an important part of the responsibility of parenthood.

That is, we can reasonably conjecture that the relative importance of the peer group in shaping the values and behaviors of a given child is inversely proportional to the competence of that child's parents (see, e.g., Mounts & Steinberg, 1995). This equation makes little difference in small, homogeneous communities, because if the parents do not do their job adequately, the neighbors and their children will do it for them. In larger, more diverse communities, an increasing proportion of the offspring of less competent parents will grow up inadequately socialized. As the example above suggests, even with all other factors constant, the incidence of delinquency might be expected to rise much faster than the increase in the size of the peer group itself. Indeed, this may help explain why the violent crime rate in the United States rose more than 250% from 1960 to 1975, while the proportion of males aged 15 to 25 (the group that commits most violent crimes) increased about 30%—the maturing of the baby boomers (Lykken, 1995, p. 196). In underclass communities, where the incidence of immature, overburdened parents (many of whom are unsocialized themselves) is very high, it is remarkable that *any* youngsters manage to grow up to be law-abiding, self-supporting adults.

The Causes of Sociopathy

> While political leaders can now feel comfortable calling for draconian measures to punish the citizens they describe as "predators," "monsters," and "punks," none has the true courage and vision to solve the problem. You might ask our political leaders, "Where do these monsters, predators, and punks come from? Did they parachute from another country? Did they emerge from a spaceship from another planet?" We know three things about these hated citizens. One, they were all born in American hospitals; two, they were all educated in American schools; and three, they were all reared by American adults. It is a rare predator indeed who has had a successful childhood.
>
> —JUDGE CHARLES D. GILL (1994, p. viii)

If sociopathy results from a failure of socialization during childhood, we must ask: What factor that might prevent the normal socialization of children has also increased sharply in recent decades? As already suggested, the increase during this period in the proportion of children who were reared without fathers may be the causal variable we seek.

Crime Risk If Reared without Fathers

The Search Institute of Minneapolis recently conducted a survey of more than 46,000 students in grades 6–12 in 111 communities across the United States (Benson & Roehlepartain, 1993). The sample did not include most large-city school systems, and, of course, youngsters who had already dropped out of school or were incarcerated were also excluded. About 8,200 of those surveyed came from single-parent families, nearly all of them marriages broken by death or divorce rather than families headed by a never-married mother. The data are reported for the sexes combined. For *all* of these reasons, this large sample greatly underestimates the frequency of delinquent behaviors, and also the expected differences between two-parent and single-parent homes.

The Search Institute found that youngsters in grades 6–8 who were living in one-parent families were twice as likely as those from two-parent families to use illegal drugs, to be sexually active, to engage in vandalism, to skip school frequently, and to steal things from stores. The single-parent children were also twice as likely to have used a weapon at least twice "to get something from another person," to have been in trouble with the police, to have been physically or sexually abused by an adult, and to plan on quitting school before graduation. Students classified as at high risk for delinquency and crime because they had engaged in five or more of the list of risk behaviors constituted 21% of those in grades 6–8 from single-parent families and 43% of those in grades 9–12 who were living with a single parent. Had the Search Institute sampled from large-city schools and used never-married mothers, in addition to divorced or widowed mothers, to make up their single-parent group, we can be confident that the differences in delinquency rates between the single-parent and two-parent samples would have been larger still.

In 1986, of the juveniles incarcerated in the United States for serious crimes, about 70% had been reared without fathers (Beck, Kline, & Greenfield, 1987). This 70% figure seems to be a magic number for much social pathology. Of the antisocial boys studied at the Oregon Social Learning Center, fewer than 30% came from intact families (Forgatch, Patterson, & Ray, 1994). Of the more than 130,000 teenagers who ran away from home in 1994, 72% were leaving single-parent homes (Snyder & Sickmund, 1995, p. 31). A 1992 study of "baby truants" in St. Paul, Minnesota—that is, elementary school pupils who had more than 22 unexcused absences in the year—found that 70% were being reared by single mothers (Foster, 1994). Nationally, about 70% of teenage girls who have out-of-wedlock babies were raised without fathers (Kristol, 1994). Seventy-two percent of adolescent murderers grew up without fathers (Cornell, 1987). A recent survey by the county attorney in Minneapolis of 135 children who had been referred for crimes ranging from arson, vandalism, and theft, to assault, burglary, and criminal sexual conduct—youngsters *aged 9 or younger*—found that 70% of these children were living in single-parent (almost always single-mother) homes (Wiig, 1995).

Children who exhibited violent misbehavior in school were 11 times as likely not to live with their fathers and 6 times as likely to have parents who were not married (Sheline, Skipper, & Broadhead, 1994). Nationally, 15.3% of children living with a never-married mother and 10.7% of those living with a divorced mother have been expelled or suspended from school, compared to only 4.4% of children living with both biological parents (Dawson, 1991). Even when race, socioeconomic status, sex, age, and ability are controlled for, high school students living with single parents are about twice as likely to drop out of school as those living with both biological parents (McNeal, 1995). According to the administrators of juvenile corrections facilities, family problems are the most common type of problem among juveniles in custody, affecting at least 76%, more common than substance abuse, peer problems, learning problems, or gang involvement (Snyder & Sickmund, 1995, p. 169).

If the base rate for fatherless rearing of today's teenagers is 25% (which is the best current estimate, although this rate is growing alarmingly) then one can calculate that the risk for social pathologies ranging from delinquency to death is about *seven times* higher for youngsters raised without fathers than for those reared by both biological parents, as shown below:

$$(.25R_{NF})/(.75R_F) = .70/.30$$

$$\text{Thus: } R_{NF}/R_F = .525/.075 = 7.0$$

where R_{NF} is the risk for delinquency of children reared without fathers, R_F is the risk for those reared by both biological parents, and .70 is the proportion of all serious delinquents reared fatherless. Computed separately for African American males, the increased risk for those reared without fathers is also about 7:1 (Lykken, 1996).

How Many Sociopaths Are There?

"[There were] 5.5 million people on probation, in jail or prison, or on parole at year end 1996—nearly 2.9% of all U.S. residents" (Bureau of Justice Statistics, 1998). A few of these are best classified as psychopaths; another few are victims of circumstance or even innocent; but most of them are sociopaths. There are undoubtedly many additional sociopaths who do not happen to be in the criminal justice system at the present time. Therefore, a *very* conservative estimate of the number of sociopaths in the present U.S. population would be 5 million, most of whom were reared without fathers. We know from birth records that in 1994 there were about 18.5 million males aged 15–25 in the United States, of whom 2.5 million or 13.4% were born out of wedlock. In that same year, there were about 21.9 million little boys aged 0 to 10 years, of whom twice as many—5.8 million or 26.5%—were being reared by unmarried mothers (National Center for Health Statistics, 1993a). The proportions in both groups reared without the active participation of their biological fathers is at least twice as high as these figures suggest, due to homes broken by divorce (National Center for Health Statistics, 1993b).

But if fatherless boys are seven times more likely than two-parent boys to grow up unsocialized, then this doubling in the proportion of the current 0- to 10-year-olds who are illegitimate indicates that the number of sociopathic young males aged 15 to 25 in the year 2011 will be at least double the number that we are now contending with. and it will double again in another 10 years, because the rates of both divorce and illegitimacy continue to rise rapidly. It is important to see that these predictions too are conservative and optimistic; they do not take into account the contagion effect of sociopathy discussed above, nor do they include any allowance for the fact that sociopaths father (but do not nurture or parent) more than their share of offspring (Lynn, 1995), who will be at especially high risk for sociopathy or psychopathy themselves.

The Costs of Sociopathy

Child psychiatrist Jack Westman (1994) has worked out careful estimates of what the typical sociopath costs our society during each year of life. Taking into account welfare costs, hospital emergency room costs, the expenses of juvenile corrections, policing, the costs of trials, public defenders, probation officers, and imprisonment costs,[2] not to mention costs to any victims of predation, Westman's estimate runs to about $50,000 per sociopath per year. Corroborating Westman's estimate, among those 135 child felons studies recently in Minneapolis, a single 9-year-old "cost the public $239,551 over four years for repeated child protection visits and placements, economic assistance, and Medicaid" (Wiig, 1995, p. 25). And Westman's figure does not include those costs resulting from the fact that sociopaths tend to breed carelessly and are bad parents, and thus are likely to produce additional debits in the next generation.

If there are at least 5 million sociopaths among us today, this means that they are costing U.S. taxpayers at least $250 *billion* annually right now. If we continue on our present course, this outlay will increase to some $1 *trillion* minimally per year by 2021, aggregating at least $15 trillion in current dollars. If we could think of ways to reduce the number of sociopaths being produced on American assembly lines each year, rather than tolerating the current positively accelerated increase in their numbers, this might be a way to save what even politicians would recognize as "real money."

PREVENTION

> The fact itself, of causing the existence of a human being, is one of the most responsible actions in the range of human life. To undertake this responsibility—to bestow a life which may be either a curse or a blessing—unless the being on whom it is to be bestowed will have at least ordinary chances of a desirable existence, is a crime against that being.
> —JOHN STUART MILL (1859/1956, p. 124)

More important even than the prodigious dollar drain cited above are the social costs of the current epidemic of sociopathy. These include the costs to the victims of crime and the fears and constricted life space of those citizens not yet victimized. But it includes especially the costs to those children whose birthrights of "life, liberty, and the pursuit of happiness" are being abrogated by feckless, incompetent, or sociopathic rearing. Judge Gill, cited earlier, points out that the place to fight crime is in the cradle.

From an evolutionary point of view, it seems probable that most children of our species would become adequately socialized if they could grow up within a stable extended-family structure similar to that of our ancestors during the Pleistocene, or to, say, the Amish culture of today. Reared in the modern way by two parents working alone—parents who have had little opportunity to learn parenting skills during their own growing-up period—a higher proportion of youngsters will be inadequately socialized, and the crime rate will increase. Reared by a single mother, with no equally committed biological father present to share the load, to provide a male role model, and to exercise paternal authority, the incidence of failed socialization *must* substantially increase. The relationship between single parenthood and juvenile crime rate is so strong that "controlling for family configuration erases the relationship between race and crime and between low income and crime" (Kamarck & Galston, cited in Moynihan, 1993, p. 24).

At least 10 million children under the age of 11 are being raised in the United States by divorced women whose ex-husbands have essentially abandoned their parental responsibilities. Another 6 million U.S. children have been born out of wedlock, and many of these are being reared by mothers who are immature, poorly educated, and poorly socialized themselves. If such children *avoid* a career of social dependency and crime, they deserve our wonderment and special approbation. In the United States today, it can be said that we are operating a veritable factory of crime.

Reversing the current trend, in which increasing proportions of young Americans are growing up unsocialized, is a major—I would say *the* major—social problem of our time. Solving this problem will be difficult and expensive, yet not nearly so expensive as not solving it. if my analysis is correct, the essence of the solution is to reduce the numbers of youngsters being reared by incompetent, indifferent, or unsocialized parents.

Parental Guidance

The solution, I believe, has three parts. The first component involves providing guidance and help to those struggling parents who are motivated to rear their children successfully but who lack the skills and resources. We know already that halfway measures do not work; nor do programs that involve only the children—programs like Head Start or even the expensive Milwaukee project (Jensen, 1989), from which the children daily return to still-pathogenic home environments. Approaches such as Patterson's (Patterson et al., 1992; Dishion, Duncan, Eddy, Fagot, & Fetrow, 1994) or the promising FAST Track program (Conduct Problems Prevention Research Group, 1992), which involve parents and school teachers as well as the children and their peers, are very expensive. We must remember, however, that sociopaths cost society at least $3 million apiece over their first 60 years. Therefore, an investment of as much as $300,000 in each of 10 high-risk youngsters, if it succeeds in turning just two potential criminals into socialized wage earners, will leave us financially ahead at the end of the day.

Alternative Rearing Environments

The second component of a workable solution to sociopathy is to provide alternative rearing environments for the many youngsters whose parents cannot or will not make effective use of help and guidance. Competent parenting is one of the most difficult—and plainly one of the most important—jobs that any of us ever undertake, and yet it is one of the most unappreciated and underpaid. One reason children are left too long with abusive or incompetent parents is that social workers have been taught to believe that the biological relationship compensates somehow for almost all deficiencies of parental commitment or skill. The much-touted "family preservation" movement, which has dominated thinking in this area since the 1970s, has been based on wishful thinking and a cruel refusal to face the facts of life on the urban streets (MacDonald, 1994). Because of this policy, for example, nearly all of those 135 child felons under age 10 in Minneapolis are once again residing with the parent or parents whose abuse and neglect led to their criminal precocity (J. Wild, Assistant Hennepin County Attorney, personal communication,

June 19, 1996). The fact that at least one prominent former exponent of this view has recently published an account of how and why he came to repudiate this policy (Gelles, 1996) may be regarded as encouraging.

Another reason why our children are left too long at risk, however, is that foster homes are in such short supply. In my own county, children taken from abusive parents (more than 90% of whom are single mothers) sometimes have to be placed with known criminals (Hennepin County social worker who prefers to remain anonymous, personal communication, January 1995). Moreover, both the licensure requirements and the supervision of the existing placements are generally negligible. Because a good foster home can often prevent the production of a sociopath, and thus avoid a $3 million debit in society's balance sheet, surely it would be a sound investment to pay a trained foster mother as much as she would make in a full-time office job. And surely in these times when most couples feel they need two incomes to make ends meet, there must be many people who would prefer to work as professional foster parents at home rather in in most conventional jobs outside—if the compensation were adequate. We know enough about parenting, about what works and what does not, to devise courses of instruction—say, at the community college level—that could be used as prerequisites to licensure for foster parents. Social workers would be needed to inspect and monitor these homes regularly, as well as to organize periodic group meetings of foster parents where they can discuss problems and compare notes. But an adequate foster home structure would also free up a lot of time that social workers now expend in dreary and largely ineffectual contacts with incompetent biological parents. The professionalization of foster care would be a cost-effective and salutary step in the right direction.

Another option, suitable especially for older boys, would be the establishment of boarding schools as suggested by J. Q. Wilson (1991; see also DiIulio, 1995, pp. 39, 40). This is foster care on a communal scale—in some ways, more like the extended-family system of socialization to which our species is evolutionarily adapted. It is also a method of socialization that has served the upper classes of most developed societies for generations. They should probably be single-sex schools, on the grounds that these are high-risk youngsters and it is wiser to keep the nitro and the glycerin in separate containers until the mixture can be handled with at least some degree of safety. Girls in coeducational schools mature earlier and are more likely to become delinquent than girls in same-sex schools (Moffitt, Caspi, Belsky, & Silva, 1992). Since girls most often commit their delinquencies in the company of boys, and since boys often commit their delinquencies either to impress or to possess girls, segregation in single-sex schools seems a sensible precaution for high-risk youngsters. We should need mostly boys' schools, because boys constitute the biggest problem, and most of the residents would be boys whose fathers were not resident at home. Does a boarding school sound too luxurious? It costs considerably more to keep a youngster in my county's juvenile corrections center than it would cost to send him to Groton School or Phillips Exeter Academy.

Most Anglophones, more familiar with Dickens's *Oliver Twist* than with contemporary realities, think of large-scale foster care or orphanages with dismay and dread. The economics professor Richard McKenzie (1996a, 1996b) has done us all a service by recounting his experiences during the 1950s in a typical American orphanage in North Carolina, and by reporting the results of his survey of the adult circumstances of many of the youngsters who shared those experiences with him. Although most of them were brought into this world by unfit or unfortunate parents—hence their consignment to "The Home"—he and many of his fellow "orphans" have achieved greater worldly success and better psychological adjustment than many of their more fortunate contemporaries who were reared by their birth parents.

Parental Licensure

> It still remains unrecognized, that to bring a child into existence without a fair prospect of being able, not only to provide for its body, but instruction and training for its mind, is a moral crime, both against the unfortunate offspring and against society; and that if the parent does not fulfill this obligation, the State ought to see it fulfilled, at the charge, as far as possible, of the parent.
> —JOHN STUART MILL (1859/1956, p. 121)

All of these programs, if properly implemented, could reduce the production of new sociopaths and thus improve the safety and the quality of life for some of them and all of us. But, by themselves, such programs would constitute only a temporary expedient. Opponents of abortion ask with sincere anguish, "What about the babies?", but we should be at least equally concerned about those babies' long and perilous journey after birth. It may be time for us directly to confront the painful problem of weighing the procreative rights of adults against the basic rights of their potential children.

Suppose we come to a river and find it full of children being swept down by the current, thrashing and struggling to keeps their heads above water. We can leap in and save a few, but they keep coming, and many drown in spite of our best efforts. This is Harris's (cited in Shanker, 1993) analogy for attempts to socialize children in the public schools. It is time to go upstream, Harris insists, to see what is pushing all those children into that river of no return. What we shall find upstream is increasing numbers of immature, indifferent, unsocialized, or incompetent people, most of them unmarried and many economically dependent, who are having children whom they cannot or will not competently rear. The licensure of parenthood is the only real solution to the problem of sociopathy and crime.

Prior to World War II, most developed countries maintained what amounted to a tradition of parental licensure. The ancient taboo against out-of-wedlock births led most young people to understand that if they wished to produce a keep a baby, they must first get married, and for that a license was required from the state. A child's jingle from that time said it all: "First comes love, then comes marriage, then comes baby in a baby carriage." But the sexual revolution of the 1960s discarded that bit of ancient wisdom, and the institution of "no-fault" divorce (which is often faulty in the extreme when children are involved) compounded the problem. It is time, I believe, to consider legislation designed to redress the balance—to place the rights of children once again ahead of the procreative rights of prospective parents.

In most jurisdictions, children are given for adoption only to mature married couples who are self-supporting and neither criminal nor incapacitated by psychiatric illness. If only these minimal requirements were made of persons wishing to retain custody of a child they have produced biologically, millions of American children would be saved each year from Harris's maelstrom, and hundreds of billions of tax dollars would be saved with which to make their world a better place. It is something to think about.

Robert: Executed at 11

Although Robert Sandifer was just a diminutive 11-year-old, he had been wanted for three days in the slaying of a 14-year-old girl. He was found Thursday lying in a pool of blood, believed to have been the victim of the gang he had embraced. (McMahon, 1994, p. 1)

This news report poignantly illustrates the kind of thing that we shall find upstream in Harris's river. Robert was always a difficult child, aggressive and hard to discipline (resembling in this his father, who is currently in prison); most 11-year-old boys would not be as reckless and venturesome as Robert, even if allowed to run loose as Robert was. His mother, Lorina, was 18 when Robert was born and only 15 when she had her first illegitimate child (the first of seven; Robert was her third). Lorina or her boyfriend responded to Robert's difficult temperament by abusing the toddler. His grandmother, Jannie Fields, had herself been just 16 when she gave birth to Robert's mother; with Aid to Families with Dependent Children and other government assistance, she has had 13 more children. (*One-third* of all U.S. births in 1993 were to parents on Medicaid; National Center for Health Statistics, 1995.) In addition to child abuse, Lorina has some 30 criminal convictions, mostly for drug and shoplifting offenses; thus we know that Jannie's own track record as a parent was a poor one. Nevertheless, for reasons reviewed earlier, county social workers placed the 3-year-old Robert and several of his siblings in her feckless care when Robert was found covered with bruises, scratches, and cigarette burns.

The grandmother provided "no discipline" at all, and Robert was arrested eight times between the ages of 9 and 11 for felonies including burglary, arson, car theft, and armed robbery. By age 10, he had a tattoo on his arm signifying membership in the Black Disciples street gang. Then one Sunday in August 1994, apparently on orders from older gang members, Robert fired a gun several times at some boys in the street, permanently crippling one of them. Three hours later and two blocks away, Robert started shooting again, this time accidentally killing a 14-year-old girl. Robert eluded a police search for 3 days until two gang comrades, aged 14 and 16, put two bullets in Robert's brain and left him under a bridge.

According to the *New York Times* story (Terry, 1994), the neighbors blamed the gangs and the guns in Robert's neighborhood, and one cannot deny that an 11-year-old is a lot more dangerous with a gun in his hand and older gang members telling him where to point it. But it is obvious that the real problem was two (or more) generations of incompetent parenting. The Cook County Public Guardian, Patrick Murphy, got it right: "'This kid was a time bomb waiting to explode,' Mr. Murphy said. 'He was turned into a sociopath by his family'" (Terry, 1994, p. A10).

Although there are thousands of juvenile murderers in the United States, Robert was unusual and newsworthy, whereas Robert's parents and grandparents are commonplace: Millions of indifferent or incompetent mothers hold parental rights over millions of fatherless children. Not all of these, perhaps, but millions still are growing up like wild things, in environments of filth, chaos, violence, substance abuse, child abuse, and crime. Juvenile corrections agencies, child protection agencies, probation and parole officers, the adult prison system—all are overwhelmed. The cases that get into the newspapers are the tiny tip of the iceberg.

Mike Royko (1994), the late Chicago columnist, asked despairingly what we can do to prevent the manufacture of juvenile sociopaths: "Robert's dad is a criminal and . . . his mother is a drug user and a fool. . . . Obviously, these two boobs should not have had children. But how do we stop them? Tie her tubes? Snip his organs? No, because that's unconstitutional and will remain so unless we become a totalitarian state" (p. 3). I think, however, that Royko was unduly pessimistic about the possibilities of a long-term solution.

What is constitutional and what is not is decided in the end by the U.S. Supreme Court, and usually on the basis of contemporary social realities. From the child's point of view, the licensure of parenthood would constitute a libertarian rather than a totalitarian step. No average couple would be discommoded by a statute that required biological parents to meet the criteria demanded of persons who wish to adopt a child. Fifteen-year-old Lorina and her then-boyfriend, however, would find themselves up on charges. She would be required to name the father (or the possible fathers, if, indeed, she had ever known their names), and modern DNA analyses would make it possible to prove parenthood. If she wished to carry her baby to term, Lorina might be required to spend those months in a compassionate maternity home providing good nutrition and medical care, individualized counseling, and job training, as well as supervision by night, to ensure that the infant got a healthy start in life. The baby would be taken into foster care at birth and the mother sent back to school or work. The father's wages (if he could be identified) would be taxed until he had paid off the costs of the confinement. If either Lorina or the boyfriend were to be involved in a second unlicensed pregnancy, they would have to submit to the implantation of a long-acting antifertility drug.

A society that enforces parental licensure, but one in which mature married couples who are self-supporting, law-abiding, and not psychiatrically incapacitated can expect to receive a license if they want one, would surely be a safer, happier one for children to grow up in. It would also be one in which the incidence of 11-year-old murderers would be negligible.

ACKNOWLEDGMENT

Portions of this chapter are adapted from Lykken (1995). Copyright 1995 by Lawrence Erlbaum Associates. Adapted by permission.

NOTES

1. At least 346 homicides during 1987–1991 were committed in Florida by felons after early release (DiIulio, 1994, p. 12). Patsy Jones, the 20-year-old who became a celebrity in 1993 after shooting a German tourist on a Miami expressway, had been released from jail only 5 days earlier; she had pulled a gun when arrested for shoplifting, but due to the press of more serious offenses, the charges were dropped (Associated Press, 1993).

2. Annual operating costs of U.S. prisons are currently $30 billion and rising fast (Tonry, 1996).

REFERENCES

Anderson, D. C. (1997, February 5). Why crime is down. *The New York Times Magazine*, pp. 47–52.

Associated Press. (1993, September 27). Killer of Miami tourist had been in police custody just 5 days earlier. *Minneapolis Star-Tribune*, p. 3.

Beck, A., Kline, S. & Greenfeld, L. (1987). *Survey of youth in custody*. Washington, DC: Bureau of Justice Statistics.

Beck, A., et al. (1993). *Survey of state prison inmates.* Washington, DC: Bureau of Justice Statistics.

Benson, P. L., & Roehlepartain, E. C. (1993). *Youth in single-parent families.* Minneapolis: The Search Institute.

Bouchard, T. J., Jr., Lykken, D. T., McGue, M., Segal, N., & Tellegen, A. (1990). Sources of human psychological differences: The Minnesota Study of Twins Reared Apart. *Science, 237,* 985–991.

Bureau of Justice Statistics. (1994). *Criminal victimization in the United States: 1973–92 trends.* Annapolis, MD: Bureau of Justice Statistics Clearinghouse.

Bureau of Justice Statistics. (1998). Corrections statistics [Online]. Available: http://www.ojp.us-doj.gov/bjs/correct.htm [1998, February 21].

Cleckley, H. (1941). *The mask of sanity.* St. Louis, MO: C. V. Mosby.

Cloninger, C. R., & Gottesman, I. I. (1987). Genetic and environmental factors in antisocial behavior. In S. A. Mednick, T. E. Mofitt, & S. A. Stack (Eds.), *The causes of crime: New biological approaches* (pp. 92–109). Cambridge, England: Cambridge University Press.

Conduct Problems Prevention Research Group. (1992). A developmental and clinical model for the prevention of conduct disorder: The FAST Track Program. *Development and Psychopathology, 4,* 509–527.

Cornell, D. (1987). Characteristics of adolescents charged with homicide. *Behavioral Sciences and the Law, 5,* 11–23.

Dash, L. (1996). *Rosa Lee: A generational tale of poverty and survival in urban America.* New York: Basic Books.

Dawson, D. (1991). Family structure and children's well-being: Data from the 1988 National Health Survey. *Journal of Marriage and the Family, 53,* 234–241.

DiIulio, J. J., Jr. (1994, Fall). The question of black crime. *The Public Interest,* pp. 3–32.

DiIulio, J. J., Jr. (1995, Winter). White lies about black crime. *The Public Interest,* pp. 30–44.

DiLalla, L. F., Gottesman, I. I., & Carey, G. (1993). Assessment of normal personality traits in a psychiatric sample: Dimensions and categories. In L. J. Chapman, J. P. Chapman, & D. C. Fowles (Eds.), *Progress in experimental personality and psychopathology research* (Vol. 17, pp. 145–162). New York: Springer.

Dishion, T. J., Duncan, T. E., Eddy, J. M., Fagot, B. I., & Fetrow, R. (1994). The world of parents and peers: Coercive exchanges and children's social adaptation. *Social Development, 3,* 255–268.

Eckholm, E. (1992, July 26). Solutions on welfare: They all cost money. *The New York Times,* p. 1.

Federal Bureau of Investigation (FBI). (1993). *Age-specific arrest rates and race-specific arrest rates for selected offenses, 1965–1992.* Washington, DC: U.S. Department of Justice.

Federal Bureau of Investigation (FBI). (1994). *Uniform crime reports for the United States, 1993.* Washington, DC: U.S. Department of Justice.

Forgatch, M. S., Patterson, G. R., & Ray, J. A. (1994). Divorce and boys' adjustment problems: Two paths with a single model. In E. M. Hetherington, D. Reiss, & R. Plomin (Eds.), *Stress, coping, and resiliency in children and the family* (pp. 96–110). Mahwah, NJ: Erlbaum.

Foster, E. (1994, April 17). Baby truants at record high in St. Paul. *Minneapolis Star-Tribune,* pp. 1, 8.

Fowles, D. C., & Missel, K. (1994). Electrodermal hyporeactivity, motivation, and psychopathy: Theoretical issues. In D. C. Fowles, P. Sutker, & S. Goodman (Eds.), *Progress in experimental personality and psychopathology research* (Vol. 18, pp. 263–283). New York: Springer.

Fuchs, V. R., & Reklis, D. M. (1992). America's children: Economic perspectives and policy options. *Science, 255,* 41–46.

Gelles, R. J. (1996). *The book of David: How preserving families can cost children's lives.* New York: Basic Books.

Gill, C. D. (1994). Foreword. In J. C. Westman, *Licensing parents.* New York: Insight Books.

Gray, J. A. (1987). *The psychology of fear and stress.* Cambridge, England: Cambridge University Press.

Grove, W. M., Eckert, E. D., Heston, L., & Bouchard, T. J., Jr. (1990). Heritability of substance abuse and antisocial behavior: A study of monozygotic twins reared apart. *Biological Psychiatry, 27,* 1293–1304.

Harris, J. R. (1995). Where is the child's environment: A group socialization theory of development. *Psychological Review, 102,* 458–489.

Horowitz, M. (1993, December). In search of Monster. *The Atlantic Monthly,* pp. 28–37.

Jensen, A. R. (1989). Raising IQ without increasing g? A review of the Milwaukee Project: Preventing mental retardation in children at risk. *Developmental Review, 9,* 234–258.

Kagan, J. (1994). *Galens' prophecy.* New York: Basic Books.

Kochanska, G. (1991). Socialization and temperament in the development of guilt and conscience. *Child Development, 62,* 1379–1392.

Kochanska, G. (1993). Toward a synthesis of parental socialization and child temperament in early development of conscience. *Child Development, 64,* 325–347.

Kraepelin, E. (1907). *Clinical psychiatry* (A. R. Diefendorf, Trans.). New York: Macmillan.

Kristol, I. (1994, November 3). Children need their fathers. *The New York Times,* p. 3.

Lemann, N. (1993). *The promised land: The great black migration and how it changed America.* New York: Knopf.

Lindsey, R. (1979). *The Falcon and the Snowman.* New York: Simon and Schuster.

Lindsey, R. (1983). *The flight of the Falcon.* New York: Simon & Schuster.

Loeber, R., & Dishion, T. (1983). Early predictors of male delinquency: A review. *Psychological Bulletin, 104,* 68–99.

Lykken, D. T. (1957). A study of anxiety in the sociopathic personality. *Journal of Abnormal Psychology, 55,* 6–10.

Lykken, D. T. (1995). *The antisocial personalities.* Hillsdale, NJ: Erlbaum.

Lykken, D. T. (1996). The American crime factory. *Psychological Inquiry, 8,* 261–270.

Lynn, R. (1995). Dysgenic fertility for criminal behavior. *Journal of Biosocial Science, 27,* 405–408.

Lyons, M. J. (1996). A twin study of self-reported criminal behavior. In G. R. Bock & J. A. Goode (Eds.), *Ciba Foundation Symposium on genetics of criminal and antisocial behavior* (pp. 61–70). Chichester, England: Wiley.

MacDonald, H. (1994, Spring). The ideology of "family preservation." *The Public Interest,* pp. 45–60.

McKenzie, R. (1996a). *The home.* New York: Basic Books.

McKenzie, R. (1996b, Spring). Orphanages: The real story. *The Public Interest,* pp. 180–184.

McMahon, C. (1994, September 4). Robert: Executed at 11. *Chicago Tribune,* p. 1.

McNeal, R. B. (1995). Extracurricular activities and high school dropouts. *Sociology of Education, 68,* 62–81.

Mill, J. S. (1956). *On liberty.* New York: Liberal Arts Press. (Original work published 1859)

Moffitt, T. E. (1993). Adolescence-limited and life-course-persistent antisocial behavior: A developmental taxonomy. *Psychological Review, 100,* 674–701.

Moffitt, T. E., Caspi, A., Belsky, J., & Silva, P. A. (1992). Childhood experience and the onset of menarche: A test of a sociobiological model. *Child Development, 63,* 47–58.

Mounts, N. S., & Steinberg, L. (1995). An ecological analysis of peer influence on adolescent grade point average and drug use. *Developmental Psychology, 31,* 915–922.

Moynihan, D. P. (1969). America. In D. P. Moynihan (Ed.), *On understanding poverty* (pp. 42–65). New York: Basic Books.

Moynihan, D. P. (1993). Defining deviancy down. *The American Scholar, 62,* 17–30.

Murphy, J. M. (1976). Psychiatric labeling in cross-cultural perspective. *Science, 141,* 1019–1028.

Murray, C. (1993, October 29). The coming white underclass. *The Wall Street Journal,* pp. 1, 2.

National Center for Health Statistics. (1993a). *Vital statistics of the United States, 1989: Vol. 1. Natality* (DHHS Publication No. PHS 93-1100). Washington, DC: U.S. Government Printing Office.

National Center for Health Statistics. (1993b). *Vital statistics of the United States, 1989: Vol. 3. Marriage and divorce* (DHHS Publication No. PHS 93-1103). Washington, DC: U.S. Government Printing Office.

National Center for Health Statistics. (1995) *Report to Congress on out-of-wedlock childbearing.* Hyattsville, MD: U.S. Department of Health and Human Services.

Newman, J. P., Kosson, D. S., & Patterson, C. M. (1992). Delay of gratification in psychopathic and nonpsychopathic offenders. *Journal of Abnormal Psychology, 101,* 630–636.

Patterson, G. R. (1982). *Coercive family process.* Eugene, OR: Castalia.

Patterson, G. R., Reid, J. B., & Dishion, T. J. (1992). *Antisocial boys.* Eugene, OR: Castalia.

Plomin, R., & Bergeman, C. S. (1991). The nature of nurture: Genetic influences on "environmental" measures. *Behavioral and Brain Sciences, 14,* 373–427.

Plomin, R., & Daniels, D. (1987). Why are children in the same family so different from one another? *Behavioral and Brain Sciences, 10,* 1–16.

Plomin, R., DeFries, J. C., & Loehlin, J. C. (1977). Genotype–environment interaction and correlation in the analysis of human behavior. *Psychological Bulletin, 84,* 309–322.

Raine, A. (1993). *The psychopathology of crime.* San Diego: Academic Press.

Rowe, D. C. (1994). *The limits of family influence: Genes, experience, and behavior.* New York: Guilford Press.

Royko, M. (1994, September 2). Who's to blame?: The obvious targets. *Chicago Tribune,* p. 3.

Rubinstein, D. (1992, November 9). Joblessness and crime. *The Wall Street Journal,* p. 1.

Rush, B. (1812). *Medical inquiries and observations upon the diseases of the mind.* Philadelphia: Kimber & Richardson.

Rutter, M. (1996). Concepts of antisocial behavior, of cause and of genetic influences. In G. R. Bock & J. A. Goode (Eds.), *Ciba Foundation Symposium on genetics of criminal and antisocial behavior* (pp. 1–20). Chichester, England: Wiley.

Scarr, S. (1992). Developmental theories for the 1990s: Development and individual differences. *Child Development, 63,* 1–19.

Scarr, S., & McCartney, K. (1983). How people make their own environments: A theory of genotype–environment effects. *Child Development, 54,* 424–435.

Shakur, S. (a.k.a. Monster Kody Scott). (1993). *Monster: The autobiography of an L.A. gang member.* New York: Atlantic Monthly Press.

Shanker, A. (1993, July 5). A million drowning children. *New Republic,* p. 21.

Sheline, J. L., Skipper, B. J., & Broadhead, W. E. (1994). Risk factors for violent behavior in elementary school boys. *American Journal of Public Health, 84,* 661–663.

Silberg, J., Meyer, J., Pickles, A., Simonoff, E., Eaves, L., Hewitt, J., Maes, H., & Rutter, M. (1996). Heterogeneity among juvenile antisocial behaviors: Findings from the Virginia Twin Study of Adolescent Behavioral Development. In G. R. Bock & J. A. Goode (Eds.), *Ciba Foundation Symposium on genetics of criminal and antisocial behavior* (pp. 76–86). Chichester, England: Wiley.

Snyder, H. N., & Sickmund, M. (1995). *Juvenile offenses and victims: A national report.* Washington, DC: Office of Juvenile Justice and Delinquency Prevention.

Terry, D. (1994, September 9). When children kill children: Boy, 11, is wanted in Chicago. *The New York Times,* pp. A1, A10.

Tonry, M. (1996). *Sentencing matters.* New York: Oxford University Press.

U.S. Bureau of the Census. (1995). *Statistical abstract of the United States.* Washington, DC: U.S. Government Printing Office.

Westman, J. C. (1994). *Licensing parents.* New York: Insight Books.

Wiig, J. K. (1995). *Delinquents under 10 in Hennepin County.* Minneapolis: Hennepin County Attorney's Office.

Will, G. F. (1992, January 18). Windows on a stressful future. *The Washington Post,* p. 18A.

Wilson, J. Q. (1991). Boarding schools might help today's "warrior class." *American Enterprise Institute Newsletter,* No. 3.

Wilson, J. Q., & Herrnstein, R. J. (1985). *Crime and human nature.* New York: Simon & Schuster.

Wright, R. (1994). *The moral animal: Evolutionary psychology and everyday life.* New York: Pantheon Books.

Zahn-Waxler, C., & Kochanska, G. (1988). The origins of guilt. In R. A. Thompson (Ed.), *Nebraska Symposium on Motivation* (Vol. 36, pp. 76–131). Lincoln: University of Nebraska Press.

9

Psychopathy or Antisocial Personality in Forensic Settings

HANS TOCH

Robert Hare, in a 1996 article entitled "Psychopathy: A Clinical Construct Whose Time Has Come," writes:

> Unfortunately, in my view, resources have been targeted primarily at programs and projects that eschew the politically incorrect idea that individual differences in personality are as important as determinants of crime as are social forces. As the title of this article implies, the situation is changing rapidly. . . . In the next few years, indices of psychopathy almost certainly will become a routine part of the assessment batteries used to make decisions about competency, sentencing, diversion, placement, suitability for treatment, and risk for recidivism and violence. Because psychopaths with a history of violence are a poor risk for early release, more and more will be kept in prison for their full sentence. (p. 49)

A different perspective on the same trend is provided by John Mortimer,[1] in an interview with the British newspaper *Inside Time*. The final paragraph of this interview reads as follows:

> [Mortimer] summed up the crux of his anxieties with a description of where our society seemed to be moving: "There is a dangerously erroneous attitude which suggests that there are a respectable number of people who don't commit crimes who live in a kind of castle around which a moat should be dug; and outside there is the enemy forming up *who are totally different from those inside the castle and for whom they have no responsibility—except to catch them and lock them up for good.* If this happens we will no longer be one society. That would be a tragedy." (Billington, 1996; emphasis added)

The same concern is expressed by Jerome Miller (1991), who commented that "I learned long ago that these diagnoses are more than anything else social prescriptions. I

144

judge labels by the treatments they demand, and current preoccupations with issues like the criminal personality, the criminal mind, and the career criminal are more ominous than hopeful" (p. 243).[2] Miller added that

> Those who so glibly construct hurtful and defeating labels—"psychopath," "sociopath," "criminal personality," all diagnoses which ensure neglect, hostility, mishandling and brutality—might first thoroughly know and respect another's life history. It takes unusual arrogance to dismiss a fellow human being's lost journey as irrelevant. (p. 246)

In this chapter I shall highlight some of the themes that emerge with the inception of the psychopathy construct, and consider the impact of these themes on forensic populations. I shall specifically argue that the effects of (l) pathologizing chronic offense careers, (2) depathologizing other problems of the same offenders, (3) furthering (and later resuscitating) a link between violence and psychopathy, (4) advancing the notion of a criminal personality entity, and (5) postulating the nonamenability to intervention of chronic offenders, have been to provide scientific support for a psychologically dichotomous view of the human race (as suggested by John Mortimer) and to promote a prescriptive inference that calls for the exiling or warehousing of serious delinquents and felons (as noted by Hare as well as Miller and Mortimer).

I also believe that the focus on psychopathy has foreclosed questions that ought to be asked about the dynamics of offense behavior, especially in cases where offenses are serious, patterned, or repetitive. Such questions can only be asked if we center on the motives and perspectives of individual offenders, rather than assuming that criminals are essentially alike. Robert Hare's views (see also Hare, Chapter 12, this volume) notwithstanding, the phrase "individual differences in personality" presupposes that there are differences among all offenders, which very much include differences among those who are now labeled psychopathic or antisocial.

PREHISTORY OF THE PSYCHOPATHY CONSTRUCT

Ironically, the construct of psychopathy did not originate as a way of denoting a qualitative difference between recidivistic offenders (or similarly disposed shady entrepreneurs) and the rest of law-abiding humanity. Nor was the notion at first that of pinpointing a subgroup of obdurate and violence-disposed criminals who are fated (unless incapacitated) to continue their damaging predations by virtue of a biologically ordained pathological constellation of traits. Instead, the concept was created to highlight violent conduct that did not appear to be accompanied by the delusional thinking that early alienists had defined as mental disorder. Thus Prichard (1837/1973) noted that "it seems, then, to have been the prevalent judgment of both medical and legal writers in this country, that *delusion,* or as medical writers express themselves, illusion and hallucination constitutes the essential character of insanity" (p. 272; emphasis in original).

Labels such as "mania without delirium" or (more mellifluously) "*la folie raisonnante*" suggested an exception to the prevailing rule. The mania at issue, according to Pinel (1801/1977), involved no cognitive dysfunction; instead, it was "marked by abstract and sanguinary fury, with a blind propensity to acts of violence" (p. 156). Patients manifesting the disorder were described as engulfed by rage and other strong feelings, under the governance of which they assaulted other persons or themselves. A mechanic studied by Pinel, for example, was one day seized by a furious paroxysm in his own house. He instantly gave warning to his wife, to whom he was tenderly attached, and advised her by an immediate flight to avoid certain death. At Bicêtre he experienced similar accessions of periodic fury, and his propensity to acts of atrocity was sometimes directed even against the governor, to whose compassionate attention and kindness he never appeared insensible. . . . He one day seized the cutting knife of the hospital shoemaker, and wounded himself deeply in the right breast and arm. The consequence was a violent haemorrhage. Close confinement, and the strait-waistcoast were employed to prevent the execution of his bloody project. (pp. 153–154)

Prichard (1837/1973), who reluctantly endorsed Pinel's observations, drew the following distinction between manifestations of destructive impulsivity—defined as "moral insanity"—and mental disorder as conventionally defined:

There are instances of insanity in which the whole disease, or at least the whole of its manifestations, has consisted in a liability to violent fits of anger breaking out without cause, and leading to the danger or actual commission of serious injury to surrounding persons. The characteristic feature of this malady is extreme irascibility depending on a physical morbid cause. . . . When this is connected with the false belief of some personal injury actually sustained, the case does not fall under the head of moral insanity. It involves hallucination or erroneous conviction of the understanding; but when the morbid phenomena include merely the expressions of intense malevolence, without ground or provocation actual or supposed, the case is strictly one of the nature above described. (p. 27)

Despite Prichard's nomenclature, he did not deal with presumptively pathological unlawful behavior. He was instead concerned with "excessive intensity of passion" (p. 29) and with variations of mood and excitation, including bipolar disorders (which had not been invented yet, or at least described as such). But given Prichard's interest in violent impulsivity, "moral" also meant "acts which under a sane condition of mind would be accounted atrocious crimes" (p. 27).

It is obvious that Pinel's and Prichard's taxonomy represented an expansion of the realm of psychopathology to behavior that had not previously been defined as mental illness. The behavior may have been dangerous (i.e., antisocial), but that was *not* the reason for adjudging it pathological. Rather, the point was that the person's acts were not under volitional control; hence the person was disturbed. The case studies that were cited were redolent with requests from patients for assistance to help them deal with unwelcome (or alien) urges or impulses.

Moreover, once this conception had been accepted the diagnosis implied exculpation, because the person's violence had been defined as not being under his or her governance *as a result of mental illness.* Hence, the proper and logical place for the "morally insane" was deemed to be the asylum.

TRANSITION TO THE MODERN CONSTRUCT

Prichard (1837/1973) felt that moral insanity should be accepted as a legal defense, and complained that juries were not giving credence to reputable expert testimony. The same complaint was later advanced by Henry Maudsley (1897/1977). Maudsley concurred that it made no sense to punish those who could not control their conduct, but also thought that prisons would not produce rehabilitative change. "If we are satisfied," he wrote with obvious irony, "that our prison system is the best that can be devised for the prevention of crime and the reformation of the criminal, we may rest satisfied that it is the best treatment for the sort of insanity which criminals suffer" (p. 27). Maudsley classed "criminal psychosis" as "an intractable malady," and asked, "How can that which has been forming through generations be *re*-formed within a single life?" (p. 33).

Maudsley's pessimism was related to his assumption that a subcategory of offenders was "marked by a defective physical and mental organization . . . which really determines their destiny in life, being an extreme deficiency or complete absence of moral sense" (1897/1977, p. 32). This deficiency, which Maudsley referred to as "moral imbecility," manifested itself as precocious criminality. He wrote:

> When we find young children, long before they can possibly know what vice and crime means, addicted to extreme vice, or committing great crimes, with an instinctive facility, and as if from an inherent proneness to criminal actions . . . and when experience proves that punishment has no reformatory effect upon them—that they cannot reform—it is made evident that moral imbecility is a fact, and that punishment is not the fittest treatment of it. (p. 179)

For Maudsley, moral imbecility, moral insanity, and criminal psychosis were concepts applicable to what he saw as a criminal class—chronic offenders of lower-class origin that any practitioner could spot. Given the possibly enduring relevance of this concept, it may be worth quoting Maudsley (1897/1977) in detail:

> All persons who have made criminals their study, recognize a distinct criminal class of beings, who herd together in our large cities in a thieves' quarter, giving themselves up to intemperance, rioting in debauchery, without regard to marriage ties or the bars of consanguinity, and propagating a criminal population of degenerate beings. For it is furthermore a matter of observation that this criminal class constitutes a degenerate or morbid variety of mankind, marked by peculiar low physical and mental characteristics. They are, it has been said, as distinctly marked off from the honest and well bred operatives as "black-faced sheep are from other breeds," so that an experienced detective officer or prison official could pick them out from any promiscuous assembly at church or market. . . .
>
> As a class, they are of mean and defective intellect, though excessively cunning, and not a few of them are weak-minded and imbecile. The women are ugly in features, and without grace of expression or movement. The children, who become juvenile criminals, do not evince the educational aptitude of the higher industrial classes: they are deficient in the power of attention and application, have bad memories, and make slow progress in learning; many of them are weak in mind and body, and some of them actually imbecile (pp. 29–30)

Earlier, in the United States, Benjamin Rush (1812/1962) a signer of the Declaration of Independence, wrote that "in the course of my life, I have been consulted in three cases of the total perversion of the moral faculties. . . . In all these cases of innate, preternatural moral depravity, there is probably an original defective organization in those parts of the body, which are occupied by the moral faculties of the mind." He added that "such persons are, in a pre-eminent degree, objects of compassion, and . . . it is the business of medicine to aid both religion and law, in preventing and curing their moral alienation of mind" (pp. 359–360). Rush felt that offenders with psychological defects were more humanely dealt with in medical then in custodial settings, but he thought that well-run prisons could be therapeutic. Of the Pennsylvania prison system, he wrote, "May this Christian system [of] criminal jurisprudence spread, without any of its imperfections, throughout the world!" (p. 366).

Subsequent psychiatrists were less optimistic about prisons, and less charitably disposed toward those whom they diagnosed as morally insane. Krafft-Ebing (1904), in a redoubtable textbook, adjudged treatment for such patients "without prospect of success," and wrote that "these savages in society must be kept in asylums [presumably, for life] for their own and the safety of society" (p. 626). Case material that documented his assertions emphasized the chronicity of psychopathic dispositions. Krafft-Ebing (1904) described one of his female patients as follows:

> On account of her dissolute life she frequently had encounters with the police, for she offended public decency and gave no attention to police regulations. She found nothing improper in her manner of life. . . . She played the injured innocent, paid no attention to the regulations of the house, incited other patients to mischief, had constantly explosions of anger in her great irritability, always about her affair with the police. The police were her enemies, and tried to injure her, though she had never done wrong. Of her moral defect and her inability to direct herself she had no idea. . . . The patient is impossible, coarse to brutality, afraid of work, tries to persuade others not to work, goes about disturbing and scolding others, trying to attract men, and demands her discharge; but she cannot say what she will do when she is put at liberty. The patient was transferred to an institution for [the] chronic insane. (p. 627)

It is noteworthy that Krafft-Ebing's vignette ends with the words "the patient was transferred to an institution for [the] chronic insane." By his time, the emerging construct had translated continuing misconduct into chronic pathology, calling for lifetime sequestration in mental health settings that offered no hope of remediation or cure.

THE ANTISOCIAL PERSONALITY CONSTRUCT

The most recent edition of the *Diagnostic and Statistical Manual of Mental Disorders* (DSM-IV; American Psychiatric Association [APA], 1994) has transmuted earlier diagnoses into that of Antisocial Personality Disorder, which is defined as an obdurate penchant for engaging in negativistic and destructive conduct starting early in life and continuing through adulthood (p. 645). In order to qualify for the diagnosis, a person has to show persistent patterned misconduct—that is, early evidence of conduct disorder. Another requisite is that the misconduct not occur during the course of schizophrenic or manic episodes.

The first of the diagnostic criteria that are listed in the DSM-IV involves behavior that violates the law and can get one arrested (p. 649). The last entails failure to manifest remorse for antisocial transgressions, including property offenses (p. 650). The APA understandably anticipated high prevalence rates in the diagnoses of inmates of forensic settings such as substance abuse treatment programs and prisons (p. 648).

In general, the APA points out that "when the DSM-IV categories, criteria, and textual descriptions are employed for forensic purposes, there are significant risks that diagnostic information will be misused or misunderstood. . . . The use of DSM-IV in forensic settings should be informed by an awareness of the risks and limitations [of misuse] discussed above" (p. xxiii).

The risks with respect to antisocial personality disorder do not end with the first and last diagnostic criteria. Another criterion is "consistent irresponsibility, as indicated by repeated failure to sustain consistent work behavior or honor financial obligations" (p. 650). Descriptively, patients "may fail to be self-supporting, may become impoverished or even homeless, or may spend many years in penal institutions" (p. 647). The APA cautions accordingly that "in assessing antisocial traits, it is helpful to the clinician to consider the social and economic context in which the behaviors occur" (p. 647), but it does not specifically indicate what the clinician is to do once he or she has considered the offender's social class. The diagnostician is left to ponder the fact that "Antisocial Personality Disorder appears to be associated with low socioeconomic status and urban settings" (p. 647).

With respect to differential diagnosis in the prison, the APA suggests that "lack of empathy, inflated self-appraisal, and superficial charm" (p. 647) may provide relevant cues. However, since only three diagnostic criteria suffice for a defensible diagnosis, a juvenile record and an offense career, aggressivity, impulsivity, a checkered work history, and/or lack of demonstrable repentance—which can be found in any prison dossier chosen at random—are more than enough for formal diagnostic purposes.

In other words, *almost any offender in a correctional setting is hypothetically entitled to a diagnosis of antisocial personality disorder.* The fact that a prior diagnosis (of conduct disorder) has to be applicable is of no mitigating help, because the behaviors subsumed under that diagnosis—fighting and aggressivity, violation of rules, impairment of academic functioning, mugging or robbery, early onset of sexual behavior, drinking, smoking and use of illegal substances—are prevalent patterns among delinquents.[3] In fact, the APA points out in DSM-IV that "concerns have been raised that the Conduct Disorder diagnosis may at times be misapplied to individuals in settings where patterns of undesirable behavior are sometimes viewed as protective (e.g., threatening, impoverished, high-crime)" (p. 88). This caution is revealing, because the diagnosis in question is often an admission criterion into the settings at issue, and an exclusion criterion from more conventional settings (such as classrooms).

The conduct disorder diagnosis can therefore become a prophecy that is partly self-fulfilling. Children who are singled out for being aggressive and obnoxious can be dealt with in a manner that is not calculated to improve the sunniness of their dispositions. The children's resentment in turn may create added rejection by others that the children find off-putting. The outcome of a degenerating sequence of this sort—reactions to responses that can lead to more reactions and responses—can be personal demeanor that is plausibly classifiable as antisocial behavior. Robins (1978) writes of future psychopaths:

> If one considers that in response to their early antisocial behaviour, parents beat them, schools expel them, and police chase them, their subjective experience of the world as unfriendly and dangerous may not be wholly irrational. Once they perceive the world in these terms, the chances that they will continue deviant behaviour may be greatly increased. It may be that the very fact of deviance beginning early in childhood makes a succession of interconnected problems highly probable. Early truancy leads to leaving school before graduation, which in turn creates job problems, which then encourages theft, which leads to jail, which alienates spouse and relatives. Thus the definition of antisocial personality as a multiproblem disorder with subjective symptoms of alienation and hostility could simply be another way of saying that we are talking about the consequences of severe antisocial behaviour occurring early in childhood. (pp. 269–270)

HARE'S PSYCHOPATHY CONSTRUCT

Robert Hare has marketed an alternative to the DSM-IV diagnosis. Hare (1996) distinguishes psychopathy, as operationalized by his instrument (currently the Psychopathy Checklist—Revised, or PCL-R; Hare, 1991) from the antisocial personality disorder diagnosis, which can "identify individuals who are persistently antisocial, most of whom are not psychopaths" (p. 34). Hare points out that given the possibility of indiscriminate diagnoses of antisocial personality disorder in prisons and forensic hospitals, clinicians in such settings are likely to supplement DSM guidelines with impressions of "personality traits indicative of psychopathy" (p. 35). But Hare also asserts that "there are no methodologically sound treatments or 'resocialization' programs that have been shown to work with psychopaths" (p. 41). Prison clinicians who share this conclusion can make their prognosis (the presumption of untreatability) an additional diagnostic criterion.

As indicated, Robert Hare contends that his inventory defines and measures "psychopathy." This construct, unlike most idioms in the psychological lexicon, has entered common parlance as a term of derogation. Webster's dictionary defines "psychopathic personality" as "an emotionally and behaviorally disordered state characterized . . . often by the pursuit of immediate personal gratification in criminal acts, drug addiction, or sexual perversion" (p. 951).

Since psychopathy is a pejorative label, honest and open encounters with subjects of classification are precluded. Materials relating to Hare's checklist carry the acronym PCL or PCL-R, so that those being assessed cannot infer the purpose of assessment (Hare, 1991, p. 1). Interviews are part of the assessment process, but Hare feels that "valid ratings can be made based on collateral information if there is sufficient high-quality information available" (p. 3). In other words, an offender can be adjudged a psychopath based on data in his or her dossier without being encountered in person.

Hare's checklist combines items from Hervey Cleckley's clinical psychopathy profile (Cleckley, 1982, p. 204) and other sources. The comprehensive version of Hare's instrument involves judgments about the extent to which a person demonstrates the 20 traits: glibness or superficial charm, "grandiose" sense of self-worth, boredom or need for stimulation, pathological lying, conning and manipulation, lack of remorse or guilt, shallow affect, callousness or absence of empathy, a "parasitic" lifestyle, inadequate behavioral controls, sexual promiscuity, early behavior problems, paucity of "realistic" long-term goals, impulsivity, irresponsibility, failure to accept responsibility, multiple marital relations, juvenile delinquency, violations of conditional release, and criminal versatility (Hare, 1991).

A review of the categories in Hare's roster confirms that many items involve adverse judgments about the person being rated. Some describe non-middle-class or unconventional mores, but most items apply specifically or felicitously to offenders (juvenile delinquency, lack of remorse, poor behavioral controls) or recidivistic offenders (early behavior problems, violations of conditional release, criminal versatility). Many of the items, in fact, can only be documented with information in offender files, and raters are repeatedly referred to such files (Hare, 1991).

The Hare checklist has good psychometric properties, and it can lay claim to empirical validation, including studies demonstrating its predictive validity. Such findings are not unexpected, given the material on the basis of which the index is derived. The best predictor of future misbehavior is past misbehavior—especially if the misbehavior is habitual and the miscreant is young. The Hare rater spends "several hours" (Hare, 1996, p. 31) poring over dossiers that are cursorily perused by others. Prediction studies are conducted in correctional and forensic psychiatric settings with high recidivism rates, using indirect measures of recidivism and items that gauge crime-related motivational recalcitrance.

The predictive validity of offense-related content obviously cannot validate a personality construct that Hare, Cleckley, and others stress is prevalent among nonoffenders living in civilian society. Cleckley (1982), in fact, contended that "the typical psychopath, as I have seen him, usually does not commit murder or other offenses that promptly lead to major prison sentences" (p. 150). Cleckley wrote:

> Many people, perhaps most, who commit violent and serious crime fail to show the chief characteristics that so consistently appear in the cases we have considered. Many, in fact, show features that make it very difficult to identify them with this group. The term *psychopath* (or *antisocial personality*) as it is applied by various psychiatrists and hospital staffs sometimes become so broad that it might be applied to almost any criminal. Granting the essential vagueness of the term, and disputing no one's right to it, I (who am using it only for convenience) maintain that the large group of maladjusted personalities whom I have personally studied and to whom this diagnosis has been consistently applied differs distinctly from a group of ordinary criminals. (p. 150)

To the extent to which Cleckley (1982) is to be taken seriously, the studies of Hare and his colleagues cannot validate his version of the psychopathy construct. Cleckley himself used case studies by way of documentation, as have his predecessors and early successors. In such documentation, validation consists of the "fit" (confirmed by the reader) between the clinical profile and the facts of the case, as exhaustively and dispassionately presented. For Cleckley (1982), direct interviews with patients did not themselves undergird diagnoses, because psychopathy is presumed "masked" (p. 258).

Validity of diagnosis is crucial with respect to psychopathy, because of the prescriptive inferences Hare, Cleckley and others draw from their portrayals. Thus Cleckley (1982), for instance, tells us that "if such patients could be evaluated in terms of their behavior and committed, like other psychiatric patients, not to limited terms of confinement but for indeterminate periods, the community would obviously obtain far better protection" (p. 277). Indeterminacy in this context implies lifetime confinement, because "there is, we must conclude, no evidence to demonstrate or to indicate that psychiatry has yet found a therapy that cures or profoundly changes the psychopath" (p. 280).

PSYCHOPATHY AS COUNTERTRANSFERENCE

Diagnoses of psychopathy are advanced—as are other psychiatric diagnoses—with advertised dispassion and scientific neutrality. But the content of the diagnoses is not morally neutral, which raises doubts about the diagnostician's dispassion. Psychopathy is a wildly pejorative designation because individuals described with this designation are presumptively sleazy, unsavory, repugnant, and dangerous. The fact that some persons by consensus can be described as loathsome, untrustworthy, and reprehensible is no help. It still leaves open the question of the extent to which the loathsomeness, untrustworthiness, and reprehensibility of such persons are intrinsic psychological qualities, as opposed to transactions between attributes and reactions to these attributes by observers. If loathsomeness can be partly in the eyes of a disapproving beholder, would it not follow that its diagnosis can describe the observer as much as the observed? In other words, could it not be validly alleged that " 'a psychopath is somebody you don't like' "? (Leo Kanner, quoted in McCord and McCord, 1964, p. 2).

The hypothesis that psychopathy is a term of clinical disapprobation can be confirmed in retrospects of early usages of the diagnosis. The excerpts from the writings of Maudsley and Krafft-Ebing quoted earlier in the chapter, as well as the writings of other psychiatrists of their generation, show moralistic, class-related biases that are obvious to us today, given the historical differences in perspective. In DSM-IV, the APA wisely enjoins us to consider contextual factors, such as socioeconomic class membership and forensic status; moreover, two subcultural criteria in DSM-III (irresponsible parenting and failure to sustain a monogamous relationship) have been deleted from the DSM-IV diagnosis. One of these items unfortunately survives in the Hare checklist—as does sexual promiscuity, which was a prominent concern of Krafft-Ebing in the vignette quoted above.

The issue of biases arises expressly in forensic settings, in which DSM-IV diagnoses have to be selectively deployed—of necessity, given the indiscriminateness of the diagnostic criteria. Thus, the experience "I sense an effort to manipulate me, and I resent it" can translate into a patient's adjudged trait of "manipulativeness," and "I feel frustrated because you won't confess your culpability when I cross-examine you" can become "lack of remorse"; similarly, "I can't get you to discuss your feelings with me when I invade your privacy" translates into "You can't have any feelings since you won't discuss them with me," *ergo,* "callousness." Other inferences can be drawn from personal reactions to the offense, or from perceptions of uncongeniality or uncooperativeness with authorities.

The situation is compounded by clinicians' role as gatekeepers in the delivery of mental health services. Because psychopathy is generally equated with untreatability, offenders that clinicians do not want to deal with can be turned away by adjudging them psychopathic, and hence unamenable to treatment. In other words, psychopathy is featured in what Vicky Agee (1979) has called the "diagnostic game"—the use of diagnoses to shuttle clients from one's own turf to other jurisdictions.[4] Psychopathy (or antisocial personality disorder) unsurprisingly becomes a salient diagnosis in the discharge summaries of hospitals who send patients back to prison after cursory review (Toch, 1982). Psychotic patients who are difficult to manage often come to carry dual diagnoses, despite provisions in DSM-IV that make this practice illegitimate. Cleckley (1982, p. 262) quotes Thompson, the author of one study:

> The administrative officers of penal institutions attempt to have such individuals transferred to mental hospitals because they believe them to be mentally ill. Knowing how little they can do for them and what difficult problems they are, the superintendents of mental hospitals attempt to get rid of them as soon as possible and transfer them back to the prison as "not psychotic." Pushed from prison to hospital and back again, wanted in neither, the psychopathic delinquent is essentially the orphan of both penology and psychiatry.

Evidence of subjectivity in diagnoses in forensic settings is provided by Gail Flint Stevens (1994) in a study of prison clinicians' use of the DSM-III diagnostic label. Stevens found that the point of the diagnosis, as far as the clinicians was concerned, was to raise a red flag about an inmate's clinical portrait. She writes:

> Respondents to the survey were asked what they hope to convey to other clinicians or staff about the inmates they diagnose as [having] antisocial personality [disorder]. Clini-

cians who were interviewed were asked the same question. The three most common responses of the respondents and the interviewees are that they hope to convey that the inmate is very difficult to treat, has very little regard for others resulting in continuous deviant behavior, and . . . [is very likely to] attempt to manipulate others to [the inmate's] own advantage. (p. 179)

Two-thirds of the clinicians in Stevens's study told her that they used the diagnosis of antisocial personality disorder in more than half of their diagnosable cases, and opined "that the diagnosis could be used in these percentages with the entire inmate population" (p. 182). Assuming such prevalence, the diagnosis is no longer a clinical description, but instead becomes a prescriptive message to others. In the words of Stevens (1994),

Perhaps most disturbingly, the diagnosis antisocial personality is given mainly to convey to others supposedly negative characteristics of inmates so diagnosed and not in the hopes of possible treatment or understanding of the diagnosis. . . . The criminal justice system has already designated [these inmates as] offenders, and, therefore, another label indicating essentially the same thing seems unnecessary. . . . The person so designated is generally considered not only a serious, violent criminal, but also someone who is fated to continue a life of criminal behavior and hopelessness. (pp. 183–184)

The Stevens study illustrates the observation that psychopathy is a label used by clinicians to distinguish run-of-the-mill offenders from offenders considered serious, obdurate, and refractory to treatment. In the process, the latter offenders are also sharply differentiated from most nonoffenders. The premise is that the offenders exhibit a distinct set of personality traits (or characterological deficits) that predispose them toward long-term criminality. This personality structure makes the offender more "bad" (morally reprehensible) than other offenders and all nonoffenders—the obverse of the distinction implied when the psychopathy construct was invented.

No other diagnostic category has the attribute of being a nonpathological condition deemed to *enhance* culpability, and this makes it reasonable to "consider whether psychopathy could ever be posited within a traditional psychiatric–medical framework . . . and whether a more flexible and accurate formulation than is possible in terms of either medicine or law may be provided by viewing it as an ethical category" (Holmes, 1991, p. 81). To see psychopathy in this way would mean that the clinician who writes about a patient, "This man is a psychopath," could admit that he or she was actually saying, "I think this individual is morally reprehensible, untrustworthy, and dangerous, which is not my area of expertise." The disclaimer would be an act of rare and disarming honesty, and a refreshing change from the status quo.

PSYCHOPATHIC PERSONALITY AND PATHOLOGY

During the early days of psychiatry, the hypothesis was entertained that offenders in general were mostly disturbed. Later, criminological science made the pathologizing of crime unfashionable as well as implausible, and crime became largely the purview of sociologists. With the acceptance of psychopathy as a construct, psychopathy experts claimed to have identified a category of psychologically predisposed offenders; but ironically, as mental health professionals, they disclaimed any jurisdiction over the offenders.

With the advent of psychopathy, in fact, the need for mental health services appeared reduced. Once offenders were diagnosed as psychopaths, their conventional mental health problems (such as depression, anxiety, or psychotic symptoms) could be downgraded or dismissed. Psychopaths by definition were manipulators, and anything they said about themselves was presumptively a means to some self-serving (and usually nefarious) end. This perception dovetailed with the desire of ambitious offenders to be seen as pragmatic, level-headed, devoid of feeling, free of anxiety, aloof, self-sufficient, and goal-oriented. Many such offenders, when in the depth of despair, have tended to present dismissively casual and superficial accounts of their problems. Serious crises, including suicide attempts and self-injuries, have routinely inspired such explanations as "I want to be transferred" or "I wanted attention," making it difficult to discover the depth of the individuals' suffering or the occasions for it (Toch, 1992a). In such instances, a clinician could easily classify the offenders as calculating malingerers desirous of improving their condition with the assistance of overly sympathetic (and naive) staff members.

When psychopathy was used with other diagnoses it tended to overshadow the latter, especially in the minds of practitioners who had limited time and resources. Given choice, ameliorative ministrations were more likely to be directed at patients whose self-reports were deemed reliable, who would not abuse trust or show ingratitude, and who might rapidly improve.

MYTH AND REALITY

Psychopathy has unquestionably benefited from the fact that it is "a clinical construct whose time has come" (Hare, 1996). Prevailing safety concerns among members of the public ensured influence for any model that sharpened the borders and enhanced the contrasts between offenders and nonoffenders. There was and is a political market for a designation that highlights criminal recidivism, dangerousness, and unresponsiveness to intervention. High-risk assessments simplify the question of what to do with the offender, and provide security to the public that is relieved of the offender's presence.

The name of the game is *incapacitation*. In the past, the goal of incapacitation had been a side benefit of other objectives. For example, in corrections, offenders were incapacitated as a corollary of being punished. The assumption was that punishment must be fairly and squarely arrived at, for offenses of which the offenders had been convicted. (People were to be punished for what they had *done*, not for what they might or might not do.) A similar principle applied to hospitals, where incapacitation was a requisite of treatment. People could be committed against their will (i.e., incapacitated) if they needed treatment for a disease that made them dangerous. They were committed to hospitals because hospitals are staffed by experts in curing diseases. If the persons did not suffer from a condition that hospital staff members could address, it was assumed that there would be no point in sending them to a hospital. Mental health settings were not considered either storage depots or places of preventive detention. They were not created for healthy persons who struck others as reprehensible and alarming, nor for prisoners whom others wanted to keep confined beyond the terms of their sentence. Such were the assumptions that the psychopathy advocates implicitly questioned, and legislators and the courts have to date backed and supported them.

One reason the public and the system have found the psychopathy construct attractive is because if its plausibility. Psychopathic personality traits (callousness, lack of remorse, promiscuous destructiveness) seemed to describe the perpetrators featured in publicized offenses. And the offenders committing the offenses seemed to be getting younger. Their life histories—the early inception of their delinquency, their violence, and its extreme chronicity—were clearly those of prototypical psychopaths, as described in the literature.

But the psychopathy literature evenhandedly stigmatized almost any offender (or type of offender) about whom there was concern or trepidation. Early on, there was the "sexual psychopath," who is now being reinvented as the "sexually violent predator" (Morier, 1996).[5] Drug abuse offenders have consistently been described as overwhelmingly psychopathic or antisocial. Serial murderers have been perennial candidates for "psychopaths of the year." The following is a typical nomination for membership that could have captured the attention of Philippe Pinel:

> Few of them can be said to be driven by delusions or hallucinations; almost none of them talks to demons or hears strange voices in empty rooms. Though their crimes may be sickening, they are not sick in either a medical or a legal sense. Instead, the serial killer is typically a sociopathic personality who lacks internal control—guilt or conscience—to guide his own behavior, but has an excessive need to control and dominate others. He definitely knows right from wrong, definitely realizes he had committed a sinful act, but simply doesn't care about his human prey. The sociopath has never internalized a moral code that prohibits murder. Having fun is all that counts. (Levin & Fox, 1985, pp. 229–230)

Though persons demonstrating constellations of traits subsumed under the psychopathy construct unquestionably exist, too many persons exist under too many constellations of psychopathic traits, and groups of such persons may have little in common with each other. Predatory delinquents are infrequently glib or manipulative, and manipulators are rarely impulsive or predatory. Offenders described by the behavioral criteria in DSM-IV or the PCL-R overlap imperfectly with those manifesting personality traits. And chronic offenders—as Cleckley (1982) points out—are not what he originally had in mind in constructing his clinical profile.

Subcategorizations of psychopathy have been suggested (e.g., by Lykken, 1995), but have had narrow appeal. And viewing psychopathy as ordinal (rather than categorical) strikes some as the counterpart of degrees of pregnancy. The demand that psychopathy must meet is to help us draw distinctions between qualitatively different groups of offenders.

A third problem is the atheoretical nature of the psychopathy construct.[6] The literature that illuminates the attributes, perspectives, and traits of so-called psychopaths lies in studies of such subjects as social learning, psychological maturation, levels of cognitive and moral development, the sociology of delinquent subcultures, the psychoanalytic literature on the formation of egos and superegos,[7] and the criminological literature on violent delinquency. The psychopathy syndrome highlights personality traits, but does not enable us to understand them.

Lastly, though individuals who fit the designation of psychopathy are recognizably encountered in settings such as prisons and academia, the label rarely describes the core attributes of such persons once we get to know them.[8] I have myself been associated with prison inmates and violent offenders most of my working life (Toch, 1992b; Toch & Adams, 1994; Toch & Adams with Grant, 1989). I can testify as a conclusion to this chapter that I recall not a single instance in which my understanding of an offender I have known would have benefited from adjudging the person a psychopath.

NOTES

1. John Mortimer is president of the Howard League for Penal Reform. His mystery novels about "Rumpole of the Bailey" have won international acclaim and have been serialized on television.

2. Jerome Miller gained fame when as head of the juvenile justice system of Massachusetts he decarcerated and closed the state's reformatories, and returned their inmates to community supervision.

3. In the words of Melton and Pagliocca (1992),

> It is difficult to imagine a youth whose behavior is sufficiently objectionable to remain in the juvenile justice system who would not meet the DSM-IIIR criteria for conduct disorder . . . a thief who sometimes lies and initiates fights would fit the criteria. . . . Taking the point a step further, it is difficult to imagine that such a youth would not be classified as seriously emotionally disturbed [SED]. The National Institute on Mental Health criteria for classification as SED require only a diagnosable condition (e.g., conduct disorder), involvement in two or more service systems (e.g., education and juvenile justice), and evidence of persistent problems. Because the latter two criteria are generally satisfied by involvement in the juvenile justice system itself, the fact that most delinquent and status offending youth could be diagnosed as having a mental disorder means that virtually all youth who are more than transient clients of the juvenile justice system are SED. In short, the definitional criteria for conduct disorder and SED are such that the identification of emotionally disturbed youth in juvenile justice is virtually a search for a tautology! (pp. 109–110)

4. Agee (1979) writes:

> Many mental health professionals feel that the place for all character disorders is some sort of correctional setting. . . . This implication can be couched in very sophisticated mental-health-ese. . . . [The] differentiation can be carried to the absurd to the point that youths who act out or have behavior problems are excluded from treatment because they have no "underlying emotional disturbance"—which would presumably indicate that their behavior is more or less motivated by an empty organism, with no feelings or thought processes. (pp. 15–16)

5. A case recently before the U.S. Supreme Court reversed a lower court's decision striking down a Kansas law that permitted the commitment of "sexually violent predators" who had completed prison sentences. In its decision, the court held that "a finding of dangerousness, *standing alone,* is ordinarily not a sufficient ground upon which to justify indefinite involuntary commitment" (*Kansas v. Hendricks,* 61 CrL 2187, emphases added, here and below); however, "the precommitment requirement *of a 'mental abnormality' or 'personality disorder'* is consistent with the requirements of . . . statutes that we have upheld, in that it narrows the class of persons eligible for confinement to those who are unable to control their dangerousness" (61 CrL 2187). The Court also noted that "we have never held that the Constitution prevents a State from civilly detaining those *for whom no treatment is available,* but who nevertheless pose a danger to others" (61 CrL 2189).

In other words, Hendricks—the subject of the litigation—was to be indeterminately warehoused, suffering from the precise condition that had been described by Prichard and Pinel in the early 19th century, in the hope that it could be medically addressed.

6. This atheoretical focus is a relatively recent development, and was not characteristic of earlier works, such as that of McCord and McCord (1964). Postwar studies of psychopathy focused on bonding failure (e.g., Bowlby, 1952) and on the effects of affectless childhood (e.g., Jenkins, 1960; Bender, 1947). The most recent editions of the DSM avoid theory as a matter of policy; other current writings have resuscitated the "bad seed" emphasis of the moral insanity school by alluding to a variety of neurological dysfunctions that can modify the way individuals respond to their environments. Lykken (1995) has noted that "there seems to be an irresistible tendency for psychopatholo-

gists to assume that underlying every syndrome there must be a lesion, that there must be something qualitatively wrong with the psychopath's brain" (p. 155). Lykken has originated a theory of psychopathy (premised on the assumption that children who have a predisposition to fearlessness will be resistant to socialization), but reports that this theory "has not been taken seriously, even by researchers whose own findings have contributed to its empirical support" (p. 155)

7. Psychoanalysis is not congenial to all psychopathy experts. Lykken (1995), for instance, has confessed that "I do not attempt to characterize these theories further because I frankly do not understand them" (p. 186). To make the case, he quotes a passage containing the phrases "a predominate, archetypal identification with the stranger selfobject," "object fusions within the grandiose self-structure," and "primary narcissistic attachment to the grandiose self." Possibly less obscure might be the following excerpt:

> There is a wrinkle to the concept of "ego," which we have spared the reader, but must now mention. This wrinkle consists of the discovery that ego development—like a poorly directed army—can be disharmonious, that the ego can advance on one flank, while remaining firmly entrenched, or retreating, on another. The condition is one that is particularly apt to face us among delinquents, and it has practical consequences. . . . "Weak" ego components are areas where the delinquent needs help, but "strength" *translates into being skillful at being delinquent and showing ingenuity in resisting resocializing influences.*
>
> The ego's deficits are primarily vested in its control system. This faces us with unchecked impulsivity, low boiling points, impatient, urgent hereness and nowness, anxiety, and helplessness. The "strong" ego, however, locates temptations, enlists delinquent allies, finds alibis and excuses, manipulates, bullies, cajoles. It is this "subcompartment"—the "delinquent ego"—which "tests" us, "cons" us, fights, defies, circumvents, and *attempts to sustain the "weak" ego's pattern of impulsivity.* In resocialization we must "reach" the offender's "weak" ego, we must buttress and cement his control system, without having the delinquent ego "reach" us by posing tasks for us which, *given our own ego deficits,* we sometimes fail. (Redl & Toch, 1979, pp. 193–194; emphasis added).

8. I would venture to uncloak a prediction of my own. Ask any large sample of forensic clinicians to respond to items such as "In working with offenders, I try to relate to them closely and intimately," "I try to understand offenders who I work with by perceiving the world as they do," or "I enjoy relaxed and scintillating conversations with offenders," and I believe that emphatic negative responses to these items would be correlated with a propensity to classify offenders as psychopaths. The converse would presumably hold as well.

REFERENCES

Agee, V. L. (1979). *Treatment of the violent incorrigible adolescent.* Lexington, MA: D.C. Heath.

American Psychiatric Association. (1994). *Diagnostic and statistical manual of mental disorders* (4th ed.). Washington, DC: Author.

Bender, L. (1947). Psychopathic behavior disorders in children. In R. Linder & R. Seliger (Eds.), *Handbook of correctional psychology.* New York: Philosophical Library.

Billington, R. (1996, Spring). If you were Home Secretary: Interview with John Mortimer. *Inside Time,* p. 10.

Bowlby, J. (1952). *Maternal care and mental health.* Geneva: World Health Organization.

Cleckley, H. (1982). *The mask of sanity* (7th ed.). St. Louis, MO: C. V. Mosby.

Hare, R. D. (1991). *The Hare Psychopathy Checklist—Revised.* Toronto: Multi-Health Systems.

Hare, R. D. (1996). Psychopathy: A clinical construct whose time has come. *Criminal Justice and Behavior, 23,* 25–54.

Holmes, C. A. (1991). Psychopathic disorder: A category mistake? *Journal of Medical Ethics, 17,* 77–85.

Jenkins, R. L. (1960). The psychopathic or antisocial personality. *Journal of Nervous and Mental Disease, 131,* 318–334.

Kansas v. Hendricks, 117 S. Ct. 2072 (1997).

Krafft-Ebing, R. von. (1904). *Textbook of insanity* (C. G. Chaddock, Trans.). Philadelphia: F. A. Davis.

Levin, J., & Fox, J. A. (1985). *Mass murder: America's growing menace.* New York: Plenum Press.

Lykken, D. T. (1995). *The antisocial personalities.* Hillsdale, NJ: Erlbaum.

Maudsley, H. (1977). *Responsibility in mental disease.* University Publications of America. (Original revised work published 1897)

McCord, W., & McCord, J. (1964). *The psychopath: An essay on the criminal mind.* Princeton, NJ: Van Nostrand.

Melton, G. B., & Pagliocca, P. M. (1992). Treatment in the juvenile justice system: Directions for policy and practice. In J. J. Cocozza (Ed.), *Responding to the mental health needs of youth in the juvenile justice system.* Seattle, WA: National Coalition for the Mentally Ill in the Juvenile Justice System.

Miller, J. G. (1991). *Last one over the wall.* Columbus, OH: Ohio State University Press.

Morier, D. (1996, August). What treatment for sex offenders? *APA Monitor,* p. 28.

Pinel, P. (1977). *A treatise on insanity.* Bethesda, MD: University Publications of America. (Original work published 1801)

Prichard, J. C. (1973). *A treatise on insanity and other disorders affecting the mind.* New York: Arno Press. (Original work published 1837)

Redl, F., & Toch, H. (1979). The psychoanalytic perspective. In H. Toch (Ed.), *Psychology of crime and criminal justice.* New York: Holt, Rinehart & Winston.

Robins, L. N. (1978). Aetiological implications in studies of childhood histories relating to antisocial personality. In R. D. Hare & D. Schalling (Eds.), *Psychopathic behavior: Approaches to research.* Chichester, England: Wiley.

Rush, B. (1962). *Medical inquiries and observations upon the diseases of the mind.* New York: New York Academy of Medicine/Hafner. (Original work published 1812)

Stevens, G. F. (1994). Prison clinicians' perceptions of antisocial personality disorder as a formal diagnosis. *Journal of Offender Rehabilitation, 20,* 159–185.

Toch, H. (1982). The disturbed disruptive inmate: Where does the bus stop? *Journal of Psychiatry and Law, 10,* 327–349.

Toch, H. (1992a). *Mosaic of despair: Human breakdowns in prison.* Washington, DC: American Psychological Association.

Toch, H. (1992b). *Violent men: An inquiry into the psychology of violence.* Washington, DC: American Psychological Association.

Toch, H., & Adams, K. (1994). *The disturbed violent offender.* Washington, DC: American Psychological Association.

Toch, H., & Adams, K., with Grant, J. D. (1989). *Coping: Maladaptation in prisons.* New Brunswick, NJ: Transaction.

Webster's ninth new collegiate dictionary. (1983). Springfield, MA: Merriam-Webster.

II

TYPOLOGIES

10

Ten Subtypes of Psychopathy

THEODORE MILLON
ROGER D. DAVIS

As the chapters of this book will attest, psychopaths have been described as having a parade of characteristics. Some observers see psychopaths as impulsive, immature, naive, aimless, and flighty; others view them as sly, cunning, and well educated, capable of clever long-range plans that deceive and exploit others. On the one hand, psychopaths have commonly been noted for their cruel aggressiveness and for the keen pleasures they derive from disrupting and intimidating others; on the other, these individuals are sometimes pictured as lacking in hostile intentions and are believed to experience extreme discomfort when their actions prove harmful or upsetting to others.

Such diametrically opposed conceptions stem in part from a failure to recognize that psychopathic behaviors spring from appreciably different personality patterns. That is, social deviation may arise as a consequence of fundamentally different styles of life—each of which may lead, however, to similar repugnant actions. In this chapter, we will differentiate the disorder into the several personality subtypes that we believe lie at its foundations. To highlight these different pathways to psychopathy, we will describe 10 variants of this disorder, each of which is found primarily in one or another of the DSM's, ICD's, and other systems' personality disorders. We believe that these types account for the great majority of those currently classified as psychopathic. Since we are concerned with differentiating subtypes, our focus is on discriminant characteristics. However, all psychopaths exhibit certain commonalities, notably a marked self-centeredness and disdain for the needs of others. In addition to this central core, they often display in common several subsidiary features that make differential diagnoses extremely difficult. Nevertheless, it is instructive for pedagogical purposes to highlight their more discriminable clinical characteristics and personality backgrounds.

THE UNPRINCIPLED PSYCHOPATH

The unprincipled psychopath is seen most frequently in conjunction with narcissistic personality patterns. These individuals are often successful in keeping their activities just within the boundaries of the law, and infrequently enter into clinical treatment.

These psychopaths exhibit an arrogant sense of self-worth, an indifference to the welfare of others, and a fraudulent social manner. There is a desire to exploit others, or at least to expect special recognitions and considerations without assuming reciprocal responsibilities. A deficient social conscience is evident in the tendency to flout conventions, to engage in actions that raise questions of personal integrity, and to disregard the rights of others. Achievement deficits and social irresponsibilities are justified by expansive fantasies and frank prevarications. Descriptively, we may characterize this psychopath as devoid of a superego—that is, as evidencing an unscrupulous, amoral, and deceptive approach to relationships with others. More than merely disloyal and exploitive, these psychopaths may be found among society's con artists and charlatans, many of whom are vindictive toward and contemptuous of their victims.

The unprincipled psychopath often evidences a rash willingness to risk harm and is usually fearless in the face of threats and punitive action. Malicious tendencies are projected outward, precipitating frequent personal and family difficulties, as well as occasional legal entanglements. Vengeful gratification is often obtained by humiliating others. These narcissistic psychopaths operate as if they have no principles other than exploiting others for their personal gain. Lacking a genuine sense of guilt and possessing little social conscience, they are opportunists who enjoy the process of swindling others, outwitting them in a game they enjoy playing, in which others are held in contempt because of the ease with which they can be seduced. Relationships survive only as long as this type of psychopath has something to gain. People are dropped with no thought to the anguish they may experience as a consequence of the psychopath's irresponsible behaviors.

These psychopaths display an indifference to truth that, if brought to their attention, is likely to elicit an attitude of nonchalant indifference. They are skillful in the ways of social influence, are capable of feigning an air of justified innocence, and are adept in deceiving others with charm and glibness. Lacking any deep feelings of loyalty, they may successfully scheme beneath a veneer of politeness and civility. Their principal orientation is that of outwitting others—"Do unto others before they do unto you." A number of these psychopaths attempt to present an image of cool strength, acting arrogant and fearless. To prove their courage, they may invite danger and punishment. But punishment only verifies their unconscious recognition that they probably deserve to be punished for their unprincipled behaviors. Rather than having a deterrent effect, it only reinforces their exploitive behaviors.

In many ways, the unprincipled psychopath is similar to the disingenuous psychopath, to whom we will turn next. They share a devious and guileful style, plotting and scheming in their calculations to manipulate others. However, the disingenuous psychopath, a variant of the histrionic personality, continues to pursue a strong need for attention and approval—characteristics not present in the unprincipled psychopath, who exhibits a basic self-centeredness and an indifference to the attitudes and reactions of others. Unprincipled psychopaths prey on the weak and vulnerable, enjoying their dismay and anger; disingenuous psychopaths, by contrast, seek to hold the respect and affection of those they put aside in their pursuit of new sources of love and admiration.

THE DISINGENUOUS PSYCHOPATH

The disingenuous psychopath's behavior is typified by a veneer of friendliness and sociability. Although making a superficially good impression upon acquaintances, this psychopath frequently shows a more characteristic unreliability, impulsive tendencies, and deep resentments and moodiness among family members and other close associates. A socially facile lifestyle may include persistent seeking of attention and excitement, often expressed in seductive behaviors. Relationships are shallow and fleeting, frequently disrupted by caustic comments and impulses that are acted upon with insufficient deliberation—characteristics typically found among histrionic personalities, which the disingenuous psychopath most resembles.

Others often see this subtype as irresponsible and undependable, exhibiting short-lived enthusiasms and immature stimulus-seeking behaviors. Notable also among these disingenuous psychopaths are tendencies to be contriving and plotting; to exhibit a crafty and scheming approach to life; and to be insincere, calculating, and deceitful. Not likely to admit responsibility for personal or family difficulties, this psychopath manifests a cleverly defensive denial of psychological tensions or conflicts. Interpersonal difficulties are rationalized, and blame is projected upon others. Although self-indulgent and insistent on attention, the disingenuous type provides others with erratic loyalty and reciprocal affection.

A flagrant deceitfulness is a principal prototypal characteristic of this variant of psychopathy. These individuals are more willful and insincere in their relationships, doing everything necessary to obtain what they need and want from others. Moreover, and in contrast to other psychopaths, they seem to enjoy seductive play, gaining gratification in the excitement and tension thus engendered. Often they are calculating and guileful when someone else has what they covet, be it the attention of a person or some tangible possession. Developmentally, their need for the approval of others gradually erodes over time, and is replaced by the means used to achieve approval. In the end, only a manipulative and cunning style remains.

The deceitfulness of the disingenuous psychopath is extended to the self. The attention and commendation of others are always perceived as consequences of the psychopath's own plotting and scheming behaviors; rarely are they seen as expressions of unconditional regard. Beneath the surface, such psychopaths' greatest fear is that no one will care for or love them unless they are made to do so. Despite this recognition, they attempt to persuade themselves that their intentions are basically good, and that their insincerely motivated scheming is appreciated for its intrinsic worth. Throughout these mixed internal messages, nevertheless, the disingenuous psychopaths persist in seeking what is most important to themselves, always angling and maneuvering to acquire it. These psychopaths are no less self-deceptive about their motives than they are about those whom they deceive.

Although their weak points are usually concealed through veils of deceitfulness, disingenuous persons are often fearful that others may see them as indecisive or soft-hearted. When mildly crossed, subject to minor pressures, or faced with potential embarrassment, these psychopaths may be quickly provoked to anger, often expressed in a revengeful or vindictive way. The air of superficial affability is extremely precarious, and they are ready to depreciate anyone whose attitudes touch a sensitive theme. When the thin veneer of sociability is eroded, there may be momentary upsurges of abuse and rage, although these are infrequent.

THE RISK-TAKING PSYCHOPATH

The next type of psychopath often engages in risk taking for itself—for the excitement it provides, and for the sense of feeling alive and involved in life, rather than for such purposes as material gain or defense of reputation. Many individuals respond before thinking, act impulsively, and behave in an unreflective and uncontrolled manner. Beyond such simple impulsiveness, however, the risk-taking psychopaths are in addition substantially fearless, unblanched by events that most people experience as dangerous or frightening. Practiced to this degree, their venturesomeness seems foolhardy, not courageous; they appear blind to the potential consequences of serious physical harm. Unwilling to give up their need for autonomy and independence, lacking habits of self-discipline, and unsure that they can ever achieve or fulfill the emptiness they feel within themselves in the real world, they are tempted to prove themselves against new and exciting ventures, traveling on a hyperactive and erratic course of hazardous activity. Descriptively, we may characterize these psychopaths as being dauntless, intrepid, bold, and audacious. Thus, this subtype represents an admixture or commingling of both antisocial and histrionic personality features.

In contrast to many psychopaths, whose basic motivations are largely aggrandizement and revenge, these individuals are driven by the need for excitement and stimulation, for adventures that are intrinsically treacherous. They are, in effect, thrill seekers, easily infatuated by opportunities to prove their mettle or open their possibilities. The factors that make them psychopathic are the undependability and irresponsibility of their actions, and their disdain for the effects of their behaviors on others as they pursue a restless chase to fulfill one capricious whim after another.

THE COVETOUS PSYCHOPATH

In the covetous psychopath, we see in its most distilled form an essential feature of the DSM's antisocial personality disorder and the ICD's dyssocial personality disorder: aggrandizement. These individuals feel that life has not "given them their due"; that they have been deprived of their rightful level of love, support, or material rewards; that others have received more than their share; and that they personally never were given the bounties of the good life. Thus, they are driven by envy and a desire for retribution—a wish to take back what they have been deprived of by destiny. Through acts of theft or destruction, they compensate themselves for the emptiness of their own lives, dismissing with smug entitlement their violations of the social order. They act on the rationalization that they alone must restore the karmic imbalance with which life has burdened them.

For those who are merely somewhat resentful, and for whom some conscious controls remain intact, small transgressions and petty acquisitions often suffice to blunt the expression of more extreme characteristics. For the more severely disordered, however, the usurpation of others' earned achievements and possessions becomes the highest reward. Here, the pleasure lies in taking rather than in having. Like hungry animals pursuing prey, covetous psychopaths have an enormous drive, a rapaciousness. They manipulate others and treat them as pawns in their power games. Although they have little compassion for the effects of their behaviors, feeling little or no guilt for their actions, they remain at heart quite insecure about their power and their possessions; they never feel that enough has been acquired to make up for earlier deprivations. Regardless of their achievements, they remain ever jealous and envious, pushy and greedy, presenting ostentatious displays of materialism and conspicuous consumption. For the most part, they are completely self-centered and self-indulgent, often profligate and wasteful, unwilling to share with others for fear that they will take again what was so desperately desired in early life. Hence, such psychopaths never achieve a deep sense of contentment. They feel unfulfilled, empty, and forlorn, regardless of their successes, and remain forever dissatisfied and insatiable. Believing they will continue to be deprived, these psychopaths show minimal empathy for those who are exploited and deceived. Some may become successful entrepreneurs, exploiters of others as objects to satisfy their desires.

Although similar in certain central characteristics to the unprincipled psychopathic personality, the covetous variant manifests a smug or justified, rather than benign, entitlement. Here an active exploitiveness, manifested through greed and the appropriation of others' possessions, becomes a central motivating force. The narcissistic psychopaths feel a sense of intrinsic superiority, of being more than others. The covetous psychopaths, however, experience not only a deep and pervasive sense of emptiness—a powerful hunger for the love and recognition not received early in life—but also an insecurity that they perhaps really are intrinsically less than others, somehow deserving of life's marginal dispensations.

THE SPINELESS PSYCHOPATH

Some psychopaths are habitually powerful and vicious tormentors of others. The explosive type (described next) acts in this manner periodically, and then is troubled and contrite about the conscionability of such irrational actions. In contrast, another variant is deeply insecure and irresolute, perhaps even faint-hearted and cowardly. Psychopathic aggression in this variant represents a paradoxical response to felt dangers and fears, intended to show persecutors that one is *not* anxious or weak, and will *not* succumb to external pressure or coercion. In our typology, such craven and cowardly individuals are spineless psychopaths. These personalities commit violent acts as a means of overcoming fearfulness and of securing refuge. For them, aggression is not intrinsically rewarding, but is instead essentially a counterphobic act. Anticipating real danger, projecting hostile fantasies, spineless types feel it is best to strike first, hoping thereby to forestall their antagonists.

The dynamics of the spineless psychopath are derivative of the avoidant and dependent personalities. Here, others are fantasized as powerful, aggressive, sadistic enemies. In contrast, the self is viewed as a precariously and helplessly undefended target. Experiencing panic, spineless psychopaths seek to head off inevitable annihilation by engaging in the very acts most deeply feared as a form of preemptive attack. By public and strong display of the opposite of their deep fear, they present a facade of formidable strength. Their behavior is counterphobic, as noted above, and as the analysts have pointed out so clearly. Not only does this mechanism serve to enable them to master their personal fears, but it serves to divert and impress the public by a false sense of confidence and self-assurance. Some turn inward as soon as the invaders have been repelled. In others, however, we see the publicly swaggering spineless type, a belligerent and intimidating variant; these individuals want the world to know that they "cannot be pushed around." As with many other psychopaths, public aggressiveness is not a sign of genuine confidence and personal strength, but a desperate means to try to *feel* superior and self-assured. Neither naturally mean-spirited nor intrinsically violent, these spineless variants become caricatures of swaggering "tough guys" and petty tyrants.

Many spineless psychopaths join militaristic groups that search for a shared scapegoat—a people or ethnic population that has been "sanctioned to hate," or so-called "outsiders" of all varieties, who invariably embody the very weaknesses that these psychopaths feel within themselves. In a perverse twist of psychic logic, these psychopaths assault their scapegoats in order to destroy the very elements within themselves that they wish and seek to deny. Throughout history, these individuals have often banded together to become the "executioners" of totalitarian power structures: the inquisitors of the medieval Catholic Church, the slavedrivers of the American South, the brownshirts of Nazi Germany, and the bureaucrats of Soviet Communism, to name just a few examples.

THE EXPLOSIVE PSYCHOPATH

The explosive psychopath is differentiated from other psychopathic variants by the unpredictable and sudden emergence of hostility. These "adult tantrums," characterized by uncontrollable rage and fearsome attacks upon others, occur frequently against members of the psychopath's own family.

Such explosive behavior erupts precipitously, before its intensive nature can be identified and constrained. Feeling thwarted or threatened, these psychopaths respond in a volatile and hurtful way, bewildering others by the abrupt change that has overtaken them, saying unforgivable things, striking unforgettable blows. As with children, tantrums are instantaneous reactions to cope with frustration or fear. Although the explosive behavior is often effective in intimidating others into silence or passivity, it is not primarily an instrumental act, but rather an outburst that serves to discharge pent-up feelings of humiliation and degradation.

Disappointed and feeling frustrated in life, these persons lose control and seek revenge for the mistreatment and deprecation to which they feel subjected. In contrast to other psychopaths, explosive individuals do not move about in a surly and truculent manner. Rather, their rages burst out uncontrollably, often with no apparent provocation. In periods of explosive rage, they may unleash a torrent of abuse and storm about defiantly, cursing and voicing bitter contempt for all. This quality of sudden and irrational belligerence, as well as the frenzied lashing out, distinguishes these psychopathics from the other subtypes. Many are hypersensitive to feelings of betrayal or may be deeply frustrated by the futility and hopelessness of their lives.

When explosive psychopaths are faced with repeated failures, humiliations, and frustrations, their limited controls may be quickly overrun by deeply felt and undischarged resentments. Once released, the fury of the moment draws upon memories and emotions of the past that surge unrestrained to the surface, breaking out into a wild, irrational, and uncontrollable rage. From the preceding descriptions, it would not be unreasonable to hypothesize that explosive psychopaths possess beneath their surface controls a pattern similar to that of individuals described as "sadistic borderlines." Usually under control, but lacking the cohesion of psychic structure to maintain controls across all situations, these individuals periodically erupt with precipitous and vindictive behaviors that signify their psychopathic style.

Whether justified or not, certain persons come to symbolize for explosive psychopaths the sense of frustration and hopelessness that sparks their explosive reactions. As the psychopaths see it, these symbolic figures must be obliterated. Many such psychopaths have established "safe partners" for abuse—individuals who have come to symbolize their failures and frustrations, who "know" their inadequacies. The mere presence of these symbolic individuals stirs deep feelings of failure and reminds them of the ways life has violated their hopes and their integrity. Because they are unable to resolve the real sources of their resentment and frustration, they come to feel that these symbols of futility and hopelessness must be removed from the scene. Confronted by their inadequacies, explosive psychopaths may be provoked into panic and blind rage. The resulting violence is a desperate, lashing-out act against symbols rather than reality.

When physical assaults are directed against persons other than safe partners, they are often the product of verbally unskilled psychopaths' seeking to terminate altercations in which they feel incapable of responding effectively. Unable to verbalize what they feel and why, feeling outmaneuvered and humiliated, the psychopaths respond in the only way possible to remove the irritation. Thus impotence and personal failure become the source of these aggressive acts, which serve to release accumulated tensions. Because these explosive psychopaths may be provoked by otherwise innocuous interactions, their victims often seem rather incidental and arbitrarily selected. The explosions are not so much a social response as an emotional release.

THE ABRASIVE PSYCHOPATH

In contrast to other psychopaths, who exhibit a struggle between doing the bidding of others and expressing their frustrations in a passive and indirect manner, the abrasive psychopath acts in an overtly and directly contentious and quarrelsome way. To the abrasive psychopath, everything and everyone is an object available for nagging and assaulting, a sounding board for discharging inner irritabilities, or even a target for litigious action. More than merely angry in a general way, these persons are intentionally abrasive and antagonistic. Abrasive psychopaths have incessant discords with others, magnifying every minor friction into repeated and bitter struggles. They may have few qualms and little conscience or remorse about demeaning even their most intimate associates. The following adjectives may be used to characterize this abrasive type: contentious, intransigent, fractious, irritable, caustic, debasing, quarrelsome, acrimonious, and corrosive. Not surprisingly, many exhibit features usually associated with the negativistic and paranoid personality disorders.

Some abrasive psychopaths insist that their quarrelsomeness is dedicated to certain high principles; though a kernel of truth may be found in their beliefs, these higher principles invariably correspond to positions they themselves hold. Others are unquestionably wrong, and they are unquestionably right. Fault-finding and dogmatic, these psychopaths achieve special delight in contradicting others. They take less pleasure in the legitimacy and logic of their reasoning than in its use to frustrate and undermine their opponents.

Not surprisingly, the behavior of the abrasive personality resembles that of adolescents who, seeking to establish their separateness and individuality, act in ways that clearly oppose their parents. Thus, the children of deeply committed conservatives will favor highly liberal or socialistic values, whereas those of liberal parents may adopt intensely conservative points of view. But the rebellion of adolescents against parental customs and standards is usually time-limited—a stage of development in which strategies of self-assertion are appropriate. Once a sense of independence is achieved, oppositional teenagers are likely to drop this style of behavior, often reverting to the very customs previously opposed. In contrast, the hostile and opposing manner of abrasive psychopaths is part of the core of their being. Their knack of belittling and denigrating anyone in the name of whatever principle they happen to espouse is well rehearsed and persistent. Criticism of others as "good for them" may even be viewed as an essential corrective mechanism. Believing that they take no personal satisfaction in telling people off or in having ulterior motives for doing so, these individuals feel unconstrained, free to say and do anything they please "to set people right."

Those with whom abrasive psychopaths relate know their pretensions of principled behavior to be but a thin veneer. Faced with any opposition, especially from persons they consider of lesser stature than themselves, these persons spew forth bitter complaints of how they are utterly unappreciated and ill treated. Anything personal they have done to others does not really reflect their character, but is merely a justified reaction to the uncaring treatment to which they have been exposed. Thus, they are justified in what they say and do, with no qualms of conscience or remorse for having acted in the most obnoxious way. As the argument is joined, the deeper origins of their personality style are perpetually reactivated and refueled.

THE MALEVOLENT PSYCHOPATH

The malevolent subtype is one of the least attractive of the psychopathic variants. These individuals are particularly vindictive and hostile; their retributive impulses are discharged in a hateful and destructive defiance of conventional social life. Distrustful of others and anticipating betrayal and punishment, they have acquired a cold-blooded ruthlessness, an intense desire to gain revenge for the real or imagined mistreatment to which they were subjected in childhood. Here we see a sweeping rejection of tender emotions and a deep suspicion that others' efforts at goodwill are merely ploys to deceive and undo them. They may assume a chip-on-the-shoulder attitude, a readiness to lash out at those whom they wish to destroy or can use as scapegoats for their revengeful impulses. Many are fearless and guiltless, inclined to anticipate and search out betrayal and punitiveness on the part of others. The primary psychopathic characteristics of these individuals blend with those of the sadistic or paranoid personality (or both), reflecting not only a deep sense of deprivation and a desire for compensatory retribution, but also an intense suspiciousness and hostility. Many murderers and serial killers fit this psychopathic pattern. Such persons might be described as belligerent, mordant, rancorous, vicious, malignant, brutal, callous, truculent, and vengeful.

To "prove" their courage, malevolent psychopaths may even court punishment. Rather than serving as a deterrent, however, punishment often reinforces their desire for retribution. In positions of power, they often brutalize others to confirm their self-image of strength. If they are faced with persistent failure, beaten down in efforts to dominate and control others, or finding aspirations far outdistancing their luck, their feelings of frustration, resentment, and anger mount to a point where their controls give way to raw brutality or secretive acts of vengeful hostility. Spurred by repeated rejection and driven by an increasing need for retribution, aggressive impulses will surge into the open. At these times, the psychopaths' behaviors may become outrageously and flagrantly antisocial. Not only do they show minimal guilt or remorse for their violent acts, but they may instead display an arrogant contempt for the rights of the others.

What distinguishes malevolent psychopaths is their capacity to understand guilt and remorse, if not necessarily to experience it. Although they are capable of giving a perfectly rational explanation of ethical concepts—that is, they know the difference between right and wrong—they seem nevertheless incapable of feeling it. These psychopaths often relish menacing others, making them cower and withdraw. They are combative and seek to bring more pressure upon their opponents than their opponents are willing to tolerate or to bring against them. Most make few concessions and are inclined to escalate as far as necessary, never letting go until others succumb. In contrast to other subtypes, however, malevolent psychopaths recognize the limits of what can be done in their own self-interest. They do not lose self-conscious awareness of their actions, and press forward only if their goals of retribution and destructiveness are likely to be achieved. Accordingly, their adversarial stance is somewhat contrived and works as a bluffing mechanism to ensure that others will back off. Infrequently, actions are taken that may lead to misjudgment and counterreaction in these matters.

THE TYRANNICAL PSYCHOPATH

Along with the malevolent type just described, the tyrannical psychopath stands among the most frightening and cruel of the psychopathic subtypes. Both relate to others in an attacking, intimidating, and overwhelming way; are frequently accusatory and abusive; and are almost invariably destructive.

Unlike the malevolent psychopaths, however, the tyrannical psychopaths seem to be stimulated by resistances or weaknesses, which encourage attack rather than deter it or slow it down. Some are crudely assaultive and distressingly vulgar, whereas others are physically restrained, but overwhelm their victims by unrelenting criticism and bitter tirades. This variant derives a special sense of satisfaction from forcing victims to cower and submit. Among those who are not physically brutal, we see verbally cutting and scathing commentaries that are both accusatory and demeaning. Many intentionally heighten and dramatize their surly, abusive, inhumane, and unmerciful behaviors. Although these individuals are in many respects the purest type of classical psychopaths, they do exhibit features of several personality disorders, most notably the DSM-III-R's sadistic and the DSM-IV's negativistic personality disorders.

Especially distinctive is this type of psychopath's desire and willingness to go out of the way to be unmerciful and inhumane. Often calculating and cool, tyrannical psychopaths are selective in their choice of victims, identifying individuals who are likely to submit rather than to react with counterviolence. Quite frequently, they display a disproportionate level of abusiveness and intimidation, in order to impress not only their victims but those who observe the psychopaths' unconstrained power. More than any other subtype, these individuals derive deep satisfaction in creating suffering and in seeing its effect on others. In contrast to the explosive psychopaths, for whom hostility serves primarily as a discharge of pent-up feelings, the tyrannical psychopaths employ violence instrumentally as a means to inspire terror and intimidation. These experiences then become the object of self-conscious reflection, providing the psychopaths with a sense of deep satisfaction. Many other subtypes, by contrast, have second thoughts and feel a measure of contrition about their actions.

Much of what drives tyrannical psychopaths is their fear that others may recognize their inner insecurities and low sense of self-esteem. To overcome these deeply felt inner weaknesses, they have learned that they can feel superior through overwhelming others by the force of their physical power and brutal vindictiveness.

THE MALIGNANT PSYCHOPATH

Malignant psychopaths represent structurally defective variants of the psychopathic pattern. Their features frequently blend with those of the paranoid personality disorder. They are characterized best by their autocratic power orientation and by their mistrust, resentment, and envy of others. Underlying these features is a ruthless desire to vindicate themselves for past wrongs by cunning revenge or callous force, if necessary.

In contrast to the other subtypes, the malignant psychopaths have found that their efforts to abuse and tyrannize others have only prompted the others to inflict more of the hostility and harsh punishment experienced in childhood. The psychopaths' strategy of arrogance and brutalization has backfired too often, and they now seek retribution, not as much through action as through fantasy. Isolated and resentful, they increasingly turn to themselves, to cogitate and mull over their fate. Left to their own ruminations, they begin to imagine a plot in which every facet of the environment plays a threatening and treacherous role. Moreover, through the intrapsychic mechanism of projection, they attribute their own venom to others, ascribing to them the malice and ill will they feel within themselves. As the line between objective antagonism and imagined hostility becomes thin, the belief takes hold that others are intentionally persecuting them. Not infrequently, persecutory delusions combine with delusions of grandeur; however, these latter beliefs play a secondary role among malignant psychopaths, in contrast to their primacy among fanatic paranoid personalities.

Preeminent among malignant psychopaths is their need to retain their independence and cling tenaciously to the belief in their own self-worth. The need to protect their autonomy and strength may be seen in the content of their persecutory delusions. Malevolence on the part of others is viewed as neither casual nor random; rather, it is seen as designed to intimidate, offend, and undermine the individuals' self-esteem. "They" are seeking to weaken the psychopaths' "will," to destroy their power, to spread lies, to thwart their talents, to control their thoughts, and to immobilize and subjugate them. These psychopaths dread losing their self-determination; their persecutory fantasies are filled with fears of being forced to submit to authority, of being made soft and pliant, and of being tricked to surrender their self-determination.

SUMMARY

In this chapter, we have described 10 psychopathic subtypes. Difficult as it may be to discriminate among several of these subtypes, we believe there is value, especially in this chaotic era, in attempting to distinguish the many varieties of those whose character and acts incline them to be antisocial, criminal, and violent. Note, however, that the number 10 is by no means special. The types have been synthesized inductively, through clinical observation and experience, clinical lore, and a reading of the research literature. Taxonomies may be put forward at levels that are more coarse or more fine-grained. Although other authors might have chosen 8, 9, or 11 types, we believe that those explicated herein are approximately comparable in their level of abstraction. Furthermore, we hope that by noting relationships between psychopathy and the personality patterns of the DSM, ICD, and other nosologies, we have made it clear that "psychopathic behavior" need not refer only to the classic psychopath of tradition, but may instead be broadened to include other clinically relevant and useful organizing principles.

11

Psychopathy and the Five-Factor Model of Personality

THOMAS A. WIDIGER
DONALD R. LYNAM

Personality disorders, including psychopathy, may represent extreme variants of common personality traits (Costa & Widiger, 1994). This hypothesis has been supported by studies that have indicated a close association of the dimensions of the five-factor model (FFM) of normal personality functioning with personality disorder symptomatology (Widiger & Costa, 1994). The purpose of this chapter is to indicate more precisely how the diagnosis and pathology of psychopathy can be understood from the perspective of the FFM. We begin with a brief description of the FFM and then discuss each of the features of psychopathy, the factor structure of the Hare Psychopathy Checklist—Revised (PCL-R; Hare, 1991), and alternative models of the pathology for psychopathy, from the perspective of the FFM.

THE FIVE-FACTOR MODEL OF PERSONALITY

The FFM consists of five broad domains of personality: (1) neuroticism (or negative affectivity); (2) extraversion (or positive affectivity); (3) openness to experience (or unconventionality); (4) antagonism versus agreeableness; and (5) conscientiousness (or constraint) (McCrae & Costa, 1990; Tellegen & Waller, in press). Each of these broad domains can be differentiated into underlying facets. Table 11.1 presents the facets identified by Costa and McCrae (1995). For example, facets of agreeableness (vs. antagonism) are trust (vs. mistrust, suspiciousness), modesty (vs. arrogance), altruism (vs. exploitation), compliance (vs. oppositionality, aggression), tender-mindedness (vs. tough-mindedness, low empathy), and straightforwardness (vs. deception, manipulation).

The FFM was developed on the basis of the compelling rationale that "those indi-

TABLE 11.1. Five-Factor Model (FFM) of Personality: Domains and Facets

Neuroticism

Anxiousness: fearful, apprehensive versus relaxed, unconcerned, cool
Angry hostility: bitter, angry versus even-tempered
Trait depression: pessimistic, glum, despondent versus optimistic
Self-consciousness: timid, embarrassed versus self-assured, glib, shameless
Impulsiveness: tempted, reckless versus controlled, restrained
Vulnerability: fragile, helpless versus stalwart, brave, fearless

Extraversion (vs. introversion)

Warmth: affectionate, attached versus cold, aloof, reserved, indifferent
Gregariousness: sociable, outgoing versus withdrawn, isolated
Assertiveness: enthusiastic, forceful versus unassuming, quiet, resigned
Activity: active, energetic, vigorous versus passive, lethargic
Excitement seeking: adventurous, rash versus cautious, monotonous, dull
Positive emotions: high-spirited versus placid, anhedonic

Openness (vs. closedness)

Fantasy: imaginative, dreamer, unrealistic versus practical, concrete
Aesthetic: aesthetic versus unaesthetic
Feelings: emotionally responsive, sensitive versus unresponsive, constricted
Actions: novelty-seeking, eccentric versus routine, habitual, stubborn
Ideas: curious, odd, peculiar, strange versus pragmatic, rigid
Values: broad-minded, tolerant versus traditional, dogmatic, biased

Agreeableness (vs. antagonism)

Trust: trusting, gullible versus skeptical, cynical, suspicious, paranoid
Straightforwardness: honest, confiding versus cunning, manipulative, deceptive
Altruism: giving, sacrificial versus selfish, stingy, greedy, exploitative
Compliance: cooperative, docile versus oppositional, combative, aggressive
Modesty: self-effacing, meek versus confident, boastful, arrogant
Tender-mindedness: concerned, compassionate, empathic versus callous,
    ruthless

Conscientiousness

Competence: efficient, perfectionistic versus lax, negligent
Order: organized, methodical, ordered versus haphazard, disorganized, sloppy
Dutifulness: dutiful, reliable, dependable, rigid versus casual, undependable
Achievement striving: purposeful, ambitious, workaholic versus aimless
Self-discipline: industrious, devoted, dogged versus negligent, hedonistic
Deliberation: reflective, thorough, ruminative versus careless, hasty

Note. The descriptions here are derived from Costa and McCrae (1992) and Tellegen and
Waller (in press).

vidual differences that are the most significant in the daily transactions of persons with each other will eventually become encoded into [this] language" (Goldberg, 1982, p. 204). The relative importance of a trait would be indicated by the number of terms that have been developed to describe its various nuances and range of expression, and the structure of the traits would be evident from the relationships among the terms. To the extent that a person is describing an important dimension of personality, it should then be evident within the FFM. Alternative models of personality, such as the interpersonal circumplex (McCrae & Costa, 1989), have indeed been consistently identified as subsets or constellations of FFM domains and facets (Digman, 1990; John, 1990).

FEATURES OF PSYCHOPATHY

Hare (1991) developed the PCL-R to assess the personality disorder of psychopathy as it was originally described by Cleckley (1941). The PCL-R includes 20 items. We discuss below how each of the constructs assessed by the PCL-R items relate conceptually to domains and facets of the Costa and McCrae (1995) FFM.

1. Glib and Superficial Charm

Glib and superficial charm is described by Hare (1991) as the tendency to be smooth, engaging, charming, slick, and verbally facile. This feature of psychopathy is essentially the absence of self-consciousness, one of the facets of FFM neuroticism (Costa & McCrae, 1995). The average person has a degree of self-consciousness and will be, at least to some extent, sensitive to ridicule, prone to embarrassment, socially anxious, awkward, or insecure (McCrae & Costa, 1990). As indicated by Lykken (1995), most persons lack psychopathic charm because they are "a little shy, a bit self-conscious, afraid to say the wrong thing, afraid to alienate, a little tongue-tied, inclined to get a bit rattled when it is [their] turn to say something" (p. 136). The psychopath, on the other hand, is extremely low in self-consciousness: "More than the average person, he is likely to seem free from social or emotional impediments, from the minor distortions, pecularities, and awkwardness so common even among the successful" (Cleckley, 1941, p. 205).

2. Grandiose Sense of Self-Worth

Hare (1991) describes the second feature of psychopathy as involving a grossly inflated view of one's abilities and self-worth. Persons with a grandiose sense of self-worth are characterized by the PCL-R as being self-assured, opinionated, and even cocky braggarts (Hare, 1991). This feature of PCL-R psychopathy is captured by the arrogance (vs. modesty) facet of FFM antagonism. Arrogant persons "believe they are superior people and may be considered conceited or arrogant by others" (Costa & McCrae, 1992, p. 18).

3. Need for Stimulation or Proneness to Boredom

Hare (1991) describes this third aspect of psychopathy as involving an excessive need for novel, thrilling, and exciting stimulation. It is nominally equivalent to the excitement seeking facet of FFM extraversion. FFM excitement seeking is the disposition to "crave excitement and stimulation" (Costa & McCrae, 1992, p. 17). The PCL-R likewise refers to taking chances and doing things that are exciting and risky (Hare, 1991).

However, the disposition to crave excitement and stimulation may at times provide only a secondary contribution to the occurrence of this PCL-R item, as more emphasis does appear to be given in the PCL-R description to facets of low conscientiousness, particularly the facet of low self-discipline. "By this [low self-discipline] we mean the ability to begin tasks and carry them through to completion despite boredom and other distractions" (Costa & McCrae, 1992, p. 18). Behavioral indicators of low self-discipline, rather than high excitement-seeking, are often used by Hare (1991) to assess PCL-R proneness to boredom, such as the failure to work at the same job for any length of time, or a failure to finish tasks that are considered to be routine or dull. The PCL-R assessment of this item emphasizes in particular an undependability, unreliability, lack of commitment, and laxness in the person's employment, training, work, and school record.

4. Pathological Lying

The PCL-R's pathological lying is represented explicitly within the FFM by the antagonism facet of manipulation/deceit (versus straightforwardness/honesty). Persons are distinguished in the FFM by the extent to which they are characteristically straightforward versus deceptive or dishonest (Costa & McCrae, 1995). Persons who are moderately low in straightforwardness will be shrewd, crafty, cunning, sly, and clever; persons who are at the most extreme variants of this disposition will be characteristically deceptive, deceitful, underhanded, unscrupulous, manipulative, and dishonest (Goldberg, 1990; John, 1990).

5. Conning and Manipulativeness

The fifth feature of PCL-R psychopathy relates closely to pathological lying, but it is concerned more specifically with the use of deceit and deception to cheat, con, or defraud persons for personal gain (Hare, 1991). As such, it is a combination of the FFM antagonism facets of deceit/manipulation and exploitation. Hare (1991) also indicates in his description of this item that the schemes and scams are often executed without any feelings or concerns for the victim. A lack of concern for the feelings and suffering of one's victims involves an additional antagonism facet of tough-mindedness (i.e., callous ruthlessness). Persons who are at the most extreme variants of the antagonism facets of deceitfulness, exploitation, and callousness would clearly display the PCL-R psychopathic feature of being conning and manipulative.

6. Lack of Remorse or Guilt

Hare (1991) also includes lack of feelings or concern for the losses, pain, and suffering of victims as a distinct PCL-R item. As noted above, lack of remorse or guilt is the most extreme variant of FFM antagonistic tough-mindedness, or the tendency to be unconcerned, dispassionate, coldhearted, and unempathic. Moderate levels of tough-mindedness would be characterized by the tendency to be "hardheaded and less moved by appeals to pity" (Costa & McCrae, 1992, p. 18), whereas the most extreme variant is the tendency to be characteristically contemptuous, callous, disdainful, and ruthless (Goldberg, 1990; John, 1990).

7. Shallow Affect

Shallow affect is the most difficult feature of PCL-R psychopathy to place within the FFM and, not coincidentally, it may also be the most difficult PCL-R item to understand and assess. If shallow affect is understood to be an emotional poverty or a limited range or depth of feelings (Hare, 1991, 1993), it is closely related to the FFM introversion facets of low positive emotionality and interpersonal coldness (vs. warmth, attachment). However, prototypical psychopathic persons lack other facets of introversion. They are not withdrawn or isolated, and may actually be quite gregarious. As indicated by the first

PCL-R item, they will be charming and engaging, and may have many friends. However, these "friendships" will lack warmth, intimacy, depth, or emotional closeness.

Shallow affect is also described by Hare (1991) in a manner that suggests a facet of antagonism: a callous indifference in the shallow manner in which the psychopathic person treats, relates to, and feels about others. In fact, Goldberg (1990) and John (1990) place interpersonal coldness (vs. warmth) within the domain of antagonism rather than introversion, and the Revised NEO Personality Inventory's Warmth scale has a substantial loading on agreeableness versus antagonism (Costa & McCrae, 1992).

8. Callousness and Lack of Empathy

The eighth feature of psychopathy is another explicit representation of FFM tough-mindedness. The PCL-R's unempathic callousness overlaps explicitly with its lack of feelings of remorse or guilt item, although unempathic callousness could be said to be directed toward people in general, whereas lack of remorse or guilt would apply more specifically to victims of one's antagonistic exploitation. Moderate levels of tough-mindedness include being impersonal, insensitive, cold, inconsiderate, and tactless, whereas the most extreme variants include such descriptors as ruthless, cruel, callous, and contemptuous (Goldberg, 1990).

9. Parasitic Lifestyle

Parasitic lifestyle is another complex feature of PCL-R psychopathy, as it involves facets of both low conscientiousness and antagonism. On the one hand, Hare (1991) describes a parasitic lifestyle as an intentional, manipulative, selfish, and exploitative financial dependence on others. As such, a parasitic lifestyle would reflect facets of antagonism. Hare (1991) even refers to the use of threats and coercion in the parasitic obtainment of support and help from others. However, a parasitic lifestyle can also include a lack of ambition, lack of motivation, low self-discipline, and inability to begin or complete responsibilities; these aspects are described well as excessively low conscientiousness (i.e., excessively low in striving for achievement and in self-discipline).

10. Poor Behavioral Controls

Poor behavioral controls, as assessed by the PCL-R, constitute another complex item. On the one hand, Hare (1991) emphasizes in particular an inadequate control of anger and temper that would correspond to FFM angry hostility and antagonistic aggression (Costa & McCrae, 1992). The PCL-R description of poor behavior control is confined largely to expressions of irritability, annoyance, impatience, threats, aggression, and verbal abuse (Hare, 1991).

However, poor behavioral control also suggests the disinhibition of low conscientiousness. Hare (1991) indicates that in using the PCL-R one needs to assess whether the assaults tend to be sudden, spontaneous, or unprovoked. To the extent that these sudden, unprovoked, and spontaneous acts reflect failing to consider future consequences, acting first and thinking later, or acting hastily, they would also reflect low deliberation, which is a facet of low conscientiousness. "At best, low scorers [on deliberation] are spontaneous and make snap decisions" (Costa & McCrae, 1992, p. 18).

11. Promiscuous Sexual Behavior

The 11th feature of psychopathy is a mixture of low conscientiousness and antagonism. On the one hand, Hare (1991) describes promiscuous sexual behavior as constituting a variety of brief, superficial relations, numerous affairs, and an indiscriminate selection of sexual partners. This aspect of promiscuity reflects a lack of conscientiousness, particularly a hedonistic lack of self-discipline, deliberation, and moral dutifulness. Persons with these facets of low conscientiousness will be undependable, unreliable, spontaneous, and incautious across a variety of activities, including (but not limited to) sexual relationships (Costa & McCrae, 1992).

The PCL-R's promiscuity measure, however, can at times also reflect an antagonistic exploitation, coercion, and/or manipulation of others, particularly as it is described in the PCL-R. PCL-R promiscuous sexual behavior includes frequent infidelities and the maintenance of several relationships at the same time (Hare, 1991). These behaviors will often demonstrate a manipulation, egocentricity, deception, and exploitation of sexual partners, rather than simply a lack of conscientious deliberation and dutifulness. Hare (1991) in fact includes a history of convictions or charges of sexual assault and efforts to coerce others into a sexual activity in his description of sexual promiscuity. Rape, sexual coercion, and sexual assault are clearly expressions of exploitative and aggressive antagonism.

12. Early Behavior Problems

The next PCL-R item includes a wide variety of behaviors prior to the age of 13, including lying, theft, cheating, vandalism, bullying, sexual activity, fire-setting, glue-sniffing, alcohol usage, and running away from home (Hare, 1991). As such, it is not really a specific personality trait. It is instead a behavioral description of psychopathy prior to the age of 13, quite analogous to the conduct disorder criterion for DSM-IV antisocial personality disorder (American Psychiatric Association, 1994).

Early behavior problems will be an expression of both antagonism and low conscientiousness. The contribution of antagonism (deception/manipulation, exploitation, and tough-mindedness) is particularly evident in such behaviors as lying, cheating, and bullying; low conscientiousness (low discipline, dutifulness, and deliberation) is particularly evident in such behaviors as running away from home, school failure, cheating, fire setting, substance abuse, and truancy (Moffitt, 1993). Low conscientiousness will also be evident in overtly antagonistic or exploitative acts that are committed without reflection, deliberation, or consideration of consequences.

13. Lack of Realistic, Long-Term Goals

The 13th feature of psychopathy corresponds directly with facets of low conscientiousness, as it concerns an inability or persistent failure to develop and execute long-term plans and goals (Hare, 1991). Persons with this feature of psychopathy are said to live day to day, they do not give much thought to the future, they are not interested in a steady job, and they may even lead a nomadic existence (Hare, 1991). These behaviors describe well a person low in conscientiousness, particularly the facets of achievement striving and discipline. Persons low in achievement striving "lack ambition and may seem aimless, but they are often perfectly content with their low levels of achievement" (Costa & McCrae, 1992, p. 18). They are neither diligent nor purposeful; they lack a direction in life; and they may even be aimless. Persons low in discipline are unable to motivate themselves to get jobs completed. They procrastinate, are easily discouraged, and are often eager simply to quit.

14. Impulsivity

Hare (1991) describes psychopathic impulsivity as the occurrence of behaviors that are unpremeditated and that lack reflection or planning. PCL-R impulsivity has an explicit representation within the FFM in the impulsivity facet of neuroticism. However, impulsivity as defined by Hare (1991) is broader than (neuroticism) impulsivity as defined by Costa and McCrae (1992). Neuroticism impulsivity refers to the inability to resist temptations, frustrations, and urges (Costa & McCrae, 1992). Lacking in reflection, lacking forethought, and being spontaneous are, in distinction, indicative of low conscientiousness, specifically a lack of deliberation. Persons low in deliberation "are hasty and often speak or act without considering the consequences" (Costa & McCrae, 1992, p. 18). Descriptors of this FFM domain include being foolhardy, rash, unpredictable, erratic, and reckless (Goldberg, 1990; John, 1990).

Considering impulsivity to include aspects of low conscientiousness is also consistent with alternative descriptions of the FFM (John, 1990). Tellegen and Waller (in press) identify this domain of the FFM as constraint rather than as conscientiousness to emphasize a rash, reckless lack of self-control. Empirically, lack of control is also more closely associated with conscientiousness than with neuroticism (Church, 1994). It is for this reason that some theorists would place impulsivity within the conscientious domain of the FFM rather than within neuroticism (John, 1990).

15. Irresponsibility

Irresponsibility is described by Hare (1991) as a repeated failure to fulfill or honor obligations and commitments. PCL-R behavioral indicators of this are confined largely to situations involving work and finances, including defaulting on loans, not paying bills, performing tasks in a careless or sloppy manner, often being absent from or late to work, and failing to honor contractual agreements (Hare, 1991). Irresponsibility is essentially low conscientiousness (whether it occurs at work or at home), particularly the facets of dutifulness and competence. Persons who are very low in competence would be lax and negligent, and persons very low in dutifulness will be irresponsible, undependable, and unreliable (Costa & McCrae, 1992).

16. Failure to Accept Responsibility for Own Actions

A failure to accept responsibility for one's own actions is in part a manifestation of low conscientiousness, particularly the facet of dutifulness. Persons low in dutifulness lack a sense of responsibility and are irresponsible and undependable. However, there are also clear indications of antagonistic manipulation and callous tough-mindedness in the PCL-R description of this construct. For example, the PCL-R assessment of this item places more emphasis on a lack of willingness to accept responsibility than on a casual, neglectful irresponsibility. Hare (1991) describes how the person may baldly deny or refuse to accept responsibility even when there is overwhelming and obvious evidence of guilt. A conscious denial of responsibility and an effort to manipulate others through this denial are manifestations of antagonism (tough-mindedness and deception/manipulation) rather than simply low conscientiousness.

17. Many Short-Term Marital Relationships

The 17th feature of psychopathy overlaps substantially with PCL-R promiscuous sexual behavior (see item 11), but it can lack the overt exploitation and coercion of the latter item, at least as it is described in the PCL-R (Hare, 1991). The occurrence of many short-term marital relationships refers more specifically in the PCL-R to a lack of commitment to a long-term relationship, which is largely a reflection of low conscientiousness, particularly dutifulness. Persons with this trait will be inconsistent, undependable, and unreliable with respect to many commitments in life, including marital (Costa & McCrae, 1992).

18. Juvenile Delinquency

Juvenile delinquency is comparable to early behavior problems, but it concerns adolescent rather than childhood antisocial behavior (Hare, 1991). In addition, only behaviors that involve violations of the law are included in the PCL-R assessment of juvenile delinquency (Hare, 1991), such as murder, attempted murder, manslaughter, rape, serious assault, robbery, auto theft, kidnapping, arson, fraud, trafficking in drugs, major driving violations, and escape. As in the case of early behavior problems, most of these behaviors clearly involve aspects of antagonism—particularly exploitation, aggression, deception/manipulation, and a callous, ruthless tough-mindedness. However, many aspects of juvenile delinquency will also reflect the irresponsibility, recklessness, negligence, rashness, hedonism, and aimlessness of low conscientiousness (Moffitt, 1993). This will be particularly evident in acts of delinquency that reflect a tendency to behave rashly, unreflectively, without deliberation, hastily, and without consideration of harmful, negative consequences.

19. Revocation of Conditional Release

Revocation of conditional release overlaps substantially with the next and final PCL-R item, criminal versatility, because it presumes a prior history of criminal activity (i.e., the person must have been on probation for some prior criminal act in order to have revoked a conditional release). The revocation of a conditional release will often occur as a result of new, additional criminal activity, but it may also occur as a result of a technical, noncriminal breach of parole (e.g., drinking while on parole or failing to appear as ordered). To the extent that the behavior reflects such technical violations, it will be most strongly related to low conscientiousness, including the carelessness of low deliberation, the lax negligence of low competence, the lack of motivation of low self-discipline, or the irresponsibility of low dutifulness. To the extent that the revocation occurs as a result of a new criminal act, it will also reflect antagonism (e.g., exploitation and/or deception/manipulation).

20. Criminal Versatility

The PCL-R's criminal versatility is to a large extent the adult version of early behavior problems and juvenile delinquency. However, emphasis is given in this case to a diversity of types of offenses (Hare, 1991). PCL-R criminal versatility refers to the occurrence of different types of criminal activity that the person has been convicted of, has been charged with, or has admitted to having committed (Hare, 1991). The list of offenses can include (but are not limited to) theft, possession of stolen property, loitering, robbery, drug possession, drug trafficking, murder, manslaughter, possession of weapons, sexual offenses, criminal negligence, fraud, forgery, escape, kidnapping, arson, obstruction of justice, perjury, assault, treason, tax evasion, smuggling, vandalism, and causing a disturbance (Hare, 1991). Most of these offences involve facets of antagonism, particularly exploitation, deception/manipulation, aggression, and ruthless tough-mindedness. However, many will also involve low conscientiousness, particularly the facets of low dutifulness and deliberation (e.g., criminal negligence, reckless driving, driving while intoxicated, loitering, and tax evasion). Being caught for a criminal act may itself be correlated with low conscientiousness (e.g., careless execution of a fraud or forgery).

FACTOR ANALYSIS

It is evident from the discussion above that all of the features of PCL-R psychopathy have a close correspondence with one or more facets of the FFM of personality. None of the PCL-R items involve personality traits that are not included within the FFM. Some of the items in fact have a quite specific association (e.g., the linkage of grandiose sense of self-worth with arrogance, of pathological lying with deception, and of irresponsibility with low dutifulness). However, it is equally evident that most PCL-R items fail to have a distinct or specific representation within the FFM.

The complexity of the association is due to a variety of factors. First, the PCL-R items themselves vary in the extent to which they refer to traits or to behaviors, and in the specificity of the respective traits or behaviors that are being described (Clark, 1992; Shea, 1992). For example, callousness is a relatively specific personality trait, but parasitic lifestyle, juvenile delinquency, and promiscuous sexual behavior refer to broad sets of behaviors that can occur for a variety of reasons. For example, PCL-R promiscuous sexual behavior is said to include frequent infidelities by a person who is married, frequent casual liaisons by a person who is single, prostitution as a means of financial support, manipulative sexual seductions by a predatory male, participation in a wide variety of paraphilic-like sexual acts, and sexual assault (Hare, 1991). It is perhaps self-evident that such a diverse set of sexual behaviors will not likely be the result of a single personality trait.

Many of the PCL-R items also lack particularly specific or distinct descriptions. Their differentiation is at times difficult. For example, schemes "carried out with no concern for their effects on victims" (Hare, 1991, p. 20) is included within the description of being conning and manipulative (item 5) rather than lacking in empathy (item 8); and taking "great pride in discussing sexual exploits" (Hare, 1991, p. 23) is presented as an indicator of promiscuous sexual behavior (item 11) rather than arrogance (item 2). Many of the PCL-R items explicitly overlap in their description and assessment. For example, charges and convictions that are the basis for juvenile delinquency (item 18) are also used for the assessment of criminal versatility (item 20). A sexual assault is included in the assessment of criminal versatility (item 20), promiscuous sexual behavior (item 11), juvenile delinquency (item 18) if the assault occurred prior to the age of 18, and the revocation of a conditional release (item 19) if it occurred while the person was on probation (Hare, 1991).

Harpur, Hakstian, and Hare (1988) conducted a widely cited and influential factor analysis of Psychopathy Checklist (PCL) items. Their analyses converged on a two-factor solution, the PCL-R items for which are presented in Table 11.2. The interpretation of the two factors, however, has been somewhat unclear and confusing. At times, the two factors are provided simply with a methodological (trait vs. behavior) distinction. Factor 1 is said to refer to personality traits, whereas Factor 2 is described (somewhat derogatorily) as simply a collection of socially deviant behaviors (e.g., Hare, 1991; Harpur et al., 1988). Harpur et al. (1988) indicated in their original derivation of the two factors that "clinical judgment and inference from interview impressions play an important role in scoring most of the [Factor 1] items" (p. 745). "Several [Factor 1] items reflect discrepancies between what an individual says and what he does" (Harpur et al., 1988, p. 745). In contrast, "most of the items in Factor 2 were scored on the basis of file information" (Harpur et al., 1988, p. 745).

However, this is not a particularly satisfying interpretation of the two factors if psychopathy is to be understood as a constellation of personality traits. This interpretation suggests that the two factors are to a large extent artifacts of the method by which psychopathy is being assessed, with the source of Factor 1 being impressions that develop during an interview, and the source of Factor 2 being the results of a file review. Lilienfeld (1994) has asked (somewhat rhetorically but cogently) that if the first factor refers to the core personality traits, then "is an individual with very high scores on the first PCL factor (who, according to Harpur et al., possess[es] the major personality traits of psychopathy), but with very low scores on the second PCL factor, a psychopath?" (p. 28).

The two factors have also been provided with more substantive interpretations. Factor 1 is said to concern a "selfish, callous, and remorseless use of others," and Factor 2 a "chronically unstable and antisocial lifestyle" (Harpur et al., 1988, p. 745). This is a

TABLE 11.2. Two Factors of the PCL-R from the Perspective of the FFM

Factor 1: Antagonism

2. Grandiose sense of self-worth (antagonism)
4. Pathological lying (antagonism)
5. Conning/manipulative (antagonism)
6. Lack of remorse or guilt (antagonism)
8. Callousness/lack of empathy (antagonism)
16. Failure to accept responsibility for own actions (antagonism)
1. Glib and superficial charm (low neuroticism)
7. Shallow affect (introversion and antagonism)

Factor 2: Low conscientiousness and antagonism

15. Irresponsibility (low conscientiousness)
13. Lack of realistic, long-term goals (low conscientiousness)
9. Parasitic lifestyle (low conscientiousness and antagonism)
12. Early behavior problems (antagonism and low conscientiousness)
18. Juvenile delinquency (antagonism and low conscientiousness)
19. Revocation of conditional release (antagonism and low conscientiousness)
14. Impulsivity (low conscientiousness and high neuroticism)
3. Need for stimulation/proneness to boredom (extraversion)
10. Poor behavioral controls (high neuroticism, low conscientiousness, and antagonism)

Note. Items 11 (promiscuous sexual behavior), 17 (many short-term marital relationships), and 20 (criminal versatility) from the PCL-R (Hare, 1991) are not included.

more substantive interpretation, but it still fails to be particularly clear or specific. The factors are being defined extensionally by simply listing a sample of the items that are included, rather than specifying a single domain of functioning that is common to them. In addition, the descriptions of each factor are incomplete, with the description of the first factor failing to recognize the presence of arrogance, and the description of the second factor failing to recognize the presence of impulsivity, proneness to boredom, and sensation seeking (Salekin, Rogers, & Sewell, 1996). "An alternative explanation of Harpur and colleagues' findings is that both PCL factors represent personality traits, but the traits assessed by the second factor are more highly associated with antisocial behavior" (Lilienfeld, 1994, p. 28)—more specifically, behaviors of delinquency, drug usage, poor employment, and criminal arrests.

We would suggest that some clarity is provided by an FFM interpretation of psychopathy. Table 11.2 also provides the FFM domain that is represented in each respective PCL-R item, as indicated by the descriptions of the items given above. A rather clear distinction from the perspective of the FFM emerges. Factor 1 appears to be confined largely to facets of antagonism (with a minimal representation of neuroticism and extraversion), and Factor 2 is dominated by the items that are a mixture of low conscientiousness and antagonism. This FFM description is not entirely distinct, but some lack of clarity will be a necessary, unavoidable result of the lack of clarity of the PCL-R items themselves, the inconsistency in the level of abstraction of the items (contributing to some method artifact), and the substantial correlation that often occurs between the two factors. The two factors identified by Harpur et al. (1988) are not in fact themselves particularly distinct from one another, as they typically correlate at a level of .50 (Hare, 1991). The presence of facets of antagonism within the second factor may in fact be the major source of the correlation between them. In any case, the FFM interpretation of the two PCL-R factors does appear to be a substantially more precise and conceptually meaningful personological description than the interpretations that are typically provided.

PATHOLOGY OF PSYCHOPATHY

Substantial efforts have been made over the past 50 years to identify a pathology that is specific or unique to persons with psychopathy (Sutker, Bugg, & West, 1993); these efforts are consistent with the presumption that the disorder is a homogeneous condition, qualitatively distinct from normal personality functioning (Lilienfeld, 1994; Meehl, 1995). However, the result has been a generation of diverse and often divergent set of alternative models of pathology. We suggest that the pathologies may instead be on a continuum with normal personality functioning (Fowles & Missel, 1994; Patrick, 1994), and that the diversity among the alternative models can be clarified to some extent by the domain of the FFM that is being emphasized, consistent with the presence of different domains of personality functioning within the PCL-R description of psychopathy.

Poor Fear Conditioning/Hypoarousal to Negative Stimuli

The pathology referred to as "poor fear conditioning" (Lykken, 1957; Patrick, 1994) or as a "hypoarousal to negative stimuli" (Fowles, 1993) is concerned primarily with the domain of neuroticism, particularly the facets of low anxiousness and low vulnerability. Poor fear conditioning was first reported in a classic paper by Lykken (1957). In this study, Lykken employed a conditioning paradigm with electric shock as the unconditioned stimulus (UCS) and electrodermal responses (EDRs) as the conditioned response (CR). Prison inmates who met Cleckley's (1941) criteria were labeled "primary sociopaths," whereas those who did not were designated as "neurotic sociopaths." During the conditioning phase, primary sociopaths displayed smaller EDRs to the conditioned stimuli (CSs) than those displayed by normal (noninmate) controls, but not smaller ones than those of the neurotic sociopaths. During the extinction phase, however, the neurotic sociopaths showed even greater resistance to extinction than the normal controls, which Lykken attributed to the perseveration of the anxiety response. Lykken concluded that primary sociopaths are deficient in the ability to develop anxiety responses.

Lykken (1995) subsequently developed a questionnaire to assess this pathology, titled the Activity Preference Questionnaire (APQ), in which subjects choose between two negative events. The alternatives are equated with respect to their general unpleasantness, but differ in the extent to which there is a threat or danger. The APQ is clearly a measure of low anxiousness or low vulnerability; "someone whose general fearfulness was lower than average should more frequently choose the frightening experiences as preferable to the onerous but nonfrightening alternatives" (Lykken, 1995, p. 146). Lykken has attempted to distinguish the APQ from FFM neuroticism by identifying persons high in neuroticism but low in fearfulness. Such persons can be identified and will provide different results than will persons low in all of the facets of neuroticism, but this is simply because neuroticism is a broader domain than the particular facet of anxiousness. It includes other aspects of functioning, such as angry hostility, depression, and self-consciousness (Costa & McCrae, 1995).

Since Lykken's original study, dozens of replications have been published, using conditioning paradigms, countdown procedures, and the presentation of stimuli with inherent aversive signal value (Fowles, 1993). When strong (usually aversive) stimuli are involved, psychopaths (persons low in FFM anxiousness) frequently manifest EDR hyporeactivity during a time period prior to an anticipated stressor.

Patrick, Bradley, and Lang (1993) have provided the most recent demonstration of this hyporeactivity, using a measure different from the EDR—the fear-potentiated startle response. They found that subjects who were low and moderate in psychopathy showed the greatest startle magnitude in response to probes while viewing unpleasant slides (e.g., mutilations), the next greatest magnitude while viewing neutral slides (e.g., household objects), and the least startle in reponse to probes while viewing positive slides (e.g., opposite-sex nudes). On the other hand, highly psychopathic subjects showed less startle when probed while viewing unpleasant slides than while viewing neutral slides. The authors interpreted these results as indicating an abnormality in the processing of emotional stimuli—in particular, a deficit in their fear response.

Patrick (1994) has specifically related this deficit to a broad domain of normal personality functioning. Citing the research of Cooke, Stevenson, and Hawk (1993), he indicated that "subjects high in negative affectivity [neuroticism] showed dramatic startle potentiation during unpleasant imagery whereas low negative emotionality subjects showed no such effect" (p. 324). He added, "This work is important because it establishes a link between temperament and individual differences in startle potentiation" (Patrick, 1994, p. 324). From this perspective, the pathology of psychopathy is not a deficit that is qualitatively distinct from normal personality functioning; it is an extreme variant of a common, fundamental dimension of personality. "The observed absence of startle potentiation in psychopaths (Patrick et al., 1993) may reflect a temperamental deficit in the capacity for negative affect" (Patrick, 1994, p. 325).

Response Modulation

Newman and his colleagues have developed a theory of psychopathy that targets the processes underlying the regulation of immediate response inclinations or dominant response sets (Newman & Wallace, 1993; Patterson & Newman, 1993). According to these authors, the psychopath has a deficit in the ability to suspend a dominant response set in order to assimilate feedback from the environment. Most recently, these investigators have placed more emphasis on the role of shifting attention from the organization and implementation of behavior to its evaluation. In either case, the pathology would contribute to an excessively low conscientiousness, particularly the facets of deliberation and discipline. Persons low in discipline are impaired in their "ability to begin tasks and carry them through to completion despite boredom and other distractions," and persons low in deliberation are "hasty and often speak or act without considering the consequences" (Costa & McCrae, 1992, p. 18). The description of the attentional deficit by Newman and colleagues is certainly more specific and precise than the description of discipline and deliberation by Costa and McCrae (1992), but it is apparent that Newman's group is describing an aspect of and a basis for being very low in conscientiousness.

Patterson and Newman (1993) have elaborated a four-stage model to explicate the response modulation process. The psychopathic deficit in response modulation is traced to a disposition for disinhibition over reflectivity at the third stage. Several studies support this conclusion. Newman, Patterson, and Kosson (1987) demonstrated that psychopaths, relative to comparison subjects, perseverated in a dominant response set on a card-playing task whose odds grew worse across time. In another study, Newman, Patterson, Howland, and Nichols (1990) used a discrimination task in which a subject used the feedback after each response to determine which stimuli were positive (response resulted in reward) and which were negative (response resulted in punishment). They found that comparison subjects paused for 1.8 seconds longer after punishment than after reward and committed fewer than 9 passive avoidance errors (failure to withhold a response to a negative stimulus), whereas psychopaths paused only 0.9 seconds longer and made more than 14 passive avoidance errors. These results again suggested that psychopaths are less likely to pause following negative feedback and therefore learn less well.

Finally, Newman, Wallace, Schmitt, and Arnett (1997), in an attempt to demonstrate that the deficit was attentional, used a retroactive interference task in which a stimulus associated with punishment in the first task was used as a distractor in the second task. These authors found that despite adequate performance on the first task (e.g., learning the association), psychopaths, unlike controls, showed no interference from the CS on the second task. Again, psychopaths appear to have difficulty making use of "peripheral" information that might otherwise influence their goal-directed behavior.

Patterson and Newman (1993) have discussed individual-difference variables that are operative at the various stages. They refer to the Stage 3 individual-difference variable as a "response modulation bias," or cognitive deficits within the domain of conscientiousness. "That which is modulated is the overt goal-directed behavior. . . . Disinhibited persons often fail to alter their response set in accordance with changing environmental events and contingencies: they do not pause, process, and then go on" (Patterson & Newman, 1993, p. 721). It is a deficit in the deliberation, planfulness, and judgment of conscientiousness (Costa & McCrae, 1992). There is "a lack of prospective reflection or, in other words, a lack of planful thought and sound judgment" (Patterson & Newman, 1993, p. 722).

Semantic Dementia/Abnormal Affective Processing

In his classic description of the psychopath, Cleckley (1941) hypothesized that the underlying deficit is a failure to process the emotional meaning of language, or a "semantic dementia." His description of this deficit relates closely to the most extreme variants of antagonistic tough-mindedness, or the virtual absence of any feelings of empathy. Persons who are excessively tender-minded are unable to close their feelings to the pain and suffering of those around them; persons who are excessively tough-minded fail to grasp, understand, or appreciate how others feel. "The psychopath's disorder, or defect, or his difference from the whole or normal or integrated personality consists of an unawareness and a persistent lack of ability to become aware of what the most important experiences of life mean to others. . . . [It is] the common substance of emotion or purpose . . . from which the various loyalties, goals, fidelities, commitments, and concepts of honor and responsibility of various groups and various people are formed" (Cleckley, 1941, p. 229).

Several investigators have pursued this hypothesis, using a variety of behavioral and psychophysiological methods. For example, Williamson, Harpur, and Hare (1990) asked psychopathic and nonpsychopathic subjects to read several sets of word triads and to group the two words from each triad that were closest in meaning. Psychopaths made less use of connotation (affective meaning) than did nonpsychopaths. In a later task that required matching clauses or pictures on inferred emotional meaning, psychopaths confused emotional polarity (good vs. bad). Williamson, Harpur, and Hare (1991) tested psychopaths' use of the connotative aspects of language in a lexical decision task involving emotional and neutral words. Subjects were required to indicate, as quickly as possible, whether or not a letter string formed a word; most individuals can make a lexical decision more quickly when the letter string is an emotional word than when it is a neutral word. Overall, there were no group differences between psychopaths and nonpsychopaths in accuracy. The analysis of reaction time, however, indicated that the controls responded more quickly to emotional than to neutral words. In addition, the psychopaths' event-related potentials (ERPs) to the emotional words were indistinguishable from their potentials to the neutral words.

Social Information-Processing Deficits

Dodge and his colleagues have developed a social information processing model that is explicitly related to facets of antagonism (Dodge & Crick, 1990). Models of social information processing describe how individuals encode, represent, and process social (e.g., interpersonal) circumstances. "With regard to conduct disorder [or early behavior problems within the PCL-R], it is hypothesized that early experiences of physical abuse[,] . . . exposure to aggressive models[,] . . . and insecure attachment relationships . . . lead a child to develop memory structures of the world as a hostile place that requires coercive behavior to achieve desired outcomes" (Dodge, 1993, p. 579).

The model specifies a five-stage sequence of information processing: (1) encoding of social cues, (2) interpretation of the cues, (3) search for responses to the interpeted situation, (4) selection of a response, and (5) enactment of the chosen response. The model proposes that individuals differ in their characteristic styles of processing at each stage, and that these differences in processing style are related to individual differences in aggression (Dodge, 1993). At Stage 1, aggressive individuals attend to fewer cues generally and attend selectively to aggressive cues (e.g., Dodge, Pettit, Bates, & Valente, 1995). At Stage 2, aggressive individuals are biased to interpret ambiguous and benign situations in aggressive ways. Aggressive individuals generate fewer competent responses and more manipulative and aggressive responses at Stage 3. At Stage 4, aggressive individuals evaluate the outcomes of their possible responses less fully, and they expect more positive instrumental and intrapersonal outcomes and fewer sanctional outcomes for aggressive responses.

In other words, Dodge and his colleagues place less emphasis on a pathology of low negative affectivity (Patrick, 1994) or low conscientiousness (Patterson & Newman, 1993), arguing instead for a more direct, overt modeling and reinforcement of a cognitive schema of antagonism—specifically, the facets of mistrust, manipulation, and aggression. The excessive attention to hostile cues, hostile attributional bias, and generation of manipulative and aggressive responses describe explicitly the antagonism facets of low trust (cynicism, suspicion), low straightforwardness (deception, manipulation), and low compliance (oppositionalism, aggression).

CONCLUSIONS

"Psychopathy as assessed by the PCL is perhaps the most reliable and well-validated diagnostic category in the field of personality disorders" (Harpur, Hart, & Hare, 1994, p. 169). This may indeed be true. Harpur et al. suggest further that it is then difficult to understand how psychopathy could involve such a collection of facets from different domains of personality functioning, as suggested in this chapter. However, the social and clinical interest in this particular collection of personality traits is understandable, as one could hardly construct a more virulent constellation of traits than high antagonism, low conscientiousness, and low anxiousness. Persons with this constellation will invariably be of immediate and substantial concern to other members of society, as they will be irresponsible, hedonistic, aggressive, exploitative, ruthless, unempathic, deceptive, fearless, and un-self-conscious. Identifying this profile with a specific term, "psychopathy," is useful to focus social and clinical attention, as long as one recognizes that the profile is indeed a collection of personality traits rather than a homogeneous, qualitatively distinct condition.

The complexity of the FFM description of psychopathy is also helpful in explaining the factor structure of the PCL-R and the diversity of models for its pathology. The proposed models of pathology do appear to differ in part by the domain of personality functioning that is emphasized. One model emphasizes low neuroticism (Lykken, 1995; Patrick, 1994); another places more emphasis on low conscientiousness (Patterson & Newman, 1993); and still another places more emphasis on antagonism (Dodge, 1993; Hare, 1993). Psychopathy does not appear to be a "distinct type of personality organization that is qualitatively different from that seen in nonpathological subjects" (Hare et al., 1994, p. 170). It appears instead to be on a continuum with normal personality functioning, with different pathologies reflecting the different facets of personality that are involved.

REFERENCES

American Psychiatric Association. (1994). *Diagnostic and statistical manual of mental disorders* (4th ed.). Washington, DC: Author.

Church, A. T. (1994). Relating the Tellegen and five-factor models of personality structure. *Journal of Personality and Social Psychology, 67,* 898–909.

Clark, L. A. (1992). Resolving taxonomic issues in personality disorders. *Journal of Personality Disorders, 6*, 360–376.

Cleckley, H. (1941). *The mask of sanity*. St. Louis, MO: C. V. Mosby.

Cooke, E. W., Stevenson, V. E., & Hawk, L. W. (1993, October). *Enhanced startle modulation and negative affectivity*. Paper presented at the Annual Meeting of the Society for Research in Psychopathology, Chicago, IL.

Costa, P. T., & McCrae, R. R. (1992). *Revised NEO Personality Inventory (NEO-PI-R) and NEO Five-Factor Inventory (NEO-FFI) professional manual*. Odessa, FL: Psychological Assessment Resources.

Costa, P. T., & McCrae, R. R. (1995)., Domains and facets: Hierarchical personality assessment using the Revised NEO Personality Inventory. *Journal of Personality Assessment, 64*, 21–50.

Costa, P. T., & Widiger, T. A. (Eds.). (1994). *Personality disorders and the five-factor model of personality*. Washington, DC: American Psychological Association.

Digman, J. M. (1990). Personality structure: Emergence of the five-factor model. *Annual Review of Psychology, 41*, 417–440.

Dodge, K. A. (1993). Social-cognitive mechanisms in the development of conduct disorder and depression. *Annual Review of Psychology, 44*, 559–584.

Dodge, K. A., & Crick, N. R. (1990). Social information processing bases of 32 aggressive behavior in children. *Personality and Social Psychology Bulletin, 16*, 8–22.

Dodge, K. A., Pettit, G. S., Bates, J. E., & Valente, E. (1995). Social information processing patterns partially mediate the effect of early physical abuse on later conduct problems. *Journal of Abnormal Psychology, 104*, 632–643.

Fowles, D. C. (1993). Electrodermal activity and antisocial behavior: Empirical findings and theoretical issues. In J. C. Roy, W. Boucsein, D. C. Fowles, & J. Gruzelier (Eds.), *Progress in electrodermal research* (pp. 223–237). London: Plenum Press.

Fowles, D. C,. & Missel, K. A. (1994). Electrodermal hyporeactivity, motivation, and psychopathy: Theoretical issues. In D. C. Fowles, P. Sutker, S. Goodman (Eds.), *Progress in experimental personality and psychopathology research* (Vol. 18, pp. 263–283). New York: Springer.

Goldberg, L. R. (1982). From ace to zombie: Some explorations in the language of personality. In C. D. Spielberger & J. N. Butcher (Eds.), *Advances in personality assessment* (Vol. 1, pp. 203–234). Hillsdale, NJ: Erlbaum.

Goldberg, L. R. (1990). An alternative "description of personality": The Big Five factor structure. *Journal of Personality and Social Psychology, 59*, 1216–1229.

Hare, R. D. (1991). *The Hare Psychopathy Checklist—Revised*. Toronto: Multi-Health Systems.

Hare, R. D. (1993). *Without conscience: The disturbing world of the psychopaths among us*. New York: Pocket Books.

Harpur, T. J., Hakstian, A. R., & Hare, R. D. (1988). Factor structure of 33 the Psychopathy Checklist. *Journal of Consulting and Clinical Psychology, 56*, 741–747.

Harpur, T. J., Hart, S. D., & Hare, R. D. (1994). Personality of the psychopath. In P. T. Costa & T. A. Widiger (Eds.), *Personality disorders and the five-factor model of Personality* (pp. 149–173). Washington, DC: American Psychological Association.

John, O. P. (1990). The "Big Five" factor taxonomy: Dimensions of personality in the natural language and in questionnaires. In L. A. Pervin (Ed.), *Handbook of personality: Theory and research* (pp. 66–100). New York: Guilford Press.

Lilienfeld, S. O. (1994). Conceptual problems in the assessment of psychopathy. *Clinical Psychology Review, 14*, 17–38.

Lykken, D. T. (1957). A study of anxiety in the sociopathic personality. *Journal of Abnormal and Clinical Psychology, 55*, 6–10.

Lykken, D. T. (1995). *The antisocial Personalities*. Hillsdale, NJ: Erlbaum.

McCrae, R. R., & Costa, P. T. (1989). The structure of interpersonal traits: Wiggins' circumplex and the five-factor model. *Journal of Personality and Social Psychology, 56*, 586–595.

McCrae, R. R., & Costa, P. T. (1990). *Personality in adulthood*. New York: Guilford Press.

Meehl, P. E. (1995). Bootstraps taxometrics: Solving the classification problem in psychopathology. *American Psychologist, 50*, 266–275.

Moffitt, T. E. (1993). Life-course-persistent and adolescence-limited antisocial behavior: A developmental taxonomy. *Psychological Review*, 100, 674–701.

Newman, J. P., Patterson, C. M., Howland, E. W., & Nichols, S. L. (1990). Passive avoidance in psychopaths: The effects of reward. *Personality and Individual Differences, 11,* 1101–1014.

Newman, J. P., Patterson, C. M., & Kosson, D. S. (1987). Response perseveration in psychopaths. *Journal of Abnormal Psychology, 96,* 145–148.

Newman, J. P., & Wallace, J. F. (1993). Psychopathy and cognition. In K. Dobson & R. Kendall (Eds.), *Psychopathology and cognition* (pp. 293–349). San Diego, CA: Academic Press.

Newman, J. P., Wallace, J. F., Schmitt, W. A., & Arnett, P. A. (1997). Behavioral inhibition system functioning in anxious, impulsive, and psychopathic individuals. *Personality and Individual Differences, 23,* 583–592.

Patrick, C. J. (1994). Emotion and psychopathy: Startling new insights. *Psychophysiology, 31,* 415–428.

Patrick, C. J., Bradley, M. M., & Lang, P. J. (1993). Emotion in the criminal psychopath: Startle reflex modulation. *Journal of Abnormal Psychology, 102,* 82–92.

Patterson, M. C., & Newman, J. P. (1993). Reflectivity and learning from aversive events: Toward a psychological mechanism for the syndromes of disinhibition. *Psychological Review*, 100, 716–736.

Salekin, R. T., Rogers, R., & Sewell, K. W. (1996). A review and meta-analysis of the Psychopathy Checklist and Psychopathy Checklist—Revised: Predictive validity of dangerousness. *Clinical Psychology: Science and Practice, 3,* 203–215.

Shea, M. T. (1992). Some characteristics of the Axis II criteria sets and their implications for assessment of personality disorders. *Journal of Personality Disorders, 6,* 377–381.

Sutker, P. B., Bugg, F., & West, J. A. (1993). Antisocial personality disorder. In P. B. Sutker & H. Adams (Eds.), *Comprehensive handbook of psychopathology* (2nd ed., pp. 337–369). New York: Plenum Press.

Tellegen, A., & Waller, N. G. (in press). Exploring personality through test construction: Development of the Multidimensional Personality Questionnaire. In S. R. Briggs & J. M. Cheek (Eds.), *Personality measures: Development and evaluation* (Vol. 1). Greenwich, CT: JAI Press.

Widiger, T. A., & Costa, P. T. (1994). Personality and personality disorders. *Journal of Abnormal Psychology, 103,* 78–91.

Williamson, S., Harpur, T. J., & Hare, R. D. (1990). *Sensitivity to emotional polarity in psychopaths*. Paper presented at the annual meeting of the American Psychological Association, Boston.

Williamson, S., Harpur, T. J., & Hare, R. D. (1991). Abnormal processing of affective words by psychopaths. *Psychophysiology, 28,* 260–273.

12

Psychopaths and Their Nature: Implications for the Mental Health and Criminal Justice Systems

ROBERT D. HARE

Psychopathy is a socially devastating disorder defined by a constellation of affective, interpersonal, and behavioral characteristics, including egocentricity; impulsivity; irresponsibility; shallow emotions; lack of empathy, guilt, or remorse; pathological lying; manipulativeness; and the persistent violation of social norms and expectations (Cleckley, 1976; Hare, 1993). It began to emerge as a formal clinical construct in the last century, but references to individuals we now readily recognize as having been psychopathic can be found in biblical, classical, medieval, and other historical sources (Cleckley, 1976; McCord & McCord, 1964; Millon, 1981; Rotenberg & Diamond, 1971).

However, like most clinical constructs, psychopathy has been and continues to be the subject of considerable debate, scientific and otherwise. Some commentators—perhaps influenced by belief systems intolerant of clinical and behavioral constructs, or overwhelmed by the inconsistent, fuzzy, and legalistic ways in which the term is often used—have even suggested that the disorder is mythological or, at the very least, not clinically or theoretically useful. These views typically have an armchair quality about them, and are held with surprising certitude and tenacity, given the wealth of clinical and empirical support for the construct of psychopathy now readily available in the literature. For example, several years ago I gave the opening and closing addresses, as well as a 1-day workshop, at an international conference on psychiatry, psychology, and law. Following my final address, a forensic psychiatrist was asked to provide a commentary on my presentations. He cautioned the participants not to be fooled by the large amount of data and by the pretty figures and pictures I had presented over a period of some 10 hours, for "it was bad science." That was it, the sum total of his comments; he gave no explanation for the basis of his stark assertion. Apparently his views were fixed and impervious to empirical data.

The fact is that psychopathy is one of the best-validated clinical constructs in the realm of psychopathology, and arguably the single most important clinical construct in the criminal justice system. Indeed, a meeting of leading researchers on personality disorders organized by the National Institute of Mental Health in Washington, DC, in June 1992 concluded that the convergence of biological, psychological, and behavioral paradigms in the theory and research on psychopathy was a useful model for the construct validation of other personality disorders (see Stoff, Breiling, & Maser, 1997).

It is true that the etiology, dynamics, and conceptual boundaries of the disorder are the subject of debate and research, but at the same time there is a consistent clinical tradition concerning its core affective, interpersonal, and behavioral attributes. Interestingly, this traditional view of psychopathy cuts across a broad spectrum of groups, including psychiatrists, psychologists, criminal justice personnel, and experimental psychopathologists, as well as the lay public (e.g., Albert, Brigante, & Chase, 1959; Cleckley, 1976; Davies & Feldman, 1981; Fotheringham, 1957; Gray & Hutchinson, 1964; Livesley, 1986; Livesley, Jackson, & Schroeder, 1992; Livesley & Schroeder, 1991; McCord & McCord, 1964; Meloy, 1988; Millon, 1981; Rogers, Dion, & Lynett, 1992; Tennent, Tennent, Prins, & Bedford, 1990). Nevertheless, until recently the lack of psychometrically sound procedures for operationalizing the construct has hindered the development of a body of replicable, theoretically meaningful research findings, as well as society's acceptance of psychopathy as an important clinical construct with practical implications.

THE ASSESSMENT OF PSYCHOPATHY

DSM-II, DSM-III, and DSM-III-R Criteria

The second edition of the American Psychiatric Association's *Diagnostic and Statistical Manual of Mental Disorders* (DSM-II) appeared in 1968. In line with clinical tradition, it described psychopaths (referred to as persons exhibiting an antisocial personality) as unsocialized, impulsive, guiltless, selfish, and callous individuals who rationalize their behavior and fail to learn from experience (American Psychiatric Association, 1968). However, DSM-II did not provide explicit diagnostic criteria for the disorder, and in the 1970s many researchers attempted to operationalize the disorder in other ways (see review by Hare & Cox, 1978). For example, my colleagues and I made global ratings of psychopathy based on clinical accounts of the disorder (especially those by Cleckley, 1976). Other researchers used scales derived from self-report inventories, such as the Minnesota Multiphasic Personality Inventory (Dahlstrom & Welsh, 1960) and the California Psychological Inventory (Gough, 1969). The psychometric properties of most of these procedures as indicants of psychopathy were unclear, and the tenuous relationships they bore to one another made it difficult or impossible to generate a solid body of replicable research findings (Hare, 1985).

With the publication of DSM-III (American Psychiatric Association, 1980), the diagnostic situation improved in one respect but worsened in another. The improvement was the introduction of a list of explicit criteria for psychopathy, now referred to as antisocial personality disorder (APD). Unfortunately, these criteria consisted almost entirely of persistent violations of social norms, including lying, stealing, truancy, inconsistent work behavior, and traffic arrests. Among the main reasons given for this dramatic shift away from the use of clinical inferences were that personality traits are difficult to measure reliably, and that it is easier to agree on the behaviors that typify a disorder than on the reasons why they occur. The result was a diagnostic category with good reliability but limited validity—a category that lacked congruence with traditional conceptions of psychopathy. This "construct drift" was not intentional, but rather the unforeseen result of reliance on a fixed set of behavioral indicators that simply did not provide adequate coverage of the construct they were designed to measure. The problems with DSM-III and DSM-III-R, its revision (American Psychiatric Association, 1987), as well as the need to bring traditional symptoms of psychopathy back into the diagnosis of APD, were widely discussed in the clinical and research literature. The issues were not simply academic, for the past decade has provided ample evidence that in forensic populations, diagnoses of APD have far less utility with respect to treatment outcome, institutional adjustment, and predictions of postrelease behavior than do careful assessments of psychopathy based on the traditional use of inferred personality traits. This will be discussed further below.

DSM-IV Criteria

Because of the problems with the DSM-III and DSM-III-R diagnosis of APD, the American Psychiatric Association carried out a multisite field trial in preparation for DSM-IV (Hare, Hart, & Harpur, 1991; Widiger & Corbitt, 1993). The field trial evaluated three criteria sets: the DSM-III-R criteria for APD; a 10-item psychopathic personality disorder (PPD) criteria set (Hare, Hart, Forth, Harpur, & Williamson, 1993), derived from the Hare Psychopathy Checklist—Revised (PCL-R; Hare, 1991) and from an early draft of its screening version (PCL:SV; Hart, Cox, & Hare, 1995); and the ICD-10 criteria for dyssocial personality disorder (World Health Organization, 1992). The PPD items were as follows: "lacks remorse," "lacks empathy," "deceitful and manipulative," "glib and superficial," "inflated and arrogant self-appraisal," "early behavior problems," "adult antisocial problems," "poor behavioral controls," "impulsive," and "irresponsible." The results of the field trial were described in detail by Widiger et al. (1996).

Many researchers and clinicians hoped that the field trial would bring the diagnosis of APD back on track, but it did so only in a limited sense, and certainly not explicitly or formally. The DSM-IV criteria for APD (American Psychiatric Association, 1994) remain problematic (see Hare & Hart, 1995). Most of the personality traits that reflect the traditional symptoms of psychopathy—the PPD and the ICD-10 items—were at least as reliable as the more behaviorally specific DSM-III-R items, thus invalidating the original premise for excluding personality from the diagnosis of APD/psychopathy. Inclusion of several of these psychopathy items would have improved greatly the content validity of APD without sacrificing reliability. One of the reasons for leaving these items out was that analyses of the field trial data indicated that their inclusion did not significantly increase correlations with several "external validators," including self-report measures of empathy, anxiety, and Machiavellianism. This is not surprising, given the relatively weak correlations typically found between self-report inventories and clinical rating scales for psychopathy, such as the PCL-R (Hare, 1985). Yet the PPD set was more strongly correlated with clinicians' ratings of psychopathy than was the DSM-III-R set. Other aspects of validity, including predictive validity, were not investigated.

In any case, the DSM-IV adult criteria for APD were not actually evaluated in the field trial. It was the DSM-III-R adult criteria—not the seven items listed in the DSM-IV adult criteria for APD—that were evaluated. The 7-item DSM-IV set was derived from the 10-item DSM-III-R set. We have no idea of how reliable or valid this 7-item adult set is, given that it was not actually used in the field trial. The scientific flavor of the field trial notwithstanding, it tells us little about the reliability or validity of the APD criteria adopted for use in DSM-IV.

DSM-IV presents clinicians working in the criminal justice system with an additional problem. The term "psychopathy" was absent in DSM-III-R. The DSM-IV text now says that APD "has also been referred to as psychopathy, sociopathy, or dyssocial personality disorder" (p. 645), thereby making it easier for forensic clinicians to use the construct of psychopathy in their reports or court testimony. Indeed, the text makes many references to the personality traits traditionally associated with psychopathy. However, the listed diagnostic criteria for APD actually identify individuals who are persistently antisocial, most of whom are not psychopaths. The problem is compounded by the following statement in the DSM-IV text for APD: "Lack of empathy, inflated self-appraisal, and superficial charm are features that have commonly been included in traditional conceptions of psychopathy and may be particularly distinguishing of Antisocial Personality Disorder in prison or forensic settings where criminal, delinquent, or aggressive acts are likely to be nonspecific" (p. 647). What this statement implies is that a clinician may conclude that an offender or forensic patient who meets the formal criteria for APD may not really have APD unless he or she also exhibits some of the key personality traits associated with psychopathy. Curiously, clinicians are left entirely on their own when it comes to whether and how to assess these traits; no guidelines are provided, nor are clinicians referred to an instrument (such as the PCL-R) that does provide explicit criteria for each symptom.

It seems that DSM-IV has perhaps inadvertently established two different sets of diagnostic criteria for APD, one for the general public and one for forensic settings. Individuals diagnosed with APD outside of forensic settings might not be so diagnosed once they find themselves in prisons or forensic hospitals, unless they also exhibit personality traits indicative of psychopathy. The inclusion of such traits in the forensic diagnosis of APD apparently is a matter of judgment for the individual clinician; as a result, a given offender or defendant might be diagnosed as having APD by a clinician who chooses to use only the listed criteria, and as *not* having APD by one who chooses to include psychopathic personality traits in the diagnosis. In each case, the diagnostic strategy would be consistent with DSM-IV guidelines—a situation that should provide some interesting courtroom debates.

In my view, DSM-IV not only failed in its stated intention to bring the diagnosis of APD back into line with clinical tradition and ICD-10; it also exacerbated the very problems that it ostensibly set out to rectify. The question is, why did this happen? One possibility is that the Axis II Work Group adopted an unusually conservative threshold for making substantive changes to APD, in effect ensuring that both DSM-III-R and DSM-IV would identify much the same individuals as having APD (Widiger & Corbitt, 1995). The formal and explicit inclusion in DSM-IV of traditional symptoms of psychopathy would have altered substantially who receives a diagnosis of APD. At the same time, results of the field trial and the clinical and empirical criticisms of the DSM-III-R criteria could not be ignored completely, and some symptoms of psychopathy were admitted through the back door, primarily for use in forensic settings. Given the apparent reluctance of the DSM-IV Work Group to make significant and logically consistent changes to the criteria for APD, the purpose of the field trial remains uncertain, in my view. Perhaps DSM-V will set things right—if not by adopting the items listed in the PCL-R, then perhaps by selecting an appropriate combination of features from those that currently describe APD and the narcissistic and histrionic personality disorders.

Meanwhile, an unfortunate consequence of the approach adopted in DSM-IV is that now, more than ever, researchers and clinicians will be confused about the relationship between APD and psychopathy—sometimes using them interchangeably, and other times treating them as separate clinical constructs. Perhaps most serious will be situations in which a clinician diagnoses an offender or forensic patient as having APD according to the formal DSM-IV criteria, and then uses the research literature on psychopathy to make statements about treatability, likelihood of reoffending, and risk for violence (Hare, 1996a). As I indicate below, the predictive validity of psychopathy as measured by the PCL-R is impressive, but has little direct relevance to APD.

The Psychopathy Checklist and Its Revision

In 1980 I first described a research tool for operationalizing the construct of psychopathy (Hare, 1980). Later referred to as the PCL, it was revised in 1985 and formally published several years later as the Hare PCL-R (Hare, 1991; see also Hart, Hare, & Harpur, 1992). The PCL-R is a 20-item clinical construct rating scale completed on the basis of a semistructured interview and detailed collateral or file information. Each item is scored on a 3-point scale according to specific criteria. The total score, which can range from 0 to 40, provides an estimate of the extent to which a given individual matches the proto-typical psychopath, as exemplified, for example, in the work of Cleckley (1976). The PCL-R's psychometric properties are well established with male offenders and forensic patients (Cooke & Michie, 1997; Hare, 1991; Harpur, Hare, & Hakstian, 1989; Hart & Hare, 1989, 1997; Heilbrun et al., in press). Fulero (1995) has described the PCL-R as the "state of the art . . . both clinically and in research use" (p. 454).

There is also increasing evidence of the reliability and validity of the PCL-R with female offenders and psychiatric patients (Cooke, 1995; Douglas, Ogloff, & Nicholls, 1997 (Hare, Strachan, & Hemphill, 1998; Neary, 1990; Piotrowski, Tusel, Sees, Banys, & Hall, 1996; Rutherford, Cacciola, Alterman, & McKay, 1996; Salekin, Rogers, & Sewell, 1997). With only slight modifications (see Forth, Kosson, & Hare, in press), the PCL-R is proving as useful with adolescent offenders as with adult offenders (Brandt, Kennedy, Patrick, & Curtin, 1997; Chandler & Moran, 1990; Forth, 1996; Forth, Hart, & Hare, 1990; Gretton, McBride, O'Shaughnessy, & Hare, 1997; Toupin, Mercier, Dery, Cate, & Hodgins, 1996; Trevethan & Walker, 1989).

Indices of internal consistency (alpha coefficient, mean interitem correlation) and in-terrater reliability are generally high, and evidence for all aspects of validity is substantial. Mean PCL-R scores in North American male and female offender populations typically range from about 22 to 24, with a standard deviation of from 6 to 8. Mean scores in North American forensic psychiatric populations are somewhat lower at around 20, with about the same standard deviation. For research purposes, a score of 30 is generally considered indicative of psychopathy, although some investigators have obtained good results with cutoff scores as low as 25. Cross-cultural research by David Cooke and Christine Michie (see Cooke, Chapter 16, this volume; Cooke, 1996, 1998; Cooke & Michie, 1997) attests to the generalizability of the construct of psychopathy and of the PCL-R as its operational measure. However, the metric equivalent of the scores obtained with North American samples may be somewhat lower in some European samples. An item response theory (IRT) analysis of the PCL-R indicated that it showed that its performance in different settings and cultural groups "reveals remarkable consistency. . . . There is no evidence detectable in these comparatively large samples that suggests that the tests biased due to race or presence of mental disorder" (Cooke & Michie, 1997, p. 10).

The high internal consistency of the PCL and PCL-R indicates that they measure a unitary construct; yet factor analyses of each version consistently reveal a stable two-factor structure (Hare et al., 1990; Harpur et al., 1989). Factor 1 consists of items having to do with the affective/interpersonal features of psychopathy, such as egocentricity, manipulativeness, callousness, and lack of remorse—characteristics that many clinicians consider central to psychopathy. Factor 2 reflects those features of psychopathy associated with an impulsive, antisocial, and unstable lifestyle, or social deviance. The two factors are correlated about .50 but have different patterns of correlations with external variables. These patterns make theoretical and clinical sense. For example, Factor 1 is correlated positively with prototypicality ratings of narcissistic and histrionic personality disorder, self-report measures of narcissism and Machiavellianism, risk for recidivism and violence, and unusual processing of affective material (see below). It is correlated negatively with self-report measures of empathy and anxiety. Factor 2 is most strongly correlated with diagnoses of APD, criminal and antisocial behaviors, substance abuse, and various self-report measures of psychopathy. It is also (weakly) correlated negatively with socioeconomic level, education, and IQ. The PCL-R factors appear to measure two facets of a higher-order construct, namely psychopathy. However, IRT analyses conducted by Cooke and Michie (1997) indicate that Factor 1 items are more discriminating and provide more information about the construct than do Factor 2 items. Factor 1 items occur at high levels of the construct and in the most extreme cases, whereas Factor 2 items are present at low levels of the construct.

Comparisons between the PCL-R and the DSM-III-R category of APD are illuminating and help to explain why the PCL-R played an important role in the DSM-IV field trial for potential revisions of the criteria for APD. Although PCL-R scores are significantly correlated with diagnoses of APD in forensic populations, the association is an asymmetric one. This is because in these populations the base rate for psychopathy, as defined by the PCL-R, is much lower (15% to 25%) than the base rate for APD (50% to 75%). Most psychopathic offenders and patients also meet the criteria for APD, but most of those with APD are not psychopaths. This is because APD is defined largely by antisocial behaviors, and consequently taps the social deviance components of psychopathy (Factor 2) much better than it does the affective/interpersonal components of the disorder (Factor 1). APD more or less leaves out the personality traits necessary to differentiate between psychopathic and other criminals (Cooke & Michie, 1997).

Although my colleagues and I have taken great pains to differentiate between psychopathy and APD, some clinicians and investigators use the labels as if the constructs they measure were interchangeable. They are not, and the failure to recognize this simple fact results in confusion and misleading conclusions (Hare, 1996a).

The Psychopathy Checklist: Screening Version

The PCL-R takes several hours to complete—too long for the average clinician working in acute psychiatric and mental health facilities. Several years ago John Monahan asked if it would be possible to develop a brief version of the PCL-R for use in the John D. and Catherine T. MacArthur Foundation project on the prediction of violence in the mentally disordered. With generous support from the Foundation, we began development of the 12-item PCL:SV (Hart et al., 1995; Hart, Hare, & Forth, 1993). The Hare PCL:SV is conceptually and empirically related to the PCL-R, and can be used as a screen for psychopathy in forensic populations or as a stand-alone instrument for research with non-criminals, including civil psychiatric patients (as in the MacArthur Foundation project).

It has the same factor structure as the PCL-R, with the affective/interpersonal and socially deviant components of psychopathy each being measured by six items. The Total score can range from 0 to 24, and a cutoff score of 18 is considered equivalent to a score of 30 on the PCL-R. There is rapidly accumulating evidence for the construct validity of the PCL:SV, including its ability to predict aggression and violence in offenders and forensic psychiatric patients (e.g., Douglas et al., 1997; Hill, Rogers, & Bickford, 1996).

Psychopathy in Children

Most clinicians and researchers are reluctant to speak of psychopathic children; however, it is likely that the personality traits and behaviors that define adult psychopathy begin to manifest themselves in childhood (Frick, 1998; Lahey & Kazdin, 1990; Lynam, 1996; McBurnett & Pfiffner, 1998; Moffitt, 1993; Robins, 1966; Robins & Rutter, 1990). If so, early intervention is essential if we are ever to have any hope of influencing the development and behavioral expression of the disorder. The problem, however, is complicated by general failure to differentiate the budding psychopath from other children who exhibit serious emotional and behavioral problems, particularly those children diagnosed with conduct disorder, attention-deficit/hyperactivity disorder, or oppositional defiant disorder (Frick, 1998; McBurnett & Pfiffner, 1998; Lynam, 1996).

Frick, O'Brien, Wooten, and McBurnett (1994) modified the PCL-R items so that they were suitable for children and could be rated by parents and teachers. In a sample of clinic-referred children between the ages of 6 and 13 years, the items identified much the same two-factor structure as that found with adults (Harpur et al., 1989). One dimension was associated with impulsivity and conduct problems (similar to PCL-R Factor 2); the other was linked with the interpersonal and motivational aspects of psychopathy, such as lack of guilt, lack of empathy, and superficial charm (similar to PCL-R Factor 1). These two dimensions, labeled "conduct problems" and "callous–emotional traits," respectively, have different patterns of associations with a variety of external variables, including conduct disorder. An important implication of their findings is that children with conduct disorder constitute a small subset with, and a larger subset without, psychopathic features. Presumably, each subset has a different developmental history and requires different treatment strategies (Frick, 1996; Wootton, Frick, Shelton, & Silverthorn, 1997).

Psychopathy: Continuum or Discrete Category?

One of the questions often raised by clinicians, researchers, and the public is this: Do psychopaths differ from the rest of us in degree or in kind? Many researchers (e.g., Blackburn, 1993; Livesley, 1998; Livesley & Schroeder, 1991; Widiger, 1998) prefer dimensional conceptualizations of personality disorders, whereas formal diagnostic systems, such as DSM-IV, make it difficult to adopt anything other than a categorical view (i.e., that an individual either does or does not have APD).

Harris, Rice, and Quinsey (1994) used extensive file information to obtain PCL-R scores for 653 male forensic patients, in order to determine whether the dimensional PCL-R reflected a dimensional or a categorical construct. Using four different taxonometric methods, they obtained results consistent with the hypothesis that psychopathy is a discrete category, or taxon. Their procedures allowed for the emergence of only two groups or classes of patients: those in the psychopathy taxon and those not in the taxon. They concluded that the optimal PCL-R score for inclusion in the psychopathy taxon was about 25, somewhat lower than the cutoff score of 30 recommended for research purposes (Hare, 1991). More recently, David Cooke (personal communication, November 21, 1994) analyzed two large sets of PCL-R scores—one from male offenders who had taken part in research conducted by my laboratory, and the other from his own stratified random sample of the Scottish prison population. Cooke's analyses differed from those of Harris et al. (1994) in two important ways: His PCL-R scores were based on both semistructured interviews and file information, and his taxonometric procedures allowed for the emergence of more than two classes of offenders. Each of his two samples yielded three classes, one clearly being a psychopathy taxon. The optimal PCL-R score for inclusion in this taxon was between 28 and 32, in line with the recommended cutoffs for the diagnosis of psychopathy.

The results of these studies are certainly suggestive, and it is quite possible that psychopathy is best characterized as an emergent entity formed by particular numbers and combinations of features that, by themselves and in other combinations and degrees, occur in many individuals and clinical conditions. On the other hand, cogent arguments can be made that psychopathy is better represented by multidimensional models or that it consists of maladaptive variants of common personality traits found in everyone (e.g., Blackburn, 1998; Livesley, 1998). We (Harpur, Hart, & Hare, 1994) and, more recently, Widiger (1998; see also Widiger & Lynam, Chapter 10, this volume) have described attempts to map the PCL-R items onto the five-factor ("Big Five") multidimensional model of personality.

PSYCHOPATHY AND THE CRIMINAL JUSTICE SYSTEM

Over the past two decades, one of the more dramatic changes in our view of psychopathy has been in its significance to the criminal justice system, particularly with respect to the assessment of risk for recidivism and violence. Guze (1976), for example, noted that once a person had been convicted of a felony, psychiatric diagnoses, including sociopathy, were not very helpful in predicting criminal activities. This view, though, was compromised by the use of diagnostic criteria at that time that permitted almost 80% of felons to receive a diagnosis of sociopathy. By way of contrast, there is now an extensive literature indicating that current assessments of psychopathy, either by themselves or as part of risk equations, are highly predictive of treatability, recidivism, and violence (see Hart & Hare, 1997). This literature is based almost entirely on research involving the use of the PCL-R. For this reason, each of the studies referred to in the rest of this chapter used the PCL-R for the assessment of psychopathy, unless otherwise indicated.

Psychopathy and Crime

Although some psychopaths manage to ply their trade with few formal contacts with the criminal justice system, their personality is clearly compatible with a propensity to violate many of society's rules and expectations. The crimes of the psychopaths who do break the law run the gamut from petty theft and fraud to cold-blooded violence (Hare & McPherson, 1984; Hart & Hare, 1997; Kosson, Smith, & Newman, 1990; Wong, 1984). However, it is primarily the violence of psychopaths that captures the headlines, particularly when it ends in an apparently senseless death. The ease with which psychopaths engage in instrumental and dispassionate violence (Cornell et al., 1993, 1996; Dempster et al., 1996; Serin, 1991; Williamson, Hare, & Wong, 1987) has very real significance for society in general and for law enforcement personnel in particular. For example, a recent study by the Federal Bureau of Investigation (1992) found that almost half of the law enforcement officers who died in the line of duty were killed by individuals who closely matched the personality profile of the psychopath.

The Psychopath as Predator

The biological and environmental factors responsible for development and maintenance of psychopathy are not well understood (see Hare, 1993; Lykken, 1995; Mealey, 1995). However, psychopathy is likely to be the product of complex interactions between biological predispositions and social forces (Hare, 1993; Livesley, 1998). Whether it is viewed as a mental disorder or as an evolved "cheater" strategy (Harpending & Sobus, 1987; MacMillan & Kofoed, 1984; Mealey, 1995), psychopathy is clearly associated with what most societies would consider to be aggressive and antisocial behavior. Elsewhere (Hare, 1993), I have described psychopaths as intraspecies predators who use charm, manipulation, intimidation, and violence to control others and to satisfy their own selfish needs. Lacking in "conscience" and in feelings for others, they cold-bloodedly take what they want and do as they please, without the slightest sense of guilt or regret. In spite of their small numbers—perhaps 1% of the general population—they constitute a significant proportion of our prison populations and are responsible for a markedly disproportionate amount of serious crime, violence, and social distress. Furthermore, their depredations affect virtually everyone at one time or another, for they are found in all races, cultures, ethnic groups, and socioeconomic levels. They are well represented by persistent criminals, serial killers and rapists, drug dealers, spouse and child abusers, swindlers and con artists, mercenaries, corrupt politicians, unethical lawyers and doctors, terrorists, cult leaders, black marketeers, high-pressure salesmen and stock promoters, gang members, and radical political activists. They are active in the business and corporate world, particularly where rules and their enforcement are lax and where accountability is difficult to determine (Babiak, 1995).

The behavioral expressions of psychopathy, as well as the degree to which they stand out from the behaviors of others, are influenced by societal and cultural structures and norms. Psychopaths often are to be found at the edges of society, where they "sparkle with the glitter of personal freedom, the checks and reins of the community are absent, and there are no limits either in a physical or a psychological sense" (Lindner, 1944, p. 13). For example, in "frontier" societies, such as the American "Wild West" in the late 1800s, the behavior of psychopaths was not considered particularly unusual. Indeed, many became "folk heroes," and some were even charged with enforcing the law as sheriffs or marshals. Similarly, in societies experiencing social, economic, and political upheaval (e.g., Rwanda, the former Yugoslavia, and the former Soviet Union), it is not uncommon for psychopaths to emerge as leaders and "patriots" who wrap themselves in a flag of convenience and enrich themselves by callously exploiting ethnic, cultural, or racial tensions and grievances. Of course, psychopaths are not the only ones who take advantage of such opportunities. Criminals in general, individuals who are socially and economically disadvantaged, and those with a grudge against society or a tendency to "go along with the crowd" are all likely to engage in antisocial behavior during breakdowns in law and order.

It is more difficult to determine how psychopaths express themselves in societies that are highly structured and in which there are strong traditions to conform to group standards. We might expect that only those whose propensities to satisfy their own needs are strongest, and whose inhibitions against doing so are weakest, will break through restrictive societal controls, conventions, and expectations. These individuals are most likely to be psychopaths. Put another way, I would expect that a significant proportion (if not most) of those in structured, traditional societies who engage in persistent antisocial and criminal activities are psychopaths. I would also argue that when such societies sanction an activity such as war, the psychopaths will still stand out from the other participants. Compared with others, the psychopaths will find it easier to dehumanize and brutalize the enemy. To paraphrase what I wrote elsewhere (Hare, 1993), if crime, violence, and predation are part of the job description, the psychopath is the perfect candidate.

Crime across the Lifespan

One important symptom of psychopathy is persistent, frequent, and varied asocial and antisocial behavior, starting at an early age (Hare, 1993; Hart & Hare, 1997). Although psychopathy is closely linked to antisocial and illegal behavior, it should not be confused with criminal behavior in general. Criminal behavior is much more common in society than is psychopathy. It may even be normative for people to engage in isolated instances of less serious criminal conduct. For example, studies of teenage boys in North America and the United Kingdom have found that more than 50% admit to having committed one or more criminal offenses in the past (see Andrews & Bonta, 1993; Blackburn, 1993). Although many psychopaths engage in chronic criminal conduct and do so at a high rate, only a small minority of those who engage in criminal conduct are psychopaths. Psychopaths are qualitatively different from others who routinely engage in criminal behavior, and different even from those whose criminal conduct is extremely serious and persistent. They have distinctive "criminal careers" with respect to the number and type of antisocial behaviors they commit, as well as the ages at which they commit them. Furthermore, it appears that the antisocial behavior of psychopaths is motivated by different factors from those that motivate nonpsychopaths, with the result that the behavioral topography of their criminal conduct (i.e., their victimology or *modus operandi*) is also different. The personality and social-psychological factors that explain antisocial behavior in general (see Andrews & Bonta, 1993; Gottfredson & Hirschi, 1990; Wilson & Herrnstein, 1985) may not be applicable to psychopaths. Any comprehensive examination of crime must include a discussion of the distinctive role of psychopathy.

Although the typical criminal career is relatively short, there are individuals who devote most of their adolescent and adult lives to delinquent and criminal enterprises (Blumstein, Cohen, Roth, & Vishner, 1986). Many of these career criminals become less grossly antisocial in middle age (Blumstein et al., 1986; Robins, 1966). About half of the criminal psychopaths we have studied showed a relatively sharp reduction in criminality around age 35 or 40, primarily with respect to nonviolent offenses (Hare, McPherson, & Forth, 1988). This does not mean that they gave up crime completely, only that their level of general criminal activity decreased to that of the average persistent offender. Moreover, it appears that the propensity for psychopaths to engage in violent and aggressive behavior decreased very little with age—a finding also reported by Harris, Rice, and Cormier (1991).

A question we might ask is this: Are age-related reductions in the criminality of psychopaths paralleled by changes in core personality traits, or have these individuals simply learned new ways of staying out of prison? Although I share the view of many clinicians that the personality structure of psychopaths is too stable to account for the behavioral changes that sometimes occur in middle age, empirical, longitudinal evidence is needed to resolve the issue. Meanwhile, a cross-sectional study of 889 male offenders provides a clue to what we might expect (Harpur & Hare, 1994). The offenders ranged in age from 16 to 70 at the time they were assessed with the PCL or the PCL-R. Scores on Factor 2 (socially deviant features) decreased sharply with age, whereas scores on Factor 1 (affective/interpersonal features) remained stable with age. These results are consistent with the view that age-related changes in the psychopath's antisocial behavior are not necessarily paralleled by changes in the egocentric, manipulative, and callous traits fundamental to psychopathy. This point is illustrated in the following brief anecdote. A prison psychologist at one of my talks told of a psychopathic offender with a history of violence who had become "born again and resocialized in prison" and was released on parole. For several years he appeared to be a model parolee, but recently it had come to the attention of his parole officer that the former inmate had been living with a disturbed woman whose only functions were to be available as a sex object and a punching bag. Believing that she deserved the abuse, she didn't report him to the police. This man certainly was no less psychopathic than when he was in prison; he simply employed a different set of antisocial and callous behaviors.

Recidivism and Risk for Violence

Perhaps the most dramatic change over the past few decades is in the perceived—and actual—importance of psychopathy to the criminal justice system has been in its predictive validity. Various actuarial systems generally do a fairly good job in predicting criminal behavior, but the use of personality tests usually results in little or no incremental validity. As a psychopathy researcher, I have always found this situation perplexing. I could not understand, for example, how two individuals with much the same scores on some actuarial device (based on similar criminal and demographic characteristics), but one egocentric, cold-blooded, and remorseless and the other not, could possibly present the same risk. That they do not is clearly indicated by the results of many recent studies, only a sampling of which can be presented here (see reviews by Hart, 1996; Hemphill, Hare, & Wong, 1998; Salekin, Rogers, & Sewell, 1996).

Adult Male Offenders

In the first of these studies, we administered the PCL to 231 adult male offenders prior to their conditional release from a federal prison (Hart, Kropp, & Hare, 1988). Overall, 46.3% of the offenders violated the conditions of their conditional release and were returned to prison. The PCL scores correlated .33 with release outcome (success or failure), and made a significant contribution to the prediction of outcome over and beyond that made by relevant features of criminal history and demographic variables. We also performed a survival analysis in which survival—that is, not being returned to prison—was plotted as a function of time following release. Within 3 years, about 75% of the nonpsychopaths but only about 20% of the psychopaths, were still out of prison.

Serin, Peters, and Barbaree (1990) administered the PCL-R to 93 male offenders released on unescorted temporary absence (UTA). The failure rate on UTA typically is very low, but the failures are sometimes spectacular and receive much media coverage. The failure rate was 0% for the nonpsychopaths and 37.5% (6 of 16) for the psychopaths. Seventy-seven of the offenders were subsequently paroled; the failure rate was 7% for the nonpsychopaths and 33% for the psychopaths. Psychopathy was more predictive of outcome than were (1) a combination of criminal history variables and demographic variables, and (2) several standard actuarial risk instruments, including the Base Expectancy Scale (Gottfredson & Bonds, 1961) and the Salient Factor Score (Hoffman & Beck, 1974). In another study, Serin and Amos (1995) followed 299 male offenders for up to 8 years after their release from federal prison. Within 3 years, about 65% of the psychopaths and 25% of the nonpsychopaths were convicted of a new crime. The difference was even greater for convictions for violent crimes: about 40% for psychopaths and fewer than 10% for nonpsychopaths.

Harris, Rice, and Quinsey (1993) found that 31% of 618 offenders released from a maximum security unit and a pretrial assessment center recidivated violently. They subjected 12 variables to regression analysis and produced a 9-point risk scale for the prediction of violence. The multiple correlation between scores on the risk scale and outcome was .46; the single most important predictor was the PCL-R, with a correlation of .34 with outcome. Individuals at the upper end of the risk scale were almost certain to recidivate violently, whereas those at the lower end were almost certain not to recidivate violently. Details on the practical use of this Violence Risk Appraisal Guide (VRAG) have been provided by Webster, Harris, Rice, Cormier, and Quinsey (1994).

Although Rice and Harris (1997) have recently cross-validated and extended the use of the VRAG to sex offenders, I should note that the samples used to develop and cross-validate the instrument came primarily from a particular maximum-security forensic psychiatric facility in Ontario. Furthermore, the predictor variables, including the PCL-R, were scored from file information—much of it rather old, as reflected in the identification of several DSM-III diagnoses as predictors. With the exception of the PCL-R, which appears to have predictive value with diverse populations, the value of many of the VRAG's predictor variables may be specific to the samples used in its development. As a general rule, jurisdictions that plan to adopt risk assessment instruments developed elsewhere should first ensure that the instruments in question generalize to their populations. A useful guide in determining which variables are likely to be of practical value in developing a local prediction scheme is the 20-item Historical/Clinical/Risk Management scheme (HCR-20; Webster, Douglas, Eaves, & Hart, 1997). Suggestions for the development and validation of violence risk assessment are provided by Borum (1996) and Hart (1996).

Although the prevalence of psychopathy is lower in forensic psychiatric populations than in offender populations, the presence of psychopathic attributes in forensic patients is a risk factor for recidivism and violence. For example, Rice and Harris (1992) found that the correlation between PCL-R scores and recidivism was .33 in a sample of 96 male not-guilty-by-reason-of-insanity schizophrenics and .30 in a sample of 96 nonpsychotic offenders. Hart and Hare (1989) found that only 10 patients in a sample of 80 consecutive admissions to a forensic psychiatric hospital were psychopaths, although the mean PCL-R score for the sample (22.0, $SD = 6.8$) indicates that many patients exhibited a significant number of psychopathic symptoms. In a recent survival analysis of recidivism in this sample, Wintrup (1994) found that more than 60% of patients with a PCL-R score of 30 or above recidivated within 5 years, whereas only about 20% of the other patients did so.

Several studies have found that the PCL:SV is predictive of institutional aggression and violence in forensic psychiatric hospitals (Hill et al., 1996; Heilbrun et al., in press). The PCL:SV also appears to predict violence following release from a psychiatric institution. Douglas et al. (1997) assessed postrelease community violence in 279 patients (167 males, 112 females) who had been involuntarily committed to a civil psychiatric facility. Although very few of the patients had a score high enough to warrant a diagnosis of psychopathy, the PCL:SV nevertheless was highly predictive of violent behaviors and arrests for violent crimes. When the distribution of PCL:SV scores was split at the median, the odds ratio for a violent crime was 9.9 times higher for patients above the median than it was for those below the median.

Female Offenders

Recidivism rates among female psychopathic offenders appear to be as high as they are among their male counterparts. Zaparniuk and Paris (1995) performed a survival curve analysis on 75 female offenders assessed with the PCL-R. Within 1 year, approximately 60% of the psychopaths and 25% of the other offenders had recidivated.

Adolescent Offenders

Psychopathy is a strong predictor of recidivism and violence in adolescent offenders. Gretton et al. (1997) examined the predictive validity of the PCL-R in a sample of 359 young offenders (aged 12 to 18; $M = 15.3$), 209 of whom had been convicted of a sexual crime. The PCL-R scores ($M = 21.8$, $SD = 7.1$) were used to divide the sample into groups that were low (0–17; $n = 124$), medium (18–27; $n = 172$), and high (28–40; $n = 63$) in psychopathy. In the follow-up period, which averaged 6 years, 72% of the offenders committed at least one crime, 41% committed at least one violent crime, and 16% committed at least one sexual crime. The percentages of offenders in the low, medium, and high groups who committed at least one crime were 55%, 69%, and 82%, respectively—a highly significant difference. The group differences for sexual and other violent crimes were more striking. Thus, 11%, 18%, and 25% of the low, medium, and high groups, respectively, committed a sexual crime in the follow-up period. The percentages of offenders in the low, medium, and high groups who committed a violent crime in the follow-up period were 26%, 46%, and 61%, respectively. Hierarchical logistic analysis indicated that even when relevant demographic and criminal history variables were taken into account, the PCL-R made a substantial and significant contribution to the prediction of general, sexual, and other violent offending. One of the conclusions drawn from this study was that adolescent psychopaths tend to be generalized offenders.

Sex Offenders

The last few years has seen a sharp increase in the public and professional attention paid to sex offenders, particularly those who commit a new offense following release from a treatment program or prison. It has long been recognized that psychopathic sex offenders present special problems for therapists and the criminal justice system. Indeed, some jurisdictions make provision for designating convicted sex offenders as psychopaths and for sentencing them to indefinite terms of detention. In the state of Minnesota, for example, a sex offender can be so committed if it is determined that he or she is a "psychopathic personality." In a recent case (CO-94-1367), the Minnesota Court of Appeals upheld the trial court's decision to commit a sex offender with a record of sexual violence and a high PCL-R score as a psychopathic personality. In June 1997, the U.S. Supreme Court ruled that it is constitutional to confine sexual offenders to a state forensic hospital if they suffer from a mental or personality disorder likely to lead to violence.

The prevalence of psychopathy—defined by a PCL-R score of at least 30—appears to be relatively high among convicted rapists. Forth and Kroner (1994) reported that in a federal prison, 26.1% of 211 rapists, 18.3% of 163 mixed sex offenders (including child molesters), and 5.4% of 82 incest offenders were psychopaths. Forth and Kroner's (1994) sample of sex offenders included 60 who were either serial rapists or rapists who killed their victims; 35% of these offenders were psychopaths. The prevalence of the disorder seems to be particularly high among offenders adjudicated by the courts as "sexually dangerous." For example, Prentky and Knight (1991) found that 45.3% of 95 rapists and 30.5% of 59 child molesters in the Massachusetts Treatment Center for Sexually Dangerous Persons at Bridgewater met the PCL criteria for psychopathy.

Sex offenders are generally resistant to treatment (Quinsey, Harris, Rice, & Lalumiere, 1993), but the psychopaths among them are most likely to recidivate early and often. For example, Quinsey, Rice, and Harris (1995), in a follow-up of 178 treated rapists and child molesters, concluded that psychopathy is a general predictor of sexual and violent recidivism. In a survival analysis, they found that within 6 years of release from prison, more than 80% of the psychopaths but only about 20% of the nonpsychopaths had violently recidivated. Many, but not all, of the psychopaths' offenses were sexual in nature. In a more recent follow-up of 288 sex offenders, Rice and Harris (1997) reported similar results. In addition, however, they found that sexual recidivism (as opposed to violent recidivism in general) was strongly predicted by a combination of a high PCL-R score and phallometric evidence of deviant sexual arousal, defined as any phallometric test "that indicated an absolute preference for deviant stimuli (children, rape cues, or nonsexual violence cues)."

The implications of psychopathy are just as serious among adolescent sex offenders as among their adult counterparts. Preliminary results from a longitudinal study of adolescent sex offenders (aged 13 to 18) released after treatment at a forensic facility in Vancouver revealed that the mean PCL-R score for 193 male sex offenders was 21.4 (*SD* = 7.0), with about 18% meeting our criteria for psychopathy (O'Shaughnessy, Hare, Gretton, & McBride, 1994). Survival analyses indicated that the reconviction rate for sexual offenses in the first 36 months following release was low (i.e., less than 10%) and unrelated to psychopathy. However, the pattern for other types of offenses was quite different. Thus, within 36 months of release, about 70% of the psychopaths and 40% of all other offenders had been convicted of a nonsexual offense. The results were most striking within the first 12 months of release; the reconviction rate for nonsexual crimes was about 55% for psychopaths but only about 15% for all other offenders. Thirty-one percent of the psychopaths and only 14% of the other offenders had been convicted for a nonsexual violent offense within 12 months of release. One conclusion is that following release, many of our adolescent sex offenders, and most of the psychopathic ones, were more likely to be convicted of a nonsexual than a sexual offense. Many of these individuals were not so much specialized sex offenders as they were offenders, and their misbehavior—sexual and otherwise—was presumably a reflection of a generalized propensity to violate social and legal expectations. If so, it may be as important to target their antisocial tendencies and behaviors as it is to treat their sexual deviancy.

Recidivism Following Treatment

In many jurisdictions, it is not uncommon for a trial judge to accept expert testimony that a defendant convicted of a serious crime is a psychopath, and then to sentence the defendant to a prison where he or she "can receive treatment." The uninformed views of such judges and the anecdotal evidence of those who run prison programs notwithstanding, there is little convincing evidence that psychopaths respond favorably to treatment and intervention (see Dolan & Coid, 1993; Hare, 1993; Losel, 1996, 1998; Suedfeld &

Landon, 1978). This does not mean that the egocentric and callous attitudes and behaviors of psychopaths are immutable, only that there have been no methodologically sound treatment or "resocialization" programs that have been shown to work with psychopaths (see the next section). Unfortunately, both the criminal justice system and the public are routinely fooled into believing otherwise. As a result, many psychopaths take part in all sorts of prison treatment programs, put on a good show, make "remarkable progress," convince the therapists and parole board of their reformed character, are released, and pick up where they left off when they entered prison.

Several recent studies illustrate the point. For example, Ogloff, Wong, and Greenwood (1990) reported that psychopaths, defined by a PCL-R score of at least 30, derived little benefit from a therapeutic community program designed to treat personality-disordered offenders. The psychopaths stayed in the program for a shorter time, were less motivated, and showed less clinical improvement than did other offenders. It might be argued that even though the psychopaths did not do well in this program, some residual benefits could conceivably show up following their release from prison. However, in a survival analysis, Hemphill (1991) found that the estimated reconviction rate in the first year following release was twice as high for the psychopaths (83%) as for the other offenders (42%).

In a well-known study, Rice, Harris, and Cormier (1992) retrospectively scored the PCL-R from the institutional files of patients of a maximum-security psychiatric facility. They defined psychopaths by a PCL-R score of 25 or more, and nonpsychopaths by a score below 25. They then compared the violent recidivism rate of 166 patients who had been treated in an intensive and lengthy therapeutic community program with 119 patients who had not taken part in the program. For nonpsychopaths, the violent recidivism rate was 22% for treated patients and 39% for untreated patients. But the violent recidivism rate for treated psychopaths was higher (77%) than was that for untreated psychopaths (55%). How could therapy make someone worse? The simple answer is that group therapy and insight-oriented programs may help psychopaths to develop better ways of manipulating, deceiving, and using people, but do little to help them to understand themselves. As a consequence, following release into the community, they may be more likely than untreated psychopaths to continue to place themselves in situations where the potential for violence is high. However, before we spend too much effort in trying to determine why therapy makes psychopaths worse, we need more evidence that it fact does so. The findings by Rice et al. (1992), though intriguing and suggestive, were based on research with a particular population of mentally disordered offenders (see my comments above about the VRAG) and with an unusual, complex, and controversial treatment program.

Management of Psychopaths

The view that psychopaths are not amenable to treatment is understandable. Unlike most other offenders, they suffer little personal distress, see little wrong with their attitudes and behavior, and seek treatment only when it is in their best interests to do so (such as when seeking probation or parole). It is therefore not surprising that they derive little benefit from traditional prison programs, particularly those aimed at the development of empathy, conscience, and interpersonal skills. What then? Do we simply keep them in prison until they are old enough to pose little risk to society? Or do we increase our efforts to explore new ways of motivating them to become more prosocial in their attitudes and behaviors?

Recently I met with a group of inmates who had volunteered to participate in an intensive program for violent offenders. Because of prison policy, most of the men in the group had some idea about their percentile ranks on the PCL-R, and several were quite candid about describing themselves as psychopaths. We spent about 2 hours discussing the implications that a diagnosis of psychopathy had for them. The discussion was rather heated and consisted for the most part of a concerted attack on me and the impact that the PCL-R was having on their lives. Many of the points made by these offenders were valid, particularly their concern that parole boards relied too heavily on PCL-R scores when making decisions about early, conditional release. Some asserted that high PCL-R scores served to "flush their lives down the drain." I protested that parole boards do not make decisions on the basis of a single instrument, and that, besides, their PCL-R scores merely reflected the way they were—their personality, attitudes, and behaviors. I also argued that the PCL-R was only one risk variable that should be taken into account. They countered that their scores were based largely on historical factors that were not susceptible to change, and that parole boards tended to discount any therapeutic gains they might have made, on the grounds that "everyone knows" that psychopaths "merely go through the motions" in therapy sessions. Their feeling was that no matter what they did to change themselves, and no matter what progress their therapists credited them with, a high PCL-R score was all a parole board needed to justify "warehousing" them.

There is no simple solution to this dilemma. At present, we ask psychopaths to participate in treatment programs that have little chance of success, and that fool them and us into thinking that the exercise is worthwhile and of practical benefit to them. It would be better for all concerned if we were to mount a concerted effort to develop innovative procedures designed specifically for psychopathic offenders (Dolan & Coid, 1993; Hare, 1993; Losel, 1996, 1998).

Several years ago the Correctional Service of Canada (CSC), which is responsible for all federal offenders, asked me to design a program that would have a reasonable chance of modifying the attitudes and behaviors of offenders at high risk for violence, including psychopaths. With the help of an international panel of experts, the broad outline of such a program was developed (Hare, 1992). In brief, we proposed that relapse prevention techniques be integrated with elements of the best available cognitive-behavioral correctional programs. The program would be less concerned with developing empathy and conscience or effecting changes in personality than with convincing participants that they alone are responsible for their behavior and that they can learn more prosocial ways of using their strengths and abilities to satisfy their needs and wants. It would involve tight control and supervision, both in the institution and following release into the community, as well as comparisons with carefully selected groups of offenders treated in standard correctional programs. The experimental design would permit empirical evaluation of its treatment and intervention modules (what works and what doesn't work for particular individuals). That is, some modules or components might be effective with psychopaths but not with other offenders, and vice versa. We recognized that correctional programs are constantly in danger of erosion because of changing institutional priorities, community concerns, and political pressures. To prevent this from happening, we proposed stringent safeguards for maintaining the integrity of the program. The CSC chose not to adopt our recommendations, with the result that psychopathic offenders continue to participate in programs that are ill suited to their problems and needs.

Recently, Losel (1996, 1998) provided a thoughtful analysis of the issues involved in the treatment and management of psychopathic offenders, and has outlined in some detail the requirements for an effective program. Although he was unaware of the program

I described above, his conclusions and recommendations were remarkably consistent with mine.

COGNITIVE NEUROSCIENCE AND THE CRIMINAL JUSTICE SYSTEM

Among the things that I have found most interesting about psychopaths are the apparent conceptual and empirical connections between their cold-blooded, predatory behavior and underlying neurobiological mechanisms (see Hare, 1998).

Much of the early theory and research on psychopathy was influenced by prevailing theories of learning, emotion, and motivation. We learned much about the biological (especially the autonomic) correlates of psychopathy, and about the role of rewards and punishments in establishing and maintaining psychopathic behavior. Though scientifically valuable, much of this work had little practical impact on the general public or on forensic and mental health workers. The situation is beginning to change dramatically, primarily because of the increasing use of procedures and paradigms from cognitive psychology and neuroscience (see Hare, 1998; Newman, 1998; Newman & Wallace, 1993). Research on cognition and emotion is particularly interesting because of its potential implications for the issue of criminal responsibility.

Clinicians have long maintained that the cognitions, language, and life experiences of psychopaths lack depth and affect. Recent laboratory research provides neurophysiological support for this view. Space prevents anything more than brief references to some of this work. Perhaps the most interesting findings are that psychopaths seem unable or unwilling to process or use the deep semantic meanings of language; their linguistic processes appear to be relatively superficial, and the subtle, more abstract meanings and nuances of language escape them (Intrator et al., 1997; Williamson, Harpur, & Hare, 1991). Furthermore, behavioral, electrocortical, and brain imaging research adds weight to the clinical belief that psychopaths fail to appreciate the emotional significance of an event or experience (Intrator et al., 1997; Larbig, Veit, Rau, Schlottke, & Birbaumer, 1992; Patrick, 1994; Williamson et al., 1991). In short, psychopaths appear to be semantically and affectively shallow individuals. Presumably, the deep semantic and affective networks that tie cognitions together are not well developed in these individuals (Hare, 1993).

Why do these cognitive and linguistic problems typically go undetected? For one thing, psychopaths use their own attributes to put on a good show. Intense eye contact, distracting body language, charm, and a knowledge of the listener's vulnerabilies are all part of the psychopath's armamentarium for dominating, controlling, and manipulating others. We pay less attention to what these individuals say than to how they say it—style over substance. Because it is so easy to become sucked in by psychopaths, my research group routinely videotapes all of our interviews for later, more detached analysis. We advise others to do likewise.

The cognitive, linguistic, and behavioral attributes of psychopaths (Hare, 1993; Newman & Wallace, 1993) may be related to cerebral dysfunction, particularly in the orbito-ventromedial frontal cortex (Gorenstein & Newman, 1980; Hare, in press; Intrator et al., 1997; Lapierre, Braun, & Hodgins, 1995). This dysfunction need not actually involve organic damage, but could reflect structural or functional anomalies in the brain mechanisms and neural circuitry—including the orbito-ventromedial frontal cortex, medial temporal cortex, and amygdala, and their neurotransmitter systems—responsible for the coordination of cognitive and affective processes (Intrator et al., 1977). Behavioral and neuroimaging studies indicate that damage to these regions can produce a dissociation of the logical/cognitive and affective components of thought (Damasio, Grabowski, Frank, Galaburda, & Damasio, 1994), or even what Damasio, Tranel, and Damasio (1987) refer to as "acquired sociopathy."

The relevance of this to the criminal justice system is that very little of what we do is based solely on logical appraisals of situations and their potential ramifications for us and others. In most cases, our cognitions and behaviors are heavily laden with emotional elements. As Damasio (1994) recently put it, "emotion is integral to the process of reasoning" (p. 144). I would argue that it is also an essential part of "conscience." However, it is this very element that is missing or seriously impaired in psychopaths; their "conscience" is only half formed, consisting merely of an intellectual awareness of the rules of the game. The powerful motivating, guiding, and inhibiting effects of emotion play little role in their lives, presumably not so much by choice as because of what they are. In effect, their internalized rulebooks are pale, abridged versions of those that direct the conduct of other individuals.

In most jurisdictions, psychopathy is considered to be an aggravating rather than a mitigating factor in determining criminal responsibility. This is the way it should be, in my view. However, I've been asked whether research evidence of the sort described above—affective deficit, thought disorder, brain dysfunction—might lead some to view psychopathy as a mitigating factor in a criminal case. As one psychiatrist put it, perhaps psychopathy will become "the kiss of life rather than the kiss of death" in first-degree murder cases. This would be disturbing, given that psychopaths are calculating predators whose behavior must be judged by the rules of the society in which they live. However, the issue is really one for the judicial system to settle. If psychopathy was to be used as a defense for a criminal act, though, the flip side of the coin would be that the disorder is currently untreatable, and any civil commitment would probably be more or less permanent.

A more serious problem is the apparent ease with which many psychopaths are able to malinger mental illness—that is, to fake psychotic symptoms in order to avoid prison (Gacono & Sheppard, 1994; Hare, 1993). They present a particularly difficult dilemma for the mental health and criminal justice systems, typically bouncing back and forth between prisons and forensic psychiatric facilities. While in the latter, they are a disruptive influence on other patients, a nuisance and danger to the staff, and a high escape risk.

CONCLUSIONS

Even those opposed to the very idea of psychopathy cannot ignore its potent explanatory and predictive power—if not as a formal construct, then as a static risk factor. Indices of psychopathy are rapidly becoming a routine part of the assessment batteries used to make decisions about competency, sentencing, diversion, placement, suitability for treatment, and risk for recidivism and violence. Because psychopaths with a history of violence are a poor risk for early release, more and more will be kept in prison for their full sentence, whereas many other offenders will be released early with little risk to society. However, unless we are content simply to warehouse high-risk offenders, we must develop innovative programs aimed at making their attitudes and behaviors less self-serving and more acceptable to the society in which most eventually must function.

Following publication of a book written for the general public (Hare, 1993), many people asked why I devoted so much space to psychopathic criminals, and so little to the psychopaths with whom they daily lived and worked and who somehow always managed to stay out of prison. Many of these correspondents seemed caught up in emotionally damaging and dangerous situations from which there apparently was no escape (see Meloy, 1992). Their plight raises an issue that urgently needs to be addressed and researched: the prevalence of psychopathy in the general population, and its expression in ways that are personally, socially, or economically damaging but that are not necessarily illegal or that do not result in criminal prosecution. We study incarcerated offenders for two reasons: The base rate for psychopathy is high, and we have access to enough solid information to make reliable assessments. However, we must find ways of studying psychopaths in the community if we are ever to provide some relief for their victims—which is to say, all of us.

ACKNOWLEDGMENTS

This chapter is a revised and updated version of a paper that first appeared in *Criminal Justice and Behavior* (Hare, 1996b).

Preparation of this chapter and some of the research described herein were supported by the Medical Research Council of Canada, the British Columbia Health Research Foundation, the British Columbia Research Services Foundation, and the Program of Research on Mental Health and the Law of the John D. and Catherine T. MacArthur Foundation.

I would like to express my deep appreciation to the graduate students who have worked with me over the years. The importance of their contributions is reflected in their authorship of many of the papers cited.

REFERENCES

Albert, R. S., Brigante, T. R., & Chase, M. (1959). The psychopathic personality: A content analysis of the concept. *Journal of General Psychology, 60,* 17–28.

American Psychiatric Association. (1968). *Diagnostic and statistical manual of mental disorders* (2nd ed.). Washington, DC: Author.

American Psychiatric Association. (1980). *Diagnostic and statistical manual of mental disorders* (3rd ed.). Washington, DC: Author.

American Psychiatric Association. (1987). *Diagnostic and statistical manual of mental disorders* (3rd ed., rev.). Washington, DC: Author.

American Psychiatric Association. (1994). *Diagnostic and statistical manual of mental disorders* (4th ed.). Washington, DC: Author.

Andrews, D. A., & Bonta, J. (1993). *The psychology of criminal conduct.* Cincinnati, OH: Anderson.

Babiak, P. (1995). When psychopaths go to work. *International Journal of Applied Psychology, 44,* 171–188.

Blackburn, R. (1993). *The psychology of criminal conduct.* Chichester, England: Wiley.

Blackburn, R. (1998). Psychopathy and personality disorder: Implications or interpersonal theory. In D. J. Cooke, A. E. Forth, & R. D. Hare (Eds.), *Psychopathy: Theory, research, and implications for society* (pp. 169–302). Dordrecht, The Netherlands: Kluwer.

Blumstein, A., Cohen, J., Roth, J. A., & Vishner, C. A. (Eds.). (1986). *Criminal careers and "career criminals."* Washington, DC: National Academy Press.

Borum, R. (1996). Improving the clinical practice of violence risk assessment: Technology, guidelines, and training. *American Psychologist, 51,* 945–956.

Brandt, J. R., Kennedy, W. A., Patrick, C. J., & Curtin, J. J. (1997). Assessment of psychopathy in a population of incarcerated adolescent offenders. *Psychological Assessment, 9,* 429–435.

Chandler, M., & Moran, T. (1990). Psychopathy and moral development: A comparative study of delinquent and nondelinquent youth. *Development and Psychopathology, 2*, 227–246.

Cleckley, H. M. (1976). *The mask of sanity* (5th ed.). St. Louis, MO: C. V. Mosby.

Cooke, D. J. (1995). Psychopathic disturbance in the Scottish prison population: Cross-cultural generalizability of the Hare Psychopathy Checklist. *Psychology, Crime, and Law, 2*, 101–118.

Cooke, D. J. (1996). Psychopathic personality in different cultures: What do we know? What do we need to find out? *Journal of Personality Disorders, 10*, 23–40.

Cooke, D. J. (1998). Psychopathy across cultures. In D. J. Cooke, A. E. Forth, & R. D. Hare (Eds.), *Psychopathy: Theory, research, and implications for society* (pp. 13–46). Dordrecht, The Netherlands: Kluwer.

Cooke, D. J., & Michie, C. (1997). An item response theory analysis of the Hare Psychopathy Checklist. *Psychological Assessment, 9*, 3–13.

Cornell, D., Warren, J., Hawk, G., Stafford, E., Oram, G., & Pine, D. (1996). Psychopathy in instrumental and reactive violent offenders. *Journal of Consulting and Clinical Psychology, 64*, 783–790.

Cornell, D., Warren, J., Hawk, G., Stafford, E., Oram, G., Pine, D., Weitzner, I., & Griffiths, R. (1993, August). *Psychopathy and anger among instrumental and reactive violent offenders.* Paper presented at the annual meeting of the American Psychological Association, Toronto.

Dahlstrom, W. M., & Welsh, G. S. (1960). *An MMPI handbook: A guide to use in clinical practice and research.* Minneapolis: University of Minnesota Press.

Damasio, A. (1994, October). Descartes' error and the future of human life. *Scientific American,* p. 144.

Damasio, A., Tranel, D., & Damasio, H. (1987). Individuals with sociopathic behavior caused by frontal damage fail to respond autonomically to social stimuli. *Behavioral Brain Research, 41*, 81–94.

Damasio, H., Grabowski, T., Frank, R., Galaburda, A. M., & Damasio, A. R. (1994). The return of Phineas Gage: Clues about the brain from the skull of a famous patient. *Science, 264*, 1102–1105.

Davies, W., & Feldman, P. (1981). The diagnosis of psychopathy by forensic specialists. *British Journal of Psychiatry, 138*, 329–331.

Dempster, R. J., Lyon, D. R., Sullivan, L. E., Hart, S. D., Smiley, W. C., & Mulloy, R. (1996, August). *Psychopathy and instrumental aggression in violent offenders.* Paper presented at the annual meeting of the American Psychological Association, Toronto.

Dolan, B., & Coid, J. (1993). *Psychopathic and antisocial personality disorders: Treatment and research issues.* London: Gaskell.

Douglas, K. S., Ogloff, J. R. P., & Nicholls, T. L. (1997, June). *Personality disorders and violence in civil psychiatric patients.* Paper presented at the 5th International Congress on the Disorders of Personality, Vancouver, British Columbia.

Federal Bureau of Investigation. (1992). *Killed in the line of duty.* Washington, DC: U.S. Department of Justice.

Forth, A. E. (1996). Psychopathy in adolescent offenders: Assessment, family background, and violence. In D. J. Cooke, A. E. Forth, J. P. Newman, & R. D. Hare (Eds.), *Issues in criminological and legal psychology: No. 24. International perspectives on psychopathy* (pp. 42–44). Leicester, England: British Psychological Society.

Forth, A. E., Hart, S. D., & Hare, R. D. (1990). Assessment of psychopathy in male young offenders. *Psychological Assessment, 2*, 342–344.

Forth, A. E., Kosson, D., & Hare, R. D. (in press). *The Hare Psychopathy Checklist: Youth Version.* Toronto: Multi-Health Systems.

Forth, A. E., & Kroner, D. (1994). *The factor structure of the Revised Psychopathy Checklist with incarcerated rapist and incest offenders.* Unpublished manuscript.

Fotheringham, J. B. (1957). Psychopathic personality: A review. *Canadian Psychiatric Association Journal, 2*, 52–74.

Frick, P. J. (1996). Callous–unemotional traits and conduct problems: A two-factor model of psychopathy in children. In D. J. Cooke, A. E. Forth, J. P. Newman, & R. D. Hare (Eds.), *Issues in criminological and legal psychology: No. 24. International perspectives on psychopathy* (pp. 47–51). Leicester, England: British Psychological Society.

Frick, P. J. (1998). Callous–emotional traits and conduct problems: Applying the two-factor model of psychopathy to children. In D. J. Cooke, A. E. Forth, & R. D. Hare (Eds.), *Psychopathy: Theory, research, and implications for society* (pp. 161–188). Dordrecht, The Netherlands: Kluwer.

Frick, P. J., O'Brien, B. S., Wooton, J. M., & McBurnett, K. (1994). Psychopathy and conduct problems in children. *Journal of Abnormal Psychology, 103,* 700–707.

Fulero, S. M. (1995). Review of the Hare Psychopathy Checklist—Revised. In J. C. Conoley & J. C. Impara (Eds.), *Twelfth mental measurements yearbook* (pp. 453–454). Lincoln, NE: Buros Institute.

Gacono, C. B., & Sheppard, K. (1994, August). *An analysis of insanity acquitees who malinger.* Paper presented at the annual meeting of the American Psychological Association, Los Angeles.

Gorenstein, E. E., & Newman, J. P. (1980). Disinhibitory psychopathology: A new perspective and a model for research. *Psychological Review, 87,* 301–315.

Gottfredson, D. M., & Bonds, J. A. (1961). *A manual for intake base expectancy scoring.* Sacramento: California Department of Corrections.

Gottfredson, M. R., & Hirschi, T. (1990). *A general theory of crime.* Stanford, CA: Stanford University Press.

Gough, H. (1969). *Manual for the California Psychological Inventory.* Palo Alto, CA: Consulting Psychologists Press.

Gray, K. C., & Hutchinson, H. C. (1964). The psychopathic personality: A survey of Canadian psychiatrists' opinions. *Canadian Psychiatric Association Journal, 9,* 452–461.

Gretton, H. M., McBride, H. L., O'Shaughnessy, R., & Hare, R. D. (1997, June). *Sex offender or generalized offender?: Psychopathy as a risk marker for violence in adolescent offenders.* Paper presented at the 5th International Congress on the Disorders of Personality, Vancouver, British Columbia.

Guze, S. B. (1976). *Criminality and psychiatric disorder.* New York: Oxford University Press.

Hare, R. D. (1980). A research scale for the assessment of psychopathy in criminal populations. *Personality and Individual Differences, 1,* 111–119.

Hare, R. D. (1985). Comparison of procedures for the assessment of psychopathy. *Journal of Consulting and Clinical Psychology, 53,* 7–16.

Hare, R. D. (1991). *The Hare Psychopathy Checklist—Revised.* Toronto: Multi-Health Systems.

Hare, R. D. (1992). *A model program for offenders at high risk for violence.* Ottawa: Correctional Service of Canada.

Hare, R. D. (1993). *Without conscience: The disturbing world of the psychopaths among us.* New York: Pocket Books.

Hare, R. D. (1996a). Psychopathy and antisocial personality disorder: A case of diagnostic confusion. *Psychiatric Times, 13,* 39–40.

Hare, R. D. (1996b). Psychopathy: A clinical construct whose time has come. *Criminal Justice and Behavior, 23,* 25–54.

Hare, R. D. (1998). Psychopathy, affect, and behavior. In D. J. Cooke, A. E. Forth, & R. D. Hare (Eds.), *Psychopathy: Theory, research, and implications for society* (pp. 105–138). Dordrecht, The Netherlands: Kluwer.

Hare, R. D., & Cox, D. N. (1978). Clinical and empirical conceptions of psychopathy, and the selection of subjects for research. In R. D. Hare & D. Schalling (Eds.), *Psychopathic behavior: Approaches to research* (pp. 107–144), Chichester, England: Wiley.

Hare, R. D., Harpur, T. J., Hakstian, A. R., Forth, A. E., Hart, S. D., & Newman, J. P. (1990). The Revised Psychopathy Checklist: Descriptive statistics, reliability, and factor structure. *Psychological Assessment, 2,* 338–341.

Hare, R. D., & Hart, S. D. (1995). A commentary on the Antisocial Personality Disorder Field Trial. In W. J. Livesley (Ed.), *The DSM-IV personality disorders* (pp. 127–134). New York: Guilford Press.

Hare, R. D., Hart, S. D., Forth, A. E., Harpur, T. J., & Williamson, S. E. (1993, January–February). Psychopathic personality characteristics: Development of a criteria set for use in the DSM-IV Antisocial Personality Disorder Field Trial. *DSM-IV Update* (Office of Research, American Psychological Association), pp. 6–7.

Hare, R. D., Hart, S. D., & Harpur, T. J. (1991). Psychopathy and the DSM-IV criteria for antisocial personality disorder. *Journal of Abnormal Psychology, 100,* 391–398.

Hare, R. D., & McPherson, L. M. (1984). Violent and aggressive behavior in criminal psychopaths. *International Journal of Law and Psychiatry, 7,* 35–50.

Hare, R. D., McPherson, L. E., & Forth, A. E. (1988). Male psychopaths and their criminal careers. *Journal of Consulting and Clinical Psychology, 56,* 710–714.

Hare, R. D., Strachan, C., & Hemphill, J. (1998). *Psychopathy in female offenders.* Manuscript in preparation.

Harpending, H., & Sobus, J. (1987). Sociopathy as an adaption. *Ethology and Sociobiology, 8,* 63–72.

Harpur, T. J., Hakstian, R., & Hare, R. D. (1988). Factor structure of the Psychopathy Checklist. *Journal of Consulting and Clinical Psychology, 56,* 741–747.

Harpur, T. J., & Hare, R. D. (1994). The assessment of psychopathy as a function of age. *Journal of Abnormal Psychology, 103,* 604–609.

Harpur, T. J., Hare, R. D., & Hakstian, R. (1989). A two-factor conceptualization of psychopathy: Construct validity and implications for assessment. *Psychological Assessment, 1,* 6–17.

Harpur, T. J., Hart, S. D., & Hare, R. D. (1994). Personality of the psychopath. In P. T. Costa & T. A. Widiger (Eds.), *Personality disorders and the five-factor model of personality* (pp. 149–173). Washington, DC: American Psychological Association.

Harris, G. T., Rice, M. E., & Cormier, C. A. (1991). Psychopathy and violent recidivism. *Law and Human Behavior, 15,* 625–637.

Harris, G. T., Rice, M. E., & Quinsey, V. L. (1993). Violent recidivism of mentally disordered offenders: The development of a statistical prediction instrument. *Criminal Justice and Behavior, 20,* 315–335

Harris, G. T., Rice, M. E., & Quinsey, V. L. (1994). Psychopathy as a taxon: Evidence that psychopaths are a discrete class. *Journal of Consulting and Clinical Psychology, 62,* 387–397.

Hart, S. D. (1996). Psychopathy and risk assessment. In D. J. Cooke, A. E. Forth, J. P. Newman, & R. D. Hare (Eds.), *Issues in criminological and legal psychology: No. 24. International perspectives on psychopathy* (pp. 63–67). Leicester, England: British Psychological Society.

Hart, S. D., Cox, D. N., & Hare, R. D. (1995). *The Hare Psychopathy Checklist: Screening Version.* Toronto: Multi-Health Systems.

Hart, S. D., & Hare, R. D. (1989). Discriminant validity of the Psychopathy Checklist in a forensic psychiatric population. *Psychological Assessment, 1,* 211–218.

Hart, S. D., & Hare, R. D. (1997). Psychopathy: Assessment and association with criminal conduct. In D. M. Stoff, J. Brieling, & J. Maser (Eds.), *Handbook of antisocial behavior* (pp. 22–35). New York: Wiley.

Hart, S. D., Hare, R. D., & Forth, A. E. (1993). Psychopathy as a risk marker for violence: Development and validation of a screening version of the Revised Psychopathy Checklist. In J. Monahan & H. Steadman (Eds.), *Violence and mental disorder: Developments in risk assessment* (pp. 81–98), Chicago: University of Chicago Press.

Hart, S. D., Hare, R. D., & Harpur, T. J. (1992). The Psychopathy Checklist: Overview for researchers and clinicians. In J. Rosen & P. McReynolds (Eds.), *Advances in psychological assessment* (Vol. 8, pp. 103–130). New York: Plenum Press.

Hart, S. D., Kropp, P. R., & Hare, R. D. (1988). Psychopathy and conditional release from prison. *Journal of Consulting and Clinical Psychology, 56,* 227–232.

Heilbrun, K., Hart, S. D., Hare, R. D., Gustafson, D., Nunez, C., & White, A. (in press). Inpatient and post-discharge aggression in mentally disordered offenders: The role of psychopathy. *Journal of Interpersonal Violence.*

Hemphill, J. (1991). *Psychopathy and recidivism following release from a therapeutic community treatment program.* Unpublished master's thesis, University of Saskatchewan, Saskatoon, Saskatchewan, Canada.

Hemphill, J., Hare, R. D., & Wong, S. (1998). Psychopathy and recidivism: A review. *Legal and Criminological Psychology, 3* 141–172.

Hill, C. D., Rogers, R., & Bickford, M. E. (1996). Predicting aggressive and socially disruptive behavior in a maximum security forensic psychiatric hospital. *Journal of Forensic Sciences, 41,* 56–59.

Hoffman, P., & Beck, J. L. (1974). Parole decision-making: A salient factor score. *Journal of Criminal Justice, 2,* 195–206.

Intrator, J., Hare, R. D., Stritske, P., Brichtswein, K., Dorfman, D., Harpur, T. J., Bernstein, D., Handelsman, L., Schaefer, C., Keilp, J., Rosen, J., & Machac, J. (1997). A brain imaging (SPECT) study of semantic and affective processing in psychopaths. *Biological Psychiatry, 42,* 96–103.

Kosson, D. S., Smith, S. S., & Newman, J. P. (1990). Evaluating the construct validity of psychopathy on black and white male inmates: Three preliminary studies. *Journal of Abnormal Psychology, 99,* 250–259.

Lahey, B., & Kazdin, A. (Eds.). (1990). *Advances in clinical child psychology* (Vol. 13). New York: Plenum Press.

Lapierre, D., Braun, C. M. J., & Hodgins, S. (1995). Ventral frontal deficits in psychopathy: Neuropsychological test findings. *Neuropsychologia, 33,* 139–151.

Larbig, W., Veit, R., Rau, H., Schlottke, P., & Birbaumer, N. (1992, October). *Cerebral and peripheral correlates of psychopaths during anticipation of aversive stimulation.* Paper presented at the annual meeting of the Society for Psychophysiological Research, San Diego, CA.

Lindner, R. (1944). *Rebel without a cause.* New York: Grune & Stratton.

Livesley, W. J. (1986). Trait and behavioral prototypes of personality disorder. *American Journal of Psychiatry, 143,* 728–732.

Livesley, W. J. (1998). The phenotypic and genotypic structure of psychopathic traits. In D. J. Cooke, A. E. Forth, & R. D. Hare (Eds.), *Psychopathy: Theory, research, and implications for society* (pp. 69–80). Dordrecht, The Netherlands: Kluwer.

Livesley, W. J., Jackson, D. N., & Schroeder, M. (1992). Factorial structure of traits delineating personality disorders in clinical and general population samples. *Journal of Abnormal Psychology, 101,* 432–440.

Livesley, W. J., & Schroeder, M. (1991). Dimensions of personality disorder: The DSM-III-R Cluster B diagnoses. *Journal of Nervous and Mental Disease, 179,* 320–328.

Losel, F. (1996). Mangement of psychopaths. In D. J. Cooke, A. E. Forth, J. P. Newman, & R. D. Hare (Eds.), *Issues in criminological and legal psychology: No. 24. International perspectives on psychopathy* (pp. 100–106). Leicester, England: British Psychological Society.

Losel, F. (1998). Treatment and management of psychopaths. In D. J. Cooke, A. E. Forth, & R. D. Hare (Eds.), *Psychopathy: Theory, research, and implications for society* (pp. 303–354). Dordrecht, The Netherlands: Kluwer.

Lykken, D.T. (1995). *The antisocial personalities.* Hillsdale, NJ: Erlbaum.

Lynam, D. R. (1996). Early identification of chronic offenders: Who is the fledgling psychopath? *Psychological Bulletin, 120,* 209–234.

McBurnett, K., & Pfiffner, L. (1998). Comorbidities and biological correlates of conduct disorder. In D. J. Cooke, A. E. Forth, & R. D. Hare *Psychopathy: Theory, research, and implications for society* (pp. 189–204). Dordrecht, The Netherlends: Kluwer.

McCord, W., & McCord, J. (1964). *The psychopath: An essay on the criminal mind.* Princeton, NJ: Van Nostrand.

MacMillan, J., & Kofoed, L. (1984). Sociobiology and the antisocial personality: An alternative perspective. *Journal of Nervous and Mental Disease, 172,* 448–457.

Mealey, L. (1995). The sociobiology of sociopathy: An integrated evolutionary model. *Behavioral and Brain Sciences, 18,* 523–599.

Meloy, J. R. (1988). *The psychopathic mind: Origins, dynamics, and treatments.* Northvale, NJ: Jason Aronson.

Meloy, J. R. (1992). *Violent attachments*. Northvale, NJ: Jason Aronson.

Millon, T. (1981). *Disorders of personality: DSM-III, Axis II*. New York: Wiley.

Neary, A. (1990). *DSM-III and Psychopathy Checklist assessment of antisocial personality disorder in black and white female felons*. Unpublished doctoral dissertation, University of Missouri–St. Louis.

Newman, J. P. (1998). Psychopathic behavior: An information processing perspective. In D.J. Cooke, A.E. Forth, & R.D. Hare (Eds.), *Psychopathy: Theory, research, and implications for society* (pp. 81–104). Dordrecht, The Netherlands: Kluwer.

Newman, J.P., & Wallace, J.F. (1993). Psychopathy and cognition. In P. Kendall & K. Dobson (Eds.), *Psychopathology and cognition* (pp. 293–349). New York: Academic Press.

Ogloff, J., Wong, S., & Greenwood, A. (1990). Treating criminal psychopaths in a therapeutic community program. *Behavioral Sciences and the Law, 8*, 81–90.

O'Shaughnessy, R., Hare, R. D., Gretton, H., & McBride, M. (1994). [Psychopathy and adolescent sex offending]. Unpublished raw data.

Patrick, C. J. (1994). Emotion and psychopathy: Some startling new insights. *Psychophysiology, 31*, 319–330.

Piotrowski, N., Tusel, D. J., Sees, K. L., Banys, P., & Hall, S. M. (1996). Psychopathy and antisocial personality disorder in men and women with primary opioid dependence. In D. J. Cooke, A. E. Forth, J. P. Newman, & R. D. Hare (Eds.), *Issues in criminological and legal psychology: No. 24. International perspectives on psychopathy* (pp. 123–126). Leicester, England: British Psychological Society.

Prentky, R., & Knight, R. (1991). Identifying critical dimensions for discriminating among rapists. *Journal of Consulting and Clinical Psychology, 59*, 643–691.

Quinsey, V. L., Harris, G. E., Rice, M. E., & Lalumiere, M. L. (1993). Assessing treatment efficacy in outcome studies of sex offenders. *Journal of Interpersonal Violence, 8*, 512–523.

Quinsey, V. L., Rice, M. E., & Harris, G. T. (1995). Actuarial prediction of sexual recidivism. *Journal of Interpersonal Violence, 10*, 85–105.

Rice, M. E., & Harris, G. T. (1992). A comparison of criminal recidivism among schizophrenic and nonschizophrenic offenders. *International Journal of Law and Psychiatry, 15*, 397–408.

Rice, M. E., & Harris, G. T. (1997). Cross-validation and extension of the Violence Risk Appraisal Guide for child molesters and rapists. *Law and Human Behavior, 21*, 231–241.

Rice, M. E., Harris, G. T., & Cormier, C. A. (1992). An evaluation of a maximum security therapeutic community for psychopaths and other mentally disordered offenders. *Law and Human Behavior, 16*, 399–412.

Robins, L. N. (1966). *Deviant children grown up*. Baltimore: Williams & Wilkins.

Robins, L. N., & Rutter, M. R. (Eds.). (1990). *Straight and devious pathways from childhood to adulthood*. New York: Cambridge University Press.

Rogers, R., Dion, K. L., & Lynett, E. (1992). Diagnostic validity of antisocial personality disorder. *Law and Human Behavior, 16*, 677–689.

Rotenberg, M., & Diamond, B. L. (1971). The biblical conception of the psychopath: The law of the stubborn and rebellious son. *Journal of History of Behavioral Sciences, 7*, 29–38.

Rutherford, M. J., Cacciola, J. S., Alterman, A. I., & McKay, J. R. (1996). Reliability and validity of the Revised Psychopathy Checklist in women methadone patients. *Assessment, 3*, 43–54.

Salekin, R., Rogers, R., & Sewell, K. (1996). A review and meta-analysis of the Psychopathy Checklist and Psychopathy Checklist—Revised: Predictive validity of dangerousness. *Clinical Psychology: Science and Practice, 3*, 203–215.

Salekin, R., Rogers, R., & Sewell, K. (1997). Construct validity of psychopathy in a female offender sample: A multitrait–multimethod evaluation. *Journal of Abnormal Psychology, 106*, 576–585.

Serin, R. C. (1991). Psychopathy and violence in criminals. *Journal of Interpersonal Violence, 6*, 423–431.

Serin, R. C., & Amos, N. L. (1995). The role of psychopathy in the assessment of dangerousness. *International Journal of Law and Psychiatry, 18*, 231–238.

Serin, R. C., Peters, R. D., & Barbaree, H. E. (1990). Predictors of psychopathy and release outcome in a criminal population. *Psychological Assessment, 2,* 419–422.

Stoff, D. M., Breiling, J., & Maser, J. (Eds.). (1997). *Handbook of antisocial behavior.* New York: Wiley.

Suedfeld, P., & Landon, P. B. (1978). Approaches to treatment. In R. D. Hare & D. Schalling (Eds.), *Psychopathic behavior: Approaches to research* (pp. 347–376). Chichester, England: Wiley.

Tennent, G., Tennent, D., Prins, H., & Bedford, A. (1990). Psychopathic disorder: A useful concept? *Medicine, Science, and the Law, 30,* 38–44.

Toupin, J., Mercier, H., Dery, M., Cate, G., & Hodgins, S. (1996). Validity of the PCL-R for adolescents. In D. J. Cooke, A. E. Forth, J. P. Newman, & R. D. Hare (Eds.), *Issues in criminological and legal psychology: No. 24. International perspectives on psychopathy* (pp. 143–145). Leicester, England: British Psychological Society.

Trevethan, S. D., & Walker, L. J. (1989). Hypothetical versus real-life moral reasoning among psychopathic and delinquent youth. *Development and Psychopathology, 1,* 91–103.

Webster, C.D., Harris, G.T., Rice, M.E., Cormier, C., & Quinsey, V.L. (1994). *The violence prediction scheme: Assessing dangerousness in high risk men.* Toronto: University of Toronto, Center of Criminology.

Webster, C. D., Douglas, K. S., Eaves, D., & Hart, S. D. (1997). *HCR-20: Assessing risk for violence, Version 2.* Burnaby, British Columbia: Simon Fraser University.

Widiger, T. A. (1998). Psychopathy and normal personality. In D. J. Cooke, A. E. Forth, & R. D. Hare (Eds.), *Psychopathy: Theory, research, and implications for society* (pp. 47–68). Dordrecht, The Netherlands: Kluwer.

Widiger, T. A., Cadoret, R., Hare, R. D., Robins, L., Rutherford, M., Zanarini, M., Alterman, A., Apple, M., Corbitt, E., Forth, A., Hart, S., Kulterman, J., & Woody, G. (1996). DSM-IV Antisocial Personality Disorder Field Trial. *Journal of Abnormal Psychology, 105,* 3–16.

Widiger, T. A., & Corbitt, E. (1993). Antisocial personality disorder: Proposals for DSM-IV. *Journal of Personality Disorders, 7,* 63–77.

Widiger, T. A., & Corbitt, E. (1995). The DSM-IV antisocial personality disorder. In W. J. Livesley (Ed.), *The DSM-IV personality disorders* (pp. 103–126). New York: Guilford Press.

Williamson, S. E., Hare, R. D., & Wong, S. (1987). Violence: Criminal psychopaths and their victims. *Canadian Journal of Behavioral Science, 19,* 454–462.

Williamson, S. E., Harpur, T. J., & Hare, R. D. (1991). Abnormal processing of affective words by psychopaths. *Psychophysiology, 28,* 260–273.

Wilson, J. Q., & Herrnstein, R. J. (1985). *Crime and human nature.* New York: Simon & Schuster.

Wintrup, A. (1994). *The predictive validity of the PCL-R in high risk mentally disordered offenders.* Unpublished manuscript, Simon Fraser University, Burnaby, British Columbia, Canada.

Wong, S. (1984). *Criminal and institutional behaviors of psychopaths: Programs branch users report.* Ottawa: Ministry of the Solicitor-General of Canada.

Wootton, J. M., Frick, P. J., Shelton, K. K., & Silverthorn, P. (1997). Ineffective parenting and childhood conduct problems: The moderating role of callous unemotional traits. *Journal of Consulting and Clinical Psychology, 65,* 301–308.

World Health Organization. (1992). *International classification of diseases and related health problems* (10th ed.). Geneva: Author.

Zaparniuk, J., & Paris, F. (1995, April). *Female psychopaths: Violence and recidivism.* Paper presented at conference on "Mental Disorder and Criminal Justice: Changes, Challenges, and Solutions," Vancouver, British Columbia, Canada.

III

ETIOLOGY

13

Genetics and Antisocial Personality Disorder

PETER McGUFFIN
ANITA THAPAR

Many forms of behavior, both abnormal and normal, run in families. These range from comparatively rare single-gene disorders such as Huntington's disease to common behaviors such as choice of religious denomination and career that are almost certainly strongly influenced by family environment. In between are a great many different traits and syndromes where there is evidence that both genes and environment play a role, and where the genetic component is likely to consist of multiple genes' acting in concert rather than single genes' having a major effect (Plomin, Owen, & McGuffin, 1994). These traits and syndromes include cognitive ability as reflected in IQ test scores; personality as measured by paper-and-pencil tests; and disorders such as schizophrenia, bipolar disorders, and personality disorders (McGuffin, Owen, O'Donovan, Thapar, & Gottesman, 1994).

The evidence pointing to a genetic contribution to antisocial personality comes from three main sources. First, studies on animals suggest that some components of temperament, including emotionality and aggression, have a genetic basis. Second, studies of personality within the normal range, using classical methods of study based on twins and adoption, suggest that most traits (including antisocial traits) are moderately heritable. Third, studies of the aggregation of criminality or antisocial behavior within families, together again with twin and adoption studies, consistently indicate genetic influence. In this chapter we will briefly review each of these areas and then go on to consider developmental aspects, covering the relationship between conduct disorder in childhood, juvenile delinquency, and adult antisocial behavior. Finally, we will consider what prospects molecular genetics has to offer in furthering our understanding of the biological basis of antisocial personality.

ANIMAL STUDIES

Differences in temperament between strains of domestically bred animals such as dogs or horses have long been recognized, as has the fact that it is possible to carry out artificial selection for certain behaviors. Aggression in dogs is a clear example of a type of behavior that shows differences between breeds. Selection studies in the laboratory have provided more quantifiable evidence for a range of observable behaviors, from alcohol preference to activity levels (Plomin 1990). For example, in rodents, inbred strain experiments (where brother–sister matings are carried out over many generations) result in ultimate loss of heterozygosity at all loci, producing strains of animals that are genetically identical. Genetic influences on behavior can be detected by making comparisons between inbred strains under the same environmental conditions. One such strain of rats has been selected for showing high emotional responsivity. "Maudsley Reactive" rats, when placed in a brightly lit enclosure, are seen to "freeze" and to defecate more frequently than "nonreactive" rats selected for low emotional responsivity (Wimer & Wimer, 1985).

The advent of molecular-genetic techniques is now carrying animal behavior genetics a stage further by enabling the location and identification of genes affecting temperament. For example, a recent study suggests that most of the measurable variation in emotionality in mice (measured in similar ways to that in Maudsley Reactive rats) can be attributed to three so-called "quantitative trait loci" (QTLs; Flint et al., 1995). This work takes advantage of the availability of a detailed map of DNA markers. This effectively provides a set of closely spaced reference points all the way along the genome (i.e., the set of chromosomes carrying the genetic material), so that it is possible to cross strains of animals with high and low emotionality, and then to carry out further crosses of their offspring to track which markers assort with which types of behavior. We will return to the issue of searching for QTLs later in this chapter, and will discuss whether genetic linkage analysis can be applied to quantitative traits in humans.

A different type of molecular-genetic study that is not applicable in humans, but that nevertheless may shed some light on the molecular genetics of abnormal personality, is the transgenic experiment. Essentially, such experiments are of two types: Either a gene from another species is introduced into a laboratory animal (most usually a mouse), or the working copies of a gene are disrupted or "knocked out" (Campbell & Gold, 1996). Two types of "knockout" mice have been created recently that show high levels of aggressive behavior. In one strain there is a lack of brain nitric oxide synthase (Nelson et al., 1995), and in the other the gene encoding for the 5-HT1b receptor is absent (Saudou et al., 1994). In both cases the abnormal behavior is seen in homozygous knockouts; that is, animals are first engineered that are effectively heterozygous, with one working copy and one disrupted copy of the gene, and the heterozygotes are then crossed to produce homozygous offspring with no working copies. It can be argued that such an engineered loss of function does not necessarily tell us much about the biological basis of naturally occurring aggression, and certainly it should not be assumed that either the nitric oxide synthase gene or the gene for 5-HT1b receptors is "*the* gene for aggression." However, it maybe that spontaneously occurring variations in these genes have a role in aggressive behavior in mice, and, by extrapolation, that they have some role in antisocial behavior in humans. For example, a transgenic mouse in which the monoamine oxidase A genes are fortuitously deleted has been found to show increased aggression (Cases et al., 1995). Interestingly, a mutation in the monoamine oxidase A gene in humans, which maps to the X chromosome, has been shown to be a rare cause of violent behavior associated with mild mental retardation (Brunner et al., 1993).

PERSONALITY AND ANTISOCIAL TRAITS

There is good evidence that self-rated and even informant rated questionnaire measures of personality are influenced by genetic factors (Eaves, Eysenck, & Martin, 1989; Heath, Neale, Kessler, Eaves, & Kendler, 1992), and there have now been many studies using twin or adoption designs where the initial aim is to partition the sources of variation in personality test scores. That is, it is assumed that the phenotype—in this case, a personality dimension such as extraversion or neuroticism—results from a combination of genotype and the environment to which the genotype is exposed. It is further assumed that there are two main types of environmental influence: shared environment, which tends to make members of the same family resemble each other, and nonshared or residual environment, which causes dissimilarities. Obviously, as we have already suggested, a trait or disorder may run in families because of genes, shared environment, or a combination of both. Family studies alone cannot tease these apart, but twin studies and adoption studies can. A special form of twin study is the study of twins reared apart, but most commonly the classic method of studying twins reared together is used. Here the basic assumption is that monozygotic (MZ) twins share all of their genes plus a shared environment, whereas nonidentical or dizygotic (DZ) twins share on average 50% of their genes, but again share their environment to roughly the same extent as MZ twins. This leads to some fairly straightfoward predictions about the pattern of correlations in twin studies (McGuffin et al., 1994). An MZ correlation that is bigger than the DZ correlation is expected if there is a genetic influence on a trait. Twice the difference between the MZ and the DZ correlation gives an approximate measure of heritability, or variation accounted for by genetic influence. Finding that the MZ correlation is more than twice the DZ correlation suggests that there are no common environmental affects, but finding that the MZ and DZ correlations are similar suggests that shared environment is the only source of familiarity (see Falconer, 1989, and McGuffin et al., 1994, for further discussion). Although there are criticisms of the "equal-environments assumption" that underpins these predictions, for most practical purposes it holds up reasonably well (Plomin, Owen, & McGuffin, 1994).

Twin studies of personality are very consistent in showing that most questionnaire-based measures have a heritability, or proportion of total variation accounted for by additive genetic effects, of between 35% and 50% (Martin & Jardine, 1986; Eaves et al., 1989). Perhaps more surprisingly, the data are also virtually completely consistent in showing that all the rest of the variation, the environmental component, is attributable to nonshared factors. That is, MZ correlations are at least twice the DZ correlations, suggesting that family environment contributes little or nothing to variation in personality within the normal range.

This general pattern seems also to apply consistently to personality measures that have a relationship to antisocial personality disorder. Goldsmith and Gottesman (1996) have recently reviewed twin studies that have used the Psychopathic Deviate (*Pd*) scale of the Minnesota Multiphasic Personality Inventory (MMPI), the Aggression scale of the Multidimensional Personality Questionnaire (MPQ), and a variety of other aggression scales. The *Pd* scale of the MMPI consists of items that distinguish psychopaths from other comparison groups, and the MPQ Aggression scale consists of items verified by factor analysis that concern acts of aggression, retaliation, and vengefulness. For MZ twins reared together the correlations ranged from .46 to .57, while in DZ twins the correlations were between .18 and .28. In general, MZ correlations were about double or slightly more than double the DZ correlations, suggesting that shared environment has little or no role. This was supported by a study of twins reared apart (Tellegen et al., 1988), which showed that with respect to the MPQ Aggression scale, the correlation for MZ twins reared apart was slightly larger (.46) than that of twins reared together (.43).

Also using the MMPI *Pd* scale, the Texas Adoption Project (Willerman, Loehlin, & Horn, 1992) compared scores at similar ages for biological mothers of adopted-away offspring and adopting relatives. The observed correlation for a biological mother and offspring was .27, whereas for an adoptive mother and offspring it was .10. Even lower correlations were seen between biologically unrelated but reared-together siblings (.02) and between an adoptive father and child (.07). The results therefore again point to moderate heritability and no contribution from shared environment. A rough estimate of heritability can be obtained by doubling the biological mother–offspring correlation (since mothers pass on half of their genes to each of their children). The result at .54 is close to that seen in the study of twins reared apart, as well as the broad heritability estimates that can be obtained from the other studies of twins reared together, derived by doubling the difference in the MZ and DZ correlations (Falconer, 1989). Later, in the section of this chapter on developmental aspects, we will look in more detail at estimates of heritability that take a more rigorous approach to biometric model fitting. For now, we can conclude that personality in general, as well as personality traits within the normal range that have a bearing on antisocial personality, are at least moderately influenced by genes.

ANTISOCIAL PERSONALITY DISORDER

One of the difficult and controversial issues surrounding the whole area of antisocial personality disorder is the question of how best to define it. Indeed, for genetic studies it becomes crucial to consider whether antisocial personality disorder is a discrete entity at all, or whether (in common with many other abnormal behaviors) there is a continuum between the obviously pathological and the blatantly normal, with no clear-cut line of demarcation. As we see it, most of the genetic evidence suggests that there is a continuum, and the pattern of results overall makes most sense if it is reviewed with this in mind. Nevertheless, for some types of studies it is both convenient and practical to consider antisocial personality disorder as a dichotomous or present–absent trait; there are some clear-cut, albeit imperfect, markers that can be used in such studies, of which the most obvious is conviction for a criminal offense. Clearly, criminality is a social or legal concept rather than one that is biologically defined. Thus it may place the petty recidivist, the serial killer, and Nelson Mandela in the same crude category. Criminality may also fail to include those with antisocial personality who have never transgressed the law of their land or have never been apprehended.

Therefore, given the clumsiness of the definition, it is remarkable that the data are actually very consistent. The combined results of twin studies of adult criminality from North America, Japan, and Europe give a pairwise concordance rate of 52% in a total of 229 MZ pairs, compared with 23% in 316 DZ pairs (Goldsmith & Gottesman, 1996). Results from the largest single study to date are summarized in Table 13.1. In this study, Cloninger and Gottesman (1987) attempted to tackle one of the problems that is faced in

TABLE 13.1. Details of Concordance and Correlation for Registered Criminality in a Danish Twin Sample

Zygosity	Pairing: Proband–twin	n of pairs	n of affected	n of concordant pairs	Probandwise rates Freq./n	%	Tetrachoric correlation
MZ	Male–male	365	73	25	50/98	51.0	.74 ± .07
MZ	Female–female	347	15	3	6/18	33.3	.74 ± .12
DZ	Male–male	700	146	26	52/172	30.2	.47 ± .06
DZ	Female–male	2,073	30	7	7/30	23.3	.23 ± .10
DZ	Male–female	2,073	198	7	7/198	3.5	.23 ± .10
DZ	Female–female	690	28	2	4/30	13.3	.46 ± .11

Note. The data are from Cloninger and Gottesman (1987).

applying a quantitative genetic model to criminality. This is that in nearly all societies, many more men than women are "affected." Cloninger and Gottesman adopted a threshold model of criminality, where it is assumed that liability to show criminal behavior is contributed to by multiple genetic and environmental factors, such that the distribution of liability in the general population will tend to be normally distributed. Only those individuals whose liability at some stage exceeds a certain threshold become classified as "affected." This is a general model first put forward by Falconer (1965) to explain the inheritance of common familial disorders. In most of these disorders, "liability" is an unobserved variable in the portion of the population that is unaffected and below the threshold. However, the model is also readily applicable to a trait such as criminality or antisocial personality disorder if the trait is considered to be one end of a spectrum of behaviors, some of which may be measurable within the normal range.

Cloninger and Gottesman applied an extension of the Falconer model to include two thresholds: one for a broad (or commoner) form of disorder, and the other for a narrow (or rarer) form (Reich, James, & Morris, 1972; Reich et al., 1979). In the most straightforward form of such a model, it is predicted that the relatives of narrow-form index cases will be more commonly affected than the relatives of broad-form cases. This is because narrow-form disorder occupies a more extreme position on the liability continuum and thus includes cases with more genetic and/or environmental risk factors. In this case, the broad form was male criminality and the narrow form was criminality in females. A model of this type, where the correlations between the sexes (male–female) are the same as those within each sex (male–male and female–female), provides a satisfactory fit to the data suggesting that criminality is equally heritable in men and women; it gives an estimate of heritability of about .54. Furthermore, in contrast with "normal" psychopathic traits or aggression measured by personality scales, the data suggest substantial shared environmental effect, accounting for about 20% of the variance.

Evidence for a genetic contribution to antisocial personality disorder or criminality has also been provided by adoption studies. These can be described as consisting of three types. Studies of adoptees themselves compare the rates of criminality in the adopted-away offspring of criminal parents with the rate in control adoptees who do not have a criminal biological parent. Studies of adoptees' families compare the rates of criminality or antisocial personality among the biological and adopted families of subjects who were adopted away early in life and have been convicted as criminals. Finally, cross-fostering studies compare the rates of criminality in the adopted-away offspring of criminal biological parents raised by noncriminal adoptive parents, with the rates in the offspring of noncriminal biological parents raised by criminal adopting parents. Studies of the first type—that is, studies of adopted-away offspring of offending versus nonoffending mothers—have shown higher rates of antisocial personality, as well as significantly more convictions, arrests, and imprisonments for offenses, among this group compared with controls (Crowe, 1972, 1974).

In a study of psychopathy in adoptees' families in Denmark, the rate of disorder was significantly higher among the biological relatives of adoptees who were psychopathic, compared with adoptive relatives and controls (Schulsinger, 1972). Similarly, a genetic influence on antisocial behavior and antisocial personality was found in a series of studies of adoptees' families in the United States (Cadoret, 1978; Cadoret & Cain, 1980; Cadoret, O'Gorman, Troughton, & Heywood, 1985). By contrast, the initial results of a Swedish adoption study suggested that genetic factors had little or no influence on antisocial behavior (Bohman, 1978). However, later reanalyses that allowed for the confounding effects of alcohol abuse showed that genetic influences were important for petty crime, but that violent repetitive crime appeared to be more related to alcoholism (Bohman, Cloninger, Sigvardsson, & von Knorring, 1982; Cloninger, Sigvardsson, Bohman, & von Knorring, 1982). Both this study and a subsequent Danish study (Mednick, Gabrielli, & Hutchings, 1984) suggest that although criminality is influenced by genes, it is heterogeneous, with genetic factors' being more influential for property crimes and petty recidivism and less important for violent crimes against persons.

Just as twin studies provide important evidence that criminality and antisocial personality are not entirely genetically determined, adoption studies have pointed to some of the environmental factors that may be influential. Thus, in Swedish studies (Sigvardsson, Cloninger, Bohman, & von Knorring, 1982), men who had been in multiple temporary placements and whose adoptive homes were of low socioeconomic status were at higher risk for criminality. In women, prolonged institutional care and urban rearing appeared to be important risk factors.

A cross-fostering study based on the National Criminal Register in Denmark enabled Mednick et al. (1984) to investigate genetic and environmental factors simultaneously. In this study, in cases where neither the biological nor the adopting parents had a criminal record, 13.5% of adoptees had a history of conviction. This compared with a rate of 14.7% among adoptees whose adoptive fathers were "known to the police" but whose biological parents were noncriminal. The difference between these two rates was nonsignificant. However, the rate for adopted-away offspring of biological criminal fathers raised by noncriminal parents was elevated at 20%, and the highest rate of criminality, 24.5%, was found in the adoptees whose biological *and* adoptive fathers had a police record. Thus the results suggest both a genetic contribution to criminal behavior and the possibility of an interaction between genetic and environmental factors.

The question of interaction (as opposed to a simple additive combination of genes and environment) was not formally tested in the Danish adoption study, but has now been tested and found to be present in a recent study in the United States (Cadoret, Yates, Troughton, Woodworth, & Stewart, 1995). Here 95 men and 102 women who were separated at birth from their biological parents were studied. A comparison was made between those adoptees whose biological parents had a documented history (in prison or hospital records) of antisocial personality and/or alcohol abuse, and those whose biological parents had no known history of psychopathology. In addition to assessing antisocial behaviors in adulthood, the investigators inquired about adolescent aggression and conduct disorder in the adoptees. The main findings were that a biological background of antisocial personality disorder predicted increased adolescent aggression, conduct disorder, and antisocial behavior. Adverse adoptive home environment, which included marital or legal problems, psychiatric disorder, or substance abuse, also predicted increased adult antisocial behaviors. Furthermore, there was a significant interaction between adverse adoptive home environment and a biological background of antisocial personality disorder, increasing the rate of aggression and conduct disorder in adoptees. An adverse adoptive home environment did not increase the risk of aggression or conduct disorder in the absence of a biological background of antisocial personality.

An attempt to take a longitudinal perspective and investigate both adolescent symptoms and behaviors during adult life in the same sample was also made in a very large study of antisocial traits in 3,226 pairs of male twins, identified via a register of men who had served in the armed forces of the United States during the Vietnam era (i.e., May 1965 to August 1975) (Lyons et al., 1995). All subjects were interviewed by telephone, according to a structured schedule. Genetic models were fitted, and a summary of the main findings with regard to symptoms in adult life is shown in Table 13.2. Eight of the adult symptoms were significantly heritable, and only one ("no regard for the truth") was significantly influenced by shared environment. However, the pattern of findings in the same subjects before the age of 15 years was rather different and is worth considering

TABLE 13.2. Antisocial Symptoms in Adults: Vietnam-Era Twin Register Study

Symptom	Prevalence (%)	Tetrachoric correlations r_{MZ}	r_{DZ}	Variance components (%)[a] Genetic (A)	Shared environment (C)	Unique environment (E)
Inconsistent work[b]	16.1	.34	.15	34	—	66
Fails to conform to social norms[b]	20.5	.49	.32	52	—	48
Aggressive[b]	38.5	.50	.27	50	—	50
Fails to honor financial obligations[c]	5.1	.39	.20	38	—	62
Impulsive[c]	7.0	.41	.23	41	—	59
No regard for truth[d]	2.7	.15	.28	—	77	23
Reckless[b]	47.8	.47	.31	48	—	52
Irresponsible parent[e]	1.2	.22	—	—	—	—
Never monogamous[c]	4.2	.30	.19	31	—	69
Lacks remorse[c]	4.0	.22	.14	22	—	78

Note. ACE is a model including all possible effects—that is, additive genetics (A), shared environment (C), and nonshared environment (E). Reduced models (e.g., AE, CE) are testing the effects of dropping A or C or both. Adapted from Lyons et al. (1995). Copyright 1995 by the American Medical Association. Adapted by permission.

[a]Best-fitting model. In no cases did a model with sibling interaction and additive genetic, shared environmental, and unique environmental effects provide a better fit to the data than a model without sibling interaction. In all cases, a model (E) with only unique environmental influences on the phenotype was rejected by a goodness-of-fit x^2.

[b]The AE model was not rejected against the full model, while the CE model was rejected.

[c]Neither an AE nor a CE model was rejected against the full ACE model. However, the goodness-of-fit x^2 of the AE model was less than that of the CE model.

[d]Neither an AE nor a CE model was rejected against the full ACE model. However, the goodness-of-fit x^2 of the CE model was less than that of the AE model.

[e]A tetrachoric correlation could not be computed because of an empty cell.

in the general context of antisocial symptoms in childhood. Therefore we will now discuss developmental issues and the genetic relationship between conduct disorder, juvenile delinquency, and adult antisocial behavior.

CONDUCT DISORDER, JUVENILE DELINQUENCY, AND DEVELOPMENTAL ASPECTS

In contrast with a consistent pattern of higher MZ concordances than DZ concordances for adult criminality, juvenile delinquency (again defined in terms of recorded transgressions of the law) tend to show little difference between MZ and DZ concordance rates (McGuffin & Gottesman, 1985). The results of twin studies of juvenile delinquency from North America, Japan, and England (except the self-report data from the Vietnam-era twin registry) have been combined by Goldsmith and Gottesman (1996). As in the earlier McGuffin and Gottesman (1985) review, the pairwise concordance rates in both MZ and DZ twins were high, at 91% in 55 MZ pairs and 73% in 44 DZ pairs. We may therefore infer that there is a very substantial effect of shared environment and only a small genetic effect, since the MZ-DZ differences are small.

If we go back earlier in life and broaden the phenotype further to include conduct disorder in younger children, the findings as a whole suggest that there is familiality, but again this largely results from shared environment. Two British twin studies have used the Rutter A Parents Scale (Rutter, Tizard, & Whitmore, 1970), from which Antisocial and Neurotic subscale scores can be derived. The scale has previously been used extensively in epidemiological research. In a study of 13-year-old twins (Stevenson & Graham, 1988), genetic factors appeared to be of some importance in influencing neurotic but not antisocial symptoms. We have recently found a similar pattern in a sample of 198 same-sex pairs of twins, spread over a wider age range of 8–16 years (Thapar & McGuffin, 1996). For antisocial symptoms (consisting of a composite score of parents' endorsement of items on stealing, destruction of property, disobedience, telling lies, and bullying), there was evidence only of shared environmental factors. Socioeconomic status was also found to have a significant influence on antisocial behavior, although this accounted for only a small proportion of the variance included within shared environmental factors.

We have also found from previous work with this sample, based on the Cardiff Twin Register, that the factors influencing psychiatric symptoms in childhood and adolescence are not static. For example, we have previously found (Thapar & McGuffin, 1994) that depressive symptoms show no significant influence from genetic factors in younger children, but that these symptoms become substantially heritable in adolescents (within the age range of 11–17 years). It is worth considering whether the same phenomenon might be observed for antisocial symptoms. We therefore carried out further analyses that address this issue (McGuffin & Thapar, 1997).

In the Cardiff twins as a whole for whom we have parent ratings on the Rutter A scale, the correlations for antisocial scores (after taking log transformations to achieve normality) are about the same for MZ and DZ twins, at .50. Thus our model fitting suggests that shared environment accounts entirely for familiality. If, however, we divide the sample and look at just those twins older than 11 years of age, the correlations begin to diverge, with the MZ correlation holding constant at about .48 and the DZ correlation dropping to .39. If we progress further up the age range and examine just the log-transformed antisocial scores for those age 14 or more (roughly the oldest third of the sample), the MZ correlation rises slightly again to .54, while the DZ correlation drops further to .34. In view of this, it seemed worth carrying out a more detailed analysis (McGuffin & Thapar, 1997) focusing on the adolescent sample, for whom we have self-report data on a wider range of antisocial items taken from a questionnaire that focuses specifically on antisocial behavior (Olweus, 1989). We restricted our analyses here to common items endorsed by 15% or more of our subjects. These are listed in Table 13.3.

The observed intraclass correlation coefficients were .81 for MZ twins ($n = 43$) and .29 for DZ twins of the same sex ($n = 38$). Although the sample is now greatly reduced from its original size (because we are just focusing on adolescents and ignoring opposite-sex DZ pairs), the difference in the MZ and DZ correlations immediately begins to suggest that we are now dealing with a more heritable trait. We have fitted a simple genetic model, as described in greater detail elsewhere (McGuffin et al., 1994; Thapar & McGuffin, 1994). Essentially, a structural equation modeling approach has been taken to partition the sources of variation into heritability (h^2), the variance explained by shared environment (c^2), and that explained by residual environment. Nested models can be compared using a likelihood ratio test. This depends on the fact that minus twice the difference in log likelihood is a chi-square, with degrees of freedom equal to the difference in the number of parameters in the two models. The results are summarized in Table 13.4. As might be predicted with an MZ correlation greater than twice the size of the DZ correlation, there is no evidence of a shared environmental effect, and c^2 has become fixed at 0 during the model fitting. In such circumstances, it is reasonable to explore whether there is any dominance variance (d^2). Although allowing for dominance variance increases the maximum log likelihood, the likelihood ratio chi-square is nonsignificant. We therefore conclude that common forms of antisocial symptoms in adolescence are substantially heritable, with no evidence of common environmental effects. There is a suggestion that nonadditive (i.e., dominant) genetic effects may also be operating, but given the small sample size, it is impossible to draw any definitive conclusions.

It is of interest to compare our findings in the adolescent sample and the apparent childhood-to-adolescence change with results from recent studies elsewhere. In a population-based twin study in the United States that also used the Rutter A scale, genetic and environmental factors were found to influence antisocial scores, although shared environmental factors were found to be of greater importance for younger girls (Silberg et al., 1996). In another twin study based on the Child Behavior Checklist, although genetic influences appeared to be important for aggressive behavior, shared environmental

TABLE 13.3. Frequently Endorsed Antisocial Items on the Olweus (1989) Behaviour and Activities Questionnaire

Item	Frequency (%)
Arrived late for school	41
Yelled at parent	32
Skipped classes	24
Got drunk	24
Kept after school by teacher	21
Been sent to head teacher	19
Skipped school	18
Yelled at teacher	17
Written graffiti	17
Got into fights	15

Note. The data are from McGuffin and Thapar (1997).

TABLE 13.4. Model-Fitting Results Using Data on Common Antisocial Symptoms in Adolescent Twins

Model	h^2	(SE)	c^2	(SE)	d^2	(SE)	$-2\ln L$
(1) Additive genes and shared environment	.814	(.005)	0*		[0]		0.999
(2) Additive genes only	.814	(.005)	[0]		[0]		0.999
(3) Shared environment only	[0]		.806	(.005)	[0]		40.321
(4) Additive genes and dominance	.362	(.205)	[0]		.452	(.21)	0.000

Note. The data are from McGuffin and Thapar (1997). h^2, heritability; c^2, proportion of variance explained by shared environment; d^2, dominance variance; $-2\ln L$, $-2 \times$ log likelihood; [0], fixed parameter; *, fixed during iteration.

Model (2) is accepted on grounds of parsimony and best fit, since likelihood ratio chi-squares are as follows:

(1) – (2) = 0.0 (n.s.)
(1) – (2) = 38.59 ($p < .001$)
(1) – (3) = 0.999 (n.s.)

effects were detected for delinquent behavior (Edelbrock, Rende, Plomin, & Thompson, 1995).

If we return to the study of antisocial traits by Lyons et al. (1995) based on the Vietnam era twin registry, we see a pattern of results that is mixed but not incompatible with our own findings. The Vietnam-era subjects were asked to report on "juvenile" symptoms (i.e., before the age of 15 years). Significant heritabilities were found for some fairly prevalent items (such as truancy, fighting, or cruelty to animals), whereas for other common self-report items (such as lying, stealing, or damaging property), shared environmental effects seemed to be more important. Apart from the difference in sample size, which would make us place more confidence in the model-fitting results of the Lyons et al. study than in our own, there are other methodological differences. We have simply computed antisocial scores by adding up symptoms rather than carrying out analyses of individual symptoms. However, we have the advantage of self-report about recent behaviors, rather than retrospective report about juvenile symptoms from subjects in their middle age. In summary, the trend that emerges in both studies is that at least some aspects of antisocial behavior in adolescence are genetically influenced, and our data suggest that heritable components probably increase as adolescents grow older.

Lyons et al. (1995) carried out further analyses, using a bivariate model to examine the continuities between juvenile and adult antisocial behaviors. Interestingly, these showed that although additive genetic factors explained about six times more variance overall in adult than in juvenile traits, the juvenile genetic determinants overlapped completely with genetic influences on adult traits. This might again be compatible with the view that delinquent or antisocial behavior in adolescence generally shows important environmental influences, but that as adolescents emerge into adulthood, persistent antisocial behavior is more likely to occur in those who have a genetic predisposition toward it.

MOLECULAR GENETICS AND THE BIOLOGICAL BASIS OF ANTISOCIAL PERSONALITY

All of the evidence we have reviewed so far suggests that despite difficulties in defining the phenotype, there is a definite genetic contribution to antisocial personality. The crucial question, therefore, is this: Can we progress further and pinpoint mutations or genetic variations that predispose individuals to antisocial behavior? We have already mentioned that some single-gene defects—for example, a mutation in the monoamine oxidase A gene (Brunner et al., 1993)—are associated with aggression. However, such defects are rare and may not have any general relevance to antisocial behavior as a whole, which is common. Similarly, there has been much interest in the past as to whether chromosomal anomalies such as XYY aneuploidy predispose individuals to antisocial acts. Epidemiological data suggest that it might (Witkin, Mednick, & Schulsinger, 1976). However, as we have reviewed in greater detail elsewhere (Thapar & McGuffin, 1993), the XYY syndrome occurs in only about 1 in 1,000 males and so is unlikely to explain much criminality. Furthermore, surveys of prisons or forensic psychiatric units identify only a tiny minority of XYY males, so that presumably the vast majority never transgress the law.

Although the findings from cytogenetics in the 1960s and 1970s failed to live up to initial expectations in explicating the genetic basis of antisocial personality, it is worth considering in a measured way whether progress in molecular genetics during the 1980s and 1990s can offer better prospects. The general strategy of positional cloning has produced dramatic advances in our understanding of the genetics of single-gene disorders. Although the details are complicated, the process of positional cloning has a simple, ruthless logic. That is, one starts out with a disease where little or nothing is known about the pathogenesis other than its genetic mode of transmission. Genetic markers are then used in families containing multiple affected individuals to find which, if any, markers track with the disorder. Linkage analysis is facilitated by the existence of detailed maps of the 23 pairs of human chromosomes, provided by a type of DNA markers known as "microsatellites" or "simple sequence repeats" (Dib et al., 1996). Detection of linkage means that a marker lies close to the disease gene on the same chromosome, and hence points to the chromosome and the chromosomal region that carry the gene. The next task is to refine the location by looking for more closely spaced markers and applying methods of physical mapping. Ultimately the gene itself can be identified and cloned; once its sequence and structure are understood, it is possible to study gene products and the consequences of mutation. The single-gene disorder that is perhaps of greatest relevance to psychiatry, and in which much progress has been made by positional cloning, is Huntington's disease (Huntington's Disease Collaboration Research Group, 1993). However, what is at issue here is whether the same broad principles might be applied to other conditions, where the mode of inheritance is more complex. Furthermore, does positional cloning have any applicability to antisocial personality disorder, which might be considered a collection of traits of dimensions rather than a single definable disease?

Some headway has certainly been made in using modern molecular-genetic techniques to map susceptibility loci contributing to common non-Mendelian disorders, such as diabetes or multiple sclerosis (Strachan & Read, 1996). The same strategies are currently being applied in psychiatric disorders such as schizophrenia and bipolar disorders, where, although the results so far are less tangible, the prospects for progress look promising (McGuffin, Owen, & Farmer, 1995). Neither schizophrenia nor bipolar disorders are ideal phenotypes for genetic analysis, but these disorders do at least lend themselves to being considered as present–absent dichotomies. It has also proved possible in many centers to identify families containing multiple affected members, which can then be used in linkage analysis. However, we think it unlikely that this approach will prove feasible or sensible in studying the molecular-genetic basis of antisocial personality disorder. The reasons for this are twofold. First, it would seem unlikely that a reasonable sample of intact, multiply affected families with antisocial personality disorder could be assembled. Second, even though the strategy of looking for single-gene subforms of complex disorder has been successful for some diseases, such as breast cancer and Alzheimer's disease, this is unlikely to be the case with antisocial personality disorder except for some very rare mutations (such as that mentioned earlier affecting the monoamine oxidase A gene). Indeed, even in bipolar disorders and schizophrenia, where families with a Mendelian-like appearance exist, the results so far suggest that multiple genes are operating and that these disorders will turn out to be polygenic (caused by many genes) or oligogenic (caused by several genes acting together) (McGuffin & Owen, 1996).

Molecular-genetic studies of antisocial personality will therefore need to adopt strategies that (1) are capable of detecting genes of small effect, and (2) can be used to map genes contributing to continuous traits—those that we have already referred to as QTLs. Attempts to map QTLs in *Drosophila* began in the 1960s and were continued by plant geneticists working, for example, on such characteristics of maize (corn) such as weight, dimensions of the crop, and counts of plant parts (Stuber, 1995). However, the area of QTL mapping has begun to come to fruition since 1990, with the advent of dense and detailed marker maps. These, both in experimental plants and animals and in humans, have resulted largely from the discovery of microsatellite DNA markers.

The mouse genome has been intensively studied; because of this, plus the fact that mice are easy to handle and cheap to house, the mouse has become an important model organism in QTL mapping (Frankel, 1995). Although model organisms such as the mouse are compliant with geneticists' breeding programs, humans inevitably follow breeding programs of their own design. For single-gene disorders or complex disorders where Mendelian subforms are suspected, the usual strategy is to study families where the disorder is segregating in multiple sibships over several generations. For reasons that we have already discussed, this is neither feasible nor appropriate for a disorder such as antisocial personality. An alternative approach that has been most commonly used in attempting to map common oligogenic disorders such as diabetes is to adopt allele-sharing methods on sibling pairs. Here the aim is to detect sharing of marker alleles at a rate more frequent than that expected by chance. For any given marker locus, the expectation of sharing zero, one, or two alleles is respectively ¼, ½, or ¼. Any significant departure from expectation in the direction of increased sharing of alleles suggests that the marker is close to (i.e., linked with) a susceptibility gene contributing to the disease. Genome scans using closely spaced microsatellite markers have been successful in implicating several loci in the etiology of insulin-dependent diabetes mellitus (Cordell & Todd, 1995). A similar strategy is currently being employed in other complex diseases, including schizophrenia and bipolar disorders.

Analysis of sibling pairs can also be applied to quantitative traits, based on the notion that there is a degree of similarity between siblings for phenotypic scores, related to the degree of allele sharing at a QTL. The approach is already being applied to behavioral traits; for example, a gene contributing to reading disability has been localized to the short arm of chromosome 6 (Cardon et al., 1994). This approach is therefore obviously promising, and there is no reason in theory why it should not be applied to studies of sibling pairs to investigate traits that might be related to antisocial behavior, such as aggression or impulsivity. The main drawback of the sibling pair approach to detecting QTLs is that it is capable only of detecting genes that account for a fairly large proportion of total phenotypic variation. QTLs that contribute less than 10% of total phenotypic variation are unlikely to be detectable unless the sample size is enormous, running into several thousand pairs (Fulker & Cardon, 1994). Although it is possible that genes of this effect size may contribute to antisocial behavior, we would need to assume (given that heritabilities are 50% or less) that only four or five genes are involved. If there is a larger number of genes involved in the genetic contribution to any such trait, we will need to apply approaches capable of detecting smaller effects.

A complementary approach, which is already being applied in studies of personality and of IQ, is to search for allelic association (Daniels, McGuffin, & Owen, 1996; Plomin, McClearn, et al., 1994). Allelic association studies compare the frequencies of marker alleles in subjects who exhibit a certain trait and subjects who do not, or, alternatively, compare these frequencies in those who score high versus low on a quantitative measure. Allelic association arises because of linkage disequilibrium, pleiotropy, or population stratification. "Linkage disequilibrium" is a phenomenon whereby a pair of loci are very tightly linked, such that pairing of alleles is undisturbed over many generations. "Pleiotropy" is a rather different phenomenon, in which the marker itself has some direct effect upon the trait. Thus both pleiotropy and linkage disequilibrium can be put to useful effect in dissecting the molecular genetics of a disorder. "Population stratification," on the other hand, is an obstacle to understanding. This is the phenomenon whereby, in recent admixtures of human populations, the component subpopulations have different distributions of allele frequencies. If the subpopulations also differ in the frequencies with which they show a particular trait or disease, allelic association studies of the population as a whole may result in spurious positive findings. It is therefore important in association studies to match patient and control groups (or high- vs. low-scoring groups) for ethnic origin.

At present, probably the most promising approach to the study of personality is to carry out allelic association studies searching for pleiotropy—that is, focusing on candidate genes. For example, there has been rapid recent progress in identifying and cloning most of the genes involved in serotonergic and dopaminergic neurotransmission. In addition to its probable role in psychosis, dopaminergic transmission is known to be involved in normal behaviors such as reward seeking. Two recent studies (Benjamin et al., 1996; Ebstein et al., 1996) have investigated an allelic variation in the dopamine D4 receptor gene and have found evidence that it has an influence on the trait of novelty seeking. Although these interim results require replication elsewhere, novelty seeking, which is akin to thrill seeking and negatively correlated with conscientiousness, may well have some bearing on antisocial behaviors. These studies therefore represent a first step in what will undoubtedly be a long and complicated road toward discovering a molecular-genetic basis for antisocial personality disorder.

REFERENCES

Benjamin, J., Li, L., Patterson, C., Greenberg, B. D., Murphy, D. L., & Hamer, D. H. (1996). Population and familial association between the D4 dopamine receptor gene and measures of novelty seeking. *Nature Genetics, 12,* 81–84.

Bohman, M. (1978). Some genetic aspects of alcoholism and criminality: A population of adoptees. *Archives of General Psychiatry, 35,* 267–276.

Bohman, M., Cloninger, R., Sigvardsson, S., & von Knorring, A. (1982). Predisposition to petty criminality in Swedish adoptees: I. Genetic and environmental heterogeneity. *Archives of General Psychiatry, 39,* 1233–1241.

Brunner, H. G., Nelen, M. R., Van Zandvoort, P., Abeling, N. G. G. M., Van Gennip, A. H.,

Wolters, E. C., Kuiper, M. A., Ropers, H. H., & Van Oost, B. A. (1993). X-linked borderline mental retardation with prominent behavioral disturbance: Phenotype, genetic localization and evidence for disturbed monoamine metabolism. *American Journal of Human Genetics, 52,* 1032–1039.

Cadoret, R. J. (1978). Evidence for genetic inheritance of primary affective disorder in adoptees. *American Journal of Psychiatry, 135,* 463–466.

Cadoret, R. J., & Cain, C. (1980). Sex differences in predictors of antisocial behavior adoptees. *Archives of General Psychiatry, 37,* 1171–1175.

Cadoret, R. J., O'Gorman, T. W., Troughton, E., & Heywood, E. (1985). Alcoholism and antisocial personality: Interrelationships, genetics and environmental factors. *Archives of General Psychiatry, 42,* 161–167.

Cadoret, R. J., Yates, W. R., Troughton, E., Woodworth, G., & Stewart, M. A. (1995). Genetic-environmental interaction in the genesis of aggressivity and conduct disorders. *Archives of General Psychiatry, 52,* 916–924.

Campbell, I. L., & Gold, L. H. (1996). Transgenic modeling of neuropsychiatric disorders. *Molecular Psychiatry, 1,* 105–120.

Cardon, L. R., Smith, S. D., Fulker, D. W., Kimberling, W. J., Pennington, B. F., & DeFries, J. C. (1994). Quantitative trait reading disability on chromosome 6. *Science, 266,* 276–279.

Cases, O., Seif, I., Grimsby, J., Gasper, P., Chen, K., Pournin, S., Muller, O., Aguet, M., Babiner, C., Shih, J., & De Maeyer, E. (1995). Aggressive behavior and altered amounts of brain serotonin and norepinephrine in mice lacking MAOA. *Science, 268,* 1763–1766.

Cloninger, C. R., & Gottesman, I. I. (1987). Genetic and environmental factors in antisocial behavior disorders. In S. A. Mednick, T. E. Moffitt, & S. A. Stack (Eds.), *Causes of crime: New biological approaches* (pp. 92–109). Cambridge, England: Cambridge University Press.

Cloninger, C. R., Sigvardsson, S., Bohman, M., & von Knorring, A. (1982). Predisposition to petty criminality in Swedish adoptees: II. Cross-fostering analysis of gene–environment interaction. *Archives of General Psychiatry, 39,* 1242–1253.

Cordell, H. J., & Todd, J. A. (1995). Multifactorial inheritance in type 1 diabetes. *Trends in Genetics, 11,* 499–504.

Crowe, R. R. (1972). The adopted offspring of women criminal offenders: A study of their arrest records. *Archives of General Psychiatry, 27,* 600–603.

Crowe, R. R. (1974). An adoption study of antisocial personality. *Archives of General Psychiatry, 31,* 785–791.

Daniels, J., McGuffin, P., & Owen, M. (1996). Molecular genetic research on IQ: Can it be done? Should it be done? *Journal of Biosocial Sciences, 28.*

Dib, C., Faure, S., Fizames, C., Samson, D., Drouot, N., Vignal, A., Millasseau, P., Marc, S., Jazan, J., Seboun, E., Lathrop, M., Gyapay, G., Morissette, J., & Weissenbach, H. (1996). A comprehensive genetic map of the human genome based on 5264 microsatellites. *Nature, 380,* 152–154.

Eaves, L. J., Eysenck, H. J., & Martin, N. (1989). *Genes, culture and personality.* New York: Academic Press.

Ebstein, R. P., Novick, O., Umansky, R., Priel, B., Osher, Y., Blaine, D., Bennett, E. R., Nemanov, L., Katz, M., & Belmaker, R. H. (1996). Dopamine D4 receptor (D4DR) exon III polymorphism associated with the human personality trait of novelty seeking. *Nature Genetics, 12,* 78–80.

Edelbrock, C., Rende, R., Plomin, R., & Thompson, L. A. (1995). A twin study of competence and problem behavior in childhood and early adolescence. *Journal of Child Psychology and Psychiatry, 36*(5), 775–785.

Falconer, D. S. (1965). The inheritance of liability to certain diseases, estimated from the incidence among relatives. *Annals of Human Genetics, 29,* 51–76.

Falconer, D. S. (1989). *Introduction to quantitative genetics* (3rd ed.). Edinburgh: Churchill Livingstone.

Flint, J., Corley, R., DeFries, J. C., Fulker, D. W., Gray, J. A., Miller, S., & Collins, A. C. (1995). A simple genetic basis for a complex psychological trait in laboratory mice. *Science, 269,* 1432–1435.

Frankel, W. N. (1995). Taking stock of complex trait genetics in mice. *Trends in Genetics, 11*(12), 471–476.

Fulker, D. W., & Cardon, L. R. (1994). A sub-pair approach to interval mapping of quantitative trait loci. *American Journal of Human Genetics, 54,* 1092–1103.

Goldsmith, H. H., & Gottesman, I. I. (1996). Heritable variability and variable heritability in developmental psychopathology. In M. Lenzenweger & J. Haugaard (Eds.), *Frontiers in developmental psychopathology* (pp. 5–43). Oxford: Oxford University Press.

Heath, A. C., Neale, M. C., Kessler, R. C., Eaves, L. J., & Kendler, K. S. (1992). Evidence for genetic influences on personality from self-reports and informant ratings. *Journal of Personality and Social Psychology, 63,* 85–96.

Huntington's Disease Collaboration Research Group. (1993). A novel gene containing a trinucleotide repeat that is expanded and unstable on Huntington's disease chromosomes. *Cell, 72,* 971–983.

Lyons, M. J., True, W. R., Eisen, S. A., Goldberg, J., Meyer, J. M., Faraone, S. V., Eaves, L. J., & Tsuang, M. T. (1995). Differential heritability of adult and juvenile antisocial traits. *Archives of General Psychiatry, 52,* 906–915.

Martin, N., & Jardine, R. (1986). Eysenck's contributions to behavior genetics. In S. Modgil & C. Modgil (Eds.), *Hans Eysenck: Consensus and controversy* (pp. 13–47). Philadelphia: Falmer.

McGuffin, P., & Gottesman, I. I. (1985). Genetic influences on normal and abnormal development. In M. Rutter & L. Hersov (Eds.), *Child and adolescent psychiatry: Modern approaches* (pp. 17–33). Oxford: Blackwell Scientific.

McGuffin, P., & Owen, M. J. (1996). Molecular genetic studies of schizophrenia. *CSHL Press Symposium on Quantitative Biology, 61,* 815–822.

McGuffin, P., Owen, M. J., & Farmer, A. E. (1995). Genetic basis of schizophrenia. *Lancet, 346,* 678–682.

McGuffin, P., Owen, M. J., O'Donovan, M. C., Thapar, A., & Gottesman, I. I. (1994). *Seminars in psychiatric genetics.* London: Gaskell.

McGuffin, P., & Thapar, A. (1997). The genetic basis of bad behaviour in adolescents. *Lancet, 350,* 411–412.

Mednick, S. A., Gabrielli, J. F., & Hutchings, B. (1984). Genetic influences in criminal convictions: evidence from an adoption court. *Science, 224,* 891–894.

Nelson, R. J., Demas, G. E., Huange, P. L., Fishman, M. C., Dawson, V. L., Dawson, T. M., & Snyder, S. H. (1995). Behavioral abnormalities in male mice lacking neuronal nitric oxide synthase. *Nature, 378,* 383–396.

Olweus, D. (1989). Prevalence and incidence in the study of antisocial behaviour: Definitions and measurements. In M. W. Klein (Ed.), *Cross national research in self-reporting crime and delinquency* (pp. 187–201). Dordrecht, The Netherlands: Kluwer.

Plomin, R. (1990). The role of inheritance in behavior. *Science, 248,* 183–188.

Plomin, R., McClearn, G. E., Smith, D. L., Vignetti, S., Chorney, M. J., Chorney, K., Venditti, C. P., Kasarda, S., Thompson, L. A., Detterman, D. K., Daniels, J., Owen, M., & McGuffin, P. (1994). DNA markers associated with high versus low IQ: The IQ QTL project. *Behavior Genetics, 24*(2), 107–118.

Plomin, R., Owen, M. J., & McGuffin, P. (1994). The genetic basis of complex human behaviours. *Science, 264,* 1733–1739.

Reich, T., Cloninger, C. R., Wette, R., & James, J. (1979). The use of multiple thresholds and segregation analysis in analyzing the phenotypic heterogeneity of multifactorial traits. *Annals of Human Genetics, 42,* 371.

Reich, T., James, J. W., & Morris, C. A. (1972). The use of multiple thresholds in determining the mode of transmission of semicontinuous traits. *Annals of Human Genetics, 36,* 163–184.

Rutter, M., Tizard, J., & Whitmore, K. (1970). *Education, health and behaviour.* London: Longman.

Saudou, F., Amara, D. A., Dierich, A., Lemew, M., Ramboz, S., Segh, L., Buhot, M. C., & Hen, R. (1994). Enhanced aggressive behavior in mice lacking 5-HT1b receptor. *Science, 265,* 1875–1878.

Schulsinger, F. (1972). Psychopathy, heredity and environment. *International Journal of Mental Health, 1,* 190–206.

Sigvardsson, S., Cloninger, C. R., Bohman, M., & von Knorring, A. L. (1982). Predisposition to petty criminality in Swedish adoptees: III. Sex differences and validations of the male typology. *Archives of General Psychiatry, 39,* 1248–1253.

Silberg, J., Rutter, M., Meyer, J., Simonoff, E., Hewitt, J., Loeber, R., Pickles, A., Maes, H., & Eaves, L. (1996). Genetic and environmental influences of the covariation of hyperactivity and conduct disturbance in juvenile twins. *Journal of Child Psychology and Psychiatry, 37,* 807–816.

Stevenson, J., & Graham, P. (1988). Behavioral deviance in 13-year-old twins: An item analysis. *Journal of the American Academy of Child and Adolescent Psychiatry, 27,* 791–797.

Strachan, T., & Read, A. (1996). *Human molecular genetics.* Oxford: Bios.

Stuber, C. W. (1995). Mapping and manipulating quantitative traits in maize. *Trends in Genetics, 11,* 477–481.

Tellegen, A., Lykken, D. T., Bouchard, T. J., Wilcox, K. J., Segal, N. L., & Rich, S. (1988). Personality similarity in twins reared apart and together. *Journal of Personality and Social Psychology, 54,* 1031–1039.

Thapar, A., & McGuffin, P. (1993). Is personality disorder inherited?: An overview of the evidence. *Journal of Psychopathology and Behavioural Assessment, 15*(4), 325–345.

Thapar, A., & McGuffin, P. (1994). A twin study of depressive symptoms in childhood. *British Journal of Psychiatry, 165,* 259–265.

Thapar, A., & McGuffin, P. (1996). A twin study of antisocial and neurotic symptoms in childhood. *Psychological Medicine, 26,* 1111–1118.

Willerman, L., Loehlin, J. C., & Horn, J. M. (1992). An adoption and a cross-fostering study of the Minnesota Multiphasic Personality Inventory (MMPI) Psychopathic Deviate scale. *Behavior Genetics, 22,* 515–529.

Wimer, R. E., & Wimer, C. C. (1985). Animal behavior genetics: a search for the biological foundations of behavior. *Annual Review of Psychology, 36,* 171–218.

Witkin, H. A., Mednick, S. A., & Schulsinger, F. (1976). Criminality in XYY and XXY men. *Science, 193,* 547–555.

14

Neurobiology in Psychopathy

LARRY J. SIEVER

Although there are intriguing leads pointing to neurobiological substrates of psychopathy, there has been relatively little systematic study of psychopathy from a neurobiological perspective, in contrast to mental disorders such as schizophrenia or bipolar disorders. In part, the dearth of clinical research may reflect the lower likelihood that psychopathic individuals will find themselves in a clinical psychiatric setting. They may be identified more commonly in a forensic context, but defining psychopathy is problematic, and variability in the construct could ultimately result in heterogeneous findings in neurobiological studies in any context. Thus, the second difficulty in studying the neurobiology of psychopaths is identifying a relatively coherent construct that would lend itself to systematic study. Unfortunately, the term "psychopathy" is a controversial one, with a lack of consensus as to its legitimacy as a distinct disorder or its most suitable borders (Blackburn, 1988). Indeed, at one time "psychopathy" was a broadly applied term and appeared to cover a range of personality disorders marked by some degree of social deviance and weakness of character. In the United States, antisocial behavior became the defining yardstick of this broad rubric of disorders, and the explicit concept of psychopathy is not specifically embodied as a distinct entity in the DSM system. The DSM criteria for antisocial personality disorder focus on disregard for the law, aggressive behaviors, and violations of social norms; they emphasize relatively less the lack of empathy and the glibness associated with most concepts of psychopathy.

Cleckley was perhaps most influential in initially defining current concepts of psychopathy. He emphasized social deviance, but highlighted particularly the superficial charm, lack of remorse, incapacity for love, and impersonal, unresponsive relational style (Cleckley, 1976). Hare developed this concept for empirical research by devising a research scale for psychopathy, the Psychopathy Checklist (PCL; Hare et al., 1990), which has since been revised as the PCL-R. This scale has been shown to be reliable and has been validated in terms of its predictive power for recidivism in criminal populations. A factor analysis of the PCL-R suggests a two-factor structure. The first factor, consists of personality traits such as glibness, lack or remorse or guilt, shallow affect, callousness, lack of empathy, and failure to accept responsibility; the second factor consists of antisocial traits and impulsive/aggressive behaviors. This distinction parallels the clinical tradition of considering these as two partially independent constructs. The first factor, reflecting callousness and lack of empathy, might be considered a "core" psychopathy factor, whereas the second factor might be considered an impulsive/aggressive factor.

In this context, a neurobiological approach to psychopathy becomes more plausible. This area has been reviewed previously (Dolan, 1994) for a broadly defined construct of psychopathy. Neurobiological investigation in the area of personality disorder research may be more likely to be successful when targeted at specific traits or dimensions that are coherent and perhaps closer to a neurobiological underpinning (Siever & Davis, 1991). Rather than exploring the neurobiology of a broader but fuzzier construct, in this chapter I will review the neurobiology of psychopathy in terms of neurobiological substrates of the "core" psychopathy factor (Factor 1) and the impulsive/aggressive (Factor 2)—a strategy consistent with the clustering of findings of neurobiological studies to date.

NEUROBIOLOGICAL SUBSTRATES OF "CORE" PSYCHOPATHY

Genetic Studies

Although genetic studies are reviewed elsewhere in this volume (see McGuffin & Thapar, Chapter 13), there has been little work addressing potential differences between aspects of "core" psychopathic personality and antisocial behaviors. Thus, most genetic studies are focused on antisocial personality disorder and criminality. For antisocial behaviors, heritability is substantial (McGuffin & Gottesman, 1985).

Neurological Abnormalities

Neurological lesions with multiple etiologies (particularly those affecting frontal and temporal lobes) may result in personality shifts, including development of traits that might be considered psychopathic or antisocial (Benson & Blumer, 1975). None of these pictures may exactly mimic, however, the naturalistic presentation of the psychopath. On the other hand, delinquents with psychopathic features have an increased prevalence of head injuries (Yeudall, 1977). Although these studies show an association under some circumstances between neurological insult and psychopathic behaviors, they are by no means convincing evidence that psychopathy necessarily reflects an underlying neurological abnormality. In general, neurological "soft signs" have been more closely associated with aggressive behavior, history of attention-deficit/hyperactivity disorder (ADHD), and antisocial behavior than with the "core" psychopathy factor (Woods & Eby, 1982; Satterfield, 1978; Wender, Reimherr, & Wood, 1981; Dolan, 1994). Although ADHD is often a precursor of adult antisocial behavior, its precise relationship to the core construct of psychopathy is less clear.

Electroencephalographic Abnormalities

The presence of electroencephalographic (EEG) abnormalities in psychopathy may also point to neurobiological underpinnings, but the available data are somewhat inconsistent and difficult to interpret. Differences in the populations tested also contribute to the lack of homogeneity in the findings. Numerous studies have focused on the EEG of aggressive psychopaths, which may demonstrate temporal spiking activity (Monroe, 1978) and will be considered later with neurobiological substrates of aggression. Although the EEG correlates of psychopathy have been reviewed recently (Dolan, 1994), the consensus appears to be that there are no consistent EEG abnormalities associated with psychopathy (Blackburn, 1979), although slow-wave activity has been observed in temporal areas (Howard, Fenton, & Fenwick, 1984).

Evoked Potentials and Attentional Function

One study has suggested that psychopaths can deploy their attention differently from other people by focusing on stimuli and screening out irrelevant information (Jutai & Hare, 1983). In this study, both evoked potential and electrodermal activity were reported in inmates with high and low ratings of psychopathy on the PCL. The N100 component of the auditory evoked potential was employed as an attentional index of response to the tone pips, and the smaller N100 response to the pips in the high-psychopathy group suggested that the psychopaths screened out these stimuli while attending to the primary task of the video games. There were no differences in response in the passive condition when subjects were not engaged in the task. These findings are consistent with the possibility of altered attentional deployment suggested previously (Yochelson & Samenow, 1976; Jutai & Hare, 1983). Baseline passive attention also appears to be normal in other paradigms (Wood et al., 1984).

Autonomic Abnormalities

Although it originally appeared that autonomic hypoarousal in psychopaths reflected a low resting skin conductance that was less variable (than normal Schalling, 1978; Hare, 1978a), more recent studies have suggested that this may not be the case (Hare, 1978b; Blackburn, 1979). Similarly, there is no convincing evidence of differences in skin conductance or response to stimuli between psychopaths and comparison groups (Hare & Cox, 1978). Interestingly, there are suggestions of diminished increments in skin conductance and heart rate when psychopaths are anticipating adverse stimuli (Hare & Cox, 1978), although this finding is not entirely consistent (Raine & Venables, 1988). Alterations in the recovery time following stimulation have also been reported (Levander, Schalling, Lidberg, Bartfai, & Lidberg, 1980; Robinson & Zahn, 1985). Again, the evidence is not so much suggestive of baseline differences; rather, the temporal and stimulus-dependent modulation of autonomic arousal suggests different reactivity to the environment, and particularly different reactivity to potential future punishment.

Neuropsychological Abnormalities

In general, it appears that psychopathic individuals have normal intellectual and neuropsychological functioning as reflected in responses to standardized batteries (Hare, 1993; Hare et al., 1990). Some studies have suggested alterations in frontal and temporal areas, although these have relied primarily on antisocial subjects (Yeudall, 1977; Dolan, 1994).

Cerebral Asymmetry

Some evidence exists for altered laterality in psychopathic patients. Normally, negative emotional words are processed preferentially by the right rather than the left hemisphere;

psychopaths appear to have problems processing affectively charged words in the right hemisphere, and shift this function to the left hemisphere (Ogloff & Wong, 1990). Right-sided advantage in information processing has been reported in dichotic listening tasks (Hare & McPherson, 1984) and in visual processing during performance of a semantic categorization task (Jutai & Hare, 1983; Hare & Jutai, 1988). These findings cumulatively suggest altered lateralization, particularly with regard to affectively charged stimuli, in psychopaths.

Language and Affective Processing

Perhaps the most convincing data for altered cortical function in psychopaths comes from studies evaluating the language of psychopaths and their processing of neutral and emotional words. Cleckley (1976) believed that abnormalities in language processing were the primary, although not the sole, manifestations of an underlying brain pathology. It has been observed that emotion is like a "second language" to psychopaths (Gillstrom & Hare, 1988). Their use of language without underlying deep affect has prompted an analogy to their "knowing the words but not the music" (Johns & Quay, 1962). Processing of neutral and emotional words can be evaluated by the lexical decision task, in which subjects are presented with randomized lists of words and nonwords (the latter are composed of strings of letters with no meaning) and are asked to circle the real words. Normal individuals seem to process emotionally charged words on a "fast track," so that their lexical decision—that is, deciding whether a string of letters constitutes a word or not—is made more rapidly, and evoked potentials evaluated during this decision are greater and more persistent. In one study, nonpsychopathic criminals showed the expected differentiation in reaction time and evoked potential response between affect-laden and neutral words, whereas psychopathic criminals did not show this difference (Williamson, Harpur, & Hare, 1991). It appeared that the psychopathic criminals processed and responded to the emotionally charged words as if they were neutral words and could not distinguish them in terms of processing.

Altered processing of emotionally charged events also seems to occur at the level of attention and memory. Again, psychopaths do not seem to process stimulation differently under emotional and neutral conditions. This may represent a deficit in "fast-track" emotional responding. Similar results were found using a blink startle paradigm (Patrick, Bradley, & Lang, 1993). Blink startle responses to noise are generally attenuated during positive emotional states and augmented during negative emotional states. The normally observed pattern was observed in subjects low in psychopathy, while the psychopaths appeared to show attenuation with both positive and negative emotional states; this suggested that their affective state was not influencing their startle response and affective arousal in an appropriate or normal manner.

Brain Imaging Studies

Although many studies have examined brain imaging in individuals with antisocial behavior, most have focused on subjects primarily defined by their aggressive or violent histories. One study to date has also focused on "core" psychopathy syndrome as defined by Hare. In this study (Intrator et al., 1997), differences in regional cerebral blood flow were evaluated by single-photon emission computed tomography (SPECT) imaging during the lexical decision task, as utilized by Williamson et al. (1991) in the study cited above. Although the selection of experimental subjects was not specifically based on Factor 1 psychopathy, the choice of individuals who scored higher than 25 on the PCL-R suggested that these patients were selected by virtue not just of aggressive and/or antisocial acts, but also of "core" psychopathic symptoms. Subjects were selected from a population of substance abusers, who were divided into those that met the criteria for psychopathy and those that did not meet these criteria but were matched for duration of cocaine, alcohol, and heroin use. Their SPECT scans were inspected for gross ischemic and hemorrhagic lesions. A normal control group was also studied in the same paradigm. There was a significant group × condition interaction that was significant for the left and right frontal temporal regions, both superficial and deep. Although the two control groups (the nonpsychopathic substance abusers and the normal control group) did not differ from each other in their relative activation between the emotional and neutral conditions, the psychopaths did differ from the control groups and appeared to show relatively greater cerebral blood flow during the emotional word list than during the neutral word list. Given data suggesting that deeply ingrained or easily processed tasks may be associated with less of a metabolic or cerebral blood flow increase (Gur, Roland, & Gur, 1992), the greater increases in blood flow in the emotional task in the psychopathic subjects may suggest a lack of facility in processing emotionally charged words on the "fast track," or a relative inefficiency in affective language processing. This study raises the possibility that alterations in frontal temporal function may underlie the affective language disturbances, which is one of the better-documented neuropsychological abnormalities associated with "core" psychopathy.

NEUROBIOLOGY OF IMPULSIVE AGGRESSION

There are considerably more data available supporting a neurobiological substrate for impulsive aggression. Aggression may not be linked specifically with the psychopathy syndrome, but may also be associated with other personality disorders (e.g., borderline personality disorder), a wide variety of criminal behaviors, and even forms of self-directed impulsive aggression (e.g., those observed in suicide attempts). The most robust neurobiological correlate of these behaviors is reduced serotonergic activity, although neurological, electrophysiological, and imaging correlates have been reported as well.

Genetic Studies

As noted earlier, twin studies and adoption studies of antisocial individuals suggest heritability for antisocial personality disorder. In most cases, specifically violent aggression was not examined as an independent factor. However, in subjects with borderline personality disorder, impulsivity was found to be more concordant in monozygotic than in dizygotic twins (Torgersen, 1992).

Neurological Factors

Minor neurological abnormalities have been reported to be increased in incidence in particularly hyperactive or aggressive populations (Woods & Eby, 1982), raising the possibility that perinatal injury may contribute to these aggressive traits. In two studies of Danish birth cohorts, perinatal complications were associated with violent criminal behavior, but not more broadly with antisocial personality disorder; again, this suggests the differentiation of antecedents of specifically aggressive or violent behaviors from those of other antisocial or psychopathic characteristics (Kandel & Freed, 1989).

Frontal lobe lesions or injuries have been associated with violent behavior (Brickner, 1934; Volvaka, 1995; Casanueva, Villaneuva, Penalua, & Cabezas-Cerrato, 1984; Heinrichs, 1989; Yeudall, 1977). The orbital frontal cortex specifically has been associated with poorly socialized, irritable, hostile behavior—a hypothesis reinforced by a modern reconstruction of the injury of Phineas Gage, a railroad worker who was transformed from a gentle, well-functioning man to a dyssocial, hostile, and verbally aggressive individual. His injury was found to involve lesions of the orbital frontal cortex, as well as anterior sections of the cingulate and anterior mesial aspects of the frontal cortex near the orbital cortex (Damasio, Grabowski, Frank, Galaburda, & Damasio, 1994).

Lesions of the temporal lobe are also associated with susceptibility to violent behavior, although only a small proportion of these patients actually develop truly violent behaviors. Among violent subjects, unexpectedly high numbers of anterior inferior temporal lobe tumors have been reported (Tonkonogy, 1991). Electrical stimulation of temporal and subcortical related regions has suggested that these regions are involved in the regulation of aggression. For example, electrical stimulation of the amygdala has been associated with rage attacks (Mark, Sweet, & Ervin, 1975), although studies are not consistent in this regard (Treiman, 1991). These studies cumulatively suggest that lesions in frontal and temporal areas may be associated with aggression, but that the relationships are far from monolithic in this regard.

Electrophysiological Studies

Violent behavior has been reported during frontal lobe seizure activity as measured by EEG (Gedye, 1989), during frontal lobe seizures in subjects with habitual violence (Williams, 1969), and also in conjunction with temporal lobe seizures (DeVinsky & Bear, 1984). However, only a small proportion of patients with temporal lobe epilepsy demonstrate violent behavior (Ramani & Gumnit, 1981; Delgado-Escueta et al., 1981; King & Ajmone Marsan, 1977; Currie, Heathfield, Henson, & Scott, 1971). Conversely, positive spiking activity has been found in approximately 40% of impulsive/aggressive psychopaths (Kurland, Yaeger, & Arthur, 1963). Other studies have supported this relationship (Williams, 1969; Monroe, 1978).

Brain Imaging Studies

Decreased blood flow in the left temporal cortex was found in four psychiatric patients with significant histories of violence, and in half of these patients decreased blood flow in the frontal cortex was found as well. In a study of murderers, bilateral decreases in glucose metabolism in both superior and interior mesial frontal cortex, as well as a trend toward decreased metabolism in orbital frontal cortex, were found in the murderers as compared to normal subjects (Raine, Sheard, Reynolds, & Lencz, 1992). In a study of patients with personality disorders, an inverse relationship between lifetime history of "aggressive impulsive behavior" in regional glucose metabolism was found in orbital frontal cortex, as well as in the right temporal lobe. Patients meeting criteria for borderline personality disorder had decreased metabolism in middle inferior frontal areas corresponding to mesiofrontal cortex just above the orbital cortex (Goyer et al., 1994). These studies cumulatively suggest that frontal temporal regions, particularly orbital frontal cortex, may be involved in the modulation of aggressive behavior.

Neurochemistry

Serotonergic System

Metabolite Studies. Decreased concentrations of the serotonin metabolite 5-hydroxy-indoleacetic acid (5-HIAA) have been associated with impulsive/aggressive behaviors in criminal offenders (Virkkunen, Nuutila, Goodwin, & Linnoila, 1987), armed services personnel (Brown, Goodwin, Ballenger, Goyer, & Major, 1979), and normal volunteers (Asberg, Schalling, Traskman-Bendz, & Wagner, 1987).

Fenfluramine Challenge. Fenfluramine, which releases serotonin, blocks its reuptake, and acts directly on serotonergic receptors, causes an increase in prolactin that can be antagonized by serotonergic antagonists. As such, it serves as a possible index of serotonergic activity. Prolactin responses to fenfluramine were found to be blunted in male patients with borderline personality disorder, compared to other personality disorder patients and normal controls (Coccaro et al., 1989). The group difference appeared to be attributable to the impulsive/aggressive criteria for borderline personality disorder: Blunted prolactin responses to fenfluramine were associated with the criteria "self-damaging acts," "impulsivity," and "suicidal gestures and attempts," but not to criteria related to affective or interpersonal difficulties. Prolactin responses to fenfluramine were highly negatively correlated with the Assault and Irritability subscales of the Buss–Durkee Hostility Inventory (BDHI), but not to other BDHI subscales such as Suspiciousness or Resentment, or to global psychopathological indices of anxiety or depression. Covarying for impulsive/aggressive criteria abolished the group differences between borderline and other personality disorder patients, suggesting that these differences were due to the presence of these particular criteria in the borderline personality disorder diagnosis. Although blunted responses to fenfluramine were not associated in this study with any Axis II diagnoses other than borderline personality disorder, other impulsive personality disorders such as antisocial personality disorder were not highly represented. In another study, blunted prolactin responses were observed in male subjects with sociopathy or antisocial personality disorder (O'Keane, Moloney, O'Neill, & O'Connor, 1992). In a different series of subjects with heterogeneous diagnoses marked by impulsive features, impulsive personality disorder patients demonstrated reduced prolactin responses to *d*-fenfluramine, compared to a nonimpulsive comparison group (Coccaro, Kavoussi, & Hauger, 1995). Substance abusers defined by their antisocial behavior demonstrated a correlation between impulsivity and prolactin responses to fenfluramine as well (Moss, Yao, & Panzak, 1990), while in another population of substance abusers with heterogeneous diagnoses, there was a positive relationship between impulsive aggression and prolactin responses to fenfluramine (Fishbein, Lozovsky, & Jaffe, 1989).

The reduced serotonergic activity may be closer than the behavior of impulsivity itself to the heritable substrate, as a blunted prolactin response to fenfluramine in personality disorder probands was a better predictor of impulsivity in their relatives than were impulsive traits in the probands themselves (Coccaro, Silverman, Klar, Horvath, & Siever, 1994). More direct evidence for an association between serotonergic abnormalities and impulsive aggression at a genetic level has been derived in a pilot study from our center, in which subjects with a genotype ("LL") of tryptophan hydroxylase, which has been associated with suicide attempts in Finnish violent criminal offenders with alcoholic histories, was found to have increased Irritability and Assault subscale scores on the BDHI (New, Trestman, Benishay, Coccaro, & Siever, 1995). The latter study suggests the possibility that alterations in regulatory genes in the serotonergic system may contribute to variance in impulsive aggression, as well as to suicide attempts in populations of subjects with impulsive/aggressive histories.

Other Serotonergic Indices. Reduced concentrations of plasma tryptophan have been reported in alcoholics with a history of aggressive or suicidal behavior (Branchey, Branchey, Shaw, & Lieber, 1984), and reductions of imipramine binding sites, which are linked to serotonin reuptake sites, are correlated with aggression and conduct disorder in adolescents (Stoff, Pollack, & Vitello, 1987). Paroxetine binding sites have also been associated inversely with impulsive aggression in personality disorder patients (Coccaro et al., 1995). Other types of challenges have not been examined in relation to aggressive behaviors in psychiatric or forensic populations.

Implications. Various preclinical studies also suggest that the serotonergic system plays an important role in the modulation of impulsive/aggressive behavior. Rats that were lesioned in the raphe nuclei (where serotonergic neurons are located) showed dramatic increases in muricidal or mice-killing behavior (Valzelli, 1981), consistent with a failure of suppression of aggressive behaviors. Lesions of the serotonin system in rats also lead to their being ineffective in suppressing behaviors that might lead to punishment or aversive consequences (Gray, 1982). These findings have raised the possibility that these animals do not "learn" from punishment, prompting parallels to sociopathic human adults. If lesioned rats are raised with mice that are later presented after the rats are lesioned in the raphe, so that they are familiar with the mice prior to the lesion, the rats do not display the characteristic muricidal behavior. These results suggest that novelty and reactivity to the environment may also be important in stimulating aggression.

The serotonergic system plays an important role in regulating behavior. Increased serotonergic activity, as reflected in increased firing rates of serotonergic neurons, is associated with rhythmic, self-directed behaviors, whereas decreases in serotonergic activity occur when the organism is presented with novel or threatening stimuli (Jacobs, 1987). The serotonergic system appears to have broad modulatory actions and plays a role in appetite, temperature, and mood regulation. Reductions in serotonergic activity may impair an individual's capacity to suppress aggressive behaviors or behaviors that will ultimately result in punishment. Serotonergic neurons project widely through the brain and richly innovate prefrontal and temporal regions. High concentrations of serotonergic receptors, particularly 5-HT_2 receptors, have been identified in frontal cortex (Arango et al., 1990), and concentrations of cerebrospinal fluid 5-HIAA in patients with frontal temporal contusions are significantly lower than in patients with diffuse cerebral contusions (VanWoerken, Teelken, & Minderhoud, 1977). In primates, variability in 5-HT_2 receptor activity has been associated with individual differences in aggressive behavior. Specifically, the numbers of 5-HT_2 receptors in posterior orbital frontal cortex, medial frontal cortex, and amygdala were inversely related to aggressive behavior, but this relationship was not observed elsewhere in the brain. In contrast, increases of 5-HT_2 receptor numbers in posterior orbital frontal cortex, posterior temporal pole, and amygdala were directly correlated with prosocial behavior (Raleigh & Brammer, 1993). These results support the hypotheses that regionally specific effects of serotonin receptor activity in orbital frontal cortex promote cooperative grooming behavior, whereas decreased levels of activity may contribute to aggression. Because serotonergic challenges like fenfluramine have been demonstrated to increase cerebral metabolism in frontal temporal regions, including frontal temporal cortex (Kapur, Meyer, Wilson, Houle, & Brown, 1994;

Malone, Campbell, Shuhua, & Mann, 1995), it is now possible to evaluate increases in metabolism in these regions to determine whether they are reduced in impulsive/aggressive subjects. Ongoing studies are underway in our center to evaluate this possibility.

Noradrenergic System

In contrast to the serotonergic system, the noradrenergic system is activated when an organism is confronted with novel or threatening stimuli; it serves to increase vigilance and to heighten the contrast of incoming information in preparation for active responses to these stimuli (Aston-Jones & Bloom, 1981; Siever, 1987). In this way it may play a complementary role to the serotonergic system by mediating activation/arousal, as opposed to the suppressive/restitutive role of the serotonergic system.

The noradrenergic system, like the serotonergic system, can be evaluated by measures of its metabolite (in this case, 3-methoxy-4-hydroxy phenyl glycol) or through responses to challenge. For example, clonidine, an alpha$_2$-adrenergic receptor located both presynaptically and postsynaptically, induces increases in growth hormone secretion by its action on adrenergic receptors. Thus, the magnitude of the growth hormone increase may reflect the responsiveness of postsynaptic alpha$_2$-adrenergic receptors. In general, the growth hormone response to clonidine has been found to be blunted in depressed patients, whether they are acutely ill or in remission (Siever et al., 1990). In contrast, growth hormone responses to clonidine appear to be heightened in association with irritability in personality disorder patients (Coccaro et al., 1991). In this latter study, there were direct correlations between growth hormone responses to clonidine and irritability in the personality disorder sample.

It is clear that these monoamine regulatory systems do not act in isolation from each other. Although responses to these challenges have not been correlated, suggesting that they are not tapping into the same underlying psychological substrate, they may interact with each other. Such an interaction may explain an apparent paradox in studies of the prolactin response to fenfluramine in depressed and personality disorder patients in our center. As discussed previously, an inverse correlation is seen between prolactin responses to fenfluramine and impulsive aggression in personality disorder patients; yet, there is no apparent correlation between impulsive aggression and prolactin responses to fenfluramine in remitted depressed patients (Coccaro et al., 1989; Siever et al., 1993). Perhaps the depressed patients, who are likely to exhibit a blunted response to clonidine (reflecting reduced noradrenergic activity), may be less irritable in response to the environment, consistent with the relative autonomy of mood observed in more serious forms of depression. Their aggression, when expressed, is manifested as suicide attempts, which are observed in both personality disorder and depressed patients studied in our center (Coccaro et al., 1989; Siever et al., 1993). In contrast, in impulsive personality disorder patients, increases in noradrenergic responsiveness may be associated with greater engagement with and reactivity to the environment; thus, such individuals are highly reactive to environmental stimuli and also have difficulty in suppressing aggressive behavior, making it more likely that they will respond aggressively to any provocation. Indeed, in studies to date noradrenergic measures seem more closely correlated with sensation seeking, risk seeking, hostility, and irritability, whereas the serotonergic measures are more closely correlated with direct physical manifestations of aggression. Thus, the different systems may play different roles in the development of impulsive/aggressive behaviors.

Monoamine Oxidase

Although they are not directly related to impulsive aggression, abnormalities in monoamine oxidase (MAO) activity in platelets have been associated with novelty-seeking and risk-taking behavior. Individuals with low platelet MAO are more likely to seek stimulation, to be socially engaged, and to be vulnerable to a variety of affective disturbances (Siever et al., 1984). Studies of MAO have been confounded by effects of nicotine and other confounding artifacts. However, the relationship of MAO to traits such as impulsivity and aggression has been rekindled by the report of a linkage between MAO-A deficiency and a syndrome of aggression and criminality in a large pedigree in the Netherlands (Brunner, Nelen, Breakefield, Ropers, & Van Oost, 1993).

A MODEL FOR PSYCHOPATHY

Although I have discussed the potential neurobiological substrates of "core" psychopathy or Factor 1 of the PCL-R separately from the substrates of impulsive aggression or Factor 2, it is clear that they are closely related constructs clinically. A parallel close relationship at the physiological level is suggested by the fact that serotonergic neurons heavily innervate frontal temporal regions, which are implicated in both psychopathy (as reflected in altered processing of emotional stimuli) and impulsive aggression. Although the basis of the altered cortical processing in psychopaths is not clear, it is possible that a neurodevelopmental aberration stemming from genetic and/or early environmental influences (e.g., nutritional deprivation) may contribute to the altered processing of affective stimuli in these vulnerable cortical regions. Serotonergic modulation of these regions may determine whether psychopathy is manifested in manipulativeness and petty "con artist"-type crimes on the one hand, or in remorseless, violent crime on the other. Serotonergic deficits in the absence of the cortical processing deficits seen in psychopaths may be more likely to result in impulsive/aggressive features in patients with borderline and narcissistic personality disorders, who feel guilt about their aggressive behaviors and wish to change or modulate these behaviors. These are the patients who are more likely to seek treatment, and who may respond, for example, to selective serotonin reuptake inhibitors. Psychopaths without such violent behavior may have cortical but not serotonergic abnormalities and are unlikely to seek clinical treatment, although they may enter the forensic arena because of illegal acts. Perhaps violent murderers who show no remorse for their behavior and may even kill repeatedly represent an extreme prototype of the potentially deleterious affects of a cortically based psychopathy interacting with reduced serotonergic modulation. Although these considerations are speculative, they may be testable, as discussed below.

FUTURE DIRECTIONS

Psychopathy has received only limited investigative attention from the standpoint of neurobiology, in contrast, for example, to schizophrenia. Paralleling psychopathy, schizophrenia may represent the convergence of several interacting factors: a core schizotypal factor, reflecting abnormalities of cortical processing of information and attention, analogous to the affective-language-processing difficulties of the psychopath; and psychosis, particularly mediated by neuromodulator systems such as the dopamine system, analogous to impulsive aggression (which is modulated by another monoamine system, the serotonin system). A neurodevelopmental aberration is likely to result in the altered cortical structure–function disturbances observed in the schizophrenia spectrum (Siever, Steinberg, Trestman, & Intrator, 1994), while subcortical dopaminergic activity may modulate this diathesis toward or away from extreme psychosis. Similarity, the interaction of "core" psychopathy with impulsive aggression may modulate the severity of antisocial behavior observed.

However, with regard to psychopathy, careful histopathological postmortem studies, neurochemical studies, and functional and instructional imaging studies have yet to be initiated. Studies examining frontal and temporal regions of interest with regard to volume and functional activity during relevant tasks are called for. Postmortem studies such as those conducted with schizophrenics are not available. Such studies need to be undertaken with caution, however. Studies of heterogeneous populations (e.g., criminals) are likely to confound the multiple factors leading to antisocial behavior, both within the syndrome of psychopathy and outside of it. The best studies of psychopathy have been those that have differentiated between psychopathic and nonpsychopathic populations, whether they have been drawn from general psychiatry clinics, substance abuse clinics, or forensic settings. Studies of largely heterogeneous groups of these populations are likely to lead to relatively less interpretable results; yet many studies in the field have not taken the appropriate controls of investigating both psychopathic cohorts and nonpsychopathic cohorts from the same population.

The possible etiological antecedents of these biological findings should also be explored with the ancillary use of family history information, nutritional history, history of trauma and abuse, parental bonding assessment, and so forth. More definitive exploration of genetic factors should include candidate gene association studies as well as sibling pair studies. Positive results might suggest measurement of neurobiological correlates as intermediate variables between genetic factors and phenomenonology, to clarify the biological mechanisms involved. Prospective and longitudinal studies of the impact of adverse environmental factors on psychopathy, and of their biological and psychosocial sequelae, are also crucial. It is important to recognize that neurobiological substrates may reflect both genetic and environmental factors. Environmental factors may include early organic influences such as the effects of nutrition on the developing fetus, viral infection, lead exposure, infection, and other factors associated with adverse environmental conditions, as well as psychosocial factors including parental neglect or abuse.It must be appreciated that psychopathy appears to be a multifactorial disorder in its etiology, and that the neurobiological approach offers but one perspective from which to evaluate the mechanisms of generation of psychopathy.

Neurobiological approaches may also ultimately be integrated into psychodynamic and cognitive-behavioral conceptions of the disorder. For example, an inability to preferentially process affectively charged stimuli and appreciate their nuances could seriously impair the capacity to empathize with or experience in parallel fashion the feelings of others, and thus could contribute to the apparent callousness of psychopaths. Such an impairment may interfere with the internalization processes necessary to develop an ego ideal and ultimately a more realistic view of self and others in an object relations context. Excessive impulsivity and aggression could contribute to a need for harsher parental controls, internalized as a more primitive, harsh superego. Difficulty in suppressing behaviors that are later punished may make more problematic the internal psychological structures of ego and superego, which are necessary for the experiences of guilt, remorse, and sacrifice for others. Although at one level psychopaths can cognitively appreciate the possibility of future punishment for their behavior, their inability to internalize these strictures may mean that the prospect of punishment has little inhibitory effect unless it is highly immediate.

These considerations may have important implications for treatment. Clearly, evidence of serotonergic deficits calls for investigation of effects of serotonin-enhancing agents, such as the serotonin reuptake inhibitors. Indeed, a number of preliminary open and controlled trials suggest therapeutic efficacy for these agents (Norden, 1989; Cornelius, Soloff, Perel, & Ulrich, 1991; Coccaro, Gabriel, & Siever, 1990; Markovitz, Calabrese, Schulz, & Meltzer, 1991; Kavoussi, Liu, & Coccaro, 1994), as well as for serotonergic receptor agonists such as buspirone or serenic compounds. (For a review of pharmacological treatments, see von Knorring & Ekselius, Chapter 23, this volume.) On the other hand, excessive enhancement of noradrenergic activity might have detrimental effects; this would be consistent with some empirical evidence, but has not yet been systematically tested. Psychotherapeutic interventions, whether they be psychodynamic, cognitive-behavioral, or milieu-oriented, must address the underlying affective processing difficulties and impulsive tendencies in psychopathic patients, and must appreciate the likely impact of these vulnerabilities in the course of therapeutic work. Whether in the context of dynamic work in the interpersonal sphere of psychodynamic therapy or of thought and behavior restructuring in the course of cognitive-behavioral therapy, acknowledgment of these vulnerabilities may facilitate the slow but incremental reworking of psychological structures. Clearly, deficits in affective processing may make the therapeutic process more problematic and in some cases impossible, whereas impulsivity and aggression in the context of better affective processing may have a more favorable prognosis. These considerations call for more integration of neurobiological measures into the ongoing evaluation of psychosocial treatments in these problematic subjects. Ideally, further knowledge will improve our interventions as well as point to the limits of their effectiveness. Promising developments in pharmacological and psychosocial treatments have gone hand in hand with an increased investigative focus on schizophrenia; if similar progress is to be made in the treatment of psychopathic or antisocial individuals, a similar research perspective must be encouraged.

ACKNOWLEDGMENTS

The contributions of Joanne Intrator, MD, and Antonia New, MD, are appreciated.

REFERENCES

Arango, V., Ernsberger, P., Marzuk, P. M., Chen, J. S., Tierney, H., Stanley, M., Reis, D. J., & Mann, J. J. (1990). Autoradiographic demonstration of increased serotonin 5-HT2 receptors and beta-adrenergic receptor binding sites in the brain of suicide victims. *Archives of General Psychiatry, 47,* 1038–1047.

Asberg, M., Schalling, D., Traskman-Bendz, L., & Wagner, A. (1987). Psychobiology of suicide, impulsivity, and related phenomena. In H. Y. Meltzer (Ed.), *Psychopharmacology: The third generation of progress* (pp. 655–668). New York: Raven Press.

Aston-Jones, G., & Bloom, F. E. (1981). Norepinephrine-containing locus coeruleus neurons in behaving rats exhibit pronounced responses to non-noxious environmental stimuli. *Journal of Neuroscience, 1,* 887–890.

Benson, D. F., & Blumer, D. (1975). Personality changes with frontal and temporal lobe lesions. In

D. F. Benson & D. Blumer (Eds.), *Psychiatric aspects of neurological disease* (pp. 151–170). New York: Grune & Stratton.

Blackburn, R. B. (1979). Cortical and autonomic arousal in primary and secondary psychopaths. *Psychophysiology, 16,* 143–150.

Blackburn, R. B. (1988). On moral judgements and personality disorders: The myth of the psychopathic personality revisited. *British Journal of Psychiatry, 153,* 505–512.

Branchey, L., Branchey, M., Shaw, S., & Lieber, C. S. (1984). Depression, suicide, and aggression in alcoholics and their relationship to plasma amino acids. *Psychiatry Research, 12,* 219–226.

Brickner, R. M. (1934). An interpretation of frontal lobe function based upon the study of a case of partial bilateral lobectomy. *Research Publications of the Association for Research in Nervous and Mental Disease, 13,* 259–351.

Brown, G. L., Goodwin, F. K., Ballenger, J. C., Goyer, P. F., & Major, L. F. (1979). Aggression in human correlates with cerebrospinal fluid amine metabolites. *Journal of Psychiatric Research, 1,* 131–139.

Brunner, H. G., Nelen, M., Breakefield, X. O., Ropers, H. H., & Van Oost, B. A. (1993). Abnormal behavior associated with a point mutation in the structural gene for monoamine oxidase A. *Science, 262,* 578–580.

Casanueva, F. F., Villanueva, L., Penalua, A., & Cabezas-Cerrato, J. (1984). Depending on the stimulus, central serotonergic activation by fenfluramine blocks or does not alter growth hormone secretion in men. *Neuroendocrinology, 38,* 302–308.

Cleckley, H. M. (1976). *The mask of sanity* (6th ed.). St. Louis, MO: C. V. Mosby.

Coccaro, E. F., Gabriel, S., & Siever, L. J. (1990). Buspirone challenge: Preliminary evidence for central 5-HT-1 receptor function in impulsive aggressive behavior in humans. *Psychopharmacology Bulletin, 26,* 393–405.

Coccaro, E. F., Kavoussi, R. J., & Hauger, R. L. (1995). Physiological responses to d-fenfluramine and ipsapirone challenge correlate with indices of aggression in males with personality disorder. *International Clinical Psychopharmacology, 10,* 177–179.

Coccaro, E. F., Lawrence, T., Trestman, R. L., Gabriel, S., Klar, H. M., & Siever, L. J. (1991). Growth hormone responses to intravenous clonidine challenge correlates with behavioral irritability in psychiatric patients and in healthy volunteers. *Psychiatry Research, 39,* 129–139.

Coccaro, E. F., Siever, L. J., Klar, H., Maurer, G., Cochrane, K., Cooper, T. B., Mohs, R. C., & Davis, K. L. (1989). Serotonergic studies in affective and personality disorder patients: correlates with suicidal and impulsive aggression. *Archives of General Psychiatry, 43,* 587–599.

Coccaro, E. F., Silverman, J. M., Klar, H. M., Horvath, T. B., & Siever, L. J. (1994). Familial correlates of reduced central serotonergic system function in patients with personality disorders. *Archives of General Psychiatry, 51,* 318–324.

Cornelius, J. R., Soloff, P. H., Perel, J. M., & Ulrich, R. F. (1991). A preliminary trial of fluoxetine in refractory borderline patients. *Journal of Clinical Psychopharmacology, 11*(2), 116–120.

Currie, S., Heathfield, K. W., Henson, R. A., & Scott, D. F. (1971). Clinical course and progress of temporal lobe epilepsy: A survey of 666 patients. *Brain, 94,* 173–190.

Damasio, H., Grabowski, T., Frank, R., Galaburda, A. M., & Damasio, A. R. (1994). The return of Phineas Gage: Clues about the brain from the skull of a famous patient. *Science, 264,* 1102–1105.

Delgado-Escueta, A. V., Mattson, R. H., King, L., Goldensohn, E. S., Spiegel, H., Madsen, J., Crandall, P., Dreifuss, F., & Porter, R. J. (1981). The nature of aggression during epileptic seizures. *New England Journal of Medicine, 305,* 711–716.

DeVinsky, O., & Bear, D. (1984). Varieties of aggressive behavior in temporal lobe epilepsy. *American Journal of Psychiatry, 141,* 651–656.

Dolan, M. (1994). Psychopathy: A neurobiological perspective. *British Journal of Psychiatry, 165,* 151–159.

Fishbein, D. H., Lozovsky, D., & Jaffe, J. H. (1989). Impulsivity, aggression, and neuroendocrine response to serotonergic stimulation in substance abusers. *Biological Psychiatry, 25,* 1049–1066.

Gedye, A. (1989). Episodic rage and aggression attributed to frontal lobe seizures. *Journal of Mental Deficiency Research, 33,* 369–379.

Gillstrom, B. J., & Hare, R. D. (1988). Language-related hand gestures in psychopaths. *Journal of Personality Disorders, 2,* 21–27.

Goyer, P. F., Andreason, P. J., Semple, W. E., Clayton, A. H., King, A. C., & Compton-Toth, B. A., Schulz, S. C., & Cohen, R. M. (1994). Positron-emission-tomography and personality disorders. *Neuropsychopharmacology, 10*(1), 21–28.

Gray, J. A. (1982). *The neuropsychology of anxiety.* Oxford: Oxford University Press.

Gur, R. C., Roland, J. E., & Gur, R. E. (1992). Neurobehavioral probes for physiologic neuroimaging studies. *Archives of General Psychiatry, 49,* 409–414.

Hare, R. D. (1978a). Psychopathy and electrodermal responses to nonsignal stimulation. *Biological Psychology, 6,* 237–246.

Hare, R. D. (1978b). Electrodermal and cardiovascular correlates of psychopathy. In R. D. Hare & D. Schalling (Eds.), *Psychopathic behaviour: Approaches to research.* Chichester, England: Wiley.

Hare, R. D. (1993). *Without conscience: The disturbing world of the psychopaths among us.* New York: Pocket Books.

Hare, R. D., & Cox, D. N. (1978). Psychophysiological research on psychopathy. In W. H. Reid (Ed.), *The psychopath: A comprehensive study of antisocial disorders and behaviors* (pp. 209–222). New York: Brunner/Mazel.

Hare, R. D., Harpur, T. J., Hakstian, A. R., Forth, A. E., Hart, S. D., & Newman, J. P. (1990). The Revised Psychopathy Checklist: Descriptive statistics, reliability, and factor structure. *Psychological Assessment, 2,* 338–341.

Hare, R. D., & Jutai, J. W. (1988). Psychopathy and cerebral asymmetry in semantic processing. *Personality and Individual Differences, 9,* 329–337.

Hare, R. D., & McPherson, L. (1984). Psychopathy and perceptual asymmetry during verbal dichotic listening. *Journal of Abnormal Psychology, 93,* 141–149.

Heinrichs, W. (1989). Frontal cerebral lesions and violent incidents in chronic neuropsychiatric patients. *Biological Psychiatry, 25*(2), 174–178.

Howard, R. C., Fenton, G. W., & Fenwick, P. B. (1984). The contingent negative variation, personality and antisocial behavior. *British Journal of Psychiatry, 144,* 463–474.

Intrator, J., Hare, R., Stritzke, P., Brichtswein, K., Dorfman, D., Harpur, T., Bernstein, D., Handelsman, L., Schaefer, C., Keilp, J., Rosen, J., & Machac, J. (1997). A brain imaging (SPECT) study of semantic and affective processing in psychopaths. *Biological Psychiatry, 42*(2), 96–103.

Jacobs, B. L. (1987). Central monoaminergic neurons: Single-unit studies in behaving animals. In H. Y. Meltzer (Ed.), *Psychopharmacology: The third generation of progress* (pp. 159–169). New York: Raven Press.

Johns, J. H., & Quay, H. C. (1962). The effect of social reward on verbal conditioning in psychopathic and neurotic military offenders. *Journal of Consulting and Clinical Psychology, 26,* 217–220.

Jutai, J. W., & Hare, R. D. (1983). Psychopathy and selective attention during performance of a complex perceptual–motor task. *Psychophysiology, 20,* 146–151.

Kandel, E., & Freed, D. (1989). Frontal lobe dysfunction and antisocial behavior: A review. *Journal of Clinical Psychology, 45,* 404–413.

Kapur, S., Meyer, J., Wilson, A. A., Houle, S., & Brown, G. M. (1994). Activation of specific cortical regions by apomorphine: A [^{15}O] H_2O PET study in humans. *Neuroscience Letters, 176,* 21–24.

Kavoussi, R. J., Liu, J., & Coccaro, E. F. (1994). An open trial of sertraline in personality disordered patients with impulsive aggression. *Journal of Clinical Psychiatry, 55*(4), 137–141.

King, D. W., & Ajmone Marsan, C. (1977). Clinical features and ictal patterns in epileptic patients with EEG temporal lobe foci. *Annals of Neurology, 2,* 138–147.

Kurland, H. D., Yaeger, C. T., & Arthur, R. J. (1963). Psychophysiological aspects of severe behavior disorders. *Archives of General Psychiatry, 8,* 599–604.

Levander, S. E., Schalling, D. S., Lidberg, L., Bartfai, A., & Lidberg, Y. (1980). Skin conductance recovery time and personality in a group of criminals. *Psychophysiology, 17*(2), 105–111.

Malone, K., Campbell, C., Shuhua, L., & Mann, J. J. (1995). *A comparison of neuroendocrine and regional brain responses to serotonin release in depressed patients*. Paper presented at the 34th Annual Meeting of the American College of Neuropsychopharmacology, San Juan, PR.

Mark, V. H., Sweet, W., & Ervin, F. R. (1975). Deep temporal lobe stimulation and destructive lesions in episodically violent temporal lobe epileptics. In W. S. Fields & W. H. Sweet (Eds.), *Neural bases of violence and aggression* (pp. 379–391). St. Louis, MO: C. V. Mosby.

Markovitz, P. J., Calabrese, J. R., Schulz, S. Z. C., & Meltzer, H. Y. (1991). Fluoxetine treatment of borderline and schizotypal personality disorder. *American Journal of Psychiatry, 148,* 1064–1067.

McGuffin, P., & Gottesman, I. I. (1985). Genetic influences on normal and abnormal development. In M. Rutter & L. Hersov (Eds.), *Child and adolescent psychiatry: Modern approaches* (2nd ed., pp. 17–33). Oxford: Blackwell Scientific.

Monroe, R. R. (1978). The medical model in psychopathy and dyscontrol syndromes. In W. H. Reid (Ed.), *The psychopath: A comprehensive study of antisocial disorders and behaviors* (pp. 190–208). New York: Brunner/Mazel.

Moss, H. B., Yao, J. K., & Panzak, G. L. (1990). Serotonergic responsivity and behavioral dimensions in antisocial personality disorder. *Biological Psychiatry, 28,* 324–338.

New, A. S., Trestman, R. L., Benishay, D. S., Coccaro, E. F., & Siever, L. J. (1995). *Self-injurious behavior in personality disorders*. Paper presented at the 148th Annual Meeting of the American Psychiatric Association.

Norden, M. J. (1989). Fluoxetine in borderline personality disorder. *Progress in Neuropharmacology and Biological Psychiatry, 13,* 885–893.

Ogloff, J. R., & Wong, S. (1990). Electrodermal and cardiovascular evidence of a coping response in psychopaths. *Criminal Justice and Behavior, 17,* 231–245.

O'Keane, V., Moloney, E., O'Neill, H., & O'Connor, A. (1992). Blunted prolactin responses to d-fenfluramine in sociopathy. *British Journal of Psychiatry, 160,* 643–646.

Patrick, C. J., Bradley, M. M., & Lang, P. J. (1993). Emotion in the criminal psychopath: Startle reflex modulation. *Journal of Abnormal Psychology, 102*(1), 82–92.

Raine, A., Sheard, C., Reynolds, G. P., & Lencz, T. (1992). Pre-frontal structural and functional deficits associated with individual differences in schizotypal personality. *Schizophrenia Research, 7,* 237–247.

Raine, A., & Venables, P. H. (1988). Skin conductance responsivity in psychopaths to orienting, defensive, and consonant vowel stimuli. *Journal of Psychophysiology, 2,* 221–225.

Raleigh, M. J., & Brammer, G. L. (1993). Individual differences in serotonin-2 receptors and social behavior in monkeys. *Society for Neuroscience Abstracts, 19,* 592.

Ramani, V., & Gumnit, R. J. (1981). Intensive monitoring of epileptic patients with a history of episodic aggression. *Archives of Neurology, 38,* 570–571.

Robinson, T. N., & Zahn, T. P. (1985). Psychoticism and arousal: Possible evidence for a linkage of P and psychopathy. *Personality and Individual Differences, 6,* 47–66.

Satterfield, J. H. (1978). The hyperactive child syndrome: a precursor of adult psychopathy. In R. D. Hare & D. Schalling (Eds.), *Psychopathic behaviour: Approaches to research* (pp. 329–346). Chichester, England: Wiley.

Schalling, D. (1978). Psychopathy related personality variables and the psychophysiology of socialization. In R. D. Hare & D. Schalling (Eds.), *Psychopathic behaviour: Approaches to research*. Chichester, England: Wiley.

Siever, L. J. (1987). Role of noradrenergic mechanisms in the etiology of the affective disorders. In H. Y. Meltzer (Ed.), *Psychopharmacology: The third generation of progress* (pp. 493–504). New York: Raven Press.

Siever, L. J., Coursey, R. D., Alterman, I. S., Buchsbaum, M. S., & Murphy, D. L. (1984). Impaired smooth-pursuit eye movement: Vulnerability marker for schizotypal personality disorder in a normal volunteer population. *American Journal of Psychiatry, 141,* 1560–1566.

Siever, L. J., & Davis, K. L. (1991). A psychobiologic perspective on the personality disorders. *American Journal of Psychiatry, 148,* 1647–1658.

Siever, L. J., Keefe, R. S. E., Bernstein, D. P., Coccaro, E. F., Klar, H. M., Zemishlany, Z., Peterson, A., Davidson, M., Mahon, T., Horvath, T., & Mohs, R. (1990). Eye tracking impairments in clinically identified schizotypal personality disorder patients. *American Journal of Psychiatry, 147,* 740–745.

Siever, L. J., Steinberg, B., Trestman, R. L., & Intrator, J. (1994). Biological markers in personality disorder. In J. Gorman & L. Papp (Eds.), *Annual review of psychiatry* (Vol. 13, Section II, pp. 253–290). Washington, DC: American Psychiatric Press.

Siever, L. J., Trestman, R. L., Amin, F., Keefe, R. S. E., Harvey, P., Mohs, R., & Davis, K. L. (1993). *Dopamine and cognition in schizotypal personality disorder.* Paper presented at the 32nd Annual Meeting of the American College of Neuropsychopharmacology, Honolulu.

Stoff, D. M., Pollack, L., & Vitello, B. (1987). Reduction of [^{3}H]-imipramine binding sites on platelets of conduct-disordered children. *Neuropsychopharmacology, 1,* 55–62.

Tonkonogy, J. M. (1991). Violence and temporal lobe lesion: Head CT and MRI data. *Journal of Neuropsychiatry, 3*(2), 189–196.

Torgersen, S. (1992). *The genetic transmission of borderline personality features displays multidimensionality.* Paper presented at the 31st Annual Meeting of the American College of Neuropsychopharmacology, San Juan, PR.

Treiman, D. M. (1991). Psychobiology of ictal aggression. *Advances in Neurology, 55,* 341–356.

Valzelli, L. (1981). *Psychobiology of aggression and violence.* New York: Raven Press.

VanWoerken, T. C. A. M., Teelken, A. W., & Minderhoud, J. M. (1977). Difference in neurotransmitter metabolism in frontotemporal-lobe contusion and diffuse cerebral confusion. *Lancet, 1,* 812–813.

Virkkunen, M., Nuutila, A., Goodwin, F. K., & Linnoila, M. (1987). Cerebrospinal fluid metabolite levels in male arsonists. *Archives of General Psychiatry, 44,* 241–247.

Volvaka, J. (1995). Neurological, neuropsychological, and electrophysiological correlates of violent behavior. In *Neurobiology of violence* (pp. 77–122). Washington, DC: American Psychiatric Press.

Wender, P. H., Reimherr, F. W., & Wood, D. R. (1981). Attention deficit disorder (minimal brain dysfunction) in adults. *Archives of General Psychiatry, 38,* 449–456.

Williams, D. (1969). Neural factors related to habitual aggression. *Brain Research, 92,* 503–520.

Williamson S., Harpur, T. J., & Hare, R. D. (1991). Abnormal processing of affective words by psychopaths. *Psychophysiology, 28*(3), 260–273.

Wood, C. C., McCarthy, G., Squires, N. K., Vaughan, H. G., Woods, D. L., & McCallum, W. C. (1984). Anatomical and physiological substrates of event-related potentials. *Annals of the New York Academy of Sciences, 425,* 681–721.

Woods, B. T., & Eby, M. O. (1982). Excessive mirror movements and aggression. *Biological Psychiatry, 17,* 23–32.

Yeudall, L. T. (1977). Neuropsychological assessment of forensic disorders. *Canadian Mental Health, 25,* 7–15.

Yochelson, S., & Samenow, S. (1976). *The criminal personality* (Vol. 1). New York: Jason Aronson.

15

Psychopathic Children: Indicators of Organic Dysfunction

NIELS PETER RYGAARD

The adult psychopathic personality (antisocial personality disorder) has been described by a number of authors—in the North American tradition, through analysis of behavior and somatic patterns, mostly in imprisoned populations (Hare, 1985; Doren, 1987; Meloy, 1988); in the European tradition, through clinical analysis of personality organization (Vanggaard, 1968; Østergaard, 1965; Larsen, 1975). Concerning the etiology of psychopathy, these two traditions indicate, respectively, a high frequency of organic deficits (such as epilepsy and arousal system deficits) and a lack of mutual bonding between mother and child in the first years of life, resulting in a lack of object representation in the psychological structure of the child's personality. The concept of "early emotional frustration" (EEF) is a diagnostic term used in Scandinavian child psychiatry for a small number of children to indicate the likelihood of their developing a psychopathic adult character. In a survey, Rutter (1995) has found a definite link between childhood conduct disorders and adult psychopathy (and, to a lesser degree, other severe adult behavior disorders).

Defining EEF and providing guidelines for its treatment have been hindered by the small number of studies that have found clear links between etiology and adult psychopathy. The term "psychopathic" has also been considered a negative psychiatric label for a decade or two; explanations for behavior have been sought in the structure of society, and group dynamic/sociological theories have defined psychopathy as a socially induced negative role, rather than as a characteristic personality. However, the need to understand this supposed particular personality structure has become acute in the current era of social change, where more rigid child-rearing patterns (often producing neurotic children) are being replaced by the amonie caused by poverty and/or parental value conflicts (often producing poorly socialized, externalizing, aggressive children). The question of EEF is also raised by the higher survival rates among premature children in recent years. Finally, the EEF syndrome calls for study in regard to war-traumatized children, as

247

well as the children found in Eastern Europe (e.g., Romania) to be living in orphanages or foster homes and suffering from severe deprivation.

Apart from the low-frequency of the EEF syndrome, failure in treating both EEF children after age 3 and adult psychopaths has challenged the common theoretical frameworks of personality organization, based on normal personality development and family structure. In Denmark, firm milieu therapy and permanent foster homes have been criticized as treatment methods in general for both economic and ethical reasons, leaving space for psychotherapeutic methods and short-term family therapy. However, these methods apparently fail, and do not answer two questions. First, can psychotherapy (e.g., play therapy) be used with unstable, unmotivated clients who experience no intrapersonal conflict or "problem" and are hostile toward therapists? Second, can a child's personality development be changed through short-term family therapy programs, when the social and personal history of the family members is a chronicle of disruption and instability, producing parents who are incapable of fulfilling even the simplest need of their child (if, indeed, any parents are present)? It is a general experience that even the most loving foster home usually fails to produce attachment if an EEF child is placed there after age 3 (Thormann, 1990); however, psychotherapeutic methods have also usually not produced positive results, whether used on an individual basis or in family programs.

The problem still seems to be how to define the problem. Does the EEF diagnosis simply describe the consequences of utmost poverty, or do EEF children have definite traits in common, separating them from others to a degree that justifies the use of a specific diagnostic category? If so, what are the relations among social events (e.g., mother–child relations), intrapersonal events (e.g., the experience of trauma), and somatic events (e.g., events describing the child's ability to experience or practice contact, such as organic trauma)—and of course—genetic events?

A SHORT SURVEY OF ADULT SYMPTOMS

From a literature survey, the most notable symptoms of adult psychopathy have been transferred to child psychiatry to define the EEF syndrome. The adult symptoms can be grouped into personality characteristics defined according to the European tradition (Vanggaard, 1968; Østergaard, 1965; Larsen, 1975; Meloy, 1988) and behavior characteristics defined according to the North American tradition (Doren, 1987; Hare, 1985, 1988a, 1988b; McCord, 1982; Meloy, 1988; Reid, Dorr, Walker, & Bonner, 1986).

Personality Characteristics (the European Tradition)

1. Low frustration tolerance; weak ego and superego functioning.
2. Short-lived emotion and motivation.
3. Absence of intrapersonal conflict (due to weak superego and ego functioning), leaving only interpersonal conflict and abreaction as means of resolution. Usually, no experience of anxiety or fear in dangerous situations.
4. Defective, absent, or immature object relations.
5. Defense strategies: denial, projective identification of aggression, splitting, fight-or-flight behavior, imitation.
6. The overall personality functioning as the symptom (in contrast to the neurotic, who is fairly normal and mature, *except* for the symptom).

Behavior Characteristics (the North American Tradition)

1. Tension-creating and novelty-seeking behavior.
2. Absence of or delayed reactions to experimentally provoked fear/anxiety (e.g., changes in cardiac rate, galvanic skin response, and arousal); learning only slowly from experience.
3. Immediate conversion of induced frustration to impulsive, outward, and often aggressive behavior.
4. Diminished ability to discriminate (e.g., contacts strangers uncritically, has difficulty in face recognition, engages in promiscuous sexual behavior).
5. Imitation of any face values or behavior patterns in present milieu (as a defense strategy without internalization).
6. Extreme field dependency; short and superficial attention and memory span.
7. Tendency to manipulate and control others.
8. Criminal record (delinquency, violence, fraud, robbery).

HYPOTHESES FROM DIFFERENT FIELDS

Genetic Hypotheses

In psychiatry, biological and heredity-based models have prevailed, although specific genetic characteristics have not been isolated. Schulsinger (1972) compared two groups of adults adopted before age 1. Those developing adult psychopathy had biological parents with a similar psychiatric record more often than children in the control group did. In addition, Schulsinger suggested a link between schizophrenia and psychopathy, since the two diagnoses often were seen within biological families (in the present investigation, 3 out of 44 mothers had a previous schizophrenia diagnosis). Schalling (1988) has suggested that the tendencies toward externalizing and aggressive behavior in psychopathic clients may be determined in part by inherited tendencies toward abnormally low or unstable serotonin production.

Neurological and Neuropsychological Hypotheses

In recent years, neurology and neuropsychology have contributed to the understanding of psychopathic development (McCord, 1982). Electroencephalographic methods have been refined, and in some cases, immature slow-wave activity patterns have been found in adult psychopaths (McCord, 1982). Moreover, certain forms of epilepsy can cause aggressive behavior that is easily confused with (or perhaps even part of) psychopathic behavior (Doren, 1987; concerning children, see Holowach, 1961). Different brain functional systems have been examined. Interest has centered on the reticular activation system (and arousal level), the hypothalamus (retention/automatization of social behavior patterns and the ability to link stimuli and emotional response), the limbic system (and emotional dysfunction), and the frontal lobes (inhibition problems and the ability to integrate internal and external stimuli on higher levels).

Malnutrition during pregnancy and the first year of life may produce a partial loss of brain development and thus result in EEF, according to several authors (Lou, 1976; Zachau-Christiansen, 1975). In children of mothers who drink to excess, fetal alcohol syndrome and fetal alcohol effects include organic damage, resulting in sensorimotor deficits and hypersensitivity in the neonates (Thormann, 1990), which in turn can reduce parent–child contact. In a large Danish study, low birth weight seemed closely connected to later poor performance in school, which included a higher frequency of disorderly conduct and diminished learning abilities, the latter measured by the Wechsler Intelligence Scale for Children—Revised (WISC-R) (Kruuse, 1984). Hansen (1977) concluded after a study of 110 children admitted to a child psychiatric ward that children who suffer from both minor organic dysfunction/immaturity and poor social conditions are most frequently given the EEF label in the subsequent process of observation and diagnosis. Hansen has suggested the term "organic psychosyndrome."

Psychological Hypotheses

In developmental psychology, several authors (Bowlby, 1988; Mirdal, 1976; Bernth, 1972) have emphasized the concepts of insufficient attachment and the loss of early maternal care as pivots in psychopathic development. Also, symbiotic mother–child relationships have been held responsible by several authors (e.g., Felding & Møller, 1990).

Blatt (1988a, 1988b, 1988c) unifies Piagetian (cognitive) and psychoanalytic developmental theories by means of the term "constancy"—the stabilization of emotional and intellectual perception into constant, organizing concepts during the first 5 years of life. From the study of adult personality disorders, Blatt retrospectively finds differences in the degree of ability to maintain internal and external object constancy on four levels of development:

1. Mother–child contact initially produces "evocative constancy" or "figure–background constancy" in the child (i.e., the ability to recognize the mother figure against shifting backgrounds). This faculty is transferred to general object perception a little later. This function apparently fails to develop in a child who later becomes psychotic.

2. "Recognition constancy"— recognition of the mother in detail (and later of other objects)—then normally develops. If it does not, the child will experience the milieu as unreal and disappearing from consciousness, and must compensate for this by seeing others as hostile and aggressive. Therefore, the adult will develop paranoid, rigid, controlling patterns and emotional distance in order to maintain fragile boundaries.

3. Next, the normal child develops the ability to maintain "object constancy." Even when the mother is physically absent (giving no sensory input), the concept of her is retained, and later the child can imagine objects. The child can now experience internal conflict, feeling shame or guilt. When this process fails, the borderline personality, which is unstable and hypersensitive to loss and separation, evolves.

4. Finally, the child sees itself as a separate entity and part of a family system, and experiments with conscious interaction. That is, the child attains "social constancy"— consciousness of itself, its role, and its impact in a social context. If this process fails, the adult will be overly narcissistic in an attempt to receive extra feedback and maintain social constancy.

In Blatt's model, the psychopathic child will advance no further than between the first and second levels of constancy development. The psychopathic adult is unable to maintain an idea of others unless they are physically present, and has no conscious idea that he or she is an active part of the social field: "It" just happened, and others are to blame for everything.

In clinical practice, it is generally agreed that constant stress or multiple stressors (violence, deprivation, and/or emotional neglect) before age 3 are often part of the etiology of EEF, whereas later stress or a single emotional trauma is supposed to have less global effects on personality development (neurosis, phobia, psychosomatic symptoms).

I was inspired to conduct this study after clinical practice in an institution convinced me that children developing psychopathic personalities have had significant minor organic dysfunction and other problems during pregnancy and birth. I have described the development of therapeutic methods and settings elsewhere (see Rygaard, 1991, 1997).

A POSSIBLE COMMON DENOMINATOR IN EEF DEVELOPMENT: CONTACT DISRUPTION BEFORE AGE 3

From this multitude of viewpoints, the problem of EEF may be reframed. Apparently the maintenance of constant early contact between mother and child is somehow crucial to personality (and thereby social) development. Although this contact is emotional in nature, it must somehow be mediated through physical contact between mother and child, especially at early stages, including pregnancy. The quality of early contact may be defined over a longer time span, if the physical aspects of contact are included in this concept. How does physical contact help the child to organize itself (especially the central nervous system [CNS]), so as to become receptive to and able to exchange emotional contact? The phenomenon of contact may be studied as a process of ever-growing complexity—from conception, pregnancy, and birth, through initial sensory contact between mother and child, to contact in a symbolic, psychological sense based on object constancy and resulting in mutual, flexible social contact patterns.

The broader hypothesis from this angle is as follows: Constancy on higher levels (social constancy) cannot be attained if contact is disrupted or terminated when the child is forming constancy on lower levels (i.e., CNS constancy). And, if a critical point is passed, the sheer number of disruptions will increase the possibility of arrested emotional (and consequently social) constancy development.

For present purposes, "contact disruption" can be defined as an absence, interruption, or withdrawal of mutual matter/stimulation exchange on any developmental level before age 3. This of course includes a lack of nutrition or stimulation, but also overstimulation (such as birth trauma or exposure to violence, resulting in reduced receptivity), exposure to substances toxic to CNS development (such as alcohol), and monotonous or disorganized stimulation (such as that received in an incubator or from a schizophrenic mother unable to give empathic care).

The study to be described in the remainder of this chapter is based on the broad concept that mother–child contact produces internal constancy; my assumption is that this concept will permit a more coherent view of contact disruption and its possible effects on EEF development. From this viewpoint, somatic aspects of contact disruption are most important early in life, and psychological and social aspects gain importance with age.

AIMS AND APPROACH OF THE STUDY

My hypotheses were that a group of EEF children would have been exposed to contact-disrupting events at a higher rate than a control group of normal children, and thus that the EEF children would deviate significantly from the control children in their performances on the WISC-R. Specifically, my aims were to examine whether the EEF children as a group would display a high frequency of characteristics known to increase the probability of organic dysfunction later in life, such as extremely low or high maternal age at birth, maternal substance abuse during pregnancy (a factor that proved to be impossible to determine with certainty—see below), prematurity, extremely high or low birth weight, and/or high frequency of birth complications. I then wished to determine whether the EEF children would differ from the control children at test and retest by more than 2 points on average single WISC-R subtest scores, and whether their total WISC-R profile would differ. Finally, I wished to examine the links between the characteristics mentioned above and the WISC-R results.

SAMPLE

The EEF group consisted of children (n = 48) admitted between January 1985 and December 1989 to a Danish institution (Himmelbjerggården) specializing in the treatment of EEF children. The average duration of treatment was 30 months, 24 hours a day; the duration of stay ranged from 18 to 39 months. Beforehand, the children had been diagnosed as EEF elsewhere, usually on child psychiatric wards or by clinical school psychologists. They were reassessed by experienced staff members when they were admitted to the institution.

Criteria for admission, were severe and long-standing behavior problems in home, foster home, or school; these were often combined with severe family problems, such as criminality, alcoholism, drug abuse, violence, and/or sexual abuse. At the end of 1989, none of the biological fathers were present in the families. The families were characterized by isolation from or conflict with their local milieu, and moved or migrated very often. Twelve children were admitted from foster homes that were unable to cope with the children's severe behavior problems. Often attempts to establish close emotional contact had resulted in episodes of pyromania, killing pets, violence toward other children, or the like.

PROCEDURE

In 1990, the county government allowed birth data to be used in the present investigation, and permission was given by the Danish National Files (Rigsarkivet) to collect birth data from the National Health Board (Sundhedsstyrelsen). The data consisted of copies of neonatal records, including sex, weight, length, anesthetic procedures and other artificial aids employed at birth, estimated gestational age, and eventual complications. The results were compared to those for a control group and to figures from the Danish Institute for Statistics (Danmarks Statistik, 1975–1979).

Mothers were evaluated concerning their relatively recent alcohol and drug abuse. Sources of information were institutional records and the personal knowledge of the institution's two social workers, who had regular contact with mothers during and after treatment. In 23 cases, there was certain knowledge of abuse for more than 2 years prior to visitation. However, this of course only indicates possible abuse during pregnancy; reliable data concerning substance abuse during pregnancy proved impossible to obtain. Therefore, this characteristic is not considered further in the presentation of results, though it must be borne in mind as a possible factor complicating those results.

I tested children in the EEF sample with the WISC-R 2 months after admission, and 24 were retested after an average of 21 months (± 2 months). The 24 children in the control group were tested by clinical psychologists in county school psychological offices all over Denmark, in order to obtain a geographic profile similar to that of the EEF sample. From a questionnaire, parents in the control group were interviewed concerning birth weight and birth complications.

RESULTS

Maternal Age Characteristics

A total of 44 mothers of EEF children were examined (one mother had three children and two mothers had two children in the sample). Mother's ages at birth of the children in the sample ranged from 17 years, 5 months to 36 years; the mean age was 25 years, 6 months. These ages did not differ significantly from average Danish figures.

The most common characteristic of these mothers seemed to be personality dysfunction. The mothers' childhood records included stories of sexual abuse, violence, and early disconnection from biological parents—stories quite similar to the EEF children's own. Prior to visitation, other authorities had diagnosed the mothers as follows: 9.3% were judged to suffer from psychosis (three were schizophrenic and one was manic–depressive); 55.8% were diagnosed as psychopathic; 23.3% were diagnosed as borderline (two of these had had psychotic episodes at the birth of the children in question, and one was also an epileptic); the remaining 11.6% were apparently normal or neurotic, with common life stories, social relations, and jobs. In these cases, the children's behavior and rearing problems were mainly due to organic deficits in the children (e.g., encephalitis, birth complications). These latter mothers had given up regulation of their children's behavior very early, and had been poorly helped by different authorities' defining the causes as psychological and not as neurological. These organic deficits in the children had severely disrupted the early mother–child contact.

Except for the "normal or neurotic" group, the general traits in maternal behavior were as follows:

1. *Heightened vulnerability to and overreaction to or withdrawal from, physical and social contact.* The contact patterns of the mothers were few, superficial, and stereotypic. Either outward imitation of staff members' values, or perpetual conflict with the staff, was common.

2. *Inability to organize practical daily tasks.* The few mothers capable of solving such tasks seemed to do so in a very tense, rigid, and restricted manner in order not to lose control. The ability to set priorities and concentrate on a subject or task was poor, and in conversation they were easily distracted by random associations or external stimuli.

3. *Role form replacing role content.* The mothers were very keen on questions of rights and demands, and often entered into conflict with others over minor items. Role shifting was common (taking a new partner, moving into a new apartment, concentrating on another child if one was difficult to cope with, regarding a child as an adult or patronizing the child, etc.). In practice, parents would act like children, and children would have adult responsibilities and tasks. Idealization, splitting, denial, paranoid tendencies, and fight–flight behavior were frequent defense mechanisms.

Children's Birth Weight and Birth Complications

Compared to all children born in Denmark in 1981 (Sundhedsstyrelsen, 1985), the EEF sample had a lower average birth weight (general population, 3,344 grams; EEF, 3,028 grams). The control group's average birth weight was 3,292 grams—again, a notable difference from that of the EEF sample. Furthermore, 34% of the EEF children weighed under 3,000 grams, compared to 23% of the general population; 17% of the EEF children weighed under 2,500 grams, compared to 6% of the general population; and none of the EEF children weighed over 4,000 grams, compared to 10.8% of the general population. The tendency toward lower birth weight in the EEF sample applied equally to children of both genders.

Fifty percent of the EEF children were noted in the official birth records as having had major birth complications (noted under the heading of "complications" or "preterm" in the copies of the birth registers). Preeclampsia and preterm birth were frequent events in the sample (the preterm births, however, did not explain the generally tendency toward lower birth weight). Notably, none of the EEF children were born postterm, compared to four in the control group. Less frequent postnatal complications in the EEF sample (occurring in only one or a few cases each) included epileptic seizures immediately after birth, encephalitis within 12 months of birth, smallness for gestational age, respiratory complications, and blood poisoning. When the use of artificial birth aids (Caesarian section, forceps, episiotomy, membrane rupture or puncture, incubator, etc.) was examined, it was found the EEF children did not receive such aids more often than the general population or control children; only a postnatal incubator stay was a possible source of deprivation.

WISC-R Results

The WISC-R (Wechsler, 1981, 1983) has been revised and standardized for use in Denmark. The Verbal section consists of six subtests (Information, Comprehension, Arithmetic, Similarities, Vocabulary, and Digit Span). The Performance section consists of five subtests (Picture Completion, Picture Arrangement, Block Design, Object Assembly, and Coding).

WISC-R Results and Birth Weight

The only physiological factor that seemed significantly linked to WISC-R results was birth weight. Birth complications and artificial birth aids were so different in nature that they did not permit the identification of other possible agents. A series of *t* tests showed significant positive correlations between high scores and high birth weight in both the EEF sample and the control group for some areas: the Verbal section as a whole, the Performance section as a whole, and the Block Design subtest. Some differences between the two groups were that birth weight affected the score on the Information subtest in the control group, but the scores on the Comprehension and Similarities subtests in the EEF sample.

The difference in general test profile between the control group and the sample (see below), however, was not affected by birth weight. Consequently, lowered birth weight alone is not likely to result in the EEF syndrome, unless it is combined with other contact-disrupting factors, such as deprivation after birth.

IQ and Subtest Profile in the Sample and the Control Group

The average IQs in the EEF sample were at the lower end of normal scores (Verbal, 99.7; Performance, 102.7). A retest of 24 of the children after 22 months of intensive treatment showed a similar IQ profile, although the Performance IQ improved somewhat (Verbal, 101.6; Performance, 111.3). These results suggest that the EEF IQ profile is stable over time, and that Verbal development in particular demonstrates stagnation: The slight unevenness in the Verbal–Performance profile at initial test was accentuated at retest.

In the control group, average IQs were generally higher (Verbal, 116.5; Performance, 114.9). The standard deviations were higher in the sample than in the control group. A multivariate analysis of covariance showed strong differences on most subtests between the sample and the control group (except for Comprehension, Digit Span, Picture Assembly, and Object Assembly), and no effect of preterm birth. A series of *t* tests showed that control children scored significantly higher than sample children on the Verbal section as a whole, Arithmetic, Coding, and Block Design.

A rotated factor matrix analysis indicated that scores in the EEF sample were low on tests requiring the ability to reorganize elements (Object Assembly, Coding, Block Design); they were relatively higher on tests where few simultaneous factors are involved, and where stereotypes learned by heart (reproducing a known, invariable sequence) influence the score positively (Information, Comprehension, Vocabulary, Similarities). Also, scores on subtests requiring figure–background construction (Arithmetic, Block Design, Coding) were lower in the sample, suggesting a high degree of field dependency in sample.

A careful interpretation of these findings could be that EEF children perceive, solve tasks, and use strategies in ways that are characteristic of earlier stages of development. A tendency toward strong field dependency, the use of stereotypic sequences learned by heart, problems in maintaining a figure when the background changes (rigidity), and a restricted ability to overlook more elements at the same time—all seem to be traits common at age 1–3, but prevailed among our EEF children despite their age (7–14 years) when tested. The different profile in the control group suggests, that normal children have developed more refined, flexible, and simply different strategies, belonging to a higher level of psychological development.

DISCUSSION

Generally, children who later develop the EEF syndrome often seem to suffer from stresses during pregnancy and birth that are known to cause organic dysfunction. The hypothesis of extremely high or low birth weight in EEF children can be adjusted to generally lower birth weight in EEF children. Maternal substance abuse during pregnancy could not be confirmed, but our estimates suggest this problem in roughly 50% of pregnancies; thus, this issue calls for further study. In regard to prematurity and high frequency of birth complications, the EEF sample displayed a more than doubled number of preeclampsia causes and preterm births, whereas the use of artificial birth aids did not exceed what was common. The range of other complications during and after birth was too broad (compared to the small sample) to allow other certain events to be proved important in EEF syndrome development.

The hypothesis that the total WISC-R profile of the sample would differ from that of the control group was confirmed, including a generally lower IQ result in the sample. Also, the theory suggested by Blatt and described earlier in the chapter (i.e., that the child learns to organize sensation from maternal contact, and that deprivation or erratic stimulation will hinder the development of conceptualization abilities) seems to be supported by the WISC-R results.

These results suggest that early preventive measures aimed at minimizing the chances of neurological damage in fetuses and supporting mothers at risk should be considered. Lier, Gammeltoft, and Knudsen (1995) report good results when psychopathic/psychotic mothers are separated from mothers undergoing normal birth preparation procedures and provided with additional intervention.

As a tool for practitioners, a checklist for identifying children at high risk for developing psychopathy, based on my colleagues' and my clinical experience and the results described above, is provided as an Appendix to this chapter.

APPENDIX

The Psychopathy Risk Checklist: Common Traits in the Background and Behavior of Psychopathic Children

Family Items

1. Mother was exposed to early deprivation, violence, and/or sexual abuse as a child.

2. Mother is single (partners change quickly), has superficial and short relationships, and/or shows a tendency toward isolation from or perpetual conflict with environment.

3. Mother has a tendency toward psychopathy, psychosis, or epileptic seizures; or, less frequently, a normal mother is exposed to crisis in child's two first years that hinders motherhood; or organic deficits in the child (e.g., blindness or fetal alcohol syndrome) hinder the child's awareness of aspects of maternal care.

4. The family often moves around or migrates. The family role pattern is disorganized; with no limits are set on child behavior, or sudden, inconsequent restrictions are applied; often sexual abuse occurs because of low sexual discrimination ability in parents. Sometimes rigid and empty roles are emphasized in order to control the underlying chaotic state.

5. Mother is unable to uphold stable practical and emotional contact with child. Child is often looked after at random, and by many persons. There is a lack of daily rhythm in family life. Mother projects adult motives and emotions into child (e.g., "He doesn't like me"). Mother lacks empathy and blames environment for child's abnormal development. Mother displays no self-criticism, doubts, second thoughts, feelings of guilt or remorse. Or mother is psychotic.

Organic Dysfunction Items

1. Mother is a substance abuser and/or malnourished during pregnancy.

2. Low birth weight, premature birth, and/or birth complications.

3. Frequent hospitalization and/or diseases after birth (e.g., epileptic seizures, febrile convulsions, meningitis, early otitis).

4. Abnormal sensorimotor development.

Hyper- or hyposensitivity to stimulation and pain; abnormal reactions to touch; early hypoactivity turning into hyperactivity at age 1–3; extreme field dependency for age.

Often sensory extraversion (ignores internal body and skin signals, is extremely alert to external stimuli, is easily distracted).

Low discrimination ability.

Disturbed basic body rhythms (sleep, eating, breathing, pulse, and attention rhythms).

Failure to make eye contact when touched or caressed.

Emotional Items

1. Oral fixation: Perceives people and things as objects to be consumed. Contact pattern resembles early stages of development.

2. Absence of separation anxiety and of fear of strangers.

3. Absolute and self-reinforcing emotions (joy becomes hysteria, anger becomes rage, etc.). Emotions depend on immediate stimulation, and disappear with stimulation source.

4. Low frustration tolerance: Cannot delay satisfaction; regresses quickly when exposed to stress.

5. No or rigid borders toward environment. Will uncritically imitate the behavior and mood of anyone present or exhibits fight or flight behavior in contact. May have psychotic episodes when close emotional or physical contact is offered.

Behavior and Profile in Test Situation

1. Behavior

    Wants to score better than others. Stimulated by new events; easily bored by routines.

    Exhibits fight–flight–freeze behavior and attempts to manipulate examiner if unable to solve problem.

    Answers quickly without doubt, self-criticism, or second thoughts. Many and uncritical associations.

    Generalizing, vague, or omnipotent answers to difficult questions. Gives answers to questions even when ignorant. Rigid, stereotypic, and infantile strategies.

    Concrete thinking in spite of abstract terminology (imitates adolescent language, no emotional response to "emotional" words).

    Short attention span; is easily distracted by irrelevant stimuli.

    Cannot concentrate on interviewer, theme, task, or goal for long.

    Blocks when presented with unstructured and vague material, such as Rorschach blots and loosely defined situations.

2. WISC-R test profile

    Relatively high scores: Comprehension, Similarities, Picture Completion, Picture Arrangement.

    Relatively low scores: Arithmetic, Digit Span (second part), Block Design, Coding.

    Lower scores in Verbal section than in Performance section of test.

    Has problems in tasks involving deeper analysis, emotional meaning of words, changing strategies, seeing a problem from more than one angle, understanding proportions and connections between elements and the whole.

REFERENCES

Bernth, I. (1972). *Institutionsbørn og hjemmebørn.* Copenhagen: Munksgaard.

Blatt, S. J. (1988a). *A cognitive morphology of psychopathology.* Plenary lecture presented at the First Congress of the International Society for the Study of Personality Disorders, Copenhagen.

Blatt, S. J. (1988b). *Differential cognitive disturbances in three types of borderline patients.* New Haven, CT: Yale University.

Blatt, S. J. (1988c). Disturbances of object representation in schizophrenia. *Psychoanalysis and Contemporary Science, 4,* 235–287.

Bowlby, J. (1988). *A secure base: Clinical applications of attachment theory.* London: Routledge.

Danmarks Statistik. (1975–1979). *Befolkningen i kommunerne 1. Januar.* Copenhagen: Author.

Doren, D. M. (1987). *Understanding and treating the psychopath.* New York: Wiley.

Felding, J., & Møller, N. (1990). Det antisociale syndrom. *Nordisk Psykologi, 42,* 313–333.

Hansen, N. (1977). Cerebro-organic pathogenesis in 110 children followed up subsequent to admission to a child psychiatric ward. *Acta Psychiatrica Scandinavica, 46,* 399–412.

Hare, R. D. (1985). *The Psychopathy Checklist.* Vancouver: University of British Columbia.

Hare, R. D. (1988a). Language-related hand gestures in psychopaths. *Journal of Personality Disorders, 2*(1), 21–27.

Hare, R. D. (1988b). Psychopathy and language. In T. E. Moffitt & S. A. Mednick (Eds.), *Biological contributions to crime causation.* Dordrecht, The Netherlands: Nijhoff.

Holowach, J. (1961). Psychomotor seizures in childhood: A clinical study of 120 cases. *Pediatrics, 59,* 339–345.

Kruuse, E. (1984). Skoleforløbet for børn med lav fodselsvægt. Copenhagen: Dansk Psykologisk Forlag.

Larsen, K. L. (1975). *Psykopatibegrebet.* Copenhagen: Munksgaard.

Lier, M., Gammeltoft, M., & Knudsen, I. J. (1995). Early mother–child relationship: The Copenhagen model of early preventive intervention towards mother–infant relationship disturbances. *Arctic Medical Research, 54*(Suppl. 1), 15–23.

Lou, H. C. (1976). *Neurologi og udvikling.* Copenhagen: Gyldendal.

McCord, W. (1982). *The psychopath and milieu therapy: A longitudinal study.* New York: Academic Press.

Meloy, J. R. (1988). *The psychopathic mind.* London: Jason Aronson.

Mirdal, G. M. (1976). *Det ufødte barn—det nyfødte barn.* Copenhagen: Munksgaard.

Østergaard, A. (1965). Differentialdiagnose mellem neurose og psykopati i barnealderen. *Ugeskrift for Læger, 127,* 241–248.

Reid, W. H., Dorr, D., Walker, J., & Bonner, J. (eds.). (1986). *Unmasking the psychopath: Antisocial personality disorder and related syndromes.* New York: Norton.

Rutter, M. (1995). Relationships between mental disorders in childhood and adulthood. *Acta Psychiatica Scandinavica, 91,* 73–85.

Rygaard, N. P. (1991). *Tidlig frustration—selvorganisering hos svært belastede børn.* Copenhagen: Munksgaard.

Rygaard, N. P. (1997). *The psychopathic child: Causes, symptoms and treatment.* Manuscript in preparation.

Schalling, D. (1988). *Personality self-report scales and biological markers for aggressivity and lack of behavioral constraints.* Plenary lecture at the First Congress of the International Society for the Study of Personality Disorders, Copenhagen.

Schulsinger, F. (1972). *Nogle undersøgelser til belysning af sammenhængen mellem arv og miljø i psykiatrien.* Copenhagen: Foreningen af danske laegestuderende.

Sundhedsstyrelsen. (1985). *Medicinsk fødselsstatistik 1981: Vitalstatistik I, 13.* Copenhagen: Statens Informationstjeneste.

Thormann, I. (1989). Når du drikker, gor dit ufodte barn det også. *Dansk Psykolognyt, 13,*

Thormann, I. (1990). *Rapport fra Skodsborg Observationshjem.* Copenhagen: Skodsborg Observationshjem.

Vanggaard, T. (1968). Neurose og psykopati. *Nordisk Psykiatrisk Tidsskrift, 22,* 277—287.

Vanggaard, T. (1985). Om amerikanisering i europæisk psykiatri belyst ved et svensk eksempel.
Nordisk Psykiatrisk Tidsskrift, 39, 167–172.

Wechsler, D. (1981). *Wechsler Intelligence Scale for Children—Revised.* New York: Psychological
Corporation.

Wechsler, D. (1983). *WISC standardisering 1974.* Copenhagen: Dansk psykologisk forlag.

Zachau-Christiansen, B. (1975). *Babies: Human development during the first year.* Chichester,
England: Wiley.

16

Cross-Cultural Aspects of Psychopathy

DAVID J. COOKE

Perhaps of all psychological disorders, psychopathy remains one of the most elusive and the most contentious in regard to its identification and description. Both the nature and the breadth of the defining features of the disorder have created fertile ground for noso-logical dispute (e.g., Blackburn, 1988; Hare, Hart, & Harpur, 1991; Holmes, 1992). Indeed, Gunn (Chapter 2, this volume) has contended that the concept of psychopathy cannot be regarded as a useful construct either from a clinical or from a theoretical perspective. Gunn contends that the use of the term "psychopathy" is misleading, as it reifies the disorder. This is perhaps the traditional British perspective; another authority, Blackburn, has famously described psychopathy as a "mythical entity" (Blackburn, 1988; see also Chapter 4, this volume). This position is hard to defend in light of the compelling North American evidence regarding both the clinical value of the construct and its theoretical coherence. It may be the case that differences between the North American and British perspectives reflect differences in both the prevalence and the presentation of the disorder in the different settings.

This chapter explores the extent to which the North American construct of psychopathy can generalize to British samples and beyond. I argue that the cross-cultural generalizability of the personality disorders is a neglected area—an area that we neglect at our peril. The cross-cultural perspective can provide important clinical and conceptual dividends. Mere acceptance of the North American models is not appropriate: There is a significant danger that the dominant North American models of personality disorder may fail to capture the cross-cultural variation in the psychological phenomena that characterize personality disorders (Fiske, 1995; Lewis-Fernandez & Kleinman, 1994). It has been argued that unlike the major mental disorders such as depression and schizophrenia, the personality disorders are less likely to have a well-crystallized "pan-cultural core" (Draguns, 1986, p. 333).

MEASURING PSYCHOPATHY

The Psychopathy Checklist—Revised (PCL-R; Hare, 1991) is a symptom construct rating scale in which information from files and interviews is combined to rate individuals on 20 characteristics that are thought to define the disorder. These characteristics, for example, include "glibness/superficial charm," "Conning/manipulative," "Callous/lack of empathy" and "Impulsivity." Each item is scored on a 3-point scale (0 = the item does not apply; 1 = the item applies to a certain extent or there is uncertainty that it applies; 2 = the item definitely applies. The 20 items can thus produce a maximum score of 40. (See Hare, Chapter 12, this volume, for a more detailed account of the PCL-R.)

Hare's conceptualization of the disorder, underpinned by the PCL-R (Hare, 1991), is fast gaining currency within forensic practice in North America. This is not surprising. The measure has been shown to have significant clinical value: indeed, it was argued recently that "There is no doubt that the PCL-R is the 'state of the art' in this area, both clinically and in research use" (Fulero, 1995, p. 454). Clinically, the PCL-R is a central tool in risk assessment, not only in its own right (Salekin, Rogers, & Sewell, 1996) but also as an integral feature of a growing number of risk assessment procedures (e.g., Webster, Harris, Rice, Cormier, & Quinsey, 1994; Webster, Eaves, Douglas, & Wintrup, 1995; Kropp, Hart, Webster, & Eaves, 1994; Borum, 1996).

Clinical utility is underpinned by theoretical coherence. There is compelling evidence that Hare's construct of psychopathy has validity. The validity of a clinical construct is not easily quantified. It has to be evaluated in relation to a wide range of criteria, including reliability; the presence of a coherent latent trait underpinning the features thought to characterize the construct; predictive utility in terms of treatment outcome or follow-up; evidence of a diathesis; and, finally, evidence of covariation between the construct and abnormalities of a psychological, physiological, or biochemical nature (e.g., Blashfield & Draguns, 1976; Kendell, 1989; Robins & Guze, 1970).

The PCL-R performs well against these criteria. In terms of interrater reliability, it is clear that psychopathy can be diagnosed as reliably as most acute mental disorders (and more reliably than other personality disorders) in a range of clinical and research settings (Hare, 1991; Widiger et al., 1996). Both factor analysis and item response theory (IRT) modeling demonstrate that the diverse manifestations of the disorder—the affective, behavioral, and interpersonal manifestations—are underpinned by coherent latent traits (Hare et al., 1990; Cooke, 1995b; Cooke & Michie, 1997; Cooke, Michie, Hart, & Hare, 1996).

In terms of predictive utility, the construct has value in relation to predicting future antisocial behavior (not merely offending behavior), and it also has utility in the prediction of the instability of interpersonal relationships and the instability of employment (Hart, Kropp, & Hare, 1988; Salekin et al., 1996; Hart & Hare, 1997). Moreover, the evaluation of therapeutic communities has indicated that those who score high on the PCL-R show a distinctly negative response to treatment (e.g., Rice, Harris, & Cormier, 1992). Indeed, Rice et al. (1992) found an interaction effect in which treated psychopaths recidivated at a *higher* rate than those who did not receive treatment; by way of contrast, nonpsychopaths demonstrated significant benefits from treatment.

Preliminary results from Livesley (1995) suggested that there is evidence of a diathesis for this disorder. Using a self-report psychopathy scale developed from the PCL, and examining a sample of twins, Livesley found strong evidence for heritability of the trait: Scores for the monozygotic twins had a heritability of .74, and scores for the dizygotic twins had a heritability of .18.

There is also compelling evidence for the validity of the construct measured by the PCL-R in terms of the last criterion alluded to above—namely, covariation with measures of basic psychological and physiological processes (see Hare, 1991, 1996, for detailed summaries of this research). Two strands of research are worthy of particular note. First, psychopaths appear to display unusual autonomic activity: They display anticipatory heart rate acceleration while awaiting an inevitable, aversive stimulus, but they do not display any significant increases in electrodermal responses (Hare, 1978). Second, research within a variety of paradigms (including behavioral, electrocortical, and brain imaging paradigms) illustrates that psychopaths' processing of the affective components of language is poor; the deeper affective meaning of language appears to be obscure to them (e.g., Intrator et al., 1997; Williamson, Harpur, & Hare, 1991; Patrick, Bradley, & Lang, 1993).

The argument that the construct of psychopathy does not have theoretical coherence and clinical utility is not tenable, at least within the North American context. Nonetheless, the vast majority of research using the PCL-R has been carried out in North America, and it necessary to consider the impact of culture on the nature and expression of this disorder. Indeed, one of the greatest tests of the theoretical coherence and clinical validity of a syndrome is the extent to which that syndrome can be generalized across countries and across cultures (Fiske, 1995).

PSYCHOPATHY ACROSS TIME AND ACROSS CULTURES

Various commentators provide evidence suggesting that psychopaths can be identified in a range of societies and at different points in historical time (Mealey, 1995). Psychopathic individuals are regarded as distinct individuals; the diagnosis is not, as some would allege, merely a mechanism for identifying those who do not fit with the expectations of modern industrialized societies. Three examples may illustrate this point.

Cleckley (1976) formed the view that Alcibiades, the Athenian general of the 5th century B.C., was a prototypical psychopath. Alcibiades was described by Plutarch and Plato as having charm but lacking principle; these traits assisted him in the manipulation of others. Although Alcibiades was talented, he did not apply his talent in any consistent manner. He also failed to honor his commitments and failed to adhere to the mores of his times. From an early age, his behavior could be characterized as reckless, violent, and impulsive.

Murphy (1976) examined the more recent existence of psychopathic-like characteristics in two contrasting nonindustrialized cultures—namely, the Yorubas of rural Nigeria and the Inuit of northwest Alaska. Murphy (1976) found that these communities have a term to describe schizophrenia, but that, in addition, they distinguish schizophrenia from a disorder that is cognate with Western concepts of psychopathy. Murphy (1976) described the Yorubas concept of *aranakan* as "a person who always goes his own way regardless of others, who is uncooperative, full of malice, and bullheaded" (p. 1026), and the Inuit concept of *kunlangeta* as a person whose "mind knows what to do but [who] does not do it" (p. 1026). Murphy (1976) elaborated on the definition of *kunlangeta* by noting:

> This is an abstract term for the breaking of the many rules when awareness of the rules is not in question. It might be applied to a man who, for example, repeatedly lies and cheats and steals things and does not go hunting and, when the other men are out of the

village, takes sexual advantage of many women—someone who does not pay attention to reprimands and who is always being brought to the elders for punishment. (p. 1026)

It is interesting—and consistent with the commonly held belief in Western psychology and psychiatry (e.g., Blackburn, 1993)—that the shamans and healers Murphy interviewed in the Inuit and Yorubas communities did not believe that this condition was amenable to change. Historically, the Inuit's management strategy for *kunlangeta* was to invite the sufferer to go hunting, and, when no one was looking, to push him off the ice (Murphy, 1976).

CROSS-CULTURAL VARIATION IN THE PREVALENCE OF PSYCHOPATHY

Major progress has been made during the last three decades in our understanding of the cross-cultural variations of major psychiatric disorders, including schizophrenia and major depression (World Heath Organization, 1973, 1983). By contrast, information concerning the distribution of psychopathy across cultures is extremely limited.

Because of the low prevalence of psychopathy in general populations, much of the information concerning the prevalence of psychopathy is based on prison studies. Prevalence estimates based on such studies are fraught with difficulties. A recent review of prison prevalence studies revealed gross variation in the reported prevalence of psychological disorder among prison samples; the rates ranged from 2% to 78% (Cooke, 1995a). At least five factors lead to such a wide range in the estimates: the source of the data (e.g., direct interviews with prisoners vs. official statistics); the definition of psychological disturbance that is applied; the type of prison and the type of prisoners sampled; the stages of the prisoners' sentence; and, finally, the point of historical time (Cooke, 1995a). These barriers obstruct not only cross-sample comparisons but also cross-cultural comparisons of the prevalence of psychopathy. It is hard to know what the estimates mean.

Given the quality of the data available, previous studies can only provide pointers. British estimates of the prevalence of psychopathy in prisons tend to be low; they range from 8% (Roper, 1950) through 10% (Gunn, Maden, & Swinton, 1991), 13% (Bluglass, 1966), and 18% (Cooke, 1995b) to 22% (Gunn, Robertson, Dell, & Way, 1978). By contrast, North American estimates include Guze's (1976) figure of 78%, and Hare's (1991) estimate (from a range of samples using the comparatively strict PCL-R-based definitions) of 28% psychopaths (i.e., PCL-R scores of 30 or above), with a further 44% displaying significant psychopathic traits (i.e., scoring between 20 and 29 on the PCL-R). On balance, this evidence suggests that a cross-cultural difference may exist; at the very least, it suggests that the possibility should be considered.

Investigators must be extremely cautious when coming to conclusions about cross-cultural differences in the rates of psychiatric disorders, since method factors may distort the true picture. It is a salutary lesson that the alleged differences in the rates of schizophrenia and depression between the United Kingdom and the United States diminished substantially when standardized sampling frames, interviewing procedures, and diagnostic criteria were introduced (Cooper et al., 1972). Nonetheless, the accumulation of evidence suggests that there is a *prima faciae* case in support of a cross-cultural difference in the prevalence of psychopathy.

CROSS-CULTURAL ASPECTS OF THE
PSYCHOPATHY CHECKLIST—REVISED

Given the compelling evidence for the validity of the PCL-R (Hare, 1980, 1991), it can be argued that it represents the most appropriate tool with which to pursue the question of cross-cultural variation in the rate of psychopathy. Within North America, the majority of published studies have focused on white adult male prisoners; however, some researchers have studied the PCL and PCL-R in subcultural groups within North America. These groups have included Francophone Canadian prisoners (Hodgins, Cote, & Ross, 1992), Native Indian Canadian prisoners (Wong, 1984), and black prisoners in the United States (Kosson, Smith, & Newman, 1990). It is noteworthy that these studies have shown considerable cross-group consistency in the psychometric characteristics of the PCL-R.

Within Europe, studies using the PCL and PCL-R have been few; those that have been published have been characterized by small and often unrepresentative samples. The PCL-R (or PCL) has been used with a sample of prisoners in a high-security prison (Raine, 1985), prisoners in a Scottish "special unit" for violently disruptive prisoners (Cooke, 1989, 1997), nonviolent Finnish prisoners (Haapasalo & Pulkkinen, 1992), and Swedish community residents (af Klinteberg, Humble, & Schalling, 1992). Overall, the pattern of results from these studies suggests that there may be cross-cultural differences in the prevalence of psychopathy, as measured by the PCL-R, between North America and Europe. Unfortunately, as was the case with the prison studies alluded to above, the evidence is patchy and inconclusive.

A DETAILED COMPARISON BETWEEN SCOTLAND
AND NORTH AMERICA

The opportunity to carry out more detailed cross-cultural comparisons arose when the PCL-R was used as part of the interview procedure in a study of the rate, nature, and etiology of psychological disturbance within Scottish correctional establishments (Cooke, 1994, 1995a).[1] A total of 307 prisoners were assessed.

Differences in the Prevalence of Psychopathy

The PCL-R can be used either as a continuous measure of psychopathy or as a categorical diagnostic measure. Hare (1991) indicated that a cutoff score of 30 on the PCL-R should be used to classify individuals as psychopathic. Individuals with scores in the 20–29 range may be considered to have "moderate" levels of psychopathy, while those with a PCL-R score of less than 20 can be regarded as nonpsychopathic. As noted above, Hare (1991) presented data from a variety of North American adult male prisoner samples and indicated that the mean prevalence of psychopathy in these samples was approximately 28%, with 44% of the prisoners falling in the "moderate" group. These rates are in sharp contrast to those found in Scotland. Only 3% of Scottish adult male prisoners were classified as psychopathic, with 15% falling in the "moderate" category (Cooke, 1995b). Examining the data in another way, by comparing the mean scores of adult males in North America (23.63) and those in Scotland (13.82), emphasizes the presence of a substantial difference ($t = 15.08$, $p < .001$). Is this putative difference real, or is it merely an artifact of the measurement process?

Are Different Constructs Being Measured?

Fundamental to any cross-cultural comparison is the availability of a common measure to assess the construct of interest. Traditionally, the cross-cultural comparability of any psychometric instrument has been assessed (1) through evaluating the extent to which the factor structures underpinning the instrument are similar in different settings; (2) by determining whether the scoring of specific items requires to be modified in the new setting; and (3) by determining whether a common set of unbiased items can be identified that will allow comparison of mean trait levels across cultures (e.g., Barrett & Eysenck, 1984; Arrindell et al., 1992).

The factor structure underpinning the PCL-R in a variety of North American samples has been examined in great detail (Harpur, Hare, & Hakstian, 1989; Hare et al., 1990). The converging evidence has demonstrated that North American ratings on the PCL-R are underpinned by two distinct yet correlated factors. The first factor, which may be characterized as representing the "selfish, callous, and remorseless use of others," is specified by core personality traits including superficiality, habitual lying, manipulativeness, and callousness, together with a lack of affect, guilt, remorse, and empathy. The second factor, which may be characterized as "chronically unstable and antisocial lifestyle," is specified by characteristics including the need for stimulation, poor behavioral controls, lack of realistic long-term goals, impulsivity, and juvenile delinquency.

What factor structure underpins the Scottish data? Oblique factor analysis, using the same extraction and rotation criteria as Hare et al. (1990), revealed a high degree of factor congruence between the North American and the Scottish data (Factor 1 = .92, Factor 2 = .93; Cooke, 1995b). These results imply that the same constructs are being measured in the two settings.

More detailed analysis demonstrated that the PCL-R has considerable similarity across settings in terms of the standard classical test theory (CTT) indices, including Cronbach's alpha for the total score and individual factor scores, and the amount of variance explained by each of the two factors. At the level of items, considerable similarity was observed in corrected item-to-total correlations and in the rank order of item means across settings. The identification and comparison of a common set of items—items that performed in a similar manner in Scotland and North America—suggested the presence of a difference in prevalence.

Although the evaluation of CTT criteria of this type can determine whether the same construct is being assessed in different settings, it cannot determine whether the same measurement scales or metrics are being used. For example, with CTT methods it is not possible to determine that the critical cutoff score of 30 represents the same level of the trait in Scotland as it does in North America (Hulin, Dragsow, & Parsons, 1983; Reise, Widaman, & Pugh, 1993). Other approaches are required.

Using IRT Models to Examine Cross-Cultural Differences

The Advantages of IRT Models over CTT Models

The cross-cultural generalizability of personality and other psychometric scales has historically been assessed via the procedures of CTT (e.g., Barrett & Eysenck, 1984; Kosson et al., 1990). However, these CTT approaches are not without their critics; proponents of IRT argue that IRT models may be more appropriate methods for assessing differential item and differential test functioning across different cultures (Bontempo, 1993; Ellis,

Becker, & Kimmel, 1993; Hulin, 1987; Holland & Wainer, 1993; Hulin et al., 1983; Reise et al., 1993).

IRT models are mathematical expressions of the relationship between an individual's score on an item and an underlying latent trait or construct. A mathematical function specifies a trace line that represents the manner in which the probability of an item score varies with the level of the underlying trait. Figure 16.1 contains the item characteristic curves (ICCs) for the probability of scoring 0, 1, and 2 on the PCL-R item "lack of remorse" for North American samples (Cooke & Michie, 1997). Examination of the figure reveals that the probability of a score or response of 0 decreases as the underlying strength of the trait increases, whereas the probability of a 2 response increases as the trait strength increases. The probability of a 1 response increases and then decreases as the strength of the underlying trait increases. The curves for 0 and 2 responses are steep, indicating that this item is a good measure of the underlying trait.

The performance of an item and its relationship to the underlying latent trait can be assessed graphically, as above, or can be summarized by two parameters: a_i and b_i. The a_i parameter is a measure of the discriminating power of the item; the higher the value of a_i, the more accurately the item discriminates between low and high values of the trait. The b_i parameter is a measure of extremity; as the value of b_i increases, the degree of item difficulty or extremity increases. In the example above, the value of b_2 (the slope for a score of 2) is 0, indicating that the item has maximum discrimination around the mean trait level. Effective measures of trait strength should have items that discriminate across the whole range of the trait, whereas diagnostic measures should have items for which maximum discrimination occurs around the diagnostic cutoff point. In both the North American data sets and the Scottish data sets, the PCL-R items demonstrate a good spread in the values of b_i—a spread across the whole range of the trait. This demonstrates that the PCL-R is a good measure of the trait (Cooke & Michie, 1997, in press).

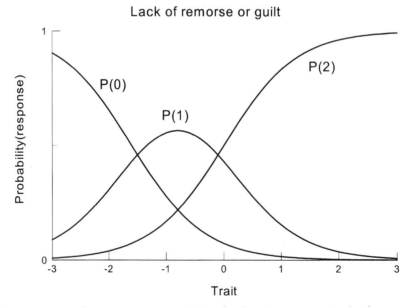

FIGURE 16.1. Item characteristic curves (ICCs) for the PCL-R item "Lack of remorse or guilt," derived in the North American samples.

Parenthetically, it is interesting to note that in all the IRT analyses so far conducted, there is a statistically significant tendency for Factor 2 items (the more behavioral items) to discriminate at low levels of the trait, whereas Factor 1 items (the items that pertain to personality and interpersonal style) to discriminate at higher levels of the trait. Factor 1 items are more prototypical of the disorder, suggesting that the continued emphasis on the behavioral characteristics in the definition of antisocial personality disorder (APD) may be misleading. (See Cooke & Michie, 1997, and Cooke, 1998, for a fuller discussion.)

A primary strength of IRT models is that the parameters and thereby the trace lines are not dependent on the sample used to generate the curve (Hambleton, 1989; Mellenbergh, 1996). By way of contrast, the key indicators of CTT are heavily dependent on the characteristics of the sample used in their generation; item difficulty, item-to-total correlations, alpha reliability, and the optimum cutoff are all sample-dependent (Nunnally & Bernstein, 1994; Hambleton, 1989; King, King, Fairbank, Schlenger, & Surface, 1993; Reise et al., 1993). The sample-dependent nature of these indices reduces their value in cross-cultural comparisons.

Cross-cultural comparison, or indeed the comparison of any two distinct groups, is directed at assessing whether the same characteristic is being measured and in the same way (Reise et al., 1993). To compare estimates of the prevalence of psychopathy in two different settings, it is necessary not only to establish that the same trait is being measured, but also to establish that it is measured on the same measurement scale (i.e., to establish metric equivalence). The Fahrenheit and Celsius scales both measure temperature, but they are not metrically equivalent because they do not have the same zero points and their scale intervals are different. Clearly, if a scale does not display measurement invariance across groups, then cross-group comparisons of prevalence are essentially meaningless. It is not possible to determine whether measurement invariance exists with CTT approaches, but procedures for this purpose do exist in IRT (Hulin et al., 1983; Reise et al., 1993; Cooke & Michie, 1997).

An IRT Comparison of PCL-R Data from Scotland and North America

Detailed IRT analyses comparing the North American and Scottish data were carried out with Multilog VI (Thissen, 1991); this program can be used to estimate the item parameters simultaneously in two or more groups, using maximum-likelihood methods. These procedures were used with PCL-R data from a sample of 307 Scottish prisoners and 2,067 North American prisoners; they revealed interesting differences in item and test performance (Cooke & Michie, 1996). Overall, the PCL-R items did not differ in terms of their a_i parameters across settings; thus, the items have equal discriminating power in relation to psychopathy in Scotland and North America. However, examination of the b_i parameters revealed interesting differences.

Figure 16.2 contains the ICCs for two PCL-R items, "Conning/manipulative" and "Irresponsibility." Examination of the ICCs for "Conning/manipulative" reveals no statistically significant differences across the two settings; the curves are essentially identical, with scores of 2 providing good discrimination at moderately high levels of the trait. By contrast, the ICCs for the item "Irresponsibility" display substantial differences in their b_i parameters. That is, the Scottish prisoners had to have higher levels of the trait before "Irresponsibility" became apparent. This was not the only item to show such differences; there were considerable differences in the b_i parameters for the item "Glibness and superficial charm." As with "Irresponsibility," Scottish prisoners had to be high on

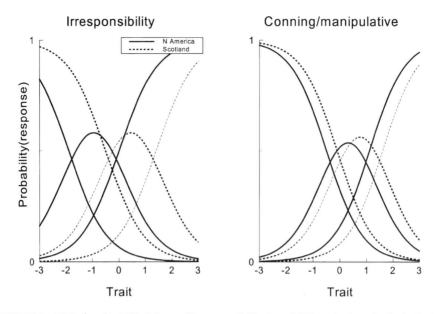

FIGURE 16.2. ICCs for the PCL-R items "Irresponsibility" and "Conning/manipulative": Scottish and North American curves compared.

the underlying trait before displaying this characteristic. This fits my own clinical impression (I have met few charming psychopaths in Scottish prisons).

What effects do these differences on individual items have on overall scores? IRT methods allow diagnostic cutoffs to be standardized across settings. When such methods were used to ensure metric equivalence, it was determined that a lower diagnostic cutoff should be applied in Scottish prisons. A PCL-R score of 25 in Scotland is metrically equivalent to the diagnostic cutoff score of 30 within North America. Even with this lower diagnostic cutoff, the prevalence of psychopathy in Scottish prisons is only 8%—still substantially lower than the prevalence in these North American samples (i.e., 29%) (Cooke & Michie, 1996).

In summary, traditional CTT methods imply greater similarity across settings than is perhaps warranted. IRT methods indicate that although the PCL-R successfully taps the same traits in both settings, practically important and theoretically interesting differences exist in the performance of the test across settings.

WHY ADOPT A CROSS-CULTURAL PERSPECTIVE?

All of the previous discussion begs the question: Why adopt a cross-cultural perspective? Is it merely an academic exercise, or does it have any intrinsic value? In broad terms, a cross-cultural perspective can be supported from both a pragmatic and an empirical point of view. From the pragmatic point of view, the PCL-R has been shown to be a useful instrument for clinical, forensic, and experimental purposes in North America (Harris, Rice, & Cormier, 1991; Hare, Forth, & Strachan, 1992; Hart et al., 1988; Hare & McPherson, 1984; Fulero, 1995). The demonstration that the instrument generalizes across cultures would obviate the need for either the reformulation or recalibration of the instrument; the current value of the PCL-R would thus be further enhanced.

Without detracting from the pragmatic perspective, it is perhaps at the level of theory that a cross-cultural perspective becomes most interesting and most valuable. Butcher (1982) and Berry, Poortinga, Segall, and Dasen (1992), for example, have argued that a cross-cultural perspective will not only increase our understanding of the generality of findings, and perhaps encourage the isolation of psychological universals; it may also highlight the role of sociocultural factors in the etiology of disorders.

A common pathway in the development of our understanding of psychopathology is that which leads from the description and classification of a disorder toward the study of its etiology. The cross-cultural path may be one path toward increasing our understanding of part of the etiological processes that lead to psychopathy. Any discussion of etiology must perforce be speculative; it is necessary to explore different disciplines (including cross-cultural psychology and psychiatry, sociobiology, and anthropology) in search of hypotheses and data. This is the challenge of the problem.

Clarifying the Role of Sociocultural Factors

Paris (1993; see also Chapter 17, this volume) has indicated that the etiology of personality disorders is unlikely to be underpinned by simple, linear, monocausal processes; complex interactive processes among variables derived from various conceptual domains are likely to be at the core of the etiology. Indeed, in his review, Paris (1993) extracts evidence from the biological, psychological, and social domains, and proposes a comprehensive biopsychosocial model for the development of personality disorders. Broad cultural factors may be important. The cross-cultural approach in psychology is predicated on the conviction that cultural transmission through both enculturation and socialization leads to the development of behavioral similarities within cultures and behavioral differences across cultures.

With regard to socialization, Ekblad (1988), for example, has indicated that cultures vary in the extent to which they permit children to express aggressive behavior, and that boys in particular are at risk of becoming aggressive if the home environment is too permissive. Her cross-cultural comparison of aggressive behavior among children in Sweden and China revealed not only substantial differences in the rate of aggressive behavior, but also substantial differences in the methods adopted by parents to deal with this aggressive behavior.

Lykken (1995; see also Chapter 8, this volume), in his account of the development of the syndrome he describes as sociopathy, has contended that the interplay between basic temperament and socialization is of central importance. He believes that variations in aspects of temperament—in particular, fearlessness and impulsivity—interact with the quality of parenting experienced in the ontogenesis of the antisocial individual. Lykken (1995) has argued that those children who are hard to socialize will emerge as sociopaths unless they are fortunate enough to experience highly competent parenting, whereas temperamentally easy children will emerge well socialized despite the incompetence of their parents.

One behavioral characteristic frequently associated with psychopathy—namely, aggression—demonstrates significant cross-cultural variation. Although there is ample evidence to indicate that aggressive behavior occurs in nearly every society, there is also substantial evidence of cross-cultural variation in norms and values concerning violence and aggression (Ekblad, 1988, 1990; Moghaddam, Taylor, & Wright, 1992). Moghaddam et al. (1992) have noted that cultural groups such as the Inuit of the Arctic, the Blackfoot nation of North America, and the Pygmies of Africa rarely engage in physical violence; they prefer to deal with disputes through withdrawal or negotiation. This behavior contrasts starkly with the behavior of the Yanomano of the upper Amazon (Chagnon, 1974). Chagnon's account indicates that there is not only constant warfare between villages, but also constant fighting and argument within villages. A male's status within his village is determined by his level of aggressiveness; his affection for his wife is determined by the harshness of the beatings she receives.

Cross-cultural variation in the level of violence is not a peculiarity of so-called primitive groups. Groups such as the Mennonites, the Amish, and the Hutterites exist within contemporary North American society, where rates of aggression are generally high; however, they display low levels of aggression, presumably as a consequence of their strong norms and values against aggression (Bandura & Walters, 1963).

Both the processes of enculturation and the processes of socialization influence levels of observed aggression. In some cultures or subcultures, violence is the norm. Glasser (1987) has provided a graphic account of his early life and the enculturation of violence in the Gorbals area of Glasgow—an area once notorious for its violence:

> We grew up with violence. It simmered and bubbled and boiled over in street and close, outside the pubs, at the dance halls . . . violence settled private accounts, transgressions of codes, the spilling over of grievance or spleen. It was so closely intertwined with everyday life, its inescapable rough edge, logical, cathartic, that its occurrence, like rain and cold and frequent shortage of food, was recognized with equal fatalism. (p. 61)

Hare (1993) has argued that cultural processes may be of great significance in the emergence of psychopathy. He contends that the acceptance and promotion of certain values may influence the development of psychopathic traits. North American society, Hare feels, "is moving in the direction of permitting, reinforcing, and in some instances actually valuing some of the traits listed in the Psychopathy Checklist—traits such as impulsivity, irresponsibility, lack of remorse, and so on" (1993, p. 177). Other commentators have expressed similar views: Leyton (1989) contends that American culture propagates and maintains "the nobility of violence" (p. 363), while Lasch (1979) has argued that the logical end result of individualistic cultures is "a narcissistic preoccupation with the self" (p. 21).

Indeed, there is some evidence in support of this position. As noted above, IRT analysis suggests that APD may be a less severe form of psychopathy, with the behavioral features of the disorder being evident at lower levels of the trait than the interpersonal and affective features (Cooke & Michie, 1996, 1997; Cooke et al., 1996). Robins, Tipp, and Przybeck (1991), using data from the Epidemiologic Catchment Area study, argued that the estimated prevalence of APD is likely to increase from 3.7% to 6.4% by the time the youngest cohort reaches the age range of 30–44 years. This implies that this aspect of the psychopathy syndrome is influenced by cultural pressure.

Cultural Pressure toward Psychopathy: Psychopathy as an Extreme Manifestation of the Individualistic Culture?

A central explanatory construct in cross-cultural psychology is the "individualistic–collectivist" dimension (Berry et al., 1992). Individualistic cultures emphasize competitiveness and self-confidence; independence from others is encouraged, and temporary or short-lived relationships are common. By way of contrast, within collectivist cultures an individual's contribution and subservience to the social group are emphasized, the acceptance of authority is paramount, and continuous and stable relationships are common. The predominant North American culture may be regarded as prototypically individualistic, whereas the predominant Scottish culture is less extreme in this regard.

Extreme manifestations of the behavior thought to be characteristic of individualistic societies can be regarded as elements of the syndrome of psychopathy. It may be argued, on the one hand, that within individualistic societies cultural transmission is likely to enhance grandiosity, glibness, and superficiality; promiscuity, multiple marital relationships, and a lack of responsibility for others will also flourish. On the other hand, cultural transmission within collectivist societies will bear down on self-expression and promote stable family and group relationships. It has been argued not only that the competitiveness inherent in individualistic societies produces higher rates of criminal behavior, but also that competitiveness leads to an increased use of Machiavellian behavior—in particular, an increase in the use of deceptive, manipulative, and parasitic behavior (Christie & Geis, 1970; Mussen & Eisenberg-Berg, 1977; Wilson & Herrnstein, 1985).

Evidence suggests that these modes of behaving are strongly influenced by the processes of enculturation and socialization (Berry et al., 1992). Once again, the evidence is slight and speculation must reign. One piece of evidence that is consistent with this speculation, however, is provided by Compton et al. (1991). Chinese societies are generally regarded as collectivist, whereas North American societies are considered individualistic (Berry et al., 1992). Compton et al.'s (1991) finding of substantial differences between the United States and Taiwan in the rate of APD is consistent with differing pressures of cultural transmission in these societies.

Differences in prevalence may be underpinned by more than variations in socialization and enculturation across cultures. Sociobiology suggests that that sociocultural factors may play a role in the etiology of those personality traits and behaviors that are consonant with a diagnosis of psychopathy. Sociobiologists are concerned, in part, with the processes leading to genetic fitness ("genetic fitness" relates to an individual's total genetic representation in the next genetic pool). Broadly speaking, there are two strategies that may be adopted to maximize genetic fitness. The first strategy entails investing a large amount of parental effort in a few children, while the second strategy entails investing a large amount of effort in reproduction but little effort in parenting. Males who adopt the second strategy may achieve their goal by having multiple female partners, by misleading their partners about both their willingness and their ability to provide parenting resources, and/or by taking no responsibility for their children—all behaviors that are consonant with the behavior of psychopathic individuals (Raine & Venables, 1992).

This line of argument emerges in other disciplines. Anthropologists such as Harpending and Draper (1988) have argued that the antisocial trait is favored in cultures where male competitiveness is high and where parental effort is low. In pursuit of this thesis, Harpending and Draper (1988) have described nonindustrial societies that are polar extremes on these two dimensions: the !Kung Bushmen and the Mundurucu. The !Kung Bushmen live in an inhospitable desert and live by foraging for food and by hunting cooperatively. They also form nuclear families in which male–female relationships are egalitarian, the number of children produced is low, and parental effort is both high and long-term. Harpending and Draper (1988) note: "In societies of this type the contexts for the anti-social trait are unfavorable. There will be no pay-offs for anti-social behavior and the bearer of the trait will be readily detected and ostracised" (p. 297).

By way of contrast, the Mundurucu live in a land of plenty and exist as *swiddeners*—that is, as low-intensity gardeners. Among the Mundurucu there is limited contact between the sexes, with male–female relationships being characterized at best by disdain and at worst by hostility. The men share a large house and only sleep in their family homes when they are ill. Daily male activity is associated with gossiping, planning raids, and fighting. They hunt, but their efforts contribute little to the total calorific intake of the group; game is often used to trade for sexual intercourse rather than to feed their offspring. By way of contrast with the !Kung Bushmen, the Mundurucu may be characterized as engaging in a reproductive strategy that entails high reproductive effort but low parenting effort. Harpending and Draper (1988) argue that antisocial characteristics would be favored in this setting: "A successful male would be brave, even fearless, skilled at fighting and raiding, but even more skilled at bluff and bravado that might obviate the necessity for real battle. He would be good at interpersonal manipulation and status gamesmanship—manipulating other men in face-to-face dominance struggles and manipulating females as a seducer if not a rapist" (p. 298).

Although the Mundurucu and the !Kung Bushmen may represent extreme and unusual adaptations to particular environmental pressures, parallels for these behaviors can be observed in modern Western industrialized societies.

CONCLUSION

In conclusion, there appears to be evidence in support of the hypothesis that cross-cultural variation in the incidence of psychopathy exists. Studies based on the PCL-R may provide a productive approach to increasing our understanding of the problem (see Cooke, 1996, 1997, for a more detailed account of methodologies for improving cross-cultural understanding). A cross-cultural perspective provides not only a pragmatically useful perspective in relation to the greater generalizability of the PCL-R, but also a useful theoretical perspective in relation to our thinking about the etiology of the disorder. Although we are only starting out on the path toward understanding the cross-cultural variation in psychopathy, all the indications are that it will be a productive path.

NOTE

1. The Scottish prison system holds all Scottish prisoners, both those on remand and those who are sentenced. There is no distinction between provincial/state and federal establishments—on the basis of either jurisdiction or length of sentence—equivalent to the distinctions within the United States and Canada.

REFERENCES

af Klinteberg, B., Humble, K., & Schalling, D. (1992). Personality and psychopathy of males with a history of early criminal behaviour. *European Journal of Personality, 6,* 245–266.

Arrindell, W. A., Perris, C., Eisemann, E., Granell de Aldaz, J., Van der Ende, D., Kong Sim Guan, J., Richter, J., Gaszner, P., Iwawaki, S., Baron, P., Joubert, N., & Prud'homme, L. (1992). Cross-national transferability of the two-factor model of parental rearing behaviour: A contrast of data from Canada, the Federal Republic of Germany, Hungary, Japan, Singapore and Venezuela with Dutch target ratings on the EMBU. *Personality and Individual Differences, 13,* 343–353.

Bandura, A., & Walters, R. (1963). *Social learning and personality development.* New York: Holt, Rinehart & Winston.

Barrett, P., & Eysenck, S. B. G. (1984). The assessment of personality factors across 25 countries. *Personality and Individual Differences, 5,* 615–632.

Berry, J. W., Poortinga, Y. H., Segall, M. H., & Dasen, P. R. (1992). *Cross-cultural psychology: Research and applications.* Cambridge, England: Cambridge University Press.

Blackburn, R. (1988). On moral judgements and personality disorders: The myth of psychopathic personality revisited. *British Journal of Psychiatry, 153,* 505–512.

Blackburn, R. (1993). Clinical programmes with psychopaths. In K. Howells & C. R. Hollins (Eds.), *Clinical approaches to the mentally disordered offender* (pp. 179–210). Chichester, England: Wiley.

Blashfield, R. K., & Draguns, J. G. (1976). Evaluative criteria for psychiatric classification. *Journal of Abnormal Psychology, 85,* 140–150.

Bluglass, R. (1966). *A psychiatric study of Scottish convicted prisoners.* Unpublished doctoral dissertation, University of St. Andrews, St. Andrews, Scotland.

Bontempo, R. (1993). Translation fidelity of psychological scales: An item response theory analysis of an Individualism–Collectivism Scale. *Journal of Cross-Cultural Psychology, 24,* 149–166.

Borum, R. (1996). Improving the clinical practice of violence risk assessment. *American Psychologist, 51*(9), 945–956.

Butcher, J. N. (1982). Cross-cultural research methods in clinical psychology. In P. C. Kendall & J. N. Butcher (Eds.), *Handbook of research methods in clinical psychology* (pp. 273–308). New York: Wiley.

Chagnon, N. A. (1974). *Studying the Yanomano.* New York: Holt, Rinehart & Winston.

Christie, R., & Geis, F. L. (1970). *Studies of Machiavellianism.* New York: Academic Press.

Cleckley, H. (1976). *The mask of sanity* (5th ed.). St. Louis, MO: C. V. Mosby.

Compton, W. M., Helzer, J. E., Hwu, H.-G., Yeh, E.-K., McEvoy, L., Tipp, J. E., & Spitznagel, E. L. (1991). New methods in cross-cultural psychiatry: Psychiatric illness in Taiwan and the United States. *American Journal of Psychiatry, 148,* 1697–1704.

Cooke, D. J. (1989). Containing violent prisoners: An analysis of the Barlinnie Special Unit. *British Journal of Criminology, 29,* 129–143.

Cooke, D. J. (1994). *Psychological disturbance in the Scottish prison system: Prevalence, precipitants and policy.* Edinburgh: Scottish Home and Health Department.

Cooke, D. J. (1995a). Psychological disturbance in the Scottish prison system: A preliminary account. In G. Davie, S. Lloyd-Bostock, M. McMurran, & C. Wilson (Eds.), *Psychology, law and criminal justice: International developments in research and practice.* Berlin: de Gruyter.

Cooke, D. J. (1995b). Psychopathic disturbance in the Scottish prison population: The cross-cultural generalisability of the Hare Psychopathy Checklist. *Psychology, Crime and Law, 2,* 101–108.

Cooke, D. J. (1996). Psychopathic personality in different cultures: What do we know? What do we need to find out? *Journal of Personality Disorders, 10*(1), 23–40.

Cooke, D. J. (1997). The Barlinnie Special Unit: The rise and fall of a therapeutic experiment. In E. Cullen, L. Jones, & R. Woodward (Eds.), *Therapeutic communities in prison.* Chichester, England: Wiley.

Cooke, D. J. (1998). Psychopathy across cultures. In D. J. Cooke, A. E. Forth, & R. D. Hare (Eds.), *Psychopathy: Theory, research and implications for society* (pp. 101–120). Dordrecht, The Netherlands: Kluwer.

Cooke, D. J., & Michie, C. (1997). An item response theory analysis of the Hare Psychopathy Checklist. *Psychological Assessment, 9,* 3–13.

Cooke, D. J., & Michie, C. (in press). Psychopathy across cultures: An item response theory comparison of Hare's Psychopathy Checklist—Revised. *Journal of Abnormal Psychology.*

Cooke, D. J., Michie, C., Hart, S. D., & Hare, R. D. (1996). *The functioning of the Clinical Version of the Psychopathy Checklist: An item response theory analysis.* Manuscript submitted for publication.

Cooper, J. E., Kendell, R. E., Gurland, B. J., Sharpe, L., Copeland, J. R. M., & Simon, R. (1972). *Psychiatric diagnosis in New York and London.* Oxford: Oxford University Press.

Draguns, J. G. (1986). Culture and psychopathology: What is known about their relationship? *Australian Journal of Psychology, 38,* 329–338.

Ekblad, S. (1988). Influence of child-rearing on aggressive behavior in a transcultural perspective. *Acta Psychiatrica Scandinavica, 78,* 133–139.

Ekblad, S. (1990). The Children's Behaviour Questionnaire for completion by parents and teachers in a Chinese sample. *Journal of Child Psychology and Psychiatry, 31,* 775–791.

Ellis, B. B., Becker, P., & Kimmel, H. D. (1993). An item response theory evaluation of an English version of the Trier Personality Inventory (TPI). *Journal of Cross-cultural Psychology, 24,* 133–148.

Fiske, A. P. (1995). The cultural dimensions of psychological research: method effects imply cultural mediation. In P. E. Shrout & S. T. Fiske (Eds.), *Personality research method and theory: A Festschrift honoring Donald W. Fiske* (pp. 271–294). Hillsdale, NJ: Erlbaum.

Fulero, S. M. (1995). Review of the Hare Psychopathy Checklist—Revised. In J. C. Conoley & J. C. Impara (Eds.), *Twelfth mental measurement yearbook* (pp. 453–454). Lincoln, NE: Buros Institute.

Glasser, R. (1987). *Growing up in the Gorbals.* London: Pan.

Gunn, J., Maden, A., & Swinton, M. (1991). Treatment needs of prisoners with psychiatric disorders. *British Medical Journal, 303,* 338–341.

Gunn, J., Robertson, G., Dell, S., & Way, C. (1978). *Psychiatric aspects of imprisonment.* London: Academic Press.

Guze, S. B. (1976). *Criminality and psychiatric disorders.* New York: Oxford University Press.

Haapasalo, J., & Pulkkinen, L. (1992). The Psychopathy Checklist and non-violent offender groups. *Criminal Behaviour and Mental Health, 2,* 315–328.

Hambleton, R. K. (1989). Principles and selected applications of item response theory. In R. L. Linn (Ed.), *Educational measurement* (pp. 147–200). London: Collier MacMillan.

Hare, R. D. (1978). Electrodermal and cardiovascular correlates of psychopathy. In R. D. Hare & D. Schalling (Eds.), *Psychopathic disorder: Approaches to research* (pp. 107–143). Chichester, England: Wiley.

Hare, R. D. (1980). A research scale for the assessment of psychopathy in criminal populations. *Personality and Individual Differences, 1,* 111–119.

Hare, R. D. (1991). *The Hare Psychopathy Checklist—Revised.* Toronto: Multi-Health Systems.

Hare, R. D. (1993). *Without conscience: The disturbing world of the psychopaths among us.* New York: Pocket Books.

Hare, R. D. (1996). Psychopathy: A clinical construct whose time has come. *Criminal Justice and Behavior, 23,* 25–34.

Hare, R. D., Forth, A. E., & Strachan, K. E. (1992). Psychopathy and crime across the life span. In R. D. Peters, R. J. McMahon, & V. L. Quinsey (Eds.), *Aggression and violence thoughrout the life span* (pp. 285–300). Newbury Park, CA: Sage.

Hare, R. D., Harpur, T. J., Hakstian, A. R., Forth, A. E., Hart, S. D., & Newman, J. P. (1990). The Revised Psychopathy Checklist: Descriptive statistics, reliability, and factor structure. *Psychological Assessment: A Journal of Consulting and Clinical Psychology, 2,* 238–341.

Hare, R. D., Hart, S. D., & Harpur, T. J. (1991). Psychopathy and the proposed DSM-IV criteria for antisocial personality disorder. *Journal of Abnormal Psychology, 100,* 391–398.

Hare, R. D., & McPherson, L. M. (1984). Violent and aggressive behavior in criminal psychopaths. *International Journal of Law and Psychiatry, 7,* 35–50.

Harpending, H., & Draper, P. (1988). Antisocial behavior and the other side of cultural evolution. In T. E. Moffitt & S. A. Mednick (Eds.), *Biological contributions to crime causation* (pp. 110–125). Boston: Nijhoff.

Harpur, T. J., Hare, R. D., & Hakstian, A. R. (1989). Two-factor conceptualization of psychopathy: Construct validity and assessment implications. *Psychological Assessment: A Journal of Consulting and Clinical Psychology, 1,* 6–17.

Harris, G. T., Rice, M. E., & Cormier, C. A. (1991). Psychopathy and violent recidivism. *Law and Human Behavior, 15,* 625–637.

Hart, S. D., & Hare, R. D. (1997). Psychopathy: Assessment and association with criminal conduct. In D. M. Stoff, J. Maser, & J. Brieling (Eds.), *Handbook of antisocial behavior* (pp. 22–35). New York: Wiley.

Hart, S. D., Kropp, P. R., & Hare, R. D. (1988). The performance of male psychopaths following conditional release from prison. *Journal of Consulting in Clinical Psychology, 57,* 227–232.

Hodgins, S., Cote, G., & Ross, D. (1992). Predictive validity of the French version of Hare's Psychopathy Checklist.*Canadian Psychology, 33,* 300. (Abstract).

Holland, P. W., & Wainer, H. (1993). *Differential item functioning.* Hillsdale, NJ: Erlbaum.

Holmes, C. A. (1992). Psychopathic disorder: A category mistake. *Journal of Medical Ethics, 17,* 77–85.

Hulin, C. L. (1987). A psychometric theory of evaluations of item and scale translation: Fidelity across languages. *Journal of Cross-Cultural Psychology, 18,* 115–142.

Hulin, C. L., Drasgow, F., & Parsons, C. K. (1983). *Item response theory: Application to psychological measurement.* Homewood, IL: Dow Jones–Irwin.

Intrator, J., Hare, R. D., Stritske, P., Brichtswein, K., Dorfman, D., Harpur, T., Bernstein, D., Handelsman, L., Schaefer, C., Keilp, J., Rosen, J., & Machac, J. (1997). A brain imaging (SPECT) study of semantic and affective processing in psychopaths. *Biological Psychiatry, 42,* 96–103.

Kendell, R. E. (1989). Clinical validity. *Psychological Medicine, 19,* 45–55.

King, D. W., King, L. A., Fairbank, J. A., Schlenger, W. E., & Surface, C. R. (1993). Enhancing the precision of the Mississippi Scale for Combat-Related Posttraumatic Stress Disorder: An application of item response theory. *Psychological Assessment, 5,* 457–471.

Kosson, D. S., Smith, S. S., & Newman, J. P. (1990). Evaluating the construct validity of psychopathy in black and white male inmates: Three preliminary studies. *Journal of Abnormal Psychology, 99,* 250–259.

Kropp, P. R., Hart, S. D., Webster, C. D., & Eaves, D. (1994). *Manual for the Spousal Assault Risk Assessment Guide.* Vancouver: British Columbia Institute for Family Violence.

Lasch, C. (1979). *The culture of narcissism: American life in an age of diminishing expectations.* New York: Warner.

Lewis-Fernandez, R., & Kleinman, A. (1994). Culture, personality and psychopathology. *Journal of Abnormal Psychology, 103,* 67–71.

Leyton, E. (1989). *Hunting humans: The rise of the modern multiple murderer.* London: Penguin Books.

Livesley, W. J. (1995, November–December). *Phenotypic and genotypic structure of psychopathic traits.* Paper presented at the NATO Advanced Study Institute on Psychopathy, Alvor, Portugal.

Lykken, D. T. (1995). *The antisocial personalities.* Hillsdale, NJ: Erlbaum.

Mealey, L. (1995). The sociobiology of sociopathy: An integrated evolutionary model. *Behavioral and Brain Sciences, 18,* 523–599.

Mellenbergh, G. J. (1996). Measurement precision in test score and item response models. *Psychological Methods, 1*(3), 293–299.

Moghaddam, F. M., Taylor, D. M., & Wright, S. C. (1992). *Social psychology in cross-cultural perspective.* New York: Freeman.

Murphy, J. M. (1976). Psychiatric labeling in cross-cultural perspective: Similar kinds of disturbed behavior appear to be labeled abnormal in diverse cultures. *Science, 191,* 1019–1028.

Mussen, P., & Eisenberg-Berg, N. (1977). *Roots of caring, sharing and helping.* New York: Freeman.

Nunnally, J. C., & Bernstein, I. H. (1994). *Psychometric theory* (3rd ed.). New York: McGraw-Hill.

Paris, J. (1993). Personality disorders: A biopsychosocial model. *Journal of Personality Disorders, 7,* 255–264.

Patrick, C. J., Bradley, M. M., & Lang, P. J. (1993). Emotion in the criminal psychopath: Startle reflex modulation. *Journal of Abnormal Psychology, 103,* 82–92.

Raine, A. (1985). A psychometric assessment of Hare's checklist for psychopathy on an English prison population. *British Journal of Clinical Psychology, 24,* 247–258.

Raine, A., & Venables, P. H. (1992). Antisocial behaviour: Evolution, genetics, neuropsychology, and psychophysiology. In A. Gale & M. W. Eysenck (Eds.), *Handbook of individual differences: Biological perspectives* (pp. 280–312). Chichester, England: Wiley.

Reise, S. P., Widaman, K. F., & Pugh, R. H. (1993). Confirmatory factor analysis and item response theory: Two approaches for exploring measurement invariance. *Psychological Bulletin, 114,* 552–566.

Rice, M. E., Harris, G. T., & Cormier, C. A. (1992). An evaluation of a maximum security therapeutic community for psychopaths and other mentally disordered offenders. *Law and Human Behavior, 16,* 399–412.

Robins, E., & Guze, S. B. (1970). Establishment of diagnostic validity in psychiatric illness: Its application to schizophrenia. *American Journal of Psychiatry, 126,* 983–987.

Robins, L. N., Tipp, J., & Przybeck, T. (1991). Antisocial personality. In L. N. Robins & D. A. Regier (Eds.), *Psychiatric disorders in America* (pp. 258–290). New York: Free Press.

Roper, W. F. (1950). A comparative study of the Wakefield Prison population in 1948: Part 1. *British Journal of Delinquency, 1,* 243–270.

Salekin, R. T., Rogers, R., & Sewell, K. W. (1996). A review and meta-analysis of the Psychopathy Checklist and Psychopathy Checklist—Revised: Predictive validity of dangerousness. *Clinical Psychology: Science and Practice, 3,* 203–215.

Thissen, D. (1991). *Multilog user's guide* (version 6). Mooresville, IN: Scientific Software.

Webster, C. D., Eaves, D., Douglas, K., & Wintrup, A. (1995). *The HCR-20 scheme: The assessment of dangerousness and risk.* Vancouver, BC: Simon Fraser University and Forensic Psychiatric Services Commission of British Columbia.

Webster, C. D., Harris, G. T., Rice, M. E., Cormier, C., & Quinsey, V. L. (1994). *The Violence Prediction Scheme: Assessing dangerousness in high risk men.* Toronto: University of Toronto.

Widiger, T. A., Cadoret, R., Hare, R. D., Robins, L. N., Rutherford, M. J., Zanarini, M., Alterman, A. I., Apple, M., Corbitt, E., Forth, A. E., Hart, S. D., Kultermann, J., & Woody, G. (1996). DSM-IV Antisocial Personality Disorder Field Trial. *Journal of Abnormal Psychology, 105,* 3–16.

Williamson, S., Harpur, T. J., & Hare, R. D. (1991). Abnormal processsing of emotional words by psychopaths. *Psychophysiology, 28,* 260–273.

Wilson, J. Q., & Herrnstein, R. J. (1985). *Crime and human nature.* New York: Simon & Schuster.

Wong, S. (1984). *Criminal and institutional behaviours of psychopaths.* Ottawa: Ministry of the Solicitor-General of Canada.

World Health Organization. (1973). *International pilot study of schizophrenia.* Geneva: Author.

World Heath Organization. (1983). *Depressive disorders in different cultures.* Geneva: Author.

17

A Biopsychosocial Model of Psychopathy

JOEL PARIS

All cultures, in some form or other, recognize a form of mental abnormality character-ized by callousness and criminality (Murphy, 1976). However, these patients only began to be treated by psychiatrists in Europe during the early 19th century. As remains largely true today, the majority of cases were handled by the criminal justice system, whereas those whose symptoms were judged to be more bizarre were admitted to mental hospi-tals, where they might merit a diagnosis of "moral insanity" (Berrios, 1993). This term reflected the beginning of the idea that criminal behavior can be the outward manifesta-tion of a major mental disorder.

In modern times, as the scope of psychiatry has widened, the idea that criminality is a form of psychopathology has gained greater credence. Cleckley's (1964) clinical de-scriptions of psychopathic patients emphasized that they exhibited more than just bad behavior, and that they suffered from a disorder characterized by deficits in empathy and an inability to manage interpersonal relationships. Yochelson and Samenow (1976), in a monumental review of the subject, made observations similar to those of Cleckley.

More recently, the DSM-IV (American Psychiatric Association, 1994) has signifi-cantly narrowed this broad construct of psychopathy into the diagnosis of antisocial per-sonality disorder (APD), in which criminality is the predominant feature. ICD-10 (World Health Organization, 1992) describes dyssocial personality disorder, which has very sim-ilar criteria. However, APD may be based too much on overt evidence of criminality. It fails to consider an independent personality dimension marked by manipulativeness in interpersonal relations (Hare, 1983). Factor-analytic studies suggest that there are two el-ements in psychopathy, one describing criminality, the other describing pathological in-terpersonal behavior; when both factors are considered, only a minority of criminals meet diagnostic criteria for psychopathy (Harpur, Hart, & Hare, 1994). Moreover, since consistent criminal behavior has become a crucial criterion, between two-thirds and three-quarters of male prison populations meet the present definition of APD (Hare, 1983; Côté & Hodgins, 1990). However, since delinquency and criminality can readily be measured, they are useful markers for APD in epidemiological research.

For the purposes of this chapter, we will generally use the term "psychopathy" to describe this form of psychopathology, except where researchers have specifically used other constructs, such as "sociopathy," "antisocial personality," or "criminality."

THE ORIGINS OF PSYCHOPATHY

Biological Factors

There is consistent evidence that genetic factors influence criminality. Of course, the fact that criminal behavior runs in families (Rutter & Madge, 1976) could be due to either genetic or environmental mechanisms. However, twin studies show that criminality shows significant levels of heritability (Cloninger, Reich, & Guze, 1978), while adoption studies show that criminality in a biological parent is a risk factor for criminality in a child (Mednick, Gabrieli, & Hutchings, 1984; Crowe, 1974).

There are several problems with interpreting research in which behaviors, rather than diagnoses, are the outcome variables. Criminality can be confounded with alcoholism, which often accompanies criminal behavior and has a strong genetic component (Bohman, Sigvardsson, Cloninger, & von Knorring, 1982). Criminality itself is heterogeneous, and it has been shown that violent criminal behavior and petty criminality are separately heritable (Plomin, 1994). In a study of Swedish adoptees (Cloninger, Sigvardsson, Bohman, & von Knorring, 1982), theft and fraud (which are more characteristic of APD than is violent crime) show a small genetic effect, but substantial environmental risk factors.

Moreover, criminality is not equivalent to psychopathy. There have been no twin studies using specific diagnostic criteria. Some reports suggest the presence of biological markers in psychopathic patients, with the most consistent findings involving differences on neuropsychological testing (Sutker, Bugg, & West, 1993). Another consistent finding is that psychopaths fail to develop conditioned responses to stimuli related to fear (Hare, 1980; Mednick & Moffitt, 1985). These observations are in concordance with clinical reports that psychopathic patients have a lack of normal fearfulness and fail to learn from negative experiences (Cleckley, 1964). They are also consistent with a theory developed by Eysenck (1977) that reduced conditionability constitutes the diathesis for criminal behavior. As suggested by Beck, Freeman, and Associates (1990), there are conditions under which fearlessness can be adaptive. This is why psychopathic individuals in the military may sometimes function well in combat, but end up in jail during peacetime (Yochelson & Samenow, 1976).

Kagan (1994) has labeled the constitutional factor in psychopathy "uninhibited temperament." This temperamental variation would not be sufficient by itself to cause criminality, but it might be a necessary precondition for its development. The converse trait, an inhibited temperament, is protective *against* criminality (Farrington, 1991).

Still another biological factor in psychopathy could involve comorbidity with attention-deficit/hyperactivity disorder (ADHD). Long-term follow-ups of hyperactive children show that about a third of ADHD cases develop criminality (Weiss & Hechtman, 1993; West & Farrington, 1973). However, there have been no systematic studies measuring how frequently adult psychopaths have had a history of ADHD.

There is a strong gender difference in the prevalence of psychopathy. There is some evidence that the genetic factors are different in males and females (Sigvardsson, Cloninger, Bohman, & von Knorring, 1982). The higher rates in males may, however, be an artifact of greater aggression in men. Higher levels of physical aggression constitute the most consistent gender difference between male and female children (Maccoby & Jacklin, 1974). Female patients with the same temperament may develop a completely different set of symptoms, such as somatization disorder (Winokur, Clayton, & Reich, 1969). Another possibility is that men with an impulsive predisposition become psychopathic, whereas women with the same predisposition develop borderline personality disorder (Paris, 1994, 1997).

Psychological Factors

Thirty years after its publication, Robins's (1966) large-scale prospective study of children at risk for psychopathy is still the most important source of data on the psychological factors in this disorder. One of Robins's principal findings was that *only* those children whose delinquency had begun prior to adolescence could be diagnosed later as "sociopathic." This observation was later confirmed in a British study (West & Farrington, 1973). This is the reason why the DSM requires a prior diagnosis of conduct disorder (CD) during childhood for a diagnosis of APD in adults. Nonetheless, only a third of children with CD develop APD (Zoccolillo, Pickles, Quinton, & Rutter, 1992).

CD is unique among psychiatric disorders for having low heritability, with its environmental variance being attributable to shared rather than unshared factors, pointing to the importance of family dysfunction in its etiology (Cadoret, Yates, Troughton, Woodward, & Stewart, 1995). One possible explanation of the relationship is that genetic factors are involved in the most severe cases of CD (which are most likely to go on to psychopathy), whereas environmental factors predominate in the majority of cases (in which children grow out of their earlier delinquency). This hypothesis is supported by evidence that earlier onset and greater severity of CD make an outcome of APD more likely (Zoccolillo et al., 1992).

Robins also found that parental pathology predicted psychopathy. The most important factor, which accounted for most other risks, was antisocial behavior in the *father*. In a different sample, Pollack et al. (1990) reported that childhood physical abuse, in conjunction with parental alcoholism, predicted adult antisocial behavior. These findings suggest that pathological parenting makes psychopathy more likely, but they could also be interpreted as reflecting common genetic factors.

The family structure of children who develop psychopathy has been shown to be characterized by parents' failure to discipline and supervise their children (Robins, 1966; West & Farrington, 1973). Separation from or loss of a parent also seems to be an independent risk factor (Robins, 1966), and only one-third of the cases in the Robins cohort were raised by two parents—an unusual rate at the time when the children were originally assessed (70 years ago). Finally, Robins found a strong relationship between sociopathy and large family size.

Studies examining the risks for delinquency and crime have presented a similar picture. In one prospective study (McCord, 1978), the most powerful predictor of delinquency was parental instability, whereas the presence of a relationship to a stable and affectionate parent was a strong protective factor. In another prospective study (West & Farrington, 1973), the risk factors were low family income, large family size, parental criminality, low intelligence, and lack of discipline and control from parents.

These findings all point to family dysfunction as the most important psychological risk factor for psychopathy. The most likely mechanism by which dysfunctional families promote psychopathy is through a decreased frequency or inconsistency of punishment, with an absence of clear consequences and limits for children's behavior (Kagan, 1994).

Social Factors

The clear-cut behavioral criteria for APD have made it practical to examine its prevalence in epidemiological research (Cadoret, 1986). APD was the only personality disorder included in two large-scale U.S. surveys: the Epidemiologic Catchment Area (ECA) study (Robins & Regier, 1991), and the National Comorbidity Survey (Kessler et al., 1994). The results of both surveys showed that prevalence is strongly correlated with demographic variables: age, gender, and socioeconomic status. Both studies found that antisocial behavior is far more common in younger individuals, in males, and in the lower socioeconomic classes. An association with male gender is the most consistent finding, the disorder being five to seven times more common in men than in women.

APD does not show differential prevalence by race. Nor are there differences between ethnic groups living in the same U.S. cities. The ECA study did report an increased prevalence in urban as opposed to rural sites, and one city (St. Louis) had a particularly high rate. Kessler's group did not confirm these urban–rural differences, but found that APD was more common in the Western states—regional differences that might be attributable either to the migration of antisocial individuals, or to the effects of social risk factors.

Using the Diagnostic Interview Schedule developed in the ECA study, investigators have found the prevalence of APD to be similar in several English-speaking countries. In the two U.S. surveys, the ECA study and the National Comorbidity Survey, it was, 2.4% and 3.5%, respectively. In a Canadian study (Bland, Newman, & Orn, 1988), it was 3.7%. In a New Zealand study (Oakley-Browne, Joyce, Weiss, Bushnell, & Hornblow, 1989), it was 3.1%.

Although psychopathy is seen in all societies (Robins, 1978), there are important cross-cultural differences in its prevalence. Some of these differences are very striking, and are unlikely to be due to problems in the translation of instruments; in fact, these differences provide powerful evidence for the role of social factors in APD. The most important data come from east Asia. Samples from urban and rural areas of Taiwan (Hwu, Yeh, & Change, 1989; Compton et al., 1991) found an unusually *low* prevalence of APD, ranging from 0.03% to 0.14%. There are some reasons to believe that these low rates might also apply to mainland China (Cheung, 1991), although no systematic studies have been carried out there. In a primary care setting in Japan (Sato & Takeichi, 1993), APD was also very rare. A low prevalence of APD is not, however, universal in east Asian societies. In South Korea, where alcoholism is also frequent, there is a high prevalence of APD (Lee, Kovac, & Rhee, 1987). Psychopathy may have different prevalences even in societies with similar cultures (Cooke, 1996; see also Cooke, Chapter 16, this volume).

A second important line of epidemiological evidence pointing to the importance of social factors in psychopathy is that APD is increasing dramatically in prevalence in North America. The ECA findings showed that the lifetime prevalence of APD in the United States nearly doubled among young people in 15 years—results later confirmed by Kessler et al. (1994). These rapid increases in prevalence of mental disorders over short periods of time can only be accounted for by changes in the social environment.

In summary, cross-cultural differences in prevalence, as well as the recent increase in the prevalence of APD in North America, point to a crucial role for social pathology in this disorder. We need to consider the possible mechanisms for these effects of social factors on prevalence.

Social structures affect the prevalence of personality disorders by lowering or raising the threshold at which other risks influence their development (Paris, 1996). Thus, the east Asian cultures with a low prevalence have cultural and family structures that are strongly protective *against* psychopathy. The low rates in Taiwan are most probably due to the high levels of cohesion in traditional Chinese families. These families have characteristics that present a veritable mirror image of the risk factors for psychopathy: Fathers are strong and authoritative, expectations of children are high, and family loyalty is prized. In the Robins (1966) study, there was also a particularly low rate of APD found in Jewish subjects, which she attributed to their strong family structures. Although highly traditional families have their own difficulties, since their repressive style could make children susceptible to other forms of mental disorder, children raised with clear boundaries and limits are at low risk for psychopathy.

Contrary to popular opinion, poverty does *not* explain the prevalence of psychopathy. Robins (1966) found no relationship between lower socioeconomic status and sociopathy, independent of the presence of criminality in the father. Poverty is not related to crime when families are functioning well. As Vaillant and Vaillant (1981) found in a long-term follow-up of an inner-city sample of young males, most people raised in poverty work hard to make their lives better, and never turn to crime.

In fact, the greatest increase in the prevalence of both criminality and psychopathy took place in Western countries in the decades following World War II, in the face of unprecedented prosperity (Rutter & Rutter, 1993). Family dysfunction, acting as a mediating factor for social influences, is probably responsible for the increasing prevalence of psychopathy. This conclusion is concordant with another finding from Robins (1966), who noted that membership in gangs was a risk factor only in those children who already came from dysfunctional families.

The impact of social factors can be best understood if the *vulnerability* to psychopathy is more widely distributed than is overt antisocial behavior. In fact, the more widely distributed a biological predisposition is, the more likely it is to be susceptible to the effects of psychosocial risk factors (Paris, in press). In particular, impulsive traits will not attain dysfunctional proportions if they can be "contained" by strong families and by strong social structures. Overt antisocial behavior will only emerge when predispositions are uncovered by family dysfunction.

Even a combination of biological predisposition and family dysfunction is not necessarily a sufficient condition for the development of psychopathy. One of the most striking findings of research on children at risk is that resilience is the rule, not the exception (Rutter & Rutter, 1993). In part, resilience may be biological, in that less adaptive traits may coexist with more adaptive traits. Another explanation is that children who are at high risk because of family dysfunction find compensating attachments in their extended family and in their community (Kaufman, Grunebaum, Cohler, & Gamer, 1979). Thus, psychopathy is more likely when family breakdown is accompanied by the breakdown of structures outside the family that might have provided community support for children at risk.

OUTCOME OF PSYCHOPATHY

Psychopathic patients tend to improve over time. In the ECA study (Robins & Regier, 1991), there was a striking decrease in the prevalence of APD after age 44. There have only been a few published follow-up studies of psychopathic patients, treated either in psychiatric clinics and hospitals (Maddocks, 1970; Guze, 1976; Black, Baumgard, & Bell, 1995), or in forensic settings (Arbodela-Florez & Holley, 1991). The most consistent improvements over time are in criminal behavior. On the whole, "recovered" patients continue to demonstrate considerable pathology.

In the most extensive follow-up study of psychopathy to date (Black et al., 1995), 71 patients were assessed after a mean of 29 years following initial hospitalization. The findings were that fewer than 10% of patients met criteria for APD by middle age. On the other hand, the vast majority of patients continued to show some of the features of their initial disorder, particularly chronic instability in interpersonal relationships.

These findings are similar to those obtained in research on the outcome of borderline personality disorder (McGlashan, 1986; Paris, Brown, & Nowlis, 1987; Stone, 1990). "Burnout" in middle age may be the natural outcome of impulsive personality disorders (Paris, 1993a). This observation may be understood in the light of longitudinal research on defense styles during adulthood. Reductions in impulsivity occur in many types of character structures (Vaillant, 1977). The mechanism of this change may be, in part, biological. There is continuous brain maturation during adulthood, which may also be associated with changes in levels of specific neurotransmitters. Improvements in neurochemical balances, particularly those related to the serotonergic system, might decrease impulsivity. But there could also be a psychological mechanism for "burnout" in APD. However slow they are to benefit from experience, psychopathic individuals may eventually undergo at least some degree of social learning.

APPLYING A BIOPSYCHOSOCIAL MODEL

The research findings reviewed above are all consistent with a biopsychosocial model of the personality disorders (Paris, 1993b, 1996). This model builds on a psychobiological theory proposed by Siever and Davis (1991), as well as on models derived from personality theory (Widiger, Trull, Clarkin, Sanderson, & Costa, 1994), which propose that diagnosable personality disorders are pathological exaggerations of personality traits.

Behavior-genetic research (Livesley, Jang, Schroeder, & Jackson, 1993; Plomin, 1994) shows that personality traits are under strong genetic influence. As suggested by Siever and Davis (1991), an unusually high intensity of certain personality traits may predispose individuals to develop personality disorders. However, a great deal of evidence indicates that psychosocial factors are crucial in determining how traits become amplified to the level of disorders (Paris, 1996).

Applying this model to psychopathy, research measuring personality dimensions in these patients can help to identify which traits underly the disorder. For example, using his tridimensional schema, Eysenck (1977; see also Eysenck, Chapter 3, this volume) found high scores on psychoticism and extraversion in psychopaths. Using the five-factor model, Widiger et al. (1994; see also Widiger & Lynam, Chapter 11, this volume) found low neuroticism, low agreeableness, and low conscientiousness in APD. Using a different tridimensional schema, Cloninger (1987) found high scores on novelty seeking, low scores on reward dependence, and low scores on harm avoidance. Since all of these dimensions of personality have a genetic component, these findings demonstrate the temperamental factors behind psychopathy.

Siever and Davis (1991; see also Siever, Chapter 14, this volume) have proposed that antisocial personality derives from a combination of temperamental abnormalities: impulsivity (modulated by low levels of serotonin) and increased behavioral activation (modulated by high levels of monoamines). Thus far, there have been no specific studies to support this hypothesis; there is evidence, however, that men with a trait defined as "impulsive aggression" have unusually sluggish central serotonin activity (Coccaro et al., 1989). Siever and Davis's psychobiological model predicts that psychopathy can *only* develop when these personality traits are present. However, the traits, by themselves, would not be sufficient to produce psychopathy. Only an interaction between biological and psychological risk factors could account for the development of a personality disorder.

Although social factors have been hypothesized to play an important role in borderline personality (Paris, 1992; Millon, 1993), they have been relatively neglected in the personality disorder literature. The most parsimonious interpretation of the epidemiological findings quoted above is that psychopathy can be rare unless specific social risk factors are present. These risks involve the breakdown of both family and social structures, and have been termed "social disintegration" (Leighton, Harding, & Macklin, 1963). Social disintegration involves interactions between social and psychological factors, in that social breakdown makes abnormal and chaotic family structures more likely, while children are at greater risk from abnormal families in the presence of social breakdown. In fact, children exposed to the psychological risk factors associated with psychopathy do not develop the disorder if these protective factors intervene (Rutter & Rutter, 1993). Protective factors also help to explain why most children with CD do not go on to develop adult criminality.

In summary, a biopsychosocial model hypothesizes that psychopathy will only develop in those individuals who are already vulnerable by virtue of their personality traits—specifically, high impulsivity and high behavioral activation. If such individuals are also exposed to antisocial parents and/or to chaotic family environments, the risk for psychopathy should be further increased. However, a diagnosable disorder should only appear when the social environment is sufficiently pathological that it fails to provide protection against these biological and psychological risks.

CLINICAL IMPLICATIONS

Of all the personality disorders, psychopathy offers the most pessimistic prospects for treatment. Attempts to manage psychopathic patients have generally involved either individual and group psychotherapies, or artificial environments in the form of "therapeutic communities" (Yochelson & Samenow, 1976; Robins & Regier, 1991). However, there is no evidence that any of these methods has any lasting effects. Although devoted clinicians, particularly in forensic settings, continue to apply their clinical skills to psychopathic patients, there have been no convincing clinical trials showing that any method of therapy is consistently effective for this population (Dolan & Coid, 1993). The follow-up study by Black et al. (1995) confirms that most of these individuals continue to have severe deficits throughout their lives.

There may be exceptions to this principle that psychopathy is untreatable. Woody, McLellan, Luborsky, and O'Brien (1985) found that psychopathic patients who *also* met criteria for the clinical diagnosis of depression could be approached in outpatient therapy. These results define a small subpopulation at the less severe end of the psychopathic continuum, but are not generalizable to typical cases. Although 5% of these patients eventually complete suicide (Robins, 1966), major depression is not generally comorbid with psychopathy.

The difficulty in treating psychopathic patients may be related to two factors: (1) the nature of the personality traits underlying the disorder; and (2) the psychosocial factors leading to the amplification of these traits. The abnormal traits in individuals prone to psychopathy, once they are reinforced by psychosocial factors, are difficult to reverse. Even when the worst aspects "burn out" by middle age, the recovered patient has failed to undergo crucial social learning that normally occurs in adolescence and young adulthood. These experiences help individuals develop skills in attaining stable employment and establishing meaningful intimate relationships. Taken together, the effect of both these factors is to leave a psychopathic patient with a serious deficit. This may be dealt with by the continuation of antisocial behaviors at a lower level of intensity. However maladaptive in the long run, the manipulativeness of the psychopath has led to intermittent positive reinforcement in the past. It is therefore not surprising that psychopathy is difficult to treat, either when it reaches diagnosable levels in youth, or when it continues to smolder at subdiagnostic levels in later life.

What this suggests is that in the long run, we will need entirely different forms of treatments to manage psychopathy. Some of them could be psychopharmacological, which would address the biology of the traits underlying the disorder by influencing neurotransmitter levels (Masters & McGuire, 1994). Another possibility would be to develop a form of cognitive-behavioral therapy specifically designed for psychopathy (Beck et al., 1990), particularly since a similar method has been shown to be effective in patients with borderline personality disorder (Linehan, 1993). However, in a society that protects the individual's civil liberty to refuse treatment, psychopathic individuals might refuse effective therapeutic modalities even if we could develop them. Moreover, given the continuing role of social factors in psychopathy, the prevalence of the disorder can be expected to rise in the coming years (Robins & Regier, 1991).

REFERENCES

American Psychiatric Association. (1994). *Diagnostic and statistical manual of mental disorders* (4th ed.). Washington, DC: Author.

Arboleda-Florez, J., & Holley, H. L. (1991). Antisocial burnout: An exploratory study. *Bulletin of the American Academy of Psychiatry and the Law, 19,* 173–183.

Beck, A. T. Freeman, A., & Associates. (1990). *Cognitive therapy of personality disorders.* New York: Guilford Press.

Berrios, G. S. (1993). European views on personality disorders: A conceptual history. *Comprehensive Psychiatry, 34,* 14–30.

Black, C. W., Baumgard, C. H., & Bell, S. E. (1995). A 16- to 45-year follow-up of 71 men with antisocial personality disorder. *Comprehensive Psychiatry, 36,* 130–140.

Bland, R. C., Newman, S. C., & Orn, H. (1988). Lifetime prevalence of psychiatric disorders in Edmonton. *Acta Psychiatrica Scandinavica, 77*(Suppl. 338), 24–32.

Bohman, M., Sigvardsson, S., Cloninger, R., von Knorring, A.-L. (1982). Predisposition to petty criminality in Swedish adoptees: I. Genetic and environmental heterogeneity. *Archives of General Psychiatry, 39,* 1233–1241.

Cadoret, R. J. (1986). Epidemiology of antisocial personality. In W. H. Reid, D. Dorr, J. I. Walker, & J. W. Bonner (Eds.), *Unmasking the psychopath* (pp. 28–44). New York: Norton.

Cadoret, R. J., Yates, W. R., Troughton, E., Woodworth, G., & Stewart, M. A. (1995). Genetic environmental interaction in the genesis of aggressivity and conduct disorders. *Archives of General Psychiatry, 52,* 916–924.

Cheung, P. (1991). Adult psychiatric epidemiology in China in the 1980's. *Culture, Medicine, and Psychiatry, 15,* 479–496.

Cleckley, H. (1964). *The mask of sanity* (4th ed.). St. Louis, MO: C. V. Mosby.

Cloninger, C. R. (1987). A systematic method for clinical description and classification of personality variants. *Archives of General Psychiatry, 44,* 579–588.

Cloninger, C. R., Reich, T., & Guze, S. B. (1978). Genetic-environmental interactions and antisocial behavior. In R. D. Hare & D. Schalling (Eds.), *Psychopathic behavior: Approaches to research* (pp. 225–237). New York: Wiley.

Cloninger, C. R., Sigvardsson, S., Bohman, M., & von Knorring, A.-L. (1982). Predisposition to petty criminality in Swedish adoptees: II. Cross-fostering analysis of gene–environment interaction. *Archives of General Psychiatry, 39,* 1242–1253.

Coccaro, E. F., Siever, L. J., Klar, H. M., Maurer, G., Cochrane, K., Cooper, T. B., Mohs, R. C., & Davis, K. L. (1989). Serotonergic studies in patients with affective and personality disorders. *Archives of General Psychiatry, 46,* 587–599.

Compton, W. W., Helzer, J. E., Hwu, H.-G., Yeh, E.-K., McEvoy, L., & Tipp, J. E. (1991). New methods in cross-cultural psychiatry: Psychiatric illness in Taiwan and the United States. *American Journal of Psychiatry, 148,* 1697–1704.

Cooke, D. J. (1996). Psychopathic personality in different cultures. *Journal of Personality Disorders, 10,* 23–40.

Côté, G., & Hodgins, S. (1990). Co-occurring mental disorders among criminal offenders. *Bulletin of the American Academy of Psychiatry and the Law, 18,* 271–281.

Crowe, R. R. (1974). An adoption study of antisocial personality, *Archives of General Psychiatry, 31,* 785–791.

Dolan, B., & Coid, J. (1993). *Psychopathic and antisocial personality disorders.* London: Royal College of Psychiatrists.

Eysenck, H. J. (1977). *Crime and personality.* London: Paladin.

Farrington, D. (1991). Antisocial personality from childhood to adulthood. *The Psychologist, 4,* 389–394.

Guze, S. B. (1976). *Criminality and psychiatric disorders.* New York: Oxford University Press.

Hare, R. D. (1980). Psychopathy. In H. van Praag, M. Lader, O. Rafaelson, & E. Sacher (Eds.), *Handbook of biological psychiatry.* New York: Dekker.

Hare, R. D. (1983). Diagnosis of antisocial personality in two prison populations. *American Journal of Psychiatry, 140,* 887–890.

Harpur, T. J., Hart, S. D., & Hare, R. D. (1994). Personality of the psychopath. In P. T. Costa & T. A. Widiger (Eds.), *Personality disorders and the five-factor model* (pp. 149–174). Washington, DC: American Psychological Association.

Hwu, H. G., Yeh, E. K., & Change, L. Y. (1989). Prevalence of psychiatric disorders in Taiwan defined by the Chinese Diagnostic Interview Schedule. *Acta Psychiatrica Scandinavica, 79,* 136–147.

Kagan, J. (1994). *Galen's prophecy.* New York: Basic Books.

Kaufman, C., Grunebaum, H., Cohler, B., & Gamer, E. (1979). Superkids: Competent children of schizophrenic mothers. *American Journal of Psychiatry, 136,* 1398–1402.

Kessler, R. C., McGonagle, K. A., Zhao, S., Nelson, C. B., Hughes, M., Eshelman, S., Wittchen, H.-U., & Kendler, K. S. (1994). Lifetime and 12-month prevalence of DSM-III-R psychiatric disorders in the United States. *Archives General Psychiatry 51,* 8–19.

Lee, K. C., Kovac, Y. S., & Rhee, H. (1987). The national epidemiological study of mental disorders in Korea. *Journal of Korean Medical Science, 2,* 19–34.

Leighton, D. C., Harding, J. S., & Macklin, D. B. (1963). *The character of danger: Psychiatric symptoms in selected communities.* New York: Basic Books.

Linehan, M. M. (1993). *Cognitive-behavioral treatment of borderline personality disorder.* New York: Guilford Press.

Livesley, W. J., Jang, K., Schroeder, M. L., & Jackson, D. N. (1993). Genetic and environmental factors in personality dimensions. *American Journal of Psychiatry, 150,* 1826–1831.

Maccoby, E. E., & Jacklin, C. N. (1974). *The psychology of sex differences.* Stanford, CA: Stanford University Press.

Maddocks, P. D. (1970). A five year follow-up of untreated psychopaths. *British Journal of Psychiatry, 116,* 511–515.

Masters, R. D., & McGuire, M. T. (1994). *The neurotransmitter revolution: Serotonin, social behavior, and the law.* Carbondale, IL: Southern Illinois University Press.

McCord, J. (1978). A thirty year follow-up of treatment effects. *American Psychologist, 33,* 284–289.

McGlashan, T. H. (1986a). The Chestnut Lodge Follow-Up Study: Long-term outcomes of borderline personalities. *Archives of General Psychiatry, 43,* 20–30.

Mednick, S. A., Gabrieli, W. F., & Hutchings, B. (1984). Genetic influences in criminal convictions. *Science, 224,* 891–894.

Mednick, S. A., & Moffitt, T. (Eds.). (1985). *Biology and crime.* Cambridge, England: Cambridge University Press.

Millon, T. (1993). Borderline personality disorder: A psychosocial epidemic. In J. Paris (Ed.), *Borderline personality disorder: Etiology and treatment* (pp. 197–210). Washington, DC: American Psychiatric Press.

Murphy, J. M. (1976). Psychiatric labelling in cross-cultural perspective. *Science, 191,* 1019–1028.

Oakley-Browne, M. A., Joyce, P. A., Welss, E., Bushnell, J. A., & Hornblow, A. R. (1989). Christchurch Psychiatric Epidemiology Study: Six month and other period prevalences of specific psychiatric disorders. *Australian and New Zealand Journal of Psychiatry, 23,* 327–340.

Paris, J. (1992). Social factors in borderline personality disorder: A review and a hypothesis. *Canadian Journal of Psychiatry, 37,* 480–486.

Paris, J. (1993a). Treatment of borderline personality disorder in the light of the research on its long-term outcome. *Canadian Journal of Psychiatry, 38,* S28–S34.

Paris, J. (1993b). Personality disorders: A biopsychosocial model. *Journal of Personality Disorders, 7,* 255–264.

Paris, J. (1994). *Borderline personality disorder: A multidimensional approach.* Washington, DC: American Psychiatric Press.

Paris, J. (1996). *Social factors in the personality disorders.* New York: Cambridge University Press.

Paris, J. (1997). Antisocial and borderline personality disorders: Two separate diagnoses, or two aspects of the same psychopathology? *Comprehensive Psychiatry, 38,* 227–242.

Paris, J. (in press). *Nature and nurture in psychiatry.* Washington, DC: American Psychiatric Press.

Paris, J., Brown, R., & Nowlis, D. (1987). Long-term follow-up of borderline patients in a general hospital. *Comprehensive Psychiatry, 28,* 530–535.

Plomin, R. (1994). *Genetics and experience.* Thousand Oaks, CA: Sage.

Pollock, V. E., Briere, J., Schneider, L., Knop, J., Mednick, S. A., & Goodwin, D. W. (1990). Childhood antecedents of antisocial behavior: Parental alcoholism and physical abusiveness. *American Journal of Psychiatry, 147,* 1290–1293.

Robins, L. N. (1966). *Deviant children grown up.* Baltimore: Williams & Wilkins.

Robins, L. N. (1978). Sturdy childhood predictors of adult outcome. *Psychologcial Medicine, 8,* 611–622.

Robins, L. N., & Regier, D. A. (Eds.). (1991). *Psychiatric disorders in America.* New York: Free Press.

Rutter, M., & Madge, N. (1976). *Cycles of disadvantage.* London: Heinemann.

Rutter, M., & Rutter, M. (1993). *Developing minds: Challenge and continuity across the life span.* New York: Basic Books.

Sato, T., & Takeichi, M. (1993). Lifetime prevalence of specific psychiatric disorders in a general medicine clinic. *General Hospital Psychiatry, 15,* 224–233.

Siever, L. J., & Davis, L. (1991). A psychobiological perspective on the personality disorders. *American Journal of Psychiatry, 148,* 1647–1658.

Sigvardsson, S., Cloninger, R., Bohman, M., von Knorring, A.-L. (1982). Predisposition to petty criminality in Swedish adoptees: III. Sex differences and validation of the male typology. *Archives of General Psychiatry, 39,* 1248–1253.

Stone, M. H. (1990). *The fate of borderline patients.* New York: Guilford Press.

Sutker, P. B., Bugg, F., & West, J. A. (1993). Antisocial personality disorder. In P. B. Sutker & H. E. Adams (Eds.), *Comprehensive textbook of psychopathology* (pp.337–369). New York: Plenum Press.

Vaillant, G. E. (1977). *Adaptation to life.* Boston: Little, Brown.

Vaillant, G. E., & Vaillant, C. O. (1981). Natural history of male psychological health: X. Work as a predictor of positive mental health. *American Journal of Psychiatry, 138,* 1433–1438.

Weiss, G., & Hechtman, L. T. (1993). *Hyperactive children grown up* (2nd ed.). New York: Guilford Press.

West, D. J., & Farrington, D. P. (1973). *Who becomes delinquent?* London: Heinemann.

Widiger, T. A., Trull, T. J., Clarkin, J. F., Sanderson, C., Costa, P. T. (1994). A description of the DSM-III-R and DSM-IV personality disorders with the five-factor model of personality. In P. T. Costa & T. A. Widiger (Eds.), *Personality disorders and the five-factor model* (pp. 41–58). Washington, DC: American Psychological Association.

Winokur, G., Clayton, P., & Reich, T. (1969). *Manic–depressive illness.* St. Louis, MO: C. V. Mosby.

Woody, G. E., McLellan, T., Luborsky, L., & O'Brien, C. P. (1985). Psychopathy and psychotherapy outcome. *Archives of General Psychiatry, 152,* 516–518.

World Health Organization. (1992). *International classification of diseases* (10th rev.). Geneva: Author.

Yochelson, S., & Samenow, S. (1976). *The criminal personality.* New York: Jason Aronson.

Zoccolillo, M., Pickles, A., Quinton, D., & Rutter, M. (1992). The outcome of childhood conduct disorder. *Psychological Medicine, 22,* 971–986.

IV

COMORBIDITY

18

Psychopathy and Psychiatric Comorbidity

ALV A. DAHL

"Psychopathy" as a mental disorder is found neither in the DSM-IV nor in the ICD-10. It is still used, however, as a diagnostic term both professionally and by laypeople, since the term has a long historical, legal, and popular tradition. The official disorders that seem closest to psychopathy are antisocial personality disorder (APD) in DSM-IV and dyssocial personality disorder in ICD-10. Hare (Hart, Hare, & Harpur, 1993) has explicitly used the term "psychopathy" in his diagnostic instrument, the Psychopathy Checklist—Revised (PCL-R). The degree of overlap among these three concepts becomes vital for a meaningful definition of the concept of psychopathy. Widiger et al. (1996) tested these concepts together on various samples in the DSM-IV Field Trials. They used a short version of the PCL-R with 10 items (referred to here as the PCS), 7 of which had to be positive for a diagnosis, and the regular definitions of the DSM-IV and ICD-10 disorders. The agreement among the three definitions is shown in Table 18.1. Although the overlaps are only moderately good, the results give support to a core concept of psychopathy that is captured by all these definitions. It should be noted here that the studies reviewed in this chapter have been done with the DSM-III/DSM-III-R definitions of APD; with the PCL or PCL-R; or with the ICD-9 or earlier versions of the international classification.

"Comorbidity" has several meanings, as pointed out by Wittchen (1996). One meaning is the relative risk that a patient with one disorder will get another one within a given time frame (e.g., 1 year or the patient's lifetime). Another meaning is the presence of two or more disorders within a given time frame. The most commonly used meaning is the presence of two or more disorders at the same cross-sectional diagnostic examination. Comorbidity has become an important issue since the tradition of a diagnostic hierarchy with one main diagnosis was discontinued in DSM-III-R. The temporal relationships between psychopathy as a long-standing personality disorder, and various types of other mental disorders (acute, recurrent, and chronic), are shown in Figure 18.1.

Wittchen (1996) also gives a warning concerning a common way of reporting comorbidity data:

TABLE 18.1. Agreement among Sets of Criteria for Psychopathy

Criteria	% agreement	Kappa	Correlation
DSM-IV/ICD-10	75	.48	.68
DSM-IV/PCS	74	.39	.73
ICD-10/PCS	73	.36	.79

Note. The data are from Widiger et al. (1996).

This demonstrates that simple comorbidity percentages, unaccompanied by a description of the specific diagnostic method and appropriate statistical analyses that control for chance agreement, are meaningless because the greater the number of prevalent diagnoses considered in the analysis, the greater the likelihood of chance association.

Comorbidity can have several causes (Klein, Wonderlich, & Shea, 1993). Two disorders can be comorbid simply by chance, since they occur completely independently of each other. They can have a common core liability that takes on different expressions. They can both be part of a spectrum of related disorders. One disorder can predispose a person to or make the person vulnerable to the other, and one disorder can be a complication of the other. For psychopathy, all these causes of comorbidity are found.

IS CRIME A DISORDER?

The DSM-III/DSM-III-R definitions of APD have been criticized for the inclusion of too many diagnostic criteria that simply reflect various criminal activities (Frances, 1990). A diagnosis of APD or psychopathy may therefore simply reflect the fact that the person is a criminal. If, for instance, panic disorder is comorbid with APD, that could simply mean that a certain proportion of panic patients are criminals. Comorbid psychopathy is then only a term indicating that a person commits crimes, whatever his or her mental disorder may be. Actually, Hodgins and Côté (1993) report that the presence of comorbid APD increases the risk of crime in patients with major mental disorders, compared to those without such disorders. Hodgins, Mednick, Brennan, Schulsinger, and Engberg (1996), in a large cohort study from Denmark, found that persons with mental disorders had a higher risk for crime than those without such disorders. The relative risk estimate for females with APD was 6.45, and for males with APD was 5.27, during the period of 1978–1990. The risk estimates for individuals with APD were *not* higher than those for persons with several other mental disorders, however.

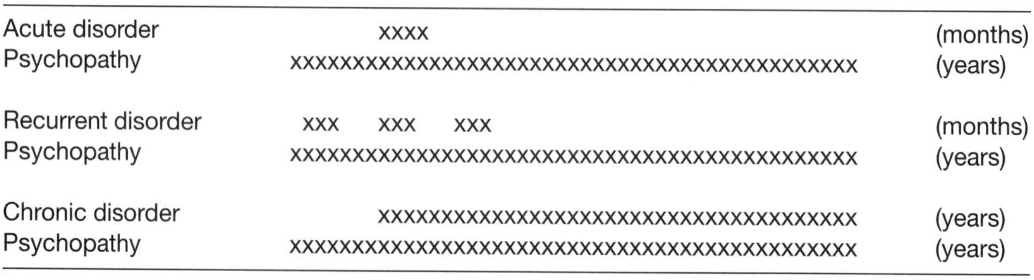

Acute disorder	xxxx	(months)
Psychopathy	xxxxxxxxxxxxxxxxxxxxxxxxxxxxxxxxxxxxxxxxxxxxxxxxx	(years)
Recurrent disorder	xxx xxx xxx	(months)
Psychopathy	xxxxxxxxxxxxxxxxxxxxxxxxxxxxxxxxxxxxxxxxxxxxxxxxx	(years)
Chronic disorder	xxxxxxxxxxxxxxxxxxxxxxxxxxxxxxxxxxxx	(years)
Psychopathy	xxxxxxxxxxxxxxxxxxxxxxxxxxxxxxxxxxxxxxxxxxx	(years)

FIGURE 18.1. Temporal relationships between psychopathy and other types of mental disorders.

The medicalization of crime has been comprehensively discussed by Raine (1993), who concludes: "Based on the definitions of disorder, it is reasonable evidence either to directly support the view that crime is a disorder or alternatively to give serious consideration to this possibility." Another alternative view, however, is that criminality is only one aspect of psychopathy. This view gets support from a factor analysis of the PCL-R (Harpur, Hart, & Hare, 1994), which defines two factors (1 and 2) that are moderately intercorrelated. Factor 1 describes interpersonal relations, whereas Factor 2 describes a general antisocial way of being. APD correlates .40 with Factor 1 and .83 with Factor 2, showing that it is more closely related to the concept of psychopathy than to criminality. Robins, Tipp, and Przybeck (1991) argue that if APD is simply a medicalization of crime, then we shall find that most patients with an APD diagnosis have a criminal history, and that most persons with a criminal history receive a diagnosis of APD. In fact, in the Epidemiologic Catchment Area (ECA) study (see below), it was found that only 47% of the persons with APD had a significant record of arrests, and that among prisoners ($n = 715$) in that study, the lifetime prevalence of APD was 32.7% (Robins et al., 1991). This prevalence is comparable to that found by Hare (1983). Jordan, Schlenger, Fairbank, and Caddell (1996) reported a lifetime prevalence of 11.9% APD among female felons entering prison. The same study found that the odds ratio for APD among these felons was 15.4 (95% confidence interval, 3.7–63.6), compared to women of the household population in the same area.

A reasonable conclusion seems to be that psychopathy and crime are not identical, but that a considerable proportion of persons with APD, especially men, have committed crimes.

PREVALENCES OF COMORBIDITY

The ECA Study

Studies agree unanimously that psychopathy is a highly comorbid disorder. Generally, comorbidity among patients studied in society is 90%, in emergency rooms 89%, and in psychiatric clinics 84% (Robins, Gentry, Munoz, & Marte, 1977). Two large epidemiological studies have systematically examined the comorbidity of DSM-III APD with other disorders. The ECA study (Robins & Regier, 1991) examined 19,182 persons at five sites. A total of 628 persons (3.3%) were found to have APD. Of these, fewer than 10% of the cases had no additional diagnosis. The ECA study gives comorbidity as prevalence ratios; the "prevalence ratio" in this case is the percentage of persons with the diagnosis among those *with* APD divided by the percentage of persons with the diagnosis among those *without* APD. For men, bipolar disorder and schizophrenia were the most common comorbid disorders, and they were among the most common for women (Table 18.2). However, the ECA study did not specify whether bipolar disorder and schizophrenia were truly concurrent disorders, or whether there were cases with these disorders whose symptoms mimicked APD, since the application of the exclusion rules of DSM-III was not reported. However, since the prevalences for both bipolar disorder (0.8%) and schizophrenia (1.3%) were low in the general population, society, the absolute number of cases with APD comorbidity must be low (see below).

The ECA study confirmed the frequent comorbidity established between APD and substance use disorders (Hasselbrock, Meyer, & Keener, 1985). The prevalence ratios were much higher for women with APD—namely, 13.1 for alcohol and 11.9 for drugs. For men, the ratios were 3.2 and 5.3, respectively. Since the prevalence in the general

TABLE 18.2. APD Comorbidity Prevalence Ratios in the ECA and
Edmonton Studies

Disorder	ECA		Edmonton (total)
	Males	Females	
Any mental disorder	—	—	3.0
Bipolar disorder	10.3	20.9	6.3
Schizophrenia	6.9	11.8	9.6
Drug abuse/dependence	5.3	11.9	6.5
Alcohol abuse/dependence	3.2	13.1	6.0
Major depression	3.2	3.5	2.5
Dysthymia	2.8	3.2	3.6
Panic disorder	2.2	4.5	3.7
Obsessive–compulsive disorder	5.3	3.5	3.7
Phobias	2.1	2.0	1.5

Note. The ECA data are from Robins and Regier (1991); the Edmonton data are from
Swanson, Bland, and Newman (1994).

population of alcohol abuse/dependence was 13.8%, and that for drug abuse/depen-
dence was 6.2%, the substance use disorders were strongly associated with APD, and the
number of cases with APD comorbidity was quite high.

The Edmonton Study

The Edmonton study (Swanson, Bland, & Newman, 1994) was designed in much the
same way as the ECA study. The overall weighted prevalence rate for APD was 3.7%,
and 90.4% of those with APD had at least one other lifetime diagnosis. The Edmonton
group also calculated the prevalence ratios of the DSM-III APD adult criteria in the persons with APD (*n* = 104) and all other persons (*n* = 3,154) (Table 18.3). The prevalence
ratios ranged from 2.8 to 25.7, with negligence toward children, and lying and the use of
aliases, as the most specific criteria for APD. The prevalence ratios for various mental
disorders found in Edmonton were quite close to those of the ECA study (see Table
18.2). The prevalence ratio for bipolar disorder was found to be higher in the ECA study,
however. The only disorders that were not found with an increased prevalence in APD

TABLE 18.3. Lifetime Prevalence Rates of DSM-III APD Adult Criteria in Persons with
and without APD in the Edmonton Study

DSM-III criterion	Prevalence rate (%)		Prevalence ratio
	APD (*n* = 104)	No APD (*n* = 3,154)	
Job troubles	91.3	32.9	2.8
Negligent toward children	15.4	0.6	25.7
Various illegal activities	59.6	4.6	12.9
Marital/relationship problems, promiscuity	60.6	15.8	3.8
Physical violence	83.7	13.5	6.2
Vagrancy	55.8	5.0	11.2
Lying, use of aliases	46.2	2.4	19.2
Traffic offenses	81.7	21.1	3.9

Note. The data are from Swanson et al. (1994).

were the three rarest in their sample—namely, schizophreniform disorder, somatization disorder, and anorexia nervosa.

The National Comorbidity Survey

The National Comorbidity Survey (NCS) differed from the ECA study by interviewing a representative sample from across the United States in order to study the comorbidity of substance use disorders with other mental disorders (Kessler et al., 1994). The NCS found the lifetime prevalence of APD to be 3.5%, and an increased prevalence was associated with male sex, younger age, less education, lower income, and residence in metropolitan areas. The comorbidity data for APD were quite close to those reported in the ECA study (Kessler, 1995).

From the epidemiological studies reviewed here, we can conclude that psychopathy is a common and highly comorbid mental disorder.

PSYCHOPATHY AND SCHIZOPHRENIA

Dunaif and Hoch (1955) coined the diagnostic term "pseudopsychopathic schizophrenia" over 40 years ago. The outstanding features of this disorder were antisocial behaviors; indeed, these were emphasized to such an extent that symptoms of psychosis were often overlooked. These authors used the broad North American concept of schizophrenia common at that time, which included most nonaffective functional psychoses. Among their differential diagnoses were "prison psychosis" and Ganser's syndrome, and they warned that such patients were often dismissed as having schizoid tendencies. Dunaif and Hoch believed that they were describing a special type of schizophrenia, but they were probably describing patients with comorbid schizophrenia and APD. An increased prevalence ratio for schizophrenia among individuals with APD was found in both the ECA study (Robins et al., 1991) and the Edmonton study (Swanson et al., 1994).

Rasmussen, Levander, and Sletvold (1995) compared aggressive and nonaggressive patients with schizophrenia. They found no differences in the schizophrenic symptomatology, but the aggressive patients had significantly higher PCL-R scores (mean = 26.6) than the nonaggressive patients (mean = 14.5).

In a study comparing schizophrenic patients with and without a criminal record, Modestin and Ammann (1996) found a significantly higher proportion of alcohol and drug abuse among the criminals. A considerably higher risk of homicide was reported by Eronen, Tiihonen, and Hakola (1996) in patients with schizophrenia and alcoholism, compared to those with schizophrenia alone. Regrettably, neither of these studies included any measure of antisocial features.

Although more studies are needed, the conclusion that comorbid APD increases the risk of violence and crime in patients with schizophrenia seems reasonable.

PSYCHOPATHY AND SOMATIZATION DISORDER

There is some evidence for an association between APD and somatization disorder (formerly called "conversion hysteria"). A higher rate of symptoms of "conversion hysteria" was found among women prisoners with APD (Cloninger & Guze, 1970). The prevalence of somatization disorder as defined by DSM-III was only 0.13% in the ECA study (Swartz, Landerman, George, Blazer, & Escobar, 1991). The DSM-III disorder required 12 of 33 symptoms in men and 14 of 37 in women. The ECA study also examined the prevalence of a "somatization syndrome," which required only 4 or more symptoms in men and 6 or more in women. The lifetime prevalence of the somatization syndrome was 11.6%. Both the disorder and the syndrome had a chronic course, and they were significantly more frequent among women.

In the ECA study, the prevalence ratio for APD in persons with somatization disorder was 2.18; for the somatization syndrome, it was 3.79 in women and 2.52 in men. These ratios are not particularly striking, and they are in contrast to earlier findings of a high degree of association between somatization/hysteria and APD, particularly in women (Lilienfeld, VanValkenburg, Larntz, & Akiskal, 1986). Two explanations for these differences were given by the ECA researchers (Swartz et al., 1991). One was differences in the definition of somatization, and the other was differences in sampling bias between clinical samples and the community samples of ECA. The second explanation seems more plausible.

However, Robins (1986) reported a striking association between the number of APD symptoms and somatization disorder symptoms in the ECA study. This is in accordance with the findings of Smith, Golding, Kashner, and Rost (1991), who reported that 8.2% of women and 25% of men with somatization disorder in primary care had comorbid APD. In their sample, no symptom group in somatization disorder was associated with APD, but patients with amnesia were more likely to have APD. However, the sample of men ($n = 20$) was small in this study. In a sample of 250 psychiatric patients, Lilienfeld et al. (1986) also reported a significant association between APD and somatization disorder for both men and women.

The clinical implication of these findings is that the frequent somatic complaints of persons with APD in prisons and other settings should be taken seriously.

PSYCHOPATHY AND MOOD DISORDERS

The ECA study reported a high prevalence ratio of bipolar disorder in persons with APD (Robins & Regier, 1991), and this was confirmed in the Edmonton study (Swanson et al., 1994). Clinically, the explanation of this comorbidity might be that under stress the narcissistic grandiosity of the psychopath is enlarged to dimensions in which reality testing is reduced and a manic episode ensues. However, further studies of this comorbidity have not been done, to my knowledge.

The prevalence ratios were moderately high for major depression and dysthymia in the ECA and Edmonton studies. Weiss, Davis, Hedlund, and Cho (1983) compared features of depression among psychopaths and matched controls; both groups were taken from first-admission inpatients and outpatients in Missouri mental health facilities between 1972 and 1980. Ratings of depression were based on the mental status reports of these patients. Among the 524 psychopaths, 131 (25.0%) had some degree of depression. Among the controls, this proportion was 30.3%, and the difference between psychopaths and controls was nonsignificant. When the psychopaths with depression ($n = 131$) were compared to those without ($n = 393$), the former were a more disturbed group. The depressed psychopaths demonstrated more "difficulties in intellectual functioning" than the nondepressed psychopaths. The items reflecting such difficulties consisted of intelligence below normal, poor abstraction, poor performance on serial 7s, inability to concentrate, paucity of knowledge, feelings of unreality, and repetitive acts. Among the depressive items, suicidal thoughts was the one that most clearly characterized the depressed psychopaths (50.4%), compared to the nondepressed psychopaths (13.0%).

A subgroup of more seriously depressed psychopaths ($n = 66$) was defined by depressive mood and suicidal ideation and compared to a subgroup of similarly depressed controls ($n = 54$). These psychopaths were both more depressed and anxious, and more likely to demonstrate impairment in intellectual functioning, than the less depressed psychopaths, but not more so than the seriously depressed controls. The seriously depressed psychopaths were perceived primarily as affectively disordered, with the antisocial characteristics regarded as much less prominent. The psychopaths with depression had longer stays in the hospital than either the nondepressed psychopaths or the depressed controls. The combination of psychopathy and depression thus appeared to complicate treatment, as has been demonstrated for personality disorders in general (Zimmerman, Pfohl, Coryell, Corenthal, & Stangl, 1991).

In a follow-up study of men with APD, Black, Baumgard, and Bell (1995) found a lifetime prevalence for major depression of 23.8%, and a lifetime prevalence for dysthymia of 9.5%. These results are comparable to those of Weiss et al. (1983).

Among 243 criminal psychopaths in the United Kingdom, Coid (1992) found that 50% of them had a lifetime diagnosis of major depressive disorder, and 23% a diagnosis of dysthymia. He also reported that 16% had bipolar disorder or atypical bipolar disorder. In a subsample of women with borderline personality disorder who also met criteria for the British legal concept of psychopathy, 71% had lifetime major depression, 26% dysthymia, and 25% bipolar disorder or atypical bipolar disorder (Coid, 1993).

The conclusion to be drawn from these studies is obvious: Mood disorders are frequently comorbid with psychopathy.

PSYCHOPATHY, SUICIDE ATTEMPTS, AND SUICIDE

Suicide attempt is not a mental disorder per se, but a serious expression of crisis and of inability to cope with stress. In her long-term follow-up study of antisocial children ($n = 94$), Robins (1996) found that 11% of the psychopaths had made suicide attempts over the years. Woodruff, Guze, and Clayton (1971) reported a suicide attempt rate of 23%, and Garvey and Spoden (1980) one of 72%, but both studies had small samples ($n < 40$).

Bagley, Jacobson, and Rehin (1976) described a "sociopathic suicide" type, characteristic of younger individuals who had experienced early disruption of family life, showed poor performance when employed, were socially isolated, and had made previous suicide attempts. The lifetime risk of suicide in APD has been estimated at 5% (Miles, 1977). The "sociopathic suicide" pattern has been confirmed to a considerable extent in subsequent studies of individuals with APD, particularly young people. Rich and Runeson (1992) compared the psychiatric diagnoses given to persons under 30 years of age who committed suicide in San Diego, California, and Gothenburg, Sweden. The proportion with APD was 15% in Gothenburg and 10% in San Diego. Almost all these persons in both countries had a substance use disorder (70% and 92%, respectively), and depression (35% and 54%, respectively). On Axis II, the comorbidity of APD and borderline personality disorder carried a particularly high risk for suicide. The finding of high suicide risk in persons with APD and comorbid substance use disorder and depression was later confirmed by Lesage et al. (1994) in a case–control study of 75 young men who committed suicide.

A research group at the National Public Health Institute in Finland studied the 53 registered suicides in youths aged 13 to 19 years during 1987–1988 (Marttunen, Aro, Henriksson, & Lönnqvist, 1994). Antisocial behavior was reported in 45% of the boys and 33% of the girls, although only 9 adolescents met the full APD criteria. Previous suicide attempts were frequent, particularly among those with more antisocial behavior. In a 19-year follow-up study of 1,056 antisocial adolescents in Sweden, 11.7% of the boys and 7.6% of the girls had died "sudden violent deaths" (Rydelius, 1988).

Taken together, the evidence shows that APD is connected with suicide attempts, suicide, and "sudden violent deaths," particularly when it is comorbid with substance use disorders, depression, and borderline personality disorder.

PSYCHOPATHY AND ANXIETY DISORDERS

Increased prevalence rates were found for panic disorder, agoraphobia, social phobia, and obsessive–compulsive disorder among persons with APD in both the ECA study (Robins & Regier, 1991) and the Edmonton study (Swanson et al., 1994). In Coid's (1992) sample of criminal psychopaths, 17% had an anxiety disorder. Hart and Hare (1989) found that 6.2% of incarcerated men had anxiety disorders, but the odds ratio of having such disorders showed no difference between men with high and low scores on the original PCL.

Weiss et al. (1983) compared features of anxiety among psychopaths and matched controls in their study. Among the 524 psychopaths, 24.2% had some degree of anxiety, and among the controls, 26.0% were somewhat anxious (n.s.). When the psychopaths with anxiety ($n = 127$) were compared to those without ($n = 397$), the former were a more disturbed group. They had higher scores on the following symptom clusters: "agitated depression," "difficulties in intellectual functioning," and "neurotic sensitivity." Suicidal thoughts were also significantly more frequent in the anxious (29.9%) than in the nonanxious (19.9%) psychopaths. Presence of anxiety did not influence the length of stay in hospital for the psychopaths, whereas those with depression had longer stays (see above).

These findings clearly demonstrate that Cleckley (1976) was wrong when he stated that psychopaths did not show manifest anxiety. On the other hand, anxiety disorders are seldom the most prominent problems of psychopaths.

PSYCHOPATHY AND OTHER PERSONALITY DISORDERS

Comorbidity among DSM-III/DSM-III-R personality disorders is a well-established fact (Oldham et al., 1992). In a sample of 171 hospitalized patients with personality disorders, I (Dahl, 1990) found 34 patients with APD (19.9%), of whom 24 (70.6%) also had comorbid personality disorders. In the comorbid patients, histrionic ($n = 13$), borderline ($n = 13$), and schizotypal ($n = 10$) personality disorders were the most frequent comorbid disorders, whereas narcissistic, avoidant, and schizoid personality disorders were infrequent. Ten patients with APD had no comorbid personality disorder, and the comorbid patients had a mean of 2.1 personality disorders each.

In his sample of criminal psychopaths, Coid (1992) found an even higher rate of comorbidity, with a mean of 3.6 personality disorders per subject. Fewer than 2% of his sample had only one personality disorder.

From these studies, we can conclude that among the more severely ill persons with APD, comorbidity with several personality disorders in Clusters A and B is very common. I have taken this (Dahl, 1990) as support for a core borderline syndrome that fulfills Kernberg's (1967) structural diagnosis of borderline personality organization. As stated above in the section on suicide, the comorbidity of APD and borderline personality disorder seems to carry a particularly high risk of suicide, especially in women.

PSYCHOPATHY AND SUBSTANCE USE DISORDERS

Clearly, the most common and complex comorbidity of psychopathy is that with substance use disorders. In the ECA study, some form of substance use disorder was reported in 83.6% of persons with APD, which gives an odds ratio of 29.6 (Regier et al., 1990; see Table 18.4). This high proportion of comorbidity should be understood in the context that substance abuse is one of the major DSM-III diagnostic criteria for APD. Substance misuse also tended to be more severe in the APD group. The odds ratio for any substance dependence was 21.1, in contrast to a ratio of 3.2 for substance abuse only. The highest odds ratio for APD was found among those using cocaine (11.0), whereas the ratios were nearly the same for those using opiates (4.8), barbiturates (4.5), and hallucinogens (5.0). The lowest odds ratios were found in persons using marijuana (2.3) and amphetamines (2.9). The Edmonton study (Swanson et al., 1994) reported approximately the same prevalence ratios for substance use disorders. Among person in prisons in the ECA study, the odds ratios were lower for substance use disorders comorbid with APD (Table 18.5), mainly due to the fact that substance use disorders were also common among prisoners without APD (Regier et al., 1990).

Looking at comorbidity the other way around, Flynn, Craddock, Luckey, Hubbard, and Dunteman (1996) found that 39.3% of 7,402 substance-dependent patients had a diagnosis of APD, with the highest prevalence in those with multiple or combined substance dependence.

The interpretation of these comorbidity findings, however, is complicated by questions about the independence of these diagnoses. Some of the diagnostic criteria for APD and substance use disorders are almost equivalent. The question of causality is also com-

TABLE 18.4. Lifetime Prevalence (%) and Odds Ratio (OR) of Substance Use Disorders in Persons with APD

Comorbid disorder	Lifetime prevalence	OR
Any substance use or dependence	83.6	29.6
Any alcohol diagnosis	73.6	21.0
Any alcohol dependence	51.5	14.7
Alcohol abuse only	22.1	5.4
Any other drug diagnosis	42.0	13.4
Any other drug dependence	30.8	15.6
Other drug abuse only	11.2	5.2

Note. The data are from Regier et al. (1990).

TABLE 18.5. Lifetime Prevalence (%) and Odds Ratio (OR) of
Substance Use Disorders in Prisoners with APD

Comorbid disorder	Lifetime prevalence	OR
Any substance use disorder	89.2	5.2
Any alcohol disorder	73.8	3.1
Any other drug disorder	73.6	3.3

Note. The data are from Regier et al. (1990).

plicated, as pointed out by Gerstley, Alterman, McLellan, and Woody (1990). Antisocial behaviors that fulfill the criteria for APD can result from a substance use disorder; should the comorbidity then just be seen as a complication of, or an expression of the severity of, the substance use disorder? DSM-III stated that the APD criteria should count "regardless of the extent to which some of the antisocial behavior may be a consequence of the Substance Use Disorder, e.g., illegal selling of drugs, or the assaultive behavior associated with Alcohol Intoxication" (American Psychiatric Association, 1980, p. 319). No revision of this statement was given in DSM-III-R. DSM-IV states:

> When antisocial behavior in an adult is associated with a Substance-Related Disorder, the diagnosis of [APD] is not made unless the signs of [APD] were also present during childhood and have continued into adulthood. When substance use and antisocial behavior both began in childhood and continued into adulthood, both a Substance-Related Disorder and [APD] should be diagnosed if the criteria for both are met, even though some antisocial acts may be a consequence of the Substance-Related Disorder (e.g., illegal selling of drugs or thefts to obtain money for drugs). (American Psychiatric Association, 1994, pp. 648–649)

ICD-10 does not specify anything concerning this problem, but the criteria for substance use disorders and dyssocial personality disorder are not equivalent to the same extent as in the DSM system.

A possible solution to the definition problem is to use the PCL-R as a measurement of psychopathy in patients with substance use disorders, since it has been shown with the original PCL that substance abuse is related to the general antisocial factor (Factor 2) but not to the interpersonal factor (Factor 1) (Smith & Newman, 1990).

Another way of looking at this problem in patients with substance use disorders is to study to what extent the patients fulfill both the child conduct criteria and the adult criteria of APD. Cottler, Price, Compton, and Mager (1995), confirming the findings of Brooner, Schmidt, Felch, and Bigelow (1992), demonstrated that 37% of patients with substance abuse fulfilled only the adult criteria for APD. They argued that this could be seen as a late-onset form of APD in patients with substance abuse, and that these patients showed a better treatment response than those who fulfilled both parts of the APD criteria set.

Generally, comorbid APD predicts a poorer prognosis in patients with substance use disorders. However, it has been demonstrated that in such comorbid patients the presence of major depressive disorder in addition improves the outcome at follow-up. This has been shown for patients who abuse alcohol (Liskow, Powell, Nickel, & Penick, 1990) and for those who are addicted to opiates (Woody, McLellan, & O'Brien, 1985).

CONCLUSIONS

This chapter has amply demonstrated the following:

- Psychopathy means that there is a high risk of comorbid mental disorders' also being present.
- The presence of comorbid disorders influences psychopathy as to prognosis, treatment response, and the risk for violence and suicide.
- Because of this, all patients with psychopathy should receive a careful examination for personality disorders, clinical syndromes (Axis I), and behavior (especially criminality, occupation, and relationships with others) (Dolan & Coid, 1993).

REFERENCES

American Psychiatric Association. (1980). *Diagnostic and statistical manual of mental disorders* (3rd ed.). Washington, DC: Author.

American Psychiatric Association. (1994). *Diagnostic and statistical manual of mental disorders* (4th ed.). Washington, DC: Author.

Bagley, C., Jacobson, S., & Rehin, A. (1976). Completed suicide: A taxonomic analysis of clinical and social data. *Psychological Medicine, 6,* 429–438.

Black, D. W., Baumgard, C. H., & Bell, S. E. A 16- to 45-year follow-up of 71 men with antisocial personality disorder. *Comprehensive Psychiatry, 36,* 130–140.

Brooner, R. K., Schmidt, C. W., Felch, I. J., & Bigelow, G. E. (1992). Antisocial behavior of intravenous drug abusers: implications for diagnosis of antisocial personality disorder. *American Journal of Psychiatry 149,* 482–487.

Cleckley, H. (1976). *The mask of sanity* (5th ed.). St. Louis, MO: C. V. Mosby.

Cloninger, C. R., & Guze, S. B. (1970). Psychiatric illness and female criminality: The role of sociopathy and hysteria in the antisocial woman. *American Journal of Psychiatry, 127,* 303–311.

Coid, J. W. (1992). DSM-III diagnosis in criminal psychopaths: A way forward. *Criminal Behavior and Mental Health, 2,* 78–94.

Coid, J. W. (1993). An affective syndrome in psychopaths with borderline personality disorder. *British Journal of Psychiatry, 16,* 641–650.

Cottler, L. B., Price, R. K., Compton, W. M., & Mager, D. E. (1995). Subtypes of adult antisocial behavior among drug abusers. *Journal of Nervous Mental Disease, 183,* 154–161.

Dahl, A. A. (1987). *Borderline disorders: A comparative sample of hospitalized patients* [Published doctoral dissertation]. Oslo: University of Oslo.

Dahl, A. A. (1990). Empirical evidence for a core borderline syndrome. *Journal of Personality Disorders, 4,* 192–202.

Dolan, B., & Coid, J. (1993). *Psychopathic and antisocial personality disorders: Treatment and research issues.* London: Gaskell.

Dunaif, S. L., & Hoch, P. H. (1955). Pseudopsychopathic schizophrenia. In P. H. Hoch & J. Zubin (Eds.), *Psychiatry and the law* (pp. 108–121). New York: Grune & Stratton.

Eronen, M., Tiihonen, J., & Hakola, P. (1996). Schizophrenia and homicidal behavior. *Schizophrenia Bulletin, 22,* 83–89.

Flynn, P. M., Craddock, S. G., Luckey, J. W., Hubbard, R. L., Dunteman, G. H. (1996). Comorbidity of antisocial personality and mood disorders among psychoactive substance-dependent treatment clients. *Journal of Personality Disorders, 10,* 56–67.

Garvey, M. J., & Spoden, F. (1980). Suicide attempts in antisocial personality disorder. *Comprehensive Psychiatry, 21,* 146–149.

Frances, A. J. (1990). The DSM-III personality disorders section: A commentary. *American Journal of Psychiatry, 147,* 1439–1448.

Gerstley, L. J., Alterman, A. I., McLellan, A. T., & Woody, G. E. (1990). Antisocial personality disorder in patients with substance use disorders: A problematic diagnosis. *American Journal of Psychiatry, 47,* 173–177.

Hare, R. D. (1983). Diagnosis of antisocial personality disorder in two prison populations. *American Journal of Psychiatry, 140,* 887–890.

Harpur, T. J., Hart, S. D., & Hare, R. D. (1994). Personality of the psychopath. In P.T. Costa & T. A. Widiger (Eds.), *Personality disorders and the five-factor model of personality* (pp. 149–173). New York: American Psychological Association Press.

Hart, S. D., & Hare, R. D. (1989). Discriminant validity of the Psychopathy Checklist in a forensic psychiatric population. *Psychological Assessment, 1,* 211–218.

Hart, S. D., Hare, R. D., & Harpur, T. J. (1993). The Psychopathy Checklist—Revised: An overview for researchers and clinicians. In J. Rosen & P. McReynolds (Eds.), *Advances in psychological assessment* (Vol. 8, pp. 103–130). New York: Plenum Press.

Hesselbrock, M. N., Meyer, R. E., & Keener, J. J. (1985). Psychopathology in hospitalized alcoholics. *Archives of General Psychiatry, 42,* 1050–1553.

Hodgins, S., & Côté, G. (1993). Major mental disorder and antisocial personality disorder: A criminal combination. *Bulletin of the American Academy of Psychiatry and the Law, 21,* 155–160.

Hodgins, S., Mednick, S. A., Brennan, P. A., Schulsinger, F., & Engberg, M. (1996). Mental disorders and crime: Evidence from a Danish birth cohort. *Archives of General Psychiatry, 53,* 489–496.

Jordan, B. K., Schlenger, W. E., Fairbank, J. A., & Caddell, J. M. (1996). Prevalence of psychiatric disorders among incarcerated women: II. Convicted felons entering prison. *Archives of General Psychiatry, 53,* 513–519.

Kernberg, O. F. (1967). Borderline personality organization. *Journal of the American Psychoanalytic Association, 15,* 641–685.

Kessler, R. C. (1995). Epidemiology of psychiatric comorbidity. In M. T. Tsuang, M. Tohen, & G. E. P. Zahner (Eds.), *Textbook in psychiatric epidemiology* (pp. 179–198). New York: Wiley.

Kessler, R., McGonagle, K. A., Zhao, S., Nelson, C. B., Hughes, M., Eshelman, S., Wittchen, H.-U., & Kendler, K. S. (1994). Lifetime and 12 month prevalence of DSM-III-R psychiatric disorders in the United States. *Archives of General Psychiatry, 51,* 8–19.

Klein, M., Wonderlich, S., & Shea, M. T. (1993). Models of relationships between personality and depression: Toward a framework for theory and research. In M. H. Klein, D. J. Kupfer, & M. T. Shea (Eds.), *Personality and depression* (pp. 1–54). New York: Guilford Press.

Lesage, A. D., Boyer, R., Grunberg, F., Vanier, C., Morisette, R., Mønard-Buteau, C., & Loyer, M. (1994). Suicide and mental disorders: A case-control study of young men. *American Journal of Psychiatry, 151,* 1063–1068.

Lilienfeld, S. O., VanValkenburg, C., Larntz, K., & Akiskal, H. S. (1986). The relationship of histrionic personality disorder to antisocial personality and somatization disorder. *American Journal of Psychiatry, 143,* 718–722.

Liskow, B., Powell, B. J., Nickel, E. J., & Penick, E. (1990). Diagnostic subgroups of antisocial alcoholics: Outcome at 1 year. *Comprehensive Psychiatry, 31,* 549–556.

Marttunen, M. J., Aro, H. M., Henriksson, M. M., & Lönnqvist, J. K. (1994). Antisocial behaviour in adolescent suicide. *Acta Psychiatrica Scandinavica, 89,* 167–173.

Miles, C. P. (1977). Conditions predisposing to suicide. *Journal of Nervous and Mental Disease, 164,* 231–246.

Modestin, J., & Ammann, R. (1996). Mental disorders and criminality: Male schizophrenia. *Schizophrenia Bulletin, 22,* 69–82.

Oldham, J. M., Skodol, A. E., Kellman, H. D., Hyler, S. E., Rosnick, L., & Davies, M. (1992). Diagnosis of DSM-III-R personality disorders by two structured interviews: Patterns of comorbidity. *American Journal of Psychiatry, 149,* 213–220.

Raine, A. (1993). *The psychopathology of crime*. San Diego, CA: Academic Press.

Rasmussen, K., Levander, S., & Sletvold, H. (1995). Aggressive and non-aggressive schizophrenics: Symptom profile and neuropsychological differences. *Psychology, Crime and Law, 2*, 119–129.

Regier, D. A., Farmer, M. E., Rae, D. S., Locke, B. Z., Keith, S. J., Judd, L. L., & Goodwin, F. K. (1990). Comorbidity of mental disorders with alcohol and other drug abuse: Results from the Epidemiologic Catchment Area (ECA) study. *Journal of the American Medical Association, 264*, 2511–2518.

Rich, C. L., & Runeson, B. S. (1992). Similarities in diagnostic comorbidity between suicide among young people in Sweden and the United States. *Acta Psychiatrica Scandinavica, 86*, 335–339.

Robins, E., Gentry, K. A., Munoz, R. A., & Marte, S. (1977). A contrast of the three more common illnesses with the ten less common in a study and 18-month follow-up of 314 emergency room patients. *Archives of General Psychiatry, 34*, 269–281.

Robins, L. N. (1966). *Deviant children grown up*. Baltimore: Williams & Wilkins.

Robins, L. N. (1986). Epidemiology of antisocial personality. In G. L. Klerman, M. M. Weissman, P. S. Appelbaum, & L. H. Roth (Eds.), *Social, epidemiological, and legal psychiatry* (pp. 231–244). Philadelphia: J. B. Lippincott.

Robins, L. N., & Regier, D. A. (Eds.). (1991). *Psychiatric disorders in America*. New York: Free Press.

Robins, L. N., Tipp, J., & Przybeck, T. (1991). Antisocial personality. In L. N. Robins & D. A. Regier (Eds.), *Psychiatric disorders in America* (pp. 258–290). New York: Free Press.

Rydelius, P.-A. (1988). The development of antisocial behaviour and sudden violent death. *Acta Psychiatrica Scandinavica, 77*, 398–403.

Smith, G. R., Golding, J. M., Kashner, M., & Rost, K. (1991). Antisocial personality disorder in primary care patients with somatization disorder. *Comprehensive Psychiatry, 32*, 367–372.

Smith, S. S., & Newman, J. P. (1990). Alcohol and drug abuse–dependence disorders in psychopathic and non-psychopathic criminal offenders. *Journal of Abnormal Psychology, 99*, 430–439.

Swanson, M. C. J., Bland, R. C., & Newman, S. C. (1994). Antisocial personality disorders. *Acta Psychiatrica Scandinavica, 89*(Suppl. 376), 63–70.

Swartz, M., Landerman, R., George, L. K., Blazer, D. G., & Escobar, J. (1991). Somatization disorder. In L. N. Robins & D. A. Regier (Eds.), *Psychiatric disorders in America* (pp. 220—257). New York: Free Press.

Weiss, J. M. A., Davis, D., Hedlund, J. L., & Cho, D. W. (1983). The dysphoric psychopath: a comparison of 524 cases of antisocial personality disorder with matched controls. *Comprehensive Psychiatry, 24*, 355–369.

Widiger, T. A., Cadoret, R., Hare, R. D., Robins, L., Rutherford, M., Zanarini, M., Alterman, A., Apple, M., Corbitt, E., Forth, A., Hart, S. D., Kultermann, J., Woody, G., & Frances, A. J. (1996). DSM-IV Antisocial Personality Disorder Field Trial. *Journal of Abnormal Psychology, 105*, 3–16.

Wittchen, H.-U. (1996). Critical issues in the evaluation of comorbidity of psychiatric disorders. *British Journal of Psychiatry, 168*(Suppl. 30), 9–16.

Woodruff, R. A., Guze, S. G., & Clayton, P. J. (1971). The medical and psychiatric implications of antisocial personality (sociopathy). *Diseases of the Nervous System, 32*, 712–714.

Woody, G. E., McLellan, T., & O'Brien, C. P. (1985). Sociopathy and psychotherapy outcome. *Archives of General Psychiatry, 42*, 1081–1086.

Zimmerman, M., Pfohl, B., Coryell, W. H., Corenthal, C., & Stangl, D. (1991). Major depression and personality disorder. *Journal of Affective Disorders, 22*, 199–210.

19

Psychopathy in the Pedophile

DARWIN DORR

This chapter presents the thesis that the majority of pedophiles are psychopathic, or manifest to a significant degree the psychological characteristics of psychopathy. Stated conservatively, there appears to be a high rate of comorbidity between the two forms of behavioral disorder. Asserted more boldly, it is argued that pedophilia may represent a special case, or subcase, of psychopathy. The primary aims of the psychopath and the pedophile are the same: to dominate, to use, and to subjugate another person in service of the grandiose self. The major difference between the two is that in the pedophile, the object of the predation is a child and the overt behavioral manifestation of the pathology is sexual. The thesis of this chapter is that the dynamics of psychopathy are clearly evident in the majority of child molesters. Extrapolation of our knowledge of the psychological dynamics of psychopathy may deepen our understanding of the pedophile, and thus may guide our diagnostic and treatment interventions.

It is notable in large numbers of works on the pedophile that the terms "antisocial personality," "psychopathy," and "psychopath"[1] are never mentioned. It would appear that many authors recognize no link between psychopathy and pedophilia whatsoever. One explanation might be that many workers in the area of pedophilia are in nonclinical fields, such as criminal justice, sociology, or counseling; thus, they are not accustomed to thinking in terms of formal diagnostic categories, or even diagnostic conceptualizations. In my view, this limits their ability to theorize about the pedophilic personality. Clinicians know much about the dynamics of the psychopath, and I am asserting that many of these elements of psychopathy are also present in the pedophile.

The position argued in this chapter is approached from four vantage points: (1) a comparison of selected general descriptions of the personality characteristics of pedophiles and psychopaths found in the extant literature on child molesters; (2) an examination of the personality characteristics of the pedophile, using a scaling procedure called Ego Function Assessment (EFA); (3) a review of psychometric assessment of pedophiles with the Minnesota Multiphasic Personality Inventory (MMPI); and (4) an expansion of

Millon's conceptualization of the antisocial personality to encompass the psychology of the pedophile.

Before beginning, some matters of definition and delineation should be addressed. First, it is acknowledged that pedophilia, like the majority of psychiatric diagnostic categories, is heterogeneous. There may be some cases of pedophilia in which psychopathic dynamics play a minimal role. For example, in the case of the regressed pedophile (Groth, 1978), wherein the perpetrator under conditions of stress and regression turns temporarily to a minor child, psychopathy may play a minimal role in the behavioral dynamics. Even in this case, though, it can be argued that some psychopathic dynamics are present.

A related matter concerns the representative model employed. This chapter uses a prototype model. According to Horowitz, Wright, Lowenstein, and Parad (1981), "a prototype is a kind of theoretical ideal, a theoretical standard against which real people can be evaluated. The more closely the person approximates this idea, the more the person typifies the concept" (p. 568). The prototype model acknowledges that some cases will be less similar to the standard of comparison than others. The approach is based on the concept of a continuum of goodness of fit and provides flexibility in determining classification.

The *Diagnostic and Statistical Manual of Mental Disorders,* fourth edition (DSM-IV; American Psychiatric Association, 1994), classifies pedophilia within the category of the paraphilias. Paraphilias are defined as sexual disorders in which there are strong, recurring sexually stimulating urges, fantasies, or behaviors usually involving (1) objects other than humans, (2) humiliation or pain for the partner or the self, or (3) children or other nonconsensual partners.

The DSM-IV diagnostic criteria for pedophilia are as follows. First, for 6 months or more, the person has had strong, recurring sexually stimulating urges, fantasies, or behaviors involving sexual activity with a child or children below the age of puberty (usually 13 years of age or younger). Second, the sexual urges, fantasies, or behaviors result in clinically meaningful difficulties or distress at work, in social contexts, or in other major areas of functioning. Third, the person is 16 years of age or older, and is at least 5 years older than the child or children in question. Individuals in late adolescence who maintain long-standing sexual relationships with 12- or 13-year-olds are not classified as pedophiles. Specifiers include the pedophile's being attracted to males, females, or both sexes; the pedophilia's being confined to incest; and the disorder's status as an exclusive type (attraction only to children) or a nonexclusive type (involvement with mature persons as well as children).

This last distinction parallels the distinction made by Groth, Hobson, and Gary (1982) between "regressed" and "fixated" pedophiles. Regressed pedophiles are described as individuals whose primary sexual orientation is toward adults of the opposite sex; under conditions of stress, however, a regressed pedophile may psychologically regress to an earlier psychosocial age and subsequently engage in sex with children. In the fixated pedophile, sexual thoughts and fantasies focus exclusively on children.

A further distinction is sometimes made (Lothstein, 1990) between "pedophilia" and "ephebophilia." Pedophiles are adults who experience sexual urges and sexually arousing fantasies regarding prepubescent children. The ephebophile is an adult who experiences recurrent sexual urges and sexually arousing fantasies regarding adolescents. The latter distinction is useful, because the DSM-IV classification does not list adult sexual involvement with an adolescent as a diagnosable condition. However, clinically, there should be as much concern about sexual abuse of teenage children by adults as there is about sexual abuse of younger children. The amount of harm done to an adolescent victim can be as great as that done to a younger child.

For the sake of simplicity, this chapter does not employ the pedophilia–ephebophilia distinction. Instead, the term "pedophilia" is used in its broad sense to encompass adult sexual involvement with any minor, whether prepubescent or adolescent. The reason for using the broader term is that in either case there has been a failure of adult responsibility and a violation of trust that can be devastating to the minor involved. This position is consistent with the general view expressed in this chapter: It is not only the sexual activity that is traumatic for the youngster, but also the violation of trust and profound failure to maintain a healthy psychological holding environment in which the child can be protected during development.

THE PSYCHOLOGICAL SEQUELAE OF CHILD SEXUAL ABUSE

The broad definition of pedophilia used in this chapter encompasses an act in which an adult—in most cases, a male (although there are female pedophiles)—presses his or her sexual desires onto a minor or, in some cases, fails to resist sexual play advances by the child. Moreover, in some cases, the child is also traumatized by actual physical harm. Often, however, the greatest damage results from the violation of a child's right to a basic trust in the environment. This first stage of Erikson's psychosocial stages pits trust against mistrust. Basic trust implies a perceived correlation between one's needs and one's world. If a child's world is reasonably predictable and orderly, the child develops a sense of balance between trust and mistrust. This in turn leads to the development of hope, a component of ego strength and a basic human virtue without which one cannot survive. Hope is the basis of faith, which is essential for the formation of healthy, mature commitments.

Psychologically healthy, mature adults generally choose adult partners, usually in the context of marriage or some enduring, committed relationship. Healthy adult love relationships are reasonably reciprocal and egalitarian, and are characterized by considerable mutuality and consent. In this light, the act of pedophilia represents a profound failure in object choice. It is impossible to argue that the pedophilic relationship is reciprocal or egalitarian, or that it is characterized by mutuality and consent. Pedophilia is the antithesis of a victimless crime and clearly represents an act of exploitation on the part of the perpetrator. The violation of basic trust, the destructive blurring of ego boundaries, and the massive failure in generativity are likely to produce trauma, whatever the age of the victim.

A case study is employed here to illustrate the position taken regarding the psychological sequelae of pedophilia. The victim was a girl of 12½ years who was just entering puberty. She had severe emotional problems, which included diagnoses of bipolar I disorder and borderline personality disorder. One manifestation of her behavioral difficulties was her failure to control her curiosity regarding sexual play. She approached her stepfather regarding sexual play. The stepfather, instead of engaging in normal, loving limit setting and thus protecting her from her own impulses, acquiesced to her request. The child was devastated—not by the sexual act, but by the failure of the adult to firmly establish a protective parental holding environment for her. After the stepfather served a period of incarceration, parole, and treatment, a plan to reunite the family was attempted. Perhaps driven by a repetition compulsion to test the stepfather's trustworthiness, the child again approached him regarding sexual play. Again he succumbed to her advances and had sex with her, and thus he again failed to establish the boundaries of the parental holding environment. Yet another opportunity to reinforce the sense of basic trust in the relationship was lost. Not surprisingly, the girl began to feel suicidal and was hospitalized. In this case, it was not the actual sex play that was traumatizing. In fact, she related that she enjoyed the sexual encounter. What overwhelmed her was the fact that once again a father figure was incapable of protecting her from her own impulses.

CHARACTERISTICS OF THE PSYCHOPATH

As this volume is devoted entirely to the study of the psychopath, the personality characteristics of the psychopath are reviewed here only briefly. DSM-IV itemizes numerous behaviors associated with the antisocial personality: not conforming to social norms, deceitfulness, lying, conning, impulsivity, not planning ahead, irritability, aggression, recklessness, irresponsibility, rationalization, and lack of remorse about harming others.

Another set of descriptors is contained in the Hare Psychopathy Checklist-Revised (Hare, 1991), which has been used extensively in research and clinical settings. Many of the Hare characteristics have been noted in descriptions of the pedophile. Some of these are pathological lying, cunning and manipulation, lack of remorse or guilt, shallow affect, callous lack of empathy, poor behavioral controls, promiscuous sexual behavior, impulsivity, irresponsibility, failure to accept responsibility for one's actions, and numerous short-term marital relationships (or, in this case, numerous short-term child liaisons).

The DSM and Hare descriptive criteria are unambiguous, are useful, and require no theoretical assumptions. Although DSM and Hare descriptors are utilized herein, I have been influenced also by the theoretical contributions of Kernberg (1984), Yochelson and Samenow (1976), Samenow (1984), and Meloy (1988), which examine the psychodynamics of the psychopathic personality. These authors outline a distinctive sequence of cognitions and emotions in the psychopath that lead to acts of predation. The crux of their work is important to the subject of this chapter in the revelation that pedophilia is most decidedly an act of psychopathic predation.

These authors describe the psychopath's obsession with mastery and being "tops" or "Number 1." The psychopath yearns to preserve this grandiose self-image, yet at some level of awareness the psychopath knows that this positive self-concept is not genuine. That is, it is not earned through competent functioning; instead, it is manufactured through fantasy and self-deception. The psychopath dreads the "opposite" of this grandiose state, which Yochelson and Samenow (1977) have labeled the "zero state." In the zero state, self-esteem plummets to rock bottom. The individual experiences a sense of worthlessness, hopelessness, and futility, in which there is a belief that his or her thoughts and feelings are transparent to others.

This inner emptiness appears to be depressive in nature, yet the primary emotion experienced in this state is actually rage. The rage is fueled by envy and greed for what others have but the psychopath does not have. Yochelson and Samenow (1977) have emphasized that the psychopath envies what others *are* (full human beings with a genuine sense of self-worth), not what others *have*. These authors have explained that "depression in the criminal is basically an angry state in which he blazes at the injustice of the world" (p. 270). The psychopath resents and covets the full humanness of others. Thus, he or she seeks to own (take, steal, possess, conquer) and/or to devalue (destroy, punish, diminish, ruin) the other. In any case, the resulting behavioral pattern is predation—the core characteristic of the psychopath. There is no concern for the fate of the object, and there is no remorse. Instead, in these conditions of anger, frustration, loneliness, and impaired self-esteem, there is a strongly felt sense of deprivation that may precipitate sexual aggression. In the case of the pedophile, it is a minor who is taken, stolen, possessed, conquered, destroyed, punished, diminished, or ruined.

REVIEW OF THE PERSONALITY CHARACTERISTICS OF PEDOPHILES

In view of space limitations, no attempt is made here to be exhaustive in this review of personality characteristics of pedophiles. Instead, well-known works are summarized, and, where appropriate, the parallels between the dynamics of pedophilia and the dynamics of psychopathy are highlighted.

Abel and Osborn (1992) have provided clear evidence that pedophilia is predation. In the examination of pedophilic acts committed by 453 offenders, these authors found that these individuals had molested 67,112 victims, resulting in 106,916 acts of child molestation. Simple arithmetic reveals that these figures yield 148 victims and 236 acts per pedophile. It would be unreasonable to suggest strongly that these acts occurred by chance. The sheer numbers suggest strongly that these perpetrators were actively preying on their intended victims.

Mayer (1985) has emphasized that the dynamics of power, including control and dominance, prevail in the psychology of child molesters. She also notes their difficulty with anger control and anger expression. In addition, Mayer has found that pedophiles view children as objects or possessions without rights. She points out that certain personality types appear to be at high risk for incestuous relationships. These include individuals with low impulse control, low frustration tolerance, frustrated dependency needs, and needs for immediate gratification of their desires. Mayer has noted as well that alcohol abuse plays a role in the cycle of sexual abuse. Furthermore, she suggests that approximately 80% of pedophiles were themselves molested as children. She theorizes that pedophiles perpetuate abuse because of their own displaced anger. That is, molesters continue to harbor anger toward the perpetrators who originally molested them, but displace this anger onto even younger children.

Mayer goes on to describe molesters' tendency to use rationalization, minimization, and denial. She observes that often pedophiles will claim that their own behavior is perfectly normal, and that frequently they will blame the children for having behaved seductively. An overall lack of social conscience in a pedophile's actions is noted, and low frustration tolerance and manipulativeness are seen as well. In addition, the pedophile's distrustfulness and inability to express guilt or remorse are described. Mayer's descriptions of the pedophile, in short, are very similar to descriptions of the psychopath.

In an assessment of the use of autobiographies in the treatment of sex offenders, Long, Wuesthoff, and Pithers (1989) note the presence of negative emotional states preceding sexual offenses. They observe that men who have committed sex offenses often describe antecedent feelings of loneliness, worthlessness, depression, anger, or resentment. Although the authors do not use Yochelson and Samenow's term "zero state," their observations appear to describe it very well.

Jenkins-Hall (1989) has argued that decision making of sexual offenders is very similar to that of criminals. Citing both Hare's and Yochelson and Samenow's work, Jenkins-Hall states: "Sexual offenders have the same flaws in their decision making as other criminals. They have problems foreseeing long-term consequences (positive or negative), they do not generate or weigh alternative solutions, and they are unaware of the impact of their behaviors on their victims" (p. 161).

In the first stage of treatment planning with a sexual offender, Jenkins-Hall generates an assessment of the offender's cognitive method of criminal decision making, including the inability to weigh pros and cons and the carefully planned course of predation. The psychopath's inability to delay gratification is compared to that of the sexual offender's similar lack of control. Jenkins-Hall does not directly articulate that sexual offenders are psychopathic. However, the descriptions of offenders and the treatments that are advocated make it evident that there is a great similarity between the characteristics of the psychopath and the characteristics of the sexual offender, including the pedophile.

Marlatt (1989) has described the inflexibility and persistent urges and cravings experienced by pedophiles in terms of "feeding the PIG" (the PIG being the "problem of immediate gratification"). Marlatt cites the case of "Bob," a repeat offender trying to follow the advice of his therapist, who had encouraged him to establish an adult dating relationship. Bob asked a convenience store clerk for a date; not altogether surprisingly, he was turned down. Instead of viewing the fact that getting a date with a stranger who works in a convenience store is a low-probability event, Bob felt that the clerk was "one up" and that he himself was "one down." He began to feel increasingly negative. He smoked marijuana and began to explore sexual fantasies in which he was a powerful seducer, virile and full of sexual prowess. Bob fantasized about overturning his "one down" status into "one up" superiority, and imagined feeling back in control, back in power. Feeling angry and aggressive, Bob left his apartment to "look for some action." He was operating fully in the predator mode as he drove by a schoolyard. The PIG had to be fed, and the result was that an 11-year-old girl was raped. Marlatt describes Bob's negative emotional states during the time when he believed he was "one down." These included feeling depressed, jealous, angry, and rejected (zero state?)—conditions that are known to "whet the PIG's appetite" (p. 228). The sequence of psychological and behavioral events would appear to be nearly isomorphic with the descriptions of the sequence and progression of cognitions and emotions typically observed in the psychopath.

Pithers, Martin, and Cumming (1989) have emphasized the failure of sexual offenders to have empathy for their victims. They explain that the victims may represent faceless, impersonal entities—objects that are devalued or, at the least, dehumanized. The common cognitive distortions employed by offenders to justify sexual aggression are also cited; for example, an incestuous father may rationalize that it would be best for his daughter to have her first sexual experience with someone who loves her. Again, these descriptions are very similar to those commonly found in accounts of psychopathic thinking and behavior.

Langevin, Hucker, Ben-Aron, Purins, and Hook (1985) have described the role of force and dominance among pedophiles, and its obverse—the need for the subservience and obedience found in the childlike state. Furthermore, they have found that pedophiles tend to rate adults as overbearing but to rate children as nonthreatening and submissive. They also note that adults wear the mantle of authority, which allows them to tell children what to do and even to hit them in the name of discipline. Pedophilia has been linked to sadism, the phenomenon of gaining pleasure in the process of dominating or controlling another person, in this case, a child. These descriptions sound similar to the descriptions of the roles of force and dominance found in psychopathic behavior, as described, for example, by Yochelson and Samenow (1977).

Prendergast (1991), citing his 30 years of working with sexual offenders, has asserted the following: "In all my years of dealing with sex offenders, both in correctional settings (convicted and sentenced) and in private practice (referred, self-referred, or on probation), I have never encountered a case where sex was the primary motivation" (p. 165). Instead, he identifies the following primary motivations, which may occur singly or in combination: power/domination needs, seductive/acceptance needs, and ritual/undoing needs. Although Prendergast never uses the term "psychopath," he describes the importance to the dynamics of the sex offender of the roles of power, assaultiveness, sexual assaults, sadism, seduction, manipulativeness, cunningness, "psyching out" victims, and undoing—all characteristics of psychopathy.

Finally, Wiederholt (1992) has boldly asserted that sex crimes are rarely sexually motivated. He maintains that sexual offenses, including pedophilia, consist of aggressive acts coupled with the intention of feeling superior to and/or feeling protected by the victim. That is, the act of sexual offense is an act of predation with the intent to defend against a "zero state."

As noted at the beginning of this section, space limitations preclude an exhaustive survey of this literature. However, even this cursory review reveals that many of the descriptions of pedophilic dynamics and behavior are strikingly similar to the descriptions of psychopathic dynamics and behavior. It seems reasonable to conclude that there is a clear overlap between the two forms of disturbance.

FAILURE IN EGO FUNCTIONS

I now assess the thesis of this chapter in the light of ego function assessment. Although many investigators view psychopathy as a failure in the strength of the superego, others (e.g., Dorr & Woodhall, 1986; Blatt & Schichman, 1981) have argued that psychopathy is not merely the result of superego deficit. At its psychological foundations, the disorder is a result of impairment in the development of basic ego functions. Bellak, Hurvich, and Gediman (1973) developed a procedure for the assessment of fundamental ego functions. Their original research with schizophrenic patients employed psychometric scaling of the most widely recognized ego functions, such as reality testing, judgment, thought processing, and object relations. We (Dorr & Woodhall, 1986) employed this scaling procedure, referred to as Ego Function Assessment (EFA), to study a sample of psychopaths well known to us. The psychopaths were found to be decidedly deficient in basic ego functions.

Several of the ego functions have relevance to our understanding of the psychology of the psychopath. A prominent one is judgment. Good judgment depends on good reality testing. If one of the components of reality testing is not adequate, judgment likely will be affected. There are three elements to the EFA Judgment scale. The first is anticipation of probable consequences. The second is exemplified by a pattern of behavior that reflects awareness of consequences. That is, one's behavior should be modified by one's cognitive appraisal of what the consequences might be. Finally, judgment involves an understanding of the appropriateness of behavior in an environmental setting.

It can be argued that pedophiles frequently and generally exhibit extremely poor judgment. The consequences for getting caught are very serious. There are mandatory reporting laws, and the fate of the imprisoned pedophile is notoriously brutal. Yet, the numbers of acts of child molestation continue to be high (Abel & Osborn, 1992)—a fact providing support for the argument that pedophiles show poor judgment.

Another prominent ego function is regulation and control of drives and affects. This dimension consists of a person's ability to tolerate anxiety, depression, disappointment, frustration, and necessity for postponing satisfaction; it refers to modulation of the expression of inner wishes, emotional strivings and urges. The ego must ultimately serve the aims of the id, but to protect the total self, it must do so in a regulated fashion. The adapted person uses cognition, imagery, logic, and the like to harness psychic energy and modulate impulsivity. Regulation requires a need to control expression of impulses. Impulse control does not seem to be a dominant characteristic among samples of pedophiles. Regulation also requires the capacity to delay and control one's behavior. By definition, pedophiles have difficulty controlling sexual and, in many cases, aggressive impulses.

A third ego function is the ability to maintain adequate and accurate object relations. Elements of this dimension are relevant to our understanding of the psychology of the pedophile. For example, one element of the EFA Object Relations scale is the capacity to perceive others as independent entities rather than as extensions of the self. The pedophile uses a child for personal gratification and generally appears to be totally oblivious to the trauma that the act of pedophilia may visit upon the child. Psychopaths have significant deficits in object relatedness, as demonstrated by their deriving pleasure from exercising power over others who are seen as extensions of their own needs and narcissism. The same argument can be made for the object relations deficits observed in the pedophile. In addition, most studies of pedophiles indicate that they do not have loving, reciprocal, healthy relationships with any adults, male or female. This highlights the pedophile's severe deficiencies in object relations.

One of the more important ego functions is reality testing. Reality testing refers to the continuous assessment—sifting, weighing, judging—of the amorphous mass of stimuli bombarding our consciousness. Obviously, there must be some concept of reality present. Reality testing requires the ability to perceive and assess one's phenomenal field accurately, with a minimum of idiosyncratic distortion. The three elements of this dimension are (1) the capacity to make accurate distinction between inner and outer reality; (2) the accuracy of perception of external events; and (3) the accuracy of perception of internal events, including a reflective awareness of the accuracy or distortion of inner reality. Our study (Dorr & Woodhall, 1986) revealed significant deficiencies in reality testing in the psychopathic sample.

In the pedophile, distortion, primitive denial, rationalization, and splitting may seriously compromise reality testing as well. For example, a pedophile I examined in my forensic practice, following an indictment for first-degree sexual intercourse with his 6-year-old stepdaughter, confessed to me with considerable enthusiasm, "She liked sex!" This simple statement revealed his extremely serious deficiency in reality testing. The finding that an adult male with no cognitive impairment believed that a 6-year-old girl would "like" first-degree sexual intercourse exposed a distortion in reality testing that approached psychotic levels. (It also exposed a profound disturbance in the object representation.)

A little-known ego function, "adaptive regression in service of the ego" (ARISE), refers to the ability of the ego to initiate a partial, temporary, and controlled lowering of its own management functions to further its primary purpose, which is adaptation. The ARISE function allows a process of controlled regression, which is followed by reintegration (usually at a higher level). In this way, the ego, or self, can rest and revive in play or nonproductive activities.

We (Dorr & Woodhall, 1986) found that the regression exhibited by our psychopaths was not adaptive. Indeed, it was highly maladaptive. In a similar way, it can be seen that the regression of the pedophile is also maladaptive. Pedophiles are generally described as childish, infantile, and impulsive, as well as maladaptive. Groth (1978) has classified pedophiles into two subtypes. One subtype, the regressed offender, is one who initially chooses adult partners for sexual gratification, but who, under situational stress, will regress and engage in pedophilic behavior as a means of coping. Hence, there is not only a failure in *adaptive* regression, but a *pathological* regression. Groth's second subtype, the fixated pedophile, is one whose pedophilic behavior is inflexible and as such is entrenched in a maladaptive regression. Thus, in both types we encounter serious deficits in adaptive regression.

Parenthetically, Kegan (1986) has proposed that the psychopath presents with a developmental delay in which cognitive, affective, and interpersonal processes are like those of a child about 10 years of age. The psychopath shows great concern for personal needs and little consideration for the needs of others. In actuality, personal needs are usually satisfied by manipulating and controlling the behavior of others. This description could easily be applied to most pedophiles as well.

Another ego function is defensive functioning. Healthy individuals are fortified by sound armamentaria of higher-level defenses, such as repression and sublimation. By contrast, lower-level defenses (e.g., splitting, primitive denial, rationalization, avoidance, and quasi-delusions, as well as acting out) are primitive defenses. These lower-level, primitive defenses are generally employed by the psychopath, and they appear prominently in pedophilic functioning as well.

In summary, a brief review of ego functions suggests multiple deficits in both the pedophile and the psychopath—deficits that are not dissimilar.

THE MMPI OF THE PEDOPHILE

In this section, I review the psychometric evidence of the relationship between psychopathy and child sexual abuse. Not surprisingly, the most common instrument used to assess this population is the MMPI (now the MMPI-2) (Hathaway & McKinley, 1967; Butcher, Dahlstrom, Graham, Tellegen, & Kaemmer, 1989). The classic MMPI profile of the psychopath is the 4-9 codetype (Lewak, Marks, & Nelson, 1990). However, the Psychopathic Deviate (4) scale alone would seem to be of considerable relevance to the understanding of the psychology of the pedophile, because of its tendency to measure impulsivity, lack of remorse, lack of foresight or judgment, failure to respond to punishment, and a host of other variables associated with psychopathy.

It is understood that the 4 scale is multidimensional and that many conditions contribute to its elevation. However, because of the extensive use of the MMPI and the utility of the Psychopathic Deviate scale in identifying global delinquent patterns, it seems reasonable to investigate the use of the MMPI with the psychopath, focusing particularly on the 4 scale.

To begin this review, we need to examine what seems to be a growing misunderstanding about the use of the MMPI with pedophiles. McAnulty, Adams, and Wright (1994) have written that their studies, together with several others (see below), have shown that the MMPI is of limited utility in identifying alleged child molesters.

These studies are of two types. The first type attempts to use the MMPI to distinguish among various kinds of sexual offenders as well as nonsexual offenders (i.e., other criminals). The second type of study attempts to identify various MMPI profiles among subtypes of pedophiles. McAnulty et al. (1994) and many others have concluded that pedophilia is heterogeneous and that the MMPI is of little use when employed with this population. According to McAnulty and colleagues,

> In summary, the findings corroborate those of other studies . . . in showing that the MMPI is of limited usefulness in identifying alleged child molesters. Attempts to identify men who display sexual attraction to children using the MMPI cannot be justified. Among accused child molesters and pedophiles, MMPI profile heterogeneity is the rule rather than the exception. The utility of the MMPI-2 . . . in the identification of paraphilic attraction to children remains to be established. (p. 184)

McAnulty et al. made this argument because the MMPI has not received high marks in distinguishing among the many variations and manifestations of pedophilia—for example, distinguishing between pedophiles who prefer boys versus girls, ones who prefer older children versus younger children, aggressive versus nonaggressive pedophiles, deniers versus admitters, regressed versus fixated pedophiles, and so forth. However, to expect that the MMPI would be capable of making these fine distinctions is totally unrealistic. This failure does not represent a failure in the test; rather, it reflects that the questions the test is expected to answer are unreasonable.

It is not the intent of this chapter to review all of the literature on the use of the MMPI with pedophiles. Instead, I briefly summarize findings in the literature. The most common finding in the vast majority of empirical articles investigating the use of the MMPI with child molesters is a substantial elevation on the Psychopathic Deviate scale. The fact that the MMPI does not discriminate among various subtypes of pedophiles, and often does not discriminate pedophiles from other forms of sexual offenders, does not negate its use with this population. No competent clinician would rely only on the MMPI or any other single test to make these very fine distinctions. In fact, it is quite unreasonable to anticipate that the MMPI could accurately identify the broad number of manifestations that pedophilia may take. Any experienced clinician will take a multitude of data points, in a clinical equivalent of a multiple-regression prediction project, when making judgments regarding the likelihood of pedophilia in any of its various forms. A brief review of selected articles on the use of the MMPI in the assessment of pedophiles now follows.

In 1978, Langevin, Paitich, Freeman, Mann, and Handy attempted to use the MMPI and the Sixteen Personality Factor Questionnaire (16 PF) to distinguish among different types of sexual abusers. Not surprisingly, they had difficulty making fine distinctions among types of offenders. However, homosexual pedophiles, heterosexual pedophiles, and incest perpetrators all had substantial elevations on the Psychopathic Deviate scale.

In 1984, Vaupel and Goeke attempted to use the MMPI to distinguish between incest perpetrators who would admit their guilt and those who would not admit it. The MMPI was not able to make this distinction. However, an examination of the mean *T* scores indicated that the Psychopathic Deviate scale was represented as the highest elevation in both the admitter and the nonadmitter groups.

Erickson, Luxenberg, Walbek, and Seely (1987) found that the Psychopathic Deviate scale was elevated in the majority of cases they examined. In examining a sample of felony sex offenders, 80% of whom were charged with molestation, they found that denial tended to lower the MMPI profile. However, in cases of partial or even full denial, the MMPI Psychopathic Deviate scale was still the highest of all the basic clinical scales.

One prominent series of studies was carried out by Hall and colleagues (Hall, Maiuro, Vitaliano, & Proctor, 1986; Hall, 1989; Hall, Graham, & Shepherd, 1991; and Hall, Shepherd, & Mudrak, 1992). In the Hall et al. (1986) study of men who sexually assaulted children, the 4 scale was the highest of the basic clinical scales, with a mean T score of 75.25 and a standard deviation of 12.19. The 11 most common 2-point codetypes were 4-8/8-4, 7-8/8-7, 2-4/4-2, 4-9/9-4, 4-5/5-4, 2-8/8-2, 5-8/8-5, 4-6/6-4, 1-4/4-1, 4-7/7-4, and 8-9/9-8. The 4 scale was well represented in the majority of these clusters.

In the Hall (1989) study, the mean score on the Psychopathic Deviate scale was 78.01, with a standard deviation of 11.77. It is notable that the Psychopathic Deviate scale was the highest of all the scales in the original basic clinical set. In the Hall et al. (1991) study, the most commonly elevated scale in various methods of clustering continued to be the Psychopathic Deviate scale, usually in combination with other scales as well. The Hall et al. (1992) study identified three clusters. The Psychopathic Deviate scale was the highest mean score in Cluster 1, with a mean of 66.17; in Clusters 2 and 3, the Psychopathic Deviate scale T scores were 80.86 and 88.78, respectively. In sum, the Psychopathic Deviate scale was consistently elevated in Hall's group's studies of pedophiles.

Duthie and McIvor (1990) analyzed 90 child molesters' MMPI profiles, which produced eight MMPI clusters. They concluded that these clusters appeared to be robust when subjected to discriminant analysis. In the first four clusters, the MMPI Psychopathic Deviate scale peaked, though in the company of other scales. Cluster 5 was labeled "normal episodic offender cluster" (i.e., not as pathological), but even in this case the 4 scale was the highest at 65, with all other scales being below 60. Cluster 6 was also a "normal cluster" and was labeled as "normal–repressed," representing 8% of the 90 offenders. Even in this case, however, the high elevations were on the 3 and the 4 scales. Only in Cluster 7 did the 4 scale not rate as one of the highest elevations. On Cluster 8, the peaks were on 2 and 8, but the Psychopathic Deviate scale was elevated beyond the T score of 70.

In 1991, Shealy, Kalichman, Henderson, Szymanowski, and McKee found four MMPI pedophile subgroups. The Psychopathic Deviate scale was not submerged in any of these subgroups and generally was either moderately or substantially elevated.

Let us now return to the McAnulty et al. (1994) study, which criticized the use of the MMPI with pedophiles. In this study, the MMPI Psychopathic Deviate scale T score was the highest elevation in both of the groups that the authors had hoped to distinguish between. Both subtypes of pedophiles showed clear psychopathic tendencies on the MMPI.

There are other studies of the use of the MMPI with various forms of child molesters. Admittedly, the MMPI does not seem to be able to make fine distinctions among different types of offenders, but a preponderance of evidence indicates that the Psychopathic Deviate scale is consistently high in pedophiles across many kinds of studies. The Psychopathic Deviate scale, of course, is elevated in all forms of delinquency and criminal behavior, but the purpose of this chapter is not to argue otherwise. Rather, the purpose is merely to argue that the Psychopathic Deviate scale has been shown repeatedly to be an important, reliable, and valid index of psychopathic tendencies, and that it is consistently elevated in samples of pedophiles.

Thus, I would argue that this psychometric evidence provides further support for the argument that psychopathic characteristics permeate the psychology and psychopathology of persons who sexually molest children.

ASSESSING THE PEDOPHILE IN LIGHT OF MILLON'S THEORY OF PERSONALITY

Theodore Millon has devoted his career to developing an integrated theory of personality and psychopathology (Millon with Davis, 1996). This theory has been extensively articulated elsewhere (Millon, 1990) and is only briefly summarized here. The two basic elements of the theory consist of (1) a system or paradigm of polarities, and (2) an integrative assessment of characteristics of various domains of personality. The prototype of the antisocial personality is an active modifier who is oriented to self, with weak polarities on accommodation and nurturance.

Millon's theory of the domains of personality is most directly relevant to our assessment of the pedophile. Millon's integrative system examines four levels of the personality: "behavioral," "phenomenological," "intrapsychic," and "biophysical." Within each level, there are one or more domains, for a total of eight. For example, the behavioral level contains two domains, "expressive acts" and "interpersonal conduct."

Expressive acts are the observable, physical, and verbal behaviors that can be readily identified by observers. The observers are able to infer or deduce from these behaviors what patients either knowingly wish to reveal about themselves or unknowingly reveal through the behaviors. One might think of the expressive acts as operant behaviors (under the control of consequent stimulus events).

The interpersonal conduct domain pertains to an individual's style of relating to others. This would consist of the manner in which people's actions may have an impact on others, intended or otherwise; attitudes that influence these actions; and methods by which persons are able to encourage others to meet their needs.

There are three domains at the phenomenological level. The first is "cognitive style," which refers to the way in which an individual thinks. In this domain, one assesses how people perceive events, focus their attention, engage in information processing, organize their thinking, and communicate their actions and ideas to other individuals. A second domain at the phenomenological level is "object relations." This domain includes internalized representations of significant others, which may be experienced in any of the sensory modalities: visual, tactile, auditory, or olfactory. This structural residue of memories, attitudes, and emotions provides an emotionally laden schema that forms an individual's understanding of significant others. A third domain at the phenomenological level is the "self-image." This domain consists of self-concept, the sense of ego, and the self, and probably contains both real and imagined self-representations.

At the intrapsychic level there are two domains. The first is "regulatory mechanisms." This domain includes the internalized processes that are used in regulating the sense of self. This domain may be thought of as the battery of defenses that an individual uses to self-regulate. A given individual may have high-, medium-, or low-level defenses. Denial and distortion may occur when the individual is faced with incompatible thoughts and feelings.

A second intrapsychic domain is "morphological organization." This domain refers to the overall architecture that provides a framework for an individual's psychic structure. The morphological organization may vary in strength from strong to weak, mature to immature, adaptive to maladaptive. Morphological organization refers to structural strength, interior congruity, and functional efficacy of the personality system.

Lastly, at the biophysical level of assessment, there is the "mood and temperament" domain. Acknowledging the work on heritability of temperament, Millon includes this domain to acknowledge the role of individual differences in mood and temperament.

Now I review Millon's description of the eight domains of antisocial personality disorder and extrapolate, where possible, to the pedophile. I argue that Millon's domain descriptors of the psychopath are very similar to common descriptors of the pedophile.

At the behavioral level, the expressive acts of the antisocial are generally described as "impulsive." Specifically, the antisocial is described in this domain as impetuous, irrepressible, acting hastily, restless, spur-of-the-moment, shortsighted, incautious, imprudent, failing to plan ahead, and heedless of consequences. Pedophiles also tend to be impulsive, or at least to exhibit poor control over their impulses. Marlatt (1989) has captured this trait of pedophiles in his concept of the PIG. They tend to act hastily; to be shortsighted, incautious, and imprudent; and to be ignorant of predictable consequences. In view of the enormous societal proscription against child molestation, a pedophile's inability or unwillingness to heed consequences is truly remarkable.

Within the interpersonal domain, the antisocial is generally described as "irresponsible." Specifically, the antisocial is described as untrustworthy, unreliable, failing to meet obligations, actively intruding upon or violating the rights of others, failing to abide by social codes, and deceitful. The interpersonal behavior of the pedophile is also clearly irresponsible. In a healthy society, adults have a responsibility to guide, protect, and nurture those who are less powerful, including children. The pedophile is untrustworthy and unable to abide by social codes, at least those governing behavior with children. A pedophile's behavior transgresses established social codes, and pedophiles are well known for their deceit in carrying out or covering up their missions, or both.

At the phenomenological level, the cognitive style is described as "deviant." Antisocial individuals construe events and relationships in accord with socially unorthodox beliefs and morals. They are disdainful of traditional ideals, fail to conform to social norms, and are contemptuous of conventional values. It is relatively easy to argue that the cognitive style of the pedophile is deviant. Much of the work on relapse prevention (see, e.g., Long et al., 1989; Jenkins-Hall, 1989; Marlatt, 1989; Pithers et al., 1989; and Marques & Nelson, 1989) focuses on distorted cognitions. Recall the forensic client described above who told me that his 6-year-old stepdaughter "liked sex!" This exemplified a remarkable cognitive deviancy.

The object representations of the antisocial are described as "debased." Internalized representations of others are degraded and diminished. These are corrupt object relations that spur vengeful attitudes and restive impulses. Antisocials are driven to subvert established cultural ideals and to devalue personal sentiments. The goal is to sully and degrade what they covet but cannot have. The object representation domain is also especially relevant to the pedophile. Note that the pedophile's internal representation of the child is debased: The child is viewed as an object to provide gratification rather than as a separate being with needs and rights. There is an enormous distortion of who the child really is. In some instances, a pedophile will physically harm a child, which represents the acting out of vengeful attitudes.

One is reminded of Bellak et al.'s (1973) EFA subcategories of object representations: (1) the degree and kind of relatedness to others; (2) the place on the continuum from primitive to mature of the object representation; (3) the extent to which the subject perceives and responds to others as independent entities, rather than as extensions of the self; and (4) the degree to which object constancy can be maintained. The first three of these, particularly the third, would appear to be unattainable for the pedophile. The child is perceived as an extension of the pedophile, who views that extension as a source of gratification, rather than seeing the child as an independent entity with a separate life and individual emotions.

The self-image of antisocial persons is described as "autonomous." They see themselves as unfettered by restrictions of social custom and constraints of personal loyalties. They value an image of being free, unencumbered, and unconfined by persons, places, obligations, or routines. This domain is somewhat more difficult to extrapolate to the pedophile. However, the literature contains many examples of pedophiles who were friends of their victims' families, and who violated personal loyalties, friendships, and social obligations by becoming sexually involved with the children.

At the intrapsychic level, the major defense or regulatory mechanism of the antisocial is "acting out." Little constraint is used to modulate expression of offensive thoughts or to control malevolent action. Socially repugnant impulses are not reshaped into sublimated forms but are discharged directly, usually without guilt or remorse. The parallel of this description to the pedophile is clear; again, consider Marlatt's (1989) discussion of the PIG. The pedophile shows little tendency to sublimate. Constraint is rarely used to modulate expression of offensive thoughts or to control malevolent action. Instead of restraining repugnant impulses, the pedophile acts them out directly, usually without guilt or remorse.

The morphological organization of the antisocial individual is described as "unruly." The internalized psychic structures that should contain drives and impulses are fragile and easily overwhelmed by impulse. There are low thresholds for hostile or erotic discharge, few subliminal channels, unfettered self-expression, and a marked intolerance for delay of frustration. By inference, we may argue that the morphological organization of the pedophile is also fragile. The pedophile readily succumbs to impulses and tends to have low thresholds for either hostile or erotic discharge, or both.

Lastly, at the biosocial level, mood is described as "callous." Antisocials are described as insensitive, irritable, and aggressive. There is a wide-ranging deficit in social charitableness. Antisocials tend to be without compassion or remorse, and there is a disregard for the safety of others. This domain is not as directly relevant to a description of the pedophile as some of the other Millon domains are. However, it can be argued that the pedophile, by definition, is deficient in social charitableness as well as in compassion and remorse for the act. Furthermore, there is, by definition, a disregard for the safety of children—and, for that matter, for the pedophile's own safety.

In summary, the characteristics of the antisocial personality outlined in Millon's domains appear to overlap considerably with common descriptors of the personality characteristics of pedophiles.

CONCLUSION

My intent in this chapter has been to assert that the behavior and psychodynamics of the pedophile have a psychopathic-like quality. The overt *modus operandi* is more specialized in the pedophile (i.e., sexual behavior with a minor), but the deeper aim—to assuage one's inner emptiness by dominating or controlling someone weaker and less able to manage the situation—seems strikingly similar to the style of the psychopath. This task has been approached here from four vantage points, each with its strengths and weaknesses. However, in each case, it has been relatively easy to defend the position being taken.

Although I believe that there is substantial merit to the argument being advanced, I am aware that it is not without flaws. Since we are dealing with two spectrum disorders, identical isomorphic overlay is unlikely. However, I have never seen a pedophile in my forensic practice who did not exhibit some psychopathic tendencies. Furthermore, I have never examined a pedophile who demonstrated tight reality testing, mature defenses, sound judgment, adaptive regression, efficient thought processes, or any other signs of mature ego functions. Instead, each one demonstrated marked character pathology of the kind seen in psychopathy. I believe that much can be learned about pedophilia by conceptualizing it as being closely related to, or a special case of, psychopathy. As we further our knowledge of this unfortunate disorder, we will improve our chances for successful treatment and improve the future for our children.

ACKNOWLEDGMENT

I would like to thank Stephanie Tilden Dorr, MA, for her editorial assistance in preparing this chapter.

NOTE

1. For simplicity, the terms "psychopath" and "antisocial personality" are used interchangeably in this chapter.

REFERENCES

Abel, G. G., & Osborn, C. (1992). The paraphilias. *Psychiatric Clinics of North America, 15*(3), 675–687.

American Psychiatric Association. (1994). *Diagnostic and statistical manual of mental disorders* (4th ed.). Washington, DC: Author.

Bellak, L., Hervich, M., & Gediman, H. K. (1973). *Ego functions in schizophrenics, neurotics and normals.* New York: Wiley.

Blatt, S., & Schichman, S. (1981). Antisocial behavior and personality organization. In S. Tuttnam, C. Kaye, & M. Zimmerman (Eds.), *Object and self: A developmental approach: Essays in honor of Edith Jacobson* (pp. 325–367). New York: International Universities Press.

Butcher, J. N., Dahlstrom, W. G., Graham, J. R., Tellegen, A., & Kaemmer, B. (1989). *Minnesota Multiphasic Personality Inventory—2 manual.* Minneapolis: University of Minnesota Press.

Dorr, D., & Woodhall, P. K. (1986). Ego dysfunction in psychopathic psychiatric inpatients. In W. H. Reid, D. Dorr, J. I. Walker, & J. W. Bonner (Eds.), *Unmasking the psychopath: Antisocial personality and related syndromes* (pp. 98–131). New York: Norton.

Duthie, B., & McIvor, D. L. (1990). A new system for cluster-coding child molester MMPI profile types. *Criminal Justice and Behavior, 17*(2), 199–214.

Erickson, W. D., Luxenberg, M. G., Walbek, N. H., & Seely, R. K. (1987). Frequency of MMPI two-point codetypes among sex offenders. *Journal of Consulting and Clinical Psychology, 55*(4), 566–570.

Groth, A. N. (1978). Patterns of sexual assault against children and adolescents. In A. W. Burgess, A. N. Groth, L. L. Holmstrom, & S. M. Sgroi (Eds.), *Sexual assault of children and adolescents* (pp. 3–24). Lexington, MA: D. C. Heath.

Groth, A. N., Hobson, W., & Gary, T. (1982). The child molester: Clinical observations. *Journal of Social Work and Human Sexuality, 1,* 129–144.

Hall, G. C. N. (1989). WAIS-R and men who have sexually assaulted children: Evidence of limited utility. *Journal of Personality Assessment, 53*(2), 404–412.

Hall, G. C. N., Graham, J. R., & Shepherd, J. B. (1991). Three methods of developing MMPI taxonomies of sexual offenders. *Journal of Personality Assessment, 55*(1), 2–13.

Hall, G. C. N., Maiuro, R. D., Vitaliano, P. P., & Proctor, W. C. (1986). The utility of the MMPI with men who have sexually assaulted children. *Journal of Consulting and Clinical Psychology, 54*(4), 493–496.

Hall, G. C. N., Shepherd, J. B., & Mudrak, P. (1992). MMPI taxonomies of child sexual and nonsexual offenders: A cross validation and extension. *Journal of Personality Assessment, 58*(1), 157–137.

Hare, R. (1985). Comparison of procedures for the assessment of psychopathy. *Journal of Consulting and Clinical Psychology, 53*, 7–16.

Hare, R. D. (1991). *The Hare Psychopathy Checklist—Revised.* Toronto: Multi-Health Systems.

Hathaway, S. R., & McKinley, J. C. (1967). *The Minnesota Multiphasic Personality Inventory manual.* New York: Psychological Corporation.

Horowitz, L. M., Wright, J. C., Lowenstein, E., & Parad, H. W. (1981). The prototype as construct in abnormal psychology: I. A method for deriving prototypes. *Journal of Abnormal Psychology, 90*, 568–574.

Jenkins-Hall, K. D. (1989). The decision matrix. In D. R. Laws (Ed.), *Relapse prevention with sex offenders* (pp. 159–166). New York: Guilford Press.

Kegan, R. G. (1986). The child behind the mask: Sociopathy as developmental delay. In W. H. Reid, D. Dorr, J. I. Walker, & J. W. Bonner (Eds.), *Unmasking the psychopath: Antisocial personality and related syndromes* (pp. 45–77). New York: Norton.

Kernberg, O. (1984). *Severe personality disorders: Psychotheraputic strategies.* New Haven: Yale University Press.

Langevin, R., Hucker, S. J., Ben-Aron, M. H., Purins, J. E., & Hook, H. J. (1985). Why are pedophiles attracted to children?: Further studies of erotic preference in heterosexual pedophilia. In R. Langevin (Ed.), *Erotic preference, gender identity, and aggression in men: New research studies* (pp. 181–210). Hillsdale, NJ: Erlbaum.

Langevin, R., Paitich, D., Freeman, R., Mann, K., & Handy, L. (1978). Personality characteristics and sexual anomalies in males. *Canadian Journal of Behavioural Science, 10*, 222–238.

Lewak, R. W., Marks, P. A., & Nelson, G. E. (1990). *Therapist guide to the MMPI and MMPI-2: Providing feedback and treatment.* Muncie, IN: Accelerated Development.

Long, J. D., Wuesthoff, A., & Pithers, W. D. (1989). Use of autobiographies in the assessment and treatment of sex offenders. In D. R. Laws (Ed.), *Relapse prevention with sex offenders* (pp. 88–95). New York: Guilford Press.

Lothstein, L. M. (1990). Psychological theories of pedophilia and ephebophilia. In S. J. Rossetti (Ed.), *Slayer of the soul: Child sexual abuse and the Catholic church* (pp. 19–42). Mystic, CT: Twenty-Third.

Marlatt, G. A. (1989). Feeding the PIG: The problem of immediate gratification. In D. R. Laws (Ed.), *Relapse prevention with sex offenders* (pp. 63–72). New York: Guilford Press.

Marques, J. K., & Nelson, C. (1989). Elements of high-risk situations for sex offenders. In D. R. Laws (Ed.), *Relapse prevention with sex offenders* (pp. 335–355). New York: Guilford Press.

Mayer, A. (1985). *Sexual abuse: Causes, consequences and treatment of incestuous and pedophilic acts.* Holmes Beach, FL: Learning.

McAnulty, R. D., Adams, H. E., & Wright, L. W., Jr. (1994). Relationship between MMPI and penile plethysmograph in accused child molesters. *Journal of Sex Research, 31*(3), 179–184.

Meloy, J. R. (1988). *The psychopathic mind.* New York: Jason Aronson.

Millon, T.(1990). *Toward a new personology: An evolutionary model.* New York: Wiley.

Millon, T., with Davis, R. (1996). *Disorders of personality: DSM-IV and beyond.* New York: Wiley–Interscience.

Pithers, W. D., Martin, G. R., & Cumming, G. F. (1989). Vermont treatment program for sexual aggressors. In D. R. Laws (Ed.), *Relapse prevention with sex offenders* (pp. 292–310). New York: Guilford Press.

Prendergast, W. E. (1991). *Treating sexual offenders in correctional institutions and outpatient clinics: A guide to clinical practice.* New York: Haworth Press.

Samenow, S. (1984). *Inside the criminal mind.* New York: Times Books.

Shealy, L., Kalichman, S. C., Henderson, M. C., Szymanowski, D., & McKee, G. (1991). MMPI profile subtypes of incarcerated sex offenders against children. *Violence and Victims, 6*(3), 201–212.

Vaupel, S. G., & Goeke, J. M. (1994). Incest perpetrator MMPI profiles and the variable of offense admission status. *International Journal of Offender Therapy and Comparative Criminology, 38*(1), 69–77.

Wiederholt, I. C. (1992). The psychodynamics of sex offenses and implications of treatment. *Journal of Offender Rehabilitation, 18*(3–4), 19–24.

Yochelson, S., & Samenow, S. (1976). *The criminal personality* (Vol. 1). New York: Jason Aronson.

20

Comorbidity of Alcoholism and Psychopathy

JOACHIM KNOP
PER JENSEN
ERIK LYKKE MORTENSEN

The interrelationship of psychopathy and substance use disorders has been an established fact for decades. It is based on both clinical experience and a substantial number of research contributions on the subject (Hesselbrock et al., 1984; Hesselbrock, Meyer, & Keener, 1985). Indeed, the two diagnostic entities are so closely interrelated that a clinical study on psychopathy will always include some consideration of the subjects' alcohol and other substance use, and vice versa: No researcher involved in a clinical study of alcoholism or other substance misuse will omit also to cover psychopathy/antisocial personality disorder (APD) in the study design, selection of variables, and so on.

Once this comorbidity was established, a series of questions arose. How are the two types of disorders interrelated in an etiological context? To single out alcoholism from among the substance use disorders (as we do in this chapter), does APD play an antecedent role for subsequent alcoholism? Or is APD a consequential factor developed after many years of drinking? Or are they epiphenomena? Our ability to answer such questions has been limited, primarily because the majority of clinical research on the subject has been based on retrospective and cross-sectional study designs.

In any discussion of the etiology and pathogenesis of a disease, the time aspect is essential to keep in mind. It is important to document the appearance of the (cluster of) symptoms over time—optimally, before diagnostic criteria for the disease are fulfilled. The time aspect is especially important to consider when we are faced with two simultaneous diagnostic entities (such as APD and alcoholism) in the same individual. In a theoretical context, the solution is simple: A research program should be designed to follow subjects at high risk for a given disease prospectively, starting at an age before signs of disease are present. However, the practical implementation of such a research program is difficult (see below).

Another important question is this: How stable are signs of future disease over time? Do they develop on a linear continuum? A pattern of stability and chronicity seems to be characteristic for both APD and substance use disorders (Chess & Thomas, 1990; Black, Baumgard, & Bell, 1995).

Concerning the etiology of alcoholism and/or APD, the essential "nature–nurture" question has engaged the scientific community for decades (Crowe, 1983). Interestingly enough, findings from the field of genetic epidemiology have contributed the most to our understanding of the etiology of APD and alcoholism. Alcoholism, APD, and criminality have all been subjects for classical genetic–environmental study designs. Twin studies have indicated that genetic (biological) factors contribute to the development of alcoholism (Partanen, Bruun, & Markkamen, 1966), APD (Lyons et al., 1995), and criminality (Dalgard & Kringlen, 1976). In particular, adoption studies (Schulsinger, 1972; Cadoret, O'Gorman, Troughton, & Heywood, 1985; Cadoret, Yates, Troughton, Woodworth, & Stewart, 1995; Goodwin, Schulsinger, Hermansen, Guze, & Winokur, 1973; Goodwin, Schulsinger, Knop, Mednick, & Guze, 1977) have demonstrated a significant biological background for development of adult APD and/or substance use disorders. (The reader is referred to McGuffin & Thapar, Chapter 13, this volume, for detailed information on the genetic aspects of APD.)

It is obvious that conditions such as APD, alcoholism, and criminality have complex etiological backgrounds that include both biological and environmental factors. But our understanding of this "nature–nurture" interplay is still limited. In this connection, the well-known vulnerability model seems relevant: Each individual is "equipped" with a special degree of sensitivity to environmental influence. As Donald Goodwin (1994) has put it concerning alcoholism, "Genes give us enzymes to metabolize ethanol, and society gives us alcohol to metabolize."

RISK FACTORS

Since research has established a considerable genetic component in the etiology of both alcoholism and APD, the next challenge is to identify potential risk factors (Stabenau, 1990). In a 1995 issue of *Archives of General Psychiatry,* several contributions highlighted the complex interplay between the biological and environmental factors that are of causal significance for APD in adulthood (Lyons et al., 1995; Cadoret et al., 1995; Gershon, 1995).

As mentioned above, two essential issues concerning risk factors have to be investigated. First, risk factors must be identified from prospectively collected data, as early in life as possible. Their predictive power for adult illness should be demonstrated. And, second, their stability–instability over time should be examined. Do they change, fade out, or fluctuate through adolescence to adulthood? Or are they necessary and/or sufficient for the development of alcoholism and APD later in life?

Recently, Michael Rutter (1996) has underlined some individual risk factors in childhood for antisocial behavior in adulthood: impulsivity, sensation seeking, low IQ, low autonomic reactivity, hyperactivity, and aggression. Either isolated or clustered in different combinations, these risk factors have been identified in long-term follow-up studies of children with conduct problems (Robins, 1978; Robins & Price, 1991). The risk factors are characterized by remarkable stability over time. Moreover, the same conduct problems in childhood/adolescence seem to have predictive power for alcoholism, APD, and criminality (Farrington, Loeber, & Van Kammen, 1990) in adulthood.

Cloninger, Sigvardsson, and Bohman (1988) have proposed a subtyping of alcoholism, based on drinking pattern, family history of alcoholism and a three-dimensional set of premorbid personality characteristics: novelty seeking, harm avoidance, and reward dependence.

Thus, in spite of different definitions of high-risk status in the child (parental alcoholism or APD, conduct problems, low IQ, hyperactivity, etc.) the majority of the studies point in the same direction: These risk factors lead to high rates of substance use problems, antisocial personality traits, criminality, and poor social functioning in adult life. In the next section, we describe a special epidemiological approach to alcohol research (the high-risk methodology) as a means of identifying particular risk factors for the development of adult alcoholism and/or APD. In the remainder of the chapter, we describe such a study that has been and is still being carried out by our research group.

THE HIGH-RISK PARADIGM

The so-called "high-risk methodology" consists of a prospective, long-term follow-up study of demographically comparable groups of subjects with well-defined high-risk and low-risk status for a given disorder in adulthood. The high-risk paradigm was introduced into psychiatric research by Moffitt and Schulsinger in 1962 (described in Moffitt, Mednick, & Cudeck, 1983), in a prospective study of children of schizophrenic mothers. This high-risk study is still in progress (Parnas et al., 1993). In addition, it is essential to perform premorbid assessments of the sample, in order to collect data of potential predictive significance.

The high-risk method's advantages and limitations have been described in detail in a review by Moffitt et al. (1983). We should emphasize here that the high-risk paradigm includes both biological and environmental risk factors for the development of illness in adulthood. Several research groups have conducted long-term high-risk studies on alcoholism (Cloninger et al., 1988; Vaillant, 1995; Schuckit & Smith, 1996). They have generated significant contributions to our understanding of the etiology of both alcoholism and APD.

A PROSPECTIVE, LONG-TERM FOLLOW-UP STUDY OF SONS OF ALCOHOLIC FATHERS

The Sample

Our subjects were selected from a cohort of children born from 1959 to 1961. The birth cohort included 8,949 consecutive deliveries in the maternity department at Rigshospitalet in Copenhagen, all examined intensively in a perinatal study. From the obstetrical records, we identified 8,440 fathers. Both fathers and mothers were screened in the Danish Central Psychiatric Register, where all psychiatric admissions (including discharge diagnoses) are registered nationwide. In this way, 488 fathers were identified as alcoholics. Their 255 sons were selected as the high-risk (HR) group. Thirty-three sons were excluded from the study due to perinatal death, family emigration, or family disappearance, leaving 222 HR sons for the study. They were matched pairwise with demographically similar low-risk (LR) subjects. That is, for each HR pair, one LR subject was selected from the remaining pool of sons without parental alcoholism ($n = 106$ for the LR group).

The Data

As Table 20.1 indicates, a great many data were systematically collected from various sources for this study. As mentioned above in our discussion of the high-risk paradigm, the selection of premorbid variables reflected a multidisciplinary approach (Knop, 1980), including both biological and environmental factors in childhood and adolescence.

Results

We now present an outline of the main results from the various premorbid assessments, and a somewhat more detailed discussion of our follow-up of the subjects at age 30 years, with special reference to APD and substance use disorders.

Pregnancy and Delivery

The two risk groups did not differ significantly on any of the scales used to assess prenatal and perinatal factors. The only difference was worse home conditions in the HR group at 1 year of age.

Schooling

We obtained data about the subjects' school careers from a structured questionnaire completed by teachers, which covered each child's intellectual, behavioral, and social functioning (Knop, Teasdale, Schulsinger, & Goodwin, 1985) As a whole, the HR boys' schooling was more difficult than that of the LR boys (disciplinary problems, repeating a grade, etc.). Most striking was the fact that 51% of the HR boys were referred to a school psychologist, compared to 34% of the LR boys. Seven *a priori* scales focusing on predicting alcohol-related characteristics were constructed from the teacher question-

TABLE 20.1. Data Sources

Years	Sources
1959–1961	Pregnancy and delivery records
	Postnatal data
1960–1962	Examination at 1 year of age
1966–1978	School physician records
	School psychologist records
	School teacher questionnaire
1979–1980	Premorbid assessment, age 19–20
	Social worker home interview
	Neuropsychological testing
	Neurophysiological testing: Electroencephalogram (EEG) and visual evoked potential (VEP) test
	Psychopathological examination
	Physical examination
	Alcohol challenge test
	Drinking history
1990–1992	30-year follow-up (see Table 20.3)
2000–?	Final follow-up
2010–2030	Registration of death causes

TABLE 20.2. Mean (± *SD*) Results from Scales of the School
Teacher Questionnaire

Scale	HR (*n* = 95)	LR (*n* = 49)
Impulsive–Restless	2.2 ± 0.75*	1.9 ± 0.74
Nervous	1.9 ± 0.87	1.6 ± 0.68
Violent	1.5 ± 0.69	1.5 ± 0.71
Independent	2.7 ± 0.70	2.9 ± 0.73
Withdrawn	2.1 ± 0.73	2.0 ± 0.61
Verbal Proficiency	2.6 ± 0.0.97*	3.0 ± 0.88
Math Proficiency	2.4 ± 0.90	2.5 ± 0.84

Note. The data are from Knop, Teasdale, Schulsinger, and Goodwin (1985).

*Mann–Whitney *U*, *p* = .02.

naire. From Table 20.2, it appears that only two of the scales separated the two risk groups significantly: the Impulsivity/Restlessness and Verbal Proficiency scales. Impulsivity, restlessness, and disciplinary problems in adolescence are well-known and characteristic precursors for APD in adulthood. In addition, these behavioral characteristics throughout the teenage period may reflect hyperactivity, attention deficits, and so forth early in childhood—difficulties that in themselves are predictive for APD and substance use problems later in life.

School medical records were collected for 83% of the HR subjects and 86% of the LR subjects. These records were based on annual examinations throughout the schooling period. Mental and central nervous system (CNS) disorders were coded (in addition to general physical problems). The HR group had significantly more language and learning disorders than the LR group did. Among CNS disorders, we only found a marginally significant excess of cranial fractures and concussions in the HR group.

Overall, the HR subjects required more specialized attention from school personnel, reflecting both educational and behavioral problems.

Findings from the 20-Year Follow-Up Study

At age 19–20 years, the subjects were invited to participate in an extensive assessment. The aim was to collect premorbid data and to test our hypotheses and selected variables by comparing the two risk groups. A total of 204 subjects (134 HR and 70 LR) completed the entire test program (see Table 20.1 for the elements of this program).

The main results from the premorbid 20-year assessment were as follows:

- Halstead Category Test: higher number of errors in the HR group (Drejer, Theilgaard, Teasdale, Goodwin, & Schulsinger, 1985).
- Wechsler Adult Intelligence Scale (WAIS) Vocabulary subtest: lower performance in the HR group (Drejer et al., 1985).
- Porteus Maze errors: higher number in the HR group (Drejer et al., 1985).
- Self-ratings of alcohol intoxication: fewer and less intense in the HR group (Pollock, Teasdale, Gabrielli, & Knop, 1986).
- EEG after ethanol: greater increase in slow-wave alpha in the HR group (Pollock et al., 1983).

- Number of stressful life events: higher in the HR group (Schulsinger, Knop, Goodwin, Teasdale, & Mikkelsen, 1986).
- Disrupted family conditions: more frequent in the HR group (Schulsinger et al., 1986).
- Number of schools attended: more in the HR group (Schulsinger et al., 1986).
- Repeating a grade in school: more frequent in the HR group (Schulsinger et al., 1986).

The psychopathological interview revealed significantly marked impulsivity and distractibility in the HR group, as opposed to ruminating and antiaggressive personality in the LR group (Schulsinger et al., 1986). The marked impulsivity in the HR group was consistent with findings from the school teacher questionnaire (Knop et al., 1985), indicating that sons of alcoholic fathers were characterized by antisocial traits, conduct problems, and social dysfunction in childhood, compared to the LR subjects. By contrast, anxiety, antiaggressiveness, and similar "acting in"—symptoms found in the LR group—may be protective factors against substance use disorders and/or APD later in life.

During the neurophysiological test program, an alcohol challenge test was performed. As noted above, the HR subjects typically reported fewer and less intense negative effects of alcohol (Pollock et al., 1986).

Because the 20-year follow-up examination was intended to be premorbid (i.e., the data were intended to be collected before any of the subjects fulfilled diagnostic criteria for alcohol or other substance dependence), evaluation of the subjects' drinking practices was essential. The mean consumption was nearly identical in both risk groups (approximately 17.5 drinks per week), and the amount was close to the mean consumption in the Danish population of males at the same age (Knop, Goodwin, Teasdale, Mikkelsen, & Schulsinger, 1984).

Findings from the 30-Year Follow-Up Study

In the mid-1990s, we completed data collection on the two risk groups at about 30 years of age. The overall aims of this follow-up were these: (1) to compare the two risk groups on a series of alcohol-related and psychopathological dimensions; (2) to determine whether risk group differences from the 20-year follow-up would continue to distinguish the risk groups at age 30; and (3) to determine whether measures from the perinatal period, childhood, and adolescence would successfully predict alcohol dependence at age 30.

A psychiatrist (Per Jensen) who was unaware of the subjects' risk status conducted home interviews covering psychopathological, neuropsychological, and psychosocial factors. It was essential to select variables that would be comparable with data collected at previous stages of the longitudinal study. In addition, we obtained access to Danish national registers covering psychiatric history, criminality, death, and military service. The interview instruments and other data sources are listed in Table 20.3. A total of 241 home interviews were conducted (161 HR and 80 LR). The number of available subjects was reduced to 304 (due to emigration, death, etc.), resulting in a participation rate of about 80%.

A few overall results, with special reference to substance use disorders and APD, are presented here (for more details, see Knop et al., 1993, and Goodwin et al., 1994).

Substance Dependence and Abuse. Substance dependence (according to DSM-III-R criteria) was significantly more frequent in the HR group, whereas substance abuse was

TABLE 20.3. Data Sources for the 30-Year Follow-Up

Psychiatric Diagnostic Interview—Revised (PDI-R)
Structured Clinical Interview for DSM-III-R, Axis II (SCID-II)
Alcohol and drug history
Neuropsychological test battery
Psychosocial, medical, family history
Tridimensional Personality Questionnaire (TPQ)
Millon Clinical Multiaxial Inventory (MCMI)
Michigan Alcohol Screening Test (MAST)
Danish Central Psychiatric Register
Danish Criminality Register
Danish Death Register
Danish Military Service Register

almost equally distributed in the two risk groups, as Table 20.4 indicates. Apart from alcohol, cannabis seemed to be the preferred drug among our subjects (particularly in the HR group).

Other Psychopathology and Substance Use. Concerning other psychopathology, the risk groups did not differ significantly in frequency of anxiety disorders, mood disorders, schizophrenia, APD, or other personality disorders. Only the difference in anxiety disorders was close to reaching significance (HR = 13%, LR = 5%; p = .055). It was particularly remarkable that the frequency of APD was very high (10–12%) in both risk groups.

However, when the sample was grouped according to severity of substance use disorders at age 30 (and not by risk status), some characteristic results appeared (see Table 20.5). The lowest rate of psychopathology was found in the no-abuse group. The highest rate was found in the dependence group, with the abuse group in between. Most striking was the comorbidity of substance dependence and APD (p = .001). And, to look at the findings the other way around, 89% of all subjects with APD had a diagnosis of substance dependence.

The course of substance dependence in all 59 subjects with dependence showed that in 32% of the cases, it was in full remission at age 30 years. In contrast, full remission was achieved by only 4% of the subjects with dependence who also had APD. These findings suggest that substance dependence in persons with APD has a significantly poorer prognosis.

Comparison of Previous Data with 30-Year Substance Dependence/APD Data. This close interrelation of substance dependence and APD led us to compare the data from previous assessments with the 30-year outcome data in some detail.

TABLE 20.4. Psychoactive Substance Use Disorders at the 30-Year Follow-Up

Disorder	HR (n = 161)	LR (n = 80)
Alcohol and/or drug abuse	19%	16%
Drug dependence	12%	6%
Alcohol dependence	19%	11%
Alcohol and/or drug dependence, total	29%*	15%

*p < .02.

TABLE 20.5. Substance Use Disorders and Other Psychiatric Disorders at the 30-Year Follow-Up

Other DSM-III-R diagnosis	No abuse (*n* = 139)	Abuse (*n* = 43)	Dependence (*n* = 59)
No diagnosis	85%	72%	31%
Anxiety disorders	6%	12%	19%
Mood disorders	5%	14%	17%
Schizophrenia	0%	0%	7%
APD	1%	5%	41%
Other personality disorders	4%	2%	15%

Note. Figures are not additive; 16 subjects had more than one diagnosis.

At age 20, as noted earlier, the subjects were asked about their drinking patterns as teenagers. Both the substance-dependent and APD groups (at age 30) began using alcohol at a significantly earlier age (the same was true for cannabis). No other measures were predictive concerning later substance dependence and APD. Similarly, objective and subjective measures from the alcohol challenge test at age 20 did not correlate with dependence or APD at age 30.

The school teacher questionnaire demonstrated significant correlations between conduct problems at about age 15 and substance dependence and APD at age 30, as Table 20.6 indicates. In this connection, the subjects' premorbid intellectual functioning is also of interest. Some preliminary data analyses demonstrated a reduced premorbid intellectual capacity among the adolescents who were later found to have substance dependence and APD at age 30 (see Table 20.7). This tendency was confirmed by significantly lower scores on the neuropsychological tests at age 30.

Social Functioning at Age 30. On the whole, the social functioning of subjects with substance dependence and/or APD at age 30 was significantly poorer than that of all other diagnostic groups. More specifically, this was true for educational level, employment situation, criminality, and subjective evaluation of mental well-being. A concrete example of this problem can be seen in the subjects' report of their social network. The APD group at age 30 reported a reduced number of close friends and an increased number of (superficial) contacts, compared with other diagnostic groups.

TABLE 20.6. Teachers' Ratings at about Age 15 and Substance Dependence/APD at Age 30

Variable (age 15)	HR–LR difference (age 30)	Substance dependence (age 30)	APD (age 30)
Impulsive	S	S	S
Spoke without thinking	S	S	S
Vocabulary	S	S	NS
Gave up easily	NS	S	S
Restless, fidgeting	NS	S	S
Easily distracted	NS	S	NS

Note. S, significant; NS, nonsignificant.

TABLE 20.7. Intellectual Capacity over Time and Substance Dependence/APD at Age 30

Variable	HR–LR difference (age 30)	Substance dependence (age 30)	APD (age 30)
Age 15: Teachers' ratings (vocabulary)	S	S	NS
Age 18: Military exam (IQ raw score)	NS	S	S
Age 20: WAIS Vocabulary	S	NS	NS
Age 30: WAIS Vocabulary	S	NS	S

Note. S, significant; NS, nonsignificant.

TABLE 20.8. Tridimensional Personality Questionnaire (TPQ) Scores and Substance Dependence/APD at Age 30

TPQ subscale	HR–LR difference	Substance dependence	APD
Harm Avoidance	NS	S	S
Reward Dependence	NS	NS	S
Novelty Seeking	NS	S	NS

Note. S, significant; NS, nonsignificant.

As noted in Table 20.3, the home interview at age 30 included the Tridimensional Personality Questionnaire (TPQ) and the Millon Clinical Multiaxial Inventory (MCMI)—both useful instruments in identifying predictive factors in alcoholism and APD (Cloninger et al., 1988; Craig, Verinis, & Wexler, 1988). As Table 20.8 indicates that scores on two of the three TPQ subscales were elevated in the group with substance dependence and in the group with APD at age 30; however, the original HR and LR groups did not differ significantly on the TPQ. The MCMI confirmed these findings and demonstrated the same predictive pattern.

CONCLUSION

The research described in this chapter has demonstrated that the prospective high-risk design is a suitable method to identify premorbid characteristics with obvious predictive value for APD and substance use disorders later in life. Our group intends to perform a final 40-year follow-up of this unique high-risk sample. Among other causal hypotheses, we will continue to focus on conduct problems in childhood and adolescence as predictors of both substance dependence and APD in adulthood.

ACKNOWLEDGMENT

This research was supported by National Institute of Alcohol Abuse and Alcoholism Grant Nos. R01-02886 and R01-08176.

REFERENCES

Black, D. W., Baumgard, C. H., & Bell, S. E. (1995). A 16- to 45-year follow-up of 71 men with antisocial personality disorder. *Comprehensive Psychiatry, 36,* 130–140.

Cadoret, R. J., O'Gorman, T. W., Troughton, E., & Heywood, E. (1985). Alcoholism and antisocial personality. *Archives of General Psychiatry, 42,* 161–167.

Cadoret, R. J., Yates, W. R., Troughton, E., Woodworth, G., & Stewart, M. A. (1995). Genetic–environmental interaction in the genesis of aggressivity and conduct disorders. *Archives of General Psychiatry, 52,* 916–924.

Chess, S., & Thomas, A. (1990). Continuities and discontinuities in temperament. In L. R. Robins & M. Rutter (Eds.), *Straight and devious pathways from childhood to adulthood* (pp. 205–220). New York: Cambridge University Press.

Cloninger, C. R., Sigvardsson, S., & Bohman, M. (1988). Childhood personality predicts alcohol abuse in young adults. *Alcoholism: Clinical and Experimental Research, 12,* 494–505.

Craig, R. J., Verinis, J. S., & Wexler, S. (1988). Personality characteristics of drug addicts and alcoholics in the Millon Clinical Multiaxial Inventory. *Journal of Personality Assessment, 49,* 156–160.

Crowe, R. R. (1983). Antisocial personality disorder. In R. E. Tarter (Ed.), *The child at psychiatric risk* (pp. 214–227). New York: Oxford University Press.

Dalgard, O., & Kringlen, E. (1976). A Norwegian twin study of criminality. *British Journal of Criminology, 16,* 231–232.

Drejer, K., Theilgaard, A., Teasdale, T. W., Goodwin, D. W., & Schulsinger, F. (1985). A prospective study of young men at high risk for alcoholism: Neuropsychological assessment. *Alcoholism: Clinical and Experimental Research, 9,* 298–302.

Farrington, D. P., Loeber, R., & Van Kammen, W. B. (1990). Long-term criminal outcomes of hyperactivity–impulsivity–attention deficit and conduct problems in childhood. In L. Robins & M. Rutter (Eds.), *Straight and devious pathways from childhood to adulthood* (pp. 62–81). New York: Cambridge University Press.

Gershon, E. S. (1995). Antisocial behavior [Editorial]. *Archives of General Psychiatry, 52,* 900–901.

Goodwin, D. W. (1994). *Alcoholism: The facts.* New York: Oxford University Press.

Goodwin, D. W., Knop, J., Jensen, P., Gabrielli, W. F., Schulsinger, F., & Penick, E. C. (1994). Thirty year follow-up of men at high risk for alcoholism. *Annals of the New York Academy of Sciences, 708,* 97–101.

Goodwin, D. W., Schulsinger, F., Hermansen, L., Guze, S. B., & Winokur, G. (1973). Alcohol problems in adoptees raised apart from alcoholic biological parents. *Archives of General Psychiatry, 30,* 238–243.

Goodwin, D. W., Schulsinger, F., Knop, J., Mednick, S. A., & Guze, S. (1977). Alcoholism and depression in adopted-out daughters of alcoholics. *Archives of General Psychiatry, 34,* 751–760.

Hesselbrock, M., Hesselbrock, V. M., Barbor, T. F., Stabenau, J. R., Meyer, R. E., & Weideman, M. (1984). Antisocial behaviour, psychopathology and problem drinking in the natural history of alcoholism. In D. W. Goodwin, K. T. Van Dusen, & A. Sarnoff (Eds.), *Longitudinal research in alcoholism* (pp. 197–214). Boston: Kluver-Nijhoff.

Hesselbrock, M. N., Meyer, R. E., & Keener, J. J. (1985). Psychopathology in hospitalized alcoholics. *Archives of General Psychiatry, 42,* 1050–1055.

Knop, J. (1980). Selection of variables in a prospective study of young men at high risk for alcoholism. *Acta Psychiatrica Scandinavica, 62*(Suppl. 285), 347–352.

Knop, J., Goodwin, D. W., Jensen, P., Penick, E. C., Pollock, V., Gabrielli, W., Teasdale, T. W., & Mednick, S. A. (1993). A 30-year follow-up study of sons of alcoholic men. *Acta Psychiatrica Scandinavica, 75*(Suppl. 370), 48–53.

Knop, J., Goodwin, D. W., Teasdale, T. W., Mikkelsen, U., & Schulsinger, F. (1984). A Danish prospective study of young males at high risk for alcoholism. In D. W. Goodwin, K. Van Dusen, & S. A. Mednick (Eds.), *Longitudinal research in alcoholism* (pp. 107–124). Boston: Kluwer-Nijhoff.

Knop, J., Teasdale, T. W., Schulsinger, F., & Goodwin, D. W. (1985). A prospective study of young men at high risk for alcoholism: School behaviour and achievement. *Journal of Studies on Alcohol, 46,* 273–278.

Lyons, M. J., True, W. R., Eisen, S. A., Goldberg, J., Meyer, J. M., Faraone, S. V., Eaves, L. J., & Tsuang, M. T. (1995). Differential heritability of adult and juvenile antisocial traits. *Archives of General Psychiatry, 52,* 906–915.

Moffitt, T. E., Mednick, S. A., & Cudeck, R. (1983). Methodology of high risk research. Longitudinal approaches. In R. Tarter (Ed.), *The child at psychiatric risk* (pp. 54–79). New York: Oxford University Press.

Parnas, J., Cannon, T. D., Jacobsen, B., Schulsinger, H., Schulsinger, F., Mednick, S. A. (1993). Lifetime DSM-III-R diagnostic outcomes of offspring of schizophrenic mothers. *Archives of General Psychiatry, 50,* 707–714.

Partanen, J., Bruun, K., & Markkamen, T. (1966). *Inheritance of drinking behaviour.* New Brunswick, NJ: Rutgers University Center for Alcohol Studies.

Pollock, V. E., Teasdale, T. W., Gabrielli, W. F., & Knop, J. (1986). Subjective and objective measures of response to alcoholism in young men at high risk for alcoholism. *Journal of Studies on Alcohol, 47,* 297–304.

Pollock, V. E., Volavka, J., Goodwin, J. D. W., Mednick, S. A., Gabrielli, W. F., Knop, J., & Schulsinger, F. (1983). The EEG after alcohol administration in men at high risk for alcoholism. *Archives of General Psychiatry, 40,* 857–861.

Robins, L. N. (1978). Sturdy childhood predictors of adult antisocial behaviour: Replications from longitudinal studies. *Psychological Medicine, 8,* 611–622.

Robins, L. N., & Price, R. K. (1991). Adult disorders predicted by childhood conduct problems: Results from the NIMH Epidemiologic Catchment Area project. *Psychiatry, 54,* 116–132.

Rutter, M. (1996, March 1). *Conduct disorder: Origins and outcome.* Paper presented at the annual meeting of the Danish Psychiatric Association, Copenhagen.

Schuckit, M. A., & Smith, T. L. (1996). An 8-year follow-up of 450 sons of alcoholics and controls. *Archives of General Psychiatry, 53,* 202–210.

Schulsinger, F. (1972). Psychopathy: Heredity and environment. *International Journal of Mental Health, 1,* 190–306.

Schulsinger, F., Knop, J., Goodwin, D. W., Teasdale, T. W., & Mikkelsen, U. (1986). A prospective study of young men at high risk for alcoholism. *Archives of General Psychiatry, 43,* 755–760.

Stabenau, J. R. (1990). Additive independent factors that predict risk for alcoholism. *Journal of Studies on Alcohol, 51,* 164–174.

Vaillant, G. E. (1995). *The natural history of alcoholism revisited.* Cambridge, MA: Harvard University Press.

21

Antisocial Personality Disorder and Narcotic Addiction

PER VAGLUM

The co-occurrence of antisocial behavior and addictions is a well-known phenomenon. In Western culture, narcotic addiction has for centuries been regarded by both laypeople and many professionals as an indication of an immoral or antisocial personality. It is therefore not surprising that when using a multiaxial diagnostic system like the DSM, one finds a high diagnostic overlap between a diagnosis of narcotic addiction (i.e., substance dependence or abuse involving a narcotic) and the diagnosis of antisocial personality disorder (APD). However, all narcotic addicts do not fulfill the criteria for APD. Adult antisocial behavior, even when it is unrelated to drug misuse, is not sufficient for this diagnosis; The person must in addition fulfill the criteria for conduct disorder (CD) before the age of 15. Narcotic addicts who fulfill the DSM APD criteria therefore constitute a subgroup of such addicts. Whether or to what degree this diagnostic overlap between narcotic addiction and APD has any specific clinical implications is still an open question, however. The aim of this chapter is to review some of our present knowledge about the nature of this diagnostic overlap and its possible clinical implications. There is an important overlap between alcoholism and APD (Sher & Trull, 1994; see also Knop, Jensen, & Mortensen, Chapter 20, this volume) as well, but this chapter will focus mainly on narcotic addiction. Since many drug addicts are alcohol misusers and vice versa, this chapter will also review some studies of polysubstance addicts.

APD (or, in the ICD, dyssocial personality disorder) is characterized by somewhat different criteria in the DSM and ICD systems. As regards drug misusers, the Research Diagnostic Criteria (RDC) and the criteria for psychopathy, as specified in the Psychopathy Checklist—Revised (PCL-R; Hare, 1991), have also been used. In this chapter, the studies reviewed are based on DSM-III or DSM-III-R criteria if nothing else is specified. The literature discussing the validity of the DSM and the ICD criteria for APD/dyssocial personality disorder is not reviewed in this chapter.

PREVALENCE OF THE OVERLAP OF APD
AND NARCOTIC ADDICTION

Verheul, van den Brink, and Hartgers (1995) have reviewed 40 studies published between 1982 and 1994 that reported empirical data on the prevalence of APD among substance misusers. The prevalence rate showed a wide variation: 3–48% among cocaine misusers, 7–48% among opiate misusers, and 1–62% among polydrug misusers. This variation seems to be most strongly related to the different research methods used. Structured interviews (e.g., the Diagnostic Interview Schedule [DIS]) gave the highest prevalence (median = 40%), and clinical assessment gave the lowest prevalence (median = 10%). There were only small variations between types of substance used (the highest median, among poly-substance abusers, was 30%), and between different settings (the highest median, in combined in- and outpatient samples, 32%). There was also a clear gender difference, the male–female ratio being at least 1.5:1.0. Verheul et al. included two studies of APD among polydrug addicts who were nonpatients. Muntaner et al. (1989), using the DIS, found a prevalence of 39%, while Zimmerman and Coryell (1989), using the Structured Interview for DSM-III Personality Disorders (SIDP), found a prevalence of 23%.

Verheul et al. (1995) concluded that the best estimate of the APD prevalence ranged from 24% to 30% in narcotic addicts (it was 18% in alcoholics). This estimate is not far from the 18% prevalence of APD among drug addicts in the U.S. Epidemiologic Catchment Area (ECA) study (Regier et al., 1990), which was not included in Verheul et al.'s review. In this epidemiological study, the lifetime prevalence of APD in the general population was 2.6%, whereas it was somewhat higher in the National Comorbidity Survey (3.5%) (Kessler, 1995). Flynn, Craddock, Luckey, Hubbard, and Dunteman (1996) found in a national, multisite, prospective study of 7,400 drug misusers in treatment that the APD prevalence was 39%. Flynn et al.'s study also illustrates the different prevalence in samples of "pure alcoholics" compared with polydrug misusers: Their "pure alcoholics" had an APD prevalence of 35%, whereas their polydrug misusers had a prevalence of 60%. A similar difference was found in our study of a nationwide representative sample of patients seeking inpatient treatment for substance misuse in Iceland (Tomasson & Vaglum, 1995). In our total sample, 28% got an APD diagnosis. Among the "pure alcoholics" the APD rate was 15%, while among the polysubstance misusers, it was 64%.

In summary, even if there are methodological and sampling problems that make comparisons difficult (see also Weiss, Mirin, & Griffin, 1992), the prevalence of APD is significantly higher among narcotic addicts than it is in the general population. It also seems clear that one can expect APD more frequently among narcotic or polydrug misusers than among "pure alcoholics," and more often among men than among women. One should also be aware of the fact that narcotic addiction and APD both independently increase the risk of having other additional serious disorders, such as schizophrenia, major depressive disorder, anxiety disorders, and borderline personality disorder. This comorbidity may have important implications for treatment and outcome, but has not been sufficiently studied yet (Drake, Bartels, Teague, Noordsby, & Clarke, 1993; Tomasson & Vaglum, 1996).

ARE APD AND NARCOTIC ADDICTION RELATED?

The co-occurrence of two different disorders or syndromes in the same person does not necessarily imply that they are related (Wittchen, 1996). First of all, the co-occurrence may be due to a chance overlap. This possibility can be ruled out here, because the prevalence of APD among drug addicts is much higher than it is in the general population.

Another reason for the high co-occurrence of APD and narcotic addiction could be a selection bias ("Bergson's fallacy"). Persons with this combination could be more likely to be referred for treatment, and the high prevalence of this combination in clinical samples could be misleading. However, while the prevalence of APD is smaller among untreated than among treated drug misusers, it is still much higher among untreated misusers than it is in the general population. How large the difference may be between addicts who are patients and addicts who are nonpatients can be illustrated as follows: Three studies (Ross, Glaser, & Germanson, 1988; van Limbeck, Wouters, Kaplan, Geerlings, & van Alem, 1982; Tomasson & Vaglum, 1995) found the prevalence of APD (according to the DIS) to be about 60% among polydrug misusers who were patients, whereas Muntaner et al. (1989), also using the DIS, found a rate of 39% among nonpatient polydrug misusers. These findings also illustrate that among polysubstance addicts, APD seems to increase motivation to seek treatment. This is a somewhat intriguing fact, since one might think that antisocial individuals would not be inclined to seek treatment. Substance-misusing persons with APD, however, may be a subgroup of persons with APD in the general population, who may believe more in getting help from others. These differences in treatment-seeking patterns among persons with APD should be explored further.

Having ruled out the possibility of explaining the co-occurrence of APD and narcotic addiction as a chance overlap or a selection bias, we are left with some other possibilities to explain the nature of this relationship: (1) APD and narcotic addiction may be the same disorder (low discriminative validity of APD); (2) APD may be a factor predisposing individuals to narcotic addiction; (3) APD may be a secondary consequence of narcotic addiction; or (4) APD and narcotic addiction may be (spuriously) linked together by a third factor. It is also possible that APD and narcotic addiction may develop in a reciprocal relationship, each increasing the further development of the other. In clinical work, it is very important to know whether the occurrence of APD influences the response to different treatment modalities and/or the course and outcome of the narcotic addiction. In the following, each of these points is discussed in somewhat more detail.

ARE APD AND NARCOTIC ADDICTION THE SAME DISORDER?

The high overlap between APD and narcotic addiction could be due to overlapping criteria, and/or in reality they may be one and the same disorder. Gerstly et al. (1989) and others (e.g., Widiger & Corbitt, 1993) have pointed out the similarities between the DSM-III/DSM-III-R criteria for APD and for substance use disorders, especially substance abuse, and have questioned the validity of this diagnostic distinction. Substance abuse is in itself considered an antisocial behavior in DSM-III, and it may also by itself induce specific behavioral problems, such as impulsivity, criminality, irritability, and poor role functioning. The DSM-III/DSM-III-R criteria for APD include such behavior as irritability, inability to sustain consistent work behavior, inability to function as a responsible parent, failure to conform to social norms with respect to lawful behavior, failure to plan ahead and to honor financial obligations, and recklessness regarding one's own safety. These are all criteria that are very similar to the criteria for substance abuse, such as theft, hazardous behavior, and failure to fulfill role functions in home, school, and work. Blackburn (1990) and others (e.g., Rutter, 1987; Hart & Hare, 1989) have also pointed out that the DSM-III/DSM-III-R APD criteria are mainly signs of social deviance and not of an antisocial (or psychopathic) personality.

Several studies have explored the discriminative validity of an APD subgroup among substance misusers. Alterman and Cacciola (1991) have reviewed this literature in regard to developmental course, treatment response, and family history of APD, and concluded that substance-misusers with APD satisfy many of the criteria that apply to establishing the validity of a clinical subtype. But they have also underlined the psychiatric heterogeneity within the APD substance-misusing group.

The importance of the CD criteria for the validity of the APD diagnosis has been explored in several recent studies. Brooner, Schmidt, Felch, and Bigelow (1992), studying a group of 237 drug misusers, compared the subgroup fulfilling only the adult APD criteria with those also fulfilling the childhood criteria. The inclusion of the childhood criteria identified a subset of misusers with important differences in extent and severity of adult antisocial behavior. Cacciola, Rutherford, Alterman, and Snider (1994) also explored whether there were any differences of clinical importance among 269 male cocaine or alcohol misusers by comparing the APD subgroup with a subgroup fulfilling only all the adult APD criteria and a non-APD subgroup. More men with APD reported arrests, illegal behavior, and chronic lying than men in the other two subgroups. The authors concluded that early onset of antisocial behavior may be a manifestation of an inherent problem, whereas adult-only antisocial behavior may be more situational (i.e., substance-use-related) behavior. Cottler, Price, Compton, and Mager (1995) also divided a drug-injecting group of 405 men and women into a group with APD and a group fulfilling only the adult APD criteria. The APD group had different scores on all childhood criteria, on adult impulsive and aggressive behavior, and on a measure of severe drug misuse.

Smith and Newman (1990) examined a sample of 360 male inmates to see whether there was a relationship between drug misuse and the two factors of the original PCL: Factor 2 (antisocial behavior) and Factor 1 (core psychopathic features, narcissism). In accordance with Hart and Hare (1989), they found a correlation only between drug misuse and Factor 2. This may indicate that among psychopaths, substance misuse is mainly linked to the disposition to engage in disinhibited behavior. This does not rule out the possibility that the core psychopathic features can have importance for treatment seeking, treatment response, or further course of substance misuse or other outcome measures among narcotic addicts. We found that narcissistic traits predicted death in a 5-year follow-up study (Ravndal & Vaglum, 1998). The importance of psychopathy and narcissism for the course of drug addiction should be further explored.

There has been some debate regarding whether the antisocial criteria for APD among addicts should be independent of the substance misuse. The RDC definition of APD specifically required that the antisocial behavior should *not* be a result of substance misuse. In fact, applying the RDC and the DSM-III criteria to the same patient samples demonstrated a difference in the prevalence of APD of between 20% and 45% (Rounsaville, Tierney, Crits-Cristoph, Weissman, & Kleber, 1982; Woody, McLellan, Luborsky, & O'Brien, 1985). However, Woody et al. (1985) also found that treatment outcome was not affected by their choice of the DSM-III criteria or the RDC. Dinwiddie and Reich (1993) compared 93 men who met APD criteria in the absence of substance-related problems with 32 subjects who got the diagnosis of APD regardless of whether the criterion symptoms occurred along with substance-related problems. Subjects with persistent antisocial behavior were indistinguishable on a variety of measures, regardless of whether the antisocial behavior occurred in the context of ongoing substance misuse or not. Their conclusion was that among those with persistent early onset of antisocial behavior, antisocial problems appeared to be more parsimoniously ascribed to APD than to substance misuse. Counting antisocial symptoms toward the APD diagnosis, regardless of substance misuse status, improved the reliability of the diagnosis without adversely affecting the diagnostic validity.

In summary, to a certain degree these studies support the discriminant validity of the APD diagnosis among narcotic addicts. It identifies a subgroup with long-standing and especially violent and criminal antisocial behavior. This subgroup is, however, not necessarily very homogeneous on other important characteristics, such as comorbid Axis I and Axis II disorders.

IS APD A FACTOR PREDISPOSING INDIVIDUALS TO NARCOTIC ADDICTION?

To study the second question, ideally we need prospective and longitudinal studies that measure antisocial behavior and the criteria for CD before the onset of use of illegal drugs. A high-risk design is also very useful. There are now several such studies in the literature. Robins (1966), in her prospective study of deviant children, found that sociopathic behavior and aggression predicted adult drug problems. Kellam, Enswinger, Simon, Turner, and Zaidi (1978) used information collected in the first grade to predict drug use at age 17, and found that aggressive behavior predated the males' but not the females' drug misuse. Zucker and De Voe (1973) found that girls who became drug users had previously tended to be antisocial and rebellious. Also, a 9-year prospective study of more than 1,000 adolescents by Kandel, Sincha-Fagan, and Davies (1986) showed delinquency as a precursor to the use of illicit drugs in young adulthood, rather than the reverse. Their results also supported the possible relationship of drug use to nonaggressive CD and to covert delinquency (Loeber & Schmaling, 1985).

Boyle et al. (1992) followed up 726 boys and girls aged 12–16 over 4 years. They found that among the psychiatric disorders at first examination, only substance use and CD made an independent contribution to predicting the use of marijuana and hard drugs. Ferguson, Lynshey, and Horwood (1993) studied a birth cohort of New Zealand children, who were examined at 6, 8, 10, 12, and 15 years of age. Conduct problems during middle childhood were significantly associated with later cannabis use. Henry et al. (1993) studied the relative importance of CD problems and depressive symptoms, measured at 11 years of age, for predicting substance use at age 15 in an unselected birth cohort from New Zealand. For males, both CD and depression predicted drug use, depressive symptoms being intermediate between CD and later drug use. Robins and McEvoy (1990) examined data from the ECA study in the United States; they found that CD increased the risk of earlier use of drugs, as well as the risk of going from drug use to drug misuse. We (Storm-Mathisen & Vaglum, 1994) followed up a clinical sample of 75 child and adolescent psychiatric patients with CD 20 years later. At this time (mean age = 34; range = 26–39), 25% had a substance use disorder; most of these had an additional anxiety disorder at the index admission.

Offord and Bennet (1994) have reviewed the literature concerning the long-term outcome of CD. In accordance with the review by Robins and Price (1991), they came to the conclusion that conduct problems or CD predates adult antisocial behavior and drug abuse/dependence, to a somewhat weaker extent in women than in men. However, not all aggressive boys become substance misusers. O'Donnell, Hawkins, and Abbot (1995) studied which factors could inhibit later drug misuse in a 3½-year prospective study of boys who were identified as aggressive by teacher reports at ages 10–11. A combination of skills for prosocial involvement, school bonding and achievement, family bonding and management practice, norms regarding substance misuse, and interactions with peers and adults significantly discriminated between boys who would and would not proceed into drug misuse.

In summary, the literature uniformly supports the notion that symptoms of CD in childhood and adolescence very often predate APD and drug misuse in adulthood. This means that a significant part of antisocial behavior among adult drug addicts is not solely a consequence of the use of drugs or of their daily lives as addicts. This has preventive implications and underlines the importance of prevention and early treatment of CD. In this connection, is it important to remember the empirical evidence showing that other childhood and adolescent disorders besides CD may be precursors of substance misuse, especially depression and attention-deficit/hyperactivity disorder. Both these disorders, independently of CD, may increase the risk of later drug addiction.

IS APD A CONSEQUENCE OF NARCOTIC ADDICTION?

Although adult antisocial behavior among narcotic addicts in many cases is secondary to childhood antisocial behavior, drug misuse, and membership in the drug addict subculture, it is without doubt also able to produce a lot of symptoms and behaviors that are identical to the adult antisocial behavior criteria for APD. In North American clinical samples, 20–40% of addicts seem to have started their antisocial behavior secondary to the use of drugs. Drug effects may lead to disinhibition and reckless behavior, as well as to poor role performance in many situations. Withdrawal effects may increase irritability, aggressiveness, and violent behavior. Adult antisocial behaviors such as these are, however, not sufficient for the APD diagnosis. Because the childhood CD criteria are demanded for the APD diagnosis, the question of whether APD is secondary to drug misuse is therefore a question of whether CD before 15 years of age is primary or secondary to drug misuse. Ideally, this question should be answered by prospective studies following children from early childhood to 15 years of age. Several such studies are under way. Still, most of the studies presently available involve clinical material on adolescents.

Loeber, Green, Keenan, and Lahey (1995) studied a sample of 177 preadolescent boys in a 6-year follow-up study, and found that substance misuse was not a predictor of CD. A recent, interesting study by Brown, Glegham, Schuckit, Myers, and Mott (1996) explored the degree to which CD symptoms predated or were secondary to polydrug misuse (mainly alcoholism) in a sample of 166 California adolescents without a DSM-III-R Axis I disorder that predated their substance misuse. Forty-seven percent were classified as "primary" CD patients, and 48% as "secondary" (i.e., they fulfilled the criteria only when delinquent behavior related to substance misuse was included). Primary CD teens reported a significant earlier age for the first CD behavior. Some of the items that discriminated best between the primary and the secondary CD groups were, interestingly enough, items that are very low in frequency in the general adolescent population (e.g., cruelty to animals, setting illegal fires). At follow-up 2 years later, the primary CD group reported significantly more APD behavior independently of substance misuse, and about 44% of the primary CD group now fulfilled the criteria for APD. Brown et al.'s sample is highly selected and difficult to generalize from. But it shows that a certain part of the CD behavior in clinical samples of adolescent drug misusers, may be secondary to the drug involvement.

In summary, these studies indicate that just as there are "primary" and "secondary" types of antisocial behavior among adult drug addicts, this is also possibly the case before the age of 15 concerning CD symptoms. In many countries, use of illicit drugs will be very moderate before 15 years, whereas use of alcohol may be more extensive. Cultural differences may therefore influence the probability of CD secondary to substance misuse before 15 years of age. The distinction between primary CD and secondary CD seems to have prognostic validity, but we need prospective, long-term studies of more representative samples than that of Brown et al. (1996). If persons with secondary CD have a different prognosis from that of APD patients with primary CD, this may explain some of the variance in the outcome between different clinical follow-up studies of APD samples. This should also remind us of the clinical heterogeneity in samples of addicts with antisocial behavior. Moffitt (1993) has underlined the importance of differentiating between antisocial behavior that persists from childhood to adulthood and antisocial behavior that is only present in adolescence (see also DiLalla & Gottesman, 1989). Not all CD children become substance misusers, and we also need to know more about the relative importance of genetic, biological, comorbid, and situational/cultural factors that influence the movement from CD to APD and substance misuse. This question is still wide open.

ARE CD/APD AND NARCOTIC ADDICTION LINKED TOGETHER BY A THIRD VARIABLE?

Theoretically, the co-occurrence of CD/APD and narcotic addiction could be due to a third variable (or to several such variables) that is (or are) strongly correlated with both. If we were to control for this variable, the correlation between CD/APD and narcotic addiction should disappear. Such third variables have as yet not been identified, but in theory they could be genetic, biological, temperamental, psychopathological, and/or environmental factors. Instead, most genetic and developmental research seems to support a developmental process model, starting with APD or hyperaggression in the biological parents, and leading to hyperaggression, oppositional defiant disorder, CD, adult APD, and eventually substance misuse in the offspring (Schubert, Wolf, Petterson, Grande, & Pendleton, 1988; Cadoret, Yates, Troughton, Woodworth, & Stewart, 1995a, 1995b). Cadoret et al. (1995a) found in their adoption study that there was an additional genetic pathway leading directly from a substance-misusing biological parent to a substance-misusing (dependent) adoptee. They also found that an interaction between adverse home environments in the adoptive families and a history of APD in the biological parents increased the rate of CD in the adoptees. Further research should give us more understanding of how biological, personality, and sociocultural variables increase the risk of proceeding from CD to APD, and later to substance misuse.

IS APD RELATED TO TREATMENT DROPOUT AND TO THE CLINICAL COURSE?

Since the APD criteria imply long-standing antisocial activity, and since illicit drug use is one form of antisocial activity, one would expect narcotic addicts fulfilling the criteria for APD to have higher risk of treatment dropout and to have poorer short- and long-term outcomes than other addicts. However, the predictive validity of APD with regard to the course of substance misuse seems to be poor; it seems to be stronger as a predictor of treatment dropout and of further criminality.

In the 1970s, before the DSM-III criteria were established, I conducted a personal 4- to 5-year follow-up study of 100 drug misusers who were treated in a drug-free therapeutic community (Vaglum, 1979). They were classified into three groups: "psychotic" (15%), "autoplastic" (61%; i.e., inhibited behavior, high on anxiety and depressive symptoms), and "alloplastic" (24%; impulsive, aggressive, reckless, and irritable behavior, low on anxiety and depression). Within the follow-up period, 64% of the alloplastic patients were sentenced to jail, in contrast with 18% in the autoplastic group and 7% in the psychotic group. At follow-up, 71% of the autoplastic patients were still using drugs, as opposed to 39% among the other groups. This alloplastic group may have resembled the nontreatable subgroup of opiate addicts in the later study of professional psychotherapy by Woody et al. (1985). These authors found that opiate addicts with a combination of APD and depression were treatable and had about the same good 7-month outcome as patients without an APD diagnosis. The opiate addicts with "pure" APD had a poor outcome, also in an ordinary drug counseling intervention. The same was found by Friedman and Glickman (1987). Gerstly et al. (1989) later re-examined the data from the Woody et al. (1985) study, and found that an early positive working alliance between a therapist and an APD addict had high predictive power concerning a good outcome.

Several other studies have examined the possible impact of APD on clinical course and treatment response, but without studying subgroups of APD addicts. Rounsaville and colleagues (Rounsaville et al., 1982; Rounsaville, Kosten, Weissman, & Kleber, 1986) followed up treatment-seeking opiate addicts for 6 months and 2½ years; they found that APD was not correlated with the course of drug use, but was somewhat correlated with later illegal activities and psychosocial adjustment. This was replicated in a study by Kosten, Kosten, and Rounsaville (1989), in which 150 treated opiate addicts were followed over 2½ years. Again, the "pure" APD group had more legal problems, but did not differ as to drug use. Cacciola and colleagues (Cacciola, Alterman, Rutherford, & Snider, 1995; Cacciola, Rutherford, Alterman, McKay, & Snider, 1996) followed up patients with different types of drug addiction over 7 months. In the first study, APD was related to continuous illegal activity; in the second, it was linked to a poor overall outcome. Again, APD was not specifically related to the course of drug use, and there were no clear differences between patients with APD and patients with borderline and histrionic personality disorders.

Failure to predict use of drugs from APD alone also occurred in a Norwegian study, in which we followed up 200 addicts in a Phoenix House program over 5 years (Ravndal & Vaglum, 1998). Self-report scores on the Millon Clinical Multiaxial Inventory (MCMI) Antisocial scale at entry did not predict the level of drug use after 5 years, but it did predict (together with narcissism) the occurrence of death during the follow-up period. In contrast to the scores on the MCMI scales measuring Cluster A and Cluster C disorders, which became more like those of normal subjects during the Phoenix House inpatient treatment, the scores regarding the Cluster B scales (the Antisocial, Narcissistic, and Histrionic scales) somewhat increased during the year addicts were abstinent and in treatment (Ravndal & Vaglum, 1991a). We also explored the influence of self-reported antisocial traits on dropout from the 1-year inpatient phase and the subsequent 6-month outpatient phase of the treatment program (Ravndal & Vaglum, 1991b). Antisocial scores at entry did not predict dropout, but a subgroup with high self-reported antisocial aggression both at entry and after the drug-free inpatient year had an increased risk of dropping out in the outpatient phase. These findings indicate that participating in the Phoenix House program did not reduce self-reported antisocial traits, and it illustrates that in such treatment programs, highly antisocial clients may "survive" without changing.

Cacciola et al. (1996) also found that APD patients left a methadone maintenance program at a higher rate than non-APD patients did. Arndt, McLellan, Dorozynsky, Woody, and O'Brien (1994) found in a 12-week random assignment placebo control trial of desipramine for the treatment of cocaine dependence that patients with APD made few gains with either medication or placebo, whereas non-APD patients made a number of gains with desipramine, but not with placebo.

In summary, these studies show that the predictive validity of the APD with regard to the course of substance misuse seems to be poor, but its predictive validity as to treatment dropout and further criminal activity seems to be stronger. These studies indicate that the possibility of reducing drug use among the APD subgroup of narcotic addicts is either as good or as poor as it is with other diagnostic subgroups. However, these findings have up to now come mainly from studies of North American methadone patients; they should be replicated in drug-free programs, with a longer follow-up period, with a longitudinal design, and on other continents. Selective attrition of the most serious psychopaths may have taken place in the follow-up studies conducted to date, and this would increase the risk of Type II errors. We should also note that the interpersonal problems of APD addicts may be the factors that lead to a higher dropout rate from treatment programs, and possibly to a poorer outcome in psychotherapy. This should lead to a more thorough evaluation of the interpersonal competence of APD addicts before they are refused therapy. Furthermore, methadone maintenance does not seem to reduce criminal behavior in APD patients as much as in other clients. This may mean that all criminal behavior is not secondary to drug misuse, and that the non-drug-related antisocial behavior is the behavior that continues. In new follow-up studies, it will therefore be important to verify this distinction. The importance of APD for treatment response and further course is still very much an open question, and the need for more research is extensive.

CLINICAL IMPLICATIONS

The general principles and practice of treating persons with APD are covered in other chapters of this book. Here, only some of the implications concerning narcotic addicts with APD are discussed.

The clinical implications of the co-occurrence of APD and narcotic addiction are still partly unclear. More studies—both prospective, longitudinal studies and experimental/quasi-experimental treatment studies—are needed. The high prevalence of APD and narcotic addiction in clinical samples underlines the importance of identifying APD and differentiating between APD and adult antisocial behavior, as well as between drug-induced and non-drug-induced criminal activity. If clinical treatment results are to be comparable, it is necessary to know the prevalence of APD in the different samples. In the evaluation of treatment programs, it is also important to clarify whether each one manages to keep APD addicts in treatment throughout the program. Since APD seems to be a predictor of dropout in some programs, monitoring of antisocial traits could be one way of identifying the clients with the highest risk of dropping out.

In treatment planning for APD addicts, it is important to remember how heterogeneous this group really is. To deny them, as a group, any type of treatment is yet not supported by empirical evidence. A clear finding emerging from the literature is that the subgroup of narcotic addicts with APD is heterogeneous in ways that may have clinical implications. This heterogeneity concerns comorbidity with other Axis I disorders (e.g., depression, schizophrenia) and other Axis II disorders (e.g., borderline and narcissistic personality disorders); It also concerns differences in self-esteem and in interpersonal and psychotherapeutic competence. Some comorbid disorders may increase treatability, and some may decrease it. There may also be a subgroup in which CD/APD is secondary to drug use, and this group may have a better prognosis. This complex heterogeneity should lead to a careful diagnostic evaluation of APD-positive narcotic addicts, and should result in differential, tailor-made psychosocial and psychopharmacological interventions. However, the importance of this heterogeneity is still not well enough understood and should be further explored.

Another important reason why it may be clinically useful to identify the subgroup of narcotic addicts with APD is that these patients usually will be those who are most strongly trying to introduce antisocial values into a treatment program and a group of patients. They may also try more often than others to become leaders within the patient group, and may try to exploit their fellow patients. Therapists should therefore be especially alert if such persons assume leadership positions within a group of patients. Because of their aggression and manipulative skills, they may more easily "survive" in therapeutic communities than more anxious and schizotypal addicts may (Ravndal & Vaglum, 1991a, 1991b).

Still another important finding from the literature is that APD does not seem directly related to the further course of drug misuse. APD is very important as a risk factor for the development of drug abuse/dependence, but once this is established, APD no longer seems to be an independent risk factor for continuing abuse/dependence. However, APD is a clear risk factor for continuing criminal activity, and drug misuse may be secondarily related to criminality. Continuing criminal activity and drug misuse may also be secondarily related to poor social skills. Social skills training, therefore, should possibly be a major part of all treatment programs for APD addicts. The drug-free therapeutic community models, such as the Phoenix House model, may be viewed as mainly forms of social and interpersonal skills training. We found in our Phoenix House study (Ravndal & Vaglum, 1998) that completion of the full 18-month program was directly related to better social functioning in the follow-up period, which in turn was related to the level of substance misuse 3½ years later.

CONCLUSIONS

• APD is a clinically valid diagnosis among narcotic addicts, and should be identified in addicts coming to treatment. Antisocial behavior may also be part of a psychopathic syndrome.

• APD is most often antecedent to substance misuse, whereas adult antisocial behavior among addicts may also be secondary to substance misuse.

• Genetic and environmental factors seem to interact in a developmental process, in which a biological parent with antisocial or hyperaggressive behavior has a child with low control of aggression and impulsive behavior. The results are CD in childhood and adolescence, adult APD, and substance misuse.

- APD is very often comorbid with other Axis I and Axis II disorders among narcotic addicts. The importance of this is still not clear, but it may have importance for treatment course and outcome in subgroups of APD addicts.

- APD is an important antecedent factor to narcotic addiction, but when the addiction is established, APD does not seem to have a direct influence on the further course of the addiction. APD seems more directly related to the further course of social functioning and criminality, and may thereby indirectly also influence the course of the substance misuse.

- In treatment programs for narcotic addicts with APD, it may be important (1) to monitor self reported antisocial symptoms; (2) to reduce other patients' risk of being exploited by APD patients who participate in the program without changing; and (3) to increase the APD participants' social skills.

- Further research is needed to clarify the role of APD and psychopathy in treatment completion and in the long-term course of substance misuse.

REFERENCES

Alterman, A. I., Cacciola J. S. (1991). The antisocial personality disorder diagnosis in substance abusers: Problems and issues. *Journal of Nervous and Mental Disease, 179,* 401–409.

Arndt, I. O., McLellan, A. T., Dorozynsky, L., Woody, G., & O'Brien, C. (1994). Despramine treatment for cocaine dependence: Role of antisocial personality disorder. *Journal of Nervous and Mental Disease, 182,* 151–156.

Blackburn, R. (1990). Treatment of the psychopathic offender. *Issues in Criminological and Legal Psychology, 16,* 54–66.

Boyle, M. H., Offord, D. R., Racine, Y. A., Szatmari, P., Fleming, J. E., & Links, P. S. (1992). Predicting substance use in late adolescence: Results from the Ontario Child Health Study follow up. *American Journal of Psychiatry, 149,* 761–767.

Brooner, R. K., Schmidt, C. W., Felch, L. J., & Bigelow, G. E. (1992). Antisocial behavior of intravenous drug abusers: Implications for diagnosis of antisocial personality disorder. *American Journal of Psychiatry, 149,* 482–487.

Brown, S. A. Glegham, A., Schuckit, M. A., Myers, M. G., & Mott, M. A. (1996). Conduct disorder among adolescent alcohol and drug abusers. *Journal of Studies on Alcohol, 57,* 314–324.

Cacciola, J. S., Alterman, A. I., Rutherford, M. J., & Snider, E. C. (1995). Treatment response of antisocial substance abusers. *Journal of Nervous and Mental Disease, 183,* 166–171.

Cacciola, J. S., Rutherford, M. J., Alterman, A. I., McKay, J. R., & Snider, E. C. (1996). Personality disorder and treatment outcome in methadone maintenance patients. *Journal of Nervous and Mental Disease, 184,* 234–239.

Cacciola, J. S., Rutherford, M. J., Alterman, A. I., & Snider, E. (1994). An examination of the diagnostic criteria for antisocial personality disorder in substance abusers. *Journal of Nervous and Mental Disease, 182,* 517–523.

Cadoret, R. J., Yates, W. R., Troughton, E., Woodworth, G., & Stewart, M. (1995a). Adoption study demonstrating two genetic pathways to drug abuse. *Archives of General Psychiatry, 52,* 42–52.

Cadoret, R. J., Yates, W. R., Troughton, E., Woodworth, G., & Stewart, M. (1995b). Genetic environmental interaction in the genesis of aggressivity and conduct disorders. *Archives of General Psychiatry, 52,* 916–924.

Cottler, L. B., Price, R. K., Compton, W. J., & Mager, D. E. (1995). Subtypes of adult antisocial behavior among drug abusers. *Journal of Nervous and Mental Disease, 183,* 154–161.

DiLalla, L. F., & Gottesman, J. J. (1989). Heterogeneity of causes of delinquency and criminality: Life span perspectives. *Development and Psychopathology, 1,* 339–349.

Dinwiddie, S. H., & Reich, T. H. (1993). Attribution of antisocial symptoms in coexistent antisocial personality disorder and substance abuse. *Comprehensive Psychiatry, 34,* 235–242.

Drake, R., Bartels, S. J., Teague, G. B., Noordsby, O. L., & Clark, R. E. (1993). Treatment of substance abuse in severely mentally ill patients. *Journal of Nervous and Mental Disease, 181,* 606–611.

Ferguson, D. M., Lynshey, M. T., & Horwood, L. J. (1993). Conduct problems and attention deficit behaviour in middle childhood and cannabis use by age 15. *Australian and New Zealand Journal of Psychiatry, 27,* 673–682.

Flynn, P. M., Craddock, S. G., Luckey, J. W., Hubbard, R. L., & Dunteman, G. H. (1996). Comorbidity of antisocial personality and mood disorders among psychoactive substance-dependent treatment clients. *Journal of Personality Disorders, 10,* 56–67.

Friedman, A. S., & Glickman, N. W. (1987). Effects of psychiatric symptomatology on treatment outcome for adolescent male drug abusers. *Journal of Nervous and Mental Disease, 175,* 425–430.

Gerstly, L., McLellan, A. T., Alterman, A. I., Woody, G. E., Luborsky, L., & Prout, M. (1989). Ability to form an alliance with the therapist: a possible marker of prognosis for patients with antisocial personality disorder. *American Journal of Psychiatry, 146,* 508–512.

Hare, R. D. (1991). *The Hare Psychopathy Checklist—Revised.* Toronto: Multi-Health Systems.

Hart, S. D., & Hare, R. D. (1989). Discriminant validity of the Psychopathic Checklist in a forensic psychiatric population. *Psychological Assessment: A Journal of Consulting and Clinical Psychology, 1,* 211–218.

Henry, B., Feehan, M., McGee, R., Stanton, W., Moffitt, T. E., & Silva, P. (1993). The importance of conduct problems and depressive symptoms in predicting adolescent substance use. *Journal of Abnormal Child Psychology, 21,* 469–480.

Kandel, D., Sincha-Fagan, O., & Davies, M. (1986). Risk factors for delinquency and illicit drug use from adolescence to young adulthood. *Journal of Drug Issues, 16,* 67–90.

Kellam, S., Enswinger, M., Simon, M., Turner, R., & Zaidi, Q. (1978). *Mental health in first grade and teenage drug use.* Chicago: Social Psychiatry Study Center, Department of Psychiatry, University of Chicago.

Kessler, R. C. (1995). Epidemiology of psychiatric comorbidity. In M. T. Tsuang, M. Tohen, & G. E. P. Zahner (Eds.), *Textbook in psychiatric epidemiology* (pp. 179–198). New York: Wiley.

Kosten, T. H., Kosten, T. R., & Rounsaville, B. J. (1989). Personality disorders in opiate addicts show prognostic specificity. *Journal of Substance Abuse Treatment, 6, 163–168.*

Loeber, R., Green, S. M., Keenan, K., & Lahey, B. B. (1995). Which boys will fare worse?: Early predictors of the onset of conduct disorder in a six year longitudinal study. *Journal of American Academy of Child and Adolescent Psychiatry, 34,* 499–509.

Loeber, R., & Schmaling, K. B. (1985). Empirical evidence for overt and covert patterns of antisocial conduct problems: A meta-analysis. *Journal of Abnormal Child Psychology, 13,* 337–353.

Moffitt, T. E. (1993). Adolescence-limited and life-course-persistent antisocial behavior: A developmental taxonomy. *Psychological Review, 100,* 674–701.

Muntaner, C., Nagoshi, C., Jaffe, J. H., Walter, D., Haertzen, C., & Fishbein, D. (1989). Correlates of self-reported early childhood aggression in subjects volunteering for drug studies. *American Journal of Drug and Alcohol Abuse, 15,* 383–402.

O'Donnell, J., Hawkins, I. D., & Abbot, R. D. (1995). Predicting serious delinquency and substance use among aggressive boys. *Journal of Consulting and Clinical Psychology, 63,* 529–537.

Offord, D. R., & Bennett, K. J. (1994). Conduct disorder: Long-term outcomes and intervention effectiveness. *Journal of the American Academy of Child and Adolescent Psychiatry, 33,* 1069–1078.

Ravndal, E., & Vaglum, P. (1991a). Psychopathology and substance abuse as predictors of program completion in a therapeutic community for drug abusers: A prospective study. *Acta Psychiatrica Scandinavica, 83,* 217–222.

Ravndal, E., & Vaglum, P. (1991b). Changes in antisocial aggressiveness during treatment in a hierarchical therapeutic community: A prospective study of personality changes. *Acta Psychiatrica Scandinavica, 84,* 524–530.

Ravndal, E., & Vaglum, P. (1998). Psychopathology, treatment completion and 5 year outcome: A prospective study of drug abusers. *Journal of Substance Abuse Treatment.*

Regier, D. A., Farmer, M. E., Rae, D. S., Locke, B. Z., Keith, S. J., Judd, L. L., & Goodwin, F. (1990). Comorbidity of mental disorders with alcohol and other drug abuse. *Journal of the American Medical Association, 264,* 2511–2518.

Robins, L. N. (1966). *Deviant children grown up.* Baltimore: Williams & Wilkins.

Robins, L. N., & McEvoy, L. T. (1990). Conduct problems as predictors of substance abuse. In L. N. Robins & M. R. Rutter (Eds.), *Straight and deviant pathways to adulthood* (pp. 182–204). New York: Cambridge University Press.

Robins, L. N., & Price, R. K. (1991). Adult disorders predicted by childhood conduct problems: Results from the NIMH Epidemiologic Catchment Area Project. *Psychiatry, 54,* 116–132.

Ross, H. E., Glaser, F. B., & Germanson, T. (1988). The prevalence of psychiatric disorders in patients with alcohol and other drug problems. *Archives of General Psychiatry, 45,* 1023–1031.

Rounsaville, B. J., Kosten, T. R., Weissman, M. M., & Kleber, H. D. (1986). Diagnostic significance of psychopathology in treated opiate addicts. *Archives of General Psychiatry, 43,* 739–745.

Rounsaville, B. J., Tierney, T., Crits-Christoph, K., Weissman, M. M., & Kleber, H. D. (1982). Predictors of outcome in treatment of opiate addicts: Evidence for the multidimensional nature of addicts' problems. *Comprehensive Psychiatry, 23,* 462–478.

Rutter, M. (1987). Temperament, personality and personality disorders. *British Journal of Psychiatry, 150,* 443–458.

Schubert, D. S., Wolf, A. W., Petterson, M. B., Grande T. P., & Pendleton, L. (1988). A statistical evaluation of the literature regarding the associations among alcoholism, drug abuse, and antisocial personality disorder. *International Journal of the Addictions, 23,* 797–808.

Sher, K. J., & Trull, T. J. (1994). Personality and disinhibitory psychopathology: Alcoholism and antisocial personality disorder. *Journal of Abnormal Psychology, 103,* 92–102.

Smith, S. S., & Newman, J. P. (1990). Alcohol and drug abuse–dependence disorders in psychopathic and non-psychopathic criminal offenders. *Journal of Abnormal Psychology, 99,* 430–439.

Storm-Mathisen, A., & Vaglum, P. (1994). Conduct disorder patients 20 years later: A personal follow-up study. *Acta Psychiatrica Scandinavica, 89,* 416–420.

Tomasson, K., & Vaglum, P. (1995). A nationwide representative sample of treatment-seeking alcoholics: A study of psychiatric comorbidity. *Acta Psychiatrica Scandinavica, 92,* 378–385.

Tomasson, K., & Vaglum, P. (1996). Psychopathology and alcohol consumption among treatment seeking alcoholics: A prospective study. *Addiction, 91,* 1019–1030.

Vaglum, P. (1979). [*Young drug abusers in a therapeutic community*] (in Norwegian). Oslo: Universitetsforlaget.

van Limbeck, J., Wouters, L., Kaplan, C. D., Geerlings, P. J., & van Alem, V. (1992). Prevalence of psychopathology in drug-addicted Dutch. *Journal of Substance Abuse Treatment, 9,* 43–52.

Verheul, R., van den Brink, W., & Hartgers, C. (1995). Prevalence of personality disorders among alchoholics and drug addicts: An overview. *European Addiction Research, 1,* 166–177.

Weiss, R. D., Mirin, S. M., & Griffin, M. L. (1992). Methodological considerations in the diagnosis of coexisting psychiatric disorders in substance abusers. *British Journal of Addiction, 87,* 179–187.

Widiger, T. A., & Corbitt, E. M. (1993). Proposals for DSM-IV. *Journal of Personality Disorders, 7,* 63–77.

Wittchen, H.-U. (1996). Critical issues in the evaluation of comorbidity of psychiatric disorders. *British Journal of Psychiatry, 168*(Suppl. 30), 9–16.

Woody, G. E., McLellan, A. T., Luborsky, L., & O'Brien, C. P. (1985). Sociopathy and psychotherapy outcome. *Archives of General Psychiatry, 42,* 1081–1086.

Zimmerman, M., & Coryell, W. (1989). DSM-III personality disorder diagnoses in a nonpatient sample: Demographic correlates and comorbidity. *Archives of General Psychiatry, 46,* 682–689.

Zucker, R., & De Voe, C. (1973). Life history characteristics associated with problem drinking and antisocial behavior in adolescent girls: A comparison with male findings. In M. Raff, R. Wist, & G. Winokur (Eds.), *Life history research in psychopathology* (Vol. 4, pp. 109–134). Minneapolis: University of Minnesota Press.

22

Sadistic Personality in Murderers

MICHAEL H. STONE

Sadistic personality disorder (SPD) made its brief appearance in the standard psychiatric nomenclature of North America by virtue of its inclusion in the 1987 edition of the DSM (DSM-III-R; American Psychiatric Association, 1987). Even then it was not accorded a place side by side with the more customary disorders of Axis II, but was relegated to an appendix of proposed categories for further study. In DSM-IV (American Psychiatric Association, 1994), SPD was omitted altogether. This omission had nothing to do with any "rarity" of sadistic personalities in the general population. The rarity of sadistic persons seeking psychotherapeutic help in overcoming their negative behavior did make it difficult to gather data concerning sadism in as methodical and scientifically reliable a way as was the case with those personality disorders for which help is ordinarily sought, such as borderline, dependent, or obsessive–compulsive personality disorders (Widiger, 1996). Fiester and Gay (1995) have, in their study of SPD, drawn attention to the few articles that have thus far appeared in the literature. They cite one such study concerning 21 sex offenders, where the prevalence rate was considered "high," though it reached only 33%. Yet four of the eight DSM-III-R criteria for SPD (numerically enough to establish the diagnosis) are that a person uses violence to establish dominance, humiliates others, takes pleasure in others' suffering, and intimidates others; these would seem to apply to rapists (the most important group of sex offenders) almost universally.

Even the largely untreatable nature of SPD did not emerge as the main reason for its exclusion from DSM-IV. Instead, as Widiger (1996) has made clear, the reason was primarily political. Precisely because there are so *many* sadistic types within the domain of forensic psychiatry and within the domain of criminal law (certainly this is the case in the United States), there was worry among some of the consultants helping to revise the DSM that various defense attorneys would seize upon a diagnosis such as SPD, claiming it to be a *mental* condition "suffered" by the violent felons who became their clients—for which these clients would therefore deserve reduced sentences on the grounds of "diminished capacity." To obviate any such misuse of the DSM, SPD was dropped.

Widiger (1996) has pointed out a paradox in this decision—namely, that the staunchest advocates of excluding SPD were feminist consultants who, though they were most ardent in condemning the sadistic practices used by certain men to subjugate women, were also the most ardent in wanting to eliminate any excuse the law might find for exculpating such men. There is a thorny philosophical problem at issue here, as Widiger reminds us: The DSM is not only a document for the mental health profession, but also a social document. The descriptions and language of DSM have an inevitable impact upon the much wider circle of the community as a whole, rather than just on the narrower circle of psychiatry. Along similar lines, Spitzer, Fiester, Gay, and Pfohl (1991) surveyed psychiatrists about SPD and found 75% of the respondents worried that if this diagnosis became official, it would have a significant potential for social or forensic misuse in lessening offenders' responsibility in child or spouse abuse cases. Inclusion of SPD might, in other words, lead to the "medicalization of evil deeds"—a step on the way to trivializing their impact and inadvertently sanitizing them by offering the excuse that they were the result of an "illness."

A BIOGRAPHY-BASED STUDY OF SADISTIC PERSONALITY IN MURDERERS

Source Material

Since it is my belief that our standard nomenclature should nevertheless be a reflection of what exists in nature, and should not be trimmed here and pruned there in the hopes of outmaneuvering excuse-hungry defense attorneys, I set about several years ago to mine the richest ore available to me in my search for sadistic personalities. Certainly my private practice of psychiatry was of little use in this connection; since 1966, fewer than 1% of the approximately 500 patients I have seen either in consultation or for therapy would meet DSM-III-R criteria for SPD. Even in my hospital work, SPD is a rarity. But in forensic work, the situation is quite different. I had occasion in 1987 to testify as an expert witness concerning the personality of Jeffrey Macdonald, an Army doctor who had stabbed to death his pregnant wife and their two daughters (McGinnis, 1983). Considering it useful to situate Macdonald somewhere along a spectrum of cruelty or inhumanity, I began reading full-length biographies of murderers and recording relevant data on six dozen variables in a computer. From this exercise in "profiling," I created a scale composed of 22 compartments, arranged in ascending degrees of inhumanity—of evil, if you will. The scale is anchored at one end by examples of justified homicide, which is neither murder nor "inhumane," and progresses through crimes of passion committed by nonpsychopathic, nonsadistic persons, all the way to the extremes of sadism committed by the most callous of psychopaths. This scale, which I call the Gradations of Evil Scale, is shown in Table 22.1.

Although I have recently supplemented this material with in-depth interviews of several murderers and serial killers in a forensic psychiatric unit, I felt I could rely on full-length biographies, since almost all of them offer detailed accounts of the evolving personalities of their subjects as they passed from childhood to their later years. By now I have analyzed data from 278 such books. These books touch on the biographies of 279 persons, since one book, concerning two cousins who became the Los Angeles "Hillside Stranglers," described two offenders.

Among the biographees are 37 "uxoricides" (men who killed their wives), 23 women who killed their husbands, 26 parenticides, and 71 instances of serial homicide

TABLE 22.1. Gradations of Evil Scale

1. [Persons who have killed but are not murderers] Those who have killed in self-defense, and do not show psychopathy.
2. Jealous lovers, nonpsychopathic, committing murder in a *"crime passionel."*
3. Willing companions of killers, impulse-ridden, with some antisocial traits.
4. Killed in self-defense but were provocative to victim.
5. Traumatized persons who killed abusing relatives and others (viz., to support a drug habit) and who show remorse.
6. Impetous hot-headed murderers without psychopathy.
7. Narcissistic murderers with a psychotic core.
8. Non-psychopathic persons with smoldering rage who kill when the rage is ignited.
9. Jealous lovers with psychopathic features.
10. Killers of people "in the way"; some psychopathic traits.
11. Clearly psychopathic killers of people "in the way."
12. Power-hungry psychopaths who killed when "cornered."
13. Inadequate rageful personalities with psychopathy also.
14. Ruthlessly self-centered psychopathic schemers.
15. Psychopathic cold-blooded spree- or multiple murderers.
16. Psychopaths committing multiple vicious acts (viz., rape) with or without murdering their victims.
17. Sexually perverse serial murderers; torture not primary motive.
18. Torture-murderers where murder was the primary motive.
19. Psychopaths driven to terrorism, subjugation, intimidation, and rape—short of murder.
20. Torture-murderers: torture the primary motive, but in psychotic persons.
21. Psychopaths preoccupied with torture in the extreme, but not known to have also committed murder.
22. Psychopathic torture-murderers, with torture their primary motive (the majority, but not all, are serial killers).

Note. From Stone (1993, p. 458). Copyright 1993 by Michael H. Stone. Reprinted by permission.

(the so-called "serial killers"). Most of the latter involve serial *sexual* homicide, as noted in 676 of the 67 male serial killers. The exception was the adopted David Berkowitz, the "Son of Sam," who shot his victims out of envy and revenge against having been abandoned by his biological mother; he did not have sex with his victims (Ressler & Shachtman, 1992).

In evaluating each biographee for the presence of SPD, I used the eight-item criterion set in Appendix A of DSM-III-R. Psychopathy was assessed according to the criteria of Hare's revision of Cleckley's checklist (Hare et al., 1990). Other personality disorders were diagnosed via DSM-III criteria (American Psychiatric Association, 1980). I paid special attention to the possible presence of schizoid, paranoid, narcissistic, borderline, and obsessive–compulsive personality disorders, since these were likely to be overrepresented in a population of murderers.

Since only celebrated murder cases inspire full-length books, the 279 biographees do not constitute a typical sample of persons who commit homicide. There are almost no lengthy accounts, for example, of the impulsive, jealous murderers who set fire to the homes of lovers who have jilted them; there are only one or two books about inner-city killers from adolescent gangs, or about psychotic vagrants who kill in the act of robbery. The blighted lives of these offenders have usually been too meager and pedestrian to capture in the telling for a large readership.

Among the serial killers known to the Federal Bureau of Investigation (FBI), some are considered chaotic and frenzied; others seem to be calm and deliberate as they go about their deadly business. The former are called the "disorganized" type and the latter the "organized" type (Ressler, Burgess, & Douglas, 1988). In the records of the police and the FBI, these types exist in approximately equal numbers. But the biographies of serial killers are more apt to focus on the organized type—individuals (usually men) who look like one's next-door neighbor, and who are the more sensational and frightening because of their greater ability to blend in with the community and to gain the confidence of their unsuspecting victims. Hence in my series there is an overrepresentation of the organized (and less easily captured) type of serial killer.

In the United States, only about one murderer in a thousand earns full-length biographical attention. Even so, aligning the cases according to the spectrum of inhumanity covered in the Gradations of Evil Scale makes it possible to determine in which compartment clear-cut psychopathy first makes its appearance, and in which categories SPD becomes a routine feature of the personality.

Results

The Presence of Sadistic Personality

Six of the 279 biographees were persons who killed in what amounted to self-defense (i.e., they fell into compartment 1 of the Gradations of Evil Scale). Several of these persons were in their teens and had endured unending brutality or incestuous molestation from parents, whom they finally killed as their only way of rescuing themselves. None of these six had any sadistic personality attributes.

Among the remaining 273 biographees, psychopathic traits, as outlined in Hare's revision of Cleckley's original list (Hare et al., 1990), were either absent or present to only a modest degree (generally not enough to warrant a diagnosis) in 16. These 16 persons, equally divided by gender, fell into the next seven compartments of my Gradations of Evil Scale (categories 2 through 8). Only 1 of the 16 (6%) had enough traits to merit a diagnosis of SPD. This was a man named Steven Ray Harper, who stalked a former girlfriend after she jilted him. He shot buckshot through her family's window, wounding his ex-girlfriend's brother. He later got hold of a chemical that causes internal bleeding, dimethylnitrosamide, and planted some in the family's lemonade (Guillen, 1995). The ex-girlfriend's new husband and their child died, but she, having drunk none of the mixture, survived. Even Charles Whitman, the ex-Marine who shot and killed 14 people from the University of Texas tower (and whom I have placed in compartment 8), had only a few sadistic and psychopathic traits.

In the much more crowded categories 9 through 22, the number of biographied murderers was 257, of whom 179 could be diagnosed as having SPD (70%). The murderers in these compartments all had significant degrees of psychopathy. If one focuses on the last six compartments (17–22), where the crimes committed all involve sexual homicide or torture or both, SPD could be diagnosed in 87 of 94 such persons (93%). Males were more likely to meet criteria for SPD than were females: 164 of 221 males (74%), as against 21 of 54 (39%) ($\chi^2 = 11.4$, $p < .01$).

The Impact of Schizoid Personality

Many of the most brutal murders or crimes of torture were carried out by offenders who were totally bereft of human feeling, and who were aloof, detached "loners" lacking any semblance of normal human relatedness, especially in the realm of intimacy. They resembled the "schizoid psychopaths" described by Gallwey (1985).

Offenders with distinct schizoid personality disorder were noted in both the nonpsychopathic section of the Gradations of Evil Scale (compartments 2–8; 3 of 16, or 19%), and in the larger psychopathic section (46 of 257, or 18%). Among those who committed crimes of a sexual or torturous nature, 35 of 94 such offenders (of either sex) were schizoid. Since all the schizoid persons in this group were male, then 35 of 85 males fit this category, or 41%.

The combination of SPD and schizoid personality disorder was noted in 5 of 163 offenders in compartments 9 through 16, but in 28 of 94 offenders in compartments 17 to 22. This difference was significant ($\chi^2 = 18.79$, $p < .001$). In the total murderer group (compartments 2–22), the presence of schizoid personality disorder did not predict SPD, or vice versa. But in the group committing serial sexual homicide or torture (with or without murder of some of their victims), the correlation between schizoid personality disorder and SPD was prominent. This correlation was prominent among the serial killers of compartment 17 (10 of 28 males, or 36%) and in compartment 22 (14 of 38 males, or 37%). But if one focuses exclusively on serial killers from compartment 17 on, 30 of 67 were schizoid, or 45%.

In this whole series, there were too few nonpsychopathic murderers to permit much statistical analysis, beyond what has been indicated above. Many of the murders that earn brief mention in the tabloids are committed by impulsive, hot-tempered men, often enough under the influence of alcohol or cocaine; the setting is usually an altercation over a drug deal gone bad, a marital jealousy situation, a barroom brawl, or a robbery where the victim resisted. Though a high proportion of such murderers are sadistic, probably only a small proportion are also schizoid. There are few data from epidemiological sources that shed light on this issue. In general, the murders of persons known to the offenders are less apt to involve killers with schizoid personality disorder, whereas the killing of strangers, especially if rape or torture are accompaniments, is more likely to involve schizoid offenders—both because the latter have few or no attachments to other persons, and because, in the more extreme instances, they lack the capacity for pity or compassion that would otherwise render impossible the commission of crimes characterized by mutilation, cannibalism, or torture. This extreme degree of callousness is a trait shared by violent psychopaths, sadists, and markedly schizoid persons. It should not be surprising that within the domain of serial sexual homicide, there is a conflation of these three personality qualities in the perpetrators.

One index of the comparative rarity of schizoid personality in persons who murder those known to them is in the rate of this personality type among spousal murderers. In my series, there were 60 examples of spousal murderers: 37 uxoricides and 23 women who killed their husbands. Schizoid personality disorder was not present in any of these 60, whereas SPD was common over in the women—especially those who cold-bloodedly poisoned their husbands in order to collect death benefits.

Comments

When murder is committed by persons who do not demonstrate sadism, death is often swift and comparatively painless. Perhaps this is more true of the United States, where handguns are readily available, and where even spousal or jealousy-fueled murders are accomplished more often by firearms than by knives or by strangulation. I would not wish to say, however, that nonsadistic murderers exact only a minor toll of mayhem and tragedy. Mass murderers, for example, can shatter the security of a whole community, as we witnessed with the killing of 16 kindergarten children and their teacher in Dunblane, Scotland, in March 1996. Little is known about the personalities of mass murderers because they almost invariably are killed or kill themselves as the police close in on them. It appears that Thomas Hamilton, the Dunblane killer, was a schizoid loner—probably paranoid, possibly homosexual, but not clearly either psychopathic or sadistic. But the magnitude and immense social ramifications of his crime had more to do with the sheer number and utter helplessness of his child victims; torture was not involved in this case.

Quite different is the variety of evil embodies in the acts of sadistic killers who subject their victims to prolonged and grotesque torture before either killing them, or (as is much less often the case) releasing them, or (as is even less often the case) failing to kill them because the victims manage to make a clever escape. The concept of evil is, I believe, justified when one is confronted with sadism at these levels, granted that mental health professionals are customarily uncomfortable about making moral judgments. Actually, sadistic killers and mental health professionals may be said to inhabit two scarcely contiguous realms. Sadists do not come to us for help, and are thus not "patients" about whom we would be making moral judgments. Rather, they are persons outside the sphere of psychiatry *as a healing art*; we take notice of sadistic tortures only insofar as psychiatry also takes on the function of diagnosing abnormal personality in the forensic setting.

In sadistic persons who subject others to torture, we see most vividly the quest for omnipotent control. As Kernberg (1967) has shown, this is a feature common to many borderline persons as well. In the case of the sadist, however, it is an omnipotent control carried to the furthest possible extreme, where (often enough) a brutish nonentity suddenly takes on the trappings of a Nero or a Caligula. The quest in the sadistic killer is for something even beyond omnipotent control: the quest is instead for the complete subjugation and the slow and painful destruction of other human beings. This has led Wilson and Seaman (1992) to refer to the psychopathology of such killers, aptly, as the "Roman Emperor syndrome."

The precise extent of SPD in a community or a country is admittedly impossible to estimate, owing to the tendency of sadistic persons to deny any sadistic behavior if interviewed in some epidemiological survey. Also, many of the victims are too intimidated to reveal such behavior to others, let alone interviewers who are strangers. This fear becomes maximal in the face of political torture, as has been documented recently by Peter Maas in his book *Love Thy Neighbor* (1996). Maas relates the terror felt by Muslim prisoners in Serbian concentration camps if they are prompted to point a finger at their tormentors, lest the latter discover this and heighten still further the cruelty of their sadistic treatment.

I hope I have shown, nevertheless, that SPD exists—certainly among the ranks of murderers, and in a high concentration among the ranks of serial killers. Furthermore, in my comparatively large series of murderers, the presence of any *two* of three disorders—psychopathy, SPD, and schizoid personality disorder—predicted the presence of the third disorder. This interrelationship was restricted to males, who constitute the vast majority of murderers (about 90%), and who are far more likely than females to exhibit sadism. In fact, the overrepresentation of females in my biographical series is a function of the shock and surprise with which the community greets the news of *any* woman committing murder—especially if her acts show cunning and scheming, and even more so if the victims happen, as in the cases of Diane Downs (Rule, 1987) and Susan Smith (Peyser, 1995), to be their own children. In any event, male psychopaths who murder are apt to be sadistic (about two-thirds of the cases); those who are in addition serial sexual killers are invariably sadistic and often (in almost half the cases) schizoid as well.

Since sadists almost never volunteer to undergo psychotherapy and since psychotherapy is ineffective in this population, we cannot expect the sort of "fieldwork" to be conducted that the authors of the DSM ordinarily require, preparatory to the inclusion of a clinical entity within its pages. As to the vast army of minor sadists who browbeat their spouses, mistreat their children, humiliate their underlings in the workplace, stalk former girlfriends (cf. Meloy, 1996), and otherwise misuse their power, I can make no guess as to their number. But SPD is the rule rather than the exception among males who murder—for which reason alone the disorder merits reinsertion into our official manual of psychiatric nosology. The willful misuse of the DSM by defense attorneys will probably continue until such time as societal values were to change in a more conservative direction. But just as the presence of SPD in a criminal does not justify the claim of "diminished responsibility," psychiatry would do well not to show a diminished responsibility of its own, in eliminating this diagnosis from the standard nomenclature.

TWO CASE EXAMPLES

To give some idea of the depths of sadism that we might find in a population of murderers, I offer the following examples of extreme SPD from among my biographees—one case involving a woman, the other a man.

Theresa Knorr

Theresa Knorr (Clarkson, 1995), who took her surname from the second of her five husbands, had six children by the time she was 24: two by her first (whom she killed, but for whose murder she was acquitted), and four by her second husband. Crazily jealous of her two daughters, she tortured and literally imprisoned them for years. She handcuffed them to pipes in closets or sinks, and forced her sons to aid her in her abusive treatment of them. In 1983 she got her sons to help her conduct one daughter, Suesan, to the foothills of the Sierra Mountains, where she then burned her alive. Later she pummeled the other, Sheila, to death in the closet where she had kept her in chains.

Before killing her daughters, Theresa regularly burned their arms with cigarette butts. Accusing Suesan of having venereal disease and of being a witch, Theresa would batter her with blunt objects and then read passages from the Bible to her or get the local priest to "exorcise" the "demons" that supposedly had taken over Suesan's body. She tried to make Suesan get fat, via overeating, so that she would not be attractive; when Suesan refused, she would have one of her sons hold the girl while Theresa punched her in the stomach. She shot Suesan in the chest with a .22, and when the girl unaccountably survived she played nurse to her, meantime permitting her no access to medical care lest the true story get out. Instead, she got the girl drunk, so that in this semianesthetized state Theresa could "operate" on her and remove the bullet. After Theresa removed the bullet, however, Suesan developed septicemia and was near death. Theresa and her sons then burned her, to destroy the evidence of the murder. As for Sheila, she was forced into prostitution to make money for her mother, who then made her confess that she had venereal disease (even though she did not). Theresa then locked the girl in a closet, chained to a pipe, till she died.

Paul Kenneth Bernardo

Paul Kenneth Bernardo (Burnside & Cairns, 1995) was the Ontario-born son of a well-to-do Canadian woman, Marilyn Bernardo, by a man with whom she had had a brief affair. In a moment of anger she blurted out, when Paul was 16, that her husband was not his real father. Already a delinquent, a tease, and a bully, Paul became more openly sadistic after this revelation. At age 18 he got into some sadomasochistic "games" with a girlfriend, whom he proceeded to beat savagely, calling her a "whore."

Paul became obsessed with sex, power, and rape fantasies, which he acted out with a number of submissive women, over whom he exercised total control and subjugation. He married a teenager, Karen Homolka, whom he set about dominating by compelling her to submit to bondage with handcuffs and by verbally abusing her (e.g., calling her "ugly" repeatedly) till she lost all self-confidence. Paul had in the meantime become a serial rapist/killer; in fact, one of his victims, Leslie Mahaffey, was discovered the day after Paul's wedding. Paul built a secret room in their house, made over into a torture chamber. There he repeatedly tortured and sexually violated Karen's younger sister, Tammy, whom he eventually killed with halothane and triazolam. He forced Karen to have lesbian sex with two women, the scenes of which he videotaped, so as to use against her if she ever broke away and told the authorities of his murders. Paul subjected Karen to ever-increasing degrees of physical abuse throughout their marriage until he was finally arrested in 1993 for rape and murder.

The progression of Paul's sadism followed the five steps that are often discernible in the life histories of sadistic killers. First, Paul had an uncanny ability to identify naive, passive, and vulnerable women—women who were ripe for being manipulated and exploited. This is Step 1. In Step 2, by behaving outwardly at first in a loving, considerate manner, the sadist wins the love of his unsuspecting victims. Paul in particular was a psychopath of the "charming con man" type, who was most adept at getting weak women to love him. In Step 3, the woman is induced to participate in sexual practices far beyond the ordinary one for her or for most women (bondage, sex photography, use of dildoes, etc.). Meantime, the sadist isolates the woman more and more from her original family. In Step 4, via possessiveness and jealousy, the sadist sets about isolating the woman from her friends and from all other outside contacts. Further control comes in such forms as giving the woman only paltry sums for transportation, groceries, and the ordinary necessities, so that she is now in a state of total subjugation. In Step 5, the woman is transformed into an object for the sadist's physical and psychological abuse, from which she is powerless to defend herself (Burnside & Cairns, 1995, p. 551).

CONCLUSIONS

I have hoped that the material presented here may help to compensate for the dearth of "fieldwork" in the domain of SPD. It is not to be expected that most persons with SPD will seek treatment and thus present themselves to clinics or other psychiatric facilities where their personality disorder can be evaluated in a methodical way. The few who do so tend to be among the milder examples: parents who have physically abused their children not very severely, and who feel genuinely remorseful about their actions; or spouses who have dealt cruelly with their mates, but who are capable of compassion and are eager to gain self-control so as not to repeat hostile behaviors. In hospital work, psychiatrists occasionally encounter patients (especially abused adolescents) who are dominated by sadistic, including murderous and sexually sadistic, fantasies, but who have not as yet passed from fantasy to action. Intensive therapy, in combined individual and group settings, will sometimes succeed in lessening the preoccupation with vengeful and otherwise sadistic fantasies, and in reducing the tendency to engage in sadistic acts. The case material presented in this chapter represents the other extreme of the sadistic spectrum—

where the accumulation of data is easier (descriptions of murderers and their acts become a matter of public record), but any hope of remediation is remote to the vanishing point.

As disagreeable as it may be to acknowledge, sadism exists, as does SPD. Although there is merit in Widiger's (1996) assertions that the DSM is in part a social document, and that the inclusion of SPD might have troublesome consequences, I believe that there would be greater merit in acknowledging this diagnosis in the next edition of the manual. Meantime, our profession needs to do what it can in the public sector both (1) to argue against the use of SPD by the legal community as exculpatory of sadistic acts or as in any way diminishing the responsibility of persons who commit sadistic acts, and (2) to promote the education, especially of young persons, to nonviolent means of resolving interpersonal differences. From the evidence thus far available, it appears that SPD owes more to nurture than to nature for its development. A history of childhood physical or emotional abuse is common in those later diagnosed with SPD (75% or more; Fiester & Gay, 1995), and a history of having come from a warm and nurturing environment is rare. The latter combination I noted, for example, in only 6 of 71 serial killers (67 males, 4 females) in my series. Since there is little hope of remediating SPD that is already fully developed in an adult, our efforts and the efforts of the community would be better directed toward making parents (and prospective parents) less punitive and less abusive to their children. This is the best way to ensure less sadistic behavior in the next generation, and, parenthetically, to minimize any adverse consequences that might arise from reinserting SPD into Axis II of the next edition of DSM.

REFERENCES

American Psychiatric Association. (1980). *Diagnostic and statistical manual of mental disorders* (3rd ed.). Washington, DC: Author.

American Psychiatric Association. (1987). *Diagnostic and statistical manual of mental disorders* (3rd ed., rev.). Washington, DC: Author.

American Psychiatric Association. (1994). *Diagnostic and statistical manual of mental disorders* (4th ed.). Washington, DC: Author.

Burnside, S., & Cairns, A. (1995). *Deadly innocence: The true story of Paul Bernardo, Karen Homolka, and the schoolgirl murders.* New York: Time Warner.

Clarkson, W. (1995). *Whatever Mother says: A true story of a mother, madness and murder.* New York: St. Martin's Press.

Fiester, S. J., & Gay, M. (1995). Sadistic personality disorder. In J. Livesley (Ed.), *The DSM-IV personality disorders* (pp. 329–440). New York: Guilford Press.

Gallwey, P. L. G. (1985). The psychodynamics of borderline personality. In D. P. Farrington & J. Gunn (Eds.), *Aggression and dangerousness* (pp. 127–152). New York: Wiley.

Guillen, T. (1995). *Toxic love: The true story of twisted passion in the "murder by cancer" case.* New York: Dell.

Hare, R. D., Harpur, T. J., Hakstian, A. R., Forth, A. E., Hart, S. D., & Newman, J. P. (1990). The revised Psychopathy Checklist: Reliability and factor structure. *Psychological Assessment, 2,* 338–341.

Kernberg, O. F. (1967). Borderline personality organization. *Journal of American Psychoanalytic Association, 15,* 641–685.

Maas, P. (1996). *Love thy neighbor: A story of war.* New York: Knopf.

McGinnis, J. (1983). *Fatal vision.* New York: Putnam.

Meloy, J. R. (1996). Stalking (obsessional following): A review and some preliminary studies. *Aggression and Violent Behavior, 1,* 147–162.

Peyser, A. (1995). *Mother love, deadly love.* New York: HarperCollins.

Ressler, R. K., Burgess, A. W., & Douglas, J. E. (1988). *Sexual homicide: Patterns and motives.* New York: Macmillan.

Ressler, R. K., & Shachtman, T. (1992). *Whoever fights monsters: My 20 years hunting serial killers for the FBI.* New York: St. Martin's Press.

Rule, A. (1987). *Small sacrifices: A true story of passion and murder.* New York: New American Library.

Spitzer, R. L., Fiester, S. J., Gay, M., & Pfohl, B. (1991). Is sadistic personality disorder a valid diagnosis? *American Journal of Psychiatry, 148,* 875–879.

Stone, M. H. (1993). *Abnormalities of personality: Within and beyond the realm of treatment.* New York: Norton.

Widiger, T. A. (1996, May 9). *Aggression: Within and beyond the DSM-IV.* Paper presented at the 149th Annual Meeting of the American Psychiatric Association, New York.

Wilson, C., & Seaman, D. (1992). *The serial killers: A study in the psychology of violence.* New York: Carol.

V

TREATMENT

23

Psychopharmacological Treatment and Impulsivity

LARS VON KNORRING
LISA EKSELIUS

Leitner and Serfling (1993) have argued that there is no specific antiborderline drug, and similar statements could probably be made in regard to all the other personality disorders as well (including antisocial personality disorder/psychopathy, on which the present volume focuses). However, Leitner and Serfling have also argued that there are identifiable drug-responsive syndromes in the specific personality disorders. Thus, for example, borderline personality disorder would include a syndrome with affective instability, responsive to carbamazepine and lithium; a syndrome with transient psychotic phenomena, responsive to major tranquilizers; and a syndrome with impulsive/aggressive behavior, responsive to serotonergic agents. If so, it will always be dangerous to draw conclusions from any study indicating an overall positive effect of a drug on a disorder consisting of several different subsyndromes.

IMPULSIVITY

Impulsivity is a prominent personality trait both in psychiatric syndromes and in personality disorders. The development of methods for measuring aspects of neurobiological functions has resulted in an increased body of knowledge about impulse control deficiency. Biological measures such as monoamine oxidase (MAO) activity in platelets, and measures related to serotonergic neurotransmission and to neuroendocrine functions, have been shown to be associated with impulsivity and vulnerability to different forms of psychopathology (Schalling, Edman, & Åsberg, 1983).

According to Eysenck's (1967) theoretical formulations, impulsivity was originally part of the extraversion concept, based on the theory of an optimal level of arousal. However, as research on the psychoticism dimension developed, it was demonstrated that much of the impulsivity trait was covered by the psychoticism dimension (Eysenck & Eysenck, 1977, 1978), whereas extraversion has become more of a measure of pure sociability. In more recent research it has been demonstrated that the psychoticism dimension is associated with psychopathy and lack of conformity to social norms (Robinson & Zahen, 1985).

Another psychobiological approach to impulsivity has been developed by Zuckerman (1979, 1991). On the basis of biological research on animals, he has developed an optimal-level-of-arousal theory of sensation seeking as a main component in disinhibitory behavior. Zuckerman (1983, 1989, 1991) has constructed a general Sensation Seeking Scale and four subscales, relating these to biological dimensions.

In the Karolinska Scales of Personality (KSP) developed by Schalling and coworkers (Schalling, 1978; Schalling et al., 1983; Schalling, Åsberg, Edman, & Oreland, 1987), two subscales concern impulsivity and sensation seeking. The latter, named the Monotony Avoidance scale, is related to Zuckerman's Sensation Seeking Scale. The Impulsivity scale is related to "subsolidity" in the system of personality dimensions described by the Swedish psychiatrist Henrik Sjøbring (1973). Impulsivity seems to be a very basic trait with a high genetic component. In an ongoing study of 196 twins from the Swedish twin register (Annas, Ekselius, Fredrikson, & von Knorring, 1996), we obtained a monozygotic intraclass correlation of .65 and a dizygotic intraclass correlation of .16 when impulsivity was measured by means of the KSP. The best available model resulted in a dominant genetic component of 58%, an additive genetic component of 7%, a unique environmental component of 36%, and a shared environmental component of 0%. Thus, it seems reasonable to believe that impulsivity may have a biological, drug-responsive substrate.

Furthermore, impulsivity is the best predictor of adult antisocial/delinquent behavior (Tremblay, Pihl, Vitaro, & Dobkin, 1994) as demonstrated in a series of prospective studies (Farrington, 1995; af Klinteberg, 1995; Tremblay et al., 1994; Fischer, Barkley, Fletcher, & Smallish, 1993; White et al., 1994). It has also been suggested by Ruegg and Frances (1995) that impulsivity may eventually be a more productive target for study than any of the currently available personality disorders. Thus, it would be of utmost importance if it could be demonstrated not only that a drug diminished impulsivity in a short-term drug study, but that this diminished impulsivity also resulted in a decreased frequency of delinquent behavior in a long-term follow-up.

DISORDERS INVOLVING IMPULSIVITY

Disorders in DSM-III-R (American Psychiatric Association, 1987) that explicitly include impulsivity or difficulty with impulse control as a criterion include, on Axis I, the "impulse control disorders not elsewhere classified" (intermittent explosive disorder, kleptomania, pyromania, pathological gambling, trichotillomania, and impulse control disorder not otherwise specified), and, on Axis II, borderline personality disorder and antisocial personality disorder (Stein, Hollander, & Liebowitz, 1993). In DSM-IV (American Psychiatric Association, 1994), they also include the predominantly hyperactive–impulsive type and combined type of attention-deficit/hyperactivity disorder (ADHD) on Axis I. However, within Axis II considerable comorbidity has been demonstrated, both within Cluster B and among the three clusters (Figure 23.1; Ekselius, Lindstrøm, von Knorring, Bodlund, & Kullgren, 1994a). Furthermore, as noted in a report of a fluoxetine trial by Markovitz (1995), borderline personality disorder may coexist with a long series of different disorders on Axes I, II, and III (Table 23.1).

If the psychopharmacological studies conducted in recent years with impulsivity as a

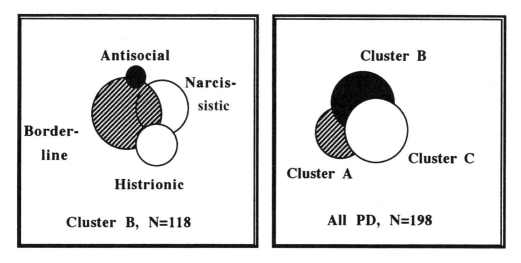

FIGURE 23.1. Comorbidity among the DSM-III-R personality disorders. The data are from Ekselius, Lindström, von Knorring, Bodlund, and Kullgren (1994).

target are taken into account, it is obvious that they cover not only the impulse control disorders per se, but a variety of other conditions. This situation may be an advantage, if a single drug is proven effective for impulsivity regardless of the Axis I, II, or III disorders studied. However, if impulsivity is reduced by a drug only in one or two of these separate disorders, there is always a risk that the main effect is an improvement in some other part of the syndrome, with secondary beneficial effects on the impulsivity.

Diagnostic categories included in psychopharmacological trials with impulsivity as a target symptom in recent years (Silver Platter, 1996) include healthy volunteers (Coull, Middleton, Robbins, & Sahakian, 1995), children with ADHD (De Sonneville, Njiokiktjien, & Bos, 1994; Handen, Janosky, McAuliffe, Breaux, & Feldman, 1994), adults with ADHD (Spencer et al., 1995), patients with borderline personality disorder (Kutcher, Papatheodorou, Reiter, & Gardner, 1995; Soloff et al., 1993), patients with depressive disorders (Dalery et al., 1995; Rampello, Nicoletti, Raffaele, & Drago, 1995), autistic children (Kolmen, Feldman, Handen, & Janosky, 1995), patients with paraphil-

TABLE 23.1. Comorbidity between DSM-III-R Borderline Personality Disorder and Axis I, Other Axis II, and Axis III Disorders in a Fluoxetine Trial

Comorbidity on Axis I	Comorbidity on Axis II	Comorbidity on Axis III
Major depression 59%	Self-defeating 82%	Premenstrual syndrome 92%
Bipolar disorder 35%	Paranoid 82%	Headache/migraine 47%
Dysthymia 6%	Compulsive 71%	Irritable bowel 41%
Generalized anxiety disorder 53%	Avoidant 65%	Fibrositis 35%
Obsessive–compulsive disorder 35%	Dependent 65%	Neurodermatitis 29%
Panic disorder 24%	Histrionic 59%	Sleep apnea 29%
Substance abuse or dependence 24%	Passive–aggressive 59%	
Anorexia 18%	Schizotypal 53%	
Phobic disorder 12%	Narcissistic 35%	
	Antisocial 35%	

Note. Adapted from Markovitz (1995). Copyright 1995 by John Wiley & Sons, Ltd. Adapted by permission.

ias (Kafka, 1995), patients with traumatic brain injury (Mandoki, 1994), patients with alcoholism (Lejoyeux & Ades, 1993), epileptic children (Mitchell, Zhou, Chavez, & Guzman, 1993), patients with HIV-1 encephalopathy (Cesena, Lee, Cebollero, & Steingard, 1995), and patients with Gilles de la Tourette syndrome (Chappell et al., 1995). From studies on such heterogeneous patient series, it is somewhat dangerous to draw firm conclusions about the effects of certain drugs on impulsivity and subsequent delinquent behavior.

DRUGS TESTED IN TRIALS WITH IMPULSIVITY AS A TARGET SYMPTOM

The fact that no single drug has yet proven to be the agent of choice for impulsivity is highlighted if we consider the drugs tested in recent years. These drugs include alpha$_1$ and alpha$_2$ receptor agonists (Chappell et al., 1995; Coull et al., 1995), stimulants (De Sonneville et al., 1994; Handen et al., 1994; Spencer et al., 1995), dopamine blockers (Kutcher et al., 1995), dopamine reuptake inhibitors (Rampello et al., 1995), antiandrogens (Kafka, 1995), naltrexone (Kolmen et al., 1995), carbamazepine (Lemke, 1995), and valproate (Stein, Simeon, Frenkel, Islam, & Hollander, 1995). They also include various serotonergic agents, such as buspirone (Mandoki, 1994), tryptophan (Cleare & Bond, 1995), MAO inhibitors (Soloff et al., 1993), lithium (Baker, 1995; Lejoyeux & Ades, 1993), tricyclic antidepressants (TCAs) (Rampello et al., 1995) and selective serotonin reuptake inhibitors (SSRIs) (Albritton & Borison, 1995; Campbell & Duffy, 1995; Dalery et al., 1995; Kafka, 1995; Poyurovsky, Halperin, Enoch, Shneiderman, & Weizman, 1995; Vartiainen et al., 1995; Silver Platter, 1996).

Positive Controlled Studies

Positive controlled drug studies relevant to impulsivity include studies of chlorpromazine in patients with "unstable character disorder" (Fink, Pollack, & Klein, 1964; Klein, 1968); flupenthixol in patients with personality disorders and parasuicide (Montgomery & Montgomery, 1982); haloperidol in patients with borderline personality disorder (Soloff et al., 1986); carbamazepine in patients with borderline personality disorder (Cowdry & Gardner, 1988); lithium in patients with unstable character disorder, prisoners with various personality disorders, and patients with borderline personality disorder (Links, Steiner, Bolago, & Irwin, 1990; Rifkin, Quitkin, Crillo, Blumberg, & Klein, 1972; Sheard, Marini, Bridges, & Wagner, 1976); and fluoxetine in patients with various personality disorders and patients with borderline personality disorder (Markovitz, 1993; Salzman, 1993).

Furthermore, there are several controlled studies concerning the anti-impulsivity effects of stimulants in both children and adults with ADHD (Elia, 1991; Gadow & Sverd, 1990; Gillberg et al., 1997; Spencer et al., 1995; Wilens, Biederman, Spencer, & Prince, 1995). In children the anti-ADHD effects of stimulants are well documented today; these effects have now also been supported in a long-term study (Gillberg et al., 1997). Sixty-two children aged 6–11 years meeting the DSM-III-R symptom criteria for ADHD participated in a parallel-groups, randomized, double-blind, placebo-controlled study of amphetamine. In the amphetamine group, children received active treatment for 15 months. Amphetamine was clearly superior to placebo in reducing inattention/hyperactivity and tended to lead to improved results on the Weschler Intelligence Scale for Children—Revised. Moreover, treatment failure rate was considerably lower and time to treatment failure longer in the amphetamine group. Finally, the results indicated that the positive effects of the stimulant drug continued 15 months after the start of treatment (Gillberg et al., 1997).

In adults with ADHD, the effects of stimulants have been more controversial. However, in a review article (Wilens et al., 1995) seven studies were found in which the effects of stimulants on the adult ADHD syndrome were studied. The seven studies included a total of 193 subjects. It was concluded that under controlled conditions, stimulants have clinically and statistically significant effects on the adult ADHD syndrome. Furthermore, in 10 studies including a total of 167 subjects, antidepressants, antihypertensives, and amino acids were evaluated. It was concluded that the antidepressants also show moderate anti-ADHD effects.

Negative Controlled Studies

There are also some negative controlled drug studies relevant to impulsivity (Table 23.2), including studies of antidepressants (Hirsch, Walsh, & Draper, 1983; Montgomery, Roy, & Montgomery, 1983), major tranquilizers (Soloff et al., 1993), buspirone (Wolff et al., 1991), and benzodiazepines (Cowdry & Gardner, 1988). In most of these studies, no significant effects were demonstrated. This absence of effects might have been attributable to small patient samples, lack of reliability, lack of compliance, too-low doses, or lack of effect of the drugs tested. However, in the study by Cowdry and Gardner (1988), alprazolam significantly increased behavioral dyscontrol in patients with borderline personality disorder. Thus, it seems reasonable to conclude that benzodiazepines ought to be avoided in this patient group.

PERSONALITY TRAITS AND BIOLOGICAL MARKERS RELATED TO IMPULSIVITY

In studies of adolescent norm breakers, high scores on the Impulsive/Sensation-Seeking Psychopathy factor of the KSP are obtained, and these are related to such biochemical deviations as high plasma cortisol, low platelet MAO activity, high dopamine, low noradrenaline, and high adrenaline levels (af Klinteberg, 1995). The most pronounced deviation is the very low platelet MAO activity, probably indicating low serotonin turnover.

In adults, impulsivity is regularly linked to central and peripheral markers indicating disturbed serotonergic function, such as deviations in tryptophan hydroxylase genotype

TABLE 23.2. Negative Controlled Drug Studies Relevant to Impulsivity

Diagnosis	Drug	Outcome	Authors
Personality disorders/ parasuicide	Mianserin	Suicide frequency unchanged	Montgomery et al. (1983)
Parasuicide	Nomifensine	Suicide frequency unchanged	Hirsch et al. (1983)
Borderline personality disorder	Alprazolam	Increased behavioral dyscontrol	Cowdry and Gardner (1988)
Borderline personality disorder	Buspirone	Unchanged global symptomatology	Wolff et al. (1991)
Borderline personality disorder	Haloperidol	No overall effect	Soloff et al. (1993)

(Nielsen et al., 1994), low plasma tryptophan (Candito, Askenazy, Myquel, Chambon, & Darcourt, 1993), low platelet imipramine binding (Simeon et al., 1992), low platelet MAO activity (Hallman, von Knorring, & Oreland, 1996), low concentrations of 5-hydroxyindoleacetic acid in cerebrospinal fluid (Virkkunen, Nuutila, Goodwin, & Linnoila, 1987; Virkkunen et al., 1994), and a blunted response to fenfluramine (Coccaro, 1993; Siever, 1993).

SEROTONERGIC DRUGS AND IMPULSIVITY

Thus, it is not surprising that the strongest hopes in recent years have been linked to the SSRIs. Several open studies, often with very few patients involved, have indicated a role for SSRIs. The majority of these studies have focused on fluoxetine. For example, for 12 twelve patients with borderline personality disorder, 5–40 mg of fluoxetine a day for 6 months resulted in improvement 75% of the subjects, mostly in regard to depression and impulsivity (Norden, 1989). In 13 patients with impulsive/aggressive behavior, 20–60 mg of fluoxetine a day for 3 weeks resulted in 100% of the patients' showing improvement (Coccaro, Astill, Herbert, & Schut, 1990). In 22 patients with borderline personality disorder, 80 mg a day for 12 weeks resulted in a decrease in the number of self-injuries (Markovitz, Calabrese, Schulz, & Meltzer, 1991). For 5 patients with borderline personality disorder, 20–40 mg a day resulted in an overall improvement (Cornelius, Soloff, Perel, & Ulrich, 1991). Marked improvements were reported for 20 patients with sexual addictions who received fluoxetine (Kafka & Prentky, 1992). For 21 mentally retarded patients, 20–40 mg of fluoxetine a day during 6–12 months resulted in marked improvement in 62%, as well as a decrease in the number of self-injuries (Markowitz, 1992). There are positive results from open trials of other SSRIs as well—for instance, fluvoxamine in patients with impulsivity, compulsions, and aggression (Poyurovsky et al., 1995); paroxetine in patients with anger in depressive syndromes (Albritton & Borison, 1995); citalopram in patients with aggression in schizophrenia (Vartiainen et al., 1995); and sertraline in developmentally disabled patients with aggression (Campbell & Duffy, 1995). However, as always, open trials must be interpreted with caution.

A further indication of the role of the effect on serotonin turnover would be if SSRIs and noradrenaline reuptake inhibitors such as paroxetine and maprotilin had different effects. In premenstrual syndrome (PMS), a syndrome including irritability, aggression, and impulsivity, paroxetine has in fact been proven to be significantly more effective than maprotilin (Eriksson, Hedberg, Andersch, & Sundblad, 1995). Moreover, in a series of clinical trials, fluoxetine has been proven effective in patients with PMS (Markovitz et al., 1991; Menkes, Taghavi, Mason, Spears, & Howard, 1992; Rickels, Sondheimer, Freeman, & Albert, 1990; Stone, Pearlstein, & Brown, 1990; Wood, Mortola, Chan, Moossazadeh, & Yen, 1992). Markovitz (1995) has concluded that the success of fluoxetine in treating this disorder has been documented.

There are also at least two separate placebo-controlled, double-blind studies of borderline personality disorder in which fluoxetine has been proven more effective than placebo. In 17 patients with borderline personality disorder and with a high frequency of comorbidity on Axes I, II, and III, 20–80 mg of fluoxetine for 3 weeks was significantly more effective than placebo (Markovitz et al., 1991). In 22 patients with borderline personality disorder, fluoxetine for 12 weeks significantly improved anger, irritability, and aggression (Salzman, 1993).

In contrast, it has been suggested in several case reports—for example, reports of six patients (two with borderline personality disorder) (Teicher, Glod, & Cole, 1990); 6 out of 42 patients with obsessive–compulsive disorder and Gilles de la Tourette syndrome (King et al., 1991); and one patient with borderline personality disorder and bulimia nervosa (Hawthorne & Lacey, 1992)—that the SSRIs can *induce* impulsive/aggressive behavior. In a meta-analysis of clinical trials, however, it was concluded that fluoxetine does not induce suicidal ideas (Burrows & Norman, 1994). One reason for the negative case reports may be that lack of efficacy in some patients with tendencies to impulsive/aggressive behavior may result in a spontaneous increase of these behaviors. There are results indicating that the SSRIs are less effective than the TCAs in the most severely ill patients with endogenous depression (Vestergaard et al., 1986, 1990), and that the lack of efficacy in these patients may result in an increased tendency toward attempted suicide. Furthermore, concomitant medication must be taken into account. It has been demonstrated that in major depression fluoxetine can reduce behavioral dyscontrol, but that this capacity is significantly reduced if benzodiazepines are added (Hantouche, Lancrenon, & Chignon, 1995).

SSRIs AND IMPULSIVE/SENSATION-SEEKING PSYCHOPATHY

In a forensic psychiatric population, we have been able to demonstrate that the Impulsive/Sensation-Seeking Psychopathy factor of the KSP is significantly increased in patients with a high degree of psychopathy and a high frequency of antisocial personality disorder (Stålenheim & von Knorring, in press).

In an ongoing trial of sertraline versus citalopram in depressed outpatients, we have demonstrated in the first 156 out of 400 patients that after 24 weeks the numbers of criteria fulfilled for narcissistic and borderline personality disorders, as determined by means of the Structured Clinical Interview for DSM-III-R, Axis II (SCID II) Screen Questionnaire, were significantly reduced (Figure 23.2; von Knorring & Ekselius, 1998). Fur-

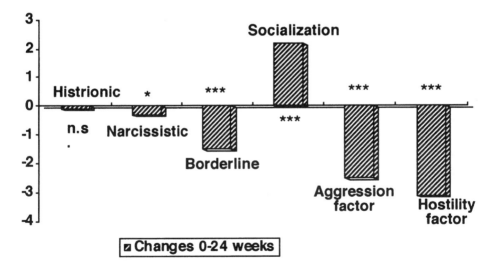

FIGURE 23.2. Changes in numbers of criteria for histrionic, narcissistic, and borderline personality disorders as determined by means of the SCID II Screen Questionnaire (Ekselius, Lindström, von Knorring, Bodlund, & Kullgren, 1994b), and in scores on the Socialization scale and the Aggression and Hostility factors of the KSP (Ekselius, Hetta, & von Knorring, 1994), during a 24-week double-blind, multicenter trial of sertraline versus citalopram (*n* = 156). The data are from Von Knorring and Ekselius, 1998.

thermore, on the KSP, the scores on the Socialization scale were significantly increased, whereas the scores on the Aggression and Hostility factors were significantly reduced. On the Impulsive/Sensation-Seeking Psychopathy factor, the scores were markedly, but not significantly, reduced.

Of course, the changes seen in the stable personality traits evaluated could have been secondary to the improvement in the depressive syndrome, but in an earlier study it was demonstrated that the scales included in the Impulsive/Sensation-Seeking Psychopathy factor (the Monotony Avoidance scale, the Impulsivity scale, and the Socialization scale) as well as all the separate scales included in the Aggression and Hostility factors (i.e., Indirect Aggression, Verbal Aggression, Irritability, Guilt, and Inhibition of Aggression), were unchanged when investigated during depression and after recovery from depression (Perris et al., 1979). In the same way, the numbers of fulfilled criteria for all four Cluster B personality disorders (Peselow, Sanfilipo, Fieve, & Gulbenkian, 1994) were unchanged when compared during depression and after recovery. Thus, it seems likely that the changes seen in our study (von Knorring & Ekselius, 1998) were a direct effect of the SSRIs on impulsivity and aggression.

CONCLUSIONS

Thus, in conclusion, there are positive controlled studies indicating that major tranquilizers, carbamazepine, and lithium may have anti-impulsivity effects. Furthermore, the anti-impulsivity effects of stimulants are well documented in both children and adults with ADHD and in children; long-term effects have also been demonstrated. However, in recent years, both a long series of studies indicating a role for serotonin in the control of impulsivity and positive results in open and controlled studies of serotonergic agents have resulted in an increased interest in the potential of the SSRIs. As stated by Markovitz (1995), "SSRIs have proved the most successful in treating impulsivity and aggression. . . . The available studies are encouraging and suggest many areas for research."

REFERENCES

af Klinteberg, B. (1995). *Biology, norms and personality: A developmental perspective*. Stockholm: Stockholm University Press.

Albritton, J, Borison, R. L. (1995). Paroxetine treatment of anger associated with depression. *Journal of Nervous and Mental Disease, 183*, 666–667.

American Psychiatric Association. (1987). *Diagnostic and statistical manual of mental disorders* (3rd ed., rev.). Washington, DC: Author.

American Psychiatric Association. (1994). *Diagnostic and statistical manual of mental disorders* (4th ed.). Washington, DC: Author.

Annas, P., Ekselius, L., Fredrikson, M., & von Knorring, L. (1996). *A twin study of personality traits as determined by means of the Karolinska Scales of Personality (KSP)*. Unpublished manuscript.

Baker, B. A. (1995). ADHD-RT and low-dose lithium: A review article and pilot study. *Journal of Neurological Orthopedics, Medicine, and Surgery, 16*, 19–27.

Burrows, G. D., & Norman, T. R. (1994). Suicide, violent behaviour and fluoxetine: Meta-analysis of clinical trials shows that fluoxetine does not cause or increase suicidal behaviour or violent acts. *Medical Journal of Australia, 161*, 404–405.

Campbell, J. Jr., & Duffy, J. D. (1995). Sertraline treatment of aggression in a developmentally disabled patient [Letter]. *Journal of Clinical Psychiatry, 56*, 123–124.

Candito, M., Askenazy, F., Myquel, M., Chambon, P., & Darcourt, G. (1993). Tryptophanemia and tyrsoinemia in adolescents with impulsive behaviour. *International Clinical Psychopharmacology, 8*, 129–132.

Cesena, M., Lee, D. O., Cebollero, A. M., & Steingard, R. J. (1995). Case study: Behavioural symptoms of paediatric HIV-1 encephalopathy successfully treated with clonidine. *Journal of the American Academy of Child and Adolescent Psychiatry, 34*, 302–306.

Chappell, P. B., Riddle, M. A., Scahill, L., Lynch, K. A., Schultz, R., Arnsten, A., Leckmna, J. F., & Cohen, D. J. (1995). Guanfacine treatment of comorbid attention-deficit hyperactivity disorder and Tourette's syndrome: Preliminary clinical experience. *Journal of the American Academy of Child and Adolescent Psychiatry, 34*, 1140–1146.

Cleare, A. J., & Bond, A. J. (1995). The effect of tryptophan depletion and enhancement on subjective and behavioural aggression in normal male subjects. *Psychopharmacology, 118*, 72–81.

Coccaro, E. F. (1993). *Fenfluramine challenge and aggression in borderline, antisocial and other personality disorders*. Paper presented at the Third Conference of the International Society for the Study of Personality Disorders, Cambridge, MA.

Coccaro, E. F., Astill, J. L., Herbert, J. L., & Schut, A. G. (1990). Fluoxetine treatment of impulsive aggression in DSM-III-R personality disorder patients. *Journal of Clinical Psychopharmacology, 10*, 373–375.

Cornelius, J. R., Soloff, P. H., Perel, J. M., & Ulrich, R. F. (1991). A preliminary trial of fluoxetine in refractory borderline patients. *Journal of Clinical Psychopharmacology, 11*, 116–120.

Coull, J. T., Middleton, H. C., Robbins, T. W., & Sahakian, B. J. (1995). Contrasting effects of clonidine and diazepam on tests of working memory and planning. *Psychopharmacology, 120*, 311–321.

Cowdry, R. W., & Gardner, D. L. (1988). Pharmacotherapy of borderline personality disorder. *Archives of General Psychiatry, 45*, 111–119.

Dalery, J., Bouhassira, M., Kress, J. P., Lancrenon, S., Tafani, A., & Hantouche, E. G. (1995). Agitated-anxious versus blunted-retarded major depressions: Different clinical effects of fluoxetine. *Encephale, 21*, 217–225.

De Sonneville, L. M. J., Njiokiktjien, C., & Bos, H. (1994). Methylphenidate and information processing: Part 1. Differentiation between responders and nonresponders; Part 2: Efficacy in responders. *Journal of Clinical and Experimental Neuropsychology, 16*, 877–897.

Ekselius, L., Hetta, J., & von Knorring, L. (1994). Relationship between personality traits as determined by means of the Karolinska Scales of Personality (KSP) and personality disorders according to DSM-III-R. *Personality and Individual Differences, 16*, 589–595.

Ekselius, L., Lindstrøm, E., von Knorring, L., Bodlund, O., & Kullgren, G. (1994a). Comorbidity among the personality disorders in the DSM-III-R. *Personality and Individual Differences, 17*, 155–160.

Ekselius, L., Lindstrøm, E., von Knorring, L., Bodlund, O., & Kullgren, G. (1994b). SCID II interviews and the SCID Screen Questionnaire as diagnostic tools for personality disorders in DSM-III-R. *Acta Psychiatrica Scandinavica, 90*, 120–123.

Elia, J. (1991). Stimulants and antidepressant pharmacokinetics in hyperactive children. *Psychopharmacological Bulletin, 27*, 411–415.

Eriksson, E., Hedberg, M. A., Andersch, B., & Sundblad, C. (1995). The serotonin reuptake inhibitor paroxetin is superior to the noradrenaline reuptake inhibitor maprotiline in the treatment of premenstrual syndrome. *Neuropsychopharmacology, 12*, 167–176.

Eysenck, H. J. (1967). *The biological basis of personality*. Springfield, IL: Charles C Thomas.

Eysenck, S. B. G., & Eysenck, H. J. (1977). The place of impulsiveness in a dimensional system of personality descritption. *British Journal of Social and Clinical Psychology, 16*, 57–68.

Eysenck, S. B. G., & Eysenck, H. J. (1978). Impulsiveness and venturesomeness: Their position in a dimensional system of personality description. *Psychological Reports, 43*, 1247–1245.

Farrington, D. P. (1995). The Twelfth Jack Tizard Memorial Lecture: The development of offending and antisocial behaviour from childhood: Key findings from the Cambridge study in delinquent development. *Journal of Child Psychology and Psychiatry and Allied Disciplines, 36,* 929–964.

Fink, M., Pollack, M., & Klein, D. F. (1964). Comparative studies of chlorpromazine and imipramine. *Neuropsychopharmacology, 3,* 370–372.

Fischer, M., Barkley, R. A., Fletcher, K. E., & Smallish, L. (1993). The adolescent outcome of hyperactive children: Predictors of psychiatric, academic, social, and emotional adjustment. *Journal of the American Academy of Child and Adolescent Psychiatry, 32,*324–332.

Gadow, K. D., & Sverd, J. (1990). Stimulants for ADHD in child patients with Tourette's syndrome: The issue of relative risk. *Journal of Developmental and Behavioral Pediatrics, 11,* 269–271.

Gillberg, C., Melander, H., von Knorring, A.-L., Janols, L.-O., Thernlund, G., Hägglöff, B., Eidevall-Wallin, L., Gustafsson, P., & Kopp, S. (1997). Long-term central stimulant treatment of children with attention-deficit hyperactivity disorder: A randomized double blind placebo-controlled trial. *Archives of General Psychiatry, 54,* 857–864.

Hallman, J., von Knorring, L., & Oreland, L. (1996). Personality disorders according to DSM-III-R and thrombocyte monoamine oxidase activity in Type 1 and Type 2 alcoholics. *Journal of Studies on Alcohol, 57,* 155–161.

Handen, B. L., Janosky, J., McAuliffe, S., Breaux, A. M., & Feldman, H. (1994). Prediction of response to methylphenidate among children with ADHD and mental retardation. *Journal of the American Academy of Child and Adolescent Psychiatry, 33,* 1185–1193.

Hawthorne, M. E., & Lacey, J. H. (1992). Severe disturbance occurring during treatment for depression of a bulimic patient with fluoxetine. *Journal of Affective Disorders, 26,* 205–208.

Hirsch, S. R., Walsh, C., & Draper, R. (1983). The concept and efficacy of the treatment of parasuicide. *British Journal of Clinical Pharmacology, 15,* 1895–1945.

Hantouche, E. G., Lancrenon, S., & Chignon, J.-M. (1995). Evaluation of discontrol change under psychotropic treatments: Preliminary evidence for an opposite effect of benzodiazepines and antidepressants on discontrol. *Encephale, 21,* 59–65.

Kafka, M. P. (1995). Current concepts in the drug treatment of paraphilias and paraphilia-related disorders. *CNS Drugs, 3,* 9–21.

Kafka, M. P., & Prentky, R. (1992). Fluoxetine treatment of nonparaphilic sexual addictions and paraphilias in men. *Journal of Clinical Psychiatry, 53,* 351–358.

King, R. A., Riddle, M. A., Chappell, P. B., Hardin, M. T., Anderson, G. M., Lombroso, P., Scahill, L. (1991). Emergence of self-destructive phenomena in children and adolescents during fluoxetine treatment. *Journal of the American Academy of Child and Adolescent Psychiatry, 30,* 179–186.

Klein, D. F. (1968). Psychiatric diagnosis and a typology of clinical drug effects. *Psychopharmacologia, 13,* 359–386.

Kolmen, B. K., Feldman, H. M., Handen, B. L., & Janosky, J. E. (1995). Naltrexone in young autistic children: A double-blind, placebo-controlled crossover study. *Journal of the American Academy of Child and Adolescent Psychiatry, 34,* 223–231.

Kutcher, S., Papatheodorou, G., Reiter, S., & Gardner, D. (1995). The successful pharmacological treatment of adolescents and young adults with borderline personality disorder: A preliminary open trial of flupenthixol. *Journal of Psychiatry and Neuroscience, 20,* 113–118.

Leitner, P., & Serfling, R. (1993). Importance of psychopharmacological medication in the treatment of the borderline personality disorder. *Psychiatrische Praxis, 20,* 207–210.

Lejoyeux, M., & Ades, J. (1993). Evaluation of lithium treatment in alcoholism. *Alcohol and Alcoholism, 28,* 273–279.

Lemke, M. R. (1995). Effect of carbamazepine on agitation and emotional lability associated with severe dementia. *European Psychiatry, 10,* 259–262.

Links, P. S., Steiner, M., Bolago, L., & Irwin, D. (1990). Lithium therapy for borderline patients: Preliminary findings. *Journal of Personality Disorders, 4,* 173–181.

Mandoki, M. (1994). Buspirone treatment of traumatic brain injury in a child who is highly sensitive to adverse effects of psychotropic medications. *Journal of Child and Adolescent Psychopharmacology, 4,* 129–139.

Markovitz, P. J. (1993). *Double blind, placebo controlled trial of SSRI in personality disorder.* Paper presented at the third Conference of the International Society for the Study of Personality Disorders, Cambridge, MA.

Markovitz, P. J. (1995). Pharmacotherapy of impulsivity, aggression and related disorders. In E. Hollander & D. Stein (Eds.), *Impulsivity and aggression* (pp. 263–287). New York: Wiley.

Markovitz, P. J., Calabrese, J. R., Schulz, S. C., & Meltzer, H. Y. (1991). Fluoxetine in borderline and schizotypal personality disorder. *American Journal of Psychiatry, 148,* 1064–1067.

Markowitz, P. I. (1992). Effect of fluoxetine on self-injurious behavior in the developmentally disabled: A preliminary study. *Journal of Clinical Psychopharmacology, 12,* 27–31.

Menkes, D. B., Taghavi, E., Mason, P. A., Spears, G. F. S., & Howard, R. C. (1992). Fluoxetine treatment of severe premenstrual syndrome. *British Medical Journal, 305,* 346–347.

Mitchell, W. G., Zhou, Y., Chavez, J. M., & Guzman, B. L. (1993). Effects of antiepileptic drugs on reaction time, attention, and impulsivity in children. *Pediatrics, 91,* 101–105.

Montgomery, S. A., & Montgomery, D. B. (1982). Pharmacological prevention of suicidal behaviour. *Journal of Affective Disorders, 4,* 291–298.

Montgomery, S. A., Roy, D., & Montgomery, D. B. (1983). The prevention of recurrent suicidal acts. *British Journal Clinical Pharmacology, 15,* 1835–1885.

Nielsen, D. A., Goldman, D., Virkkunen, M., Tokola, R., Rawlings, R., & Linnoila M. (1994). Suicidality and 5-hydroxyindoleacetic acid concentration associated with a tryptophan hydroxylase polymorphism. *Archives of General Psychiatry, 51,* 34–38.

Norden, M. J. (1989). Fluoxetine in borderline personality disorder. *Progress in Neuropsychopharmacology and Biological Psychiatry, 13,* 885–893.

Perris, C., Eisemann, M., Eriksson, U., Jacobsson, L., von Knorring, L., & Perris, H. (1979). Variations in self-assessment of personality characteristics in depressed patients, with special reference to aspects of aggression. *Psychiatria Clinica, 12,* 209–215.

Peselow, E. D., Sanfilipo, M. P., Fieve, R. R., & Gulbenkian, G. (1994). Personality traits during depression and after clinical recovery. *British Journal of Psychiatry, 164,* 349–354.

Poyurovsky, M., Halperin, E., Enoch, D., Shneidman, M., & Weizman, A. (1995). Fluvoxamine treatment of compulsivity, impulsivity, and aggression: Part 2. *American Journal of Psychiatry, 152,* 1688–1689.

Rampello L., Nicoletti G., Raffaele R., Drago F. (1995). Comparative effects of amitriptyline and amineptine in patients affected by anxious depression. *Neuropsychobiology, 31,* 130–134.

Rickels, K., Sondheimer, S., Freeman, E. W., & Albert, J. (1990). Fluoxetine in the treatment of premenstrual syndrome. *Current Therapeutic Research: Clinical and Experimental, 48,* 161–166.

Rifkin, A., Quitkin, F., Crillo, C., Blumberg, A. G., & Klein, D. F. (1972). Lithium carbonate in emotionally unstable character disorder. *Archives of General Psychiatry, 27,* 519–523.

Robinson, T. N., & Zahen, T. P. (1985). Psychoticism and arousal: Possible evidence for a linkage of P and psychopathy. *Personality and Individual Differences, 6,* 47–66.

Ruegg, R., & Frances, A. (1995). New research in personality disorders. *Journal of Personality Disorders, 9,* 1–48.

Salzman, C. (1993). *Fluoxetine in borderline personality disorder.* Paper presented at the Third Conference of the International Society for the Study of Personality Disorders, Cambridge, MA.

Schalling, D. (1978). Psychopathy-related personality variables and the psychophysiology of socialization. In R. D. Hare & D. Schalling (Eds.), *Psychopathic behaviour: (pp. 85–106). Approaches to research* Chichester, England: Wiley.

Schalling, D., Åsberg, M., Edman, G., & Oreland, L. (1987). Markers for vulnerability to psychopathology: Temperament traits associated with platelet MAO activity. *Acta Psychiatrica Scandinavica, 76,* 172–182.

Schalling, D., Edman, G., & Åsberg, M. (1983). Impulsive cognitive style and inability to tolerate boredom: Psychobiological studies of temperamental vulnerability. In M. Zuckerman (Ed.), *Biological basis of sensation seeking, impulsivity and anxiety* (pp. 123–150). Hillsdaale, NJ: Erlbaum.

Sheard, M. E., Marini, J. L., Bridges, C. I., & Wagner, E. (1976). The effect of lithium on impulsive aggressive behaavior in man. *American Journal of Psychiatry, 133,* 1409–1413.

Siever, L. J. (1993). *Predicting suicide with clonidine and fenfluramine challenges.* Paper presented ay the Third Conference of the International Society for the Study of Personality Disorders, Cambridge, MA.

Silver Platter. (1996). *Psychiatry 1/86–1/96.* Amsterdam: Excerpta Medica.

Simeon, D., Stanley, B., Frances, A., Mann, J. J., Winchel, R., & Stanley, M. (1992). Self-mutilation in personality disorders: Psychological and biological correlates. *American Journal of Psychiatry, 149,* 221–226.

Sjöbring, H. (1973). Personality: Structure and development. *Acta Psychiatrica Scandinavica, 49,* (Suppl. 244), 1–204.

Soloff, P. H., Cornelius, J., George, A., Nathan, S., Perel, J. M., & Ulrich, R. F. (1993). Efficacy of phenelzine and haloperidol in borderline personality disorder. *Archives of General Psychiatry, 50,* 377–385.

Soloff, P. H., George, A., Nathan, R. S., ,schultz, P. M., Ulrich, R. F., Perel, J. M. (1986). Progress in the pharmacotherapy of borderline disorders: A double-blind study of amitriptyline, haloperidol and placebo. *Archives of General Psychiatry, 43,* 691–697.

Spencer, T., Wilens, T., Biederman, J., Faraone, S. V., Ablon, J. S., & Lapey, K. (1995). A double-blind, crossover comparison of methylphenidate and placebo in adults with childhood-onset attention-deficit hyperactivity disorder. *Archives of General Psychiatry, 52,* 434–443.

Stålenheim, G., & von Knorring, L. (in press). Personality traits determined by means of the Karolinska Scales of Personality (KSP) in a Swedish forensic psychiatric population. *European Journal of Psychiatry.*

Stein, D. J., Hollander, E., & Liebowitz, M. R. (1993). Neurobiology of impulsivity and the impulse control disorders. *Journal of Neuropsychiatry and Clinical Neuroscience, 5,* 9–17.

Stein, D. J., Simeon, D., Frenkel, M., Islam, M. N., & Hollander, E. (1995). An open trial of valproate in borderline personality disorder. *Journal of Clinical Psychiatry, 56,* 506–510.

Stone, A. B., Pearlstein, T. B., & Brown, W. A. (1990). Fluoxetine in the treatment of premenstrual syndrome. *Psychopharmacological Bulletin, 26,* 331–335.

Teicher, M. H., Glod, C., & Cole, J. O. (1990). Emergence of intense suicidal preoccupation during fluoxetine treatment. *American Journal of Psychiatry, 147,* 207–210.

Tremblay, R. E., Pihl, R. O., Vitaro, F., & Dobkin, P. L. (1994). Predicting early onset of male antisocial behavior from preschool behavior. *Archives of General Psychiatry, 51,* 732–739.

Vartiainen, H., Tiihonen, J., Putkonen, A., Koponen, H. Virkkunen, M., Hakola, P., & Lehto, H. (1995). Citalopram, a selective serotonin reuptake inhibitor, in the treatment of aggression in schizophrenia. *Acta Psychiatrica Scandinavica, 91,* 348–351.

Vestergaard, P., Gram, L. F., Kragh-Sørensen, P., Bech, P., Reisby, N., & Bolwig, T. G. (1986). Citalopram: Clinical profile in comparison with clomipramine. A controlled multicenter study. *Psychopharmacology, 90,* 131–138.

Vestergaard, P., Gram, L. F., Kragh-Sørensen, P., Bech, P., Reisby, N., & Bolwig, T. G. (1990). Paroxetine: A selective serotonin reuptake inhibitor showing better tolerance but weaker antidepressant effect than clomipramine in a controlled multicenter study. *Journal of Affective Disorders, 18,* 289–299.

Virkkunen, M., Nuutila, A., Goodwin, F. K., & Linnoila, M. (1987). Cerebrospinal fluid monoamine metabolite levels in male arsonists. *Archives of General Psychiatry, 44,* 241–247.

Virkkunen, M., Rawlings, R., Tokola, R., Poland, R. E., Guidotti, A., Nemeroff, C., Bissette, G., Kalogeras, K, Karonen, S. L., & Linnoila, M. (1994). CSF biochemistries, glucose metabolism, and diurnal activity rhythms in alcoholic, violent offenders, fire setters, and healthy volunteers. *Archives of General Psychiatry, 51,* 20–27.

von Knorring, L., & Ekselius, L. (1998). SSRI by depression and personality disorders in primary health care. [Proceedings of the 25th Nordic Psychiatric Congress, May 7–11, 1997, Trondheim, Norway]. *Nordic Journal of Psychiatry, 52*(Suppl. 41), 100.

White, J. L., Moffitt, T. E., Carpi, A., Bartusch, D. J., Needles, D. J., & Stouthamer Loeber, M. (1994). Measuring impulsivity and examining its relationship to delinquency. *Journal of Anormal Psychology, 103*, 192–205.

Wilens, T. E., Biederman, J., Spencer, T. J., & Prince, J. (1995). Pharmacotherapy of adult attention deficit/hyperactivity disorder: A review. *Journal of Clinical Psychopharmacology, 15*, 270–279.

Wolff, M., Carreon, D., Summers, D., et al. (1991). *Lack of efficacy of buspirone in borderline personality disorders.* Paper presented at the 144th Annual Meeting of the American Psychiatric Association, New Orleans, LA.

Wood, S. H., Mortola, J. F., Chan, Y. F., Moossazadeh, F., & Yen, S. S. C. (1992). Treatment of premenstrual syndrome with fluoxetine: A double-blind, placebo-controlled, crossover study. *Obstetrics and Gynecology, 80*, 339–344.

Zuckerman, M. (1979). *Sensation seeking: Beyond the optimal level of arousal.* Hillsdale, NJ: Erlbaum.

Zuckerman, M. (Ed.). (1983). *Biological bases of sensation seeking, impulsivity and anxiety.* Hillsdale, NJ: Erlbaum.

Zuckerman, M. (1989). Personality in the third dimension: A psychological approach. *Personality and Individual Differences, 10*, 391–418.

Zuckerman, M. (1991). *The psychology of personality.* New York: Cambridge University Press.

24

The Psychotherapeutic Management of Psychopathic, Narcissistic, and Paranoid Transferences

OTTO F. KERNBERG

A contemporary psychoanalytic approach to the etiology of the antisocial personality disorder focuses on the pathological intrapsychic structures of these patients. It is assumed that the development of psychic structure in general derives from the interaction of earliest object relations with the genetic and constitutionally given activation of affect dispositions. In these patients, the pathology of early affect development and the pathology of early object relations are assumed to interact from birth on (Kernberg, 1992a). This contemporary psychoanalytic view integrates the concepts of (1) a biological predisposition to excessive aggression, derived from excessive activation of aggressive affects; (2) the influence of early trauma in inducing aggressive affect, mediated by intense and prolonged pain; and (3) the distortion of internalized object relations, under the impact of severely pathological interactions in infancy and early childhood. Abnormalities in the neurochemical systems that codetermine affect activation; deficits in early perceptive and cognitive functions derived from central nervous system pathology; and the direct influence of severe distortions in early attachment derived from the experience of physical pain, physical and sexual abuse, and early abandonment all enter this equation, as well as the more complex interaction between the infant and the parental figures that will determine the internalization of moral codes.

I have proposed in earlier work (Kernberg, 1992a) that the dual-drive theory of libido and aggression needs to be reformulated, with the drives reconceptualized as the hierarchically supraordinate integration of the corresponding series (from their most primitive to their most complex forms) of aggressive and libidinal affects. I have also proposed that the general concept of identification needs to be conceived of as the inter-

nalization not only of the representation of the other, but the simultaneous internalization of the representation of the self interacting with the representation of the other within a given affect state. In short, the construction of psychic reality is based on the internalization of dyadic units of self- and object representations linked by a dominant affect
disposition (Kernberg, 1993).

PSYCHODYNAMICS OF THE SPECTRUM OF
NARCISSISTIC DISORDERS

With this conceptual frame as a background, I now formulate, from a psychodynamic
viewpoint, the characteristic structural aspects of the antisocial personality disorder, as
well as of the entire spectrum of narcissistic pathology with antisocial behavior—ranging
from the narcissistic personality disorder proper, to the syndrome of malignant narcissism, to the antisocial personality disorder proper. I am defining "the antisocial personality disorder proper" here in the sense of Robert Hare's (Hare, Hart, & Harpur, 1991;
Hare & Hart, 1995) and my own (Kernberg, 1989) work, which reestablishes the direct
connection with Cleckley's (1941) classical description, and avoids the dilution of the
concept of the antisocial personality disorder that has occurred as a consequence of the
DSM system (American Psychiatric Association, 1980, 1987, 1994).

The Antisocial Personality Disorder Proper

The antisocial personality disorder proper as defined here constitutes the most severe
form of pathological narcissism. The essential structural characteristic of the antisocial
personality disorder proper is the marked distortion, absence, or deterioration of the
superego system. In these patients, the earliest layer of superego precursors—namely,
primitive, persecutory, aversive representations of significant others (onto whom primitive aggressive impulses have been projected)—has not been neutralized by the internalization of idealized, all-good, demanding, yet gratifying representations of significant
others, which normally constitute the second layer of superego precursors or the early
ego ideal. The absence of such idealized object representations of the ego ideal precludes
the normal toning down of the fantasied threatening prohibitions and punishments of
the first superego layer, and reinforces their defensive reprojective attribution onto the
environment. As a consequence, the realistic demands and prohibitions of the third level
of superego precursors (corresponding to the advanced Oedipal stage) cannot be assessed
realistically and internalized; instead, they are experienced in a highly distorted way under the impact of projected aggression. Thus, the third layer of superego precursors—the
internalization of realistic demands and prohibitions from the Oedipal phase—cannot
develop.

The resultant absence of a normally integrated superego (i.e., of a system of more or
less coherent internalized ethical and moral demands) brings about a total dependency of
the individual on immediate external cues for the regulation of interpersonal behavior; a
total lack of the normal support that superego functions provide to an individual's self-
experience and identity formation; and dependency upon immediate admiration from
others, or indications of triumph and dominance over the external world, for a sense of
security and self-esteem. The capacity for ethical self-regulation, and for empathy with a
moral and ethical dimension of others as a significant motivational system in interpersonal relations, is absent. By means of projective mechanisms, the selfish, suspicious,

combative attitude of a self deprived of superego regulation is attributed to all others, precluding the capacity for trust, intimacy, dependency, and gratification by the experience of love from others. The overall structural characteristics of these individuals, in summary, include the absence of a functioning, integrated superego, and the hypertrophy of a threatened, endangered, violent self geared to face an essentially dangerous, violent world. This pathological, grandiose, aggressively infiltrated self is the most primitive type of "identification with the aggressor."

To translate this pathological structural system into the language of unconscious fantasies, the world of the antisocial personality disorder reflects the pathology of internalized object relations, and thus is characterized by a basic experience of savage aggression from the parental objects. A world of violence is experienced as a constant background to all interpersonal interactions. The lack of any good, reliable object relationship results in the sense that the good are weak and unreliable; in a reaction of rage and hatred to the frustrations derived from being inevitably disappointed by potentially gratifying objects; and in unconscious envy of others who act as if they were not dominated by a violent inner world. The painful state of envy and resentment fosters the powerful defenses of devaluation and contempt that characterize these individuals' pathological grandiose self. Those who matter in the external world are only the powerful, who need to be controlled, submitted to, manipulated, and above all feared, because the powerful are also sadistic and unpredictable.

The transformation of pain into rage, and chronic rage into hatred, is a central affective development of these patients. The structural characteristics of hatred imply the relationship between an endangered self and a hateful and hated object that must be controlled, made to suffer in revenge, and ultimately destroyed. The projection of hatred brings about a basic paranoid orientation toward a world perceived as hateful, against which one must defend oneself through dishonesty, treacherousness, and aggression. Given crude self-interest as the only standard of behavior, and given the basic assumptions that impulsive rage and hatred determine the unpredictability of the dangerous behavior of powerful others, the assessment and internalization of a value system are irrelevant. Survival depends upon cautious submission and evasion, a consistent manipulation of assumed aggressors.

In other words, the basic paranoid orientation of the antisocial individual and the psychopathic defenses against it (Kernberg, 1984) interfere with any possible internalization of value systems, even the idealization of the value systems of the potential aggressor. In this regard, the antisocial personality disorder proper is different from the syndrome of malignant narcissism—in which there is at least some idealization of the value systems of the powerful; an idealization of the pathological grandiose self in terms of self-righteous aggression; and the capacity for some identification with other powerful idealized figures as part of a cohesive "gang" (Meltzer, 1977), which permits at least some loyalty and good object relations to be internalized. For the psychopath, in contrast, only power itself is reliable, and the pleasure of sadistic control is the major motivation system in a world clearly divided between the all-powerful and the despicable weak.

The clinical differentiation Henderson (Henderson, 1939; Henderson & Gillespie, 1969) made between "passive" and "aggressive" psychopaths seems to me of significant clinical value. To begin with, the passive type is much less dangerous, and therefore provides some potential "space" for a psychotherapeutic intervention, questionable as its effectiveness may be. The eminent dangerousness of the aggressive psychopath, in contrast, immediately calls for protection of the family and of society—and of the therapist—as the highest priority in dealing with such a patient. The passive type of psychopath has been able to learn to deal with the powerful through pseudosubmission and through outsmarting them—a passive, parasitic exploitiveness that at least implies the capacity to control immediate anger and rage, and to transform it into the slow-motion aggression of a "wolf in sheep's clothing." In the case of these patients, their own aggression can be denied, and the division of the world into wolves and sheep is complemented by the adaptive function of the wolf disguised among the sheep.

Whether psychopaths are predominantly aggressive or passive, the gratification they seek is exclusively linked to bodily functions—to eating, drinking, drugs, and alcohol, and to a sexuality divested of its object relations implications and thus devoid of love and tenderness. In the most severe cases of aggressive psychopathy, sexual sadism may become an invitation to murder, making these individuals extremely dangerous. Or else early aggression may dominate their emotional lives to the extent that even the sensuality of bodily contact and skin eroticism is eliminated. In this case, there is a global extinction of all capacity for sexual gratification, which is replaced by senseless physical destructiveness, self-mutilation, and murder.

Malignant Narcissism

The syndrome of malignant narcissism is a somewhat less severe form of pathological narcissism, with significant antisocial features, paranoid traits, and ego-syntonic aggression directed against self or others, but without total destruction of superego functions (Kernberg, 1989). In this syndrome, the process by which the earliest aggressive superego precursors are either projected or internalized in the form of a violent, grandiose, pathological self is modified by the capacity to internalize at least some idealized superego precursors as well. These patients have the capacity to admire powerful people, and can depend on sadistic and powerful but reliable parental images. The syndrome of malignant narcissism has the particular characteristic of the internalization of both aggressive and idealized superego precursors, leading to the idealization of the aggressive, sadistic features of the pathological grandiose self of these patients. "Justified indignation" becomes justified violence against self or others. The idealization of the powerful self goes hand in hand with the capacity for some loyalty and a certain tolerance of the third level of realistic superego demands and prohibitions.

The Narcissistic Personality Disorder Proper

The next step in this continuum from most to least severe psychopathology is the narcissistic personality disorder proper. Here, a certain degree of superego development (with internalization of the third level of more realistic demands and prohibitions) has evolved, while the pathological grandiose self constitutes, by its idealized nature, a massive defense against the awareness of unconscious aggression—particularly in its form of primitive, dominant envy. In fact, the defenses against unconscious envy represent the dominant dynamics of the narcissistic personality disorder proper, and, by the same token, signal these individuals' capacity to recognize good aspects of others that they envy and wish to incorporate. The antisocial behavior of these individuals reflects the ego-syntonic, rationalized entitlement and greed of a pathological grandiose self; potential conflicts between areas of superego deterioration and remnants of internalized value systems may evolve in the course of successful treatment.

PROGNOSTIC CONSIDERATIONS

A basic question still remains unanswered: Once a malignant intrapsychic structure has evolved—that is, a pathological grandiose self infiltrated with aggression dominates psychic functioning, in the absence of the moderating and maturing reliance on an integrated superego—can later psychosocial influences and, in particular, psychotherapeutic treatment be of help? A subset of this question relates to social influences that may promote antisocial behavior. We were made dramatically aware of the susceptibility of ordinary people to such influences through Milgram's (1963) experiments in the United States, and through Zinoviev's (1984) analysis of socialized dishonesty as a major cultural characteristic of the totalitarian system of the former Soviet Union. Edith Jacobson (1971) has pointed to the "paranoid urge to betray" that is a part of paranoid structures in general, and I have applied this analysis to the psychopathic regression of individuals in leadership positions in highly paranoiagenic organizations (Kernberg, 1992b).

Are there healing influences that may alter the psychopathic structure, either in early childhood or perhaps even in later years? We do have good clinical evidence that the narcissistic personality disorder proper with antisocial features may be effectively treated, and that even the syndrome of malignant narcissism is treatable. So far, to my knowledge, this has not yet been demonstrated for the antisocial personality disorder proper. What complicates the question of prognosis is that in many studies, the selection of individuals with antisocial behavior does not differentiate sharply between the antisocial personality disorder proper and the less severe syndromes in which antisocial behavior dominates. I believe that it is absolutely crucial that we reintroduce sharp diagnostic differentiations in this field, as a precondition for the evaluation of the effectiveness of various treatment modalities. In what follows, I shall explore some guiding principles for the clinical management of patients with severe antisocial behavior; these principles are based on the diagnostic considerations I have formulated, and on the clinical experiences derived from the psychotherapy research project on borderline conditions at the Westchester Division of the New York Hospital–Cornell Medical Center.

THERAPEUTIC STRATEGIES AND TACTICS

From a diagnostic, prognostic, and therapeutic viewpoint, it is crucial to the treatment of any case in which antisocial features are at issue to evaluate (1) the presence or absence of some form of pathological narcissism; (2) the extent to which superego pathology dominates—that is, where the patient falls in the continuum from the narcissistic to the antisocial personality disorders; (3) the intensity of ego-syntonic aggression, whether directed toward the self (in the form of suicidal, parasuicidal, and/or self-mutilating and self-destructive behavior) or against others (in the form of physical violence, homicidal tendencies, or a life-endangering sadistic perversion); (4) the severity of paranoid trends; and finally (5) the stability of reality testing (Kernberg, Selzer, Koenigsberg, Carr, & Appelbaum, 1989).

The careful assessment of the foregoing aspects make it possible to assess, first, the extent to which one can rely upon the patient's honest communication; the dangerousness of the patient to self and others, including the therapist; and the overall prognosis for the capacity to sustain a psychotherapeutic relationship, as opposed to the likelihood of early dropout from treatment. The most general prognostic psychotherapeutic rule—namely, that the degree of antisocial tendencies and the quality of object relations determine the prognosis for any psychotherapeutic treatment—thus becomes much more specific and immediately useful in planning the treatment of this particular spectrum of patients (Kernberg, 1984). The psychotherapeutic strategies I describe here derive directly from the criteria outlined earlier, and therefore depend on a careful, detailed, comprehensive diagnostic evaluation.

Setting Conditions for Treatment of Severer Forms of Narcissistic Pathology

In this discussion of setting conditions for treatment, I cover only patients with the antisocial personality disorder proper and patients with the syndrome of malignant narcissism. As I indicate later, patients with the narcissistic personality disorder proper usually show less severe antisocial behavior, so that setting conditions for their treatment is not as challenging or complex.

Patients with the Antisocial Personality Disorder Proper

The most urgent question in any case presenting with severe aggressive or self-aggressive behavior is the extent to which there is a risk to the patient's life and/or to the lives of others, including the therapist. If the diagnosis is that of an antisocial personality disorder, aggressive type, as defined above, it is crucial to take protective measures involving the patient's family, social services, and/or the law, in order to protect human life.

The prognosis for psychotherapeutic treatment of the antisocial personality disorder proper is practically zero. The main therapeutic task is to protect the family, the therapist, and society from such a patient, as well as to protect the patient from self-destructiveness. When such patients possess dangerous weapons, an immediate arrangement of protective separation from such weapons is required. For example, one patient sought a consultation because of severe hypochondriacal symptoms and turned out to be involved in homosexual seduction of men, whom he would lure into a hotel in the center city and then rob at gunpoint. The therapist demanded that the patient deliver his weapon before any further psychotherapeutic contacts were made, and the therapist consulted his own lawyer as to his legal responsibilities in the case.

If the patient fulfills the criteria for the antisocial personality disorder proper, but does not present aggressive and/or exploitative behaviors that are of immediate potential threat, the diagnostician's most urgent task is to ascertain the reason for the consultation: whether the family is searching for help; whether the consultation is exclusively geared to providing the patient with protection from impending legal action; whether the legal system is seeking help in assessing the patient's responsibility for criminal action; whether the family or social agencies have pressed for this consultation as part of an effort to deal with the threats this patient represents for the environment; or whether the patient is seen during a period of genuine psychotic regression. In regard to this last possibility, there exists a small group of patients who exhibit what traditional German psychiatry denominated "pseudopsychopathic schizophrenia" (Guttmacher, 1961)—that is, patients who experience periods of extended psychotic illness that conform to the criteria for chronic schizophrenia, interspersed with periods of recovery of reality testing, at which time the patients fulfill all the criteria for an antisocial personality disorder. These patients constitute prognostically the most ominous group within the antisocial personality disorder category, and usually can be managed only under conditions of practically permanent seclusion in specialized psychiatric hospitals or psychiatric prisons.

Patients with the passive or aggressive type of antisocial personality disorder who do not pose a serious immediate threat present the clinician with the task of protecting the family and/or the social environment from the long-term dangers posed by the patients' behavior. These patients may chronically steal from or exploit their families, may be chronically violent without actual threat to life, or may engage in behavior likely to result in involvement with the law. Protective intervention may involve the clinician in serving as consultant to the family, social agencies, and the law. It is, of course, essential that psychotherapeutic contacts not be exploited as a protection against legal procedures. In addition, the psychotherapist must take all measures to assure his or her own safety as a precondition for any interventions with the family, including getting legal advice about his or her responsibilities.

Any psychotherapist who decides to attempt to work with a patient presenting this diagnosis must, as the minimal precondition for treatment, secure the patient's agreement to discontinue any antisocial activity that is potentially threatening to the patient or others. For example, an HIV-positive male patient with a pedophilic perversion (or paraphilia) would have to commit himself to absolute abstention from any pedophilic activity as a precondition for treatment. Of course, it would be absurd to propose such a precondition in the case of a patient who had not proven honest in his communication about his behavior.

One patient with antisocial and self-mutilating behavior and chronic suicidal tendencies threatened, during an early diagnostic session, to act on the impulse to cut herself with the razor blades she carried in her purse, and to cut the therapist if she attempted to interfere. The therapist took immediate action to assure her own safety, summoning a colleague to join her until arrangements could be made for the patient's immediate hospitalization. A therapist should not attempt to carry out a diagnostic assessment alone in a closed room with a dangerous patient.

Another patient, with the diagnosis of the passive type of antisocial personality disorder, had sequestered the money allocated for taxes on his wife's business for several years. When this was discovered by the Internal Revenue Service, repayment bankrupted the business. He wanted to enter psychotherapeutic treatment as a way to demonstrate to his wife his commitment to changing his behavior in order to avoid a separation and divorce. In the course of an evaluation that included the entire family, it emerged that his wife would be willing to give him another chance only under conditions of a total separation of their financial activities. This would preclude his continued economic dependency on her, and would force him to engage in productive work commensurate with his professional background. Psychotherapy was offered to him on the condition that he would be responsible for the payment of his treatment based upon his own work, and with the understanding that the therapist's ongoing communication with the patient's wife and other family members would be an essential aspect of a long-range psychotherapeutic arrangement. Once it became clear to the patient that psychotherapy would not further his efforts to remain financially dependent on his wife and her family, he rejected the offer of treatment.

Psychotherapeutic treatment of a patient with an antisocial personality disorder who is not dangerous requires open communication with the patient and the family regarding the severity of the condition, the poor prognosis, and the need to maintain open communication with the entire family system in order to monitor the patient's compliance with the requirement that all antisocial behavior be suspended as a condition of treatment. Such arrangements increase the likelihood of success in ongoing assessment and control of potential aggression toward self and others, and of eliminating the secondary gains of entering psychotherapeutic treatment itself. These arrangements also, as in the case described above, increase the chance that the patient will reject psychotherapy, thus sparing the therapist and the family the exhaustion of their resources in pursuit of an unattainable therapeutic goal.

Chronic lying as a major presenting symptom in a patient with an antisocial personality disorder does not necessarily preclude the achievement of the preconditions for treatment mentioned above. For example, in the case of an adolescent living with and potentially under the control of the parents, the treatment arrangements should include educational contacts with the family to stress the fact that the only reliable source of information about the patient is his or her behavior. The family will need help to make it very clear to the patient that the patient's behavior and not any of his or her statements will determine how they will interact with the patient, and what rights and privileges he or she will be granted in the home. If the youngster's behavior threatens the well-being of the family (e.g., the teen continues to steal from the parents to buy drugs), institutional or foster care placement may be the only alternative.

If the only antisocial behavior is lying, parental control may be much easier. The patient's chronic lying may then be taken up in psychotherapy as the dominant or unique transferential issue until it is either resolved or demonstrated to be impossible to resolve.

Patients with Malignant Narcissism

When the diagnostic assessment is that of the syndrome of malignant narcissism (i.e., the typical combination of a narcissistic personality structure, severe antisocial behavior, paranoid trends, and ego-syntonic aggression directed against self and/or others), the prognosis is better. Again, however, a precondition for the treatment is strict control of the antisocial behavior, with the development of a treatment structure that includes open communication with the family and/or the social system; elimination of all secondary gains of treatment; and the physical, social, and legal protection of the therapist.

In our experience, most of these patients require an initial period of hospital treatment to set up the necessary treatment arrangements. Psychodynamic psychotherapy may begin in the hospital when long-term inpatient treatment is available, and may be continued on an outpatient basis once the patients are ready to take on the responsibility for fulfilling the preconditions for treatment as part of the treatment contract. There are, however, cases where outpatient treatment may be attempted from the beginning.

For example, one adolescent patient presented severe behavior problems at school, with cheating, drug dealing, and inordinate physical violence against other students and teachers; meanwhile, he lied to family members, abused alcohol and drugs, engaged in promiscuous sexual behavior, and held a leading position in a street gang. He was found to have a typical narcissistic personality structure, along with ego-syntonic aggression, severe paranoid traits, and antisocial behavior. But he was able to maintain loyalty to his gang and to individual members of it, and also evinced the capacity for nonexploitative dependency on some family members. Furthermore, he showed the capacity for authentic guilt feelings when one of his violent outbursts seriously injured another boy. I therefore agreed to attempt outpatient psychotherapy, although I made it clear to the youngster and his parents that I did not have very hopeful expectations. A tight social control system was set up, involving a psychiatric social worker who maintained ongoing contacts with the patient's family and school, strict control regarding his finances and whereabouts, and ongoing contact with the local police regarding his gang-related activities. This, along with the patient's agreement to attempt to live within these strictures, provided an adequate structure to attempt an outpatient psychotherapeutic relationship.

This patient began coming to psychotherapy sessions only under the family's threats to cut off all financial support unless he attended regularly. In the sessions, the patient alternated between berating me for being the agent of his parents and filling the hours with trivialities, while I systematically focused on his deceptiveness in his relationship with me and the functions of this deceptiveness in our interaction. The analysis of his perception of me as a corrupt agent of his parents, a foolish dispenser of quackery, and a dangerous enemy who was attempting to control his life while pretending to be on his side gradually helped to clarify the projection of the characteristics of his own pathological grandiose self onto me. His profound conviction that in a world in which everybody was everybody else's enemy, and only the powerful and the "wolves disguised as sheep" could triumph over the "suckers" who were their victims, shifted the transference from a typically psychopathic one into a paranoid one.

General Psychotherapeutic Principles

In general, if and when the therapist can establish a solid and unbreakable treatment frame that provides the space for the analysis of the antisocial psychopathology, systematic interpretation of the psychopathic transference may gradually resolve it and transform it into a predominantly paranoid transference. This may then be explored in the same way that one analyses the severe paranoid regressions in nonantisocial narcissistic personalities and in patients with borderline personality organization in general (Kernberg, 1992a).

Patients who are able to communicate honestly can provide information about their behavioral problems outside the sessions, and this, combined with the development of severely regressive behaviors in the sessions, gradually makes it possible to transform interpretively their pathological behaviors into cognitive and affective experiences in the transference. Patients whose chronic deceptiveness deprives the therapist of an accurate assessment of pathological behaviors outside the sessions require a reliable network of information that permits the therapist to bring the pathological behavior expressed in the patients' lives into the sessions. All patients with severe acting-out tendencies require the interpretive transformation of their automatic, repetitive behavior patterns into affectively invested fantasies in the transference. The exploration and working through of these fantasies is a major task during extended periods of the treatment.

Some general psychotherapeutic principles apply as to the issues to focus on in the treatment hours. First, the therapist should always consider the following as priorities for intervention, in descending order of urgency (Kernberg et al., 1989): (1) danger to self and others, (2) threats of disruption of the treatment, (3) dishonesty in communication, (4) acting out outside and inside the sessions, and (5) trivialization of the communication. Second, it is essential to look for the aspect of the total material—the patient's verbal communication, his or her nonverbal behavior, and the countertransference—that is affectively dominant. During extended periods of time in the treatment of such patients, their verbal descriptions of their subjective experience is a relatively "weak channel" for the transmission of cues as to what is affectively dominant and in need of exploration. Instead, these cues are to be found through careful evaluation of the patients' behavior and the therapist's countertransference.

Countertransference Issues in the Psychopathic Transference

This brings us to the problems of the countertransference in the treatment of patients with severely antisocial behavior. It is important, to begin with, that the therapist find some potentially likeable, authentic human aspect of such a patient—a potential area of ego growth that will constitute the initially minimal yet essential base for genuine communication from the therapist to the patient. The therapist's position of technical neutrality implies an authentic commitment to what he or she expects or hopes constitutes a still available core of ordinary humanity within the patient. When such a core of object relation investment can be found, it assures a capacity for authentic dependency and the establishment of a therapeutic relationship.

The therapist's comments start from an implicit alliance between the therapist in his or her specific role, and whatever normal aspect of the patient's personality has been preserved. It is from this initial vantage point that the therapist consistently confronts the patient's identification with primitive sadistic, corrupt, antisocial, death-desiring parts of inner life. The internal object relations world of such a patient is populated by primitive sadistic representations of self and others, and their interactions with masochistic, devalued, threatening, or corrupt enemies. At the beginning, the therapist may have to assume the existence of a somewhat normal self-representation in the middle of this nightmarish world. Such an assumption permits the therapist to systematically confront the patient's imprisonment in a destructive world, without experiencing these interpretations as an attack on the patient himself or herself.

This means that in spite of the patient's projection of his or her primitive superego precursors onto the therapist, and the consequent perception of any critical comment from the therapist as a savage attack to be fended off, it is important that the therapist remain firmly in a moral stance without becoming moralistic. The therapist must maintain a critical attitude without letting himself or herself be seduced into an identification with projected sadistic images, or tempted into a defensively seductive, mutually manipulative style of communication that reinforces mutual denial of the severe aggression rooted in the patient's internal world.

The patient, by means of provocative behavior, will attempt to move the therapist out of this position of technical neutrality and authentic human concern into the role of a sadistic persecutor, the patient's masochistic victim, or a manipulative, essentially indifferent authority, or else into a total emotional withdrawal from the patient. Paradoxically, a therapist's pseudoinvestment—a friendly surface that denies the aggression in the countertransference, or reflects a basic indifference toward the patient—may bring about an apparent "warming up" of the therapeutic relationship without a resolution of the underlying dishonesty in the patient's communication, or, more fundamentally, the possibility of resolving the severe denial and splitting processes that defend against the aggressive implication of the patient's antisocial behavior.

The therapist can maintain an honest investment in the relationship only so long as his or her objective safety is protected. Whenever the therapist feels threatened by the patient's pathology or by the patient himself or herself, the first step has to be for the therapist to assure his or her own physical, emotional, social, and legal safety. This safety must take precedence over any other consideration, because it is the very precondition for an authentic investment in the psychotherapeutic endeavor, and is therefore a basic guarantee for the survival of the therapy.

The investment I have described precludes "going out of one's way" to try to help an impossible patient, and demands the maintenance at all times of a realistic boundary of the therapist's involvement. A messianic attitude of helping and saving impossible cases—going overboard to provide such patients with a "corrective emotional experience" of total dedication, in the face of their provocative behavior—may create the risk of the therapist's denying the negative aspects of the countertransference. This can result in the gradual, unconscious, and eventually conscious accumulation and sudden acting out of the negative countertransference, which may precipitate an end to the treatment.

The Paranoid Transference

In clinical practice, the spectrum of narcissistic pathology—ranging from the narcissistic personality disorder proper with antisocial features, to the syndrome of malignant narcissism, to the antisocial personality disorder proper (in both its passive and its aggressive forms)—always includes significant paranoid features. Insofar as the combination of antisocial behavior and primitive defensive mechanisms implies a projection of these antisocial tendencies onto others, the fears of being found out, mistreated, manipulated, or exploited are frequent correlates of antisocial behavior.

Once the psychopathic transference has shifted into a predominantly paranoid one—that is, the patient's dishonest and pseudofriendly behavior has shifted into an honest suspicion and distrust of the therapist—the patient may appear much more hostile and belligerent in the sessions, but, by the same token, more honestly engaged in the psychotherapeutic relationship. Now the main question is the extent to which the structure of the treatment protects the patient, the therapist, and the treatment setting from the acting out of severe aggression. This depends on whether the patient's superego is sufficiently intact and noncorrupted to enable the patient to experience enough guilt and concern for the therapist and the therapeutic relationship to prevent him or her from threatening the therapist or the treatment with destruction.

The task now is to examine in great detail the nature of the patient's projections, the image of the therapist that emerges through them as a sadistic persecutor, and eventually the projective processes through which the patient is attributing to the therapist what he or she cannot tolerate in the self. One patient had violent temper tantrums in connection with her suspicion that the therapist had been talking about her to third parties, and assumed that the therapist was attempting to obtain confidential information from her in order to use it against her later on. In this, as the patient gradually became aware, she repeated the suspicious and enraged behavior of her mother, who would attempt to control the patient's communications with people outside the family and her private life in general. Eventually the patient became aware that she had been attributing to the therapist her own proclivity for surreptitiously spying on others in order to achieve control over them, manipulating of other people to obtain information about their social lives, eavesdropping on conversations, and participating in meetings under false pretenses in order to obtain privileged information.

A particular complication with a patient whose syndrome of malignant narcissism has evolved through psychotherapy into a severely regressive paranoid transference is the patient's acting out of primitive sadistic object relations by dragging the therapist into legal threats and involvements. At times this paranoid development takes the form of unremitting and sometimes violent provocations of the therapist, which eventually give rise to sadistic countertransference reactions. When the therapist enacts these responses, in however attenuated a form, the patient then triumphantly uses these enactments as the basis for initiating legal actions against the therapist. Or else the patient enters into a new psychotherapeutic relationship with a new idealized therapist, who may be drawn into encouraging or condoning the pursuit of legal action against the previous therapist. After some time, the new therapist is also transformed into a persecutor; the patient may now initiate legal actions against him or her, and look for a third therapist as part of this chronic pattern. The primitive, violent, sadistic internalized object relations of such a patient require the therapist's ongoing concern—not only for his or her own survival but also for the survival of efforts to liberate the patient from destructive internal tormentors. The therapist must realistically feel secure in the treatment situation in order to be able to break this vicious circle.

There are times when a patient's paranoid regression may take on frankly psychotic features, with the development of delusions in the transference. At such points, it is important, first, to maintain the rules of strict boundaries in the therapeutic situation, stressing the kind of behavior that can and cannot be tolerated both within and outside the sessions; and, second, to ascertain whether such delusion formation occurs only in the therapy hours, or also in the patients's external life. If paranoid delusion formation develops outside the hours in a patient whose diagnosis is definitely that of a borderline personality organization (i.e., a nonpsychotic disorder), it is important to provide clear structure for the patient outside the hours in order to avoid dangerous aggressive and self-destructive behavior, even before the nature of this behavior can be understood in the transference.

Once it is established that the patient's convictions are clearly delusional, the technique of "incompatible realities" may be utilized to resolve such a psychotic regression. It consists of letting the patient know that the therapist understands that the patient's conviction is unshakable, and that the therapist respects this conviction. At the same time, the therapist should explain that his or her own conviction is totally different from the patient's, so that the patient is faced with the fact that the patient and the therapist are living in different realities—or else the therapist is lying, and if the therapist were lying, what would that mean in terms of the therapeutic relationship? In any case, it is important that the therapist present his or her own conviction without attempting to convince the patient, while making it very clear that he or she will not be convinced by the patient's view either. The therapist should demonstrate, through his or her behavior, an interest in the implications of the differences in their respective convictions.

A patient who still has severe unresolved psychopathic transference may see the therapist's statement regarding "incompatible realities" as evidence that the therapist is lying. At this point, a good deal of time may have to be devoted to exploring the transference implications of a "dishonest" therapist's treating the patient before tracing those back to projective processes in the patient. In other words, this development reflects a regression from the paranoid to the earlier stage of predominantly psychopathic transference. If, on the other hand, the patient believes that the therapist is sincere but totally out of touch with reality, then the situation of being in mutually incompatible realities can be analyzed. In this way, a psychotic nucleus in the transference may be circumscribed and then examined as a particular transferential problem. This approach is very effective in reducing paranoid transference regression in essentially nonpsychotic patients, but is contraindicated in patients with a psychosis with paranoid features.

One patient became convinced that the therapist was presenting his comments in a sarcastic or otherwise provocative way, in order to get her angry enough to lose control and thus justify treating her as if she were psychotic. This perception of the therapist's sadistic, cynical, insensitive, and provocative behavior enraged her. Her vehement protest was combined with ironic mimicry of the therapist's statements, linguistic style, and accent. Her indignation escalated to the point that she was considering making formal complaints to the therapist's superiors. The therapist pointed out that he believed she was in fact convinced that he was treating her in such sadistic and provocative ways, but that, in his view, there was nothing in his behavior that objectively would warrant such an accusation. He added that his conviction that her accusations were totally unfounded required an examination of the extent to which he was honest in making such a statement. If the patient thought that he was honest, how would she understand that he would be so totally blind to the nature of his own behavior as to make such a categorical statement, in total contrast with her experience of the situation? The patient in this case did not believe that the therapist was lying, but she also could not accept that the therapist would be unaware of something so obvious as what she was describing. This led to an acute sense of confusion on the patient's part, and to her self-accusation that she was mistreating a good therapist. This enabled the therapist to point to her fear of asserting a view of him that, though perhaps not corresponding to reality, might nevertheless have an important function for herself. Eventually the patient was able to recognize in her view of the therapist the frightening experience of her "crazy" parents, savagely fighting with each other under the influence of severe drug intoxication. The therapist represented a psychotic parental couple destroying their mutual relationship while oblivious to their child (the patient) as an innocent victim of this savagery.

The working through of paranoid transference eventually leads to the patient's capacity to acknowledge the projection of his or her own aggressive needs and wishes, and to the capacity to integrate the awareness of this "persecutory" segment of self-experience with the split-off, "idealized" segment of self-experience in which the longing and capacity for a dependent relationship, for love, for gratitude, and for reciprocity of loving feelings are sequestered. This bridging of opposite self-representation and object representation units initiates the development of "depressive" transference—the advanced stage of the treatment of patients with borderline personality organization.

The Narcissistic Transference

I turn now to the treatment of patients with the narcissistic personality disorder proper. As noted earlier, this group usually shows less severe antisocial behavior, so that setting up the structure for the limitation of antisocial behavior is much less a problem. These patients' capacity for establishing a therapeutic contract is not disturbed by severe superego distortion, deceptiveness, or incapacity to accept responsibility for themselves, and thus the major proportion of their treatment can be devoted to the analysis of narcissistic transference.

The basic problem in the treatment of patients with predominantly narcissistic transference is their lack of capacity to depend on the therapist. Dependency means acknowledging the importance of the therapist, which in these patients generates intense conscious and unconscious envy, and (through projection) fears of the therapist's envious attacks on the patients, who therefore have to protect themselves. Massive devaluation of the importance of the therapist and the therapeutic relationship is an essential defense against dreaded dependency and the related unconscious envy. In a severe case, the incapacity to depend may present as the creation of an unrealistic therapeutic atmosphere, within which the therapist feels consciously (and sometimes, at first, unconsciously) excluded. As the patient's "self-analysis" goes on, the therapist, treated as a bystander, often becomes bored, restless, or sleepy during the sessions.

Another possibility is that a primitive, frail, and unstable idealization will evolve in which the patient appears to accept the therapist's understanding or interpretations eagerly, except that, in the long run, these interpretations prove to be useless. They are devalued, or "extracted" as magical comments to be appropriated by the patient and used for his or her own purposes. Such patients tend to "outguess" the therapist in order to protect themselves against attacks from the therapist, against unconscious envy, and essentially, against dependency on the therapist.

Manifestations of omnipotent control in such a case include efforts to manipulate the therapist to respond in ways the patient expects. Should the therapist react differently, and thus show that he or she has knowledge that the patient did not already have, the patient would feel either put down, humiliated, or attacked. Through a process of radical devaluation of the therapist's "unexpected" interpretations or statements, the patient neutralizes the therapist—who, in short, has to be as good as, but neither better nor worse than, the patient, and to correspond rigidly to the patient's expectations.

In a patient with significant superego pathology, even in the absence of antisocial behavior, there is a profound lack of trust in the therapist's genuine interest—a suspicion that the therapist is only interested in exploiting the patient and has no authentic knowledge to contribute, only magic, quackery, or "gimmicks" that the patient may appropriate to enhance his or her own manipulative skills. What tends to be denied in the process is the therapist's distinct reality as a different human being with his or her own internal life. It is particularly the therapist's creativity in the therapeutic process that these patients profoundly envy and unconsciously seek to destroy.

The effect of all these mechanisms may be a severe "emptying out" of the therapeutic situation—the therapist's sense that nothing is really going on and that no development is taking place in the transference. This obscures the fact that, on the contrary, intense activation of the patient's pathological grandiose self is going on in the transference relationship. In fact, the transitory idealizations of the therapist reflect the temporary projection onto the therapist of the patient's own grandiose self-image—an idealization that may be as easily withdrawn as reactivated. The patient's activations of grandiosity, omnipotent control, devaluation, and denial of dependency reflect the object relation derived from the pathological grandiose self.

When the pathological grandiose self is infiltrated with ego-syntonic aggression, the manifestations of omnipotent control, devaluation, and projective identification of undesirable aspects of the self onto the therapist become much more evident. Under these conditions, the patient may express inordinate demands; an overbearing, openly controlling behavior; and the syndrome that Bion (1968) described as a combination of arrogance, curiosity about the therapist's mind and life (not about the patient's own experience), and pseudostupidity (i.e., the apparent incapacity to listen to ordinary logic and reasoning if it does not correspond to the patient's own preset ideas). Severe narcissistic devaluation may bring about premature disruption of the treatment. This is particularly likely with patients with significant antisocial features and severe superego pathology, in whom the capacity for engaging in authentic relationships is seriously compromised. Premature ending of treatment out of narcissistic devaluation of the therapist is distinct from the often surprising late dropouts that occur precisely at the point when the patients have experienced the therapist as providing them with authentic help. The latter are negative therapeutic reactions out of unconscious envy. The therapist's awareness of the potential for such negative therapeutic reactions may permit the preventive interpretation of such reactions at points when patients seem, perhaps for the first time, to be able to acknowledge the therapist's help.

A careful analysis of particular aspects of a patient's grandiosity, arrogance, demandingness, and devaluation may gradually reveal the components of the pathological grandiose self—that is, the patient's condensed identification with idealized self- and object representations reflecting a selective takeover of those aspects of significant others that, in the patient's past, signified the possession of strength, wisdom, power, and superiority. The more severe the superego pathology, of course, the more such powerful images (particularly parental images) include sadistic and corrupt features. Often patients with severe narcissistic personality disorders who have been the victims of physical or sexual abuse or exploitation harbor a deep conscious resentment against the perpetrators of these attacks on them, while unconsciously identifying with the double role of victim and perpetrator themselves. In the transference, the activation of both victim and perpetrator status must be carefully explored, together with such a patient's unconscious activation of the idealized aspects of past representations of self and other. The careful analysis of all these component identifications in the transference permits the gradual resolution of the pathological grandiose self and of its protective function against more primitive aggression. The emergence of conflicts centering around hatred and envy tends to move the narcissistic transference toward paranoid transference. Although on the surface the paranoid transference seems much more negative than the narcissistic one, at bottom it reflects the development of a more intense and dependent object relation that lends itself to gradual working through along the lines of the elaboration of paranoid transference referred to above.

One patient tended to dismiss those comments of the therapist that did not fit with her preset views as "meaningless" or "stupid." At the same time, she was extremely curious about what the therapist might be thinking. Meanwhile she avoided talking openly about her own thoughts, fearing that honest communication would expose her to being exploited and mistreated. She was immensely curious about the therapist's relations with his family members, and went to some trouble to find out as much about them as she could. Her reaction to this information oscillated between radical devaluation of them and resentful envy of their privileges on the one hand, and a sense of relief as she communicated to the therapist whatever she had discovered that she thought might put his family in an unfavorable light on the other.

Another patient, fearful that the therapist would try to cheat him of his allotted time, carefully checked every minute of the sessions, while using whatever pretext he could to prolong them. This patient had a remarkable tendency to waste time in the sessions, with endless repetition of the same questions and enraged demands for answers. He used the "stolen" moments after the end of each session to impart the apparently important information he had withheld during the regular session. It turned out that what the therapist would give "freely" of his time and interest was worthless; only what the patient could appropriate by force would gratify his sense of envious resentment.

A particularly malignant expression of narcissistic resistance may be a patient's destroying his or her own life in a gradual, undramatic, and yet highly effective way, in fulfillment of unconscious wishes to defeat the treatment. Thus, for example, one patient neglected her academic responsibilities, repeatedly placing herself at serious risk of being expelled from her postgraduate program. She systematically withheld from her therapist the trouble she was getting into until a major crisis had reached a point at which it would be almost impossible to correct the situation. Again and again, the therapist felt called upon to carry out last-minute rescue efforts that would typically fail. It was some time before he realized how the patient was keeping information from him to prevent him from becoming aware of her self-destructive behavior in time for him to intervene successfully to help her.

This last illustration relates to a more general dangerous development—namely, "perversity" in the transference. Perversity consists of the recruitment of love in the service of aggression: The patient consciously and unconsciously evokes the therapist's dedication and commitment, and then sees to it that the therapist's attempts to help either fail or make matters worse. One patient, for example, implored her therapist to explain the nature of her problematic relationships with men. She listened to the therapist's interpretations, and seemed to be thoughtfully applying them to an understanding of her difficulties. Several weeks of work on this problem eventuated in the patient's making use of all she had learned from the therapist in a devastating attack on her current boyfriend, using distortions of the therapist's statements to reinforce her sadistic attack. She placed a massive misuse of what she had received from the therapist at the service of definitively destroying the relationship with her boyfriend. A dramatic type of perversity in the transference is an apparent demand for love that is eroticized and becomes an aggressive effort to seduce the therapist sexually, with the ultimate purpose to destroy the treatment and the therapist's professional life.

The psychodynamic psychotherapy of narcissistic transference may be frustrating to the therapist because of the enormous time required to transform the activation of the pathological grandiose self in the transference into its component transference dispositions—the primitive object relations involved—and their gradual working through. The advanced stages of the treatment of such a patients come to resemble quite closely those of other patients with borderline personality organization, and the therapist may not be aware at this point that a major breakthrough has been achieved. Furthermore, as successful work goes on in the therapy, the patient may develop an active life of engagement outside the treatment situation while the transference appears to be monotonously narcissistic. This combination of apparent behavioral improvement and the therapist's ongoing frustration in the sessions may prompt the therapist to bring the treatment to an end prematurely instead of patiently working through the narcissistic resistances; such work, however, is an essential precondition for consolidating whatever gains the patient may have made in the extratransferential field.

Summary

To summarize, the important complications arising from the combination of narcissistic, antisocial, and paranoid behaviors in a patient with borderline personality organization require an initial careful assessment of where the patient stands along the spectrum of severity of the narcissistic psychopathology; the decision whether the patient, under the present circumstances, is at all able to undergo psychodynamic psychotherapy; the setting up of realistic conditions and a frame for the treatment to proceed; and, finally, the exploration and systematic working through of the particular transference developments in these cases.

THE COGNITIVE STYLE OF ANTISOCIAL DISORDERS

Here I wish to explore the relevance of a particular cognitive style that is typical of psychopathic transference, its impact on the analyst, and the technical approach required to deal with it. This technical approach requires, in turn, a particular cognitive style in the analyst's interventions.

David Liberman (1983) has provided fundamental, path-breaking findings about possible approaches to patients with different types of transferences. Liberman describes six styles of verbal communication characteristic of various types of psychopathology.

He points to the defensive nature of these cognitive styles, as well as to their enormous influence on the transference situation and on the analyst's capacity for thinking and interpretation. He stresses the importance of the analyst's not being co-opted into responding in the same defensive style as that of the patient, and the need for the analyst to counteract the patient's defensive style with a flexible and differentiated communicative style of his or her own.

Specifically, Liberman describes the "narrative style," characteristic of patients with obsessive–compulsive illness; the "dramatic style that provokes an aesthetic impact on the analyst," typical of hysterical patients; the "epic style," typical of patients with antisocial pathology; the "lyrical style," typical of depressive–masochistic patients; the "dramatic style that creates suspense," typical of phobic patients; and the "inquisitive style that does not create suspense," typical of patients who project their own paranoid curiosity onto the analyst. Dr. Ann Appelbaum (personal communication, 1996) has suggested an additional style, the "manic style"—one that is very effective in co-opting the therapist toward a jocular, satirical, or hilarious mode of interaction.

In my view, the richness and manifold clinical implications of Liberman's findings have not yet been absorbed as fully as they should be in the recent literature on psychoanalytic technique (with the exception of Etchegoyen's [1991] text). I shall confine myself here to describe the "epic style" of the communications of patients with psychopathic transference and indicating how the therapist's use of a modified "narrative style" may counteract it, to the patients' benefit. I believe that the destructive effects of these patients' cognitive style are crucial in the diagnosis of and psychoanalytic work with psychopathic and paranoid transferences.

Liberman describes the ego-syntonicity of psychopathic patients' impulsive behavior, rationalized by their ad hoc "ethical" system. Within these patients' episodic, ego-syntonic acting out, third parties are severely damaged precisely when some collaborative interaction with them might take place. A radical devaluation of these attacked and damaged third persons protects the patients from any reflection on their own behavior. Their subtle distortions of the truth hide their tendency to impulsive action, and seduce the analyst into behaviors that the patients then interpret as in collusion with their own destructive actions.

Psychopathic patients' verbal communications seem informative, but limit the knowledge the analyst may acquire by subtly manipulating the facts, and particularly by preventing him or her from realizing that the patients may use the analyst's reaction to this information to support the patients' impulsive destructiveness. These patients function under the assumption that to survive, they must withhold and lie; to do otherwise is to court disaster. Nor do they find anything unusual in this idea—indeed, they assume that the rest of the world operates according to a similar assumption. In order to avoid being manipulated by the analyst, they build up a dossier on him or her, so as to be able later to prove that they are correct in perceiving the analyst as dishonest and manipulative. On the surface, these patients may imitate the "narrative style" that characterizes obsessive patients, but their narratives change from session to session or even from moment to moment. This creates a sense of confusion in the analyst, who may not be able to tell whether the patients or the analyst himself or herself is responsible for these shifts.

The antisocial patients' projection onto the therapist of their own dishonesty perpetuates their conviction that the analyst's communications have the same purpose as their own. Therefore, the unconscious engagement of the therapist in collusion with the patients' purposes is the only alternative to being victimized by the therapist for his or her own hidden purposes. These patients may induce the therapist to respond with certain comments that the patients carefully gather over a period of time, in order to prove eventually to themselves, the therapist, and perhaps the world at large that the therapist's behavior is contradictory, manipulative, and dishonest.

The essential characteristics of this "epic" communicative style are the patients' unconscious need to induce in the therapist a potential for action, and their inability to conceive of the therapist as reflecting on the patients' behavior in order to help the patients reflect on it themselves. If they imagine the therapist as thinking about them, they assume that this is only in order to plan ways to manipulate the patients into action.

The major danger, in Liberman's view, of the "epic style" of patients with antisocial behavior is the analyst's gradually developing inability to contain the information communicated to him or her in ways aimed to induce action rather than understanding. The analyst may become fascinated with this process and experience a growing preoccupation with the patient outside the treatment situation; as a result, the analyst may be seduced into unconscious collusion with the patients, which may end with the analyst himself or herself as the injured "third party" of the patients' ego-syntonic aggression. My experience in treating antisocial patients with psychopathic transference or a combination of antisocial and paranoid tendencies (as in malignant narcissism) has provided me with ample clinical experiences confirming Liberman's descriptions.

Liberman's recommendations for dealing with these dramatic, potentially dangerous transference developments focus on the importance of the analyst's guarding himself against any tendency to be naive. The analyst must be alert to the possibility of being seduced by these patients—especially by one he or she becomes preoccupied with beyond the treatment sessions. Liberman also advocates what we have described as "structuralization," or limit setting to protect the analytic frame. In work with borderline patients during severe regressions, our research team at the Westchester Division of the New York Hospital–Cornell Medical Center (Kernberg et al., 1989) proposes a sequence that starts with clarifying and confronting the patient with the need for setting limits on behaviors that impede the treatment process; continues with analyzing the transference under such structuralization; and is completed, under optimal circumstances, by the interpretation and analytic resolution of the need for such limit setting. Such structuralization typically includes protection of the frame regarding the time of and payment for the sessions; control of attempts to use the treatment for destructive purposes; and confrontation and control of the use of the treatment situation as a protective cover for frankly destructive antisocial behavior.

In addition, Liberman stresses the importance of the analyst's communicating with antisocial patients consistently in a "narrative style," aimed at transforming the patients' implicit manipulation of the analyst (in order to induce him or her to take action) into a narrative. This narrative is a coherent cognitive statement that retranslates an intended action into its motivating unconscious fantasy. The analyst is demonstrating through this interpretive behavior that he or she is relying upon reflection rather than action in interactions with the patients. Here, Liberman's general proposal of the need to counteract these patients' defensive cognitive style by means of a different, interpretive cognitive style is expressed explicitly in the analyst's "narrative" response to the patients' "epic" presentation. The analyst, however, must preserve his or her capacity to respond flexibly in rapidly shifting communicative styles if shifts in the transference situation warrant it. My experiences with these psychopathic transference in recent years have tended to validate the usefulness of Liberman's approach. The diagnosis of a particular "epic style" in patients with psychopathic transference, and its neutralization by a compensating "narrative style" from the therapist, may contribute to the resolution of severe psychopathic and paranoid regressions in the transference. The therapist's narrative interpretive style, free from seduction into action, may provide the most important therapeutic experience for patients who have previously consistently defended themselves against reflective narratives through inducing action in others and taking ego-syntonic, destructive actions themselves.

THE EFFECTS OF TREATMENT

I believe that the prognosis in the work with such patients—who are most frequently not considered suitable for psychoanalytic treatment, and sometimes not even for psychoanalytic psychotherapy—depends in part on the structural characteristics of their illness, and in part on developments that can be assessed only during the treatment itself (Kernberg, 1992a). If the treatment starts out with conspicuous psychopathic transferences, and if the therapist is able to diagnose these in terms of chronic mendacity and an epic style of communication, the main question is whether the analysis of these developments will permit the transformation of a psychopathic transference into an openly paranoid one. Sometimes a patient's chronic dishonesty cannot be resolved by analytic means, and the patient may abandon the treatment at a point when the failure of the psychopathic defense in the transference threatens him or her with the ascendance of severe paranoid developments. By contrast, a seduced therapist's unconscious collusion with a patient's psychopathic transference may perpetuate the treatment over many months or years, with a total lack of change in the patient's behavior outside the sessions. Under these circumstances, severe antisocial behavior that is completely dissociated from the treatment situation may evolve over time, with the treatment ending only after the consequences of such external behaviors threaten its continuity.

If the therapist is successful in transforming the dominant transference from a psychopathic into a paranoid one, the analytic work with "incompatible realities" in the transference may result in the gradual resolution of a psychotic nucleus. However, the perpetuation of a psychotic nucleus may in itself bring about complications that threaten the treatment. At that point, a primitive, sadistic object relation between a fantasied, overpowering, cruel, sadistic, and dishonest object on the one hand, and a powerless, paralyzed, humiliated, and tortured self on the other, may crystallize in the transference—with rapid role reversals, but without the possibility of being challenged by the remaining, healthy, dependent part of the patient's self. This is particularly true with patients who have experienced great trauma in the first few years of life. Typically, their physical or mental suffering has been consciously and unconsciously attributed to a sadistic and overwhelming maternal figure or a combined mother–father figure with no compensating parental figure, the idealization of which would counter a conception of a universe inhabited only by the powerfully cruel and their victims.

Severe pain in early life is transformed into primitive aggression, which is dispersed in action or defended against via massive denial and projective identification. These defenses against the transformation of aggression into symbolic thinking are all dramatically reenacted in the transference in these cases. The treatment situation becomes a power struggle in which a patient actively devalues and destroys everything that comes from the therapist, and experiences the therapist's effort to interpret this situation as an attack on the patient's autonomy. By means of projective identification, a treatment situation may be perpetuated in which the therapist is forced, mostly by means of powerful countertransference developments, to submit helplessly to victimization in an unconscious identification with the patient as a victim; or the therapist may be propelled into an identification with the aggressor, in a violent reversal of the patient's desperate efforts at omnipotent control.

I have found several approaches helpful, depending on the circumstances. What seem to be effective in cases in which significant change and resolution of the paranoid transference regression are achieved are the following elements. First, the therapist needs to be alert to the potential for paranoid regression when psychopathic transference is present. Second, the therapist must pay attention to the chronic countertransference reactions that develop under conditions of primitive defensive operations in the transference derived from the patient's inability to reflect, as well as from his or her tendency to evacuate intolerable conflicts massively through projective identification. Ongoing countertransference analysis outside the treatment sessions often permits a clear formulation of the nature of the primitive object relation activated in the transference and makes it possible to interpret this relationship.

Third, the therapist's ability to recognize a patient-induced impulse to action as material to be interpreted and contained rather than acted on will permit the therapist to refrain from action. The transformation of an "action potential" into the narrative mode may become an important aspect of the therapist's interpretive style, limited only by such structure setting as seems indispensable over a period of time. In this regard, I have made it a basic rule of thumb not to take decisions about changes in my relationship to a patient or in the structure of our treatment arrangements during a session in which such an idea or impulse for a change comes to my mind; this protects the patient and myself as much as possible from countertransference acting out. Some countertransference acting out, however, is almost unavoidable in terms of shifts in the style of the therapist's communication, and may have to be reflectively acknowledged at a later stage of the treatment.

Fourth, when acting out is acute, I believe it is helpful to interpret the total transference situation as much in depth as possible, while remaining willing to return to the "surface" of the immediate interaction between patient and therapist. This may mean returning, if necessary, to the initial contract of the treatment—that is, reminding the patient of what he or she came to treatment for, what the nature of the task is for both therapist and patient, and what both have committed themselves to do. This can be a way of reinstating a rational frame (the "normal relationship," in contrast to the transference relation) before again examining the transference in depth. Such restatement and consolidation of the treatment frame are sometimes indispensable if any analysis of the transference is to occur.

Lastly, it is important to keep in mind that some patients cannot be helped (at least in the concrete situation of any particular psychotherapeutic engagement), and that, in the end, it cannot be only the therapist who wishes to help patients whose major gratification in life is the destruction of those who are attempting to help them.

REFERENCES

American Psychiatric Association. (1980). *Diagnostic and statistical manual of mental disorders* (3rd ed.). Washington, DC: Author.

American Psychiatric Association. (1987). *Diagnostic and statistical manual of mental disorders* (3rd ed., rev.). Washington, DC: Author.

American Psychiatric Association. (1994). *Diagnostic and statistical manual of mental disorders* (4th ed.). Washington, DC: Author.

Bion, W. R. (1968). *Second thoughts: Selected papers on psychoanalysis.* New York: Basic Books.

Cleckley, H. (1941). *The mask of sanity.* St. Louis, MO: C. V. Mosby.

Etchegoyen, R. H. (1991). *Fundamentals of psychoanalytic technique.* New York: Karnac Books.

Guttmacher, M. (1961). Pseudopsychopathic schizophrenia. *Archives of Criminal Psychodynamics, 1,* 502–508.

Hare, R., & Hart, S. (1995). Commentary on antisocial personality disorder. In J. Livesley (Ed.), *The DSM-IV personality disorders* (pp. 127–134). New York: Guilford Press.

Hare, R., Hart, S., & Harpur, T. (1991). Psychopathy and the DSM-IV criteria for antisocial personality disorder. *Journal of Abnormal Psychology, 100,* 391–398.

Henderson, D. K. (1939). *Psychopathic states.* London: Chapman & Hall.

Henderson, D. K., & Gillespie, R. D. (1969). *Textbook of psychiatry: For students and practitioners* (10th ed., rev. by I. R. C. Batchelor). London: Oxford University Press.

Jacobson, E. (1971). *Depression.* New York: International Universities Press.

Kernberg, O. F. (1984). *Severe personality disorders: Psychotherapeutic strategies.* New Haven, CT: Yale University Press.

Kernberg, O. F. (1989). The narcissistic personality disorder and the differential diagnosis of antisocial behavior. *Psychiatric Clinics of North America, 12*(3), 553–570.

Kernberg, O. F. (1992a). *Aggression in personality disorders and perversion.* New Haven, CT: Yale University Press.

Kernberg, O. F. (1992b). Paranoiagenesis in organizations. *Clinica y Análisis Grupal, 14,* 9–30.

Kernberg, O. F. (1993). Psychoanalytic object relations theories. In W. Mertens (Ed.), *Key concepts of psychoanalysis* (pp. 96–104). Munich: Klett-Cotta.

Kernberg, O. F., Selzer, M., Koenigsberg, H. W., Carr, A., & Appelbaum, A. (1989). *Psychodynamic psychotherapy of borderline patients.* New York: Basic Books.

Liberman, D. (1983). *Lingüística, interacción comunicativa y proceso psicoanalítico* (2 vols.). Buenos Aires: Ediciones Kargieman.

Meltzer, D. (1977). *Sexual states of mind.* Perth, Scotland: Clunie Press.

Milgram, S. (1963). Behavioral study of obedience. *Journal of Abnormal and Social Psychology, 67,* 371–378.

Zinoviev, A. (1984). *The reality of communism.* New York: Schocken.

25

A Group-Analytic Approach to Psychopaths: "The Ring of Truth"

MURRAY COX

The editors of this book have requested that the author or authors of each chapter provide an "overview" of their field. The term "overview" implies a survey of locations; this takes us at once to the heart of the topic, because the group-analytic treatment of psychopaths can only take place where patients can safely congregate. Indeed, any discussion of such work should be framed by envisioning the setting. Descriptions of outpatient, ambulatory psychotherapy—however group-analytically "pure" it may be—cannot possibly be relevant to group participants who have been charged with such offenses as rape or homicide. This focusing frame of reference is often ignored in both professional publications and debates, and can lead to unnecessary confusion. The simple question of where therapy is conducted immediately defines the degree of presumed dangerousness of the group members. The group dynamics within an outpatient group may be identical to those of a group conducted within a secure perimeter. But the fact that patients in the former setting may travel home by public transport, whereas those in the latter know that "home" is without limit of time in the same institution, carries immense legal, clinical, and existential *gravitas*. It is for this very reason that staff members conducting outpatient psychotherapy are often exposed to far greater levels of anxiety than their colleagues who work within a secure setting. It calls for no great imaginative leap to think of a psychopathic patient who has expressed reactivated antiauthoritarian anger in an outpatient group, and who then acts out and storms out of the therapy session, only to disappear into the bowels of a public transport system. Therapists working in a special hospital or a regional secure unit do not have this particular anxiety, though they certainly experience variants on the theme.

In addition to asking for the "overview," the editors wisely discerned that "publication in the form of a book will demand a complete rewriting of your paper." Certainly, as far as this contribution is concerned, the intensity of both public and informal personal discussion served to underline the importance of some essential aspects of this work, which can so readily be taken for granted because other considerations seem to carry more weight. Issues such as outcome studies, resource implications, ethical and civil rights priorities, and many other issues of impingement between the criminal justice health system and the wider society could never be regarded as insignificant. Nevertheless, if therapists were not able to "survive" in a forensic setting (and the work involves in-depth contact with the conscious and unconscious lives of aggressive psychopaths, as well as the particularly high-voltage atmosphere of a group-analytic group), then there would be no outcome studies to consider. I do not intend to exaggerate or dramatize this issue, but I am discussing something far more pervasive than the conventional psychoanalytic connotations usually attached to the term "countertranference." At this juncture I will simply refer to the fact that effective "therapist outcome" is a much understudied topic, which should never be regarded as relatively insignificant when outcome studies are being discussed in conventional professional research debates. This theme will not be developed further here, but it is lodged at this point as a "marker" in the hope that it may generate subsequent exploration.

A further introductory comment draws attention to a personal mode of working. It seems to have particular advantages as a means of obtaining safe, nonthreatening access to the inner world of the aggressive psychopath, and to the matrix of anachronistic resonance that is always intensified in group-analytic work. I refer to the use of aesthetic access, the aesthetic imperative, the mutative metaphor, and the place of imagery—perhaps best captured by Bachelard (1969; quoted in Cox & Theilgaard, 1987, p. xiii), who writes, "But the poetic image has touched the depths before it stirs the surface." This approach has been described elsewhere (Cox & Theilgaard, 1987) and reinforced by Millon (1994), who has written that "it is of great value to pay attention to the poets, in particular Shakespeare, when considering personality theories. . . . [He] can prompt therapists in their interpretative efforts."

One of the difficulties confronting a writer, which does not challenge a speaker, is to know how to convey the subtle laminations of language, cadence, momentum, deictic stress, and the numerous paralinguistic overtones that color all our speech—but that carry particular intensification when it comes to the language of deep emotional disclosure. One of the certainties of dynamic psychotherapy with psychopaths is that, sooner or later, the therapist will come across areas of experience about which the psychopathic patient cannot be glib and dismissive. It is common knowledge that whereas such a patient may describe multiple rapes with ease (and even relish), there will always be areas of experience where the individual's self-esteem is threatened. A man with a long clinical and forensic history comes to mind whose linguistic gloss and ferocious felicity of phrasing meant that he could talk fluently about virtually everything, until it came to describing the various excuses he gave to avoid taking a shower in the presence of his school classmates because of the absence of age-specific pubic hair. I have drawn attention elsewhere (Cox, 1978) to the "compromise with chaos" when it comes to various therapeutic approaches, which may help to "increase the volume" when listening to the inaudible language of the unconscious.

Finally, there is frequent discussion as to whether group-analytic groups "work." In other words, there is debate as to whether a small group is an agent of change. But, in my experience, there is no doubt whatever that the small group—particularly when conducted in a ward of a large institution—can serve as an essential crucible in which patients' overt behavior and clues to their inner-world phenomena can be observed at close quarters. Such phenomena may so easily be overlooked as "fine print" when seen against the background of events in the ward as a whole. It was while waiting in a hospital group room for members to arrive that I overheard the following discussion: "It isn't every day you kill someone, is it?" "Just every now and then."

It is from the vantage point of this particular professional perspectival world that the ensuing material is presented. It has taken the form of a condensation of some issues and an expansion of others which, taken together, constituted the substance of my original presentation in Copenhagen. The subtitle "The Ring of Truth" carries several connotations, including a circular configuration and the resonance of veracity. It also reinforces the importance of aesthetic accuracy—in Bateson's (1979, p. 17) sense of the pattern that connects—and of poetic precision. In a volume on research, precision and accuracy are never out of place, but further fidelities are called for when one is trying to reach the inner world of psychopaths, who are doing all they can to divert attention from their affective poverty and inner isolation.

This chapter explores some of the kaleidoscopic intermingling of fantasy and fact, psychological containment, and a custodial "holding environment" that forms the dynamic crucible in which modified group-analytic psychotherapy with psychopathic patients can take place. Condensation and selection of salient features are inevitable. The numbered "marker" headings below will, I hope, provide guidance for the subsequent references, discussion, and exploration. Even so, such key topics as assessment and research are bypassed, because the variables are so numerous and complex that they resist summary. It is the clinical weight of 25 years' experience of attempting to conduct modified group-analytic psychotherapy in an English "special hospital" (maximum security) that provides a firm conceptual footing for the ensuing formulation. It could be said that I am a forensic psychotherapist on "front-line duty," reporting from the "trenches."

In Broadmoor Hospital, psychopathic patients make up approximately 25% of the patient population. The other 75% suffer from chronic psychosis—largely one of the many forensic presentations of schizophrenia. There are 500 patients *in toto,* 400 men and 100 women. All the patients are legally detained, and the analytic groups I shall discuss are composed of patients whose legal category is deemed to be "psychopathic" (Dolan & Coid, 1993). Nevertheless, from a psychodynamic phenomenological perspective, most exhibit borderline personality organization and therefore furnish evidence of the following three structural criteria: (1) identity diffusion, (2) a primitive level of defensive operations, and (3) (as a forensic codicil, particularly during micropsychotic episodes) impaired reality testing (Kernberg, 1984).

Broadmoor patients are "offender patients," which is to say that they have been charged with an index offense at the "heavy end" of the antisocial spectrum, such as homicide (sometimes repetitive, sometimes multiple), arson, or rape. Index offenses are often committed during a micropsychotic episode, which can make subsequent dynamic assessment a daunting challenge. Patients are detained "without limit of time." This implies that it is only when patients are considered psychodynamically integrated, socially stable, and "safe" that they are transferred to less secure conditions. These might prove to be a regional secure unit, a general psychiatric hospital, or even a carefully supervised return to the community.

It is against this complex medicolegal and ethical/philosophical background that the modified group-analytic treatment of psychopaths, the subject of this chapter, takes place. One final point must be emphasized before I begin: *Forensic vigilance must never be relaxed for a moment, and group-analytic treatment may need to be integrated with other relevant treatment modalities.*

1. THE FORENSIC SETTING HAS A PERVASIVE INFLUENCE

It is self-evident that group treatment of psychopaths charged with such major offenses can only be conducted in a secure setting. It could be argued that in order to be formally designated as "psychopathic," the individuals concerned must be somewhere en route within the criminal justice system. Kierkegaard's (1848/1978) familiar words may legitimately be adapted to say that "we can only meet psychopathic patients where they are." There are echoing cadences of Kierkegaard in the summary of Symington's (1980) paper "The Response Aroused by the Psychopath," except that he is talking of therapeutic presence rather than location: "The foundation for a successful treatment is to be present to the psychopath *as he is*" (emphasis added). The only place where we can meet a group-analytic group of psychopaths must be within the secure setting of a prison, a regional secure unit, or a special hospital, because it is only in such an environment that it is possible to conduct group psychotherapy with patients whose histories include homicide, arson, or rape. On the other hand, such an environment provides the therapeutic possibilities of conducting mixed-group psychotherapy, where rapists and female patients (who, in Broadmoor Hospital, often prove to be arsonists) can participate in regular analytic therapeutic sessions.

Less dangerous patients, whose destructive energies are confined to fantasy, may be found in specialized units conducting outpatient group therapy for personality disorders, such as the Portman Clinic in London (Welldon, 1993, 1996); in a therapeutic community setting, such as the Henderson Hospital in Surrey (Norton, 1996; see also Dolan, Chapter 26, this volume); or within a probation office.

Pines and Schermer (1994, p. 139) deal with the important topic of therapeutic groups where "primitive rage and destructiveness are encountered." But this is a different dynamic constellation from that of forensic patients, who embark on group therapy *because* of the previous destructiveness of their homicidal "voltage." The cardinal distinction between the therapeutic setting provided by a special hospital and all other relevant locations is that the patients are legally detained "without limit of time." This open-endedness of therapeutic possibility permeates the intricate laminations of human exchange that flourish within a secure perimeter.

2. TIME, DEPTH, AND MUTALITY ARE DEFINING DIMENSIONS

It is now over 20 years since I wrote a description of early attempts at conducting "group psychotherapy in a secure setting" (Cox, 1976). Through long-established personal proclivity, I tend to open any presentation with a brief survey of the defining dimensions (time, depth, and mutuality) in which all dynamic psychotherapy can be construed, and then provide examples from the last individual or group session I attended (Cox, 1978). Such an approach inevitably combines both a theoretical framework and a statement of the current exigency of the present moment. The original version of this chapter was written on March 10, 1996, so that the session taken to illustrate group-analytic treatment of psychopaths in "action" took place on March 8.

The group in question had six members. The moment I entered the room, one patient excitedly announced that he had just been told that he would be leaving the hospital in a matter of days—"any time now." Hard on his heels came the same message from another member. Such figures are manifestly not representative of the group process as a whole; yet time, depth, and mutuality assumed a fresh timbre. In that particular session, one-third of the group participants were coming to terms with the risky excitement and wistful poignance of termination and "moving on" to less secure conditions.

On returning to my office, I found a paper on my desk (Reiss, Grubin, & Meux, 1996) entitled "Young 'Psychopaths' in a Special Hospital: Treatment and Outcome," which was a study based on the ward in question. Synchronicity was further in evidence when the same issue of the *British Journal of Psychiatry* contained an editorial titled "Psychopathy—A Clinical and Legal Dilemma" (Reed, 1996), as well as a review article on "Psychotherapy Assessment and Treatment Selection" (Tillett, 1996). For our present purposes, there could scarcely be a more relevant trio of papers within one issue. But these publications do not directly grapple with the pros and cons of group-analytic psychotherapy with psychopaths. They deal with wider frames and other parameters. Still, they do set the scene for the ensuing concentrated material.

3. GROUP ANALYSIS "IN PURE CULTURE" IS IMPOSSIBLE

The purist will feel that the presence of security equipment, such as alarm bells or television cameras, will of necessity contaminate therapy. By contrast, those interested in mutative metaphors (Cox & Theilgaard, 1987) will reflect upon the power of such images to catalyze the group process. At Broadmoor, such unheralded events as a "spot check" for a missing knife, the interruption of a group session because staff members have been alerted to a hostage-taking risk, or a casual reference to a fire "set" in a patient's room just before the group session started causes the therapist to think in several modes simultaneously—and to do so quickly.

4. COUNTERTRANSFERENCE ISSUES ARE PIVOTAL

Glover (1960, p. 149) writes:

> No psychiatrist should ever attempt to treat a psychopath who has neither understanding of psychopathy or sufficient counter-transference to endure the psychopath's assaults on his most cherished possession, namely, his capacity to heal. In other words the prerequisite of any therapy with the psychopath is a capacity to endure repeated disappointments.

Gunn's (1994) review of Tyrer and Stein (1993) endorses this point. Glover's statement could justify an entire volume of exploration. It underlines the fact that no forensic psychotherapist will die of an overdose of gratitude. The hovering attentiveness that is more than ever demanded of those who work in the forensic field must therefore be linked to other avenues for self-esteem regulation. This is a highly personal, idiosyncratic matter; it will depend on a cosmos of concerns intricately interwoven with a personal *Weltanschauung*, and, in my view, the flexible stability of adequate gyroscopic introjects (Stierlin, 1970). Likewise, a psychopath's self-esteem regulation may well have motivated the individual's index offense. Rosen's (1996) account "Perversion as a Regulator of Self-Esteem" cannot be overvalued when one is exploring forensic psychopathology and appropriate therapeutic initiatives. Self-esteem regulation for patient and therapist are co-inherent, yet must remain separable.

Racker's (1972) distinction between "concordant" and "complementary" counter-transferance is a crucial consideration impinging upon forensic group therapy. It is relevant both in relation to the group as a whole and to each individual member.

5. CONTEXTUAL AND EXISTENTIAL CONSIDERATIONS ARE UBIQUITOUS

In addition to time, depth, and mutuality, the setting, context, and location where psychotherapy is actually conducted are always important considerations. Furthermore, existential aspects of existence and such universal questions as the nature of hope are constantly in the air. For this reason the comments of an existential theologian and philosopher (Macquarrie, 1966, pp. 59–60) are directly relevant here. Having made the point that medicine and pathology usually consider systematic disturbances, such as those of the respiratory or the genital system, Macquarrie raises the issue of a disorder of existence itself:

> The disorder of human existence can be defined more precisely as *imbalance,* and in calling it "pathological" I have implicitly compared it to *imbalances* in the physical organism. But here we are thinking of existential imbalance.... These disorders represent the retreat from possibility, decision-making, responsibility, individual liability and even from rationality.

Boss (1979, p. 121) raises other existential issues when he refers to those who have "used up their existence by actualizing all of its essential relational possibilities." In my view, one of the functions of group analysis is to restore the possibility of further "essential relational" encounters—by diminishing transference distortions secondary to abusing relationships. (In writing this chapter, I was surprised to discover the intensity with which these existential issues presented themselves. Perhaps it is because my patients vicariously carry life-and-death issues for those of us who work with them. I found that I needed to cite the wider "framing" existential and ethical parameters before even referring to Foulkes, who, as the founding father of group analysis, I would have previously guessed as being the primary reference!) Another philosopher and theologian (Raven, 1959, p. 180) has this to say of the therapist: "He is not going to make a real healer unless he has . . . not only a knowledge of human beings but a concern for them (I almost said an affection for them), an appreciation not only of their weaknesses but of their worth, not only of their diseases and defects, but of their *capacity for growth and for goodness*" (emphasis added). This reference to the capacity for growth is a tacit echoing of the capacity for the immature psychopath to "grow up," and this chapter will end with the aesthetic security of a Shakespearean statement on the matter.

6. FOULKES SPEAKS OF GROUP ANALYSIS

I intend to set two quotations from Foulkes one after the other and allow them to speak, without commentary, for themselves.

It would be of the utmost interest to study deviant groups such as delinquents, criminals or *psychopaths* in general in pure culture and see whether they, as a group or individually, do really essentially deviate from others or not. (1964, p. 298; emphasis added)

One would not offer analytic group psychotherapy to socially irresponsible or *psychopathic* patients. (1975, p. 92; emphasis added)

With exemplary simplicity Foulkes began a paper "On Group-Analytic Psychotherapy," presented in Vienna in 1968, in this way: "The best I can do is to tell you how I work today. . . . The group our patient now enters sits in a circle round a small table" (in E. Foulkes, 1975, pp. 169 and 171). Nevertheless, it might be ironically observed that to get a group of overactive aggressive psychopaths to "sit in a circle" would be no mean achievement! It may also explain why this particular chapter finds a place among a plethora of outcome studies, based on rigorous research criteria.

In the 1990 Foulkes Annual Lecture (Cox, 1993), I explored some of the forensic facets of a group-analytic approach, touching upon dynamics that are cognate with my present theme.

7. MURALITY AND OMNIFERENCE ARE KEY CONCEPTS

The terms "murality" and "omniference" convey complex issues with both precision and depth (Cox, 1993; Cordess & Cox, 1996, Vol. 2, p. 3). "Murality" refers to every quality of "wallness," regardless of whether it is literal or metaphorical, internal or external. It is a pervasive concept in the presentation of any forensic work; it has rapidly become descriptive of intrapsychic and interpersonal boundary phenomena, and of interdisciplinary demarcation, in addition to its unambiguous reference to custodial perimeters and security.

"Omniference" is a psychodynamic term and refers to the "all-carrying-allness" of a group. Foulkes (1975) described group analysis as treatment "by the group, of the group . . . including the conductor." Omniference implies that the therapist is also carried by the group as a whole, which, by definition, carries each participant. This was evident at a recent session in Broadmoor Hospital, when one group member said to another (who was much larger and frightening):

Member A: You are unapproachable . . . but I approached you.
Member B: But that was in the group.
Member A: What difference does the group make?
Member B: The group is a guarantee, isn't it?
Member A: Of what?
Member B: A guarantee of safety, of course.

In this instance, both the approacher (A) and the "unapproachable" member (B) were offered the guaranteed safety of rapprochement within the setting of the group. The group itself was the containing witness of the safe risk undertaken by a hitherto anxious man. He had previously been so anxious that homicide was his only way of responding to threats that were presumed to be in the air.

Both murality and omniference invite considerable exploration. The latter is still paradoxically operative even with reference to the "anti-group" (Nitsun, 1996), which has many forensic reifications.

8. HIGH-PROFILE CASES REQUIRE SPECIAL DISCRETION

Most of the patients admitted to Broadmoor have been "high-profile" cases, commanding huge headlines in the tabloid press. They need guaranteed immunity from salacious and malignant media encroachment. Quite apart from generic issues of professional confidentiality, it would be impossible to disguise their index offenses if they were to be described in any detail. It is for this precise reason—the totally safe discussion of details about individuals' inner world and their "index offenses"—that, long ago, I changed the focus of my teaching to the study of other "high-profile cases." Their names are well known—and, if not, they should be! They might include Lady Macbeth, Richard III, Iago, Cassius, Titus Andronicus, and other Shakespearean characters.

Thus the experience undergone by Lavinia, whose hands are cut off and whose tongue is cut out, is akin to any of the most extreme incidents relived within forensic group psychotherapy. Tricomi (1974, p. 19) writes: "Whatever our final aesthetic judgement concerning the merits of *Titus Andronicus,* we must understand that we are dealing, *not with a paucity of imagination but with an excess of dramatic witness*" (emphasis added). When writing about this passage elsewhere, a colleague and I concluded, "and from the clinical forensic arena, comes this codicil: 'But *NOT* with an excess of *CLINICAL* witness' " (Cox & Theilgaard, 1994, p. 359). In other words, we are conducting psychotherapy with patients whose sadistic offenses are sometimes no less mutilating than the injuries sustained by Lavinia.

9. PLACES OF SAFETY ARE NEEDED—IN EVERY SENSE

One of the phrases transplanted in its entirety from the 1959 to the 1983 Mental Health Act of England and Wales was the reference to "places of safety." Although this is a socially and legally necessary term, it also has wide metaphorical relevance in the field of psychotherapy. Human beings have a great need for intrapsychic safety. This would be another way of thinking of an adequate psychological defensive system. It may be only through repression or denial that an individual experiences an intrapsychic "place of safety"; even so, such safety is spurious. Dynamic psychotherapy can be regarded as a process in which "the patient is enabled to do for himself what he cannot do on his own" (Cox, 1978, p. 45), and part of this is to enable spurious safety to be turned into genuine intrapsychic safety. This can only occur when primitive defenses are relinquished, so that unconscious material has entered consciousness and been safely integrated.

10. PARADOXICAL POIESIS INFLUENCES GROUP PROCESS

Poiesis refers to the capacity to "call into existence that which was not there before"; it is a term coming from antiquity, and its homologues of musical modulation or changes in harmony may color the "shape" of a therapeutic intervention (Cox & Theilgaard, 1987, p. 23). Creativity and *poiesis* influence the crystallization, the timbre, and the cadence of an interpretation. It is referred to as "paradoxical" in this instance because it tends to reverse Strachey's (1934) concept of the mutative interpretation. By this I mean that when the therapist senses that a truly mutative interpretation is "in the air," he or she can facilitate the way in which the material is kept "free-floating" within the group matrix, somewhat in the way that a football may be "kept in play" by being passed from one player to another. No one takes full possession until the individual concerned almost *wrests* the interpretation out of the ethos and says, in effect, "This applies to me." In the same way, Titus says to silenced Lavinia:

> Thou shalt not sigh, nor hold thy stumps to heaven,
> Nor wink, nor nod, nor kneel, nor make a sign,
> But I of these will wrest an alphabet!
> And by still practice learn to know their meaning!
> *(Titus Andronicus,* III.ii.42–46)

The other members are then aware that the hitherto "free-floating" interpretation has been grasped and appropriated by one of their number. The others may also be asking themselves whether such an interpretation could apply to them too, and, ideally, to the group as a whole. I have in mind an incident already published (Cordess & Cox, 1996, Vol. 2, p. 91). It involved a female patient's reliving the experience of bravely entering a little stream at the foot of the garden at the age of 5, when the water became so deep that it flowed over the top of her brand-new Wellington boots. At the approach of two eels swimming downstream, the little girl screamed and tried to move, while experiencing a pleasant warm tickling feeling rising up between her legs. At this point in the description, she suddenly stopped in the middle of the sentence (and also in the middle of catching her breath) and asked breathlessly, "Is this why I am afraid of penises?" Such an autogenous interpretation carries an unmistakable stamp of authenticity.

11. A DISCRIMINATION MUST BE MADE BETWEEN CONSCIOUS–WITHHELD AND CONSCIOUS–DISCLOSED MATERIAL

It is necessary to distinguish between "conscious–withheld" material and that which is "conscious–disclosed." Although I have been involved in therapeutic work with psychopathic patients since 1970, it was not until some years later that I first became aware of the important differentiation between material that is conscious–withheld and its subsequent release as material that is conscious–disclosed. This is an important distinction. Material may enter a patient's consciousness and yet not be fully disclosed—except to an individual analyst, in which case it has still not become truly "public." The therapeutic group provides an intermediate *temenos* (a sacred or highly valued place) where private, shame-inducing, fragile experience may be safely ventilated so that material becomes conscious–disclosed. This echoes the previous references to the group as a "guarantee of safety" and to the phenomenon of omniference.

12. THE GROUP PROVIDES MULTIPLE TRANSFERENCE RECIPIENTS

A therapeutic group augments the number of possible recipients of projected transference responses, compared with that provided by the therapist conducting an individual session. Each individual in the group may serve as a "host" for projected transferential feelings and thoughts—for example, "John looks at me with disdain in the same way that my father did and I hate him for it." Or, in the case of mixed-group therapy, a male patient may feel that "Mary's smile is seductive and irresistible, but I know that women who look at me like this ultimately betray me." Therapists are often construed as possessing the assets or liabilities of parental figures. Furthermore, parataxic distortion frequently renders a duo of cotherapists (particularly if there is one of each gender) liable to evoke transference responses; for better or worse, these are sequential reactivations of feelings and thoughts about previous significant others, who are, of course, usually parental figures.

But in addition to the individual group members and the therapists, who form part of the overall dynamic constellation of the group matrix, the group-as-a-whole phenomenon itself may temporarily serve as a recipient for transference material. Thus, the group as a whole may seem to "behave" as one patient's father had done: "It just goes on and takes no notice of me. It ignores me." By contrast, another patient may feel that the group as a whole "is like my home before my mother died. It is warm and friendly and a nice place to be, even when nothing much seems to be happening. There is usually someone laughing about something, and I look forward to being with them."

13. CREATIVITY IN GROUP ANALYSIS: INVOLVES A PARADOXICAL MOVEMENT FROM DEPTH TO SURFACE

In formal individual psychoanalytic psychotherapy and also in group-analytic psychotherapy, there are sound reasons for the injunction that is usually expressed as follows: "Begin every interpretation from the surface" (Greenson, 1967, p. 145). Time and space do not allow for a discussion of this statement, but in the present context it is likely to be an acceptable "given." Nevertheless, some of the dynamic burden of therapy undertaken using mutative metaphors is based on the previously cited provocative statement by Bachelard: "But the poetic image has touched the depths before it stirs the surface" (quoted in Cox & Theilgaard, 1987, p. xiii). To take the crude analogy of a dental drill, access to the patient does not take the form of deeper and deeper penetration into painful material. On the contrary, there is a sense that something is safely coming to the surface within the patient, which the patient recognizes as his or her own experience and so does not try to push it away.

14. THE RIPPLE EFFECT: FORMAL THERAPY SESSION MUST BE INTEGRATED WITH A PATIENT'S TOTAL LIFE

Increasing emphasis is nowadays given to the patient's experiences *between* sessions, which make the impact of the overall context even more important. It even seems absurd to mention the fact that a patient's playing brilliantly on the football team, winning first prize in the annual poetry competition, passing some significant exam in the education department or taking part in a drama production needs to be integrated with the increasing self-knowledge that the patient gains in formal therapeutic sessions. Although much research has been done on this theme in connection with schizophrenic patients, I have no doubt that it is equally important in a secure setting for work with psychopathic patients, whose "maturational processes" are evident in many ways. Winnicott's (1965) phrase has an impact on overall therapeutic strategy that can never be exaggerated.

15. ACHIEVING TRUST STATUS IS THE GOAL—ON EVERY LEVEL

The achievement of "trust status" is a current preoccupation of National Health Service managers and administrators in Great Britain. Yet it is far more than prevailing fashion with reference to the psychotherapy of the psychopath. The language of poetry and metaphor can often convey a deeper precision than that afforded by technical terms, and is further evidence of the clinical relevance of aesthetic accuracy and poetic precision. Shakespeare offers us a complex dynamic process of internalization with this paradoxical and incongruous reference to "internal" fashion, which thus clothes the true self rather than hiding the false self:

> Sorrow so royally in you appears
> That I will *deeply* put the fashion *on,*
> And wear it *in* my heart.
> (*II Henry IV,* V.ii.51–53; emphasis added)

Many of the patients admitted to Broadmoor with a legal classification of "psychopathy" have the personality structures of borderline patients. It is therefore not surprising that so many of their index offenses are related to superego pathology and guilt-disowning projective identification. Kernberg (1992) writes:

> I have coined the term *psychopathic transference* to refer to periods in the treatment when . . . conditions of deceptiveness and their projection prevail. In my view, it is essential to explore such transferences in great detail, and to resolve them interpretatively before proceeding with other materials.

However true this may be when working with an individual patient, it is certainly a predominant theme and variations in the early phases of group-analytic psychotherapy with psychopaths. Yet even here, the mutative metaphor can provide the sort of startling and unexpected confrontation that so unsettles a psychopath. Because it is impossible to habituate to the unexpected, such patients are often taken off their guard and find that their heavily defended true selves have been brought into the open.

By way of exemplification, I have an individual patient in mind who was constantly attention-seeking and manipulative at a certain phase in the life of the group. On one occasion she sat in a "corner" of the group, which had started off in a conventional circular configuration but had soon become kidney-shaped, with Jane occupying the lower calyx. To make matters even more difficult, she had placed a vase of flowers at the angle of a table, and the vase directly interrupted the line of any possible reciprocal gaze we might have had. There was a barely concealed smile of smug satisfaction on her face. But this soon vanished when I said that this was a moment for which the entire group had been waiting for a long time. In answer to her question seeking an explanation for my opaque comment, I said, "This is the first time that 'Honesty' has come between us!"

This intervention, which initially appeared as a superficial pun, had more of the qualities of *paronomasia* (see Cox & Theilgaard, 1987, p. 114) which refers to "meaning beyond the meaning." It captured the group's struggle to be honest with itself, and the search for authenticity was augmented. Such comments also strike a note of international warning. My Danish readers will know (as my original Danish listeners knew) that the flower I have been describing, which is called "Honesty" in English, is known as "Judas Money" in Danish! It would have been an intervention of an entirely different timbre had I said to Jane, "This is the first time that 'Judas Money' has come between us!" This is undoubtedly provocative, and makes us wonder what dynamic issues would have unfolded had I said to the group as a whole, "This is the first time that you have allowed 'betrayal' to come between us." We might, in the end, also find ourselves grappling with the necessity of exploring and diminishing psychopathic transference.

CONCLUSION

I am fully aware that in this chapter many crucial concerns—such as the selection of patients, the integration with other therapeutic modalities, the necessity and repercussions of working with a cotherapist (often two cotherapists, when one is a member of the nursing staff who is in constant touch at the clinical front line), outcome studies, and other necessary research topics—have been avoided. But selection is inevitably selective! For elaboration of these and other related issues, see Cordess and Cox (1996), the first major publication on forensic psychotherapy, where 60 psychotherapists with forensic experience have grappled with such things.

It is appropriate that a chapter based on a lecture given in Denmark should find words of Kierkegaard sharing the last page with words of Shakespeare: "Hope is a passion for what is possible" (quoted in Moltmann, 1967, p. 20). This differs from the major emphasis Freud gave to wishing and wish fulfillment. Hope carries a connotation of expectation. One of the constant themes in both the overt "text" and the virtually continuous "subtext" of group-analytic psychotherapy with psychopaths is the nature of hope. In one way or another, individual members of the group and the group as a whole explore the many ramifications of this question: "What can realistically be expected of me now and in the future, in view of my disturbed and disturbing history?" As always, Shakespeare has the creative facility of enshrining such topics in poetic language that is hard to forget. He could have had an immature psychopath embarking upon a therapeutic journey in mind when he wrote:

> As dissolute as desperate, yet thro' both
> I see some *sparks of better hope*, which elder years
> May happily bring forth.
>   (*Richard II*, V.iii.20–22; emphasis added)

Had he done so, he would have caught an essential aspect of "The Ring of Truth"—the circular configuration of a group-analytic therapeutic group for psychopaths. And clinical experience would endorse this description of the acceleration of previously delayed emotional maturation. It has the ring of truth about it.

REFERENCES

Bateson, G. (1979). *Mind and nature: A necessary unity.* London: Wildwood House.

Boss, M. (1979). *Existential foundations of medicine and psychology.* New York: Jason Aronson.

Cordess, C., & Cox, M. (Eds.). (1996). *Forensic psychotherapy: Crime, psychodynamics and the offender patient* (2 vols.). London: Jessica Kingsley.

Cox, M. (1976). Group psychotherapy in a secure setting. *Proceedings of the Royal Society of Medicine, 69,* 215–220.

Cox, M. (1978). *Structuring the therapeutic process: Compromise with chaos.* London: Jessica Kingsley.

Cox, M. (1993). *The group as poetic play-ground: From metaphor to metamorphosis* (1990 Foulkes Annual Lecture). London: Jessica Kingsley.

Cox, M., & Theilgaard, A. (1987). *Mutative metaphors in psychotherapy: The Aeolian mode.* London: Tavistock.

Cox, M., & Theilgaard, A. (1994). *Shakespeare as prompter: The amending imagination and the therapeutic process.* London: Jessica Kingsley.

Dolan, B. M., & Coid, J. (1993). *Psychopathic and antisocial personality disorders: Treatment and research issues.* London: Gaskell.

Foulkes, S. H. (1964). *Therapeutic group analysis.* London: Allen & Unwin.

Foulkes, S. H. (1975). *Group analytic psychotherapy: Method and principles.* London: Gordon & Breach.

Glover, E. (1960). *The roots of crime.* London: Imago.

Greenson, R. R. (1967). *The technique and practice of psycho-analysis* (Vol. 1). London: Hogarth Press.

Gunn, J. (1994). [Review of Tyrer, P., & Stein, G. (Eds.), *Personality disorder reviewed*]. *Criminal Behaviour and Mental Health, 4,* 123–126.

Kernberg, O. F. (1984). *Severe personality disorders: Psychotherapeutic strategies.* New Haven, CT: Yale University Press.

Kernberg, O. F. (1992). Psychopathic, paranoid and depressive transferences. *International Journal of Psycho-Analysis, 73,* 13–28.

Kierkegaard, S. (1978). Points of view on my author-activity. In S. Kierkegaard, *Kierkegaard's writings* (Vol. 18, pp. 96–97). Princeton, NJ: Princeton University Press. (Original work published 1848)

Macquarrie, J. (1966). *Principles of Christian theology.* London: SCM Press.

Millon, T. (1994). Foreword. In M. Cox & A. Theilgaard, *Shakespeare as prompter: The amending imagination and the therapeutic process.* London: Jessica Kingsley.

Moltmann, J. (1967). *Theology of hope* London: SCM Press.

Nitsun, M. (1996). *The anti-group: Destructive forces in the group and their creative potential.* London: Routledge.

Norton, K. (1996). The personality-disordered forensic patient and the therapeutic community. In C. Cordess & M. Cox (Eds.), *Forensic psychotherapy: Crime, psychodynamics and the offender patient* (Vol. 2, pp. 401–421). London: Jessica Kingsley.

Pines, M., & Schermer, V. L. (Eds.). (1994). *Ring of fire: Primitive affects and object relations in group psychotherapy.* London: Routledge.

Racker, H. (1972). The meaning of uses of countertransference. *Psychoanalytic Quarterly, 41,* 487–506.

Raven, C. (1959). *Science, medicine and morals: A survey and a suggestion.* London: Hodder & Stoughton.

Reed, J. (1996). Psychotherapy—a clinical and legal dilemma [Editorial]. *British Journal of Psychiatry, 168,* 49.

Reiss, D., Grubin, D., & Meux, C. (1996). Young 'psychopaths' in a special hospital: Treatment and outcome. *British Journal of Psychiatry, 168* 99–104.

Rosen, I. (1996). Perversion as a regulator of self-esteem. In I. Rosen (Ed.), *Sexual deviation* (3rd ed.). Oxford: Oxford University Press.

Stierlin, H. (1970). The functions of inner objects. *International Journal of Psycho-Analysis, 51,* 127–159

Strachey, J. (1934). The nature of the therapeutic action of psycho-analysis. *International Journal of Psycho-Analysis, 15,* 127–159.

Symington, N. (1980). The response aroused by the psychopath. *International Review of Psycho-analysis, 7,* 291–298.

Tillett, R. (1996). Psychotherapy assessment and treatment selection. *British Journal of Psychiatry, 168,* 10–15.

Tricomi, A. H. (1974). The aesthetics of mutilation in *Titus Andronicus. Shakespeare Survey, 27,* 11–19.

Tyrer, P., & Stein, G. (Eds.). (1993). *Personality disorder reviewed*. London: Gaskell.

Welldon, E. (1993). Forensic psychotherapy and group analysis. *Group Analysis, 26*(4), 487–502.

Welldon, E. (1996). Group-analytic psychotherapy in an out-patient setting. In C. Cordess & M. Cox (Eds.), *Forensic psychotherapy: Crime, psychodynamics and the offender patient* (Vol. 2, pp. 63–82). London: Jessica Kingsley.

Winnicott, D. W. (1965). *The maturational process and the facilitating environment*. London: Hogarth Press.

26

Therapeutic Community Treatment for Severe Personality Disorders

BRIDGET DOLAN

Patients with severe personality disorders continue to be recognized as one of the more difficult clinical populations. Left untreated, personality disorders (PDs) are chronic and persistent, with high mortality rates (Martin et al., 1985; Robertson, 1987). Alongside the psychiatric disturbance, PDs are also at the root of a great amount of physical morbidity—for example, through associations with drug and alcohol misuse, HIV infection, suicide, and other self-harm (Norton, 1992a). People with PDs tend to "suck in" services in response to a crisis, and many could be described as "abusers" of services rather than "users." They are sporadic attendees at therapy and are difficult to engage in any long-term management plans (Frank, 1991). Yet, despite their lack of compliance with care plans, such patients continue to be heavy users of services, with frequent presentations at a whole range of health care, social, and criminal justice agencies. Many of the interventions offered by such agencies are aimed at containment and management rather than at treatment per se. Frequent hospitalizations of short duration are common features, and thus, because of the chronic and unremitting nature of their disorders, PD patients are very costly (Perry, Lavori, & Hoke, 1987; Menzies, Dolan, & Norton, 1993; Hyde & Harrower-Wilson, 1995). Engaging such patients in treatment is a difficult clinical task (Norton, 1996); they have high early dropout rates; and poor therapy outcomes are often reported. In addition, the presence of a personality disorder exerts a "malign and negative influence" on the outcome of therapy for concurrent mental illness (Tyrer & Seivewright, 1988; Bearden, Lavelle, Buysee, Karp, & Frank, 1996), and thus it is perhaps unsurprising that the treatability of PDs is frequently doubted by many clinicians, who are reluctant to accept PD patients into therapy (Coid & Cordess, 1992). Indeed, following a survey of clinicians' attitudes toward them, personality-disordered individuals have been termed "the patients psychiatrists dislike" (Lewis & Appleby, 1988).

   The ambivalence of professionals toward this client group is reflected in the contin-uing debate about whether personality disorders are diagnosable conditions; what is the most appropriate method of assessment; whether PDs are treatable conditions, and, if so, whether there are any effective treatments; what are suitable markers of change in PDs (let alone any notions of "cure"); and whether any of these can be accurately or ade-quately measured. Latterly in Britain, since the restructuring of the National Health Ser-vice, the issue has arisen of whether, given the cost implications, people with PDs should be offered treatment resources at all (Dolan & Norton, 1992; Dolan, Evans, & Norton, 1994b).

   Yet, despite their unpopularity with many clinicians, people with PDs frequently ex-hibit antisocial behaviors that are damaging to others, and that inevitably precipitate professional intervention in their lives. However, it often seems forgotten that, alongside these antisocial behaviors, much manifest psychological disturbance and distress are ex-perienced by PD individuals. These individuals suffer as a consequence of their disor-ders; thus, professional involvement in their care is not only unavoidable but warrant-ed.

   Although over the past decade there has been an increasing academic and clinical in-terest in PDs, it is clear from recent governmental reports and comprehensive literature reviews that our knowledge of effective treatments for PDs remains rudimentary (Quali-ty Assurance Project, 1991; Dolan & Coid, 1993; Reed, 1994; Ruegg & Frances, 1995). This lack of knowledge can lead to claims of the "untreatability" of PDs. Although PD patients are notoriously difficult to engage in treatment research studies, part of the re-sponsibility for the lack of substantial evidence of treatment efficacy must be located in the researchers themselves, rather than simply in the patients. The view that PDs are un-treatable derives from poor-quality treatment outcome studies. The design of most out-come studies is inadequate. Many have failed to adequately assess the severity of person-ality disorders; nor do they evaluate change in core personality disorders, but instead apply indirect measures of PD pathology with insufficiently described treatment condi-tions.

ASSESSING CHANGE IN PERSONALITY DISORDERS

The accurate assessment of change in core PD phenomena is hampered by the continued use of indirect measures of PDs, many of which are not conceptually linked to the focus of treatment (Norton & Dolan, 1995b). Indeed, change in any of a range of features as-sociated with PDs is erroneously equated with change in the PDs themselves; these fea-tures include Axis I diagnostic symptomatology (Fava et al., 1994), or behavioral fea-tures such as criminal activity (Serin & Amos, 1995), self-mutilation, or suicidality (Shearin & Linehan, 1994).

   One reason for researchers' reliance upon proxy measures of change is perhaps that instruments for measuring the phenomenology of personality disorders (whether based upon DSM-III-R/DSM-IV or ICD-10 classifications) are often ill equipped to act as mea-sures of change. Personality disorders are long-term patterns of functioning (American Psychiatric Association [APA], 1994); thus, demonstrating change is problematic with a short follow-up period, and on some core defining criteria change is impossible—for ex-ample, evidence of a conduct disorder before age 15 for DSM-IV antisocial personality disorder. Perhaps it is a reflection of the professionals' lack of expectation of change that very few measures have been developed to assess shifts in core PD features. In the face of such difficulties with measuring change in core features, it may be appropriate to instead evaluate those associated parameters that are considered desirable outcomes in PD patients (such as absence of offending). It is also understandable that research will favor the most easily measurable aspects of PD. However, the demonstration of change (or lack of change) in such proxy measures should not be mistaken for change (or lack of it) in core PD. It is important that measures of indirect or of associated features are construed as such and commented upon, so as to avoid confusion about what has and what has not been measured and has or has not changed.

Unfortunately, very few studies have even attempted to measure changes in core PD; indeed, many treatment outcome studies have not assessed the personality disorder pathology of their subjects at all (Fink, Derby, & Martin, 1969; Carney, 1976; Cavior & Schmidt, 1978; Stermac, 1986). Particularly in Britain, many research studies have described subjects only in terms of their legal classification of "psychopathic disorder," although there is consistent evidence that this legal term bears little relationship to any recognized clinical diagnosis of personality disorder (Chiswick, 1992; Coid, 1992); nor does it have any consistent equivalence to Hare's operationalized definition of "psychopathy" (Coid, 1993).

There are many other methodological imperfections in research designs, which indeed are common in treatment outcome research in other clinical fields. They include small sample sizes (Høglend, 1993; Digeur, Barber, & Luborsky, 1993) and uncontrolled study designs (Budman, Denby, Soldz, & Merry, 1996; Chiesa, Iacoponi, & Morris, 1996), with short lengths of posttreatment follow-up (Digeur et al., 1993). However a particular shortcoming of research in PDs is the lack of description of treatments applied in the outcome studies. With the exception of pharmacological research and therapeutic community (TC) approaches, most studies of treatment outcome for PDs do not actually describe the treatment given to patients in enough detail to allow subsequent researchers to replicate the study or interested clinicians to recreate the treatment approach in their own clinics. In most studies of PDs (particularly those studies conducted in secure environments), the only treatment variable recorded is length of stay in the institution, and the only outcome variable is offending after release. There is rarely any record of the treatment (or varieties of treatments) received by a patient during incarceration. Thus these are not studies of *treatment* outcome, but could be more accurately described as "studies of the correctness of the decision to release the patient."

The inadequacy of our methodological strategies to date means that there are few empirical data to support the "untreatability" of PD patients at all (Dolan & Coid, 1993). Indeed, the view that PDs cannot be treated may be a response to feelings elicited by these patients in therapy, rather than a response to empirical data. What results is a mood of therapeutic pessimism, rather than a healthy skepticism regarding the treatability of PDs. Yet despite this clinical dejection surrounding PDs, there is increasing evidence of the success of psychotherapeutic approaches for these disorders (Bannon, 1995; Budman et al., 1996). In particular, those units that employ a democratic TC model have shown substantial improvements following therapy in a variety of domains: improved psychological state, reduced offending, reduction of core PD pathology, and reduced usage of psychiatric services following treatment (Warren & Dolan, 1996).

This chapter first reviews evidence for the efficacy of TC treatment of PDs in a range of secure and nonsecure settings internationally. Following this, the TC model applied at Henderson Hospital in England is described in greater depth, and a recent research study that demonstrates its successful outcome with PD patients is summarized.

THE DEMOCRATIC TC MODEL

The democratic TC model was an innovative approach that arose from the changes occurring in British psychiatric hospitals after World War II. Influenced by the developments of group-analytic approaches at that time (Foulkes, 1946/1996; Dewar, 1946), the *Zeitgeist* moved away from an authoritarian to a more collaborative style of staff behavior (Bridger, 1946/1996; Bion, 1946), including, importantly, more active participation of the patients in their own treatment (Main, 1946; Davidson, 1946/1996). Thus responsibility for the day-to-day running of a TC is shared among patients known as "residents" and staff. This collaborative and democratic style, whereby the community itself is invested with an important decision-making function, forms a cornerstone of therapy—embodied in the concept of the "community as doctor" (Rapoport, 1960).

There is a flattening of the staff and resident hierarchy, and the staff and residents collaborate in a wide range of activities combining sociotherapy and psychotherapy. All interactions and relationships within the TC can be examined. The aim is that such examination will lead to a better understanding of deviant or unhealthy previous behavior (reenacted within the treatment setting), which may then result in altered interpersonal behavior and improved psychosocial functioning. Tom Main, who coined the term "therapeutic community" in 1946, suggested that it is not simply "the structure, but the culture which is decisive for the human relations on offer." As he described it, the TC is a "culture of enquiry . . . into personal and interpersonal and intersystem problems," including "the study of impulses, defences and relations, expressed and arranged socially" (Main, 1946).

Within a TC, the focus is on real tasks and development of real relationships. Thus, many of the interactions of the external world are recreated inside the institution. Therapy follows from other community members' observing, questioning, understanding, and challenging a person's reactions, emotions, and behaviors within this "real" environment. This also provides much better opportunities for patients to consider how they might respond in the external world. Such opportunities are often lost within the disempowering models of custodial institutions.

A wide variety of institutions describe themselves as TCs, although distinctions have been drawn between the "therapeutic community proper" and the "therapeutic community approach" (Clark, 1965), or the "old" and "new" TCs (De Leon, 1983). This distinction is based on the commitment to "more active, humane, caring institutions where the human rights and dignity of the inmates are recognised and respected" incorporated in the TC proper. The four core tenets (permissiveness, communalism, democratization, and reality confrontation) identified by the social anthropologist Robert Rapoport in his 1950s study of Henderson Hospital encapsulate the TC proper, in contrast to the approach used in the hierarchical concept houses or concept-based TCs developed in the United States (Rapoport, 1960). In these latter communities, the hierarchy is keener and more authoritarian (Kennard & Roberts, 1983), and the "social organisation is a family surrogate system, vertically stratified . . . authority . . . is more autocracy than democracy" (De Leon, 1983). These hierarchical TCs are particularly aimed at substance misusers; the staff members may themselves be ex-addicts, and the communities aim to keep each member "clean" by using very confrontative encounter groups. Although these very different TCs are not reviewed in this chapter, it should be mentioned that some of these communities (which are predominantly located in the United States) are particularly well researched and demonstrate good outcome results in treating substance abuse and dependence (Wexler, 1995).

Democratic TCs treating people with PDs have been established in various psychiatric and prison settings throughout the world, including day hospitals, inpatient settings, secure hospitals, and prisons. The efficacy of these units has been assessed in a variety of domains: psychological and behavioral changes (both during and following treatment), patterns of offending and service usage, and cost offset following treatment.

TCs in Prison Settings

In Britain, units adopting a TC approach have been established within several prisons, and at Her Majesty's Prison (HMP) Grendon Underwood, the entire establishment of over 200 inmates has been run as a democratic TC since 1962.

Grendon Underwood is unique in the British penal system, in that it is described as a "therapeutic prison" providing a therapeutic regimen for offenders with moderate to severe PDs. Inmates, who are usually high-tariff offenders with sentences of over 5 years, are referred to the prison specifically for voluntary treatment within the TC. Prisoners may request to return to the ordinary prison system at any time, or they may be rejected from the TC if they continually break the cardinal community rules or fail to engage sufficiently in treatment. Gray (1974) described the strength of the group values and social structure in Grendon, noting that during its first 11 years of operation there were no major incidents (such as escapes or serious violence), and that for many years Grendon has had the lowest prison offense rate of any British prison.

Early studies of psychological changes during treatment in Grendon demonstrated decreased depression, anxiety, social introversion, and hostility, and increased extraversion and ego strength, as measured by Minnesota Multiphasic Personality Inventory changes between admission and discharge. Significantly greater decreases in psychopathology were also found with the General Health Questionnaire after 9 months in a group of Grendon prisoners, compared with a group of prisoners held in other, nontherapeutic prisons (Gunn, 1978).

Despite these psychological changes, a study of men treated at Grendon in the 1970s showed little effect of admission on recidivism, with 92% of men reconvicted after 10 years (Robertson & Gunn, 1987). However, it has been suggested that this lack of impact on offending was in part due to the fact the study included a high proportion of men imprisoned on short sentences for minor acquisitive offenses. In the two decades since Robertson and Gunn's original study, Grendon has moved toward treating more dangerous, more violent, and higher-tariff offenders, and recently Cullen (1993) reported an overall 33.2% reconviction rate 2 years after discharge. Cullen (1994) has also demonstrated clear "dosage effects" of the therapy at Grendon. When prisoners were matched for offense type, sentence length, and previous convictions, only 19% of those completing 18 months or more of therapy were reconvicted within the 2-year period, compared with 50% of those receiving therapy for less than 18 months. For only those men paroled into the community directly from Grendon (rather than via ordinary prisons), the reconviction rate was far lower, at 10% for the longer-staying group and 39% for those staying less than 18 months. Indeed, the most recent Home Office figures have shown a significant reduction in offending 5 years after therapy at Grendon, when released Grendon prisoners are compared with those prisoners referred but not admitted to the unit who were matched for criminal history (Home Office Research and Planning Unit, 1996).

A report from North America also showed improvement in several personality and social variables (e.g., ego strength, social relationships, trusting others, and ideas of self), and reduction of tension, frustration, and depression, after admission to a therapeutic prison in California based on the Maxwell Jones TC model (see below). However, no differences were found in reconviction and recidivism rates when the treated group was compared with a control group from a mainstream prison (Fink et al., 1969).

A special unit established within HMP Barlinnie in Scotland uses a modified TC approach to manage those high-tariff prisoners who have presented severe control problems in the normal system. In common with findings from Grendon, it has been demonstrated that admission to the unit significantly reduced the numbers of serious prison discipline incidents (fire setting, violence, self-mutilation, and absconding). A group of 25 inmates staying in therapy for an average of 41 months was involved in only 9 such incidents, despite an expected frequency of 154 incidents based on extrapolations from preadmission behavior. This improvement in behavior was maintained after transfer back to ordinary prison, and of the 12 men released into the community, only 4 were subsequently reconvicted at follow-up (Cooke, 1989). Such positive effects upon prison discipline incidents have also been reported from an Indian prison that implemented a TC regimen for "psychopaths." During the time of the implementation of the TC regimen, no serious assaults or other incidents occurred in the prison, and 72% of inmates were judged to have improved by clinical standards (Sandhu, 1970).

The Annexe at HMP Wormwood Scrubs in London is another therapeutic unit, established within the main prison in 1973. On a voluntary basis, the Annexe admits inmates with addiction, personality problems, or persistent violence. Studies using a repertory grid approach have demonstrated improvement in self-esteem and less aggressive self-perception during treatment (Jones, 1990). Comparison with nonadmitted referrals showed lower reconviction rates 2 years after release for treated men (Sewell & Clark, 1982). A subsequent study with 122 prisoners found that where treated inmates did reoffend, in 25% of cases the reoffense was less violent, although in 17% it was more serious (Jones, 1988).

Although a positive effect from prison TCs seems widely supported, it is also suggested in some studies that "psychopaths" (as defined by the Psychopathy Checklist; Hare, 1985) do less well than "nonpsychopaths" in such regimens. In Canada, Ogloff, Wong, and Greenwood (1990) found that psychopathic inmates showed less improvement than nonpsychopathic inmates in self-assessed motivation and psychological state. However, the fact that the nonpsychopathic group stayed significantly longer in therapy was not controlled for in the data analysis. In addition, the quality of the outcome measures and the approach to data analysis may have obscured some important effects in this study (see Evans, 1994, for a detailed commentary).

A Canadian study of a prison "social therapy unit" (STU) at Penetenguishene also found no positive outcome for psychopathic inmates in terms of reoffending. When only those who spent at least 2 years in the STU were considered, recidivism rates were unaffected for psychopathic offenders, although recidivism was significantly reduced in nonpsychopaths (Harris, Rice, & Cormier, 1994). Indeed, it seems that the STU may even have had a negative effect on violent recidivism for the psychopathic group. The authors suggest that within the STU psychopaths had learned to be more self-confident criminals who could maintain high self-esteem while committing antisocial acts. This study is often cited as a demonstration of the ineffectiveness of TC treatment for psychopaths. However, there is great debate as to whether the unit can legitimately lay claim to the title of a TC (Warren, 1994; Whiteley, 1995; Harris & Rice, 1995). The program at Penetenguishene involved a very coercive regimen with "radical therapeutic techniques," including nude marathon therapy groups and drugs such as LSD and scopolamine. The program was described as heavily peer-operated and humanistic, with a charismatic leader. Although many types of institutions with varying social organizations and structures have been *called* "TCs," simply running a therapeutic program within an institution is not sufficient to constitute a TC proper (Bloor, McKeganey, & Fonkert, 1988), and thus it is suggested that the term was inappropriately applied to the Penetenguishene regimen.

Maximum-Security Psychiatric Hospital TCs

The TC approach has been most extensively used for offenders in maximum-security hospitals in the Netherlands. Encouraging outcome results are available from these institutions, which treat personality-disordered offenders under an order from the government (Feldbrugge, 1992). At the Van der Hoeven Clinic in Utrecht, reoffending rates of 22.4% were found at a 5-year follow-up for a cohort of treated prisoners discharged to the community (Jessen & Roosenberg, 1971). However, this impressively low reconviction rate relates to only those patients who had been considered well enough to be discharged by the clinical team. Van Emmerik (1987) studied all patients treated at the Van der Hoeven Clinic, including those discharged against medical advice, and found a higher overall reconviction rate of 52% over 5 years.

Within Broadmoor Special Hospital, a maximum-security hospital in England, a single ward operates a structured milieu incorporating elements of the TC approach with younger patients held under the legal category of "psychopathic disorder." In a case-note study, 49 men who had been treated on the unit for a minimum of 1 year were followed up an average of 4 years, 9 months after leaving the ward. Home Office records were used, and psychiatric supervisors and prisons were contacted in some cases. Only 28 patients had spent any time out of hospitals in the follow-up period; the remainder either had not been discharged from Broadmoor or had moved to other secure hospitals. At follow-up, 25 men were still living in the community and were judged to have "good" social interaction (16 of them now held jobs). Two men were dead (one suicide, one road accident), and 10 men had reoffended, including two serious sexual offenses and two homicides (one homicide was carried out inside a secure hospital) (Reiss, Grubin, & Meux, 1996).

Specialist TC Units in Nonsecure Health Service Settings

In Norway, Ulleval Day Hospital operates a day hospital TC for both personality-disordered and non-personality-disordered patients. Vaglum et al. (1990) used the Symptom Checklist 90 (SCL-90) and the Health and Sickness Rating Scale to measure outcome in a group of 97 patients after treatment for an average of 5.5 months. There were significant changes in scores in both the personality-disordered and non-personality-disordered groups, which were maintained up to 3 years later (Mehlum et al., 1991). However, significantly more of the non-personality-disordered group were asymptomatic after treatment. Karterud et al. (1992) have also reported on the containing function of the day unit for personality-disordered patients, as evidenced by a lowered prevalence of suicide attempts, psychotic decompensation, and transfer to other units.

The Cassel Hospital, Surrey, was one of the first inpatient TCs in Britain; it was founded by Tom Main (who had coined the term "TC" in 1946). Rosser, Birch, Bond, Denford, and Schachter (1987) reported 5-year follow-up outcome for a group of 28 admissions to this hospital in terms of clinical features and social adjustment. Unfortunately, the specific criteria for "success" in the study are not clear from the report; however, "success rates" of 64% were reported. An economic analysis based on the "estimated lifetime profiles of earning" before and after treatment suggested that benefits far outweighed the cost of treatment. More recently, Chiesa et al. (1996) have compared 1-year service usage of two separate groups of Cassel patients: a group about to be admitted for treatment, and a treated group discharged from the hospital. The treated group used significantly fewer inpatient and outpatient psychiatric services, required fewer inpatient medical and surgical beds, had fewer laboratory investigations, and used fewer minor tranquilizers than the pretreatment group. They were also significantly more likely than the pretreatment group to be employed. Unfortunately, the study had small sample sizes ($n = 26$), and the independent group design means that it is not possible to associate any of these group differences with the TC treatment per se.

HENDERSON HOSPITAL

The present-day Henderson Hospital has evolved from the psychiatric and industrial rehabilitation units established during and after World War II (Whiteley, 1980; Murto, 1991). During 1940–1945, Maxwell Jones and his colleagues created the basis for the treatment model later to be called the TC, with the central realization of the strength of peer group support in large-group situations and the value of fellow patients in passing on the culture and philosophy of treatment to new admissions (Jones, 1942, 1946; Main, 1946). In 1947 Jones took charge of a unit catering to many emotionally disturbed prisoners of war returning from the Far East and suffering from "neuroses and character disorders leading to chronic social and emotional disablement." The fear of death, hunger, torture, and isolation from friends and families had led many to acquire antisocial behaviors, adjustment problems, or obsessions with feelings of guilt. As Jones developed his group approach, it became clear that the experiment was useful not only in wartime, and that many social misfits and neurotic casualties could be helped through the work to find resources within themselves to lead more fulfilling lives (Jones, 1956). Whiteley (1980) describes how the development of the unit required internal reorganization of the traditional hospital structures to incorporate the changed status of patients; thus, the unit's treatment approach moved away from an authoritarian, hierarchical style to one that was more collaborative and democratic. Patients were expected to take an active part both in their own treatment and in that of other patients. The traditional doctor–nurse–patient hierarchy became less rigid; there was more open communication among these subgroupings, and this was facilitated by daily discussions in which the whole unit, including all its subgroups, took part (Jones, 1952). Jones (1968) later described how "by the end of the War we were convinced that people living together in hospital, whether patients or staff, derived great benefit from examining, in daily community meetings, what they were doing and why they were doing it."

As time moved on, patients were referred more frequently from the courts or through rehabilitation officers and social work agencies, and some came directly from prison to treatment. Many of the population suffered from character disorders of a kind usually considered unsuitable for psychotherapy or physical treatment methods. They were classified as "inadequate and aggressive psychopaths," "schizoid personalities," "early schizophrenics," "drug addicts," "sexual perverts," and "chronic psychoneurotics" (Jones, 1952).

Jones's unit, by now sited in South London, offered a combined psychotherapeutic and sociotherapeutic approach. In 1959 it was renamed Henderson Hospital after Professor Sir David Henderson. Henderson had been Jones's mentor for 5 years during his psychiatric training in Edinburgh. He was author of the classic text *Psychopathic States* (Henderson, 1939) and originator of the descriptors "predominantly aggressive," "inadequate," and "creative" psychopaths. The unit became renowned for its two areas of specialization: first, as the center of the TC ideology, and second, as a unique treatment unit for psychopaths.

The current treatment program and philosophy have been described at length in several books and papers. The unit is described only briefly below, as more detailed descriptions of the treatment approach can be found elsewhere (Rapoport, 1960; Whiteley, 1980; Norton, 1992b, 1992c, 1996; Norton & Dolan, 1995a).

The Residents

Active participation of patients in their own and others' treatment is central to the TC philosophy; in recognition of this, community members are called "residents" rather than "patients," to avoid the passive connotations of the latter term. The hospital has up to 29 residents at any one time. There are equal numbers of women and men, and the maximum length of stay is 1 calendar year. The majority of residents are single and unemployed at the time of admission. Typical presentations include self-damaging and suicidal behavior in the context of severe emotional and psychosocial disturbance. Substance abuse, violence, and antisocial behaviors are common. Unsurprisingly, the vast majority have long histories of inpatient and outpatient therapy in a range of settings. The early onset of their personality disturbance is shown, in that more than a quarter had psychological or psychiatric treatment as children or adolescents, and a fifth were brought up in social services' care or were fostered as children.

Henderson only accepts voluntary admissions, as an essential aspect of the model is that membership of the community and engagement in therapy are voluntary. Thus residents are never admitted under any court order of treatment or section of the 1983 Mental Health Act. At the present time, approximately 50% of admissions to Henderson have a history of adult convictions, and 20% have served a prison sentence. However, in order for the community to function and for social order to be maintained, the members must feel that they have actively chosen to collaborate in the regimen. Thus at Henderson clients on parole, suspended sentences, community supervision orders, and probation orders without attached conditions of treatment are able to join the community voluntarily.

The voluntary nature of the Henderson TC model does not necessarily preclude its application within secure settings. Although members may not be voluntarily incarcerated, TCs can be provided as a voluntary option *within* that incarceration, as shown in the similar regime at HMP Grendon Underwood (as described above). Indeed, it is noteworthy that those who have attempted TC approaches but have relied upon compulsory participation have all reported less favorable outcomes of treatment than voluntary units (Craft, Stephenson, & Granger, 1964; Fink et al., 1969; Rice, Harris, & Cormier, 1992; Harris et al., 1994).

Diagnostically, the resident group can be broadly described as having severe PDs. Indeed, Henderson residents' diagnoses are mostly classifiable into Cluster B, the dramatic, erratic group of personality disorders of DSM-III-R (APA, 1987) and DSM-IV (APA, 1994). However, in a recent study of 275 referrals to Henderson, subjects averaged six DSM-III-R Axis II diagnoses each on the self-rating Personality Disorder Questionnaire (Hurt, Hyler, Frances, Clarkin, & Brent, 1984). Although the most prominent diagnosis was borderline personality disorder (in 86%), these subcategories of the diagnostic group of personality disorders hold little meaning because of the large amount of personality disorder comorbidity found in such populations. Over 70% also had antisocial personality disorder, and of the 275 patients who took part in the study, only 3% scored within a single personality disorder cluster (Dolan, Evans, & Norton, 1995).

Alongside the personality disturbance, there was considerable neurotic symptomatic disturbance in this group. A questionnaire study that used the SCL-90-R to investigate symptomatic psychological distress in residents showed high scores on anxiety, depression, interpersonal sensitivity, psychotic symptoms, hostility, and paranoid ideation. Low self-esteem combined with high levels of irritability, anxiety, and depression are often found (Norris, 1985; Dolan & Mitchell, 1994). Eating disorders are also a common part of the presentation in both women and men, although these symptoms may be covert, particularly in men. One study found high rates of previously undiagnosed and unrecognized eating problems, with 37% of women and 9% of men scoring above the clinical cutoff point on the Eating Attitudes Test (Dolan, Evans, & Norton, 1994a).

Engagement in Therapy

Regardless of treatment method or setting, regular difficulties are encountered in treating patients with PDs. Problems center on meaningful engagement and maintenance in therapy. Thus nurturing engagement is a paramount concern, and the process of engagement begins at selection for therapy.

At Henderson, a unique selection process has evolved in keeping with the ideology of the TC approach. No individual therapy is used at Henderson, and thus selection also takes place in a group setting. In acknowledgment of the importance of the "community as doctor" (Rapoport, 1960), the community as a whole takes responsibility for those decisions that in another institution would be made by the doctor (e.g., who to admit and to discharge). Prospective residents are invited to attend a weekly selection group consisting of nine senior residents (elected by the community for the purpose) and four staff members (drawn from across the multidisciplinary team). Up to four prospective residents will meet with the group. They will be invited to talk about themselves as people, their current and past difficulties, previous treatment they have received, aspects of their childhood and adolescence, and problems they would wish to address if admitted to Henderson. Following group discussion, a vote is taken, and the majority's decision is accepted. One resident records the interview, which is presented to the entire community in a large-group meeting prior to a successful candidate's admission.

Assessment via this group situation involves the active participation of the whole resident group in the community (either by being in the group or by voting for those members who will make up the nine selection representatives). This is an important feature in the functioning of the unit, and an example of the democratization that is a core tenet of the TC approach (Rapoport, 1960).

Being given the responsibility for such major decision making serves to raise the self-esteem of community members, which has been shown to be one major beneficial effect of the TC approach (Norris, 1985). A further advantage of this approach is that the current residents can often be more challenging of defensive behaviors than professionals can. If, for example, a client has been carrying out some self-destructive behavior, the residents are able to challenge them in a way that indicates that they are not taken in by any attempt to play down or rationalize this behavior, as they have experienced it themselves. First, this confrontation has a holding function, in that the client is impressed by the honest and direct but uncritical confrontation. Second, the client feels an empathic bond with others who have experienced and understand a problem because they have been through similar events themselves. Hope is instilled on the basis that clients are exposed to people like themselves who have made some progress toward resolving their difficulties in the treatment situation on offer. An inability to respond to these approaches and to drop defensive nonverbal behavior is an indicator that a client is unlikely to benefit from a TC approach.

Of the residents, only the more senior (longer than 3 months' stay) are involved in the selection process, which itself is an important ingredient of their own treatment. During the selection group, these residents experience the weight of decision making—of being on the "authority" end of a transaction for a change. Residents see themselves and their difficulties reflected in the candidates who come for admission, and they begin to realize how they appear to others (or, at least, how they used to appear). Residents also experience some empowerment in making a decision regarding another person, which might be highly influential for that person's future. Heated discussion often results over whether to admit candidates, particularly when there are issues of sexual victimization, physical violence, arson, homosexuality, or racial prejudice (Dolan, Polley, Allen, & Norton, 1991).

Research into the selection process with the SCL-90 (Derogatis, Lipman, & Covi, 1973) has shown that those not selected (approximately one-third of candidates interviewed) tend to be more somatizing, obsessive–compulsive, and phobic in their symptomatology (Dolan, Morton, & Wilson, 1990). It appears, therefore, that the selection group is picking those who have the capacity to verbalize feelings and psychosocial difficulties and to function in a group setting (among other attributes).

Even when meaningful engagement has been established, remaining in treatment long enough to make lasting personality change is problematic. At Henderson, maintenance of engagement is facilitated via the effect of a variety of features of the hospital's internal organization and operation, resulting in a therapeutic mixture of supportive containment and reality confrontation.

Psychotherapy and Sociotherapy Program

All therapy at Henderson is group-based—from the daily community meeting (involving all residents and staff) through the small-group psychotherapy (thrice weekly) to art therapy or psychodrama (weekly) (Hamer, 1993), task-centered work groups (twice weekly), and women's and men's groups (weekly) (Collis, 1987). The weekly program is perhaps more reminiscent of a school timetable; residents are in active group therapies for a minimum of 25 hours each week.

The program has an important containment effect in the community. It is rigidly organized with fixed time boundaries, which are strictly adhered to (albeit with fixed periods of leeway). Thus, for example, 10 minutes' absence from a therapy group is the maximum that is tolerated by the community before the group is officially missed. This fact is then routinely announced at the next day's community meeting, under one of the standing items of the agenda, and the resident in question needs to account for his or her absence. Missing more than two therapy groups in 1 week means that all groups the next day must be attended in full. At the end of this, a "treatability vote" is taken by the whole community. The resident in question may be discharged from the community unless an adequate reason, show of remorse, or good intentions for the future are demonstrated and accepted. Given that readmission is unlikely, discharge is the ultimate censure, but this power depends on the resident's being sufficiently engaged with the community. Again, residents' greater numbers mean that they have greater power than staff members to decide on who leaves and when.

The employment of such a group program means that residents know they are expected to be in certain places at certain times, that their absence will be noted, and that they will be called to account over this. Although it may seem on first glance that the program has strict and complicated rules, these rules are not implemented as a means of authoritarian control, but provide a structure that the community can use to encourage residents to reflect on why a rule (e.g., the rule about missing groups) has been broken. The emphasis is on "means" rather than "ends" in these discussions—on examining why the resident felt the need to do what he or she did. Thus the "culture of enquiry" is established. Such exploration encourages the resident to develop psychological-mindedness, to think before acting, and to take into account the effect that actions have on others.

There is a good deal of variety in the structured program, and a large amount of social contact also takes place in the domestic and the unstructured time. Residents undertake responsibility for many of the domestic duties in the unit. This does not just mean cooking and cleaning, but also includes planning weekly menus, ordering food, liaising with outside wholesalers, and balancing budgets. There are many niches within the sociotherapuetic milieu into which individual residents may fit. Some demand more verbal skills, and others more practical or manual ones. However concentrating on the "healthy" abilities of residents and helping them to develop skills have an important beneficial impact on self-esteem (Norris, 1985). The importance of the sociotherapy alongside the psychotherapy program is highlighted in a study of "therapeutic factors" within the Henderson TC, in which the residents recorded that 50% of the most important events in their therapy had occurred outside formal group time (Whiteley & Collis, 1987).

Implied Treatment Contract

In agreeing to admission to Henderson, residents voluntarily elect to forgo their usual means of dealing with emotional conflict (often impulsive or violent behaviors). Admission is planned, in contrast to crisis admission. The residents are also aware of the implicit contract to live by the community's rules (in particular, no violence to self, others, or property), which are a microcosm of those in the wider society, and to participate actively in their own and others' treatment. One important result of this implicit agreement is that residents at Henderson are provided with an environment in which to experience and endure psychological tension consciously, and through this to learn more adaptive ways of coping with the difficult emotions that surround reemerging memories (often of chronic abuse or neglect in childhood), and that are evident once habitual acting-out solutions are prohibited. They thus must strive to turn to the peer group for support during emotional crisis, regardless of the time of day, and to attempt to avoid their usual means of psychic tension discharge. This involves residents in taking the risks implicit in trusting others, since human relationships cannot provide the immediate, familiar, and predictable response of the bottle, the "fix," or the (self-mutilating) blade.

Rules: Breaking and Enforcing

Breaking of the rules that proscribe violence (to self, others, and property) and illicit drugs or alcohol intake occasions automatic discharge. Rule breakers are considered by the community to have discharged themselves, but may ask for permission to stay until the community meets in full the following morning (an example of "permissiveness"— i.e., tolerance of greater deviance than is normal in society at large; Rapoport, 1960). If such consensus permission is granted (following discussion, at an emergency meeting), then the miscreant has to attend all groups the following day and then undergo a "read-mission" vote.

The resident in crisis needs to account for the rule-breaking behavior and its antecedents, and also to experience its immediate consequences, all of which are discussed and explored. The resident must also, either there and then or further on in treatment, ask for support before any further acting out becomes a temptation. This represents a very different situation from that which habitually attends rule breaking in wider "institutional" society; for example, the time delay between committing a crime and being apprehended or accounting for the behavior in a court of law, as well as experiencing its consequences, may be very great. In an analogous way, in hospitals there may be an unhelpful delay in decision making, especially when the relevant decisions are made only at the weekly ward round!

Instead of a judge and jury sitting above the rule breaker, there is at Henderson a peer group sitting on the same level, whose members nonetheless carry out a role of social censure or approval (as appropriate). At times the residents' peer group is harshly moralistic—seeming to act automatically, without reflection or empathy, to discharge one of its members and, in this way, enacting a complementary relationship. Ironically, it is the staff members who are then required to act to avert an overpunitive and nonindividualizing response by the resident group's acting upon itself; the intervention restores a balance in the feedback by preventing an oversimplified view of either victim or perpetrator. (It should be noted that the resident group has a larger say in the timing of discharge of fellow residents than does the staff group, since this is the result of a democratic, "one person, one vote" system following discussion, if a given resident is not felt to be genuinely striving to change or has broken a major rule of the community.)

It is perhaps surprising that enforcing the community's rules at Henderson is relatively easy. The major reason is that the residents themselves enforce rules, having been on the receiving end of intoxicated, disordered, violent, neglectful, or abusing others previously (i.e., rule breakers). Rule enforcement by residents gives power to people who have often been disempowered victims. The tendency is toward a harsh, unempathic, and unthinking rule enforcement, and at times staff members need to act to mitigate this effect. Inevitably, new residents will test out and challenge Henderson's novel (albeit "institutional") environment, and they attempt to involve others (peers and staff) in an interpersonal enactment of conflict—often via violence to self, others, or property. In other words, they "bump up" against the community's rules and feel the community's "counterpunch." Unavoidably, this does happen, and at times staff members need to take the major responsibility for trying to unlock the projective systems that underpin what, for example, may appear as scapegoating of a resident by his or her peers.

Response to Crisis

If an important rule (e.g., one occasioning automatic discharge) has been broken, or a resident is particularly distressed or suicidal, and a discussion of this cannot be delayed until the next day's community meeting, then the "top three" senior residents can call an emergency meeting at any time of day or night. All community members must attend or else be on a discharge vote themselves. The various resources of the community may be mobilized in order to support the resident or residents in question. At night this may entail others' sleeping in or outside an individual's bedroom (each resident has a single bedroom), or a number of residents, together with the distressed one(s), may occupy a larger room with their mattresses. Staff members, who also attend the emergency meetings, do not participate in providing this practical support, and no psychotropic medication is ever prescribed.

There is much emotional and practical support in the community for those residents viewed as being deserving, and especially for those who have previously provided such support for others or who are seen to be genuinely tackling their problems. Tolerance, however, is limited, and this fact can actually be beneficial, resulting in confrontation over the distressed role's having been overplayed and having become an act of manipulation. If fellow residents have repeatedly sat up with a disturbed member at night, for example, they will begin to expect a change from a deviant way of expressing distress and an increased use of the therapy groups during daylight hours! Thus, compared to many other settings, deviant behavior (as a way of expressing otherwise unbearable psychic pain) is not reinforced, but genuine struggling with psychological difficulties is. There is no "special treatment" by staff and therefore no endless supply of one-to-one relationships, which can tend to reinforce sick or manipulative behavior.

Disengaging from the Community

For those who stay, Henderson has often become a place of special attachment and security, and leaving is difficult. For some residents, leaving has been synonymous with expulsion in the past, and often the community will be set up by a resident (perhaps through rule breaking) in order for this pattern to be repeated. Once this strategy is seen through, however, the resident is supported, encouraged, cajoled, or shamed into owning his or her feelings in the face of leaving. Aggression is often an easier emotion to tolerate than sadness, and also a camouflage for it. Repeated working through is necessary if the resident is to "leave properly" (Wilson, 1985). In order to facilitate this, there is a weekly "leavers'" group and a thrice-weekly "welfare" group. In these groups, both practical and emotional issues are explored and (ideally) resolved in this setting. Just as the new residents have their own small group for the first 3 weeks, which involves a senior resident, so the "leavers'" group involves a nonleaving resident. Information from this group is regularly fed back into the community meeting.

OUTCOME OF TREATMENT AT HENDERSON:
A SUMMARY OF RECENT RESEARCH

Henderson Hospital has produced a range of outcome research since the 1950s, which has consistently demonstrated the efficacy of treatment in terms of psychological, behavioral, and service usage variables. However, much of the early work from Henderson suffers from the methodological flaws discussed earlier, in that it used poorly defined outcome criteria or proxy measures of personality disorders and/or lacked comparison or control samples (Rapoport, 1960; Tuxford, 1961; Taylor, 1966; Whiteley, 1970; Copas & Whiteley, 1976; Norris, 1985; Dolan, Evans, & Wilson, 1992).

One treatment outcome study completed in 1984 did include a comparison group of nontreated referrals, although recidivism and psychiatric hospital admission were used as outcome variables. It was demonstrated that 41% of admitted patients were free of reconviction or readmission at a 3-year follow-up, compared with only 23% of the nonadmitted group. Five-year follow-up rates were 36% and 19%, respectively. The study also demonstrated that outcome improved with length of stay in treatment, with 62% of those admitted for over 6 months and 71% of those who stayed over 9 months being free of reconviction or readmission at the 3-year follow-up (Copas, O'Brien, Roberts, & Whiteley, 1984).

In order to improve on previous research designs, Henderson Hospital has recently established a large outcome study that will evaluate changes in core PD alongside other measures of change (behavioral features, service usage, and cost offset evaluation). It has also been possible to use more adequate comparison samples than previously applied. The first year's follow-up results from this study are summarized here.

Sampling and Procedures

The initial sample cohort of 567 subjects consisted of all those who were referred to Henderson Hospital between September 1990 and December 1994, and who were discharged from treatment by December 1995. Eventually, 225 of these referrals were admitted for treatment. Of the 342 nonadmissions, 100 (29.2%) were deemed unsuitable for admission by the hospital; 176 (51.5%) were withdrawn, canceled, or did not attend for assessment/admission; and 66 (29.2%) had funding of their treatment refused by their local district health authority (DHA).[1]

The unit accepts referrals nationally from a wide range of health care, social, and criminal justice services; thus, the 567 patients were referred by a variety of professionals. The majority of referrers were psychiatrists (67.5%), the remainder being probation officers (8.8%), general practitioners (GPs) (5.7%), social workers (4.9%), and psychologists (3.1%). Other professionals, such as community psychiatric nurses and solicitors, made up 9.5%. Finally, 0.5% of patients were self-referred.

On referral, all patients were sent a psychological and behavioral questionnaire pack that included, among other measures, the Borderline Syndrome Index (BSI; Conte, Plutchick, Karasu, & Jerrett, 1980) and the Multi-Impulsivity Scale (MIS; Lacey & Evans, 1992). A follow-up questionnaire pack was sent 1 year after referral (for nonadmitted patients) or 1 year after discharge (for admitted patients).

One year after either referral or discharge, a short survey form was sent to each patient's referrer and/or GP. This form requested information on (1) whether the professional had had any contact with the patient in the past year—and, if so, whether the patient had been (2) admitted for inpatient, outpatient, or day patient treatment; (3) if so, for what periods; (4) whether the patient had been prescribed medication for psychological symptoms; (5) whether the patient had used any nonstatutory services; and (6) whether the patient had offended. A patient version of this form was also sent to each patient at the same time as the clinical evaluation form.

A total of 137 participants completed both a baseline and a follow-up questionnaire pack. Of this final sample, 70 had been admitted for treatment and 67 were not admitted. Of the latter, nonadmitted sample, 18 (26.9%) were refused admission by Henderson on clinical grounds; 27 (40.3%) did not attend assessment or admission ;and 22 (32.8%) had funding of their treatment refused by their local DHA.

A response from either the referrer or the GP was received for 514 (91%) of subjects. However, in 90 (15%) cases, neither professional had seen the patient since the referral. Thus a "positive trace" was recorded for 424 cases (75%), who formed the final study sample. This was 177 admitted patients and 247 nonadmitted patients (made up of 84 deemed unsuitable for admission, 119 who were canceled/withdrawn, and 44 who were refused funding).

Findings

Comparison of admissions with nonadmitted referrals showed a significantly greater improvement in the average BSI score of the admitted than of the nonadmitted group. The magnitude of the change for admitted patients was positively correlated with length of stay in treatment ($r = .38$).

However, the ideal treatment goal of Henderson (and the wish of most patients) is not simply to show an overall group average reduction in scale scores on a measure (as shown in statistical significance tests), but for the patients to return to normal functioning. Therefore, the data-analytic methods of Jacobson, Follette, and Revenstorf (1984) were used to provide a means to evaluate of the clinical relevance of the changes in individuals 1 year after leaving therapy. With this approach, it was shown that a far greater proportion of the treated group (43%) than of the nontreated group (18%) showed reliable and clinically significant improvements (this was also 18% of the nonfunded group) (Dolan, Warren, Norton, & Menzies, 1996).

One-year change scores for the MIS summarized across items were small and nonsignificant for the nonadmitted sample; however, the admitted sample showed considerable, statistically significant improvements in both impulsive urges and impulsive actions. When group comparisons were made for all 22 items individually, changes tended towards greater reductions in impulsivity in the admitted group than in the nonadmitted group. Summing these individual change scores again gave highly statistically significant and quite large group differences for urges, actions, and total scores (Warren, Evans, & Dolan, 1996).

Significantly fewer of the admitted than of the nonadmitted sample had been admitted to a hospital (25.8% vs. 34.8%) or had offended (12.4% vs. 23.5%) in the previous year; however, significantly more of the admitted group had used outpatient services (62.7% vs. 48.5%). There were no differences in the proportions of each group who had been prescribed psychotropic medication (31% vs. 30.4%) or used other treatment resources (11.3% vs. 12.6%).

When the admitted sample was divided into those 86 patients who stayed over 3 months ("treated" group) and those 91 who stayed less than 3 months ("dropouts"), there was a clear effect of length of stay. Significantly fewer of the treated group than of the dropouts had been admitted to a hospital (16.3% vs. 33.0%), and there was a nonsignificant tendency for fewer of them to have offended (7% vs. 17.6%) or to be on medication (24.4% vs. 37.4%). There were no significant differences in the proportions of each group who had been in outpatient treatment (58.1% vs. 69.2%) or used other treatment resources (11.6% vs. 11.0%).

Although those treated at Henderson used markedly fewer services than those not admitted in the following year, the approach used above cannot show *changes* in service uptake of individual residents following treatment. In a more detailed analysis of the changes in the costs of service use in a subgroup of 24 admissions to the hospital, these residents were found to have used an average of £13,966 worth of psychiatric and prison services in the one year prior to their admission to the unit but only £1,308 worth of services in the year following treatment. This annual saving of £12,600 would offset the average £25,641 cost of these patients' treatment at Henderson within 2 years (Dolan et al., 1996; Menzies et al., 1993).

DISCUSSION

These findings, all coming from a single study cohort, demonstrate that treatment at Henderson Hospital can effect changes not only in those impulsive behaviors associated with PDs and in health and penal service usage, but, importantly, in core PD features. The study, along with the outcome results from other TCs within a variety of criminal justice and health service settings (reviewed above), forms part of the growing consensus that democratic TC methods can be used successfully to treat clients with PDs.

The methodological purist will find flaws in all the studies cited earlier. Most early studies were uncontrolled, and, indeed, many did not even use comparative samples. The use of an unfunded comparison sample in the recent Henderson research allows greater confidence that the findings are not simply due to selection effects. However, the practical and ethical difficulties involved in random controlled studies mean that such approaches are unlikely in this area. The issues of methodological rigor in research into treatment for personality disorders have been discussed more thoroughly elsewhere (Norton & Dolan, 1995b; Dolan & Coid, 1993). Despite the methodological shortcomings, it is unarguable that the TC model is far better supported by research studies than are any other treatment strategies for this group. In the absence of conclusive evidence of the effectiveness of *any* treatment, we ought to protect and develop those therapies that can demonstrate some efficacy in treating PDs (Dolan & Coid, 1993).

It should not, of course, be argued that TC treatment is a panacea. The approach is unsuitable for many PD patients, as they are unable to take on the responsibilities associated with communal living or to submit to the painful examination of their feelings and behaviors that is required. However, there is still an underprovision of TC units for PD clients. A large cross-sectional survey of psychiatric illness and treatment needs in British prisoners recently assessed 5% of the total male and 25% of the total female prison population. It was estimated that 2,000 people currently in prison In England and Wales were in need of TC treatment (Maden, Swinton, & Gunn, 1994).

Even where the pure democratic TC model is inappropriate, aspects of the TC model may be applicable to dealing with PDs in other settings. The nature of the institution in question will have an important bearing on how much of, and how far, the democratic TC model might be appropriately utilized. However, certain aspects of the model that may be translated into other settings are outlined below.

Homogeneous Patient Group

In a residential setting, the clinical experience is often that a homogeneous population of personality-disordered individuals is more successfully treated in a structured therapeutic environment than is a smaller number of personality-disordered patients in a heterogeneous (e.g., acute or long-stay) psychiatric ward, which is not so structured or rich in terms of an active treatment model or so consistent in its application. Among patients with heterogeneous diagnoses, a small number of PD patients can be seriously detrimental to overall function of the ward, as is often shown by the a disproportionate demand for staff time and the curtailment of a ward's activities when a single PD patient acts out (Miller, 1989).

A Single Treatment Approach

There is a need, as far as possible, for all staff members involved in the treatment setting to agree on a single treatment approach (if not a formal treatment contract) for a given patient, or at least to discuss openly among themselves their differences of opinion so that these do not remain covert. This is much easier with a homogeneous patient group and only one treatment approach, as in the democratic TC model. Even then, however, the acting-out patient group may well exert pressure on the staff to respond with an authoritarian style and to become involved in power-based rather than empathic relationships. This can result in therapeutic staff members' being experienced as malicious "prison warders," and hence, in the minds of residents, punitive, alien, and untrustworthy. Professionals may be, in effect, set against one another by the provocative behavior of their charges, who, on the one hand, elicit sympathy and understanding (as victims) and, on the other, evoke a punitive response (as perpetrators of rule breaking via acting-out behavior). Importantly, more adaptive coping strategies or support must be offered to patients if they are to stop discharging emotional conflicts via acting out. Staff members need to be aware of the nature of the pressures exerted on them by such patients and to be able to construct their own means of mutual support and self-examination in order to minimize the effects of the divisive and polarizing "splitting" mechanisms described above. Staff groups also need to be empowered with greater responsibility and accountability for the discharge and transfer of those in their care. Only in this way can they be enabled to maintain their own capacity for mature dependence (rather than infantile dependence within a hierarchical structure) in a way that acts as a role model for patients, who are thereby potentially enabled to develop their own capacities for maturation and individualization.

Participation and Involvement of Patients

Although the participation of patients in an authentic negotiation of their own treatment goals and involvement in the treatment of fellow patients may be difficult to achieve in more secure settings than Henderson, without doubt there are ways in which progress can be made toward greater participation. This should include collaborative involvement with the staff in the day-to-day running of ward activities. For this to happen, it is important to have PD patients under one roof and to have them meet formally and regularly, together with the staff, in a large group (community) setting. This means that the given institution has to confront any fears engendered by such an idea and to be generally supportive of such a development.

Development of Horizontal Relationships

As described above, the internal organization of the institution can provide a setting in which acting-out patients are enabled to support and educate one another, at least to some degree. This allows them to develop psychosocially through more horizontal relationships with peers and staff, rather than to have reinforced authoritarian (vertical) relationships, which only serve to elicit and promote oppositional, antiauthority, and complementary behavior and relationships. This requires staff structures that are sufficiently flexible and that avoid overly hierarchical and authoritarian styles. This ideal is harder to achieve as the need for custodial security increases; however, failure to obviate the patients' need to act out often leads to a perceived need by staff members to increase the level of security of accommodation.

Appropriate Recognition of Change within a Range of Environments

Within a given community, the flow of patients through it needs to be sufficient to minimize malignant or fixed structures. These come about if too many senior patients are forced to remain in an environment that can no longer sustain their continued emotional and social development. Necessarily exploitative means of survival are found by a group of PD patients under such conditions. Patients who are genuinely developing need to move through a range of treatment settings of appropriate sophistication, ultimately leading to discharge. Therefore, a comprehensive range of facilities, is required to enable the successful patient, who manages personality maturation within a secure setting, to maintain therapeutic momentum.

Such movement should ideally be both planned and dictated or dictated by clinical needs, and not subject to time delays (e.g., those of a remote ministry of justice, as in the case of certain detained patients). Many of the existing traditional institutions function so as to provide patients with abrupt environmental transitions in terms of timing, degree of psychological maturity required, or both; they cannot be adequately prepared for such transitions, and cannot function adaptively in their new environments (especially if the demands of the new are too high—i.e., not "articulated" to those of the old). In this way, earlier psychological traumas associated with separation and loss are repeated in treatment or custodial settings—and, again, without the possibility of learning from the traumatizing experience. Attention must be paid to psychologically preparing an individual for any such move so that attendant emotions can be integrated with the event, leaving time to say a proper "goodbye." This is particularly the case if it is known that the "gap" between environments is large (in terms of the psychological maturity required of the patient to survive and flourish in it), as it is, for example, between inpatient and day patient or between day patient and outpatient settings.

CONCLUSION

In conclusion, the democratic TC approach (including adaptations of its philosophy within other institutional settings) offers great hope for the treatment of individuals with severe PDs, who have previously been deemed "untreatable" in conventional psychiatric systems. Although not all services will be able to establish a pure TC unit, some lessons concerning the institutional management of PD people who act out are reasonably clear and should not now need to be repeatedly learned (and forgotten) by successive generations of professionals.

However, it remains an issue that the whole area of personality disorder treatment research is at present hampered by methodological difficulties. If our knowledge is to progress, improved method and logic must inform future research. Our ignorance about treatability is treatable; we do now know what we need to do to correct the situation. The problem is that (like treating our clients), this will be a difficult, long-term case needing input from a variety of services and disciplines. The treatment of PDs rarely involves one treatment modality or one therapist, but is usually a multiagency reshaping procedure extending over a long period. Yet there is a noticeable absence of intersetting and interagency outcome studies. It seems now time for researchers to consider collaborative international studies, in order to share and improve all our knowledge about the treatment of this difficult client group.

NOTE

1. Since the restructuring of the National Health Service, patients' treatment in national specialist units such as Henderson must be paid for by their local DHA. Some DHAs have refused to fund admission to Henderson, although this decision is often made on financial rather than clinical grounds.

REFERENCES

American Psychiatric Association (APA). (1987). *Diagnostic and statistical manual of mental disorders* (3rd ed., rev.). Washington, DC: Author.

American Psychiatric Association (APA). (1994). *Diagnostic and statistical manual of mental disorders* (4th ed.). Washington, DC: Author.

Bannon, E. (1995). The effectiveness of psychotherapy for personality disorders: Recommendations for future study. In *Abstracts: Fourth International Congress on Personality Disorders, Dublin, Ireland.*

Bearden, C., Lavelle, N., Buysee, D., Karp, J. F., & Frank, E. (1996). Personality pathology and time remission in depressed outpatients treated with interpersonal psychotherapy. *Journal of Personality Disorders, 10*(2), 164–173.

Bion, W. R. (1946). The leaderless group project. *Bulletin if the Menninger Clinic, 10*(3), 77–81.

Bloor, M., McKeganey, N., & Fonkert, D. (1988). *One foot in Eden: A sociological study of the range of therapeutic community practice.* New York: Routledge.

Bridger, H. (1996). The Northfield Experiment. *Therapeutic Communities, 17*(2), 81–86. (Original work published 1946 in *Bulletin of the Menninger Clinic*)

Budman, S., Demby, A., Soldz, S., & Merry, J. (1996). Time-limited group psychotherapy for patients with personality disorder: Outcome and dropouts. *Internal Journal of Group Psychotherapy, 46*(3), 357–377.

Carney, F. L. (1976). Treatment of aggressive patients. In D. J. Madden & J. R. Lion (Eds.), *Rage, hate, assault and other forms of violence.* New York: Spectrum.

Cavior, H. E., & Schmidt, A. (1978). A test for the effectiveness of a differential treatment strategy. *Criminal Justice and Behaviour, 5*, 131–139.

Chiesa, M., Iacoponi, E., & Morris, M. (1996). Changes in health service utilization by patients with severe personality disorders before and after inpatient psychosocial treatment. *British Journal of Psychotherapy, 12*(4), 501–512.

Chiswick, D. (1992). The special hospitals: A problem of clinical credibility. *Psychiatric Bulletin, 6*, 130–132.

Clark, D. H. (1965). The therapeutic community: Concept, practice and future. *British Journal of Psychiatry, 11*, 947–954.

Coid, J., & Cordess, C. (1992). Compulsory admission of dangerous psychopaths. *British Medical Journal, 304*, 1581–1582.

Coid, J. W. (1992). DSM-III diagnosis in criminal psychopaths: A way forward. *Criminal Behaviour and Mental Health, 2*, 78–94.

Coid, J. W. (1993). An affective syndrome in female psycopaths with borderline personality disorder? *British Journal of Psychiatry, 162*, 641–650.

Collis, M. (1987). Women's groups in the therapeutic community: The Henderson experience. *Therapeutic Communities, 8*(1), 175–184.

Conte, H. R., Plutchick, R., Karasu, T. B., & Jerrett, I. (1980). A self-report borderline scale: Discriminant validity and preliminary norms. *Journal of Nervous and Mental Disease, 168,* 428–435.

Cooke, D. J. (1989). Containing violent prisoners: An analysis of Barlinnie Special Unit. *British Journal of Criminology, 129,* 129–143.

Copas, J. B., O'Brien, M., Roberts, J., & Whiteley, S. (1984). Treatment outcome in personality disorder: The effect of social, psychological and behavioural variables. *Personality and Individual Differences, 5(5)* 565–573.

Copas, J. B., & Whiteley, J. S. (1976). Predicting success in the treatment of psychopaths. *British Journal of Psychiatry, 129,* 388–392.

Craft, M., Stephenson, G., & Granger, C. (1964). A controlled trial of authoritarian and self-governing regimes with adolescent psychopaths. *American Journal of Orthopsychiatry, 34,* 543–554.

Cullen, E. (1993). The Grendon reconviction study, Part 1. *Prison Service Journal,* No. 90, 35–37.

Cullen, E. (1994). Grendon: The therapeutic prison that works. *Therapeutic Communities, 15(4),* 301–311.

Davidson, S. (1996). Notes on a group of ex-prisoners of war. *Therapeutic Communities, 17(2),* 100–109. (Original work published 1946 in *Bulletin of the Menninger Clinic*)

De Leon, G. (1983). The next therapeutic community: Autocracy, and other notes toward integrating old and new therapeutic communities. *Therapeutic Communities, 4(4),* 249–261.

Derogatis, L. R., Lipman, R. S., & Cori, L. (1973). SCL-90: An out-patient psychiatric rating scale—preliminary report. *Psychopharmacology Bulletin, 9(1),* 13–28.

Dewar, M. C. (1946). The technique of group psychotherapy. *Bulletin of the Menninger Clinic, 10(3).*

Digeur, L., Barber, J. P., & Luborsky, L. (1993). Three concomitants: Personality disorder, psychiatric severity and outcome of dynamic psychotherapy of major depression. *American Journal of Psychiatry, 150,* 1246–1248.

Dolan, B., & Coid, J. (1993). *Psychopathic and antisocial personality disorders: Treatment and research issues.* London: Gaskell.

Dolan, B., Evans, C., & Norton, K. (1994a). Eating disorders in male and female patients with personality disorders. *Journal of Personality Disorders, 8(1),* 17–27.

Dolan, B., Evans, C., & Norton, K. (1994b). Funding treatment for offender patients: Do financial considerations trump clinical need? *Journal of Forensic Psychiatry, 5(2),* 263–274.

Dolan, B., Evans, C., & Norton, K. (1995). The multiple Axis-II diagnosis of personality disorders. *British Journal of Psychiatry, 166,* 107–112.

Dolan, B., Evans, C. D. H., & Wilson, J. (1992). Neurotic symptomatology and length of stay in a therapeutic community. *Therapeutic Communities, 13(3),* 171–177.

Dolan, B., & Mitchell, E. (1994). Personality disorder and psychological disturbance of female prisoners: A comparison with women referred for NHS treatment of personality disorder. *Criminal Behaviour and Mental Health, 4,* 130–142.

Dolan, B., Morton, A., & Wilson, J. (1990). Selection of admissions to a therapeutic community using a group setting: Association with degree and type of psychological distress. *International Journal of Social Psychiatry, 36(4),* 265–271.

Dolan, B., & Norton, K. (1992). One year after the NHS bill: The extracontractual referral system and Henderson Hospital. *Psychiatric Bulletin, 16,* 745–747.

Dolan, B., Polley, K., Allen, R., & Norton, K. (1991). Addressing racism in psychiatry: Is the therapeutic community approach applicable? *International Journal of Social Psychiatry, 37,* 71–79.

Dolan, B., Warren, F., Norton, K., & Menzies, D. (1996). Cost-offset following therapeutic community treatment of personality disorder. *Psychiatric Bulletin, 20(7),* 413–417.

Evans, C. (1994). TC methods within the penal system: Is research on possible selection variables as simple as it sounds? Or should it be simpler? *Therapeutic Communities, 15(4),* 319–324.

Fava, M., Bouffides, E., Pava, J. A., McCarthy, M. K., Steingard, R. J., Rosenbaum, J. F. (1994). Personality disorder: Comorbidity with major depression and response to fluoxetine treatment. *Psychotherapy and Psychosomatics, 62,* 160–167.

Feldbrugge, J. T. T. M. (1992). Rehabilitation of patients with personality disorders: Patient–staff collaboration used as a working model and tool. *Criminal Behaviour and Mental Health, 2*(2), 169–177.

Fink, L., Derby, W. N., & Martin, J. P. (1969). Psychiatry's new role in corrections. *American Journal of Psychiatry, 126,* 124–128.

Foulkes, S. H. (1996). Principles and practice of group therapy. *Therapeutic Communities, 17*(2), 95–99. (Original work published 1946 in *Bulletin of the Menninger Clinic*)

Frank, A. F. (1991). The therapeutic alliances of borderline patients. In J. F. Clarkin, E. Marziali, & H. Munroe-Blum (Eds.), *Borderline personality disorder: Clinical and empirical perspectives.* New York: Guilford Press.

Gray, W. J. (1974). Grendon Prison. *British Journal of Hospital Medicine, 299*–308.

Gunn, J. (1978). The treatment of psychopaths. In Gaind & Hudson (Eds.), *Current themes in psychiatry.* London: Macmillan.

Hamer, N. (1993, Winter). Some connections between art therapy and psychodrama in a therapeutic community *Inscape,* pp. 23–26.

Harris, G. T., & Rice, M. E. (1995). Reply to Whiteley [Letter]. *Therapeutic Communities, 16*(2), 147–148.

Harris, G., Rice, M., & Cormier, C. (1994). Psychopaths: Is the therapeutic community therapeutic? *Therapeutic Communities, 15*(4), 283–300.

Henderson, D. K. (1939). *Psychopathic states.* London: Norton.

Høglend, P. (1993). Personality disorders and long-term outcome after brief dynamic psychotherapy. *Journal of Personality Disorders, 7*(2), 168–181.

Home Office Research and Planning Unit. (1996). [Unpublished report.]

Hurt, S. W., Hyler, S. E., Frances, A., Clarkin, J. F., & Brent, R. (1984). Assessing borderline personality disorder with self-report, clinical interview, or semi-structured interview. *American Journal of Psychiatry, 141,* 1228–1231.

Hyde, C., & Harrower-Wilson, C. (1995). Resource consumption in psychiatric intensive care: The cost of aggression. *Psychiatric Bulletin, 19,* 73–76.

Jacobson, N. S., Follette, W. C., & Revenstorf, D. (1984). Psychotherapy outcome research: Methods for reporting variability and evaluating clinical significance. *Behavior Therapy, 15,* 336–352.

Jessen, J. L., & Roosenberg, A. M. (1971). Treatment results at the Dr. Henri van der Hoeven Clinic, Utrecht, The Netherlands. In *Excerpta Medica International Congress Series: No. 274. Proceedings of the V World Congress of Psychiatry.* Amsterdam: Excerpta Medica.

Jones, L. (1988). *The hospital annexe: A preliminary evaluation report* (DPS Report, Series II, No. 164). London: Directorate of Psychological Services, Home Office.

Jones, L. (1990). *The use of repertory grid technique as a tool for the evaluation of a therapeutic community.* Unpublished master's thesis

Jones, M. (1942). Group psychotherapy. *British Medical Journal, ii,* 276–278.

Jones, M. (1946). Rehabilitation of forces neurosis patients to civilian life. *British Medical Journal, i,* 533–535.

Jones, M. (1952). *Social psychiatry.* London: Tavistock.

Jones, M. (1956). Industrial rehabilitation of mental patients still in hospital. *Lancet, ii,* 985–986.

Jones, M. (1968). *Beyond the therapeutic community: Social learning and social psychiatry.* New Haven, CT: Yale University Press.

Karterud, S., Vaglum, S., Friis, S. et al. (1992). A day hospital therapeutic community for personality disorder: An empirical evaluation of containment functioning. *Journal of Nervous and Mental Disease, 180*(4), 238–243.

Kennard, D., & Roberts, J. (1983). *An introduction to therapeutic communities.* London: Routledge & Kegan Paul.

Lacey, J. H., & Evans, C. (1992). The impulsivist: A multi-impulsive personality disorder. *British Journal of Addictions, 81,* 641–649.

Lewis, G., & Appleby, L. (1988). Personality disorders: The patients psychiatrists dislike. *British Journal of Psychiatry, 153,* 44–49.

Maden, A., Swinton, M., & Gunn, J. (1994). Therapeutic community treatment: A survey of unmet need among sentenced prisoners. *Therapeutic Communities, 15*(4), 229–236.

Main, T. (1946). The hospital as a therapeutic institution. *Bulletin of the Menninger Clinic, 10,* 66–68.

Martin, R. L., Cloninger, C. R., Guze, S. B., et al. (1985). Mortality in a follow up of 500 psychiatric outpatients: Cause-specific mortality. *Archives of General Psychiatry, 42,* 58–66.

Mehlum, L., Friis, S., Irion, T., et al. (1991). Personality disorders 2–5 years after treatment: A prospective follow-up study. *Acta Psychiatrica Scandinavica, 84,* 72–77.

Menzies, D., Dolan, B., & Norton, K. (1993). Are short term savings worth long term costs? Funding treatment for personality disorders. *Psychiatric Bulletin, 17,* 517–519.

Miller, L. J. (1989). Inpatient management of borderline personality disorder: A review and update. *Journal of Personality Disorders, 3*(2), 122–134.

Murto, K. (1991). *Towards a changing community ? The development of Anton Makarenko and Maxwell Jones' communities* (Jyväskylä, Finland: University of Jyväskylä Studies in Education, Psychology and Social Research No. 79).

Norris, M. (1985). Changes in patients during treatment at Henderson Hospital therapeutic community during 1977–1981. *British Journal of Medical Psychology, 56,* 135–143.

Norton, K. (1992a). The health of the nation: The impact of personality disorder on "key areas." *Postgraduate Medical Journal, 68,* 350–354.

Norton, K. (1992b). A culture of enquiry: Its preservation or loss. *Therapeutic Communities, 13*(1), 3–26.

Norton, K. (1992c). Treating personality disordered individuals: The Henderson Hospital model. *Criminal Behaviour and Mental Health, 2,* 180–191.

Norton, K. (1996). Managing difficult personality disordered patients. *Advances in Psychiatric Treatment, 2,* 202–210.

Norton, K., & Dolan, B. (1995a). Acting-out and the institutional response. *Journal of Forensic Psychiatry, 6*(2), 317–332.

Norton, K., & Dolan, B. (1995b). Assessing change in personality disorder. *Current Opinion in Psychiatry, 8,*

Ogloff, J. R. P., Wong, S., & Greenwood, A. (1990). Treating criminal psychopaths in a therapeutic community program. *Behavioral Sciences and the Law, 8,* 181–190.

Perry, J. C., Lavori, P. W., & Hoke, L. (1987). A Markow model for predicting levels of psychiatric service use in borderline and antisocial personality disorders and bipolar type II affective disorder. *Journal of Psychiatric Research, 21*(3), 213–232.

Quality Assurance Project. (1991). Treatment outlines for antisocial personality disorder. *Australian and New Zealand Journal of Psychiatry, 25,* 541–547.

Rapoport, R. (1960). *The community as doctor.* London: Tavistock.

Reed J. (1994). *Report of the Working Group on Psychopathic Disorder.* London: Department of Health, Home Office.

Reiss, D., Grubin, D., & Meux, C. (1996). Young 'psychopaths' in a special hospital: Treatment and outcome. *British Journal of Psychiatry, 168,* 99–104.

Rice, M. E., Harris, G. T., & Cormier, C. A. (1992). An evaluation of a maximum security therapeutic community for psychopaths and other mentally disordered offenders. *Law and Human Behaviour, 16,* 399–412.

Robertson, G. (1987). Mentally abnormal offenders: Manner of death. *British Medical Journal, 295,* 632–634.

Robertson, G., & Gunn, J. (1987). A ten year follow-up of men discharged from Grendon Prison. *British Journal of Psychiatry, 151,* 674–678.

Rosser, R. M., Birch, S., Bond, H., Denford, J., & Schachter, J. (1987). Five-Year Follow-up of Patients Treated with Inpatient Psychotherapy at the Cassel Hospital for Nervous Diseases. *Journal of the Royal Society of Medicine, 80,* 549–555.

Ruegg, R., & Frances, A. (1995). New research in personality disorders. *Journal of Personality Disorders, 9*(1), 1–48.

Sandhu, H. S. (1970). Therapy With violent psychopaths in an Indian Prison Community. *International Journal of Offender Therapies, 14,* 138–144.

Serin, R. C., Amos, N. L. (1995). The role of psychopathy in the assessment of dangerousness. *International Journal of Law and Psychiatry, 18*(2), 231–238.

Sewell, R., & Clark, C. (1982). *An evaluation study of "The Annexe," a therapeutic community in Wormwood Scrubs prison.* Unpublished report from the Home Office Prison Department.

Shearin, E. N., & Linehan, M. M. (1994). Dialectical behaviour therapy for borderline personality disorder: Theoretical and empirical foundations. *Acta Psychiatrica Scandinavica, 89*(Suppl. 379), 61–68.

Stermac, L. E. (1986). Anger control treatment for forensic patients. *Journal of Interpersonal Violence, 1,* 446–457.

Taylor, F. (1966). Methods of care: Henderson Hospital. In M. Craft (Ed.), *Psychopathic disorders.* Oxford: Pergamon Press.

Tuxford, J. (1961). *Treatment as a circular process.* London: Edward's Hospital Fund.

Tyrer, P., & Seivewright, N. (1988). *Personality disorders: Diagnosis, management and course.* London: Wright.

Vaglum, P., Friis, S., Irion, T., Johns, S., Karterud, S., Larsen, F., & Vaglum, S. (1990). Treatment response of severe and non-severe personality disorders in a therapeutic community day unit. *Journal of Personality Disorders, 4*(2), 161–172.

Van Emmerik, J. (1987). Detention at the government's pleasure: A follow-up study of patients released from the Dr. Henri Van Der Hoeven Clinic. In M. J. M. Brand-Koolen (Ed.), *Studies on the Dutch prison system.* Kuger.

Warren, F. (1994). What do we mean by a therapeutic community for offenders? *Therapeutic Communities, 15*(4), 312–319.

Warren, F., & Dolan, B. (1996). Treating the untreatable: TC treatment of severe personality disorder. *Therapeutic Communities, 17*(3), 205–213.

Warren, F., Evans, C., & Dolan, B. (1996). *The impact of specialist TC treatment on impulsivity in personality disorder.* Manuscript submitted for publication.

Wexler, H. K. (1995). The success of therapeutic communities for substance abusers in American prisons (review). *Journal of Psychoactive Drugs, 27*(1), 57–66.

Whiteley, J. S. (1970). The response of psychopaths to a therapeutic community. *British Journal of Psychiatry, 116,* 517–529.

Whiteley, J. S. (1980). The Henderson Hospital. *Therapeutic Communities, 1,* 38–58.

Whiteley, J. S., & Collis, M. (1987). Therapeutic factors applied to group psychotherapy in a therapeutic community. Therapeutic Communities, 8(1), 21–31.

Whiteley, S. (1995). The effectiveness of therapeutic communities for psychopaths [Letter]. *Therapeutic Communities, 16*(2), 146.

Wilson. J. (1985). Leaving home as a theme in a therapeutic community. *Therapeutic Communities, 6*(2), 71–78.

27

The Management of Dangerous Psychopaths in Prison

JEREMY W. COID

Many mental health care professionals forget that there is a subgroup of psychopaths exist whose psychopathology is so severe, and whose associated behavioral disorders are so potentially dangerous to others, that they cannot be safely contained within a therapeutic setting. Most treatment settings accommodate only those patients who have been selected as suitable for and likely to respond to the treatments they offer. Mental health legislation in many countries facilitates this process of selection. In some, it can also facilitate the transfer elsewhere of an individual who has not responded to treatment. In essence, secure hospital services can usually rid themselves of dangerous and untreatable psychopaths. Prisons, on the other hand, do not have the luxury of being able to refuse inmates.

Within the context of the prison environment, management's responsibility is to maintain good order and discipline in the day-to-day running of the institution. Staff members in prisons do not always understand the behavior of psychopathic individuals as the outward manifestation of their underlying psychopathology. Disordered behavior may be viewed more simplistically as the transgression of prison rules and that which must be contained and controlled. All penal systems have a series of punitive sanctions that can be applied following problem behaviors. In Westernized countries, this usually ranges from the withdrawal of privileges to segregation, which involves placement for varying periods in solitary confinement. Despite a punitive approach, containment and management of the most disruptive, psychopathic prisoners can still be highly stressful for the prison staff. It may also pose ethical questions over what is an acceptable level of retribution. Ultimately, a small subgroup of psychopathic prisoners will continue to remain unresponsive to all therapeutic attempts at treatment and rehabilitation, recalcitrant in the face of all punishment, and still able to exert a malign and destructive influence, even from within the most highly secure and segregated environments.

For example, two men serving life sentences were housed in adjacent special-security

431

cells in an English prison that had been built for the containment of prisoners posing exceptional risks. One had killed a total of five men, including his first victim, whose murder had led to admission to a maximum security hospital; another patient in the hospital; and three other prisoners in two different prisons, following his transfer from the hospital to serve a life sentence for the second killing. It appeared that he would take any opportunity that arose to attempt to kill another prisoner, especially when he suffered from severe mood swings. These were characterized by severe tension and profound dysphoria, and the act of killing produced a feeling of relief. This man explained that homicides had occurred when he had unsuccessfully petitioned to get himself moved to another prison and felt that his request had been ignored. (The murder of two prisoners in a single morning subsequently had the desired effect.) At other times, he claimed that he was possessed by a demon. His neighbor in the adjoining special cell had killed two fellow prisoners—the first an individual he had become convinced was spreading malicious rumors about him, and the second a homosexual rival for the affections of a younger man. This second prisoner became convinced (probably correctly) that the first man intended to kill him at the first opportunity. Luring the first man to the wire mesh that separated them, the second man told his neighbor to bring his ear as close as possible so that he could whisper without the prison officers' hearing. He then thrust a screwdriver (which he had secretly obtained and sharpened) through the mesh in an attempt to stab the first prisoner in the eye, but missed, causing only a cut.

Fortunately, such events remain rare in U.K. prisons; most prisoners serve their sentences uneventfully, conform to prison discipline, and make no attempts to escape. However, it is clear that a minority cannot be managed in ordinary prison locations because of their persistently difficult and dangerous behavior. A small subgroup are found to be psychotic, but the majority are psychopaths. This chapter will describe the psychopathology of such prisoners and will attempt to clarify their behavior. However, the chapter will first examine the notion of "severity" in determining the level of personality abnormality in the psychopath, as well as the notion of "untreatability." This will be followed by an examination of contrasting approaches to the management and containment of these individuals, both in the United Kingdom and in North America.

LEVELS OF SEVERITY AND THE CONCEPT OF UNTREATABILITY

Psychodynamic Classifications

Current classifications of psychopathic disorder are derived from the two dominant modes of conceptualizing personality: psychodynamic theory and psychological trait theory. Both include a framework in which abnormality of personality can be considered pathological to varying degrees, and within which treatment response can also demonstrate a range of possibilities. Psychodynamic therapy conceptualizes severity according to "levels" of personality functioning. The psychodynamic concepts of borderline and narcissistic personality organization are most relevant to psychopaths. These are reflected in the patient's primary characteristics, especially (1) the degree of identity integration, (2) the type of defensive operations habitually employed, and (3) the capacity for reality testing. Kernberg (1975, 1984) has proposed three broad structural organizations—neurotic, borderline, and psychotic—that stabilize the mental apparatus, mediating between etiological factors and direct behavioral manifestations of illness. Narcissistic personality organization is seen as a specific form overlapping with, or in some cases part of, borderline organization. Psychopaths can be placed at the severe end of a spectrum of severity of both these forms of personality organization.

Gunderson (1984) has suggested an alternative, narrower concept of borderline personality disorder that is in line with the diagnostic category in the *Diagnostic and Statistical Manual of Mental Disorders,* and that has described three levels. Gunderson perceives lower levels of psychological functioning emerging regressively in borderlines and acting to preserve a sense of contact with and control over major object relationships. At the third level (the level at which many psychopathic patients function), Gunderson perceives an absence or lack of any major object. As a result, these patients can experience brief psychotic episodes, panic states, or impulsive efforts to avoid panic. These can include fights and promiscuity, which are often assisted by the disinhibiting effects of drugs and alcohol, and which reflect desperate efforts to establish contact with—and revive the illusion of control over—some new object. In psychopaths, major objects are perceived as absent, and this corresponds to a sense of abandonment and results in the severest forms of separation anxiety; thus, these phenomena can be especially severe.

An understanding of the concept of pathological narcissism is highly important in making sense of the observation that certain individuals, with similar primitive defensive mechanisms and highly disturbed superego pathology, are still able to retain superficially normal social functioning in many life situations—sometimes for relatively long periods. These individuals will not demonstrate the more severe examples of anxiety, polysymptomatic neurosis, and identity diffusion observed in borderline personality organization. Examples include highly predatory sadistic killers who may otherwise lead superficially conventional lifestyles and hold jobs, or ruthless criminals who successfully portray themselves as "solid citizens" to friends and associates. To explain such phenomena, Kernberg (1975) and Kohut (1971, 1977) have proposed another group of patients who are also at a level of structural organization between neurotic and psychotic, but whose personality is not necessary borderline. Kernberg (see also Chapter 24, this volume) has argued that in the more severe or lower-order examples of narcissistic personality, the organization is in fact borderline. In these cases, the patient is protected from the intense intrapsychic conflicts more typical of borderline pathology by the development of the "pathological grandiose self." Features of narcissistic personality organization can be usefully applied to some of the individuals described in this chapter. Narcissistic personalities do not usually appear severely regressed, but present with an unusual degree of self-reference in their interactions with others. There is a contradiction between their inflated concept of themselves and an inordinate need for positive attention from others. They derive little enjoyment from life, except from tributes from others or from within their grandiose fantasies. They envy others, but idealize those who provide them with narcissistic supplies, deprecating and treating with contempt those from whom they expect nothing. Their relationships with others tend to be exploitative and sometimes parasitic. They feel that they have a right to control and possess others and to exploit them without guilt. Behind what can be a superficially charming and engaging exterior are coldness and ruthlessness.

Kernberg (1984) has described six levels of superego pathology in these individuals, ranging from those with neurotic character pathology along a continuum to psychopaths, or persons with antisocial personality disorder proper. At the more severe end of the spectrum are narcissistic personalities with antisocial features and those with malignant forms of pathological narcissism whose aggressive sense of entitlement is expressed in ego-syntonic antisocial behavior. Kernberg differentiates this group from the most severe level, in that they have some availability of idealized superego precursors.

The more severe cases of malignant narcissism, with examples of overt aggression and sadism, will merge into the most severe forms of superego pathology seen in the final group, the psychopaths. The antisocial proper, or psychopathic group, is described by Kernberg as entirely identified with a grandiose self-structure, the stranger selfobject. Their primary mode of relating is aggression, usually experienced as sadistic pleasure. They do appear to understand the moral requirements of social reality, to which they may superficially appear to conform, but do not understand that this represents an authentic system of morality that other persons have internalized. They cannot experience authentic investment of love in others or appreciate the difference between such investments others may have for them. They have a marked tendency toward ruthless exploitation and manipulation.

For instance, a highly disruptive and subversive prisoner was moved into a special unit in an attempt to stabilize his behavior after spending long periods in solitary confinement. He had been repeatedly moved from one prison to another due to difficulties in containing him. He had twice previously been successful in escaping, and on one occasion had left the United Kingdom and had been rearrested in another country, from where he was extradited. He expressed considerable pride that he had managed to break into the prison archives during one escape and to remove his case records. Within a short time, he had established himself at the top of the pecking order within the unit among a group of highly difficult and disruptive men, several of whom had already achieved formidable reputations for violence within the prison system. He subsequently began to exert his influence over a female teacher who was employed to provide education for the inmates; he exploited her own personality pathology and difficulties in her marriage. Their relationship progressed from an initial professional relationship to furtive sexual activity in the unit's art room, and ultimately to a carefully planned escape. She escorted him out of the prison disguised as a visitor and in possession of a firearm, which she had provided (and which was fortunately not used during the escape. Considering herself now in love with the prisoner, she created a diversion by sitting in a supermarket parking lot, claiming that she had been abducted and that she was sitting on a time bomb in her car. This was a dummy device that they had made together in the unit workshop. He meanwhile escaped. When subsequently interviewed following his recapture and the addition of several years to his sentence, he expressed his general disdain and distaste for the sexual attractiveness of his female accomplice, who was now also serving a sentence of imprisonment for her part in the escape. He freely admitted that he had used her to effect his escape, and he showed no concern about her current circumstances. He claimed to have found a new role as the bodyguard of a notorious older gangster serving a sentence in his current prison.

Kernberg believes that patients at this level of severity are usually too dangerous to treat in an ordinary psychotherapeutic setting. The enactment of overt sadistic triumph over the therapist through extreme deprecation, together with direct financial or other exploitation, may be a frightening experience outside of a highly secure setting. Among this group, Kernberg sees a continuum between the passive, exploitative, parasitic criminal and the frankly sadistic criminal. Even in the former, confrontation at this level of superego pathology with the individual's antisocial behavior can still trigger violent paranoid regression in the transference projected onto the therapist. In the most severe cases, the grandiose self is infiltrated with aggression and a subsequent ego-syntonic search for the gratification of sadistic urges. It is as if this type of individual identifies with the primitive, ruthless, totally immoral power that can obtain satisfaction only through the expression of unmitigated aggression. Unlike those in the previous subgroup, these individuals do not seek to morally justify their behavior and demonstrate no adherence to any consistent value other than the exercise of power. Such individuals are particularly at home in social conditions or occupations where they can freely express their primitive aggression and cruelty.

Trait-Based Classifications

Traits fit more easily into a dimensional system of classification. Within this diagnostic framework, severity of abnormality of personality can be measured along a unidimensional scale or series of scales to form a personality profile. For example, Hare's Psychopathy Checklist—Revised (PCL-R) is not a classificatory system but a unidimensional scale of psychopathy, which consists of both personality traits and antisocial behaviors (Hare, 1991). The cutoff for the PCL-R is a score of 30 or more, above which a subject is designated a psychopath for research purposes. Research with samples of Canadian and U.S. prisoners has shown a correlation between violent and aggressive behavior in these institutional settings and scores on the PCL-R. Furthermore, the instrument appears to have good predictive value, with high scores correlating with poor risk following release from a prison or the hospital environment; "risk" has been measured in terms of the number of subjects whose parole was revoked, or who reoffended, and length of time for each before a failure occurred (see review in Hare, 1991).

Severity and Categorical Classification

Categorical diagnostic systems do not lend themselves so readily to the measurement of severity. Recommendations have been made that the current diagnostic categories for the Axis II personality disorders should be replaced by dimensional scores. But most clinically trained mental health care professionals prefer the use of categories. However, when categorical classifications are used, severity can be implied in two ways. First, there is the implication that certain diagnostic categories are more severe, are more treatment-resistant, or include "lower-level" psychopathology. For example, antisocial, narcissistic, and borderline personality disorders can be contrasted with conditions such as obsessive–compulsive personality disorder, which are considered to reflect functioning at a higher level (Kernberg, 1984). This approach can involve a hierarchical model in which certain diagnoses are seen to supersede others in terms of their severity. Second, severity may be implied by multiple diagnostic labels that indicate "breadth" of psychopathy (Dolan & Coid, 1993). For example, a study of subjects in maximum-security hospitals and special units for disruptive prisoners demonstrated that they were given multiple Axis II diagnostic labels when a research diagnostic instrument was used, and that the most prevalent conditions were borderline, antisocial, narcissistic, and paranoid personality disorders (Coid, 1992).

A man serving a long sentence for the rape of two females was now serving an added sentence for the attempted murder and sodomy of another prisoner. In the first offense, he had observed the women involved in a road traffic accident and had followed them back to their home. He was perceived as one of the most dangerous men in the entire prison population, with a spectacular history of repeated assaults against other prisoners and staff, repeated offenses against discipline, and self-mutilation. At times he was placed in special-security cells and had to be restrained by the use of a body belt. His history in the community was indicative of a lifelong antisocial disposition, and his convictions for a series of acquisitive offenses dated from the age of 13. His mother had left him in the care of his criminal father, who had physically abused him, and he was subsequently transferred to the care of relatives. As he became increasingly uncontrollable, he was placed in local authorities' children's homes. At interview, he described bouts of severe irritability and anger that would come on for no understandable reason, and during which he was totally unable to control his aggression. During these episodes he could explode at the slightest provocation. He also admitted to intermittent periods of intense suspicions of those around him, during which he believed that prison staff or other prisoners were considering tormenting him or plotting against him. But he conceded that on most occasions this was subsequently found to be untrue. He described himself as a "child" who was totally unable to cope in the outside world. He was frequently on the verge of tears when describing himself and his life during the interview. At the same time, his manner was also very controlling. He was easily irritated when some of the inconsistencies in his story were questioned. He was heavily tattooed and scarred from self-mutilation and numerous fights. He was of very powerful build. Although generally cooperative and very keen to talk about himself to a psychiatrist, he was potentially explosive and could easily have become assaultive if questioned insensitively. A research diagnostic interview with the Structured Clinical Interview for DSM-III, Axis II (SCID II) revealed that he had antisocial, borderline, histrionic, narcissistic, paranoid, avoidant, and passive–aggressive personality disorders. Examination of lifetime Axis I disorders with the Schedule for Affective Disorders and Schizophrenia—Lifetime (SADS-L) revealed that he had experienced one brief hypomanic episode, chronic dysthymia since childhood with superimposed depressive episodes, and social phobia. In addition, he had experienced bulimic episodes and admitted to pedophilic fantasies.

The formidable range of psychopathology presented by this case study demonstrates the advantages of a categorical approach in indicating the prisoner's severity of personality abnormality. He scored 37 out of a maximum of 40 on the PCL-R (Hare, 1991). But it could be argued that the latter, unidimensional approach failed to reveal the true range of his psychopathology. The prisoner had never been seriously considered for transfer to a hospital setting for treatment, possibly because he was perceived as too dangerous. He posed exceptional problems of management even within a maximum-security prison, spending most of his sentence in solitary confinement. From the clinical perspective, there is considerable interaction between the various diagnostic components demonstrated with the research diagnostic instruments. Prognosis for treatment may be poor in such cases as one form of psychopathology interacts with another. Most importantly, a therapeutic approach with this prisoner could not be seriously considered until there was consistent stabilization of his severe behavioral disorders.

THE EPIDEMIOLOGY OF DISRUPTIVE AND DANGEROUS PRISONERS

Although it is reasonable to hypothesize a strong link between psychopathy and disruptive behavior, there has been surprisingly little research with prisoners to establish the connection. There is also a shortage of studies on the prevalence of personality disorders, or of psychopathy as measured with the PCL or PCL-R, among prisoners.

Prison Surveys

Few epidemiological surveys that examine the full range of DSM Axis II disorders have been carried out in community settings. Several have included the single category of antisocial personality disorder, which appears to have a lifetime prevalence of 2–3% in the United States, Canada, and New Zealand, and a considerably lower prevalence in Taiwan. The overall lifetime rate of any Axis II disorder is thought to range between 10% and 13% (see reviews by Weissman, 1993, and de Girolamo & Reich, 1993). Paranoid, schizoid, and narcissistic personality disorders seem uncommon in the general population, with a lifetime rate of less than 1%, although there is evidence that such conditions maybe considerably more prevalent in samples of criminals who have committed the most serious offenses (Coid, 1992). Table 27.1 indicates that the prevalence of antisocial personality disorder is much higher in criminal populations, but with a range of findings between different institutions. The prevalence appears higher in penitentiary settings with hardened criminals who are serving longer sentences. However, as Robins, Tipp, and Przybeck (1991) have pointed out, only a small proportion of persons with antisocial personality disorder will be found in prisons at any one time. Nevertheless, Table 27.1 indicates that there is some support for an association between antisocial personality disorder and dangerous and disruptive behavior.

PCL and PCL-R Findings in Prisoners

The PCL-R (like its predecessor, the original PCL; Hare, 1980) may not be a suitable instrument to establish the epidemiology of psychopathy in prison populations. Nevertheless, Hart, Kropp, and Hare (1988) studied 231 male prisoners prior to release and found that 30% scored 34 or more on the PCL; Serin, Peters, and Barbaree (1990) studied 93 males released from a federal prison, of whom 17% scored 31 or more on the PCL; and Forth, Hart, and Hare (1990) found that 36% young male offenders scored 30 or more on the PCL. In a study of English male prisoners on special units (Coid, 1996),

TABLE 27.1. Lifetime Rates per 100 of Antisocial Personality Disorder (DSM-III), Based on Prison Surveys and Surveys in Maximum-Security Hospitals

Author(s)	Location	Sample	Method[a]	Rate per 100
	Males			
Hodgins & Côté (1990)	Quebec penitentiary	495	DIS	61.7
Hodgins & Côté (1990)	Three U.S. penitentiaries	?	DIS	28.9–50.1
Hare (1991)	British Columbia (provincial)	75	Clinical	33.3
Hare (1991)	British Columbia (federal)	171	Clinical	41.5
Coid (1996)	U.K. prison special units	81	SCID II	84.0
Coid (1996)	Broadmoor Hospital, U.K. (psychopaths[b])	86	SCID II	83.0
	Females			
Teplin et al. (1996)	Chicago (jail detainees)	1,272	DIS	13.8
Jordan et al. (1996)	North Carolina (convicted)	805	CIDI	11.9
Coid (1996)	Three maximum-security hospitals, U.K. (psychopaths[b])	93	SCID II	44.0

[a]DIS, Diagnostic Interview Schedule; SCID II, Structured Clinical Interview for DSM-III, Axis II; CIDI, Composite International Diagnostic Instrument.

[b]Legal category of English Mental Health Act of 1983, not diagnostic category.

73% were found to score 30 or more on the PCL-R. Although Hare (1991) has estimated that 23% of adult male prisoners in North America are psychopathic according to ratings on the PCL-R, his evidence for this estimation is not entirely clear. Furthermore, when the instrument is applied to prisoners in Scotland, Cooke (1994; see also Chapter 16, this volume) has estimated that the prevalence is only 3% among adult male prisoners. Cooke (1997) has speculated that the impact of socialization and enculturation, together possibly with the drift of psychopaths from Scotland to England, account for the differences in these prevalence rates. However, these disparities may also indicate problems with using the PCL-R as an instrument to measure the epidemiology of psychopathy.

The PCL-R may be more useful in studies that examine specific associations between psychopathy and other variables, such as disruptive behavior in the prison setting. It is generally accepted as highly useful in a range of risk assessment procedures. Hare and McPherson (1984) have confirmed an association between violent and aggressive behavior in prison inmates and psychopathy scores; specifically, they demonstrated that psychopathic inmates were significantly more likely to have demonstrated a history of verbal abuse and verbal threats, to be described as easily annoyed or irritated, to be belligerent, and to have had episodes of fighting in the prison setting. Similarly, Cooke (1994) found in a Scottish prison survey that psychopathic disorder was associated with an increased likelihood of prisoners to be held in restricted conditions, to exhibit both violent and nonviolent offending behavior, and to have a history of disciplinary infractions while in custody.

CHARACTERISTICS OF DISRUPTIVE AND DANGEROUS PRISONERS

Defining "Disruptive" and "Dangerous"

Coyle (1987) has estimated that at any one time the proportion of disruptive and dangerous prisoners in the United Kingdom can vary between 0.2% and 5% of the prison population. But this will depend on the definition of "disruptive" and "dangerous." It is not clear from previous research whether the problem is actually increasing, despite prison statistics in several countries demonstrating a rise in the overall number of possible indicators (reported disciplinary infractions, etc.). The problem is complicated by changes in the collecting of statistics within penal institutions, the general enhancement of prisoners' rights; and pressures generated by overcrowding following the relentless rise of the prison population, especially in the United States and the United Kingdom. These prison populations have also shown an increase in the number of inmates serving long sentences.

A review of the factors associated with the overall level of problematic behavior within prisons does not specifically reveal a major impact of such factors as psychopathy. Within the overall population, age appears to have the strongest association with measured disciplinary infraction rates: Younger inmates are more frequently involved in disruptive behavior. Ditchfield (1990) has observed that previous offending history is strongly associated with behavioral disturbance in prison: Offenders serving sentences for robbery, aggravated burglary, attempted murder, and assault have above-average involvement in prison violence; offenders serving sentences for murder, manslaughter, sexual offenses, and drug offenses have below-average involvement; and the extent of involvement of property offenders appears to be unclear from the available research.

However, the studies reviewed by Ditchfield apply to prison populations in general, rather than prisoners who pose exceptional risks of disruptiveness and prison violence.

Toch, Adams, and Grant (1989) described four categories representing patterns of prison misbehavior over time, which were drawn from a large sample of inmates in several New York institutions. A small subgroup, which constituted 3% of a release cohort, had accounted for 12% of adjudicated disciplinary infractions and had demonstrated chronic prison misbehavior. This subgroup was characterized by having a more extensive previous history of violent crime and more experience of civil psychiatric hospitalization than the other subgroups. English prisoners who had posed exceptional control problems resulting in transfer to three special units (Coid, 1991) were older (with a mean age of 35 years), and the majority were serving sentences for homicide offenses, other serious violence, and/or robbery. However, the qualitative nature of the homicide offenses was highly unusual, and none fitted the standard picture of a "domestic" killing as implied by Ditchfield's (1990) review, where homicide was associated with a lower rate of disciplinary infractions. A subgroup of these men resembled that identified by Toch et al. (1989) and continued to suffer from mental illness, including psychotic illness, while incarcerated. But the majority were designated as "psychopaths" via the PCL-R. The evidence would therefore suggest that although some general characteristics of the overall prison population may be associated with disruptive and dangerous behavior, a subgroup exists with either chronic mental health and personality problems, or specific forms of behavior, that create a higher level of difficulty in their management and constitute potential dangerousness.

Classification of Disruptive and Dangerous Prisoners

One approach to classifying difficult and disruptive behavior is to adopt the descriptions used by prison staffs. An early example is a study by Pope (1979) in four English maximum-security prisons, where staff members in charge of each wing were asked to identify management problems and to list the kind of problems that each prisoner presented. The groupings were as follows:

1. *The antiauthority and subversive group.* This was the largest group and consisted of inmates who had been involved in behavior designed to confront or undermine the authority of the staff. The motivation behind such activities could range from concerted attempts to derive greater power for the prisoner community, to individual efforts pursued as a part of institutional cultural prescriptions. The essential problems posed by this group were control and the maintenance of stable order within the institution in the face of attempts to redress or adjust the distribution of power by the prisoners. The considerable variety of ways in which this could emerge presented major problems for the staff.

2. *The problem personality group.* This was the second largest group and included prisoners of the type who constitute the main focus of this chapter. According to the staff, these individuals demonstrated extreme "unpredictability" in their behavior, associated with perceived personality problems. The descriptions used frequently referred to "psychopathic" or "aggressive" characteristics, together with "unstable" or "hysterical" outbursts. It was not so much the activities of the group that drew attention to them, but rather their potential to harm themselves, other prisoners, or the staff. This group tended to be seen as presenting "medical" problems by the staff, even if these did not receive therapeutic management.

3. *Prisoners needing protection.* This group included sexual offenders, those who had gotten into difficulties in their relationships with other prisoners, and those who were known to have given evidence at trial against other offenders. The major problem posed by this group was one of protection.

4. *Escapees.* This group overlapped with the first group, but the motivation for their behavior was primarily escape rather than subversion, and the main problem was one of containment by the staff.

5. *A residual group without any classification.* This category included the wide range of individuals who did not fit neatly into any other category.

The Control Review Committee (CRC; Home Office, 1984) identified problem prisoners in three broad categories: (1) those who behaved in a disorderly fashion themselves, (2) those who encouraged others to misbehave, and (3) those who suffered from some form of mental disturbance (especially if it predisposed them to violence or made them easy prey for exploitation). These categories were thought to represent useful distinctions in some contexts, but were neither comprehensive nor mutually exclusive. The first category could range from institutional killers to inmates who repeatedly provoked staff and other inmates with behavior that was very difficult to cope with, but who might not present any great or immediate danger. The second category included several types of prisoners who had an influence over the inmate population and used it malignly. These individuals could extend from the "barons" who enforced their debts to prisoners who deliberately fomented riots. Prisoners in all three categories could act alone or in groups and the groups, with which they had links could range from traditional criminal groups to terrorist organizations. However, the committee recognized dangerous psychopaths as appearing in the third group; they were perceived as exhibiting mental disturbance or disability, which led them to behave in an unstable and/or aggressive manner. Some were observed to have histories including repeated or long periods of confinement in psychiatric hospitals. Others included inadequate prisoners who had been shown to be unable to cope with institutional stress and who would resort to violence and self-injury, and overtly aggressive prisoners who were both immature and inadequate but who would erupt into frequent bouts of violence. Some could still exhibit extremely bizarre and unpredictable behavior, which would put staff and other inmates under stress and create tensions that would give rise to widespread control problems involving other prisoners (who would not necessarily be involved under other circumstances). Some could be manipulated to behave dangerously by more sophisticated prisoners.

Williams and Longley (1987) carried out an empirical study in English prisons to examine the characteristics of the judgments of prison governors as to who their difficult prisoners were. Disciplinary transfers and individuals notified as having murdered another inmate were particularly likely to be identified as causing major problems. Prisoners serving prolonged periods in solitary confinement were less likely to be identified, but this was simply because they had less opportunity to be involved in disruptive behavior. The inmates who had received disciplinary transfers between prisons were compared to randomly selected comparison groups. These inmates were more likely (1) to be "Category A" prisoners (indicating that they posed the highest level of risk in the event of escape); (2) to have received more than 20 governors' reports for indiscipline; (3) to have exhibited violence toward staff and other prisoners; and (4) to have been segregated during their present sentence. Overall, prisoners who had received disciplinary transfers from one institution to another, especially on a repeated basis, were found to be the most significant group of difficult inmates in the English system.

THE ENGLISH SPECIAL UNITS STUDY

Sampling and Procedure

The English Special Units Study, which I carried out between 1987 and 1993, was a detailed psychiatric investigation of a small sample of disruptive and dangerous prisoners. Three special units were established following the report of the CRC (Home Office, 1984) which had recommended a range of small units in English prisons, operating a variety of regimens for disruptive prisoners with special needs. The aim was to devise a constructive way of managing prisoners to achieve the optimum level of behavior, but to take account of their severe limitations and the likelihood that any goals would have to be realistic. The special units were intended to offer an alternative approach to managing prisoners who could not be contained within an ordinary prison wing elsewhere, and who had established records of violence toward staff and/or other prisoners, repeated offenses against discipline, damage to property, or behavior that generally and persistently gave cause for concern (including behavior dangerous to themselves and others). A subgroup of inmates known to have a history of mental abnormality had been identified.

Prisoners were referred to a central selection committee from the prisons in which they were posing major problems. However, the movement of prisoners through the units was slow. Over the first 6 years, a total of 102 prisoners (all men) were admitted. Of this total sample, I interviewed 87 (85%) with a battery of questionnaires to establish DSM-III Axis II disorders (SCID II), lifetime Axis I diagnoses (SADS-L), and psychopathy (PCL-R). A semistructured interview was carried out to establish family and developmental history, early psychosocial environment, criminal history, history of behavioral disorders in different institutions, and psychiatric treatment. Supplementary information was obtained from the special unit file, the prison file, prison hospital case files, psychiatric hospital case notes (including case notes of relatives), and probation officers' reports. A total of 81 prisoners (79%) were able to complete all questionnaires at interview, but 6 (6%) could not do so because of active symptoms of mental illness. Of the original 102, another 11 (11%) refused and 4 could not be interviewed, 3 having been released and a further subject murdered.

The mean age of the subjects was 34 years, with a range of 22–53 years. The mean age of first court appearance was 13 years, with a range of 8–20 years. Overall, the sample had a mean of 13 previous court appearances to receive a sentence, with a range of 0–36 previous appearances to receive conviction. Their mean PCL-R score was 31. Only 2 prisoners were serving sentences of less than 5 years; 27 (33%) were serving sentences of over 5 years; and 52 (64%) were serving life sentences.

The index offenses that had led to the subjects' current period of imprisonment were not mutually exclusive. Offenses clustered among the most serious forms of violence against the person: robbery and aggravated burglary (n = 39; 48%); murder and manslaughter (n = 39, 47%); attempted murder and grievous bodily harm (n = 29, 36%); assault (n = 13, 16%); and rape, sodomy, or indecent assault (n = 10, 12%). The data, however, obscure the exceptional degree of violence that was involved in the majority of these incidents. None of the homicides arose from "domestic" disputes. One subject was a serial killer, another a contract killer, and a third a mass killer whose violence had erupted after a girlfriend had broken off their relationship. Robbery sometimes involved extreme violence to employees in commercial premises. Aggravated burglary usually involved violence to the occupants of households that had been broken into, usually at night, by the armed subjects. Some homicides had involved the beating, torture, and final murder of the victims during a burglary, in an attempt to discover the whereabouts of cash and other valuables. A subgroup of severely personality-disordered men had killed or attempted to kill sexual partners or casual pickups in circumstances that at first seemed bizarre and inexplicable. For example, three men had killed older men who had engaged them for sexual favors, in circumstances of almost unbelievable violence. One victim had been beaten to death and his body repeatedly burned with a hot iron; another offender repeatedly slashed his victim with a linoleum knife and severed his penis; the third offender had caused depressed skull fractures to his victim with a wooden mallet.

Six of the men appeared to have been overtly psychotic at the time of the index offense but had not received a hospital disposal when they appeared in court. For example, two men had stabbed complete strangers in the back as a result of delusional ideas that had not come to light at their trial, despite their having been interviewed by psychiatrists. Several men experienced intermittent compulsive homicidal urges. For some of these, the urges had continued during their sentences and had led to acts of serious violence, including the murder of other prisoners. These urges would come on without any provocation or precipitant that the prisoner could describe. They were highly compulsive, and associated with a strong urge to achieve excitement, power, and/or the relief of depression. These men strongly denied any sexual excitement or gratification from their behavior, although the urges and behavior could be accompanied by a sense of exhilaration and excitement.

The subjects received a mean of four DSM-III Axis II personality disorder diagnoses. Antisocial personality disorder was the most common diagnosis ($n = 68$, 84%), followed by paranoid ($n = 54$, 67%), narcissistic ($n = 51$, 63%), and borderline ($n = 45$, 56%). Paranoid personality disorder appeared an important component of these men's psychopathology. They would repeatedly interpret the actions of others as deliberately demeaning or threatening toward them, and would generally expect exploitation or harm from others. They were easily slighted and quick to react with anger and counterattack, many bearing grudges for long periods which sometimes had resulted in attacks on others. Despite the frequent diagnosis of narcissistic personality disorder, the more severe narcissistic personality characteristics of the PCL-R construct were more appropriate in reflecting the pathological narcissism of these ruthless, cunning, manipulative, and remorseless individuals; 59 men (73%) scored 30 or above on the PCL-R. The intense mood instability of the men with borderline personality disorder is described further below. The single individual with no Axis II personality disorder was an armed robber who had supported his legitimate business during financial difficulties from the proceeds of crime. He was held in high esteem by the other men; prison officers, however, perceived him as a profoundly disruptive influence. He presented with subthreshold narcissistic traits and admitted a craving for excitement despite his age.

Twenty men (23%) had at some time suffered from Axis I clinical syndromes. Several were psychotic at interview, with schizophrenic or paranoid illnesses. In some cases, the symptoms were unknown to the prison staff. For example, one prisoner who had seriously assaulted a female staff member at another prison described an elaborate delusional system of how female prison employees frequently behaved in deliberately indecent ways to torment prisoners like himself, and how it was necessary to teach them lessons to stop them. Another man was hypomanic and had to be reinterviewed on a later occasion. One huge, bear-like man padded the staircases and landings of a unit aimlessly, unable to engage in any meaningful activities whatsoever, despite receiving the maximum recommended levels of several antipsychotic medications.

A significant proportion of the men also showed features of mood disorder that did not amount to a diagnosis of mental illness, but resulted in fluctuating symptoms of irritability, anxiety, tension, and depression. It was sometimes necessary to choose another time to interview them, as these moods were closely related to their violent and explosive behavior. This phenomenon was associated with a diagnosis of borderline personality disorder.

In terms of lifetime prevalence, the major DSM-III Axis I mental disorder categories represented in the sample were depression (n = 37, 43%), alcohol abuse or dependence (n = 28, 32%), drug abuse or dependence (n = 27, 31%), anxiety disorders other than obsessive–compulsive disorder (n = 23, 26%), schizophrenia (n = 21, 24%), dysthymia (n = 16, 18%), biopolar disorder (n = 11, 13%), and unspecified psychosis (n = 10, 11%). Most subjects had suffered from a major depressive episode that had lasted at least 2 weeks, and the majority of these had received antidepressant treatment for this condition. A larger proportion might have experienced serious problems with substance abuse or dependence had they not received repeated periods of imprisonment.

A subgroup of men had first presented with symptoms of psychosis while serving a prison sentence. In some, the condition may have been exacerbated by stress factors. Others had spent long periods in segregation, and the psychotic symptoms had emerged in these situations, unbeknownst to the prison staff. However, it remained unclear whether deteriorating behavior as a result of slowly developing psychosis had led to prolonged periods of segregation or whether the segregation itself had acted as a stress factor leading to the psychosis. In still other cases, psychotic illness had exacerbated the individuals' already difficult, disruptive, or dangerous behavior within prison.

Difficult/Disruptive Prison Behaviors

All subjects had presented control problems of a serious nature prior to their admission. They were considered to be at the extreme end of the spectrum within the English prison system. However, there was wide variation in the different forms and motivations behind these behaviors. Violence was the most common type of behavior: specifically, violence toward other inmates (n = 55, 68%) or staff members (n = 55, 68%), and making/hoarding weapons (n = 42, 52%), were quite common. However, violent behavior was by no means the only reason for being considered difficult and disruptive. Property damage (n = 59, 73%) was the most common single problem. Another type of problem was demonstrated by a man with schizoid personality disorder who denied his gender, and whose behavior at times was so bizarre and his attitude towards other prisoners so provocative that he was in danger of being seriously assaulted.

An earlier system of classifying inmate's disordered behaviors, devised by Toch et al. (1989), described the dominant goals toward which the behaviors appeared to be directed. This system was modified for use with an English sample. Toch and colleagues grouped patterns of behavior under five headings: (1) gratifying impulses, (2) seeking refuge, (3) enhancing esteem, (4) pursuing autonomy, and (5) maintaining sanity. Certain items were added to reflect the psychopathology of the English subjects, and a number of others were omitted as they did not appear meaningful within the English context. In the end, four categories were derived: (1) mental abnormality, (2) characterological, (3) purposeful, and (4) other.

Mental Abnormality

A proportion of prisoners (n = 35, 43%) repeatedly experienced unwarranted suspicions of others to an intense degree, but not to the extent of delusions or hallucinations. These men often felt persecuted by others; they exploded when they imagined that others wished them ill or wanted to harm them. They lived for long periods in a state of considerable suspicion or unease, made worse by the hostility and fear they engendered in those around them. Others (n = 15, 19%) spent long periods in their cells deriving pleasure from ruminating on their previous violence toward others. A small group (n = 11, 14%) derived extreme pleasure and excitement from the actual carrying out of violent behavior. Nine men (11%) experienced compulsive urges to kill within prison. These urges came on without provocation from their victims, were intermittent, and took the form of obsessional intrusive thoughts.

A proportion of the men (n = 29, 36%) described severe mood swings that did not amount to a major mental illness, but that clearly related to their violent and disruptive behavior. Most described these moods as consisting of a mixture of tension, dysphoria, anger, anxiety, and irritability. They stated that these symptoms could be relieved by violent outbursts either toward others, toward property, or sometimes toward themselves in the form of self-mutilation (see Coid, 1993). An overlapping group of men (n = 29, 36%) was hyperirritable. Irritability and anger were the primary symptoms of these men's mood swings. The slightest provocation would cause them to explode into violence, although this had not been preceded or motivated by a desire to relieve these symptoms.

Characterological

Characterological features were thought to be components of the subjects' underlying personality and their typical style of relating to others. One group (n = 45, 56%) appeared to be chronically explosive in the face of any minor provocation or stress. This was not a fluctuating phenomenon, the result of an intermittent mood state, but an ingrained feature of their personality. Others (n = 32, 40%) appeared profoundly antiauthoritarian and would not accept any rules or restrictions on their behavior. A smaller group (n = 18, 22%) was prone to regressive, childlike tantrums in the face of stress or provocation. For example, one man became so angry and aroused when punched by another inmate in the exercise yard that while screaming a tirade of abuse, he simultaneously defecated in his trousers.

"Primitive self-gratification" (n = 19, 11%) referred to men who operated at a level of infancy for much of the time, engaging in repeated behaviors designed to satisfy their needs in a direct and primitive manner. For example, one inmate of low intelligence would tear up all his clothing when he was frustrated or could not obtain what he wanted. This was an ingrained pattern of behavior that had continued over many years and had not been extinguished by a range of sanctions in different prisons. Certain personality-disordered men (n = 15, 19%) were considered very dangerous and unpredictable, in the sense that they could easily be "set up" to act aggressively or to disrupt the prison regimen by other prisoners more cunning than themselves; some would inappropriately and unrealistically perceive themselves as the ringleaders and organizers of these incidents. Other men (n = 21, 26%) were obsessed with what they perceived to be the unfairness of their sentence and proclaimed their innocence (it should be noted that one such man was subsequently released, following a widely publicized miscarriage of justice). Most men denied the seriousness of their offenses, according to the official sources of information. A subgroup of these men spent long periods writing to lawyers, outside organizations, and pressure groups. Their campaigns frequently brought them into major conflicts with the prison authorities.

"Failed jailing" (n = 8, 10%) was derived from a category used by Toch et al.

(1989), who referred to individuals who pursued the "good life" in prison through accumulating illicit amenities and possessions and through bartering. However, they repeatedly ran into difficulties, making promises they could not fulfill and seriously losing "face," or else running into debts. They would then attempt to save face in a violent manner by engineering a serious or series of incidents, in order to get themselves moved to another prison so that they could escape payment. "Games turned sour" ($n = 13, 4\%$) referred to men who enjoyed setting up confrontations between other prisoners by disseminating false information, but whose machinations was easily discovered by their potential victims. It was usually necessary for these men to launch a preemptive violent attack before they themselves were attacked.

Purposeful

For some men ($n = 34, 42\%$), violence appeared the only solution to resolve difficulties, grievances, and arguments with others. In these cases, violent means of problem resolution had been typically employed within conflicts throughout their lives. Another group of men ($n = 23, 28\%$) employed violence, or the threat of violence, to avoid other prisoners. These subjects were all avoidant men who experienced symptoms of social phobia. They described mounting anxiety in the face of noise, movement, and the large number of other men around them. They found it intolerable to share a cell. It was clear that the individual attention they received from officers in the special units, and their new ability to retreat into their own space within these new locations, were essential to their stability. Most were prepared to act ruthlessly to be isolated if their demands were not met by the prison staff. Most were content to spend long periods in solitary confinement.

Some men used violence to enhance their self-esteem ($n = 27, 33\%$) or took a "macho" pride in their physical prowess and fighting ability ($n = 16, 20\%$). Yet another group ($n = 18, 22\%$) did not need to advertise this quality and had been highly effective in bullying or intimidating inmates in other institutions. Some men ($n = 14, 17\%$) would carry out preemptive, planned attacks on rivals. Two men (2%) had murdered homosexual rivals for the affections of their boyfriends. Several men ($n = 17, 21\%$) had violently assaulted others following blows to their self-esteem.

Other

Over one-third of the men ($n = 30, 37\%$) were systematically and persistently subversive, encouraging others to defy those in authority and to disrupt the prison regimen at any opportunity. Eight men (10%) were engaged in obsessive litigation, spending considerable periods of time writing to lawyers, prisoners' organizations, and the government. Some men ($n = 13, 16\%$) had organized protests involving large groups of prisoners. Further groups were at risk of assault from other prisoners due to their behavior ($n = 14, 17\%$) or the nature and circumstances of their index offenses ($n = 9, 11\%$). The latter included offenses against children and giving evidence against codefendants at trial.

Developmental History

The first-degree relatives of these men showed a high prevalence of substance abuse and personality disorders. One-third had first-degree relatives who had suffered from depression. A subgroup had a history of perinatal complications (12%), and others demonstrated features suggestive of nonspecific neuropsychiatric abnormality. One man suffered from frontal lobe syndrome following a motorcycle accident. However, the most striking feature of their histories was the severity of their early environmental disadvantage. Only two men were brought up in conventional, middle-class, "nuclear" families. However, one was now paranoid and stated that he hated his parents; the other had murdered his mother and preserved her body for some months afterward. Half of the subjects had been brought up in poverty, had delinquent siblings, and had suffered severe physical abuse during their childhood. Sixty percent had been placed in local authorities' care during childhood, and half had lost a parent by divorce or death before the age of 15. Ten percent had been sodomized by a member of the immediate family or a stepfather. Over one-third had parents who were themselves professional criminals. The men who described physical abuse during childhood described particularly extreme and unusual examples, even for a criminal sample. For example, one man had been kept in a garage by his aunt and father, where he slept on a pile of sacks until the age of 4, when he had been discovered by the local social services. Two men refused to describe in any detail what they had experienced, threatening to assault me if this line of questioning continued. It was striking that although most men would answer questions regarding their criminality and violent behavior in detail, questions regarding family life almost invariably resulted in reservation, sometimes suspicion, or even overt hostility.

The life histories of the men presented a profoundly depressing picture. Many had mentally ill or personality-disordered parents, or other family members with mental abnormality. There was evidence that some men had been temperamentally difficult from a very early age, some presenting with hyperactivity; this suggested that constitutional factors may have combined with their highly adverse family environment. Again, the sheer severity of physical abuse and emotional deprivation was striking, and many had experienced a series of different careers. Emotional disturbance characterized the early childhood of many individuals, with increasing truancy, fighting, stealing, substance abuse, and court appearances by puberty. In early adolescence, their education was usually completed in an approved school setting. By this time most subjects were spending little time in a family environment and had turned instead to a delinquent peer group, or alternatively had begun a pattern of solitary, impulsive, and sometimes bizarre offending. By their teens, their self-esteem had suffered severe damage from violent, inadequate, or mentally abnormal parents and siblings, or else they had been coached into violent behavior by these same individuals. From their midteens onward, most were increasingly being controlled, educated, and cared for in institutional settings. The length of time they spent in the community began to diminish progressively, and their criminality persisted over their late teens and into their early 20s, with increasing seriousness. By the stage of youth custody, many had been identified as control problems, with fighting and attempted escapes. From early adulthood, they had spent little time out of the penal system. Few had formed stable relationships; relationships, when formed, were usually characterized by discord and violence.

In their mid-20s, some of the men had begun to manifest severe symptoms of mental illness. The bizarre quality of their criminal behavior and behavior in prison had resulted for some in referrals to maximum-security prison hospitals. Many had committed their index offenses in their mid- to late 20s, after which they had received life imprisonment or long fixed sentences. This final imprisonment was now characterized by increasing periods of segregation and repeated movements from one prison to another. A hardened malignancy of attitude had now set in, with ingrained, repetitive patterns of behavioral disorder. Repeated punishments within the prison setting, and increasingly negative attitudes toward these individuals on the part of the prison staff, only served to cement the process. Many men and their custodians were now locked into a vicious spiral of punishment, resentment, retaliation, and more punishment, from which neither side seemed able to find a way out. Features of mental illness remained untreated in a small subgroup. But for most of the cases who presented with severe mental illness, this was superimposed on a psychopathic personality, and the underlying psychopathic personality was what rendered them unattractive to the secure hospital services. For others, the disordered behaviors had remained unchanged, despite numerous attempts at psychiatric treatment in the past. By the mean age of admission to a special unit (34 years), attempts at modifying their behaviors by sanctions and encouragement had totally failed. The move to the special units for many of these men represented the last resort in a cycle of despair and hopelessness, both for the men themselves and for the prison staff members who had to contain them.

TREATMENT, MANAGEMENT, OR CONTROL?

Safe containment and reduction of risk may be more realistic goals than routinely pursuing a treatment option. At some stage in their sentence, some prisoners will ultimately cooperate and receive individual treatment, and the omission of a review of therapeutic prison programs at the individual level from this chapter is not intended to minimize their potential benefits. However, many dangerous psychopathic prisoners will not take part in any therapeutic programs. Moreover, in many correctional settings, the necessary resources are not available.

Mental health care professionals (psychiatrists, psychologists, counselors, etc.) often have a peripheral role, and many are employed by correctional services on a contractual basis. It is important to be aware of different viewpoints taken by correction staff members when managing control problems, as well as to be aware of the wider prison context. For correctional officials in some countries, designing prison regimens for long-term inmates that permit safety, productivity, growth, and humane containment is a formidable task in the face of increasing demand from overcrowding. An increasing prison population brings with it a considerable diversity of individuals with different needs, of whom psychopathic individuals posing control problems are just a subgroup. In many cases, more limited but still highly important tasks, such as assessing and advising on suitability for specific prison regimens or for a move to a specific institution, may be an alternative but key role of the mental health care professional. A further, highly important role is the provision of support to members of the prison staff. It is primarily they who are the central agents in exerting a therapeutic or ameliorating influence on the prisoners' behavior.

THE SITUATIONAL RESPONSE TO PROBLEM BEHAVIOR

Cooke (1991) has argued that an emphasis on situational and environmental manipulation, rather than on direct interaction with individuals, is often more productive with difficult prisoners. In its simplest form, this may merely involve the transfer of a highly disruptive inmate to another penal institution, where his or her behavioral disorder may show a dramatic improvement because the staff members are more skilled in handling

the individual in the new location. Megargee (1977) has observed that characteristics of
the milieu in which a violent incident takes place are often more important than characteristics of the individual. It may be possible to change a prisoner's behavior to a
greater extent by modifying the environment than by attempting to modify psychological functioning. Cooke has emphasized the importance of the characteristics of the staff
members who deliver the regimen to prisoners and has identified key elements in this
area, including staff–inmate communication, staff training, staff experience, and staff
morale.

The quality of relationships between prisoners and outside visitors can be especially
important for certain inmates. The processes involved are complex but include the obvious factor of incentives for good behavior (Ditchfield, 1990). Glaser (1984) has also argued that disruptive behavior may be reduced by maximizing the contact between prisoners and noncriminal persons from outside. However, in terms of incentives, the
location of the prison itself can have important implications for control. Some inmates
are prepared to behave badly if they feel that this will result in their transfer to a more
accessible prison, which will allow visits from and the maintenance of contacts with
friends and relatives.

The relationship between a prison population density that leads to overcrowding
and inmate discipline has been the subject of considerable research. But it is difficult to
draw firm conclusions. Some researchers appear to have established an association (Mc-
Cain, Cox, & Paulus, 1980; Megargee, 1977; Nacci, Teitelbaum, & Prather, 1977),
while others have failed to demonstrate a relationship (Atlas, 1982; Evans & Feltham,
1980). Although a relationship may well exist, it is also likely to be complex and mediated by several other factors, such as the characteristics of the inmates. Whether psychopathic prisoners are more prone to violence in such conditions is also unclear. However,
the specific mix of prisoners may be of prime importance. In some cases it is necessary
for prisoners to be identified and separated into groups to prevent predatory behavior by
one group against another (see "Inmate Classification," below).

It is widely assumed that prisoner programs and activities promote control in prisons. Dunbar (1986) has argued that it keeps prisoners active and thereby reduces time
for other activities ("an idle prisoner is a dangerous prisoner"). Hare (1970) has suggested that psychopathic prisoners may employ manipulation or violence to "liven up" their
institution, in a search for stimulation. Ditchfield (1990) observed that poor work opportunities and the curtailment of certain facilities had contributed to subsequent mass
disturbances in certain U.K. prisons. However, research suggests that the relative levels of
facilities and privileges are what primarily concern inmates, rather than their absolute
levels. Inmates feel more threatened by a perceived deterioration in their standard of living than by a poor standard of living overall.

Administrative changes and uncertainty can also influence the level of violence. Ellis
(1984) has noted that where there is a high turnover of prisoners, then the rate of violence tends to be higher. This may be because inmates no longer have a stake in keeping
their living area under control, and also because it inhibits the establishment of staff–
inmate and inmate–inmate attachments. New prisons may be more vulnerable to violent
behavior until both staff culture and inmate culture are established. Following 120 stab-
bings over a 6-month period in a U.S. prison (Folsom Prison, California), Ward (1987)
observed that chaotic administration had contributed to the escalation in violence. Paradoxically, increasing security levels may sometimes increase the probability of violence,
as prisoners resort to violence as a means of saving face by resisting the regimen (Cooke,
1991).

INMATE CLASSIFICATION

Prison classification systems have been developed for prison officers' observations of prisoners' behaviors. These are intended to identify inmates who are frequently aggressive and who should be assigned to a particular wing or cell block—or, alternatively, to identify weaker individuals more prone to victimization who should be housed elsewhere for protective purposes. The intention of this approach is that through the process of identification and separation of particular groups of prisoners, there will be a reduction in problematic behavior.

Quay (1984) developed a classification system that divides prisoners into one of five types. Group 1 prisoners include those who currently display hostile, aggressive, and violent behavior; are resentful of rules and regulations; and crave excitement and become bored easily. They have little concern for the feelings or welfare of others and present serious disciplinary problems in institutions. They are most likely to be involved in fighting, assaults, threats of bodily harm, extortion, destruction of property, and possession of weapons. This group includes aggressive, psychopathic prisoners. Inmates in Group 2 do not have the same degree of outward aggression, but are hostile toward authority and attempt to deal with others through cunning or manipulative behavior. They may be organizers of inmate gangs or illicit enterprises within the institution, and they are generally seen by the staff as untrustworthy and unreliable. Group 3 inmates are neither excessively aggressive nor dependent, although the experience of being in prison may demoralize them. They do not have extensive criminal histories and have a low frequency of disciplinary problems. They are often the type of prisoners upon whom the staff can rely; they are cooperative and maintain some of the prison activities and industries. Prisoners in Group 4 are withdrawn, sluggish, unhappy, and passive. They are easily victimized by those in Groups 1 and 2, as they are often friendless and are perceived as weak, indecisive, and submissive. Group 5 consists of prisoners who constantly display anxiety; are easily upset and unhappy; appear sad, depressed, and tense; and are unable to relate to the prison officers. They are also easily preyed upon by others. They do not have a high rate of disciplinary infractions in the institution, but when they are involved in misconduct it is often of a serious nature, as they tend to explode when they cannot handle stress.

Quay has argued that after prisoners are separated into these groups, they should be placed in different types of regimens. For example, regimens for the first two groups should be staffed by officers who treat them in a "no-nonsense" and "by-the-rules" manner. Those in Group 3 should be treated in a "hands-off" manner. Those in Groups 4 and 5 should be treated in a supportive and highly verbal manner. The rates of inmate–staff and inmate–inmate assaults dropped significantly in a large maximum-security penitentiary during a 4-year period after the inmates were separated according to this classification.

CONVENTIONAL METHODS OF CONTROLLING DISRUPTIVE BEHAVIOR

Most Westernized countries have a formal system of prison rules whereby adjudications are held on prison misbehavior, which is dealt with by loss of privileges or (for more severe examples) by loss of remission of sentence. The most serious examples may result in further police investigations, formal charges, and a further sentence following a conviction in an outside court. However, placement in solitary confinement, for varying periods and with varying levels of privileges and facilities while confined, is a primary disincentive.

In many penal systems, individuals who appear to be mentally disturbed or highly stressed are admitted to prison hospitals for short periods, but these hospitals are usually poorly equipped to cope for long periods with highly disruptive individuals. Most countries have maximum-security psychiatric hospitals, but there can be major obstacles to be overcome before a prisoner can be transferred to such a facility. Psychopathic prisoners are routinely rejected for treatment in these facilities in many countries.

Although disruptive prisoners can be sent for periods to a segregation unit, isolated from the main part of the prison, it is often still possible for a prisoner in segregation to continue to exert a powerful influence on other prisoners. Some countries, such as the United Kingdom, operate a system of repeated transfers between establishments for the most disruptive inmates. This system is intended to provide "cooling-off" periods, and a transfer facility is usually made available for prisoners who need to be removed from their normal location because an explosive situation exists and placement in the host prison's segregation unit is inappropriate or impractical. For example, a prisoner may still exert a disruptive influence from the segregation unit or provide a focal point of prisoner unrest, so that placement in the unit could have a provocative and explosive effect on the rest of the establishment. The procedure can be a useful device in defusing potential explosive situations, yet it has little deterrent effect. It has been observed in the United Kingdom that some individuals regard the procedure as little more than a rest period, from which they subsequently return with added status in the eyes of the other inmates.

For the most extreme problems—for example, those who have killed, or present a real and continued threat that they will kill again—certain penal systems have developed special high-security cells, or even super-maximum-security prisons.

SPECIAL REGIMENS

The problems posed by dangerous and psychopathic prisoners have led to special measures and specialist facilities. These fall into two categories, with contrasting and conflicting philosophies: therapeutic units within prisons (some of which have been established on an experimental basis), and units or entire prisons, offering security without therapeutic input. Specific examples have been selected to illustrate the relevant principles in the final part of this chapter.

Grendon Underwood Prison, England

Grendon Underwood Prison was opened in 1962 and offered a therapeutic community approach to the psychiatric treatment of nonpsychotic recidivist offenders with moderate to severe personality disorders (Gray, 1974). Inmates are referred specifically for psychiatric treatment and must be willing to cooperate with the regimen. They are free to return to an ordinary prison location on request. Prisoners are initially received into an assessment unit, where those unsuitable for treatment are filtered out. This may clearly remove a number of the most difficult and disruptive individuals, although a few predatory and dangerous psychopathic prisoners do manage to settle within the Grendon regimen. Following assessment, inmates are then randomlyallocated to the four treatment wings (for a description of the assessment process, see Woodward, 1991).

For many years Grendon has had the lowest prison offense rate of any security establishment in the United Kingdom. But evaluation of the Grendon regimen by academics in the United Kingdom has centered largely on the question of whether it reduces recidivism following release. These studies have been examined and summarized elsewhere (Dolan & Coid, 1993). The more limited goal of managing the difficult prisoners during their sentence has been examined in Genders and Player's (1994) evaluation of the therapeutic process at Grendon. Using interviews and observational data, they found that the prisoners dropped the "them and us" mentality of prison culture over time. Feelings of isolation and alienation seemed to be reduced soon after admission to Grendon. With time, inmates became significantly more likely to talk to prison officers about personal matters and to approve of uniformed officers' being present in therapy groups. The longer prisoners had been at Grendon, the less likely they were to think that their problems emanated from an external factor (such as drugs or alcohol), and the more likely they were to attribute their problems to difficulties in establishing and maintaining personal relationships. Inmates also exercised more social responsibility and more control over illicit activities within the prison setting. For example, the majority who had been at Grendon for more than a year said they would intervene if they suspected the presence of heroin on the unit. Genders and Player (1994) have argued that reconviction rates per se are not the only, or even the most appropriate, measure of the success of Grendon. However, the effect of the institution on the overall level of violence and on disruptions within the system elsewhere has not been evaluated. It is also unclear what proportion of severely psychopathic individuals can be successfully managed within the therapeutic regimen of the institution.

Barlinnie Special Unit, Scotland

The Barlinnie Special Unit was opened in 1973 as an experimental unit to contain prisoners who had been seriously violent, subversive, or destructive in the main prison system. This unit has now closed. During its operation, it also functioned on principles derived from the therapeutic community model. This included some degree of loosening of the staff–inmate boundaries; prisoners would take an active part in decision making on the unit and, to some extent, were held responsible for their own behavior and that of their peers. Inmates were encouraged to express their aggressive feelings verbally and to learn to deal with their emotions in more constructive ways. Prisoners in the unit would also enjoy privileges such as frequent visits, single cells (which they could decorate themselves), and self-catering, although any of these could be withheld by a community decision if the social "rules" of the unit were infringed. The cost to the inmates was to live with generally fewer facilities than within the ordinary prison system, lack of privacy, and above all the emotional cost of facing and changing their own aggressive behavior.

Cooke (1989) has described the changes in behavior of the first 25 inmates during and after their stay at Barlinnie. These men were in the unit for an average of 41 months, and all had convictions for violent offenses (64% for murder). All had been deemed uncontainable in the normal system, as evidenced by the fact that 68% received additional sentences while in prison. Prior to transfer, the men had been responsible for 195 episodes of disruptive behavior in prison. However, ratings on the PCL-R showed that only 5 (20%) were classified as psychopaths (scores over 32). A further 14 (56%) showed significant psychopathic traits (scores of 25–32). The low scores demonstrated by these men, which contrasted with their history of highly disruptive prison behavior, may have been due to the fact that admissions were heavily influenced by self-selection of a group of professional criminals. The men in the unit tended to have high status in the Scottish criminal underworld and retained this while in the Scottish penal system. Special "abilities" in criminality may have been "transferable" to a conventional environment, resulting in certain notable examples of success, in which these men subsequently pursued law-abiding and well-paid occupations. For example, some became highly successful artists (Boyle, 1977).

Changes during and after admission to the unit were assessed according to the inmates' yearly rates of serious incidents against prison discipline before admission (such incidents included assaults, violence, disruptions, demonstrations, fire setting, self-mutilation, and absconding). By comparing the expected behavior within the unit with the behavior that actually occurred after transfer back to the ordinary system, Cooke demonstrated a dramatic fall in the observed number of incidents. This suggested that substantial change had been effected by admission, although Cooke (1989) acknowledged that the research consisted of a one-group pretest–posttest design and lacked a control sample.

CRC Special Units, England

Three special units were established initially in Parkhurst, Hull, and Lincoln Prisons in England, following the deliberations of the CRC (Home Office, 1984). The CRC did not attempt to prescribe a specific regimen or facilities, but set out what it regarded as four important principles for the special units' operations. First, that the units should not be punitive in purpose. Second, none should be regarded as a place of last resort. Third, different units should complement each other, and a unit should not be an ad hoc collection of aims and beliefs. Fourth, the prison service should be completely open about the establishment of the units and the way they operated.

The regimens are intended to include a degree of structure and have not taken the therapeutic community approach. Staff members are encouraged to operate a multidisciplinary style of working and to develop individual training plans and programs with prisoners. Identification of early signals of impending crisis is considered a high priority. Each unit operates a "personal officer" scheme, in which a named officer is expected to develop a close relationship with an inmate and to monitor the inmate's progress and behavior. This is intended to avoid communication problems that often occur, and specifically to minimize inmates' abilities to split and manipulate the staff.

Several studies (Walmsley, 1991; Bell, 1991; Boag, 1991; Bennett, 1991; Bottomley, Jepson, Elliott, & Coid, 1994) have indicated the difficulties these facilities face in balancing staff morale and effectiveness against the demands of the host prison, combined with the sustained pressure imposed by dealing with highly demanding and potentially violent inmates. The units may value professional relationships between staff and prisoners, but the rest of the prison perceives the officers as interchangeable and tends to move them around according to the institution's staffing needs, with little regard for the disruption of staff–inmate relationships. The units also cost more than other prison placements, and the governor in each host prison is under considerable pressure to spend resources more evenly.

The effectiveness of the special units has not been formally evaluated, but they have been able to contain subgroups of the most disruptive inmates in the English penal system for varying lengths of time. There continue to be three units in operation, but two have moved to other prisons.

Special Handling Units, Canada

The conceptual framework of the special handling units in the Canadian federal correctional system was developed in the Vantour (1975) report. There had been serious concerns about conditions in federal facilities; the handling of long-term, segregated prisoners; and a high level of violent incidents in Canadian institutions during the mid-1970s. It was found that a number of inmates who were considered persistent and serious threats to staff and other prisoners were being confined in segregation for 23 hours a day for many months, without the benefit of any treatment or rehabilitative programs. Although this was deemed inhumane and counterproductive, many of these inmates had been responsible for a substantial proportion of violent incidents in Canadian prisons. Two special handling units were therefore established, one for English-speaking and the other for French-speaking inmates. These were intended for prisoners presenting serious and persistent threats, rather than for those who only required short-term periods of segregation.

Unfortunately, a regimen contrary to that originally envisioned by the architects of the special handling concept took hold very quickly. There had been a wave of violence in the mid-1970s—in particular, a series of hostage-taking incidents, during one of which a prison officer was killed. Upon transfer of the three inmates involved in this incident, written instructions were given that three officers were to be present when one of their cells was opened, that only one of the three inmates could be moved at any one time, and that their hands would be handcuffed behind their backs "if and when they are allowed to exercise." This procedure set the terms for the special handling units' operating procedure (Vantour, 1991, p. 93).

Thus, a control mentality continued to prevail in the operation of the special handling units, despite the decrease in the overall rate of violence from the mid-1980s onward. Inmates were routinely moved with at least two officers accompanying them. Interviews were conducted through bars, and overhead catwalks were patrolled by armed officers. The use of handcuffs became the rule rather than the exception whenever an inmate was in the presence of the staff. Meaningful activities for prisoners became virtually nonexistent, and there was very little contact between staff and inmates.

In his assessment of these specialist facilities, Vantour (1991) concluded that the Canadian system was "floundering." There was no ready-made approach for dealing with inmates who were difficult to manage, and it appeared that without one, the system was sometimes prone to change for the sake of change. Change would usually occur following a crisis, but with each crisis security seemed to be increased further. By the late 1980s, new admission statements for the Correctional Service of Canada attempted to redefine the direction. A new approach was subsequently adopted, involving a period of assessment followed by a management program. The objective of programming within the unit was to return inmates safely to a maximum-security institution at the earliest reasonable time. This would occur through a team approach involving case management carried out by the security staff; ongoing staff training to increase awareness and understanding of violent behavior and appropriate intervention techniques; and the development of a variety of treatment programs, including psychiatric and psychological intervention, anger management, life skills, and drug and alcohol programs. These have been augmented by personal development, employment and recreational opportunities, and pastoral counseling.

The experience of the special handling units is important in demonstrating the tension that can arise between models of control and treatment in the management of dangerous and disruptive individuals. The experience also provides an example of what can go wrong when control and restraint are the only priorities and when there is a spiraling escalation of violence, punishment, and restraint. The end product can be a dehumanizing regimen where isolated inmates are only unlocked when several staff members are present and are routinely moved around the unit in handcuffs or other physical restraints. This can be demoralizing and unacceptable for staff, as well as for prisoners. Subsequently, the Correctional Service of Canada found it necessary to return to an emphasis on personal relationships as a means of influencing behavioral change, even though the environments of the special handling units have by no means been transformed into overtly therapeutic settings.

The U.S. Federal Administrative Maximum Penitentiary, Florence, Colorado

The U.S. Federal Administrative Maximum Penitentiary, Florence, Colorado, was opened in 1995 and consolidated the current U.S. Federal Bureau of Prisons policy for the management of dangerous and disruptive male inmates, especially those posing escape risks. Its approach to prisoner management represents one extreme of the spectrum in its emphasis on control. The penitentiary is the most technologically advanced in the combination of its regimen and architectural design. Although there is no therapeutic element in its policy for controlling inmates, it has attracted increasing interest from the correctional systems of many other countries and from other correctional systems within the United States, several of which have developed, or are in the process of developing, similar facilities.

The penitentiary's "state-of-the-art" architectural design, which complements its regimen, is a combination designed to limit all opportunity for inmate-on-inmate or inmate-on-staff violence, escape, or other forms of disruptive behavior. Inmate housing within the penitentiary reflects a stratified system intended to provide prisoners with incentives to adhere to improved conduct. Progress through the program is entirely dependent on good behavior. Prisoners must demonstrate periods of clear conduct without any rule infractions before they can transfer from one unit to another, and ultimately back to a maximum-security penitentiary elsewhere within the federal system. Privileges afforded to inmates are determined according to the housing unit in which they are detained, as is the number of hours an inmate spends out of his cell. Indoor and outdoor recreational facilities are provided in each individual unit, and educational programs are offered by closed-circuit black-and-white TV. The average length of stay at the penitentiary is intended to be 36 months, depending on conduct and positive participation in programs; however, it is accepted that an inmate may stay longer, depending on his behavior.

An additional "control unit" operates as a prison within the prison. An inmate is transferred to this unit as punishment following a serious act of violence that meets the criteria established for placement in the facility. For example, an inmate could spend up to 36 months in the control unit following a serious assault on another inmate with a weapon. There are further reductions of privileges in this unit, as well as an increase in the level of security. For example, inmates can only have solitary exercise for 1 hour per day and must leave their cells in leg irons, in addition to being handcuffed from behind. One officer must always restrain the prisoner, holding the handcuffs from behind, and must be accompanied by two additional officers carrying batons.

Most Florence inmates have posed special problems of control within the federal system; require special levels of security due to their risk of escape; or are high-profile criminals and/or those with considerable resources at their disposal, such as leaders of major criminal organizations or members of terrorist organizations. Prisoners who require a high level of security and individuals requiring special measures for the control of their behavior are contained in the same penitentiary.

The penitentiary has been highly effective in preventing disruptive and dangerous behavior by its inmates. However, the facility and its accompanying regimen might not be politically acceptable in certain countries. Civil libertarians have argued that the Florence regimen breaches Articles 9 and 10 of the International Covenant on Civil and Political Rights. It is also possible that the institution represents a U.S. solution to a U.S. problem. Coyle (1987) has cautioned that any considerations of penal policy in the United States must be viewed in the background of the especially high levels of violence in U.S. society which are mirrored in its prison system.

CONCLUSION

Mental health care professionals have an important role to play in the assessment and management of dangerous psychopaths in prison. Although these individuals are often rejected as unsuitable and untreatable in hospital settings, and require security levels that exceed those in a maximum-security hospital, management in the prison setting can clearly benefit from the input of professional expertise. The alternative may be a management program that has no therapeutic input and a regimen based entirely on behavioral control. Many (but not all) correctional staff members can find the latter stressful or unacceptable to work in. But unrealistically low levels of observation and inmate control would prove equally stressful, because of the high risks posed by these prisoners, and are clearly unsustainable for the most difficult individuals. Future developments that capitalize on the situational approach to problem behavior, and in which correctional staff members devise new therapeutic regimens in conjunction with mental health care professionals, are required. These settings must be safe to work in, must be safe for inmates to live in, and still must remain cost-effective in their reduction of inmates' behavioral disorders.

REFERENCES

Atlas, R. (1982). *Violence in prison: Architectural determinism* (Doctoral dissertation, Florida State University). Ann Arbor, MI: University Microfilms International. (University Microfilms No. DDJ8-17967)

Bell, R. E. (1991). Staff–inmate relations: The personal officer scheme. In K. Bottomley & W. Hay (Eds.), *Special units for difficult prisoners*. Hull, England: Centre for Criminology and Criminal Justice, University of Hull.

Bennett, P. (1991). Hull Special Unit. In K. Bottomley & W. Hay (Eds.), *Special units for difficult prisoners*. Hull, England: Centre for Criminology and Criminal Justice, University of Hull.

Boag, D. (1991). Lincoln Special Unit. In K. Bottomley & W. Hay (Eds.), *Special units for difficult prisoners*. Hull, England: Centre for Criminology and Criminal Justice, University of Hull.

Bottomley, K., Jepson, N., Elliott, K., & Coid, J. (1994). *Managing difficult prisoners: The Lincoln and Hull special units*. London: Home Office Research and Planning Unit.

Boyle, J. (1977). *A sense of freedom*. London: Pan Books.

Coid, J. W. (1991). Psychiatric profiles of difficult/dangerous prisoners. In K. Bottomley & W. Hay

(Eds.), *Special units for difficult prisoners.* Hull, England: Centre for Criminology and Criminal Justice, University of Hull.

Coid, J. W. (1992). DSM-III diagnosis in criminal psychopaths: A way forward. *Criminal Behaviour and Mental Health, 2,* 78–94.

Coid, J. W. (1993). An affective syndrome in female psychopaths with borderline personality disorder? *British Journal of Psychiatry, 162,* 641–650.

Coid, J. W. (1996). *Psychopathology in psychopaths: A study of diagnostic comorbidity and aetiology.* Unpublished doctoral dissertation, University of London.

Cooke, D. J. (1989). Containing violent prisoners: An analysis of the Barlinnie Special Unit. *British Journal of Criminology, 29,* 129–143.

Cooke, D. J. (1991). Violence in prisons: The influence of regime factors. *The Howard Journal, 30,* 95–109.

Cooke, D. J. (1994). *Psychological disturbance in the Scottish Prison System: Prevalence, precipitants and policy.* Edinburgh: Scottish Home and Health Department.

Cooke, D. J. (1997). Psychopaths: Oversexed, overplayed but not over here? *Criminal Behaviour and Mental Health, 7,* 3–11.

Coyle, A. (1987). The Management of Dangerous and Difficult Prisoners. *The Howard Journal, 26,* 139–152.

de Girolamo, G., & Reich, J. H. (1993). *Personality disorders.* Geneva: World Health Organization.

Ditchfield, J. (1990). *Control in prisons: A review of the literature* (Home Office Research Study No. 118). London: Her Majesty's Stationery Office.

Dolan, B., & Coid, J. (1993). *Psychopathic and antisocial personality disorders: Treatment and research issues.* London: Gaskell.

Dunbar, I. (1986). *A sense of direction.* London: Home Office.

Ellis, D. (1984). Crowding and prison violence: Integration of research and theory. *Criminal Justice and Behaviour, 11,* 277–308.

Evans, R., & Feltham, R. (1980). *Catastrophic monitoring on a local prison wing at Bristol, 1977–79* (DPS Report, Series II, No. 74). London: Directorate of Psychological Services, Home Office.

Forth, A. E., Hart, S. D., & Hare, R. D. (1990). Assessment of psychopathy in male young offenders. *Psychological Assessment: A Journal of Consulting and Clinical Psychology, 2,* 342–344.

Genders, E., & Player, E. (1994). *The therapeutic prison: A study of Grendon.* Oxford: Oxford University Press.

Glaser, D. (1984). Six principles and one precaution for efficient sentencing and correction. *Federal Probation, 48,* 22–28.

Gray, W. J. (1974). Grendon Prison. *British Journal of Hospital Medicine, 12,* 299–308.

Gunderson, J. G. (1984). *Borderline personality disorder.* Washington, DC: American Psychiatric Press.

Hare, R. D. (1970). *Psychopathy: Theory and research.* New York: Wiley.

Hare, R. D. (1980). A research scale for the assessment of psychopathy in criminal populations. *Personality and Individual Differences, 1,* 111–117.

Hare, R. D. (1991). *The Hare Psychopathy Checklist—Revised.* Toronto: Multi-Health Systems.

Hare, R. D., & McPherson, L. M. (1984). Violent and aggressive behaviour by criminal psychopaths. *International Journal of Law and Psychiatry, 7,* 35–50.

Hart, S. D., Kropp, P. R., & Hare, R. D. (1988). Performance of Male Psychopaths Following Conditional Release from Prison. *Journal of Consulting and Clinical Psychology, 56,* 227–232.

Hodgins, S., & Côté, G. (1990). Prevalence of mental disorders among penitentiary inmates in Quebec. *Canada's Mental Health,* March, 1–4.

Home Office. (1984). *Managing the long-term prison system: The report of the Control Review Committee.* London: Her Majesty's Stationery Office.

Jordan, B. K., Schlenger, W. E., Fairbank, J. A., & Caddell, J. M. (1996). Prevalence of psychiatric disorders among incarcerated women: II. Convicted felons entering prison. *Archives of General Psychiatry, 53,* 513–519.

Kernberg, O. (1975). *Borderline conditions and pathological narcissism.* New York: Jason Aronson.

Kernberg, O. (1984). *Severe personality disorders: Psychotherapeutic strategies.* New Haven, CT: Yale University Press.

Kohut, H. (1971). *The analysis of the self.* New York: International Universities Press.

Kohut, H. (1977). *The restoration of the self.* New York: International Universities Press.

McCain, G. V., Cox, V. C., & Paulus, P. B. (1980). *The effect of prison crowding on inmate behavior* (Final report). (Available from the National Criminal Justice Reference Service, Box 6000, Rockville, MD 20850)

Megargee, E. I. (1977). The association of population density, reduced space and uncomfortable temperatures with misconduct in a prison community. *American Journal of Community Psychology, 5,* 289–298.

Nacci, P. H., Teitelbaum, H., & Prather, J. (1977). Population density and inmate misconduct rates in the federal prison system. *Federal Probation, 41,* 27–38.

Pope, P. (1979). Prisoners in maximum security prisons: Perspectives upon management and problems. *Prison Service Journal, 22,* 1–5.

Quay, H. C. (1984). *Managing adult inmates: Classification for housing and program assignments.* College Park, MD: American Correctional Association.

Robins, L. N., Tipp, J., & Przybeck, T. (1991). Antisocial personality disorder. In L. N. Robins & D. A. Regier (Eds.), *Psychiatric disorders in America.* New York: Free Press.

Serin, R. C., Peters, R. DeV., & Barbaree, H. (1990). Predictors of psychopathy and release outcome in a criminal population. *Psychological Assessment, 2,* 419–422.

Teplin, L. A., Abram, K. M., & McClelland, G. (1996). Prevalence of psychiatric disorders among incarcerated women: I. Pretrial jail detainees. *Archives of General Psychiatry, 53,* 505–512.

Toch, H., Adams, K., & Grant, J. D. (1989). *Coping: Maladaption in prisons.* Oxford: Transaction.

Vantour, J. A. (Chair). (1975). *Report of the study group on dissociation.* Ottawa, Canada: Solicitor General.

Vantour, J. A. (1991). Canadian experience: The special handling unit. In K. Bottomley & W. Hay (Eds.), *Special units for difficult prisoners.* Hull, England: Centre for Criminology and Criminal Justice, University of Hull.

Walmsley, R. (1991). *Managing difficult prisoners: The Parkhurst Special Unit* (Home Office Research Study No. 122). London: Her Majesty's Stationery Office.

Ward, D. A. (1987). Control strategies for problem prisoners in American penal systems. In A. E. Bottoms & R. Light (Eds.), *Problems of long-term imprisonment.* Aldershot, England: Gower.

Weissman, M. M. (1993). The epidemiology of personality disorders: A 1990 update. *Journal of Personality Disorders, 7*(Suppl.), 44–62.

Williams, M., & Longley, D. (1987). Identifying control-problem prisoners in dispersal prisons In A. E. Bottoms & R. Light (Eds.), *Problems of long-term imprisonment.* Aldershot, England: Gower.

Woodward, R. (1991). Allowing people to behave well: The role of the Grendon Assessment Unit. In S. Boddis (Ed.), *Proceedings of the Prison Service Psychology Conference, October 1991.* London: Home Office.

28

Treating the "Untreatable" in Denmark: Past and Present

HEIDI HANSEN

Since its founding in 1935, the Herstedvester Detention Center in Denmark has functioned as an institution for criminals in need of psychiatric/psychological treatment. For nearly 40 years this institution was headed by the world-famous psychiatrist Georg K. Stürup, known for his 1968 book *Treating the "Untreatable."* In this book, he described his lifetime of experience as a psychiatrist at the institution.

Herstedvester is a prison, and as such it comes under the authority of the Danish Department of Prisons and Probation. Since Chief Physician Stürup's appointment in 1942, however, the institution has served as a treatment center—and, until 1982, was headed by a medical superintendent. Since then, the institution has been headed by a government official; however, an executive medical superintendent is responsible for psychiatric and psychological treatment. Over the years, the management structure has given rise to serious conflicts, which at times have made the work of treating inmates virtually impossible. Treatment and punishment are antithetical terms. The purpose of treatment is to ease suffering; the purpose of punishment is to inflict suffering. Within the terms of this dilemma, the work of treatment must be carried out. And unless doctors and jurists resolve to work with respect for each other within the terms of this dilemma, then the task is impossible.

The primary characteristic of a dilemma is the fact that there is no absolutely right or wrong solution to the problem in question; if there were, then it would not be a dilemma. Here, for example, we could choose to say that all treatment should be carried out under the auspices of the hospital service. This would relieve us of our dilemma—although much suffering would then go untreated: Patients who are being punished *would not be able* to receive treatment under the hospital service, because they would not stay there. Also, we have to consider that those responsible for treatment in a prison have a duty to ensure that their patients receive the best possible treatment at all times.

There are both advantages and disadvantages in having a jurist as the administrative head of the institution. One important advantage is that it is not a doctor who is responsible for the forced imprisonment of a patient, but a jurist. Also, the institution involves a lot more than the treatment of patients. The practical running of the institution, for example, is a considerable task for which a therapist may be quite unqualified.

The most important disadvantages, as far as I can see, are that the prison warders (rightly) consider themselves responsible to the governor of the institution, and that the administrative medical superintendent does not have a governor's power or authority. This means, among other things, that the medical superintendent has no influence in the appointment of prison staff members. When punishment and treatment come into conflict with each other—for example, when a mental patient is placed in solitary confinement—the decision to place the patient in solitary confinement is the sole responsibility of the governor. However, the medical superintendent still has responsibility for the *treatment* of the patient, and must intervene if the situation is such that the patient's doctor cannot accept this responsibility. It is obvious that only when prison staff members and therapists work together in an atmosphere of mutual respect will an institution such as Herstedvester work successfully. And such cooperation, when it is successful, also provides the best possible basis for the treatment of sometimes extremely dangerous but mentally-disordered criminals.

In *Treating the "Untreatable,"* Stürup (1968) stated: "The institution [Herstedvester] must be regarded neither as a mental hospital primarily dedicated to therapy nor as a prison dedicated to security for the most troublesome and dangerous offenders; it is a security institution, but one whose goal is rehabilitation" (p. 5). The institution is the only one of its kind in Denmark and receives offenders from all over the country. It receives offenders in need of psychiatric/psychological treatment or offenders who, because of their special mental state, cannot be placed in other prisons. Since its founding, the institution has developed a tradition of treating sexual offenders; over the years, it has thus accumulated considerable expertise in the treatment of severely recidivistic, dangerous sexual criminals (Hansen & Lykke-Olesen, 1997).

Psychiatric/psychological treatment at Herstedvester is individual and generally consists of psychodynamically oriented therapy. However, the institution also has a long tradition of influencing offenders through their day-to-day work—a tradition aimed at correcting the behavior and reshaping the attitudes of the offenders. This environmental form of treatment is carried out by the uniformed staff and the psychiatric staff in conjunction. For many years, the daily meetings of the institution's six departments have been fundamental to the work of the institution. These daily meetings take place in the respective departments. The meetings are attended by each department's uniformed staff, together with the psychiatrist, psychologist, and social advisor attached to the department. The uniformed staff members keep records on each individual inmate, and these records are discussed at the daily meeting.

The institution's psychiatric and psychological treatment varies according to the individual offender's background and the overall assessment of the case. However, all our patients have one thing in common: They have all inflicted suffering (often very great suffering) on other people. Precisely because they have inflicted suffering on often quite innocent people, a great deal of our treatment is concerned with the patients' capacity for empathy—in other words, for putting themselves in the position of others and understanding their feelings. Very often we find that patients do not know what we are talking about; it is an undiscovered country as far as they are concerned. It is not because they have repressed it, but because they have never experienced or learned or discovered what empathy is. In short, they have no capacity for empathy—they have a defect. The fact that, in addition to this, they very often have conflicts as well is another matter.

In the treatment of the mentally ill, we have a tendency to focus on drives and conflicts, and not so much on defects. Perhaps this is because it is difficult for us to accept that we cannot cure many mentally ill or afflicted patients, but can only ease their symptoms. During his time at Herstedvester, Stürup (1968) wrote: "I never say that I cure psychopaths; I do claim, however, that during their stay in Herstedvester they have been helped to become nicer psychopaths" (p. 2).

It is, of course, no mere coincidence that almost every one of the offenders at Herstedvester has endured wretched conditions from early infancy. Quite a few of our patients were, as children, forcibly removed from their parents because of neglect. Just as our motor skills are acquired, surely, in the same way, our feelings are too. And nature will always provide us with the best conditions for survival, even at the expense of skills. By this I mean, for example, that if a child has a squint in one eye and the squint is not treated, the child will be blind in that eye from the age of 6, and no amount of training will ever be able to restore sight to that eye. Perhaps the same applies to empathy—one of the qualities that is unique to humans in comparison with animals. We must assume that this quality is acquired at a very early age through contact with other people. If, however, such contact is either totally absent or of a very negative nature, we may then imagine that certain feelings will not be given the right conditions for growth and will therefore not develop. Children will protect themselves against this emotional rejection and neglect by making themselves insensitive.

It is my belief that in many psychopathic criminals, a defect may be a more dominant trait than a conflict—a defect that may be either biologically or psychologically determined. Psychopathic criminals often have developmental disturbances. A Danish child psychiatrist, Ole Sylvester Jørgensen, has written a book entitled *Mellem Autisme og Normalitet* (*Between Autism and Normality*; Jørgensen, 1994). It is in precisely this zone that many psychopathic criminals find themselves. They are of normal intelligence, but they are emotionally deficient. They have no emotional understanding of other people. They have no understanding of the fact that other people have their own subjective inner lives separate from theirs. For this reason, they often have no understanding of the suffering of their victims, and are likewise unable to appreciate the feelings of others. Just like developmentally disturbed children, they have no moral sense. They *can* learn rules, and treatment consists of (among other things) teaching them rules. This, however, cannot be achieved by an hourly visit to a therapist once a week, but only when the treatment is combined with the therapist's day-to-day contact with the department staff—in other words, when such patients are committed to an institution.

When we discuss the treatment of psychopathic criminals in general terms, we talk a lot about impulses and drives, and hence about conflicts. We talk about narcissistic rage; we talk about how impotence and total loss of identity trigger anxiety (for which the rapist, for example, compensates by gaining power and total submission from another person through the use of force). However, there are undoubtedly many sexual offenders who commit their crimes because they are emotionally defective. After talking to them, we are often left with the impression that, as Jesus Christ said of his executioners, "They know not what they do."

On the face of it, it seems as if at the outer extremes we can talk about at least two types of psychopathic criminals: the ones who commit a crime because of a conflict, and the ones who commit a crime because of a defect. And, of course, I know that in the majority of cases it is probably a question of "not only, but also." For the purposes of psychotherapeutic treatment, however, it is important to know whether we are dealing with a conflict or a defect. If we are dealing with a person with a defect, it is by no means certain that psychotherapeutic treatment can prevent the offender from committing new offenses. In some individuals, irreparable emotional damage may have been done, as a result of which the persons in question will never be able to function normally. Some people believe that if, for example, sex criminals who were sexually abused as children are given the proper treatment to overcome the mental harm caused by this abuse, then they will not commit any more sex crimes. In some cases, such a belief would be analogous to the attempts in former times to make homosexuals heterosexual. Sometimes the only possible treatment is for such persons to accept that they have a defect in their sexuality and to come to terms with it. In the case of a few dangerous sex criminals, this may mean that they have to accept medical castration—to mention the most drastic form of treatment we have at Herstedvester.

It is painful for a person to accept the fact of having an emotional defect. It is tempting to continue to visit new psychotherapists in the hope, for example, of becoming sexually normal. But what can we do if there is a defect? It is not possible to start all over again. We cannot undo the damage done in early childhood. We cannot make a new, defect-free human being. But we can try to teach the person in question to come to terms with the defect.

The world-famous Danish philosopher Søren Kierkegaard, the father of existentialism, suffered from a secret affliction (temporal lobe epilepsy? [Hansen & Bork-Hansen, 1988]) that placed him outside normal society. The whole of his literary production dealt with how it is possible for people to reconcile themselves, even with a defect, to the lives they have. Kierkegaard asserted that what is important is the way people relate to their suffering. The temptation is that they may become demonic. They may take revenge for the terrible childhood traumas that have made their emotional lives defective. As an example, Kierkegaard cited Shakespeare's Richard III, who was born a hunchback; he was an outsider from birth. Others may feel themselves to be outsiders because their emotional lives are destroyed in childhood, before they had a chance to develop. In the play, Richard III takes his revenge by becoming demonic, thoroughly evil. Many psychopathic criminals take revenge by inflicting humiliation and violence on their victims.

But Kierkegaard also suggested a different option: People can take responsibility for themselves. They can make it their life's work *not* to take revenge. They can make it their life's work, despite all the possibilities from which they are excluded, to concentrate on what is possible.

Kierkegaard taught us to understand the psychological mechanisms that operate in individuals who have to bear a defect for which they are not to blame. He taught us to understand that such persons can become demonic. And not until we understand this can we hope to help such persons. Kierkegaard stated: "Sympathy one must have, but this sympathy is genuine only when we admit deep down to ourselves that what can happen to one person can happen to all. Only then can one be of utility to oneself and to others" (1844/1963, p. 146; my translation). Later, he added: "If we truly wish to succeed in leading a person to a particular place, we must first and foremost ensure that we seek the person where he is, and start from there. That is the secret of all succor" (1848/1963, p. 96; my translation).

A therapist can only achieve this necessary understanding, this necessary sympathy, by becoming acquainted with a patient—by, among other things, hearing about the patient's childhood traumas. These childhood traumas may have resulted in the person's having not only an emotional conflict, but also an emotional defect. A neurotic person has only an emotional conflict, which can be treated. The neurotic person has a coherent self and a coherent experience of a self. The neurotic person is capable of conducting an inner dialogue. The sole task of the therapist is to interpret and correct the patient's inner dialogue, and thus to enable the patient to solve the conflict. The therapist must be neutral, objective, and withdrawn, and must provide room for the patient's inner dialogue. In theory, it is unimportant whether or not the therapist has any sympathy for the patient.

It is quite a different matter when it comes to treating psychopathic criminals. In addition to (usually) having an emotional conflict, these people have an emotional defect. They are defective in that, among other things, they do not have a coherent self or a coherent experience of a self, for which reason they are unable to conduct an inner dialogue. They are also defective in that they cannot relate naturally to other people or appreciate other people's feelings. In order to help such a patient at all, the therapist must be able to create the external conditions, the room, for a dialogue that can lead to development. This room can only be created, however, if the therapist has understanding and sympathy for the patient, and if the patient can experience this.

What development is it, then, that we can hope for? It is that such patients can learn to take responsibility for themselves. After serving their sentences, many criminals want to start all over again, to start afresh. But none of us can start all over again. We must always start from where we are. A human being is, as Kierkegaard (1849/1963) said, a synthesis of freedom and necessity—freedom to choose, but also necessity because the person has to shoulder the burden of everything that has gone before, including, for example, a defective emotional life. We may be able to find the probable reason why a person's emotional life is the way it is, but that does not necessarily mean that we can change it.

A human being embodies this necessity, but at the same time, the human being embodies freedom. Let me give a further example. A rose is a rose is a rose; it is only necessity. But a defective person is more than the defect. At the same time, the person is *also* the defect, however painful it may be to accept the fact. And yet, through this very acceptance, and because a human being also embodies freedom, this person gains an opportunity—the opportunity to take responsibility for himself or herself. What this means for the individual, only a dialogue with the individual can determine—and it is this dialogue that a therapist must be ready to take part in, because the criminal is not able to conduct an inner dialogue. I would like to conclude with an analogy: Even though we cannot teach a blind person to see, we can tell the person *what* we see. But in order for this to be of any importance, the person must believe what we say.

REFERENCES

Hansen, H., & Bork-Hansen, L. (1998). The temporal lobe epilepsy syndrome elucidated through Søren Kierkegaard's authorship and life. *Acta Psychiatrica Scandinavica, 77,* 352–358.

Hansen, H., & Lykke-Olesen, L. (1997). Treatment of dangerous sexual offenders in Denmark. *Journal of Forensic Psychiatry, 8*(1), 195–199.

Jørgensen, O. S. (1994). *Mellem autisme og normalitet: Aspergers syndrom.* Copenhagen: Hans Reitzels Forlag.

Kierkegaard, S. (1963). Begrebet angest. In S. Kierkegaard, *Samlede værker* (Vol. 3, Section 6, pp. 146–147). Copenhagen: Gyldendal. (Original work published 1844)

Kierkegaard, S. (1963). Synspunktet for min forfatter—virksomhed. In S. Kierkegaard, *Samlede værker* (Vol. 3, Section 18, pp. 96–97). Copenhagen: Gyldendal. (Original work published 1848)

Kierkegaard, S. (1849). Sygdommen til døden. In S. Kierkegaard, *Samlede værker* (Vol. 3, Section 15, p. 73). Copenhagen: Gyldendal. (Original work published 1849)

Stürup, G. K. (1968). *Treating the "untreatable."* Baltimore: MD: John Hopkins University Press.

Index